Corruption

To Isella and Sandro Bellavite Pellegrini – M.A.

To Marco – L.B.

Milano, 7 luglio 2016

Io sottoscritto Egidio Arnone, fratello e erede del dott. Marco Arnone, con la presente riconosco a tutti i fini di legge che il dott. Leonardo Borlini, è **autore esclusivo** della Parte II e delle conclusioni del libro "Corruption. Economic Analysis and International Law" (pp. 177-528, capitoli 8-17), come indicato in nota 3 a p. xix della prefazione del Prof. Gabrio Forti al medesimo libro. Inoltre, come espressamente indicato in nota 2 a p. xvii della stessa prefazione, riconosco che il dott. Leonardo Borlini è **co-autore** dell'introduzione, del capitolo 1, dei paragrafi 2.1, 2.2, 2.3, 2.4.2, 2.4.4 del capitolo 2, dei paragrafi 3.3.2., 3.7 del capitolo 3 e del paragrafo 7.4.1.2 del capitolo 7.

P.S. TUTTO AI FINI CONCORSUALI.

In fede,

dott. Egidio Arnone

'Although corruption has affected human society since its very birth with different intensity over time, it is not confined to any particular geographic region, country, social or political system or culture. Recently there has been widespread international determination to effectively curb such crime. Corruption: Economic Analysis and International Law by Marco Arnone and Leonardo Borlini reviews the richness and complexity of the ongoing research on corruption and shows the value of integrating a comprehensive economic understanding of its consequences and a critical assessment of the several legal instruments promoted by major intergovernmental organizations on this issue. This approach is particularly timely because, on the bright side, this book shows that economic crises may lead to greater social responsiveness in the face of attempts to drain public resources through corruption and bribery. The use of a wide range of economic models and the acute analysis of the contemporary evolution of traditional institutions belonging to the realm of international and European law represent two additional values of this work. Finally, the personal commitment of both authors to scientific research and professional activity related to public governance and anti-corruption reforms make this book a valuable source for further thought and analysis for scholars, public servants and practitioners.'
Giorgio Sacerdoti, Professor of International and European Law, Bocconi University and former Chairman of the WTO Appellate Body and Vice President of the OECD Working Group on Corruption

'It is now rather common to speak of 'transnational law' as an approach to legal research that transcends national frontiers and domestic regulatory policies. Such a model accepts that rules can be generated not just by governments or by international cooperation, but also by individuals, corporations and various other organizations. As clearly evidenced by this book, unfortunately, one of the most successful transnational systems is the one based on corruption. The authors however, never to be defeated, show through a rigorous legal and economic analysis how instead, to develop policies and rules to fight what is sometimes perceived as an unavoidable phenomenon. In short, an invaluable addition to the study of this still largely unexplored area.'
Andrea Biondi, Kings College London, UK

'In everyday understanding, corruption means degradation, decomposition, degeneracy, depravity. The concept is common to all cultures, and all dictionaries provide for very close descriptions. Corruption, in a specific connotation, is also defined by the statutory law of most – if not all – States as a a criminal offense: it is an illicit trade of official functions, committed betraying the very reason ('the duties') of one's office. Corruption alters, dismantles and depravates the idea of a civil society, as it critically wounds the bond of trust that lays at its very basis, and, thus, the deepest foundation of all social relations. To marginalise corruption, and heal the damage it causes to society at large, it is necessary, first, to investigate what corruption is. By thoroughly analyzing the phenomenon per se, and offering a review of possible remedies against it, this book brilliantly and with exceptional efficacy, contributes to such an indispensable goal.'
Gherardo Colombo, formerly Public Prosecutor, Milan Public Prosecutor's Office and Judge, Supreme Court of Italy

'To effectively combat corruption globally, the collection and dissemination of knowledge is crucial. This excellent book takes us a step forward in our collective efforts to better understand the causes and effects of corruption from an international perspective. Through its detailed analysis of the economic impact of corruption in a diverse range of countries, this publication provides us with a new resource to draw on in our future efforts to reduce corruption together worldwide.'
Dimitri Vlassis, United Nations Office on Drugs and Crime, Vienna, Austria

---

Marco Arnone, former Director of the Centre for Macroeconomics and Finance Research, Italy and **Leonardo S. Borlini** is at Bocconi University, Italy.

ISBN 978-1-84980-266-6

9 781849 802666

EDWARD ELGAR
A FAMILY BUSINESS IN INTERNATIONAL PUBLISHING

The Lypiatts, 15 Lansdown Road, Cheltenham, Glos GL50 2JA, UK
Tel: + 44 (0) 1242 226934 Fax: + 44 (0) 1242 262111 Email: info@e-elgar.co.uk
William Pratt House, 9 Dewey Court, Northampton, MA 01060, USA
Tel: +1 413 584 5551 Fax: +1 413 584 9933 Email: elgarinfo@e-elgar.com
www.e-elgar.com www.elgaronline.com

Marco Arnone
Leonardo S. Borlini

CORRUPTION

EE

EE

Marco Arnone
Leonardo S. Borlini

CORRUPTION
Economic Analysis and International Law

Corruption

Economic Analysis and International Law

The late Marco Arnone

Former Director, Centre for Macroeconomics and Finance Research, Italy

Leonardo S. Borlini

Bocconi University, Italy

Edward Elgar

Cheltenham, UK • Northampton, MA, USA

Published by
Edward Elgar Publishing Limited
The Lypiatts
15 Lansdown Road
Cheltenham
Glos GL50 2JA
UK

Edward Elgar Publishing, Inc.
William Pratt House
9 Dewey Court
Northampton
Massachusetts 01060
USA

A catalogue record for this book
is available from the British Library

Library of Congress Control Number: 2013943207

This book is available electronically in the ElgarOnline.com
Law Subject Collection, E-ISBN 978 1 78100 613 9

MIX
Paper from responsible sources
FSC® C013056

ISBN 978 1 84980 266 6

Typeset by Servis Filmsetting Ltd, Stockport, Cheshire
Printed and bound in Great Britain by T.J. International Ltd, Padstow

A donation has been made to the UN Refugee Agency in lieu of an author royalty

Contents

PART II BIRTH AND EVOLUTION OF A GLOBAL ANTI-CORRUPTION LEGAL STANDARD

Section 4: Cases of transnational corruption: description and legal issues

Section 5: Horizontal assessment of international hard law instruments

About the authors

The late **Marco Arnone** (1968–2012) was the Director of the Centre for Macroeconomics & Finance Research (CeMaFiR, Milan, Italy). He held an MSc (Warwick, UK) and a PhD (Pavia, Italy) both in Economics, and was visiting scholar at Stanford University (US) in 1996, with an American Study and Student Exchange Committee scholarship, and 1999. He worked as an economist in the Monetary and Financial Systems department and the African department at the International Monetary Fund, in countries such as Peru, Croatia, Sri Lanka, Lebanon, Kenya, Zambia, Angola, Mozambique, Lesotho. Dr. Arnone taught at the Catholic University of Milan, the State University of Milan, and the University of Eastern Piedmont. He published nationally and internationally on issues ranging from the economics of corruption and anti-money laundering to development finance, banking and central banking issues.

His recent books and articles (with co-authors) include: *Primary Dealers in Government Securities* (IMF, 2005), *The Cost of Corruption – Economic, Institutional and Social Effects* (Vita e Pensiero, Milan 2005 and 2007), *Il Venture Capital per lo Sviluppo* (Vita e Pensiero, 2006), *Measures of Central Bank Autonomy: Empirical Evidence for OECD and Developing Countries, and Emerging Market Economies* (IMF, 2006), *Banking Supervision Quality and Governance* (IMF, 2007), "External Debt Sustainability and Domestic Debt in Heavily Indebted Poor Countries", *Rivista Internazionale di Scienze Sociali*, 2007, "Financial Supervisors Architecture and Banking Supervision", in D. Masciandaro and M. Quintyn, *Designing Institutions for Financial Stability: Independence, Accountability and Governance* (Edward Elgar, 2007), *Anti-Money Laundering by International Institutions: A Preliminary Assessment* (EJLE, 2008), *Central Bank Autonomy: Lessons from Global Trends* (IMF, 2009), *Central Bank Independence, Accountability, and Transparency* (Palgrave Macmillan, 2009), *Economics of the Mafias: Evolution, Governance and Evaluation Criteria for Sized Assets* (Studi sulla Questione Criminale, 2009), *Anti-Money Laundering: Transnational Criminal Regulation* (Amicus Books, ICFAI, Hyderabad, 2009), *Debt Relief Initiatives: Policy Design and Outcomes* (Ashgate, 2010), *Riciclaggio e Imprese* (Vita e Pensiero 2011).

Leonardo S. Borlini is Assistant Professor of EU Law and a Research Fellow at the Baffi Center on International Markets, Money and Regulation, Bocconi University, where he is also responsible for the participation of Bocconi University in the Anti-Corruption Academic Initiative (ACAD) under the patronage and coordination of the United Nations Office on Drugs and Crimes (UNODC). Dr. Borlini holds a BA cum laude in Economics and Business Administration from Bocconi University, a BA cum laude in Law from the University of Pavia, an LLM Magister Legum from the University of Cambridge and a PhD in International Law and Economics from Bocconi University. He was visiting scholar at Wolfson College, University of Cambridge in 2008. He has been teaching in numerous academic institutions, including the State University of Milan, the Free University of Social Studies LUISS of Rome and the Free University Institute "Luigi Catteneo" of Castellanza. He has published nationally and internationally on issues ranging from the law and economics of corruption and anti-money laundering to competition policy and antitrust law, WTO and EU legal systems. Besides his academic work, Dr. Borlini carries out a number of consultancy jobs. In addition to the International Monetary Fund and the World Bank, he was a consultant for the Italian Competition Authority. At an international level, he was part of the Italian delegation at both the OECD Working Group on Bribery's meeting for the evaluation of the Italian Implementing Law of the 1997 OECD Convention on Combating Corruption of Foreign Public Officials in International Business Transactions and the V Conference of State Parties to the UNCAC in November 2013.

He has published nationally and internationally on issues ranging from the law and economics of corruption and anti-money laundering, to competition policy and antitrust law, WTO and EU legal systems. His recent books and articles include: "The Economics of Money Laundering", in P. Reichel and J. Albanese (eds.), *Handbook of Transnational Crime and Justice*, 2nd edn. (Thousand Oaks, CA: Sage Publications, forthcoming 2014), pp. 227–43; "EU Anti-Money Laundering Regime: An Assessment within International and National Scenarios", Paolo Baffi Center Research Paper No. 2012–125, Bocconi Legal Studies Research Paper No. 2144122, available at: http://papers.ssrn.com/sol3/papers.cfm?abstract_id=2144122; "International Anti-Money Laundering Programs: Empirical Assessment and Issues of Criminal Regulation", with M. Arnone, in *Journal of Anti-Money Laundering Control*, 13(2), 2010, 226–71; "Methodological Issues of the 'More Economic Approach' to Unilateral Exclusionary Conduct. Proposal of Analysis Starting from the Treatment of Retroactive Rebates", *European Competition Journal*, August 2009; "Empirical Assessment and International Criminal Aspects of Anti-Money Laundering Law", with M. Arnone, in A. Sabitha (ed.), *Anti-Money Laundering: Transnational Criminal Regulation* (Hyderabad: Amicus Books, ICFAI, 2009); "Legal and Economic Appraisal of the 'More Economic Approach' to Unilateral Exclusionary Conduct: Regulation of Loyalty-Inducing Rebates (Case C-95/04P)", in T. Tridimas and P. Eeckhout (eds.), *Yearbook of European Law*, vol. 14, 2008 (Oxford: Oxford University Press, 2009); "A Claim for 'Soft Solutions' in Interconnecting the EU and WTO Legal System – Constitutional Issues and Implementation Exceptions: Is It Time to Lift Rigid Structures", in C. Dordi (ed.), *The Direct Effect of WTO Law in the European Community Legal System and in Other Countries*, The Interuniversity Centre on the Law of International Economic Organizations (CIDOIE) (Turin: Giappichelli, 2011).

Foreword

Pier Carlo Padoan[1]

The global financial crisis has prompted a rethink about growth models in several parts of the global economy. Once the deepest phase of the recession is over and the immediate causes of fragility have been repaired, it will be impossible to go back to business as usual. Growth models will have to be reconsidered, priorities will have to be restated, behavior and incentives will have to change to make growth more sustainable, more balanced, and more equal. This will require a strong push for structural reforms, delivering better labor markets, more competition in product markets, more efficiency in public administration. Available evidence indicates that structural reforms can increase potential growth rates by significant amounts while helping achieve fiscal consolidation and minimize social exclusion.

Structural reforms deliver results if they are well designed, but, also, if implemented effectively. This is where corruption enters the stage as a key determinant of success or failure in structural adjustment. As this very comprehensive and fascinating book by Marco Arnone and Leonardo Borlini shows, corruption can undermine the economic process in several interconnected ways. When dealing with public officials, there is a risk of a conflict of interest which increases as more space is left to discretion and the opportunity for corruption increases. This is relevant in the area of public spending as well as in tax collection, where the incidence of bribery increases as the system gets more complex. Corruption also proliferates where governance is weak since weak governance in both the private and public sector increases the areas of discretion.

A finding which bears directly on the impact of corruption on growth is the evidence that, where public and private corruption proliferates, markets are dominated by distortions and inefficiencies; in turn, the malfunctioning of markets generates advantages only for privileged lobbies, who are the insiders of the corrupt structure.

---

1 Italian Minister of Economy and Finance and former OECD Deputy Secretary General and Chief Economist.

In addition to undermining competitiveness, corrupt markets do not attract international capital flows and are associated with low growth (due to additional barriers to entry and the higher risk to investment caused by corruption). In short, corrupt countries are at a disadvantage compared with others. And the book documents the negative relationship between corruption and income per capita that holds for countries worldwide, including advanced, emerging, and developing economies. Fighting corruption is also a key principle when thinking about public administration reforms. Indeed over-lengthy bureaucratic procedures are generally associated with high levels of corruption.

On the bright side, the book documents the fact that economic crises lead to greater social responsiveness in the face of attempts to conceal cases of corruption. At the same time, when the need for fiscal consolidation following a crisis is large, thus leading to a reduction in public expenditure, conflicts between companies for limited public resources are exacerbated. This generates tensions that eventually lead to collaboration with the investigating authorities or, at least, make it more difficult for agreements to be reached and sustained on what to keep hidden.

Another important element related to the financial crisis is that corruption can affect the performance of financial markets and instruments, be they sophisticated as in advanced economies or still in their infancy, as in developing countries. Also, corruption affects the financial performance of firms, be they large listed corporations or relatively small microfinance institutions. The main point is that global investors require a substantially greater return on debt when the issuer is a more corrupt country. Conversely, a well-functioning and transparent financial system is a strong antidote against corruption. Indeed corruption is negatively correlated with quality and transparency of supervision; hence, transparency-based reforms of supervision would be useful to achieve multiple objectives (better institutional governance, better supervision, and lower corruption).

The second part of the book looks extensively at the legal instruments available at national and international level to fight corruption. The reader will find this part just as fascinating and useful as the first one. I would like to mention one aspect in this respect. The absence of corruption is a public good. A corruption-free global system would be a global public good. As is well known, public good production requires strong collective action and effective international collaboration in multi-country environments. One lesson from the global financial crisis is that global governance has lagged behind market integration, making the global system more risky and the costs of the crisis larger. Building a more stable and equitable global economy requires, as mentioned, a strong effort in structural reforms and adjustment. A stronger global governance is something that requires a corruption-free environment while being, at the same time, a powerful instrument to fight corruption. This requires, among other things, strong international institutions.

International approaches to fighting corruption are already bearing fruit. For example governments that adhere to and actively enforce anti-corruption standards, such as those in the OECD Anti-Bribery Convention, send a strong message to potential foreign investors that they are committed to providing a clean and stable environment for business. But there is more to it than that. Governments that adhere to the enforcement of international standards usually encourage their companies to adopt appropriate internal controls, ethics and compliance measures. These companies can more easily enter the supply and distribution chains of larger companies that are increasingly doing due diligence when contracting with third parties to avoid liability under domestic anti-corruption legislation, such as the United States Foreign Corrupt Practices Act and the United Kingdom Bribery Act.

Let me conclude with some warm thoughts about Marco Arnone. Marco was a great economist and a very good friend. I had the privilege of sharing with him many reflections and some work in the areas which he privileged, that is the deep and complex interactions between economics and institutions. As this book demonstrates, he mastered these issues quite thoughtfully. I learned a lot from him. Thank you Marco.

Foreword

Gabrio Forti[1]

Several works, drawing on a wide range of experiences and sciences (economics, political science, law, sociology, even psychology), have dealt in the last two decades with the thorny and tangled issue of corruption. Thanks to them we have accustomed our eyes to huge sets of international and national data, together with impressive descriptions of relevant wrongdoings and a bunch of elaborate reform schemes. Thus awareness of the massive harm caused by this crime has been more than adequately diffused among politicians, academics and practitioners. For a long time, even the renowned Transparency International Index appeared annually in most popular newspapers. Some countries' low rankings on the scale have often been highlighted, thus helping to focus the attention of public opinion on the problem and confronting them with the uneasy perception by *other* countries of the low reliability of their own to attract investors and entrepreneurs.

Marco Arnone and Leonardo Borlini have aptly chosen as the epigraph for their book a sentence by the great reformer of criminal law in eighteenth century Europe, Cesare Beccaria, namely that "crimes are only to be measured by the injury done to society". The two authors actually dismiss the main traditional arguments put forward by certain economic theories that corruption serves to grease the wheels of commerce, thus reducing transaction costs and lowering the cost of capital. They extensively and convincingly show that the injury done to society by corruption is enormous; that, besides losing competitiveness, corrupt markets do not attract international capital flows and are marked by low growth. Moreover corrupt countries are at a disadvantage in comparison with others, as corruption not only reduces public revenues, but also has a negative impact on the allocative decisions of governments, heavily influenced by relationships based on patronage, to favor low productivity investment which compromises growth, as well as reducing public investment in education and health, thus compromising the standard of

---

1 Professor of Criminal Law, Catholic University of Milan, Italy.

health and human development of citizens. As put forward by Roubini (2008), and quoted in the book, when corruption extensively penetrates public and private realms, uncertainty rises in the financial system as well, nullifying the correct functioning of the market mechanism in an inherently unstable sector, with potentially destructive consequences for the whole economy.

It seems however paradoxical that, despite the huge amount of serious research put forward as evidence of the devastating injuries stemming from corruption, politicians, administrators and common citizens remain substantially unaffected or at least affected in a way quite disproportionate to the high global price that this "cancer" (according to a metaphor recurrent in seminars and conferences devoted to the evils of corruption) is bound to exact from the moral and material resources of entire populations. Even the upsurge of indignation prompted by the financial crisis hasn't yet marked a real turning point (certainly in Italy), apart from some reforms that have still not been able to inject sufficient adrenaline into the muscles to prevent corrupt practices.

As emphasized in the book, corruption is highly persistent, which means that "domestic corruption is stable over time and does not vary significantly on a year-to-year basis". A feature due to the fact that "corruption is the fruit of multiple coexisting factors, many of which are of an environmental nature, and is not significantly subject to influence from one-time, ad hoc policies with temporary effects".

The persistence of high rates of corruption in many countries offers more than a hint of well-intentioned reformers aiming at establishing good integrity standards or maintaining them in the long run also in the most virtuous countries: it should be matched by an equal and contrary "virtuous" persistence of integrity standards in economic, legal, and social policies. This is a great challenge to national and international regulatory endeavors, particularly prone to aiming at short-sighted measures, often overvalued and sold on the vociferous electoral market. The principle stated, for example in the German Federal Constitution (§ 20a), which requires the State to protect the natural conditions of life, thereby taking responsibility for future generations, should also steer any regulation aimed in the long run at preserving an "environment" of public integrity in our late-modern institutions and social lives.

We could also say that the persistence, together with the elusiveness of corruption, as clearly stated in the book, stems from the extreme difficulty "of identifying the causal direction of the dynamics on which it is based; causes and effects are strongly interconnected with feedbacks that can hardly be isolated: the 'effects' negatively influence their 'causes'". Chasing the multi-directional causal chains which make up the phenomenon and its main damaging power requires indeed the ability to combine different knowledges and competences, and, what is more, a broad cultural vision that stretches beyond the boundaries of single technical skills.

In Part I of the book,[2] Marco Arnone would seem to have been blessed with the rare ability to embrace the intricacies of corruption dynamics through a wide "vision" and to combine his understanding with the persistence to track down the many noxious vicious circles which make corruption a sort of auto-immune self-replicating disease: "where corruption is pervasive and public officials pursue their individual interests, regulations governing society reflect bad governance. In these circumstances the laws appear not to oppose corruption and low-quality institutions".

In spite of being a law scholar myself, I can only appreciate the critical remarks expressed in the book to legal experts bent on combating corruption solely or mainly with the armoury of rules and sanctions. They often seem to act within "the boundaries of a Newtonian world" and are therefore "at a loss in dealing with complexity, that is, the emergent properties of a system formed by recognizable and simple elements". I am also in full agreement that it's not enough for criminal experts to prosecute individual elements of the system or that "law-makers regulate market infrastructure", since "what we need is to understand complexity and modify our legal systems to minimize these negative impacts".

These comments sound really Machiavellian, in quite the best (and strictly etymological) meaning of the word, to the effect that they show due attention to an aspect often neglected by lawyers, legislators and economists as well, as highlighted in Chapter XV of *The Prince*, where the great Florentine thinker expounds his intent "to write something useful to whoever understands it", and then "more fitting to go directly to the effectual truth of the thing than to the imagination of it". Actually the ease with which legislators can write down their rules fatally exposes them to the lures of the imagination, as it gives rise to the delusion of fully controlling social processes just through a few blots of ink, which more often than not means they fail to grasp the quite dynamic "effectual truth" of social and economic processes. As Remo Bodei wrote recently, commenting on this Machiavellian sentence (*Il Sole – 24 ore*, 24 March 2013), the art of governing according to reason and justice and to temper conflict and order requires the ability to track down and mold such "effectual truth" (the German *Wirklichkeit*), which is a moving flow of historical energies,

---

[2] Written by Marco Arnone. Leonardo Borlini co-authored Part I, Chapter 1; Chapter 2, Sections 2.1, 2.2, 2.3, 2.4.2, 2.4.4; Chapter 3, Sections 3.3.2, 3.7; Chapter 7, Section 7.4.1.2.

absolutely not a static picture once and for all encompassed within a set framework of desultory schemes (and laws).

It is not only the absent-mindedness or limited vision of legal theory and approach that should be remedied thanks to a wider, mobile perspective. Economic theory too requires to be vigorously driven towards "the effectual truth of the thing" and away from "the imagination of it". Suffice it to mention the infamous (yet for decades rather influential) "trickle-down theory", which assumes that the benefits of economic policies can trickle down from the wealthy to everyone else, fostering for the most part, on these false premises, heavy tax cuts. As Steven Greenhouse puts it (*The Big Squeeze*, 2008) trickle-down economics didn't actually work, as revealed by a terrific worsening of income inequality, which suggested rather a trickling up of prosperity (e.g. in America, household incomes tripled for the richest 1 percent of households and grew 80 percent for the top fifth, while increasing only 6 percent for the bottom fifth).

Marco Arnone, one of the authors and the mentor of this book, was not only a clever young economist, but a true renaissance man, with his deep knowledge of various fields, curiosity about many of the humanities (whose mastery seemed to him a prerequisite for any technical and professional approach) and rare open-mindedness and readiness to listen to and learn from non-economist researchers, including lawyers and legal scholars, for whom he always displayed great respect and the genuine expectation of receiving helpful hints in finding ways to deal with economic and social problems: a trait not easily found among economists, especially in recent times.

The legal approach, with all its rigidities and limitations, is undeniably helpful in devising regulatory measures aimed at a reduction in the complexity (and opacity) of economic and, especially, financial practices, which the book deems unchecked so far and thus a source of gross instability at the macro and micro level. The strategy recommended is one equivalent to keeping a biological system in check when cells replicate, eliminating wrong and/or dangerous mutations: "if the organism fails, then cancer ensues: the strategy to fight cancer is exactly that of limiting the complexity of cancer cell replications and interactions". The role of legal and criminal experts is then particularly valued, especially within schemes aimed at prosecuting not only individuals, but also emergent properties and organizations that misbehave (as is the case with Italian law 231/2001 on the criminal-administrative responsibility of legal persons).

Actually Marco Arnone felt and expressed a deep loyalty himself to the "rule of law", thus not only understanding the paramount importance of this principle and requirement for a public life based on democracy, legality and human rights protection, but even assuming it as a kind of moral and social standard of human decency, quite opposite to that self-satisfied acquisitive attitude which Jorge Maria Bergoglio, now Pope Francis, described in 2005 (in a public address recently published) as making up the "heart of the corrupted man", resistant to redemption, being sealed up against external dialogue and respect for other people's (and also his own) dignity.

Entirely consistent with his wide-ranging humanistic and cultivated way of thinking and living, Marco Arnone particularly emphasized, among the double directions of causation deemed the most relevant, the one linking education and corruption. As he had already shown in one of his previous works (written with E. Iliopulos, *Corruption Costs*, 2005), corruption is often associated with cutting expenditure on education and thus with falling cultural standards in a country, with devastating effect on the quality of governance: "less educated citizens are inevitably less conscious voters, penalized by a weakened ability to influence the political course of the country", an argument which has gathered further support in recent empirical evidence from the United States, revealing a significant relationship between the extension of corrupt practices and the number of citizens with only a primary level of education.

Looking at Part II of the book,[3] on the "birth and evolution of an anti-corruption global legal standard", the reader is comforted by the description of the huge advances in international hard law instruments deployed in the field, but also frankly overwhelmed by the intricacies of legal issues involved in the fight against corruption, laid bare by the cases of transnational corruption discussed therein. The different ways of criminalizing the offence and sanctions among various countries, the many distinctions in conceiving corporate liability, the quite thorny jurisdictional and mutual legal assistance issues, the slow progress in asset recovery achievements, the measures and the need for sound follow-up procedures: we feel that, apart from persistent distractions, the path yet to be trodden is still very long and littered with hindrances and traps. It should however be strenuously followed, especially with the aim of reshaping a "global governance, that goes beyond the nation-State toward a bloc-sized global financial and legal management, in areas such as finance and transnational crime, further invigorating all multilateral organizations, and in particular the International Monetary Fund, the World Bank, the OECD, and the multilateral financial institutions in general".

Due to the intertwining causal chains and feedbacks which make corruption so complex a phenomenon to deal with at any level, the most

---

3 Written by Leonardo Borlini.

suitable strategy would be to target it not only through frontal onslaughts, but, with much more effectiveness, through an encirclement maneuver capable of eroding the ground and draining the sources through which this "cancer" of civil society, politics and administration draws its vital nutrition. However such an elusive, almost homeopathic, bunch of remedies, conceived to counter the elusiveness of corruption, should single out the predominant causal directions to be addressed first within long-running and wide-ranging reforms.

In a 1996 Conference on Responding to Corruption, which took place in Italy, Robert Klitgaard pleaded for the targeting of a few "big fish", whose cases should be prosecuted first. I think that any anti-corruption strategy, unwilling to be sucked into the micromanagement of the too many variables at stake, should select as its "big fish" some well-localized but also essential target areas, in other words, it should concentrate its efforts on those "jugular veins" of corruption whose cutting will obstruct the flow of the most noxious of its vicious circles.

If, according to the World Bank distinction, there are two main types of corruption – State capture and administrative corruption (where the concept of State capture concerns all illegal actions aimed at influencing the decision-making process of policy making in the different spheres of the life of a country) – the first "big fish" to be targeted should be just State capture. As aptly highlighted in the book, this kind of all-out corruption "leads to the destruction of the 'intangible goods' of society", "jeopardizes institutional credibility, legitimacy, and image in the forum of public opinion; it encourages illegal acts and, therefore, speeds up its own diffusion and enhances a self-reinforcing process". Actually governance variables have a strong causal link to corruption of any kind, as the "spreading of corruptive episodes depends on the qualitative characteristics of governance"; "good governance minimizes the conflict of interest and areas of discretion (necessary preconditions to make corruption possible); sets effective rules, creates reliable institutions and also sets in place an effective system of prevention, control and punishment of deviant behavior".

Moving from these basic premises, a crackdown on conflict of interest (and on tax evasions and tax havens, from which the resources for kickbacks are mainly drawn) appears to be the primary step towards prevention of State capture, the most noxious kind of corruption from which a large part of administrative and (comparatively) minor political corruptions (here properly) "trickle down".

In one of the most original sections of the book, jointly written by Carlo Bellavite Pellegrini and Laura Pellegrini and devoted to the impact of corruption on financial markets, the first part of the book describes how the element of "capture" can be endemic to certain economic systems, where economic entities have some degree of market power due to connections with higher political echelons. Such connections do not necessarily originate monetary transactions, but can take more indirect forms, like the trading of influences. Empirical evidence confirms that access to finance is one key factor in determining the success of new businesses and the competitiveness of new market entrants and that politically connected firms enjoy better access to finance, stronger market power and tax benefits, while, conversely, performing generally worse than other businesses. Italy (where 79 industrial and holding listed firms have been politically connected with 44 politicians from 1987 to 2006) "represents a telling example of an industrialized and democratic country, where the impact of political connections within the economic system is considerable".

We could even say that, together with the blurring of any divide between the public and private sector, the evolutionary stage of illicit practices dissolves the same distinction of roles between briber and the bribed increasingly played by the same political or economic (politics and economics cease to be separate) entities. This is the climax, the apotheosis of corruption, in the sense of confusion and loss of the original form of things which *should* be kept clearly distinct. After having reached this stage, the cancer of corruption is well planted in the pith and marrow of society and its mores. It's quite apparent therefore that such an invasive presence in a given market of politically-connected firms "cannot be effectively coped with through regulatory responses, and calls for radical systemic reforms".

Considering the great gap existing between the widespread awareness of the injuries of corruption and the real efforts to contain it, any serious anti-corruption policy could not help addressing pointedly also what I would call the "anaesthetic of corruption", namely the "weapons of mass distraction" which paralyse the ability of individuals, institutions and societies to act in accordance with such awareness.

Drawing on the ample definition of corruption provided by the book, as "an abuse of public office for private gain", we get a good first explanation of this numbing effect inherent in the wrongdoing. Corruption stems from inequality and further enlarges the areas of inequality. As the book well details, "corruption favors the interests of those who know the rules of a game in which there is a concentration of power and money". Thus "the insider-outsider structure that comes to be inevitably determined results in vicious circles that tend to favor stronger strata of society, who have access to large resources or hold strategic positions". On the one hand, "the basis of corruption dynamics consists precisely in the disparity of conditions faced by different economic actors"; on the other hand, corruption itself "can raise social inequality remarkably".

As Michael Sandel (2009) puts it, we suffer (not only in America) from a dearth of attention to inequality in contemporary politics and the most important reason to worry about the growing inequality in many societies (as confirmed also for various European countries, like Italy, by recent data developed from the Gini coefficient, used as a measure of inequality of *income* or *wealth*) is that the yawning of a huge gap between rich and poor undermines the solidarity required by democratic citizenship, leading the privileged to secede from public institutions and facilities, and thus to a kind of cultural and human desertification of those institutions that once gathered people together and served as informal schools of civic virtue.

In a few words: it brings about what has been aptly called the hollowing out of the public realm and, we could add, the hollowing out of any persistent rule of law.

Since inequality and conflict of interest are the powerful breeding grounds of corruption (besides being its damaging outcomes), targeting them at any level, through far-reaching systemic reforms, should be the primary way to break the vicious circles of the ever expanding corrupt flow. Albeit difficult, this is not mission impossible, and in any case it is inescapable for any anti-corruption policy bent on achieving good integrity standards and not merely interested in exhibiting its self-righteousness or in selling junk reforms to easily distracted (or contented) audiences.

It is greatly to the credit of Marco Arnone's friend and colleague Carlo Bellavite Pellegrini that he patiently collected and edited, together with Laura Pellegrini – both co-authors of three chapters in the first part of the book – one of his most worthy intellectual legacies, which is not only his substantial contribution to this book, but the very idea of writing and publishing it, coupling economic and legal doctrines and expertise in such a way as to provide a sound and enlightening reference work for any future anti-corruption awareness and policy.

Acknowledgements

We wish to thank colleagues and friends at the IMF, the World Bank, the Inter-American Development Bank and the United Nations Office on Drugs and Crime: Jonathan Agar, Lisa Bhansali, Pascale Dubois, Roberto De Michele, Yara Esquivel, Francisco Figueroa, Matthew R. Fowler, Marianne Mathias, Richard Messick, Roberto Manrique, Andrew Milford, Jody Myers, Marco Nicoli, Jean Pesme, Maurizio Ragazzi, Alessandro Rebucci, Juan Roderos, Kenneth Stephenson, Oliver Stolpe, Kate Sylvester, Emil J. M. Van Der Does De Willebois, Concepcion Verdugo Yepes, Dimitri Vlassis, Staurt Yikona and participants in the seminars, *Corruption: Economic Analysis and Evolution of the International Law and Institutions*, and *Corruption, Markets and Competition: a Microeconomic Analysis*, respectively, given at the World Bank (Washington, DC) on 25 May 2011 and at the International Monetary Fund (Washington, DC) on 14 January 2014 for their invaluable feedbacks and suggestions on earlier drafts of parts of this book. Extra special thanks to Francesca Recanatini and Laura Valli, and to Gianluca Esposito, Nadim Sami Kyriakos-Saad, Emmanuel Mathias, and Eric Robert for their thought-provoking observations and experience, for their wonderful hospitality at the World Bank and the International Monetary Fund and for organizing the two seminars.

We also wish to thank the Arnone Bellavite Pellegrini Foundation, CeMaFIR (Centre for Macroeconomics and Finance Research), and Carlo Bellavite Pellegrini, CEO of the Foundation, for making possible the realization of this book. We are grateful to the magistrates who participated in the conferences International Cooperation in the Fight Against Corruption and Investigative Techniques and Standards of Proof in the Area of Crimes Against the Public Sector, both given at the Higher Council for the Judiciary, Rome, on 30 May and 27 September 2012, respectively, for their stimulating feedback and suggestions on an earlier draft of Part I of this book. We are also grateful to participants in several other seminars, where early draft chapters were presented, given at the Scuola Superiore della Pubblica Amministrazione, Rome, and the University of Pisa.

We are also especially indebted to Alberto Alessandri, Andrea Biondi,

Thomas Botzios, Luigi Campiglio, Andrea Canale, Gherardo Colombo, Giuseppe Sean Coppola, Piercamillo Davigo, Luca De Matteis, Francesco De Simone, Andrea Di Stefano, Claudio Dordi, Piet Eeckhout, Gianmaria Flick, Paola Gaeta, Alessandro Gambini, Federico Ghezzi, Franzo Grande Stevens, Rodolfo Jannaccone-Pazzi, Tom Lasich, Paola Magrini, Grazia Mannozzi, Paola Mariani, Donato Masciandaro, Piergiorgio Morosini, Luz Estella Nagle, Nikos Passas, Piercarlo Padoan, Mark Pieth, August Reinisch, Lorenzo Salazar, Jack D. Smith, Francesco Testa, Gabriella Venturini, Eduardo Vetere, Takis Tridimas and members of the Catholic University of Milan Centro Studi "Federico Stella" per il diritto penale e la politica criminale (CSGP), Matteo Caputo, Francesco Centonze, Francesco D'Alessandro, Stefania Giavazzi, directed by Gabrio Forti, for discussions and suggestions on the issues addressed here and their support in pursuing this project. We would also like to extend our warm gratitude to the colleagues of the Department of Legal Studies, Bocconi University, Milan, and, especially, to Damiano Canale, Stefano Liebman and Giorgio Sacerdoti for their generous support of the last period of research dedicated to the finalization of the book.

We would also like to thank Carlo Bellavite Pellegrini for his contribution to Chapters 5 and 6; Laura Pellegrini, for her contribution to Chapters 4 and 5; Emiliano Sironi for his technical comments on these chapters and Luciano Canova for his help with the data. The dedicated work of Giulio Nessi was crucial in finalizing this publication.

Our special thanks go to our publisher Edward Elgar for the attention and professional support offered during the different phases of our work.

Finally, our gratitude goes to Josephine Fontana, Anthony Turner and Silvia Pedrini for the excellent research environment in Sarasota, Washington, DC, and Pavia respectively.

Abbreviations

ABM	Arnone, Bellavite Pellegrini, and Messa
ADB	Asian Development Bank
AfDB	African Development Bank
AML	Anti-Money Laundering
AU	African Union
BCP	Basel core principles
BNP	Banque Nationale de Paris S.A.A.
BPI	Bribe payers index
CDCJ	European Committee on Legal Co-operation
CDPC	European Committee on Crime Problems
CFA	Committee on Fiscal Affairs
CFIU	Corruption and Fraud Investigations Unit (World Bank)
CFT	Countering Financing of Terrorism
CIA	Central Intelligence Agency
COE	Council of Europe
CoECivLCC	Council of Europe Civil Law Convention
CoECLCC	Council of Europe Criminal Law Convention on Corruption
COSP	Conference of State Parties (UNCAC)
CPI	Corruption perceptions index
CPI	Consumer price index
CRPD	Company Risk Profile Database (World Bank)
DOJ	Department of Justice (US)
EAW	European Arrest Warrant
EBC	Office of Ethics and Business Conduct (World Bank)
EBRD	European Bank for Reconstruction and Development
EC	European Communities
ECB	European Central Bank
ECHR	European Court of Human Rights
ECJ	European Court of Justice
EITI	Extractive Industries Transparency Initiative
EJN	European Judicial Network in Criminal Matters
EO	Evaluation and Suspension Officer (World Bank)

EOS	Executive opinion survey
EPC	Engineering – procurement – construction
EPPO	European Public Prosecutor's Office
EU	European Union
EU Report	EU Anti-corruption Report
FATF	Financial Action Task Force
FCPA	Foreign Corrupt Practices Act (USA)
FD	Framework decision
FDI	Foreign direct investments
FE model	Fixed effect model
FIU	Financial Intelligence Unit
FSAP	Financial sector assessment program
GAC Strategy	Governance and Anticorruption Strategy (World Bank)
GCI	Global competitiveness index
GDP	Gross domestic product
GMC	Multidisciplinary Group on Corruption
GNP	Gross national product
GPA	General Procurement Agreement (World Trade Organization)
GRECO	Group of States against Corruption – Council of Europe
HRBA	Human rights-based approach to development
IAIS	International Association of Insurance Supervisors
IBRD	International Bank for Reconstruction and Development
ICJ	International Court of Justice
ICO	Integrity Compliance Officer (World Bank)
ICRG	International Country Risk Guide
ICSID	International Centre for Settlement of Investment Disputes
IDA	International Development Association
IDB	Inter-American Development Bank
IFC	International Finance Corporation
IFI	International financial institutions
IIC	Independent Inquiry Committee
IMD	International Institute for Management Development
IMF	International Monetary Fund
INT	Integrity Vice Presidency (World Bank)
IOSCO	International Organization of Securities Commissions
IRG	Implementation Review Group (UNCAC)
LC	Letter of credit

LSDV	Least square dummy variable
MDBs	Multilateral Development Banks
MESICIC	Follow-up Mechanism for the Implementation of the Inter-American Convention against Corruption
MFI	Microfinance institutions
MIGA	Multilateral Investment Guarantee Agency
MIX	Microfinance information exchange
ML	Money Laundering
NGO	Non-governmental organization
NICS	Newly industrialized countries
OAS	Organization of American States
OAS Convention	Inter-American Convention Against Corruption
OAU	Organization of African Unity
OECD	Organisation for Economic Co-operation and Development
OLAF	European Anti-Fraud Office
OLS	Ordinary least squares
ORAF	Operational Risk Management Framework
OSD	Office of Suspension and Debarment (World Bank)
PEP	Politically Exposed Person
PFI Convention	Convention on the Protection of the European Communities' Financial Interests (26.7.1995)
Procedures	World Bank Sanctions Procedures
PRGs	Partial risk guarantees (World Bank)
PSU	Preventive Services Unit (World Bank)
RE model	Random effect model
ROA	Returns on assets
ROL	Rule of law
S&P	Standard and Poor
SAE	Statement of Accusations and Evidence (World Bank)
SDO	Chief Suspension and Debarment Officer
SEC	Securities and Exchange Commission (USA)
SME	Small- and medium-sized enterprises
SOMO	State Oil Marketing Organization (Iraq)
SOX	Sarbanes-Oxley Act (USA)
StAR	Stolen asset recovery initiative (UNODC-World Bank)
TEU	Treaty on the European Union
TFEU	Treaty on the Functioning of the European Union
TI	Transparency International
UNCAC	United Nations Convention against Corruption
UNCTOC	United Nations Convention against Transnational Organized Crime

UNDP	United Nations Development Program
UNESCO	United Nations Educational, Scientific and Cultural Organizations
UNIDROIT	International Institute for the Unification of Private Law
UNODC	United Nations Office on Drugs and Crime
VAT	Value-added tax
VCLT	1969 Vienna Convention on the Law of the Treaties
VDP	Voluntary Disclosure Program (World Bank)
WB	World Bank
WEF	World Economic Forum
WEO	World Economic Outlook
WGB	OECD Working Group on Bribery
WGI	Worldwide Governance Indicators
WTO	World Trade Organization

Introduction

Crimes are only to be measured by the injury done to society
(Cesare Beccaria, *Of Crimes and Punishments*, 1764)

1. CORRUPTION: DEFINITIONS AND CHARACTERISTICS

Corruption is a multi-faceted phenomenon, even more so when it is so deeply rooted as to be considered "normal". The problem related to defining it is strictly connected with the multiplicity of aspects that mark the phenomenon and with the difficulty of distinguishing it from other kinds of illegal acts or even from behaviors which are borderline but still legal. Here we address corruption in relationships between public and private sector, but make some reference to private sector corruption; the latter is analysed further in Part II where international treaties against corruption are addressed specifically.

From a very general legal perspective, corruption can be defined as "a deterioration in the decisional process that characterizes all cases where the decider (a private or a public agent) accepts to, or asks for, deviating from the criteria that should lead his (or her) decision for his (or her) private gain; however, the reasons that lead his action cannot justify his decision" (Huber 2002). This behavioral definition focuses on key aspects of the phenomenon: the concepts of exchange of favors and abuse of power. Since our analysis is based on data collected by Transparency International (TI), we follow its definition of corruption: an abuse of public office for private gain. While acknowledging that one of the two parties needs to be a public economic agent, there is no distinction between administrative and political corruption. However, in general the episodes of corruption can involve either one agent (or more) from the public sector and one private agent (or more); or two parties within the private sector.

This study concentrates on the dynamics involved in episodes of bribery between the private and public sector; in this case, corruption does not only affect economic development but distorts the policy-making process and its enforcement. Having said that, corruption within the private sector is a significant phenomenon and has recently been the subject of legal studies (Forti 2003b).

The World Bank (2002b) makes a distinction between the two main types of corruption: State capture and administrative corruption (we also mention so-called "grand corruption", which can be defined as abuse by public officials or the theft of public resources). The latter concerns all public employees' or public officials' actions for private gain that distort the application and enforcement of existing laws or rules; generally, these actions grant exemptions or tax allowances to specific agents. Alternatively, they are aimed at giving priority access to public services to an élite of agents.

The concept of State capture concerns all illegal actions aimed at influencing the decision-making process of policy making in the different spheres of the life of a country. Public opinion is an important input in policy making: it assures that the needs of citizens are taken into account by the authorities, while keeping the latter under scrutiny (and making them accountable to their voters). On the contrary, the concept of State capture concerns all actions exploiting illegal and secret channels that aim at favoring the interests of specific groups at the expense of everybody else. These channels are clearly accessible only to a limited group of "insiders" at the expense of those who are "outsiders" and do not participate in bribery.

The dynamics of corruption can be either organized centrally, by a single central group of agents inside the institutions, or decentralized throughout the system. Easterly (2002) shows that the number of episodes of bribery tends to increase when corruption is decentralized; however, when the dynamics of corruption are centrally organized, the average value of bribes tends to be larger.

We try to identify the peculiar features of corruption and the context in which it grows and spreads out. Bribery goes deep into the structures of public administration, limiting its ability to pursue economic and institutional goals; it interferes at the decision-making level by modifying general goals to the advantage of hidden parties; it compromises plans by thwarting the effective implementation of rules set by the authorities. It also interferes with the decision-making power of individuals by twisting the principles which guide their actions. The multi-faceted features that characterize the phenomenon confer on corruption a strong elusiveness. The elusiveness of corruption makes it difficult for politicians to fully understand the complexity of this phenomenon. If, on the one hand, aspects of bribery are clearly recognizable, on the other hand, their most dangerous effects are not directly measurable and lead to the destruction of the "intangible goods" of society. Corruption jeopardizes institutional credibility, legitimacy, and image in the forum of public opinion; it encourages illegal acts and, therefore, speeds up its own diffusion and enhances a self-reinforcing process.

2. PRECONDITIONS FOR CORRUPTION

The economic and legal literature describes a whole set of preconditions which constitute breeding grounds for episodes of corruption; it is concerned with those factors which, given agents with the same moral standards, encourage this kind of behavior.

The protection of its own citizens is the primeval function of the State, and also its origin (Pirenne 2010: 120). Citizens "delegate" powers to others, who voice their needs. These latter agents, however, also have personal private interests; thus, whenever their private interests are "compared" with the public welfare, a conflict of interest can arise. Indeed, thanks to the nature of their position, public officials are in a position that facilitates the fulfillment of their personal interests.

Not all aspects of the life of a State can be codified a priori. The residual aspects are thus left to the discretion of public agents. However, their action is limited by the supervision of the judiciary, by the control of citizens via the electoral process, and by public opinion. The degrees of freedom of public officials are at the root of possible conflict of interest: the more space is left to discretion, the more conflict of interest may arise. Therefore, if conflict of interest is not controlled and limited, a breeding ground exists for the spreading of episodes of corruption.

Corruption spreads in those areas of discretion characterized by strong concentration of political and economic power given to public officials.

For instance, too large areas of discretion are at the root of the episodes of bribery that affect the process of public spending. Indeed, if the process is characterized by conflicts of interest, decisions could be directed towards private gains instead of welfare considerations: tenders for public infrastructures involve large amounts of money; they represent an important source of profit for private agents; when systems are corrupt, tenders are often linked to the payment of bribes. In turn, wrong motivations lead to unproductive investments; to have an idea of the effect of decisions led by corruption instead of public welfare, one can think of investments with useless features (the so-called "white elephants") or infrastructure placed in non-strategic locations (the so-called "cathedrals in the desert"). Similarly, one dimension of public activity where discretion is most critical is tax collection; in particular, empirical evidence (Tanzi 2002) shows that the more complex the tax system, the more the episodes of bribery.

In addition, the more the collection of taxes allows for contact between citizens and tax collectors, the more bribery occurs. Indeed, the possibility to have contact with citizens gives tax collectors some bargaining power. It should be noted that fund-raising activities that are aimed at influencing policy making are not per se classifiable as bribery. Insider-outsider dynamics arise only whenever the tools to raise funds and the channels used to affect political decisions are secret and illegal, and thus only accessible to a group of insiders.

3. GOVERNANCE

Corruption is mostly characterized by the difficulty of identifying the causal direction of the dynamics on which it is based; causes and effects are strongly interconnected with feedbacks that can hardly be isolated: the "effects" negatively influence their "causes".

The attempt to isolate cause from effect should be understood in the light of the strong limitations imposed by the presence of multi-directional causal chains. Cause and effect are recognized as such according to the predominance of the causal direction which empirical literature usually ascertains through econometric analysis.

The empirical literature recognizes governance variables as the main ones in the causal link to corruption. The actual spreading of corruptive episodes depends on the qualitative characteristics of governance. Good governance minimizes the conflict of interest and areas of discretion (necessary preconditions for the presence of corruption); sets effective rules, creates reliable institutions and also sets in place an effective system of prevention, control and punishment of deviant behavior. In this context, prevention of conflict of interest needs to be considered as a fundamental step towards prevention of corruption.

Keeping all other factors fixed, the level of domestic corruption is inversely related to the effectiveness of controls and punishment for episodes of bribery. Clearly, the larger the probability of being punished, the lower the number of episodes of corruption. Notice, however, that if on the one hand the number of illegal acts decreases, on the other hand, the amounts involved per bribery may increase (Rose-Ackerman 1997). Finally, the allocation of risks and benefits among agents depends also on their bargaining power: the more powerful the agent, the larger their benefit.

If governance is not strong enough to prevent episodes of public and private corruption, markets are dominated by distortions and inefficiencies; in turn, the mismanagement of markets generates advantages only for privileged lobbies, these being the insiders of the corrupt structure. The incentive to join these lobbies weakens governance more and more.

Besides losing competitiveness, corrupt markets do not attract international capital flows and are marked by low growth (due to additional barriers to entry and the risk to investment caused by corruption). Corrupt countries are at a disadvantage compared with others: just consider that corruption not only reduces public revenues, but also has a negative impact on allocative decisions. A corrupt government does not allocate public revenues according to a project's qualitative features, but is heavily influenced by relationships based on patronage. Public investments are then characterized by low productivity which, in turn, compromises growth. Finally, in countries marked by pervasive corruption, governments tend to reduce public investment in education and health. It is consequently a truism that corruption impacts markets, and the dynamics of public bureaucracy jeopardize the fulfillment of the primary needs of the people. Corruption compromises the standard of health and human development of citizens, via the impact on investment in public health and education; cutting expenditure on education leads to a fall in the cultural standards of a country, and this has a devastating effect on the quality of governance: less educated citizens are inevitably less conscious voters, penalized by a weakened ability to influence the political course of the country. The negative feedback on the quality of governance is then evident.

Figure I.1 depicts the economic and social effects of corruption. The solid arrows indicate the main causal direction, from governance to

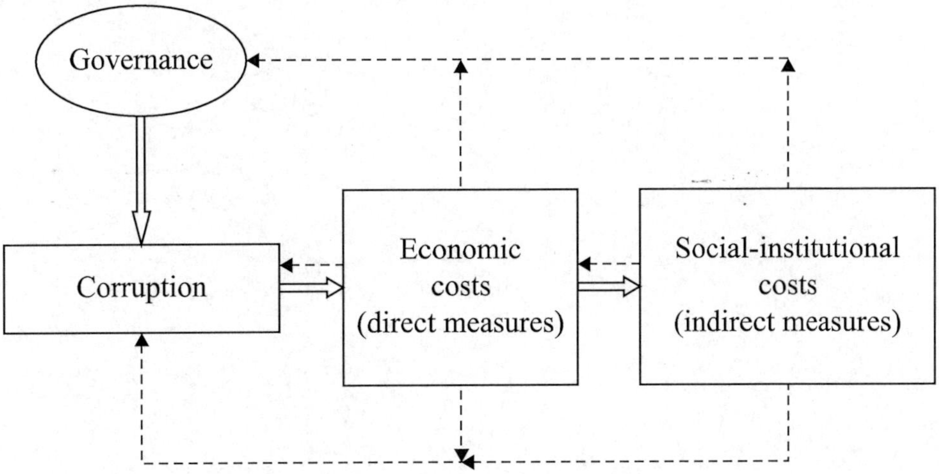

Figure I.1 Causal relationships (or interaction) between economic and social effects and governance

corruption, from corruption to economic costs (direct measures) and social-institutional costs (indirect measures). The broken lines reveal the feedback effects, which turn out to be weaker in comparison with the main causal relationships.

PART I

Economics, finance, and governance

EMERGENT PROPERTIES AND COMPLEX FINANCIAL MARKETS

When we deal with financial markets we know that they are formed by market infrastructures, individual agents, and flows of information/money. These are the basic constituents. But where does the invisible hand analogy comes from? It derives from the interactions among all these elements; the invisible hand is an emergent property of markets: the invisible hand is the structure of interactions and feedbacks in a non-linear dynamic system.

The analysis of the individual fundamentals is like Newtonian physics, where interactions are very simple, and we can do away with them. In a world of complexity, we need to analyze the emergent properties: an analogy can be drawn with statistical mechanics. In a gas, individual molecules are pretty well known, their precise behavior cannot be described simply, but only with the help of a random element. However, the aggregate behavior of the gas is an emergent property that can be described by specific and testable laws.

In a human, emergent properties are conscience, will, and creativity, derived from the interactions of billions of neurons. Alas, we still don't know how to reconstruct or replicate these properties.

In financial markets, where many humans interact, complexity is extremely high, and we have rationalized only a few emergent properties, like the metaphor of the invisible hand, equilibrium prices, and quantities. But what other emergent properties are there that we still ignore? For example, what is the threshold of stability for prices (see technical analysis, stop-loss rules in the aggregate)?

Even worse: with financial derivatives we introduce a higher degree of complexity because many of them are customized, prices are not public, contracts are not in a repository.

In this case we are no longer in the realm of a Newtonian world: we keep switching between the micro (particle physics world) and the macro (relativity), but we ignore how to go from one to the other (just as in physics, although quantum gravity theoretical physicists are trying hard).

Legal experts are still within the boundaries of a Newtonian world, so they are at a loss in dealing with complexity, that is, the emergent properties of a system formed by recognizable and simple elements. Criminal experts can prosecute an individual element of the system, a finance person that violates the law; lawmakers can draw up rules to regulate market infrastructure; they and the bureaucracy can limit what services or information can travel via this infrastructure (dirty money, derivatives, pornography). There have been only limited attempts at regulating emergent properties and reducing complexity: improved governance at the corporate, market, and country level. But this is definitely not enough. Breaking complexity (and limiting negative emergent properties) is a rough attempt. What we need is to understand complexity and modify our legal systems to minimize these negative impacts.

But what is negative and positive in this context? For 30 years financial theory has been ideologically bent on assuring everybody that the pursuit of individual utility would *necessarily* bring about the best aggregate outcome for everybody, although economists know very well about market failures.

But finance has been given a free pass on everything, by letting its players decide what is positive and negative. One cannot be a player and the rule-maker: there is a plain conflict of interest (a negative emergent property), which is the logical and operational foundation of corruption.

It is time for economists to abandon this ideological assumption depicting a Dr. Panglossian world, and for society to come to a decision about what real-life finance should aim at: this means that society should freely and democratically choose what is positive or negative in finance and its institutions (banks, hedge funds, central banks).

This means that the complexity of finance could and should be curtailed if it does not lead to measurable improvements in people's welfare. The unchecked growth of complexity has been shown to lead to gross instability at the macro and micro level. If parts of the system need to be linearized, so be it. While in the meantime adjusting our instruments to understand this complex system.

This strategy is equivalent to keeping a biological system in check when cells replicate, eliminating wrong and/or dangerous mutations; if the organism fails, then cancer ensues: the strategy to fight cancer is exactly that of limiting the complexity of cancer cell replications and interactions.

Legal and criminal experts have a role in this process: moving from prosecuting an individual to considering the possibility of *prosecuting emergent properties* and organizations that misbehave (Chapter 12). The Italian law 231/2001 for the criminal responsibility of the legal person, especially firms, together with its legislation against criminal organizations – probably the most advanced in the world – moves exactly in this direction and should be reinforced. To this end, corporate, market, and macroeconomic governance are key in managing, limiting, redressing, or fine-tuning the emergent properties of complex systems like the financial system, with its subsystems and macro-financial linkages.

In this context, there is also a key role for a reshaped global governance that goes beyond the nation-State toward a bloc-sized global financial and legal management, in areas such as finance and transnational crime, further invigorating all multilateral organizations, and in particular the International Monetary Fund, the World Bank, the OECD, and the multilateral financial institutions in general. In addition, global management is required in addressing issues of planetary impact, from environmental sustainability to resource management in the new lands freed by melting glaciers, to cosmic explorations.

Section 1:

Economics

1. Opening remarks: corruption and economic analysis[1]

The first scholarly research into the causes and the consequences of corruption date back several decades. Scott's (1972) seminal work on political corruption, for example, dealt with a wide array of aspects of corruption. Until the 1980s, however, academic research on corruption was mostly confined to the domains of sociology, political science, history, public administration, criminal law, and criminology.

Campos and Bhargava (2007a), who have reviewed the evolution of the economic analysis of corruption, emphasize that the earlier systematic studies on the economics of corruption, although extensive and enlightening, were weak on measurement and quantification. The raw material for those studies largely relied on journalism to supply the facts and their results, because there were no statistical efforts to measure the harm caused by corruption. The closest were studies by Krueger (1974) and Bhagwati (1982) that attempted to provide a cautious measure of the volume of rent-seeking and illegal transactions in international trade by making use of the two sets of books available internationally in exporting and in importing countries. Then some authors argued that there was a rather limited quantity of definitive economic analysis. Sanchez and Waters (1974: 249) explained the scarcity of definitive economic studies regarding the impact of corruption on economic performance, suggesting that: "corruption is like sex was in Victorian England: it absorbs intense activity and is the subject of much speculation, but it is seldom considered a suitable topic for serious economic analysis." Since then, an increasing number of economists have focused on this topic, largely because of its increasingly evident link to economic performance.

The economic part of our work builds on and expands the existing literature through the analysis and elaboration of an extensive data set of micro, macro, and institutional variables. It was mainly in the early 1990s that the economic community witnessed the emergence of cross-country, perception-based, quantitative assessment of country governance and

---

1 This chapter was jointly written by Marco Arnone and Leonardo Borlini.

corruption. The best-known and most referenced corruption index to date, TI's corruption perceptions index (CPI), started its annual survey in 1995. The annual CPI ranked more than 150 countries (in 2009 it included 180 countries) in terms of perceived levels of corruption, as determined by expert assessments and opinion surveys. The CPI is a questionnaire-based survey, which assesses perceived corruption on a scale of 0 to 10. Ten refers to a (perceived) corruption-free country; zero refers to countries where corruption is perceived as extremely pervasive.

Shortly afterwards, the World Bank (WB) succeeded in developing a more inclusive data set covering broader governance concerns providing a better picture of the overall state of governance in a country, which is split up into six dimensions: control of corruption, rule of law (ROL), government effectiveness, regulatory quality, voice and accountability, and political stability and the absence of violence.[2] With the aid of these data sets, researchers have achieved major strides in assessing the macroeconomic impact, and understanding the microeconomic effects, of corruption.

More to the point, the macro-level econometric findings have been able to establish a material etiological link between corruption and, more broadly, weak governance, on the one hand, and poor private investment and growth, on the other. Empirical research shows that corruption

---

2 Since corruption is often concealed (corruption is illegal, and it must therefore be kept secret) and its appreciation is inherently subjective, the measure of corruption is often a problem. Most assessments use perception-based measures of corruption. There exist many polls that measure the level of corruption. These surveys are based on different criteria. Some consist of assessments by country risk analysts based in the home country or abroad. Others are surveys of local or expatriate businessmen, while there are also methodologies based on local residents. The three most popular surveys are from the Economist Intelligence Unit, the International Country Risk Guide, and TI's CPI. Although different surveys are collected by different methods, ratings from different polls show a high degree of correspondence with each other. Treisman (2000) remarks that indices of corruption that come from surveys of businessmen conducting business in a country are highly correlated with the indices of corruption that come from surveys of the citizens in the same countries. To sum up, although the corruption indices at issue are subjective measures of individuals' perception, they appear to capture an important conceptual framework, which manifests itself in a variety of other forms in society. From the analysis of the related literature, it unambiguously emerges that the social and economic effects of corruption are significant, pervasive and generally negative. The CPI is a sort of "poll of polls", condensing composite information from up to 12 individual surveys and ratings. The respondents are business people, risk analysts, and the general public. A country must be covered by at least three surveys to be included in the CPI. Thus, we chose this index mainly because of its comprehensive coverage, and because it incorporates the outcomes of the other major indices.

affects the allocation of resources, by diverting budgetary funds toward activities where bribes and illegal commissions can more easily be made.

Overall, empirical studies exploring the efficiency implications of corruption through its effects on growth and investment, composition of government expenditure, allocation of foreign direct investment (FDI), generally find that corruption reduces growth and investment, skews expenditure towards public investment and away from operations and maintenance, and redirects FDI towards countries with lower corruption. Moreover, the economic literature provides strong evidence of significant adverse distributional effects of corruption: high and rising corruption is associated with higher income inequality and poverty.

Before starting our own inquiry, it is worthwhile to review the main theoretical arguments *in favor* of corruption which have been put forward. In the past, indeed, views on the economic effects of corruption were not unanimous, and some economists had even found some redeeming value in it. Ehrlich and Lui (1999) argue that corrupt conduct by itself does not necessarily impose a net social cost because it involves transfer payments from bribe payers to bureaucrats. Besides, bribes could even ameliorate the deadweight cost of government intervention by directing scarce resources toward higher bidders (Leff 1964, Lui 1985).

This early stream of theoretical work suggests that corruption might serve to grease the wheels of commerce, thus reducing transaction costs and lowering the cost of capital (Leff 1964, Lui 1985). (Kaufmann and Wei 1999, and Aidt 2003 offer rebuttals.) Until the 1997 financial crisis, some South East Asian countries seemed to represent a case for the view that corruption, within restricted circumstances, might promote growth. "Indonesia, Thailand and some other countries were often mentioned as countries growing fast in spite of, or even because of, perceived high level of corruption" (Tanzi 2002: 43). Notably, "this corruption was associated with a low degree of uncertainty" (Tanzi 2002: 43). Tanzi summarizes, but does not support, the main arguments in favor of the view that corruption may promote efficiency and even growth:

1) As advanced in the 1960s by Leff (1964) and Huntington (1968), corruption can be efficiency enhancing since it removes government-imposed rigidities that impede investment and interfere with other economic decisions favorable to growth. Therefore, corruption would oil the mechanism or grease the wheel, a reasoning frequently used to explain the high rates of growth in some countries of South East Asia.
2) Theoretical models, developed by Beck and Maher (1986), and Lien (1986), show that, in bidding competitions, those who are most efficient can afford to pay the highest bribes. As a consequence, bribes

could promote efficiency by assigning projects to the most efficient firms.

3) Corruption might represent a useful political glue by allowing politicians to accumulate funds that could be used to hold a country together, and that might happen to constitute a necessary precondition for growth.
4) From the starting point that time has different value for different individuals, depending on their level of income and the opportunity cost of their time, Lui (1985) argues that corruption can be efficient since it allows the saving of time by those for whom time has the greatest utility.
5) Since corruption can supplement low wages, it can allow government to maintain a lower tax burden, which can favor growth. The issue here is whether a lower tax burden is more favorable to growth than a lower degree of corruption: a classic second-best problem.

A similar pattern is supported by Eiras (2003) in commenting on the research promoted by the Heritage Foundation/*Wall Street Journal*, the primary aim of which is to account for the relationship between corruption, economic freedom, and growth. The argument starts by referring to De Soto (2000), who, focusing on the importance of access to credit for economic growth, assumes that many of the poorest in the developing world own many things which, were their property rights validated, could be used as collateral to get credit access in order to start new and, likely, innovative business activities, and ends by asserting that this legal precondition is made impossible by an excessively pervasive bureaucracy.

Eiras (2003) goes on to highlight what seems quite a simplistic etiological relation between the size of the public sector and informal economic activities: corruption, circumvention of rules, and informal economic activities would merely be symptoms of over-regulation, representing some sort of reaction to economic repression and government actions causing undesired behavior by private actors. The gist of the thesis is that informal economic conduct, including corruption, is a recurring side-effect in economic systems where public intervention is high: regulations are mainly regarded as hurdles to economic freedom, while the negative externalities of economic activities seem to be considered less relevant.

In Chapters 2 and 3 we show that the relationships between regulations, corruption and markets, on the one hand, and corruption, public and private sectors, on the other, far from being unidirectional are rather more intricate.

This efficiency-enhancing view of corruption has found little empirical support and has largely fallen out of favor (Aidt 2003). Here, it suffices to summarize how the main arguments *in favor* of corruption can easily be countered:

1) Rigidities and rules, far from being exogenous and unmovable features of a society, are created, and in fact can be intentionally created by public officials to extract bribes. In sum, "when rules can be used to extract bribes, more rules will be created" (Tanzi 2002: 44).
2) According to Tanzi, individuals and/or economic agents who can pay the highest bribes are not necessarily the most economically efficient, but rather the most successful at rent-seeking.[3] What is more, corruptors may be associated with a wide network of organized criminal groups: in this sense corruption can have a virulent impact on the legal economy to the advantage of organizations which are inclined to exploit the system.
3) Payment of speed money may constitute a material incentive for bureaucrats to reduce the speed at which most practices are carried out, hence slowing down the average time for the whole process.
4) As emphasized by the same author, whereas it might be true that corruption may work as a political glue in the short run, it is likely to cause major problems over the long run. The experience of Zaire under Mobutu is a paradigmatic case of this dynamic.

As to the link between corruption and public sector size, let us refer to Arnone and Iliopulos (2005), who recall the well-known circumstance that Scandinavian countries are characterized by significant State intervention and low corruption. To explain this commonly held view, the two economists use the level of public revenues per individual country to proxy public sector size and public intervention. By elaborating data from TI and the WB, they show how, contrary to public opinion, large public revenues are associated with low corruption.

Similar outcomes are obtained when using tax revenues to proxy the

---

[3] The existence of corruption creates the wrong set of incentives in a society. As Ehrlich and Lui (1999) point out, "since bureaucratic power holds the promise of economic rents through corruption, individuals have an incentive to compete over the privilege of becoming bureaucrats." The existing literature has referred to such activity as *rent-seeking* (e.g. Krueger 1974). Ng (2006: 828) remarks that rent-seeking is referred to as an "investment in political capital, [which] consumes economic resources that could otherwise be used for production or investment in human capital. This is the source of the social loss from corruption." Along the same lines, Murphy et al. (1991: 93) argue that rent-seeking distorts the allocation of talent away from entrepreneurship and innovation, thereby reducing growth.

degree of public intervention: higher tax revenues are associated with lower corruption. Public revenue is also a reasonable proxy for public sector size: the larger the public sector, the greater the revenues needed to finance it. The analysis goes on to graph how State revenues and corruption are inversely correlated. Given that this data set also reflects the impact of income in various countries, to control for this influence, they consider another set of more recent data for OECD countries: the "empirical evidence is not sufficient to prove causation; nevertheless, it is sufficient to reject current opinion that large public sector size helps develop corruption." Rather, "the roots of corruption are not so much in the size of the public sector, as in the discretionary powers of public officials, in the bad management of possible conflicts of interest, and in low quality governance" (Arnone and Iliopulos 2005: 78).

In Chapter 3 we also explore the relationship between economic cycles and corruption. While Akerlof and Shiller (2009) maintain with anecdotal evidence that episodes of corruption are a factor in causing or worsening economic recessions or slowdowns, with specific reference to the 2008–12 economic and financial crisis, Arnone and Davigo (2005) argue more generally that causality might also run the other way around: recessions, making resources more valuable and competition stronger, contribute to the collapse of illegal agreements. Therefore, episodes of corruption emerge more easily, facilitating investigations.

2. Firms, markets, and corruption

2.1 INTRODUCTION

Asserting that corruption is one of the most serious challenges to modern economic systems and societies sounds commonplace at best: it lacks power to evoke interest because of overuse. The present chapter and the following four chapters provide evidence that corruption, accurately labeled *the enemy within*, causes serious systemic economic, institutional and social costs, and, when it hits financial markets, affects asset prices and financial supervision. In particular, the present chapter[1] investigates the effects of corruption at the microeconomic level: the focus is on corruption as one of the most serious distortions of the competitive well-functioning of modern regulated markets, which typically creates and crystallizes asymmetric business environments, where outsiders are either excluded ex ante or forced to exit, as well as *closed* social systems, where the views of those without sufficient economic or political influence or enough visibility are simply without representation.

For corruption is not a uniform and stand-alone problem. Before turning to consider such economic effects, it is useful to establish a proper conceptual underpinning by exploring the main theoretical models accounting for its dynamic, the key incentives for corruption which have been elaborated by the economic research, along with the primary variables determining the size of such incentives. This provides us with a solid ground on which to build the following analysis of the costs of corruption in terms of poor economic performance and instability, erosion of democratic institutions, social inequality and threat to fundamental human rights. Secondly, the identification of the key determinants of widespread corruption contributes to our assessment of the existing countermeasures, and the evolution of the international anti-corruption programs and their implementation within national legal systems. To sum up, attacking corruption with effective countermeasures requires understanding and targeting its key determinants.

---

1 This chapter builds on, updates, and expands Arnone and Iliopulos (2005). Leonardo Borlini co-authored Sections 2.1, 2.2, 2.3, 2.4.2, and 2.4.4.

However, a word of caution must be expressed: one of the defining features of corruption is the extreme difficulty of establishing the causal direction of its dynamics. Arnone and Iliopulos (2005: 5) start their analysis with a pertinent admonition: "corruption is mostly characterised by the difficulty of identifying the causal direction of the dynamics on which it is based; causes and effects are strongly interconnected with feedbacks that can hardly be isolated: the effects negatively influence their causes." Any attempt to isolate and distinguish causes from effects suffers from the limitations imposed by the presence of multi-directional causal chains.

2.2 CAUSAL DYNAMICS: AGENCY MODEL AND OTHER INCENTIVES FOR CORRUPTION

Contemporary economic research on corruption began with theoretical work that built on industrial organization, public finance, and price theory to isolate the main incentives for paying and receiving bribes. The economic literature identifies a group of conditions which, either directly or indirectly, determine the size of corrupt operations. We first explain how the classical agency model and the insights of information economics have been traditionally deployed in order to explain the main causal dynamics of corruption. We then turn to the key incentives for the perpetration of corrupt operations, and, finally, explore other variables which impinge on the size of those incentives.

According to Rose-Ackerman (1999), the starting point for understanding the ample spectrum of causes, which contributes to an explanation of the dynamics of corruption, is understanding the recurring interfaces between the political and economic spheres; an interface which fosters incestuous relationships. Pathologies in the agency/principal relation lie at the heart of corrupt conduct. Traditional microeconomic research into the causes of corruption is based on information economics and agency models, more recently supplemented by empirical studies.

Information economics is grounded on two pillars: (i) not all the principals have the same amount of information on their exchange (information asymmetry) and (ii) agents' actions and their effects are not easy to observe and/or quantify. Under these assumptions, theoretical and empirical research examines potential maverick behaviors of markets and government, and suggests measures that could reduce such behaviors at the lowest possible cost.

Economists like Cartier-Bresson (2000) and Rose-Ackerman (1999) claim that principal-agent relationships and asymmetric information – along with other fundamental determinants like deep cultural, historical, and social factors – are at the heart of complex cases where a private individual bribes a public official to obtain an undue benefit. According to this viewpoint, the main causes of corruption are rooted in the delegation of power. The diverging interests of agents and principals, along with the asymmetry of information to the advantage of the agents, give rise to opportunities for corruption. Klitgaard (1988), Arnone and Iliopulos (2005), and Lambsdorff (2006) argue that opportunities for corruption depend on the size of the rents under the control of public agents, the discretion they have in allocating those rents, and, finally, their lack of a sense of responsibility towards society which will last as long as social standards do not stigmatize corruption and legal enforcement does not effectively repress and prevent corruption.

According to this model, generally corruption equals monopoly power plus the discretion of public officials minus their accountability. The first factor, the monopoly power of the public sector, indicates the degree to which the government controls and intervenes in national industries and services. The International Monetary Fund (IMF) traced much public corruption to government intervention in the economy, noting such examples as: trade restrictions, subsidies, and low wages in the civil service, setting prices for public utilities, and control of pollution emitted in a firm's production process.

However, as hinted above, corruption is not so much grounded on the size of the government's role in the economy, as on the discretion of public officials within the State's regulatory framework.

This leads us to the second broad cause of corruption, that is the discretion of public officials, which is contingent upon the control the government has over the economy: corruption heavily depends on the discretion officials have in dispensing those benefits. As clarified in the following, when States operate particular enterprises in lieu of private sector management, corrupt public officials can cause losses within an industry, especially when they are not held accountable.

Finally, the third causal element of corruption identified within the model, that is the lack of accountability of public officials, stems from the discretionary power of public officials: if public officials are able to use their discretion without threat of repercussion, then unchecked corruption could ensue. Lack of accountability corresponds to lack of market transparency, which allows inefficient practices to go undetected. Where public officials with monopoly power over discretionary decisions are not held accountable, they have the incentive to be corrupt.

It is now possible to specify when a market for corruption can exist and prosper. The conditions are well captured by Cartier-Bresson (2000: 12): such a market exists "when people trade public goods illegally against payoffs at the risk of having to pay a penalty." It goes without saying that the less likely it is that the penalty will apply, the higher the incentive to be corrupt.

However, as emphasized by Rose-Ackerman (1999: 33), "in seeking realistic reforms it is important to realize that, like all illegal activities, the efficient level of bribery is not zero. Reforms must consider the marginal costs as well as the marginal benefits of anti-corruption strategies." The author then illustrates the material circumstances which affect the possibility of applying the penalty: (1) again, information asymmetries protecting the corrupt agents; (2) as a consequence, the difficulty in identifying and proving corrupt operations; and (3) essentially, the extreme difficulty of mobilizing a large number of victims against well-organized networks of agents profiting from illegal gains.

Incentives for corrupt operations perpetrated to obtain gains are often created by the activities carried out by governments:

(1) when government buys or sells goods or services, firms might act corruptly in order to be included in the list of qualified bidders, or to be selected as the winning contractors. Again, when government acts in the marketplace as a buyer or a contractor, once a firm has been selected, it may pay to get inflated prices or to reduce quality;
(2) in most countries the government frequently engages in the provision of goods and services at prices below the market price. Often dual prices exist – a low State price and a higher free market one. This may be related to foreign exchange; credit; commodities (fuel, electricity, water); public housing; some rationed goods; access to educational and health facilities. Firms might then pay off officials for access to below-market State supplies;
(3) corruption may occur when the level of subsidies and benefits is too low to satisfy all who qualify, or when officials are endowed with material discretion when deciding who is qualified for an entitlement;
(4) processes like privatization of State-owned enterprises and provisions of concessions might create strong incentives for corruption. Since the sale of big public-sector firms is similar to tendering for large public infrastructure projects, the incentives for corruption are analogous;
(5) for all types of government programs where officials are likely to have valuable information for the outsider, private actors might be willing to pay in order to get this information sooner than their competitors;
(6) as in the context of the current global economic crisis, when massive recovery and stimulus packages, fast-track disbursement of public

funds and attempts to secure economic stability are implemented around the world.

Looking at bribes paid to avoid costs, a first incentive is represented by the firm's aim to obtain a favorable interpretation of rules or a discretionary judgment in their favor under public regulatory programs. Firms can offer bribes in order to avoid or lighten the regulatory load or to interpret in their favor the regulatory requirements when laws are numerous and unclear. Already Tacitus in his *Annales* remarked that "*corruptissima re publica plurimae leges*." Not surprisingly, business people and other private actors may collude with tax collectors to lower the sum collected.

As a general rule, a system of taxation based on clear regulations and not requiring frequent contact between taxpayers and tax inspectors is far less likely to promote acts of corruption.

According to Tanzi (1998), however, corruption is likely to be a major problem in tax and customs administration when: laws are difficult to understand and can be interpreted differently; the payment of tax requires frequent contact between tax administrators and taxpayers; the wages of tax collectors are low; acts of corruption on the part of tax administrators are not easily detectable and when discovered are penalized only mildly; the administrative procedure (e.g. the criteria for the selection of taxpayers for audits) is not transparent; the tax administration retains discretion over important decisions, such as those related to the determination of tax liabilities; selection of audits; litigation and the like.

In similar fashion, another incentive for corrupt operation is represented by customs. Here payoffs are likely to be used in order to reduce tariffs and export fees and to obtain import and export licenses. In the case of illegal business (gambling, human trafficking, weapons, and drug dealing), the incentive for corruption may be dual. On the one hand, law enforcement authorities can demand bribes to overlook violations or limit penalties. On the other hand, the illegal business runners may actively corrupt enforcement activity not only to seek immunity, but also to raid their competitors or to restrict entry. Also, in many countries informal payoffs are required to obtain expedited services.

Having described some of the main types of advantages sought by bribers, either as gains obtained or costs avoided, we now assess the variables which determine the size and the incidence of bribes. As to the level of corruption, Rose-Ackerman (1999: 38) argues that it "is a function of the honesty and integrity of both public officials and private individuals. Holding these factors constant, however, the size and incidence are determined by the overall level of benefits available, the discretionary power of officials, the riskiness of corrupt deals, and the relative bargaining power of the briber and the bribee." Thus, the two central relationships which mainly determine the incentives to bribe are: (1) the relationship between the benefits available and the actual discretion of public officials, on the one hand, and, on the other, (2) the relationship between risks and the division of gains.

1) Regarding the first relationship, since the level of benefit is not necessarily exogenous, the different corrupt dynamics may depend on how the corrupt public officials misuse their discretionary powers. The same author emphasizes that there are several ways this can be done:
   i) Public officials may be able to get some of the contractor's payoff by bringing in payment delays or devising ex post regulatory hurdles.
   ii) Public officials can arbitrarily behave in an unclear fashion to create demand for clarity/transparency. Again, they can threaten to enforce criminal and regulatory laws more strictly than is usual. Officials may also be able to work out privatization projects or natural resources concessions with a view to including a high level of monopoly profits for whoever obtains the newly privatized firm or the concession.
   iii) They can propose *white elephant* projects that are a highly inefficient way to encourage economic development or use limited budget resources or both.
   iv) A crucial factor being considered under this perspective is the competitiveness of the corrupt market. Whereas some corrupt markets are more or less competitive (for instance, routine government services can fall into this category), others are less competitive and public officials may be able to bribe-price discriminate. When corrupt officials are able to bribe-price discriminate, they can extract bribes proportional to the monopoly profits of the briber.
2) As to the second relationship which may create an incentive for corruption, the first element is the risk of the corrupt deal: if the probability of detection and penalty is high, either the supply of or the demand for bribes may fall significantly. The analysis continues much like any study for the economics of crime as traditionally designed by Becker and Stigler (1974): the expected cost of bribery is "the probability of being caught times the probability of being convicted times the punishment levied." The model goes on to consider the respective position of a risk-neutral actor, who compares the expected cost with the expected benefit and corrupts only if the balance is positive, and a risk-averse actor, who must also be compensated for the uncertainty of the opera-

tion. The basic assumptions are that the bribers are price takers and do not have any bargaining power over the level of the bribe and the benefit obtainable in return, conditions which do not often occur. This is why Rasmusen and Ramseyer (1994) and Arnone and Iliopulos (2005) elaborate more accurate bargaining models, which illustrate the likely underlying reasoning of the corruptor and the would-be officials based on the maximization of their respective utility functions weighted by the possibility of being discovered and sanctioned and assuming that both parts of the transaction have bargaining power. Indeed, as the cost of corruption rises, it is not obvious how the remaining gains are split between the corrupter and the corrupt official, this depending mainly on (i) the tolerance for risk of, respectively, the briber and the would-be corrupt officials; and (ii) the briber's willingness to pay, which, in turn, depends on the available alternatives (e.g. the ability to obtain the same benefits by relocating in another jurisdiction or country; the possibility of following legal procedures at some additional cost; access to a specialized technology or a type of financing not available to others; monopoly power in dealing with the State; the ability to use different officials for the same transaction).

Finally, some (other) general lessons on causation can be derived from the richness and complexity of the ongoing interdisciplinary research on corruption:

1) Kaufmann, Kraay, and Mastruzzi (2006) explore the issue of causation econometrically by using a set of cross-country perception data and show, along with Arnone and Iliopulos (2005) and Lambsdorff (2006), that the dominant direction of causation is from weak governance, including corruption, to weak economic performance, a relationship which finds strong support in our own study (Chapter 3).
2) After reviewing works that associate constitutional structures and voting rules with reported perception of corruption, Kunicová (2006) asks whether shifts in the democratic framework matter and concludes that presidential systems are more corrupt, on balance, than parliamentary democracies and that proportional representation systems are more corrupt than first-past-the-post systems.
3) Another primary institutional element is the complex link between decentralized government, corruption, and government accountability. Bardhan and Mookherjee (2006) inquire into this multi-layered relationship and warn against the trap of taking for granted the simple view that decentralization would reduce corruption by making it easier for ordinary people to monitor the activities of their local

government: some argue that federal States are more corrupt than unitary ones, this mainly derived from the multiplication of corruptible bodies in numerous levels of government. Furthermore, smaller polities may act as hurdles to innovation and change: they may group more uniform classes of people, and politics may result in a less competitive game, leading to increased corruption. It is worth stressing that local kleptocracy can be especially difficult to monitor and tackle in rural areas of poor countries.

4) Conventional economic wisdom may be an inaccurate guide to understanding corruption if applied to poor countries. Khan (2006) points out that traditional economic analysis assumes that corruption impedes the enforcement of "clear" legal rules. State intervention often occurs in the absence of a clear legal basis in poor and highly corrupt States, where populist politicians and clientelism are likely to be less limited and more unchecked than in countries with stronger institutions. In such a context, corruption is not designed to elude the rules; rather it determines the behavior of public officials endowed with discretionary power and political leaders in a substantial legal vacuum. Consequently, in Khan's view, the models and policy prescriptions which characterize the experience of States with strong laws and institutions are an inaccurate way of understanding corruption in weak States. Here, given the very characteristics of developing markets and high levels of political conflict, political leaders would attempt to achieve stability by allocating resources to the most powerful or dangerous factions through networks dominated by tribal/familistic forms of clientelism. This leads to widespread political corruption, which, in turn, would prevent any attempt to implement pro-poor policies and nullify the result of policies promoting greater economic transparency and accountability. Therefore, it is necessary to assess the underlying political and economic forces producing corruption in different States, before applying policy recipes tailored to the experience of more advanced markets and countries.
5) Economists, political scientists, and criminologists also group together a multitude of *indirect* factors that may further corruption, the common element of which seems to be their close relationship with the institutional system of public governance. Arnone and Iliopulos (2005) suggest the following examples: a weak system of checks and balances; poor quality among the bureaucracy; low level of public sector wages; ineffective mechanisms of institutional control over public officials' activities; inappropriate behavior by institutional, political, and economic ruling groups.
6) Della Porta and Vannucci (2007) illustrate a path-dependent model

accounting for the spread of corruption in a certain social and geographic context. They argue that the level of institutionalization in a certain corrupt market is a fundamental determinant of the proliferation of corruption, and outline the main features of the basic mechanisms for governing such a corrupt market. For the moment, it is worth emphasizing that the consolidation of a normative framework governing the behavior of corruptees and corruptors resembles Hayek's (1960) approach to the "spontaneous evolution of behavioural rules", which in the case of corruption allows those agents to obtain the desired payoff – that is, the well-organized functioning of the corrupt market – without proper preordination. The different level of evolution of such a regulative framework explains much of the variety in the scale of corruption in social and economic contexts characterized by comparable basic features.

2.3 MARKETS AND RULES

In this book (and, mainly, in our economic analysis of the phenomenon), we are predominantly concerned with corruption in the form of interaction between public and private entities, to be read in its general meaning of misuse of public power for private gains.[2] First of all, however, we need to look at the overall, fundamental relationship between markets and rules; therefore, the following arguments also apply to corruption between private entities only. It is key to go deeper into market *physiology* so that we may understand its *pathologies*.

Far from being jungles where the law of the strongest rules, markets are a set of most sophisticated relations between producers and consumers, and between production factors, technical knowledge, and organization in time and space. Furthermore, they are also a set of relations between economic actors and social, political, legal, and civil institutions. A set of rules common to all economic actors, and their enforcement, is an

---

[2] From a social and economic perspective corruption is not just about bribery. On the contrary, corruption extends beyond bribery to include other exercises of discretionary power in the public sector. In the academic literature, corruption is often defined as the misuse of public office for private gains (Shleifer and Vishny 1993, Klitgaard 1991, Transparency International 1995). As we specify in analyzing the legal and institutional evolution of the normative apparatus against corruption, the legal definition of corruption is narrower, even though some of the anti-corruption international conventions embrace a more extensive notion. See Part II.

essential precondition for the functioning of competitive markets, with their outcomes of efficient distribution and utilization of resources and optimal individual choices.

There is an abysmal distance between this idea of the market and a primitive vision – widespread and yet totally erroneous – of a market in which competition and the dynamics of birth and mortality of enterprises are mistaken for "the law of the strongest", with markets open to abuse by whoever may be wielding power.

Nothing is further from the concept of market as defined in microeconomic theory: in a competitive market those who affirm themselves are as efficient, innovative and capable of organizing resources at least as well as others, while abiding with existing laws and regulations.

Markets characterized by widespread corruption are, instead, dominated by operators with the least entrepreneurial capabilities, who need to break the rules, illegally impose their will, use (or be used by) political power to avoid competition. These operators may be good at rent-seeking, while they seek resources and parasitic advantages, but are not entrepreneurs as such.

Let us go back to the relationship between market and rules. We said that a set of commonly shared rules is required in a market, that is to say, no competitive market exists without its own proper legal order. Not all rules are at the same level. Certain regulations, principles, or single provisions are indeed subject to negotiation. This typically applies to market failures: we may think of the allocation of rights in cases where externalities are of concern, such as in the case of smoking. Once they are established, these regulations – which may change in time to reflect social and political choices – are common to all actors who take part in the economic life of a society.

However, there are some norms that are so fundamental to the very existence of a market that we may not even think about them being not enforced or systematically changed. This is the case with ownership rights and their enforcement: in a society where no such rights exist, or where they are not enforced, it is not even possible to define an Edgeworth box, an analytical instrument through which economists demonstrate that a competitive market provides efficiency and optimality; in this case we may not talk about a market at all.

The example tells us that there exist rules, which are necessary preconditions for the very existence of a market and make it a desirable means to allocate resources, satisfy individual choices, and disseminate information. Such a perspective does not claim a natural character for the market: the place where individuals are willing to buy and others are willing to sell certain goods or services – a market in its very essence – is a set of private and public rules and institutions. In other words, without such normative framework a market would not even exist.

Such fundamental rules are not up for bargaining – less so for the bargaining of few individuals rather than all, as is typical with cases of corruption. In the aftermath of the fall of the Soviet Union and the birth of new countries, ownership rights, while enjoying legal recognition, lacked de facto enforcement. Appropriation of resources became a possibility as opposed to voluntary market exchange. In such conditions no price is determined that is significant for transactions, nor is there any free market at all.

Similarly, in areas where there is strong criminality, actors in the market may come under pressure or be forced to exchange their goods or services by whoever may use threats to secure profitable businesses. Clearly, also in these conditions there are no voluntary transactions nor do prices have any economic significance.

Moreover, *dirty* players jeopardize the survival of competitors who play by the rules: a paradigmatic and, unfortunately, rather frequent case in (also developed) economies pervasively infiltrated by criminal organization is that of *hybrid conglomerates*, actors which operate in both legal and illegal markets. One who bids for a contract and has dirty money available may win that contract because dirty money costs less than clean money, and allows lower costs. In calculating the cost of that money, indeed, one has also to deduct the extra-profit represented by laundering it.

Therefore, an organization, which runs both licit and illicit activities, may be looked at as a sort of a hybrid conglomerate having a clear and substantial interest in cross-subsidizing its licit activities with the profits of its illegal business. Phrased differently, such a peculiar conglomerate has an extra-cost to take into consideration regarding its illicit branch (the cost of laundering its illicit profits) and, simultaneously, an extra-profit achievable by carrying out its licit business (the amount of money it eventually has at its disposal after laundering the illicit profit through the licit branch of its conglomerate business). By focusing on the licit part of its business, one may note that such economic actors have a wider spectrum of financial resources at their disposal than their "clean competitors": clean players do not have illicit funds being invested and laundered.[3] Hence clean players are impaired or excluded. When this happens on a regular

---

[3] In time of financial distress, these dynamics may have even more vicious effects. Limited access to finance and a relatively high cost of capital may represent relevant barriers to entry, which, in turn, may end up by consolidating the position of the incumbents, regardless of whether or not their economic performance justifies such consolidation.

basis, clean players may see their position weaken until they are driven out of business. Dirty players come to dominate the market. This market is not a competitive one.

The arguments above show how the concept of rule of law (ROL) (see Box 2.1) logically precedes that of market. Markets are (implicitly but inevitably) defined as part of an organized social context, where there are established commonly shared behavioral rules, with enforcement mechanisms that punish excessive deviations. Adam Smith defines his concept of an invisible hand in his *Wealth of Nations* – in which self-interested individuals contribute to maximize collective welfare by pursuing their own interest – later in his *Theory of Moral Sentiments* the motives are presented that drive individuals to form societies, define organized structures, and establish behavioral rules.

In a mistaken *market-biased* vision of society in which the market devours a social organization and its rules, while it violates and bends them to the (mistaken) idea that everything is exchangeable and has a price, the market destroys itself.

Also, at the same time, the logical desirability of the market as we discussed earlier – that the market is an efficient mechanism for allocating resources, an instrument to realize optimal individual choices, and a mechanism for defining prices as a synthesis of the information that is sufficient to make economic decisions – loses its foundations. Whenever players violate the rules, equality no longer exists between all players. There is no assurance that whoever emerges is the best from an economic point of view: the market no longer guarantees efficiency or optimality or informative prices.

When economists talk about competitive markets, they often take it for granted that there exists the logical prior of common, respected, and enforced rules. It is indeed of practical importance that policymakers reinforce supervisory agencies and regulators in order to protect competition and monitor individual behavior. We analyze this in Chapter 7 to clarify the context in which financial supervisory/regulatory agencies operate. If these agencies are not sufficiently well established and functioning properly, risks exist with respect to the very concept of competitive markets, efficiency and optimality. In the long run an economic system is less capable of producing wealth and improving the standard of living of actors in the economy.

Finally, in a competitive market the principle of freedom has ultimate value, embodied in the concept of consumer sovereignty: individual choices based on individual preferences and budget constraints, and freedom from third-party directions. In a market in which certain players use illegal means to secure resources and opportunities, the market might

BOX 2.1 RULE OF LAW: AN EVOLVING CONCEPT

In dealing with the notion of ROL we are well aware of its complex nature. In particular, we keep well in mind that, in spite of the plain traditional meaning of the English expression, which has usually been contrasted with the "rule of man," the ROL is an open-ended notion, the precise meaning of which varies according to the historical, geographic, and cultural environment. The concept of ROL gets a precise meaning if contextualized within common law legal systems, whereas it is frequently related to notions from other legal systems – *stato di diritto*, *état de droit*, *estado de derecho*, *rechtsstaat* – which, nonetheless, are all endowed with precise and distinguishing definitional features.

Even the main intergovernmental institutions dealing with the subject seem to have adopted a flexible approach to such a notion, while highlighting the importance of positive law and legal institutions. In trying to identify the precise notion of ROL used by the World Bank (WB), Barron (2005: 13) argues that the WB working definition "has tended to reflect the particular views of its reigning General Counsel." Accordingly, he identifies two competing subsets of definition, respectively, related to Shihata's and Tung's mandates. Ibrahim Shihata, the WB Counsel from 1983 to 1998, for example, defined the ROL as "a system, based on abstract rules which are actually applied and on functioning institutions which ensure the appropriate application of such rules" (Shihata 1991: 85). More specifically, under such a definition, the ROL requires that: (a) there is a set of rules which are known in advance; (b) such rules are actually in force; (c) mechanisms exist to ensure the proper application of the rules and to allow for departure from them as necessary according to established procedures; (d) conflicts in the application of the rules can be resolved through binding decisions of an independent judicial or arbitral body; and (e) there are known procedures for amending the rules when they no longer serve their purpose.

However, Barron (2005) observes that "the Bank's position appears to have changed, however, in recent years, and the ROL was defined in a different way by Shihata's successor as General Counsel, Ko-Yung Tung, in a speech he gave in 2002. The definition of the ROL put forward in that speech has been incorporated into the Bank's most recent publications on legal and judicial reforms.

It asserts that the ROL prevails where: (1) the government itself is bound by the law; (2) every person in society is treated equally under the law; (3) the human dignity of each individual is recognized and protected by law; and (4) justice is accessible to all. The ROL requires transparent legislation, fair laws, predictable enforcement, and accountable governments to maintain order, promote private sector growth, fight poverty, and have legitimacy" (World Bank 2002a, 2003a, 2004a).

Today, considering that the multitude of ROL concepts is likely to breed confusion and misunderstanding between donors and recipients, or even among different members of the same community, it is the Bank's website on Law and Justice Institutions which expressly warns that "overlooked in much of the dialogue about the ROL is that the term has no fixed meaning." It originated in normative writings on law and government, principally by Western authors, and each tailored the term to fit his or her vision of the *ideal* or *just* State. As a consequence, one survey (Grote 1999: 271) of how the term has been used in Germany, France, the United Kingdom, and the United States concludes that it "belongs to the category of open-ended concepts which are subject to permanent debate." Despite this multiplicity of definitions, the Bank deems that "most can be classified according to whether they emphasize formal characteristics, substantive outcomes, or functional considerations", and assesses the main advantages and flaws of such approaches. Accordingly, "formal definitions of the ROL look to the presence or absence of specific, observable criteria of the law or the legal system. Common criteria include: a formally independent and impartial judiciary; laws that are public; the absence of laws that apply only to particular individuals or classes; the absence of retroactive laws; and provisions for judicial review of government action. There is no definitive list of formal criteria, and different formal definitions may use different standards. What formal definitions have in common is that the ROL is measured by the conformity of the legal system to these explicit standards."

The analysis moves on to highlight that a first alternative "to the formal approach to the ROL is one that looks to substantive outcomes such as *justice* or *fairness*. This approach is not concerned with the formal rules, except inasmuch as they contribute to the achievement of a particular substantive goal of the legal system. Unlike the formal approach, which eschews value judgements, the substantive approach is driven by a moral vision of the good legal system, and measures the ROL in terms of how well the system being assessed approximates this ideal (Dworkin 1977)."

Finally, the Bank proceeds to describe the third approach to the ROL, which seems similar to the substantive definition, "but tries to avoid the thorny normative issues by focusing on how well the law and legal system perform some function – usually the constraint of government discretion, the making legal decisions predictable, or some combination of both (Hayek 1960). One version of this view, for example, would hold that a society in which government officials have little or no discretion has a high level of ROL, whereas a society in which they wield a great deal of discretion has minimal ROL." Interestingly enough, in commenting on the UNCAC, Freeman (2005) remarks that "the conception of the ROL and its purposes, diverges from one society to the next. Compare, for example, attitudes in Sweden and China."

fail to satisfy the demand of clean players, who will suffer a limitation on their freedom.

This discussion of rules and markets highlights the opportunity for a *dialogue* between economics and law. Also, it makes clear that, in the best interest of societies and economic actors, ethics and the concept(s) of freedom should have their say in such a dialogue.

2.4 CORRUPTION AND DISTORTIONS OF MARKETS

The mechanisms through which corruption distorts the functioning of competitive markets and allocation of resources are manifold. Here we account for some of the most remarkable.

Given the complexity of the phenomenon, no single direct cause exists that may determine widespread corruption; however, certain public sector activities may provide a suitable background for the development of corruption. Included are licensing regulations, taxes, public spending, party finance, and all activities that are inherently discretionary, or characterized by a concentration of political and economic power.

Corruption may significantly influence both resource allocation and domestic product distribution: because of this, both private and public activities may experience major efficiency losses. Market functioning may be subject to distortions that limit free competition: corruption challenges market competitiveness in terms of productive efficiency, allocative efficiency, and dynamic efficiency, which, as widely recognized by the microeconomic mainstream – Krugman et al. (2007); Fumagalli and Motta (2008); Motta and Ruta (2008); Kip Viscusi and Zeckhauser (2005) – represent the main parameters adopted by analysts to measure the health of markets.

By its very nature, it generates an asymmetric context where competitors are excluded and – like stakeholders, whose interests are the opposite of those subjects involved in corrupt operations – do not find any means of licit and substantial representation. In addition, it fosters the emergence of a corrupt market, which, in turn, augments common citizens' pervasive feelings of uncertainty, which individual actors perceive as a serious drawback of globalization.

Coming to the ultimate values at the root of competitive markets – which are realized when individual choices based on individual preferences and freedom from third-party direction – whenever certain players may resort to illegal means to secure resources and opportunities, the market is likely to fail to satisfy consumers, who will suffer a limitation to their freedom and choices.

If used to maintain a certain market or business, corruption endows dirty players with a way of excluding rivals that is potentially far more effective than the most brazen forms of hard-core cartels and attempts at monopolization: corruptors jeopardize the survival of competitors who abide by the rules, and, as a consequence, cause economic inefficiencies similar to those of serious antitrust violation.

Corruption also affects the fundamental role of government in the areas of protection of property rights and enforcement of contracts. This may not only severely distort the market mechanism, but also harm, more generally, the role of the fundamental social institutions upon which the correct functioning of the market mechanism is grounded. Nor is the damage limited to the private sector. Corruption also raises the cost of government projects through inefficient allocation processes, whereby government contracts and concessions may not be awarded to the most efficient bidders if those firms are unwilling to pay bribes.

Furthermore, corruption can lower the quality of public projects and services, since a contract is likely to be awarded so as to maximize the gain of the corrupt official instead of optimizing social benefits. The quality of service can suffer even more where contractors make payoffs to cut corners. Let us refer to the case of a corruptor who bids for a contract and has dirty money at his disposal: as explained by Arnone and Iliopulos (2005: 18), "it may win that contract because dirty money costs less than clean money, and allows lower costs enabling a successful bid. Hence clean players are excluded." Thus, any equality between players ceases to exist, and, notwithstanding the sporadic opposite view, there is no assurance that the winner of such a distorted process of rivalry is the best from an economic point of view. The market no longer guarantees efficiency, innovation and price informativeness.

The case of the TSKJ Consortium (Chapter 8) involving some of the major world oil companies, allegedly culpable of systemically paying bribes to Nigerian high officials in order to award engineering–procurement–construction (EPC) contracts in Bonny Island, is a typical case of a supranational cartel which, by means of transnational corruption, succeeds in winning the competition for highly profitable markets and excluding rivals which play by the rules.

Finally, corruption can likely cause a concealed and yet extremely inefficient and asymmetric compartmentalization of the relevant market. As is widely known, an efficient allocation of resources occurs where there is free play of market forces and risk-adjusted returns from all the various forms of economic activity are equalized at the margin. Whereas efficient allocation in this regard refers to that of the public in general, private maximization is socially efficient when market failures and externalities are insignificant. The private optimum of corruptors is socially inefficient, as corruption produces significant externalities in terms of costs upon the society. Put somewhat differently, corruption splits up the market into two segments: a hidden and highly profitable corrupt market which is restricted to a variable bunch of insiders, on the one hand, and a licit open market, the operators of which ultimately bear the costs of the former, on the other. Della Porta and Vannucci (2007) stress that the corrupt market may have a high degree of institutionalization and be endowed with rules and reliable intermediaries easing and stabilizing the relationships between its insiders at the expense of the competitiveness of the licit market.

Corrupt firms, and firms belonging to well-organized and extremely harmful criminal organizations (examples of which abound in China, Colombia, Japan, Italy, Mexico, Russia, and several African countries), may also *cross-subsidize* their economic activity in other markets by resorting to extra-profit extracted in a certain market through corrupt conduct, acting similarly to dominant firms abusing their strength in a certain market to secure the exclusion of competitors in a related market (a type of conduct familiar to antitrust scholars and practitioners). In such a case, the competitive process is distorted in two different markets.

State regulators determine many characteristics of the economic environment in which players interact. With no regulatory system to protect the functioning of free competition, markets per se may ensure no efficient resource allocation. Market failures structurally limit the possibility that the conditions necessary for efficient competition may endogenously materialize.

Also, a social ethic, chosen via a political process and requesting solidarity, inclusion, or other meta-economic characteristics, may require State intervention (e.g. in the healthcare sector; Cheng and Reinhardt 2012): competition per se may not ensure that the equity principle is upheld.

State regulation is inherently discretionary. As such, it reflects the expertise and moral qualities of lawmakers. As discretion and strong economic interests favor power abuse, those laws that should guarantee good market functioning may be designed instead to favor specific groups or individuals. Distortions arising in this respect may affect both public and private sectors and influence resource allocation, production or (re) distribution. Also, requirements or regulations that are either excessively restrictive or complex may prevent access to new market entrants.

2.4.1 Impact on New Market Entrants

The close association between low quality governance and corruption is of particular significance with regard to new market entrants. Market regulation has a strong impact on both the conduct of business and market entrance decisions: it has a role in selecting market players. Regulations and requirements that are necessary to conduct a business aim at guaranteeing that markets function with full respect for competition and the ROL.

Nevertheless, regulations in favor of individual entities have the opposite effect and are an impediment for players other than those favored. Furthermore, incumbents should generally have less of an incentive to stimulate public action against corruption, since it allows them a certain degree of protection from full market competition. In the end, corruption and economic and political inequality work as mutually reinforcing incentives which limit economic development. While players who are not favored may either exit their business or never start a new one, this has negative effects on society as a whole, slowing economic growth and development processes. Where would-be entrants are potential innovators, the consequences in terms of the impairment of dynamic efficiency and technological innovation are self-evident.

The results of an empirical study conducted jointly by the European Bank for Reconstruction and Development (EBRD) and the WB confirm that corruption represents a major obstacle curtailing access for new market entrants (Tanzi and Davoodi 2002a); their Business Environment and Enterprise Performance Survey analyzes results for a sample of 3,000 firms from transition economies. It is interesting to note that firms identify anti-competition practices and corruption as major obstacles to starting up a business. Our arguments below help illustrate these results.

New business creation and efficient market regulation are positively associated. It appears that if, on the one hand, market functioning is not ensured by the market per se and must be protected through the establishment of rules and regulations, on the other hand a non-distorted market promotes new market entrants. The support of regulations for efficient market functioning is a key element for firms and reflects a variety of distinct country-specific factors. Regulations favoring individual self-interested entities versus overall market functioning discourage new market entrants and create the opportunity for widespread corruption. Figure 2.1 illustrates the relation between State legislation in favor of new business creation and domestic corruption.

Figure 2.1 shows that lower corruption is generally associated with the number of government regulations; the evidence indicates that governance and corruption are negatively correlated.

Efficient market regulation is reflected in the quantity and quality of regulations (Figures 2.2 and 2.3, respectively). Bureaucratic requirements

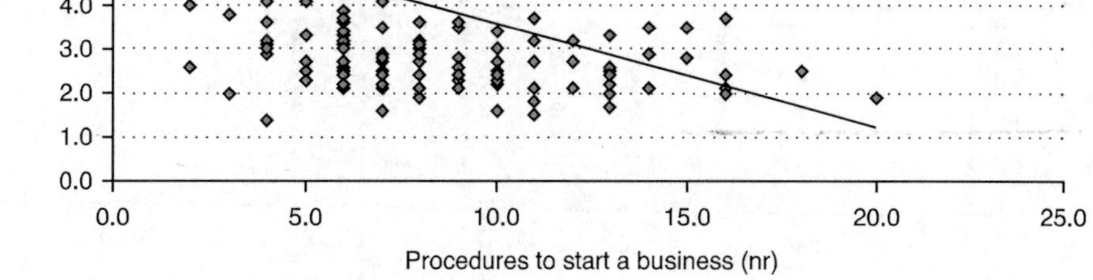

Note: CPI = 10 denotes the absence of corruption while CPI = 0 denotes the highest level of corruption.

Source: Authors' calculations based on WB Business Environment and Enterprise Performance Survey and TI data.

Figure 2.1 Corruption and procedures to start a new business, 2009

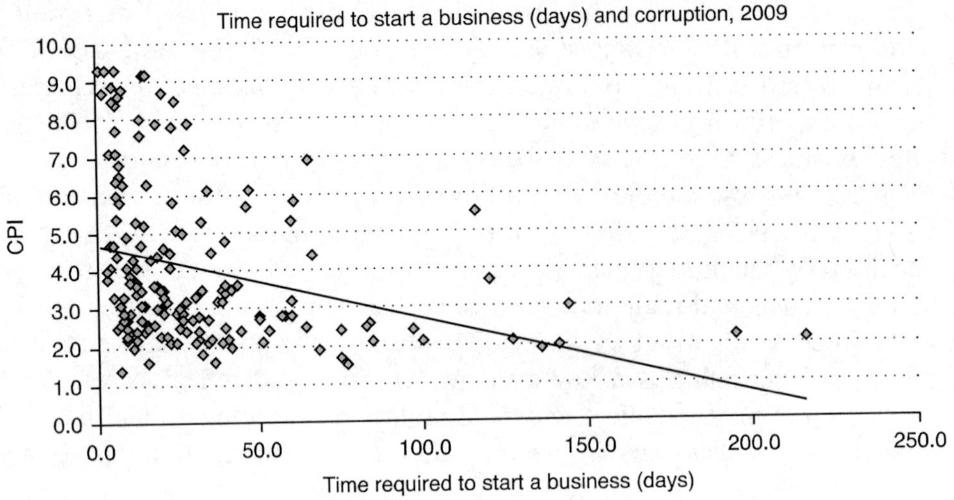

Note: CPI = 10 denotes the absence of corruption while CPI = 0 denotes the highest level of corruption.

Source: Authors' calculations based on WB and TI data.

Figure 2.2 Corruption and days required to start a new business, 2009

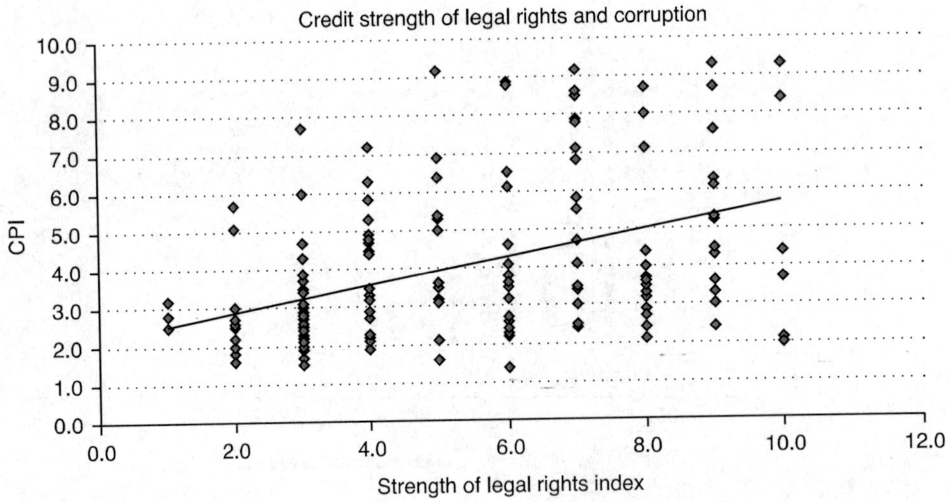

Note: CPI = 10 denotes the absence of corruption while CPI = 0 denotes the highest level of corruption.

Source: Authors' calculations based on WB and TI data.

Figure 2.3 Credit strength of legal rights and corruption, 2009

represent costs in terms of time and money; if, on the one hand, effective costs may reflect fiscal policy choices, on the other hand no policy choice justifies over-lengthy procedures: these represent a major efficiency loss. We may also note that a complex, non-transparent bureaucracy favors abuse by State officials and helps spread corruption; also, bureaucracies pervaded by corruption have an incentive to create complicated, non-transparent procedures and increase illegal rents.

In Figure 2.2 we represent a country's domestic corruption in association with how long it takes to go through the bureaucracy needed to start a new business. We use the number of days between the beginning of bureaucratic procedures and the effective beginning of business operations as a proxy for difficult and lengthy bureaucracy. Again, we use CPI as a proxy for domestic corruption.

Over-lengthy bureaucratic procedures are generally associated with high levels of corruption. With few exceptions (specifically, Spain's average corruption is associated with a number of days that are significantly higher than the industrialized country average), this relationship is strong all through our data set. It is interesting to note that in Indonesia, a country with one of the highest levels of corruption, it takes half a year before a new business can begin.

Corruption favors certain players and excludes others from access to necessary services. The inability to access services is among the principal factors militating against new business creation. An empirical study of a sample of Moscow-based firms found that management connectedness with city officials helps predict which firms will access bank finance (Tanzi 2002). Access to finance is critical to new businesses, and the granting of finance determines access of new market entrants. These results confirm empirical evidence as provided by recent studies on business-politics relations; these studies confirm that politically-connected firms enjoy better access to finance, stronger market power and tax benefits. Nevertheless, empirical evidence also shows that these businesses perform generally worse than other businesses. We deal extensively with this topic in Chapter 4.

The credit dimension of legal rights, as part of the general quality of governance, is also a primary determinant of market entry and investment decisions: extra costs are a significant obstacle to business creation. In Figure 2.3 we show that the impact of the cost of capital on the economy and domestic corruption are correlated. We may suppose that, if the cost of capital is too high, alternative (possibly uncertain and unsafe) sources of capital may be available in the economy.

Figure 2.3 shows that high corruption (low CPI) is associated with an adverse impact on the credit strength of legal rights, which in turn impacts negatively on the cost of capital. Again, the reason for this correlation may be the negative impact of bad governance on institutional decisions (which the cost of capital depends upon), risk factors or the fact that, should the cost of capital pervasively hinder their businesses, market players might use alternative, illegal practices, such as corruption. We cannot exclude the possibility that the relationship between the negative impact of high costs of capital and corruption may take effect through channels that involve such variables as economic growth and risk. We analyze below the dynamics associating corruption with economic growth and the cost of money.

2.4.2 Competitiveness: Effects of Corrupt Environments on Firms

In a market pervaded by corruption, resource allocation is distorted. The effects of corruption constitute an impediment not only to new business creation, but also to existing businesses, the interests of which are not protected. Since the difficulties for firms of operating in corrupt environments are substantial, special attention must be given to them.

2.4.2.1 Obstacles to businesses

Corruption distorts some of the main functions of government regulation. Over time there might be many instances of incumbent firms lobbying in favor of regulating their own sector since the cost of complying with the regulations may keep new companies from entering the market. When corrupt practices are added to the existing regulations, the distorting effect is intensified by the creation of new "illicit" artificial barriers. Several empirical works reveal that "in many countries (*e.g.*, Ukraine, Russia, and Indonesia) enterprises – especially small ones – are forced by public officials to pay to make things happen or even to keep bad things from happening. Often these payments must be made if the enterprise is to remain in business" (Tanzi 2002: 46).

A WB study (Kaufmann 2004) offers an analysis of channels through which corruption obstructs the activity of firms with operations in corrupt environments. This study is based on evidence from a World Economic Forum executive opinion (EOS) survey. This report analyzes the results of a survey from a sample of firms with operations in industrialized and developing countries. A question was asked to identify five factors (out of a list of 15) which most obstruct their business.

OECD's data show that in emerging economies factors with a major adverse impact are corruption, bureaucracy, political instability and finance; labor regulations, inefficient bureaucracy and taxes are critical factors in industrialized countries. We may note that these results reflect the perceptions of individual firms. Yet, this is not a good reason to underestimate these results: perceptions are at the basis of expectations and investment decisions.

If we group all 15 factors into seven sets, the governance-variables set is the most important: in particular, firms in 79 out of 104 EO-surveyed countries indicate that governance factors have a major adverse impact on their business. Corporate finance, labor market, tax regime and infrastructure rank as a second critical set. A significant gap exists between the first and second critical set.

2.4.2.2 Dangers and costs for firms

It should now be clear that corruption raises the costs and risks of doing business. To the obvious cost of paying bribes, one has to add the – more damaging in terms of overall efficiency – unnecessary delays or red-tape requirements devised by public officials in order to extract bribes. What is more, corruption is a cost for society as a whole and acts as a structural constraint. It may not be eliminated nor minimized significantly by individuals in the economy, but calls for governance reforms. Like security and crime prevention, corruption represents a fixed cost and is a major charge to corporate investment decisions. EOS results for 2004 (Kaufmann 2004) with respect to the relative costs of corruption reveal interesting issues.

OECD's data related to different institutional contexts shows that State capture is perceived as the most harmful threat according to firms in Southern Asia, Eastern Europe, Asian developing countries and the former Soviet Union. Also, it represents a major charge for firms in the G7 and OECD countries, South America and the newly industrialized countries (NICS). Only in North European countries – for which CPI scores are very good – does the impact of corruption seem negligible.

While it denotes the importance of State capture costs, we need to highlight also the importance of the costs of organized crime, including all organized corruption other than State capture. In Latin America, Eastern Europe, the former Soviet Union, Asian emerging economies, Northern Europe, and OECD countries, crime ranks second amongst all perceived costs for firms; moreover, the cost of organized crime for firms is one of the most significant for all countries, excluding Northern Europe.

Empirical evidence shows that terrorism is a significant cost in most of the areas examined, but only firms in industrialized countries perceive terrorism as a particularly dangerous threat. If we consider that State capture and organized crime are at significant levels also in this area, we may reasonably think that policymakers should widen their focus from terrorism to governance-related crimes. In the light of this argument, it may be useful to show empirical evidence from Kaufmann (2004) on a

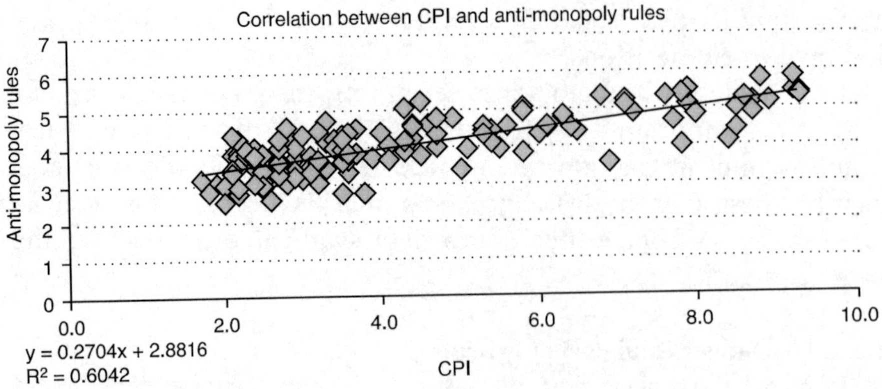

Note: CPI = 10 denotes the absence of corruption while CPI = 0 denotes the highest level of corruption.

Source: Authors' calculations based on the World Economic Forum (WEF) World Report and TI data.

Figure 2.4 Anti-monopoly rules and corruption, 2009

comparative analysis of the costs of terrorism and organized crime for firms in a specific country sample.

Organized crime appears to be a major obstacle to business in Italy and Russia. In spite of so significant an impact being more of an exception than the rule, we may note that, as in other industrialized countries including Spain, Portugal and Japan, the impact of organized crime must not be underestimated.

2.4.2.3 Regulated competition

Corruption uses governance factors to operate from inside markets and distort resource allocation (see Chapter 7 for an analysis of corruption in relation to governance variables). Opposing competitive market functioning are various obstacles, also in the form of laws to protect individual versus collective interests; the functioning of competition reflects the quality of regulations to protect it. In Figure 2.4 we show the relationship between the perceived efficient regulation of competition and CPI; well-regulated competition is associated with high CPI, or low corruption.

Inefficiently regulated markets are poorly competitive. Production processes are a priori distorted by inefficient resource allocation and a selection of market players that does not reflect quality parameters. If, on the one hand, inefficient firms or firms that are unable to meet consumer tastes can survive, provided they are favored by distortions, on the other

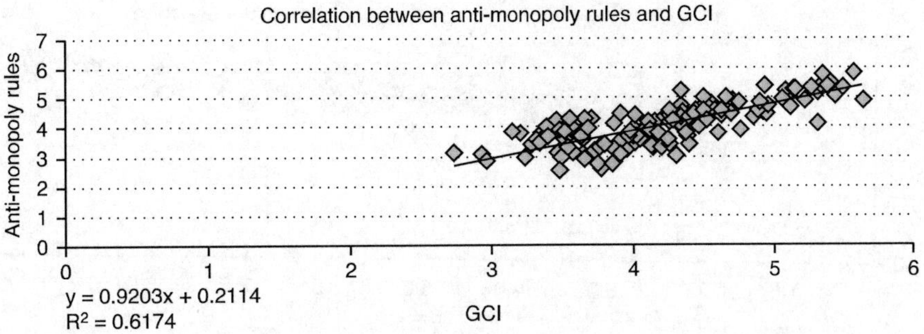

Source: Authors' calculations based on WEF and Global Competitiveness Index (GCI) data.

Figure 2.5 Anti-monopoly rules and firms' competitiveness, 2009

hand, firms not favored by regulations may be driven out of business irrespective of their quality. Such a market does not guarantee efficiency, hence it is not competitive.

This argument leads one to think that efficient regulation of competition and market competitiveness are positively associated. We analyze the evidence available to us. Figure 2.5 shows the positive and strong correlation between an index of efficient regulation and an index of firm competitiveness in individual countries.

Regulations that reflect bad market governance hinder competitive selection and favor inefficiencies. We may note that certain countries show patterns other than this general trend: while firm competitiveness is strong in the US, US regulation of competition is just above average and firms' competitiveness does not reach the highest efficiency levels.

From the fact that both country competitiveness and CPI are positively associated with the quality of competition, we may infer that competitiveness and corruption are also correlated. Based on different methodology and indicators, Kaufmann (2004) derives this relation running a regression of the GCI on the variables in his Figure 3.4. Corruption results in being the most significant explanatory variable, with a negative coefficient of *c*.0.76, measuring its correlation with competitiveness. In Figure 2.6 we show the empirical evidence that is available to us in this respect.

The data underline the fact that the higher the level of a country's competitiveness, the lower the corruption it experiences. However, within this general context, the United States shows a slightly different pattern: one of the world's most competitive economies shows low domestic corruption, but not the lowest.

This empirical evidence is particularly significant in its possible implications for economic policy. The data underline the importance of governing

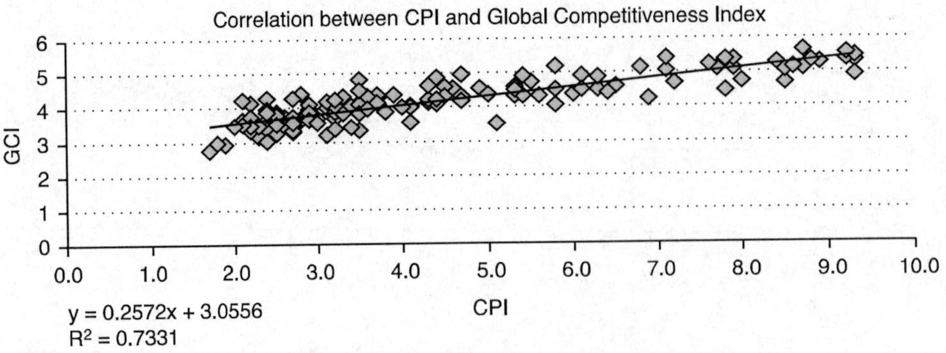

Note: CPI = 10 denotes the absence of corruption while CPI = 0 denotes the highest level of corruption.

Source: Authors' calculations based on GCI and TI data.

Figure 2.6 Competitiveness and corruption, 2009

competition clearly and efficiently; bureaucracy in excess and unnecessary State intervention cause serious inefficiency. To minimize government involvement means to eliminate discretion for State officials and inefficiencies in connection with bureaucratic regulators. Nevertheless, because markets per se may not guarantee market efficiency, there is a need for market regulation to protect the functioning of competition or to prevent a free rein for single firms, when, for reasons of economic efficiency, it is desirable to have a monopolistic or highly concentrated market structure (e.g. public utilities).

To ensure that regulations as established are correctly implemented, independent authorities are required to supervise the market. Mandated to monitor the functioning of competition, supervisory/regulatory authorities play a fundamental role in this respect. Nevertheless, the correct functioning of supervisors is threatened both by political and private pressures (the risks of political capture and private capture, respectively): to ensure that supervisors are not vulnerable to the possibility of such conditioning, it is necessary for such institutions to undertake their activities with a high degree of autonomy. Prominent examples are the independent agencies constituted worldwide in order to regulate and monitor economic sectors after their full or partial liberalization and privatization, like the network industries (e.g. energy and telecommunication). If effective autonomy cannot be granted and preserved, there may be a basis for the development of power abuse and corruption (see our further analysis of institutions and governance in Chapter 7).

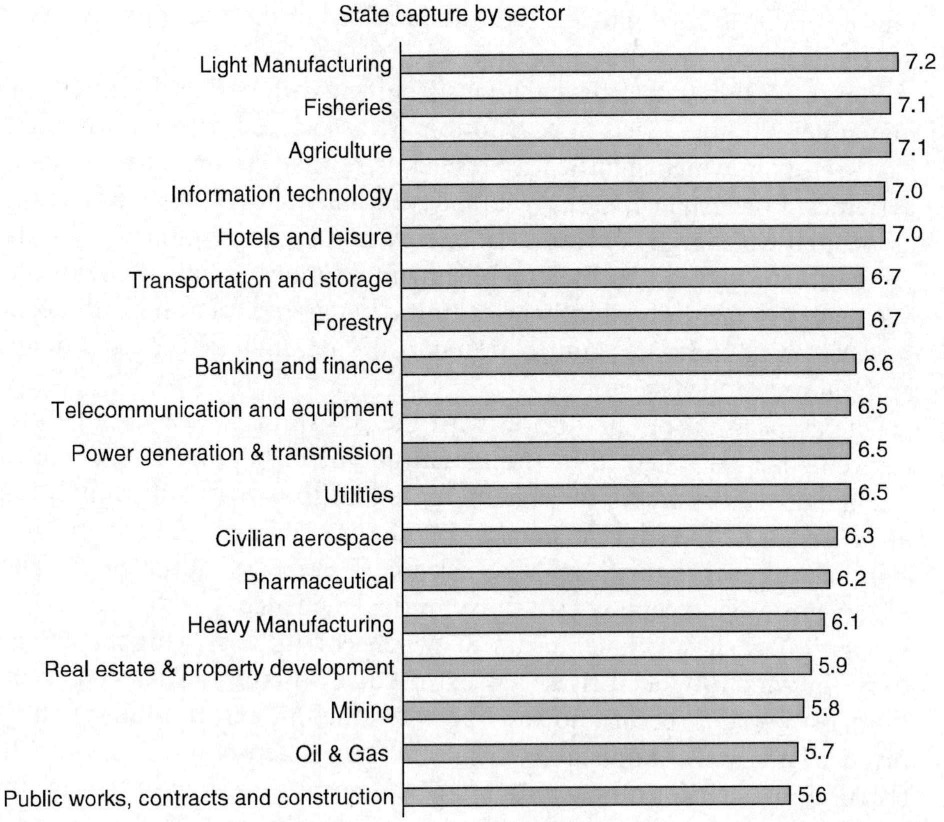

Note: 0 denotes highest perceived corruption and 10 denotes the absence of corruption.

Source: TI, BPI 2009.

Figure 2.7 Sectors where bribe payments to State officials are more frequent, 2008

2.4.3 Corruption and its Impact on Markets

Corruption has no uniform impact on all markets, or on all businesses in one market. The impact of corruption may be greater for certain businesses. Environments in which there is concentrated economic or political power largely favor the development of corruption. An incentive to corruption is that the costs of prosecution are more than compensated by illegal rents.

To analyze the impact of corruption in different sectors of the economy, we utilize the results of a study by TI. Figure 2.7 illustrates the perceptions of sampled firms in sectors where bribe payments are more frequent. Our reference index is the bribe payers index (BPI), which is calculated using a sample of emerging countries that are involved in international trade and are the recipients of foreign finance.

Figure 2.7 shows data that are consistent with our earlier discussion. We may note that high levels of corruption are associated with highly capitalized sectors in which significant State constraints exist on entrepreneurial activities. For instance, in real estate development corruption exists that is associated with large contracts. In energy and telecommunications, State regulations may lead to the establishment of monopolies or oligopolies. We may also mention all industries supplying governmental products and services only, under no competition constraints: included are the defense and pharmaceutical sectors.

The association of corruption with the possibility of earning substantial rents is also reflected in the magnitude of bribe amounts. If, on the one hand, sectors where there is the potential to extract substantial rents are corrupt to the highest degree, on the other hand, favors that earn significant benefits for those who ask may have a very high price. These arguments are in keeping with the empirical evidence.

Figure 2.8 shows that sectors in which corruption is higher are also those in which higher bribes are extorted. Construction is perceived as the most corrupt sector and the one where the highest amount is paid in bribes. This is also applicable to oil and gas, defense and energy. While corruption is close to the average, bribe amounts are low in the banking and finance sectors, as shown in Figures 2.7 (in which banking and finance rank 8) and 2.8 (in which banking and finance rank 2) respectively.

2.4.4 Small- and Medium-sized Firms

We conclude our discussion of the multi-faceted market impact of corruption with a focus on SMEs: their peculiarity is not so much that they contribute to widespread corruption, as that they may not be able to bear its additional costs.

The empirical study of OECD countries during the 1990s by Tanzi and Davoodi (2002a and 2002b) spells out a number of interesting aspects which lie behind the changing perception of the role of SMEs in the economy: even though they may comprise a smaller share of added value in the economy than large enterprises, they employ the bulk of the labor force and create most of the new jobs. Consistent with their importance in the employment share, they tend to be less capital intensive. While large firms tend to be process-innovative, SMEs tend to invest more in product-vs-process innovation (as larger firms do). They are more financially constrained than large enterprises, which have easier access to capital markets. Access to finance aside, their survival depends on

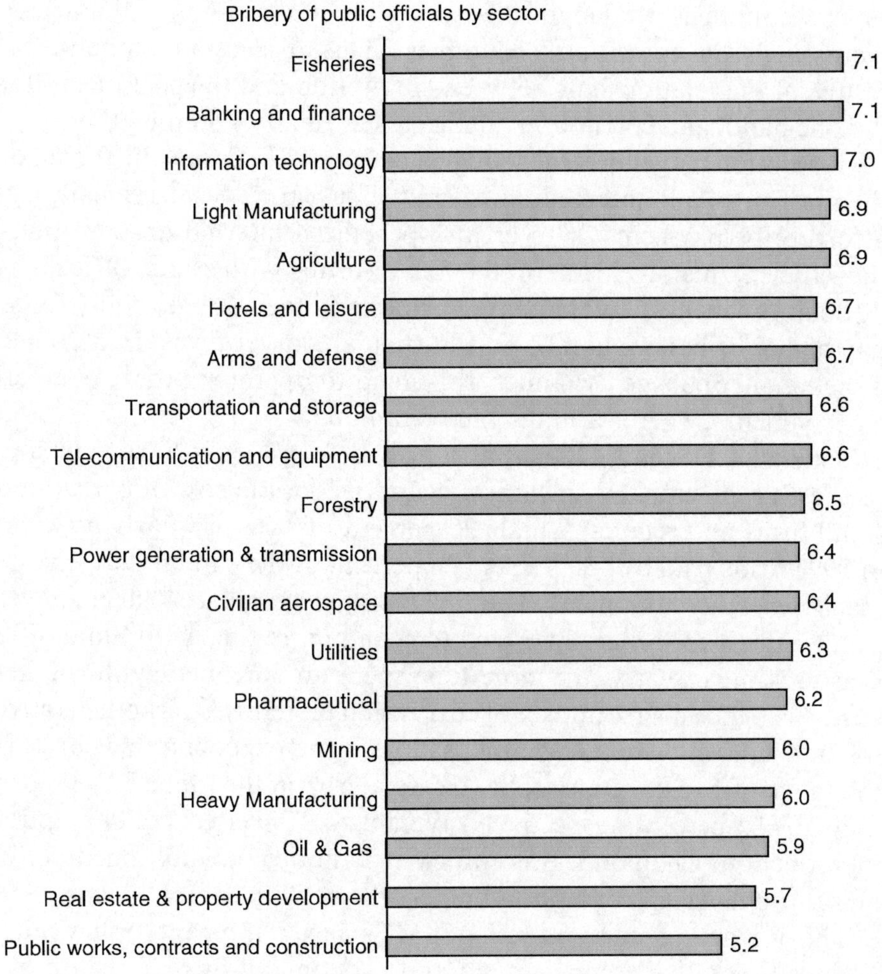

Note: Scores reflect the percentage of answers that mention a specific sector.

Source: TI, BPI 2008.

Figure 2.8 Sectors where bribe payments to public officials are higher in amount, 2008

competent entrepreneurship, talented management, and the environment they face.

The vital role of SMEs is not limited to OECD countries, but extends to transition economies and developing countries as well. Tanzi and Davoodi (2002a and 2002b) highlight that the effect of corruption is differentiated among enterprises and is particularly intense for SMEs. For this reason corruption acts as a brake on the engines that promote growth in most countries: obstacles to the creation and growth of small new enterprises cause economies to languish, especially in developing countries and increasingly in transition economies. This discussion strengthens the results of the relationships between corruption and the cost of capital, on the one hand, and corruption and access to finance, on the other.

Corruption may represent so high a cost that SMEs may be forced out of the market: small- and medium-sized (versus large) firms typically cannot afford bribe payments or to create specialized internal organizations for the efficient management of the relationship with State officials. It is difficult for them to avoid paying bribes and they are generally forced to pay higher bribes per unit of output than are larger firms. Far from experiencing oligopolistic dynamics, they tend to operate in more competitive environments, where earnings can be minimal.

Tanzi and Davoodi (2002a) also provide empirical evidence in support of these arguments. For instance, in Indonesia, the cost of corruption for small firms and retailers equals 20 percent of sales; similarly, in Uganda, in 1997 firms paid bribes of up to 28 percent of the capital they invested in machinery and equipment. There is empirical evidence that managers of smaller firms are generally forced to spend more time with State officials. Because time is scarce, the more time spent on bureaucracy the higher the cost. Also, the adverse impact of corruption on returns to capital is stronger for smaller firms: while Argentina's larger firms experience lower returns in the range of 1 to 2.5 percent, SMEs see a drop in the range 3.0–3.6 percent and 2.0–2.5 percent, respectively. We analyze the effects of corruption on investment in Chapter 3. It is sufficient to notice the multiplicity of channels through which corruption hinders the activity of small firms.

The impact of corruption on SMEs has important policy implications. SMEs drive labor demand and economic growth; because of this, economic policy should seek to eliminate obstacles to their activities to promote development. Nevertheless, our earlier discussion highlighted how corruption negatively impacts the possibility that SMEs continue their activities; hence, policy measures in their favor may prove ineffective unless attention is drawn to the costs of corruption.

A similar lesson can be drawn to that learned for the relationship between competitiveness and corruption: economic development through SMEs in corrupt economies is not generally possible unless financial sector governance undergoes major reforms.

2.5 THE ALLOCATION OF TALENTS

The existence of markets pervaded by corruption is at the same time cause and effect of the possibility that most talented individuals will prefer rent-seeking versus productive activities. Several recent studies have confirmed this trend and underlined the possible adverse implications for economic growth (Murphy, Shleifer, and Vishny 1991, Tanzi and Davoodi 2002a). Like the first one, the second study is empirical research analyzing the implications of students from 53 countries who choose to enroll in productive activities, such as engineering, versus rent-seeking-associated activities such as law. The results of regressions show that domestic corruption is adversely correlated with the choice of productive activities; there is also a major adverse impact on growth due to the allocation of talent in favor of non-productive activities. Finally, individuals from affluent social groups are more inclined to choose non-productive activities in corrupt environments; Dabla-Norris and Wade (2002) show that, if constraints exist on financial markets, individuals with income in excess of a certain critical threshold tend to favor rent-seeking. This reflects an attempt both to preserve initial wealth and, more importantly, to prevent others from appropriating this wealth.

In Chapter 3 we bring the realistic insights of the emerging field of behavioural economics into our analysis of corruption dynamics in order to understand how the economy works when people really are human, that is to say, possessed of what Akerlof and Shiller (2009) – with a clear reference to J.M. Keynes – call "all-too animal spirits", i.e. people's non-economic motives, irrational (irrational from the perspectives of the simplistic and ad hoc assumption-driven neoclassical economics) behaviors. In the context of the present paragraph, another remark is worth emphasizing: endemic corruption acts as a tremendously blocking psychological factor for those who are willing to invest in their education and talent; our view is that, when strongly rooted in a given society, it has the potential to increase fear, frustration, and anger to such an extent that it can unconsciously paralyze any plan over the mid to long run of young generations and impede them from entering into the adult phase of their own lives. The cost in terms of wasted energy and frustrated talents may be enormous. The evidence on the relationship between the number of school dropouts and corruption we provide in Chapter 3 represents the first evidence in favor of this hypothesis.

2.6 ECONOMIC DEVELOPMENT AND CORRUPTION

Corruption may impact a country's economic development not only through market dynamics, but also through the environment where those dynamics develop. A common proxy for a country's welfare, gross domestic product (GDP), measures, in fact, annual economic production. It does not, however, measure potential development. Potential growth results from a number of factors that are discussed in greater detail in Chapter 3.

Our focus is now on an index of business environment quality. The business environment index reflects a country's existing opportunities to start new businesses; it includes such sub-indexes as market potential, fiscal policies, labor conditions, infrastructure, know-how, and, finally, a sub-index for the quality of a country's political environment. While it may provide no representation of a society's overall development potential, it offers a perspective on the existing market environment. This index not only takes into account constraints imposed by market regulations, but represents a proxy for a country's infrastructure, workforce, investment potential and political environment. Empirical evidence with respect to the relationship between a country's corruption and *governance* quality, and between corruption and competitiveness, respectively, indicates that corruption also has an adverse impact on the business environment.

Arnone and Iliopulos (2005) present empirical evidence on the correlation between the business environment index and CPI. As argued above, data show that a country's business environment quality and domestic corruption are clearly related; markets favoring the development of entrepreneurial activities are clearly the least corrupt. We can go a step further by considering recent evidence from Italy. It is fair to state that historically Italy has confronted levels of political corruption higher than those found in other countries at similar levels of development. Thanks to the availability of comparative rankings according to the perceived corruption starting in the 1990s, we confidently assert that contemporary Italy is a relatively highly corrupt country. Already in 2000, Italy ranked as the world's most corrupt wealthy democracy and since then its ranking has worsened. At the same time, at least considering some of the main variables related to the political environment used by the EIU to generate the business environment index: Government policy towards business; Effectiveness of political system in policy formulation and execution; Quality of the bureaucracy; Transparency and fairness of legal system; Efficiency of legal system, performed significantly worse than the regional average (out of 18 countries: Austria, Belgium, Cyprus, Denmark, Finland, France, Germany, Greece, Ireland, Italy, the Netherlands, Norway, Portugal, Spain, Sweden, Switzerland, Turkey and the UK) over the period 2005–2009 and, on aggregate, the gap became more significant over the period 2010–14.[4] In more detail, over the period 2005–2009, Italy scored 3.0 in

4 Cfr. www.funzionepubblica.gov.it.

Government policy towards business versus the 3.9 of the regional area; 3.0 versus 3.9 in Effectiveness of political system in policy formulation and execution; 3.0 versus 3.7 in Quality of the bureaucracy; 3.0 v. 4.0 in Transparency and fairness of legal system; and, finally, 2 versus 4.2 in Efficiency of legal system. Over the period 2010–2014, Italy scored 3.0 in Government policy towards business versus the 3.8 of the regional area; 2.0 versus 3.4 in Effectiveness of political system in policy formulation and execution; 3.0 versus 3.7 in Quality of the bureaucracy; 3.0 v. 4.0 in Transparency and fairness of legal system; and, finally, 2 versus 4.2 in Efficiency of legal system. Recalling that Italy has also ranked worse and worse in terms of the main corruption perception-based indexes over the same periods, again we find a telling case to confirm the argued correlation between a country's business environment quality and domestic corruption.

This evidence provides a wider focus for our analysis. Corruption has a deep impact on society: its effects are not only of concern in several aspects of economic life, but extend to institutional dimensions (Chapter 7).

3. Corruption and macroeconomic performance

3.1 INTRODUCTION

In Chapter 2 we discussed the microeconomic effects of corruption: our analysis highlighted the fact that corruption adversely impacts society in the form of a major efficiency loss. Additionally, we noticed that a negative correlation exists between certain variables that are proxies of governance quality and a country's domestic corruption. We showed that a negative correlation also exists between corruption and domestic competitiveness. These relationships call out to policymakers as they show how corruption represents a limit for business competitiveness and a drag on economic development. Economic policies that initiate governance-enhancing reforms can be effective in promoting a country's competitiveness (Alesina and Giavazzi 2006).

The literature on the impact of corruption on economic performance is exceptionally wide: the focus of our analysis shifts now from the perspective of firms and markets to the dynamics underlying the determination of macro variables in an economic system.[1] We turn our attention to the effects of corruption on a country's income, trade, and interest rates for both industrialized and developing economies; we also discuss how corruption adversely affects macroeconomic performance indirectly via education or trade flows. The second part of this chapter is devoted to an in-depth analysis of the effects of corruption on the public sector, including its performance during economic cycles. Finally, in the last paragraph our focus broadens to the issue of the persistence of corruption over time.

1 This chapter builds on, expands, and updates Arnone and Iliopulos (2005). Leonardo Borlini co-authored Sections 3.3.2 and 3.7.

3.2 DOMESTIC PRODUCT

Corruption is not a feature of poorer countries only, but an evil that strikes advanced economies as well. Nevertheless, our arguments so far infer that poorer countries may be more easily struck; given the relationship between bad governance and corruption, to establish State organizations that are not vulnerable to corruption means committing major resources to institutional apparatuses and a good incentive system for public officials (see Chapter 7).

The direction of causation between corruption and economic wealth may not be established unequivocally because very often both variables are mutually influential. In general, poorer countries do not have the necessary means to create efficient bureaucracies or checks to fight corruption. Moreover, low income drives individuals to corruption as a way to improve their living standards. Our earlier analysis emphasized how corruption may adversely affect economic development.

One important distinction is between national production and its growth. Both GDP and GNP offer a static measure of economic size and are of no use in defining causation with respect to corruption. We will analyze later how corruption is related to economic growth, and the direction of causation.

Figure 3.1 maps GDP per capita and CPI in a cross-country data set

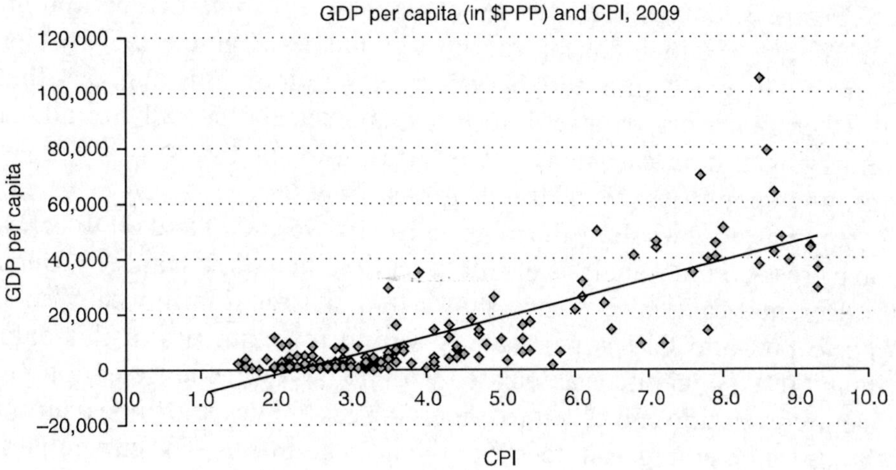

Note: CPI = 10 denotes absence of corruption while CPI = 0 denotes highest corruption level.

Source: Authors' calculations from TI and WB data.

Figure 3.1 GDP per capita and domestic corruption, 2009

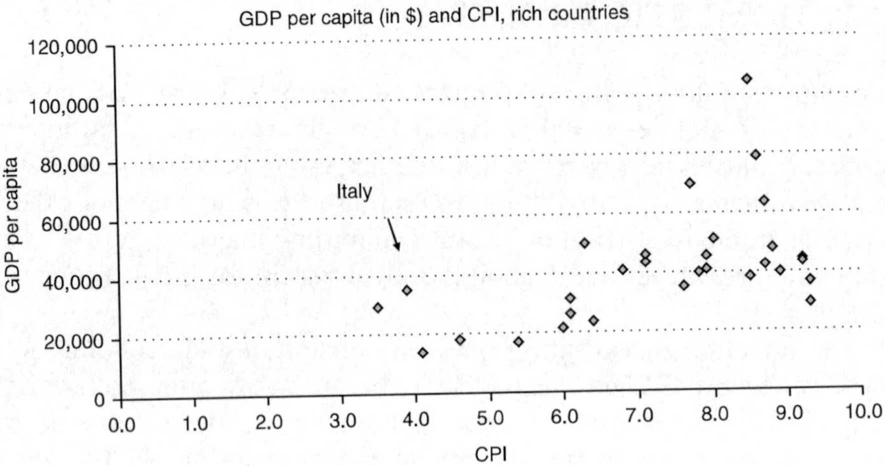

Note: CPI = 10 denotes absence of corruption while CPI = 0 denotes highest corruption level.

Source: Authors' calculations from TI and WB data.

Figure 3.2 GNP per capita and domestic corruption, 2009, advanced economies

that includes well over 120 countries. In line with our expectations, high income is generally associated with high CPI scores.

Figure 3.1 maps the adverse relationship of domestic corruption and GDP, and the high concentration of countries characterized by close to zero GDP per capita and pervasive corruption. This suggests that we further divide our data set into three data sets, specifically, of advanced, emerging and developing countries. It is now possible to verify for which group of countries this relationship is strongest.

In Figure 3.2 we show the relationship between CPI and GDP per capita in a cross-country analysis of a data set that includes advanced economies.

Recent empirical evidence shows that the relationship between GDP per capita and CPI is particularly strong for countries in this data set; high GDP per capita is associated with high CPI, i.e. low corruption. The same correlation comes out for emerging economies; the same relationship holds for emerging as it does for advanced countries. The curve that minimizes differences amongst diverse points as graphed is positively sloped.

We also note that income and CPI tend to be concentrated at very low levels in this data set. Finally, we show the relation between GDP per capita and CPI for the developing country data set.

Figure 3.4 shows a positive relationship between domestic corruption and GDP per capita in developing countries. High GDP per capita is

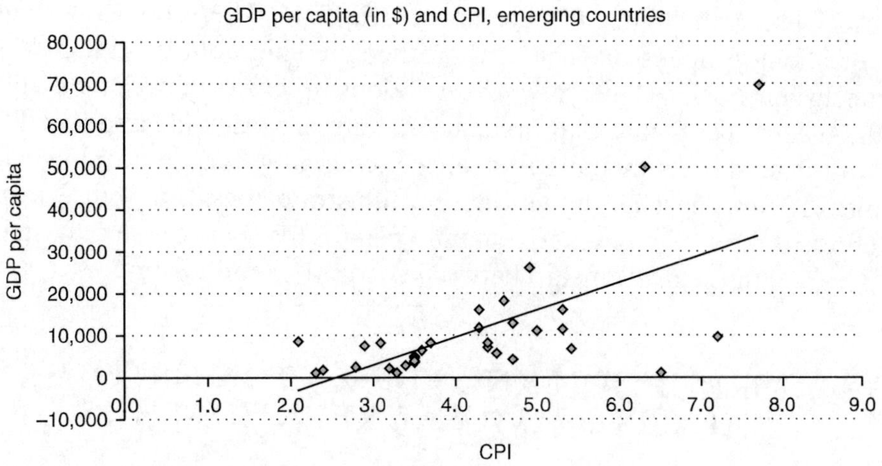

Note: CPI = 10 denotes absence of corruption while CPI = 0 denotes highest corruption level.

Source: Authors' calculations from TI and WB data.

Figure 3.3 GDP per capita and domestic corruption, 2009, emerging economies

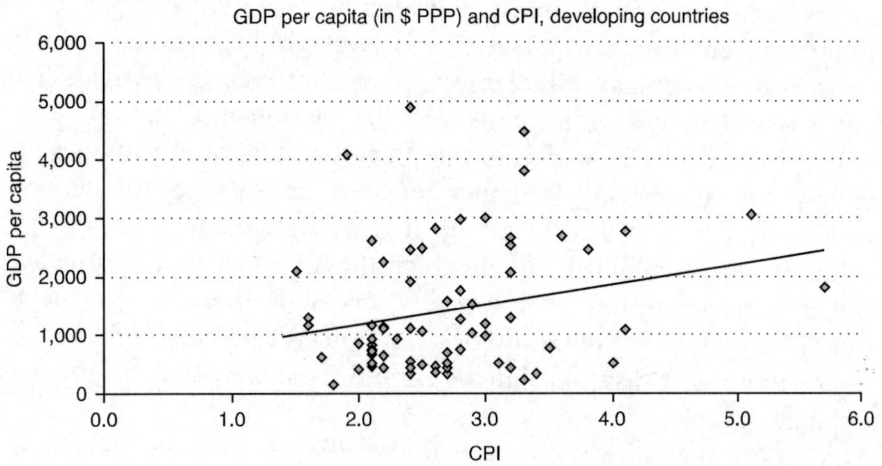

Note: CPI = 10 denotes absence of corruption while CPI = 0 denotes highest corruption level.

Source: Authors' calculations from TI and WB data.

Figure 3.4 GDP per capita and domestic corruption, 2009, developing economies

associated with high CPI, i.e. low corruption. The data show higher, more homogeneous dispersion than the emerging country data set. Our conclusion now is that a negative relationship exists between corruption and income per capita that holds for countries worldwide and is reflected in all data subsets including advanced, emerging and developing economies. The evidence as shown does not illustrate causation, but is a static representation of reality. A dynamic perspective is necessary to analyze causation in the relationship between corruption and income.

3.3 CORRUPTION AND EFFECTS ON GROWTH: AN ANALYSIS OF CAUSAL RELATIONSHIPS

The economic literature has found that domestic corruption and economic growth are inversely related. As we mentioned earlier, empirical studies (Murphy, Shleifer, and Vishny 1991) find a negative impact of corruption on growth due to resources being allocated in favor of rent-seeking activities. Mauro (1995) finds a relationship between growth and corruption based on a negative impact on investments; this is also a finding of Bardhan (1997), who focuses on distortions in investment allocation. Tanzi and Davoodi (2002a, 2002b) consider public and private investments separately and pay particular attention to small and medium firms. Finally, recent studies (Pellegrini and Gerlagh 2004) make a distinction between direct versus indirect effects of corruption on growth and conduct an empirical analysis of the causes of this relationship.

Empirical evidence shown in the previous paragraph provides no indication of the underlying dynamics nor of the causal direction between corruption and growth. It is necessary that we shift the focus of our analysis to discuss the channels through which these two variables influence each other. Because mutual dependence is very high, there is no possibility of establishing only one direction of causation. We will highlight the prevailing direction of causation, but we should remember that feedback effects are unavoidable.

A survey of empirical literature on the effects of corruption shows that, given the same moral qualities and cultural inclination to comply with the law, governance variables are the principal factors underlying domestic corruption, while the effects of other variables are secondary (Mauro 1995). This allows us to continue our study while we set aside the effects of growth on corruption. We will only consider causation as running from corruption to growth and not vice versa. Nevertheless, we recognize that economic growth may have effects on CPI, though not prevalent, primarily through an impact on institutions (Pellegrini and Gerlagh 2004).

Growth has no unequivocal impact on domestic corruption: strong and sudden growth (e.g. the result of the discovery of new natural resources or existing resources in large quantities) tends to be associated with higher domestic corruption (Leite and Weidmann 2002). Conversely, when economic growth is reflected in improved quality of institutions and equally shared higher living standards, corruption tends to decrease.

To estimate the effects of corruption, Pellegrini and Gerlagh (2004) run a regression whereby economic growth depends upon an initial level of income, domestic corruption and a vector of variables that the economic literature on growth identifies as determinants; this regression shows that the *direct* effect of corruption on growth is slightly significant. A change of one standard deviation in the corruption variable increases growth by a modest 0.20 percent. The direct effect on the growth rate of a reduction in the corruption index seems insubstantial, when compared to the contribution of any of the other independent variables. These results seem to contradict our earlier analysis and require further discussion.

3.3.1 Indirect Causation: Investments, Risk and Interest Rates

The empirical evidence of a strong relationship between corruption and growth leads us to think that, because it is not direct, this relationship must be of an indirect nature. Hence we take into consideration the variables that economic literature identifies as main determinants (Pellegrini and Gerlagh 2004) and verify whether, also based on available empirical evidence, corruption has a strong impact on them.

Firstly, we analyze gross investments. Empirical studies show that corruption significantly lowers private investment, thereby reducing growth. Mauro (1995) estimates that a one standard deviation improvement in the corruption index leads to an increase in the investment rate of 2.9 percent of GDP. Analogously, Pellegrini and Gerlagh (2004) find that a one standard deviation increase in the CPI increases investments by 2.46 percentage points; this, in turn, enhances economic growth by 0.34 percent a year. As they remark, the effect of the investment transmission channel exceeds substantially the direct corruption effect of 0.20 percent growth per year (calculated above). Robustness tests confirm the direction of causality: a high degree of corruption hinders gross investment, which, in turn, dampens growth.

The negative relationship between investments and corruption reflects the additional costs of bribery for firms. In addition to the amount of such bribes, other charges must be considered in connection with the execution of bribery-based agreements. Agreements in connection with bribe payments are obviously illegal, and no external authority exists that may be called upon to guarantee their execution. Costs may be incurred in connection with illegal activities in the event of counterparty non-performance and to maintain secrecy throughout the procedure.

We now present the relationship between investments and corruption based on recent empirical evidence. Which indicator is best suited to proxy gross investments is not an obvious choice, and must be further supplemented. We note that multiple factors cause capital movements internationally. Included are such determinants as liberalized capital movements on an international basis, access to finance and, above all, economic growth. To assess the impact of corruption on investments we measure the effect of corruption on investment risk, after controlling for other factors. This proxy allows us to determine how corruption may materially hinder investments, while we control for the direct effects of growth on investments; economic growth heavily impacts investments decisions and is difficult to isolate.

We now consider the International Country Risk Guide (ICRG). This index reflects economic, financial and political risk ratings for 140 countries and helps determine the opportunity to invest or start new businesses in a country. It includes 22 variables in the subcategories of political, economic or financial country risk ratings.[2] As an indicator of investment risk, ICRG ratings are calculated with the help of several financial institutions and firms. It is reasonable to assume that this index can proxy the cost of investment risk on a worldwide basis. This risk variable is a composite index and reflects expectations underlying investment decisions.

The data show a clear relationship between investment risk and CPI: high corruption is associated with high risk. We note that this relation is very strong and the data present a very high concentration along the line that minimizes deviations. This results in the increased significance of this relationship; we may hence conclude that risk in connection with

---

2 Political country risk rating includes such indicators as government stability, socio-economic conditions, investment profile, internal and external conflicts, corruption, military in politics, religious tensions, law and order, ethnic tensions, democratic accountability (mechanisms whereby policymakers in democratic systems are held accountable to voters) and bureaucracy quality. Financial risk indicators include foreign debt as a percentage of GDP, foreign debt service and current account as a percentage of exports, international liquidity (in months of imports) and exchange rate stability. Economic risk components are GDP per head of population, real annual GDP growth, the annual inflation rate, the budget balance as a percentage of GDP and current account as a percentage of GDP. We note that corruption is one sub-component of political risk. This suggests that domestic corruption has an impact on the relationship we are examining. Nevertheless, this effect is minimal.

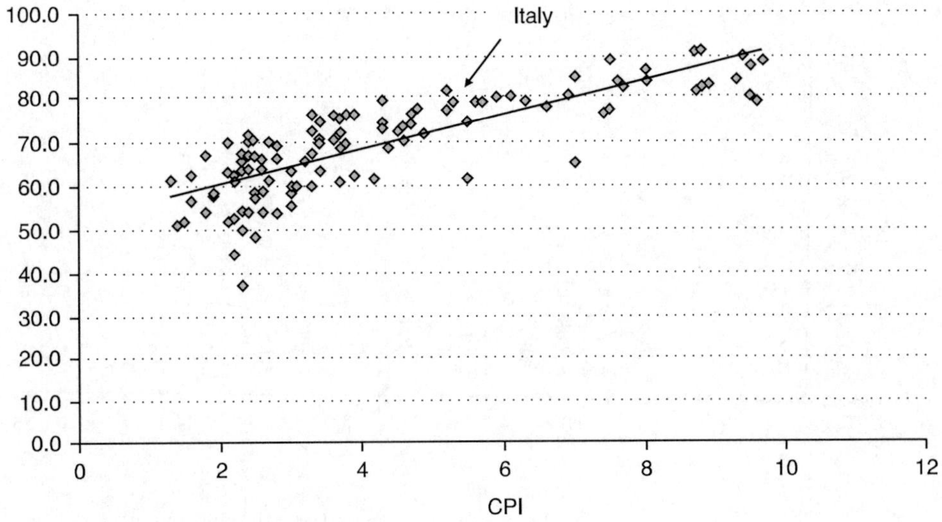

Notes:
CPI = 10 denotes absence of corruption while CPI = 0 denotes highest corruption level.
A score of 0 indicates maximum risk, 100 indicates the absence of risk.

Source: Authors' calculations from TI and IMF data.

Figure 3.5 Cost of investment risk and corruption, 2002, 2003 (Investment risk index)

investment decisions in a country is strongly correlated with domestic corruption. In a country characterized by pervasive corruption, investment risk is substantial and creates a drag on economic activity.

We now consider interest rates and verify if higher risk due to domestic corruption is reflected in a higher cost of money. If so, it would be possible to obtain an explicit measure of the macroeconomic cost of corruption. We focus our attention on the spreads between interest rates applied to deposits versus loans. This variable proxies perceived risks on bank loans: the higher the risks of a loan, the higher the premium required by banks to lend the money. It is clear that if the cost of finance is high, this creates a drag on investment. Figure 3.6 shows the relationship between CPI and interest rate spreads for a worldwide representative country data set.

Empirical evidence shows that high levels of corruption are associated with a high cost of finance for a worldwide representative data set.[3] This

[3] We note, however, that interest rate spreads are an indication not only of the degree of risk associated with money lending, but also of the degree of concentration in the banking sector.

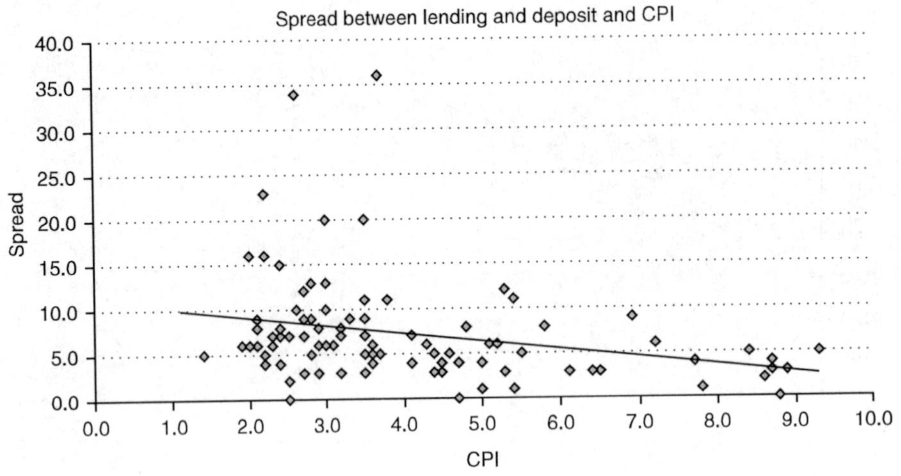

Note: CPI = 10 denotes absence of corruption while CPI = 0 denotes highest corruption level.

Source: Authors' calculations from TI and IMF data.

Figure 3.6 Interest rate spreads and corruption, 2009

result is significant and has important implications: it allows us to calculate the impact of corruption on interest rate spreads and offers an accurate measure of the cost of corruption. The impact is represented by the slope of the straight line that minimizes quadratic deviations, as in Figure 3.6; this straight line represents the relationship under consideration. Hence, we calculate the slope of the straight line that minimizes deviations and obtain the relationship between CPI and interest rate spreads.[4] The data show that the slope of the regression line (represented in Figure 3.16) has a coefficient of -1.15: for a unit increase in the CPI, spreads decrease by 1.15 percentage points. This means that a unit increase in the CPI is associated with a more than proportional increase in the cost of money; corruption causes a higher cost of finance, which we can accurately calculate.

3.3.1.1 Foreign direct investment

The impact of corruption is particularly significant for foreign direct investment (FDI). This is foreign capital flowing into low-liquidity activities as opposed to financial ones, through which foreign investors commit

4 Because there are no empirical studies that provide the value of this coefficient, we calculate it through a regression whereby interest rate spreads depend on CPI values (F-test and t-test confirm the significance of this relationship).

resources to a country on a medium-to-long-term basis. Foreign investors must look carefully at the risks of the economic environment in which they commit resources. It is evident that corruption and the costs involved are part of the decision-making process for investors on an international basis.

The role of FDI in driving growth is known in the economic literature (Tanzi and Davoodi 2002a). The significant technology and know-how that is part of FDI has a role in innovation. FDI is clearly a catalyst in improving the productivity of domestic investment. Finally, FDI represents an important means of financing investment that may not be possible without a contraction of domestic consumption.

Wei (1997) estimates that a percentage point deterioration in the CPI causes an 11 percent decrease in FDI. It is important to note that an equivalent increase of a tax on investments is estimated to have a negative impact on FDI of only 3.3 percent. Taxes are a lower cost than corruption for economic agents because there are no additional costs in connection with confidentiality and because they are established on an a priori basis, which makes them predictable. It is estimated that the less predictable corruption (the greater the dispersion of CPI) the greater the uncertainty of investors and the risk to investments (Wei 1997).

We show recent empirical evidence to confirm the relationship between corruption and FDI. To eliminate the effect of other income-related variables, we again split our worldwide data set into three subsets of advanced, emerging and developing countries, respectively.

Figure 3.7 shows that countries in which corruption is lower are characterized by higher FDI as a percentage of GDP. This means that international investors seem to prefer less corrupt countries as a destination for their lower-liquidity assets.

Figure 3.8 shows the relationship between corruption and FDI as a percentage of GDP in emerging countries. High CPI levels are associated with high FDI as a percentage of GDP also for emerging countries. We note that the data present lower dispersion than for advanced countries and are more clustered along the trend line (except for the Czech Republic, which has both a high FDI/GDP ratio and high corruption). This leads us to think that in emerging countries, for which bureaucracy, both domestically and internationally, provides fewer guarantees than for advanced countries, corruption seems to be a particularly important factor in the investment decisions of international investors.

Finally, we consider a developing country data set (Figure 3.9). We take the opportunity to emphasize that, particularly for this data set, we expect that the relationship between CPI and FDI will also be affected by variables like free capital movements and guarantees offered in individual countries. If in advanced countries open markets and solid international

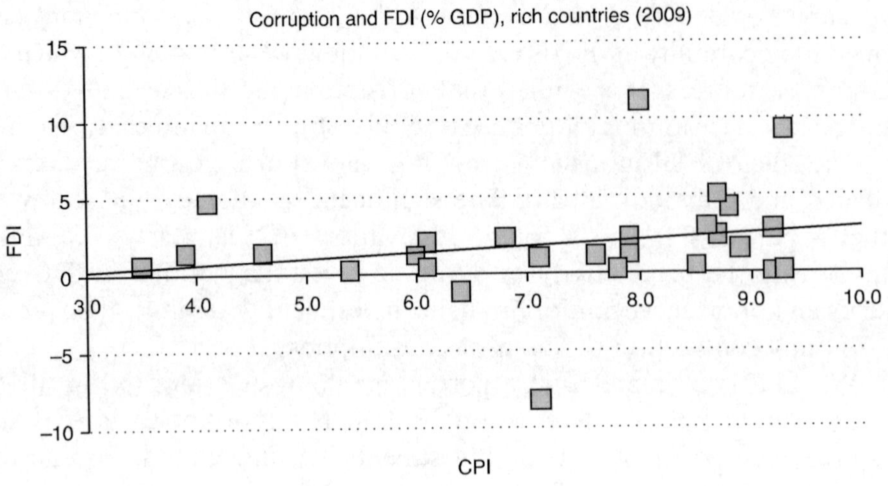

Note: CPI = 10 denotes absence of corruption while CPI = 0 denotes highest corruption level.

Source: Authors' calculations from TI and IMF data.

Figure 3.7 Corruption and FDI, 2009, advanced countries

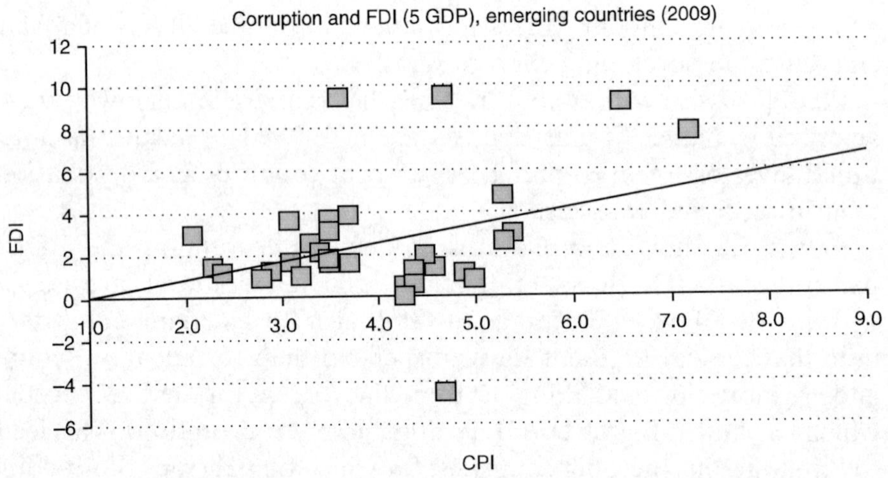

Note: CPI = 10 denotes absence of corruption while CPI = 0 denotes highest corruption level.

Source: Authors' calculations from TI and IMF data.

Figure 3.8 Corruption and FDI, 2009, emerging economies

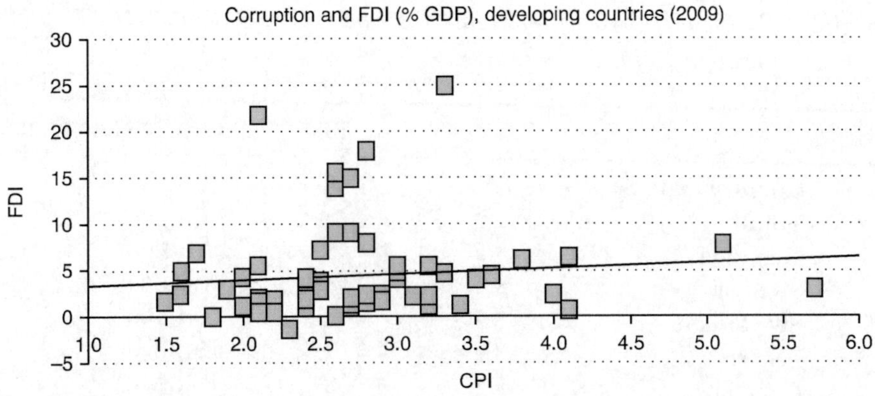

Note: CPI = 10 denotes absence of corruption while CPI = 0 denotes highest corruption level.

Source: Authors' calculations from TI and WB data.

Figure 3.9 Corruption and FDI, 2009, developing countries

guarantees were seen to be significant factors, while capital market structure and guarantees were seen to be significant factors in emerging countries, these dynamics are key in developing countries.

In line with our expectations, the relationship between CPI and FDI appears weaker and the data show higher dispersion.

3.3.1.2 Capital flows and exported corruption

The financial relations of multinational companies based in several countries have frequently brought to light factors characterizing domestic markets in countries around the world. Multinational corporations have begun to confront corruption dynamics that create obstacles to certain markets more than others, and international investors have started taking these factors into consideration when making their investment decisions. The proliferation of multinational corporations has highlighted the fact that certain countries are more inclined to export corruption than others. Certain multinational corporations are in fact more inclined than others to bribe public officials in the country where they have their operations, thus "exporting" corruption. This phenomenon involves primarily industrialized countries (that export capital worldwide) and emerging economies, for which capital flows are largely destined.

Table 3.1 lists countries from which capital flows originate, whose corporations are more inclined to self-benefiting payments. In column 1 countries are ranked based on bribe-payment proneness; we note that at the top of the list are those countries that are less prone to bribe foreign

Table 3.1 Exported corruption, countries where corporations tend to bribe public officials, 1999, 2002

Rank		2002	1999	OECD Convention
	Country Data Set, Total	835	779	
1	Australia	8.5	8.1	Ratified
2	Sweden	8.4	8.3	Ratified
3	Switzerland	8.4	7.7	Ratified
4	Austria	8.2	7.8	Ratified
5	Canada	8.1	8.1	Ratified
6	Netherlands	7.8	7.4	Ratified
7	Belgium	7.8	6.8	Ratified
8	United Kingdom	6.9	7.2	Ratified
9	Singapore	6.3	5.7	Not signed
10	Germany	6.3	6.2	Ratified
11	Spain	5.8	5.3	Ratified
12	France	5.5	5.2	Ratified
13	United States	5.3	6.2	Ratified
14	Japan	5.3	5.1	Ratified
15	Malaysia	4.3	3.9	Not signed
16	Hong Kong	4.3	–*	Not signed
17	Italy	4.1	3.7	Ratified
18	South Korea	3.9	3.4	Ratified
19	Taiwan	3.8	3.5	Not signed
20	China	3.5	3.1	Not signed
21	Russia	3.2	–**	Not signed

Notes: The question is related to the propensity for corporations from industrialized countries as listed in the table above to bribe public officials in emerging countries. A full score, which denotes no propensity to offer bribe payments, corresponds to 10.0; countries are ranked based on such score.
* not considered as part of China in 1999.
** not included in 1999.

Source: TI.

officials. At the bottom of the list we find countries whose corporations are more inclined to use bribery to obtain benefits in the foreign country where they have established their operations. Country ranking is based on country scores (see fourth and fifth columns respectively). The last column illustrates whether individual countries have ratified the OECD Convention. This is an international convention which involves a large number of countries and makes a powerful stand against corruption.

To verify if, in general, worldwide perceptions closely reflect domestic

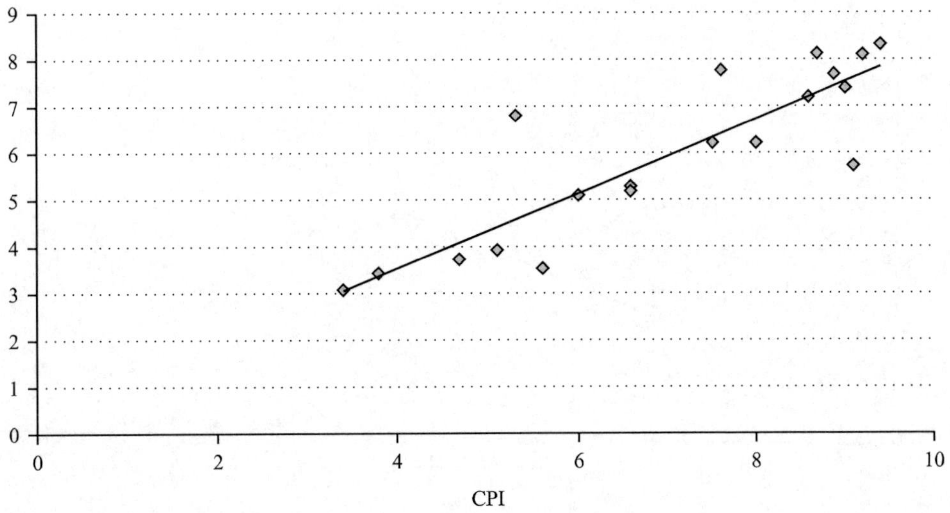

Notes:
CPI = 10 denotes absence of corruption while CPI = 0 denotes highest corruption level.
High scores for the exported corruption index denote low exported corruption.

Source: Authors' calculations from TI data.

Figure 3.10 Domestic corruption and exported corruption, 1999 (Exported corruption on vertical axis = y)

corruption, in Figures 3.10 and 3.11 we represent the relationship between the two variables. If worldwide perceived corruption approaches CPI, interesting conclusions may be drawn.

Both figures graph a positive relationship between domestic corruption and corruption exported by individual countries. This means that countries in which corruption is high tend to export this corporate culture worldwide. We note that the data present low dispersion and the relationship has a high degree of persistence. This relationship holds strongly for both 1999 and 2002.

The possibility that corrupt countries may spread corruption worldwide represents a danger for the international community as a whole. On this perspective, the role of international organizations and their commitment to combating corruption becomes of particular significance. At the same time, the fact that the domestic problems of corrupt States may reach other countries puts further pressure on countries to formulate policies to combat corruption. From this perspective, individual countries have a responsibility with respect to the costs of domestic corruption that extends internationally. The fact that domestic corruption is exported from within one country by corporations with international operations highlights the

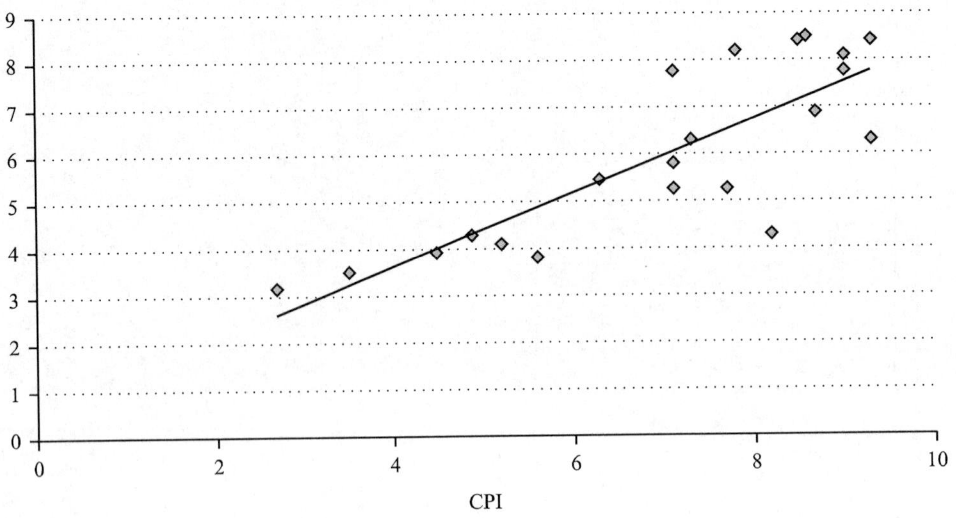

Notes:
CPI = 10 denotes absence of corruption while CPI = 0 denotes highest corruption level.
High scores for the exported corruption index denote low exported corruption.

Source: Authors' calculations from TI data.

Figure 3.11 Domestic corruption and exported corruption, 2002 (Exported corruption on vertical axis = y)

responsibility of international organizations and individual governments with respect to the possibility of an expansion of corruption (Arnone and Padoan 2008).

3.3.2 Indirect Causation: International Trade and Development Issues

Our earlier arguments on the role of foreign investment in growth may help in understanding the reason why the empirical literature identifies a positive causal relationship between economic growth and international trade; capital and trade flows generally move in parallel. Moreover, if a country participates in international trade it will have the opportunity to specialize in the activity for which it has higher comparative advantages than the rest of the world, hence gaining efficiency. Finally, access to new technology and know-how fosters innovation and improved productivity.

Deeply corrupt societies are generally characterized by constraints that tend to curtail access to foreign trade. Corrupt systems tend to favor conditions that allow personal benefits for elitist insiders to continue. Conversely, frequent relations with multinational corporations and other international investors jeopardize the secrecy that clouds bribery.

International trade increases the number of outsiders in the economy, together with the probability that bribe practices be unveiled. Finally, international trade and finance are both under the control of international supervisors, such as international trade organizations (WTO) and international financial organizations (IMF, WB, FATF), that are generally under no individual country influence and are effective controllers.

If we use the number of years that a country has had international trade operations as a proxy for an open country, it is possible to compute the effect of corruption on a country's openness to international trade. Pellegrini and Gerlagh (2004) show that a one standard deviation decrease in corruption is associated with an increase in the openness of a country of 0.19, in turn associated with an increase in growth of 0.30 percent per year.

It remains to explore a second relationship between corruption and international trade: that corruption should be looked at as a distributive rather than a trade issue. Corruption owes much of its recent salience as an international (economic) problem to a concern about what it does to foreign exporters and investors, rather than to what it does to the domestic economy and polity. Since corrupt bureaucrats have always been around, it seems debatable that the issue has somehow become more serious in recent years.

Taking as read the fact that people and institutions are paying more attention to the issue, a relevant question to be addressed is *what* is the actual rationale that legitimately justifies this shift of emphasis away from the relationship between corruption and international trade? Rodrik (1998: 109) is rather clear on this point: "the trouble to see corruption through the lens of international trade and investment rather than through the lens of development is that the issue becomes primarily one of redistribution – whether among the industrial countries, or between industrial-country exporters and developing-country importers – and of confrontation." In his opinion, this stance stems from a too simplistic and basically flawed view of corruption as a mere trade issue. Rather, it should be predominantly looked at as a developmental and distributive problem. Rodrik's case for this stance relies on a sound international economic theoretical experiment: he considers the case of a developing country with a corrupt president who invites bids for a large order of jet aircraft.

Firstly, he considers the implications of the 1977 US Foreign and Corrupt Practices Act,[5] the first piece of national legislation to criminalize

[5] Foreign and Corrupt Practices Act of Dec. 19, 1977 codified at US Code Title 15 Sections 78a, 78m, 78dd-1, 78dd-2, 78 ff (hereinafter referred to as the "FCPA or the Act"). See Chapter 9.

corruption on the part of foreign public officials. Since the president and his entourage are determined to get a kickback, the Americans soon find themselves out of the running, and the Europeans get the order. Nonetheless, the president cannot now play the Europeans off against the Americans. Thus, his bribe (from the Europeans) is likely lower than it would have been without the FCPA. According to Rodrik, part of the cost of bribing the president, moreover, is presumably passed on in the final price of the European aircraft. Rodrik then goes on to examine the implications of this operation from the perspective of global welfare. Where the European jets are reasonably close substitutes for American ones, which can plainly be assumed, the world as a whole is no worse off. In his clear words: "whatever the Americans and the corrupt president lose, the Europeans gain, and the developed country still gets the same number of jets. A lot of money changes hands, but the global outcome is a wash and there is little or no efficiency loss" (Rodrik 1999: 110).

Secondly, Rodrik considers what would happen if the Americans managed to get the Europeans on board and all exporters agreed to stop corrupt payments. As a result, the next time the developing country places an order for jet aircraft, the president does not get his bribe. Yet, if one assumes, as is likely, that there is no domestic manufacturing capability for the jets in the developing country and, consequently, that the order has to be filled either by the Americans or by the Europeans, the effects of trade are once again merely redistributive: the world as a whole is no better off.

Finally, one might consider the case where the corrupt president is overthrown and a clean government takes over. Because the Europeans and American exporters have already sworn off paying kickbacks, they are no better off. Rather, they may end up worse off if the new regime, lacking a personal profit motive in the transaction, chooses to order fewer aircraft. Also in this latter example, the final outcome is mainly redistributive: no or little efficiency gain occurred; the primary beneficiaries of the shift of welfare this time are the people of the developing country. Thus, the primary economic concern raised by corruption at the international level is most of the time a distributive and, especially, developmental issue, rather than an efficiency concern. In light of the above Rodrik (1999: 111) makes a remarkable assertion: "this puts corruption as a trade issue in the same category as, for example, trade-related intellectual property rights (TRIPS) during the Uruguay Round, and makes it quite different from the bread-and-butter concerns of the GATT/WTO system, such as reducing trade barriers."

3.3.3 Indirect Causation: Political Instability

The evaluation of the opportunity to invest in an economic activity should not be done without studying environmental characteristics; expected returns, opportunity costs and risks must be weighted and compared at the same time. Hence, it is evident that political stability is one factor that international investors must take into consideration in the course of deciding where to commit their capital. We emphasized above that political risks are part of the ICRG components relating to investment risk. On the other hand, the relationship between growth and political stability reflects the fact that political risks inhibit economic activity. Not surprisingly, a decrease in corruption by one unit is associated with an increase in political stability of 0.06 percent and a final positive effect on growth of 0.14 per cent (Pellegrini and Gerlagh 2004).

3.3.4 Indirect Causation: Education

A country's literacy level is a determinant of economic growth. Tanzi and Davoodi (2002b) show that corruption is generally associated with low public revenues. An in-depth analysis of the effects of corruption on the public sector is beyond the scope of this section (but it is addressed below). Nevertheless, it is evident that lower public revenues determine lower social expenditures. Empirical evidence shows that the higher the corruption levels, the lower the education budget (Mauro 1998; see also below). In general, the higher the level of domestic corruption, the higher the budget for public activities that allow personal benefits; major benefits are generally obtained in sectors in which there is a high concentration of economic and political power, where money circulates in large amounts. Education has no such features, and is not favored in systems in which corruption is pervasive.

Public spending on education is an economic and social policy choice: it represents the value that governments attribute to education. Given the strong relationship between economic growth and education, the importance that policymakers attribute to education systems has important implications for a country's development: public spending may generally be representative of the quality of a country's education system.

In Figure 3.12 we show public spending on education for a worldwide-representative data set. Figure 3.12 graphs the education budget in various countries. Amongst advanced economies, Denmark has the highest education budget. Conversely, at the bottom of the list, Japan's and Greece's public spending on education are the lowest, with spending levels as a percentage of GDP lower than the average in developing countries. Amongst

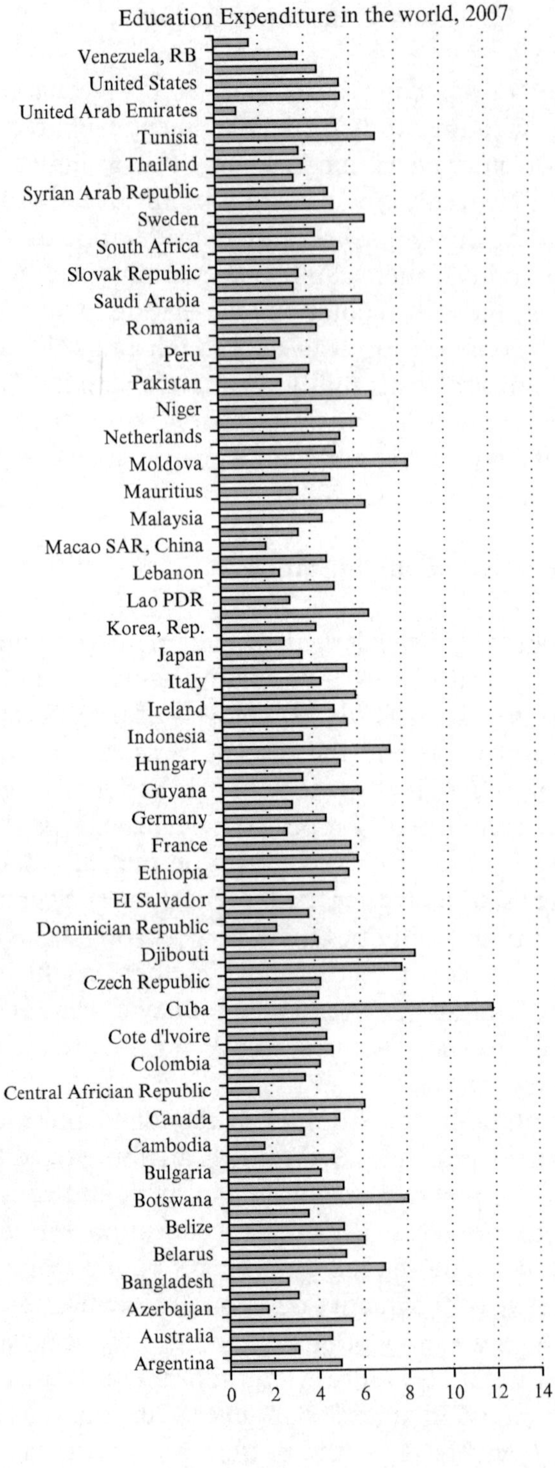

Source: WB.

Figure 3.12 Spending on education, 2007

emerging economies, Israel has the highest spending on education, with levels significantly stronger than the advanced countries' average. In the case of developing economies, Tunisia shows spending levels on education that are much higher than the average in both developing and advanced countries.

Empirical studies find that the number of years spent on specialization studies decreases as domestic corruption worsens. In particular, Pellegrini and Gerlagh (2004) find that a one standard deviation decrease in corruption is associated with an increase of half a year of schooling for people above 25 years. This, in turn, leads to an increase in growth of 0.06 percent per year. While this result is robust in terms of the direction of causation in the relationship between corruption and education, our prior arguments on the allocation of talents (Chapter 2) suggest that, in turn, very corrupt societies favor education schemes that facilitate widespread corruption thanks to rent-seeking.

3.3.4.1 Education and corruption

We turn our attention now to the direction of causation that characterizes the existing relationship between corruption and education. We have emphasized how lower public spending on education is one effect of corruption. Nevertheless, it is important that we also stress how education budgets (and education levels as such) are not affected by corruption only, but that education is one determinant of domestic corruption.

Education impacts on corruption: high education levels are associated with good quality politicians and institutions. Educated and informed citizens can choose good policy makers and monitor their activity and performance. These characteristics have a strong impact on the quality of institutions and are effective constraints on bad governance. This, in turn, acts as an incentive to improve the quality of governance, with subsequent positive effects on domestic corruption (see Chapter 7). Hence, it is reasonable to think that "correlation between development and good political outcomes occurs because more education improves political institutions" (Glaeser and Saks 2004).

Our earlier arguments find support in recent empirical evidence from the United States (Glaeser and Saks 2004). If we proxy the level of education with variables other than public spending on education, the relationship between education and corruption is confirmed again. A significant relationship exists between the number of corrupt practices and the number of citizens with a primary level of education. To highlight that the level of education is one determinant, and no mere consequence of domestic corruption, we may use alternative indicators. If we proxy schooling results with the ratio of qualifications obtained to the numbers of students

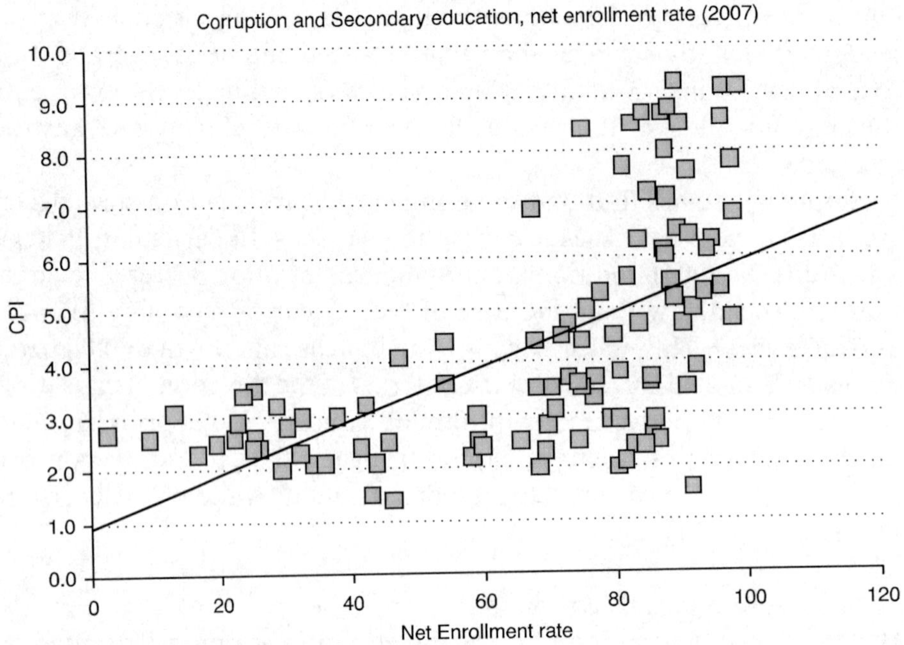

Note: CPI = 10 denotes absence of corruption while CPI = 0 denotes highest corruption level.

Source: Authors' calculations from TI and OECD data.

Figure 3.13 Corruption and population with a secondary school qualification, 2007

enrolled, this correlation is again validated. The level of schooling is finally proxied using the degree of congregationalism in several US States; these States have historically spent more on education and have higher levels of schooling today. The correlation between education and corruption is confirmed yet again. We note, however, that congregationalism may also affect corruption through causation independent of the level of education.

In Figure 3.13 we show recent empirical evidence from an OECD country data set. Figure 3.14 shows domestic corruption and the percentage of the population with a secondary school qualification. The data show that low domestic corruption is associated with a high percentage of the population with a secondary school qualification.

3.3.4.2 Direct and indirect causation: corruption and growth

Now that we have investigated both the direct and indirect effects of corruption, the latter appear as one of the most significant factors having an impact on economic growth. According to Pellegrini and Gerlagh (2004), a one standard deviation decrease in corruption leads to an increase in growth of 1 per cent per year, for a given initial income level. The long-term income level increases by 140 percent.

Finally, looking at the long term, a one standard deviation decrease in corruption levels increases the long-term level of investment by 4.86 percentage points, consistent with Mauro's (1995) findings. It further increases schooling by 2.21 years (for the population over 25 years old), increases the openness coefficient by 0.30 and increases the political instability index by 0.06.

3.4 INFLATION

With a view to providing a general analysis of the economy, we may not overlook inflation. This variable plays a fundamental role in the economy because it is an index of citizens' purchasing power. If inflation is high, prices grow at a steady pace and citizens experience lower real income, unless nominal income also grows at a steady pace in parallel. Nevertheless, negative inflation, or deflation, is not necessarily positive for the economy because deflation generally characterizes recession. These examples, albeit too few to illustrate diverse dynamics in connection with inflation, are useful to help understand the importance of the role of this variable.

When no authority controls inflation, price levels are established as a result of the interaction of demand and supply at an aggregate level; an increase in demand that is not accompanied by an equivalent increase in supply (or negative supply shocks that are not accompanied by decreases in demand) have an upward effect on prices. Positive sectoral supply shocks that are not accompanied by corresponding increases in demand (or contractions of aggregate supply) have a downward effect on prices. It is clear that, if no authority monitors it, inflation may reflect demand and supply shocks and be very volatile.

Among their goals, monetary authorities set inflation targets and pursue these through specific monetary policy instruments. This is the principal responsibility of central banks in the majority of countries[6] (Arnone, Laurens, and Segalotto 2006b, Laurens, Arnone, and Segalotto 2009). Monetary policy is an effective policy instrument with effects that are visible in the short term. Because of this, monetary policy operations

---

[6] It should be added that many central banks are also in charge of financial stability and, often, banking supervision. In these cases, the independence of the monetary authority extends to banking supervision, which we address in Chapter 7.

must be in the hands of extremely competent authorities, characterized by independence, accountability and transparency (Chapter 7).

If the monetary policy authorities are corrupt, the pursuit of objectives as established is profoundly jeopardized in the definition of the objectives and in the policy measures necessary to achieve them. It is clear that the effects of corruption are distinguished based on the goals of the entities involved and the instruments used to achieve them. Nevertheless, recent studies (Lambsdorff and Schinke 2002) emphasize that corruption generally leads to the monetary authorities having to adopt measures in favor of higher inflation through the issuance of additional base money.

Sometimes, this excess of new money is aimed at allowing self-appropriation by the same monetary authorities. This happened in 1979 with Zaire's deputy central banker. Corruption may also aim at obtaining confidential information: Lambsdorff and Schinke (2002) mention that in 1999 Brazil's central banker Francisco Lopes gave advance warning to a group of private banks before an 8 percent devaluation, so that this devaluation benefited them; the same authors mention other instances related to governor Lopes, who was charged with fraud in 2000. We may also mention situations where certain central banks are at the center of very tight connections (which should, however, be kept distinguished as such from corruption in a strict sense), as in the case of former Bank of Italy governor Antonio Fazio in 2005. In addition, Swiss National Bank president Philipp Hildebrand resigned in January 2012 over accusations of insider trading; these may cause a misuse of monetary policy instruments (e.g. open market operations, exchange rate interventions) or other distortions, especially related to banking supervision.

Sometimes it is beneficial for certain actors in the economy to lower monetary stocks. Nevertheless, "it is easier to increase one's share when the whole cake increases" (Lambsdorff and Schinke 2002). Empirical evidence confirms these arguments. In Figure 3.14 we show the relationship found between corruption and inflation. The data show that as corruption decreases (the CPI goes up), inflation decreases.

3.5 THE PUBLIC SECTOR

Our analysis so far has emphasized the effects of corruption on markets and economic growth, with particular attention to the behavior of private actors in the economy. We now shift the focus of our analysis to corruption that involves both public and private entities. In these cases corruption results in distortions that are not only a constraint on private activities, but also a charge for the public sector as such.

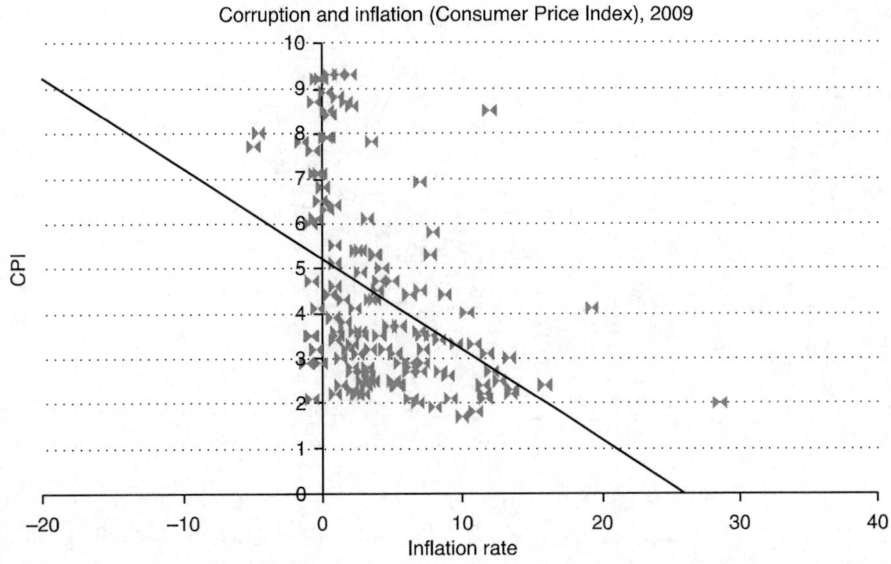

Note: CPI = 10 denotes absence of corruption while CPI = 0 denotes highest corruption level.

Source: Authors' calculations from TI and IMF data.

Figure 3.14 Corruption and inflation, 2009

3.5.1 Public Revenues and Domestic Corruption

It is reasonable to think that in bureaucracies deeply pervaded by corruption a share of public resources is appropriated by public officials. This view is supported by empirical evidence: the data show that domestic corruption is negatively correlated with public revenues. If corruption increases in a system, the risk of being caught in corrupt deals diminishes and corruption among (self-interested insider) public officials increases to the detriment of public revenues. Tanzi and Davoodi (2002b) estimate that a unit point deterioration in the corruption index causes a 1.5 percent decrease in total public revenues (as a share of GDP), a decrease in tax revenues by 2.7 percent (as a share of GDP) and an increase of 1.3 percent in non-tax-revenues (as a share of GDP).

Figure 3.15 shows the relationship between CPI and public revenues (as a percentage of GDP). The empirical evidence includes few advanced countries. CPI for advanced countries is generally higher than for other countries. CPI is also high for Singapore, an outlier with respect to the amount of public revenues as a share of GDP.

We now turn to the relationship between tax revenues and corruption.

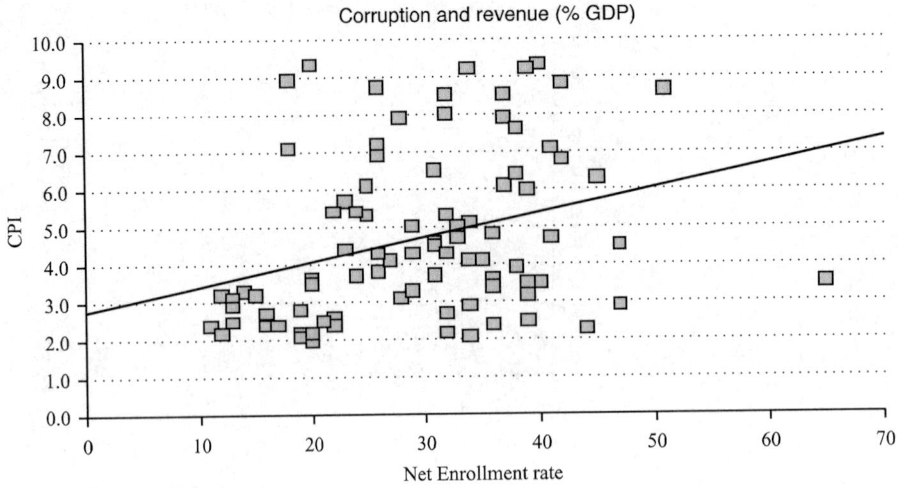

Note: CPI =10 denotes absence of corruption while CPI = 0 denotes highest corruption level.

Source: Authors' calculations from TI and IMF data.

Figure 3.15 Public revenues (as a percentage of GDP) and CPI, 2009

Fiscal revenues are part of total public revenues and include all State tax collection. Tanzi and Davoodi (2002b) suggest this is a closer relationship than between public revenues and CPI. Figure 3.16 shows recent empirical evidence.

There are some outliers to this relationship: Singapore, Canada, and New Zealand are characterized by very low corruption with respect to the ratio of tax revenues to GDP. These countries are significant exceptions compared with other countries in this data set, but belong to a group of countries with much higher GDP. The available empirical evidence is based on few advanced countries.

Certain taxes are more easily affected by domestic corruption. Sales taxes and excise taxes are established on an a priori basis and are collected centrally by the tax administration system. Individual income taxes may be more easily the subject of negotiation and are more easily affected by domestic corruption. Tanzi and Davoodi (2002a) estimate that a unit increase in corruption is associated with a decrease in income taxes (as a share of GDP) by 1.8 percent and a decrease in indirect taxes as a share of GDP) by 1.2 percent: higher corruption is associated with a higher decrease in income taxes. That income taxes decrease in favor of higher taxes other than on income is not devoid of implications for redistribution; the tax system's neutrality is brought into question and income distribution policies are strongly distorted.

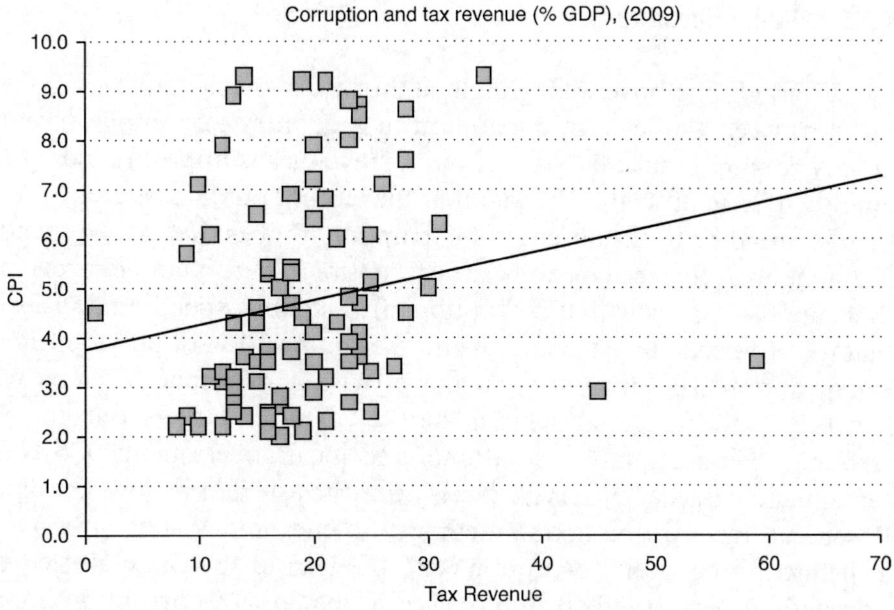

Note: CPI = 10 denotes absence of corruption while CPI = 0 denotes highest corruption level.

Source: Authors' calculations from TI and IMF data.

Figure 3.16 Tax revenues and corruption, 2009

Finally, we note that the higher the personal benefits (via tax extortion) for public officials, the more they tend to change tax collection in favor of instruments that are of advantage to them. However, in order to ensure stable tax revenues, corrupt countries tend to rely more on indirect taxes than on income tax.

There is no empirical evidence supporting the relationship between sales taxes and domestic corruption (Tanzi and Davoodi 2002a). However, the situation is more complex in the case of international trade: confirming the fact that the association of customs regulations and corruption is empirically supported, statistical evidence shows a negative relationship between domestic corruption and value-added tax (VAT) efficiency[7] (Tanzi and Davoodi 2002a). However, this relationship is statistically weak.

---

7 If we define VAT efficiency in terms of the ratio of VAT revenues and GDP divided by the VAT standard rate, we obtain a value that indicates the degree of efficiency of VAT systems.

3.5.2 Public Spending

In the paragraph above we highlighted the fact that a negative relationship exists between the level of corruption in a country and public revenues: in very corrupt countries, part of public revenues is appropriated by self-interested State officials. The fact that the level of public resources is lower than it would be in the absence of corruption implies that public spending decisions are influenced by domestic corruption. There is empirical evidence that supports the view that corruption affects public spending decisions in that it distorts resource allocation and the composition of public spending.

Corruption has an impact on the provision of public services, while it causes higher costs and limits services. This is largely due to lower resources being available to national and local governments. Costs may remain unchanged, but service quality may be affected by lower revenues. Based on diverse bribe-taking methods, Shleifer and Vishny (1993) make a distinction between corruption with theft from the State and corruption without such theft. In the first case, the cost of corruption impacts citizens because it raises the effective price of the service bribed. The case of corruption without theft is when the cost of corruption is in the form of an appropriation of public resources and has a second-round effect on citizens: through higher service prices, lower service quality or an increase in public deficit.

When public service prices increase and service quality is compromised, in both cases incentives are created that lower citizens' demand for public services. Gupta, Davoodi, and Tjongson (2002) show that countries pervaded by high degrees of corruption (and inefficient public services) have on average 26 percent more students dropping out of school (relative to less corrupt countries). Moreover, the empirical evidence is that a negative correlation exists between the quantity of public service and domestic corruption. Additionally, empirical evidence supports a further relationship between the quality of public healthcare and education, on the one hand, and corruption, on the other.

As we discussed earlier with regard to the choice of different tax instruments, an incentive exists that drives politicians to allocate collective resources where they may benefit personally, and secrecy may be better maintained with respect to corrupt deals. The possibility of profiting substantially is also at the basis of engaging in rent-seeking activities (see Chapter 2). The possibility of extracting rents in a sector exists if competition is low and exact product values are difficult to establish. This typically happens with advanced technology (Shleifer and Vishny 1993) and where the consequences of discretion by public officials are not openly visible. Supporting this argument, the empirical evidence shows a positive relationship between military spending and domestic corruption: high levels of corruption are generally associated with high military spending (Gupta, de Mello, and Sharan 2002; Gupta, Davoodi, and Tjongson 2002).

The other side of the coin of corrupt governments' tendency to allocate public resources to sectors where rent extraction possibilities are enhanced is that public service sectors in which rent extraction possibilities are lower tend to be neglected. Hence, we may infer that public spending is particularly low in these sectors. Empirical studies support this assumption and find that corrupt countries spend very little on maintenance operations (Tanzi and Davoodi 2002b). This results from lower revenue to finance these expenses or, even worse, from resource allocation that favors tenders for new projects versus maintenance works.

Healthcare and education suffer the negative effects of corruption most; these are the sectors where corrupt governments typically cut finance. Several studies confirm that a negative relationship exists between healthcare spending and corruption (Mauro 1998); and between domestic corruption and spending on education (Mauro 1998; Tanzi and Davoodi 2002b). In particular, Mauro's (1998) regression shows that a one standard deviation improvement in the corruption index leads education expenditure to rise by over 6 percentage points of total government consumption expenditure. This relationship is robust with respect to various functional forms and holds for various data subsets (Mauro 1998).

In Figure 3.17 we show the relationship between CPI and public spending on education in advanced countries; we control for income by splitting the sample: richer countries generally tend to allocate more resources than other countries. This data set is not as extensive as the data sets used earlier because internationally comparable data on fiscal policy are relatively limited.

The relationship between CPI and spending on education holds strongly in other country groups, showing the same relation for the developing countries data set (Figure 3.18): less corrupt countries spend more on education.

Figure 3.18 shows that an adverse relationship between public spending on education and the degree of domestic corruption also holds for developing countries. Nevertheless, the data show higher dispersion than for the previous subset. This reflects other factors affecting public spending on education in these countries.

3.5.3 Public Investments

Corruption and public investments have often coexisted. Large public projects and development of infrastructure create the possibility of major

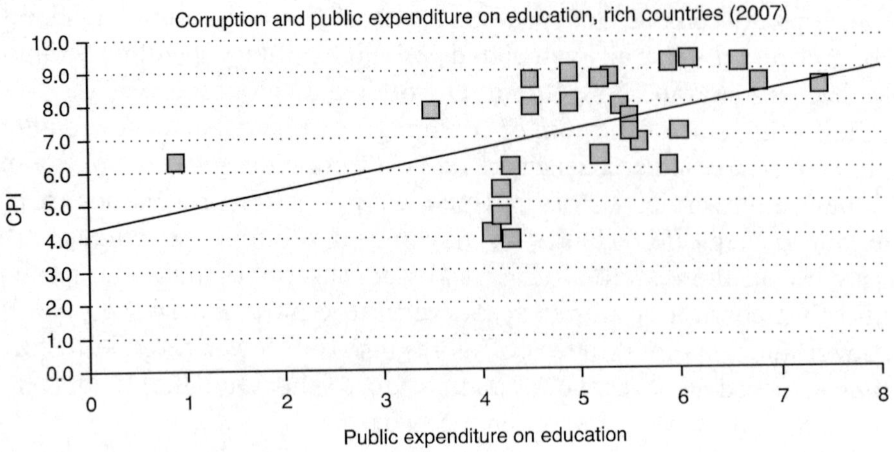

Note: CPI =10 denotes absence of corruption while CPI = 0 denotes highest corruption level.

Source: Authors' calculations from TI and IMF data.

Figure 3.17 Corruption and public spending on education, 2007, advanced countries

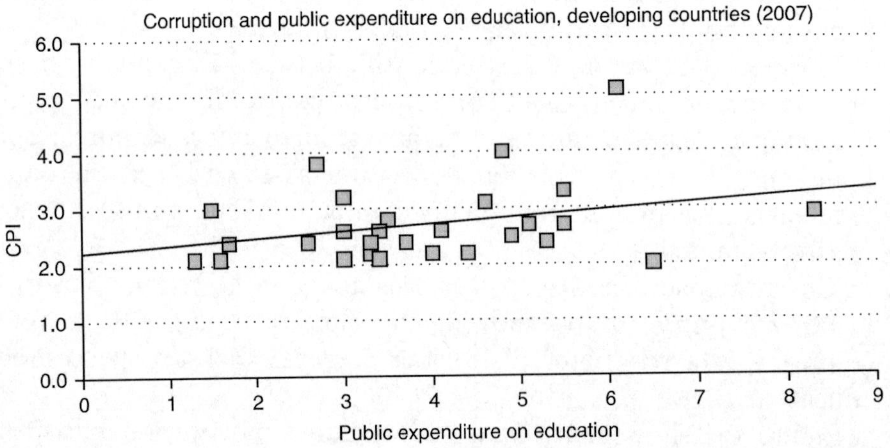

Note: CPI =10 denotes absence of corruption while CPI = 0 denotes highest corruption level.

Source: Authors' calculations from TI and IMF data.

Figure 3.18 Corruption and public spending on education, 2007, developing countries

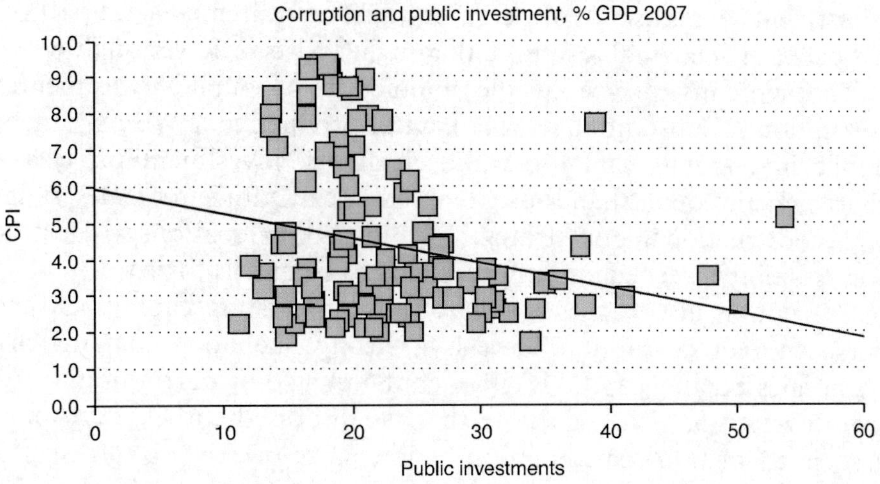

Note: CPI =10 denotes absence of corruption while CPI = 0 denotes highest corruption level.

Source: Authors' calculations from TI and WB data.

Figure 3.19 Corruption and public investments, 2007

profitability for both bid-winning private contractors and bribe-taking public officials. Public tender processes are often very complex and based on the calculation of many uncertain factors; because of this, the likelihood of cases of corruption being revealed can be very low. Empirical evidence finds a correlation between public investment spending (as a percentage of GDP) and domestic corruption; the higher the level of corruption, the higher is spending on investment (Tanzi and Davoodi 2002b).

Figure 3.19 shows that high corruption is associated with high public investment spending (as a percentage of GDP). We note that this correlation is often hidden behind a so-called investment bias (Tanzi and Davoodi 2002b), or a trend in favor of public investment projects to the detriment of public consumption spending, on the basis that investments are a driver of a country's development. Nevertheless, not all infrastructure developments are necessary investments, nor do all public contract awards reflect quality and merit criteria.

Public contracts represent earning opportunities for private contractors; this possibility is often on condition that commission is paid to public officials. As for public spending, the question arises as to who should bear this additional cost. The alternative options are whether the bid for the contract includes the cost of such commission, whether upward adjustments are allowed, or no strict quality requirements are part of the bid package. The final result is either higher costs or lower quality.

Another consequence of the interaction of public investment and corruption is substantially lower capital productivity. We may mention public investments that are white elephants, investment projects with characteristics other than those required or cathedrals in the desert, large-scale construction in non-strategic locations, or in locations where no such construction is needed and thus destined to be underutilized.

Corruption also causes lower returns on existing capital. Given the persistence of corruption there is a strong likelihood that in corrupt economies existing capital is either contaminated by corruption or results from corruption. We also note that, as discussed earlier, corruption is associated with low spending on maintenance of existing infrastructure: one implication is that returns on this capital drop drastically. Finally, we recall that there are cases where it is a deliberate choice not to execute any maintenance, causing existing infrastructure to deteriorate, so that new contracts may be awarded.

3.5.4 Size of the Public Sector

Corruption between the public and private sectors is associated with discretionary and monopoly powers of government and bureaucracy. Many, including Nobel-prize-winning economist Gary Becker, have assumed that a positive relation exists between a country's public sector size and domestic corruption. Becker went so far as to state that corruption would be eliminated completely if the State was abolished (Tanzi 2002). Setting aside the question of the impossibility of abolishing the public sector, we turn our attention to verifying whether this view is correct. It is well known that Scandinavian countries are characterized by significant State intervention and low corruption.

To assess this commonly held view, we use the level of public revenues per individual country to proxy public sector size and public intervention. Figure 3.20, presented below, shows how, contrary to public opinion, large public revenues are associated with low corruption; also, if we use tax revenues to proxy the degree of public intervention, we obtain similar results: higher tax revenues are associated with lower corruption.

Public revenue is also a reasonable proxy for public sector size: the larger the public sector, the greater the revenue needed to finance it. We have argued that the roots of corruption lie not so much in the size of the public sector, as in the discretionary powers of public officials, in the bad management of possible conflicts of interest, and in low quality governance.

Recent studies have clearly identified the (positive) impact of a transparent fiscal policy amongst all variables that affect domestic corruption. Hameed (2005) emphasizes how several effects of corruption may be curbed through transparent fiscal policy. Hameed finds that fiscal transparency has a positive impact on corruption; higher fiscal transparency is associated with greater "control of corruption" with a significant and positive coefficient. Once control variables are added, the coefficients are smaller but still significant. He shows that if countries in the lowest 10th percentile of transparency were to improve their transparency up to the highest 10th percentile average, they would see an improvement in the "control of corruption" index from -0.8 to -0.04. We note that in this regression, corruption is measured by the WB Control of Corruption Index, which is a good proxy for the CPI.[8]

Figure 3.20 shows the relationship between the fiscal transparency index and CPI, thus offering further support for the relationship between corruption and fiscal transparency. Empirical evidence confirms that an increase in corruption (a CPI decrease) is associated with lower fiscal transparency.

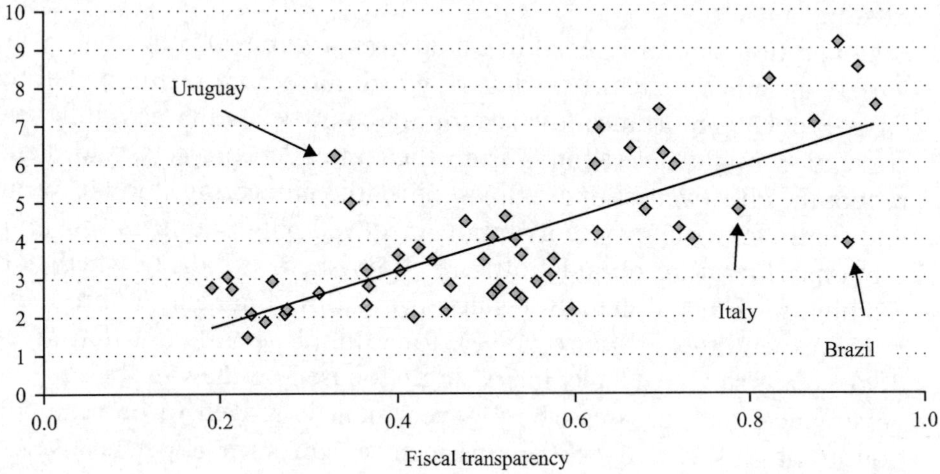

Note: CPI = 10 denotes absence of corruption while CPI = 0 denotes highest corruption level.

Source: Authors' calculations from TI and IMF data.

Figure 3.20 Corruption and fiscal transparency, 2004

[8] The "control of corruption" variable and CPI have a correlation coefficient of 0.96.

3.6 ECONOMIC INEQUALITY

Corruption favors the interests of those who know the rules of the game where there is a concentration of power and money; those who have no access to information in the hands of a close élite, nor sufficient capital to pay bribes, nor hold strategic positions, are irreparably not favored compared with those who take part in these dynamics. The insider-outsider structure that inevitably comes about results in vicious circles that tend to favor the stronger strata of society, who have access to large resources or hold strategic positions. In both cases, insiders have access to resources that outsiders are denied (outsiders are those individuals lacking personal connections, access to exchanges of favors and benefits). We may hence assume that one main characteristic at the basis of corruption dynamics consists precisely in the disparity of conditions faced by different economic actors. Given different initial conditions and rules of the game, income distribution reflects the same rules that originated it; stronger actors have access to larger resources while weaker actors are excluded. Eventually, corruption undermines social welfare by redistributing a nation's wealth in a manner that generates tensions or exacerbates existing ones.

Corruption can raise social inequality remarkably also through a wide variety of indirect channels, some of which have been mentioned above. Of particular importance for developing countries is the possibility that corruption might divert funds from their intended projects, and, hence, reduce the effectiveness of aid flows. Since the pioneering study of Wraith and Simpkins (1963) on corruption in developing countries, an ample economic literature on aid flows has flourished, exploring whether the fungibility of aid ultimately results in aid flow financing unproductive public expenditures. Mauro (1998), for example, points out that several donor countries have lately increasingly focused on the variables of good governance, and in cases where government is judged to be very poor, donors have scaled back their assistance. On such a perspective, the greatest challenge relating to corruption in economically underdeveloped countries is possibly the very fact that political power is often the main, if not the sole, source of economic benefit. Perhaps, more importantly, of corruption.

In developing countries the effects on the recipient side are particularly severe. Corruption frequently constitutes the only motive for the public authorities to enter into a contract at all. Rent-seeking may be the only reason to buy unnecessary or inadequate public goods and services. What is more, huge projects, organized and funded by bilateral or multilateral development agencies, have generated millions of dollars in bribes to government officials. This frequently not only has resulted in an explosion of foreign debt to be paid off by the next generation under conditions of austerity imposed by the same development agencies, but may enable an oligarchy to preserve its power for yet another decade with obvious consequences for the growth of a young democracy.

3.7 CORRUPTION AND ECONOMIC CYCLES

Our study aims also at stimulating further research in what seems to have become a key area for understanding some of the most treacherous pathologies of contemporary market-oriented economies. As recently emphasized by Rajan (2006), Akerlof and Shiller (2009), and Roubini (2009), the role played by perverse systems of incentives and by irrational and predatory behavior, of which corruption is one the most blatant cases, has traditionally been overlooked when addressing pathologies of market-oriented economies, whilst those attitudes explain much of the variation through time in the extent of activities which have, in turn, demonstrably contributed to the crashes and failures disrupting the modern financial economy at long intervals or hidden places.

Also, Kaufmann (2009) reminds us that, insofar as we include acts that may be legal in a strictly narrow sense, but are the outcomes of capture of the supervisory, regulatory and political power, corruption is intimately related to the current global crisis. He remarks that corruption is a major challenge also for industrialized countries: economies where private markets become more widespread and efficient are seriously impaired by corruption. Tanzi and Davoodi (2000) and Roubini (2009) argue that when corruption penetrates both public and private realms extensively, uncertainty rises in the economy, nullifying the correct functioning of the market mechanism with potentially destructive consequences for the whole economy. Furthermore, as we show in Section 2, the economic impact of corruption on industrialized countries during economic downturns is similar in kind to that on developing economies. It is, therefore, worth exploring the relationship between economic cycles and corruption in greater detail.

In their *Animal Spirits* Akerlof and Shiller (2009) emphasize that the role played by irrational and predatory behaviors in the thought patterns animating people's ideas and feelings have constantly been overlooked when addressing pathologies of market-oriented economies, whilst those attitudes explain much of the variation through time in the extent of corrupt activities. In turn, according to these two American economists, corruption demonstrably contributed to the crashes and failures that have disrupted the modern financial economy at long intervals or hidden places. In order to cope with the 2008–12 economic and financial crisis, originating in turmoil in financial markets, policymakers must consider how the economy works when people really are human, that is to say possessed by all-too *animal spirits* – people's non-economic motives, irrational behaviors.

Thus, realistic insights in behavioral economics are brought into our analysis of corruption dynamics. Elaborating on this expression – originally coined by the great British economist J.M. Keynes (1936) – Akerlof and Shiller describe five different animal spirits (among them corruption) and explore how they affect economic decisions. By drawing on their acknowledgment of the temptation toward corrupt, antisocial, and predatory behaviors (the economy's sinister side) and their role in the modern financial economy, Akerlof and Shiller maintain with anecdotal evidence (referring to the crises of 1990–91, 2001, and 2007) that episodes of corruption are a factor in causing or worsening economic recessions or slowdowns. More precisely, these cases "illustrate that the business cycle is connected to fluctuations in personal commitments to principles of good behavior and to fluctuations in predatory activity, which in turn is related to changes in opportunities for such activity" (Akerlof and Shiller 2009: 38).

With complementary arguments, Davigo and Mannozzi (2007) suggest that there is a feedback effect from cycles to corruption: recessions, which shrink available resources and strengthen competition, help the collapse of illegal agreements. Therefore, episodes of corruption emerge more easily, facilitating investigations.

Preliminary analyses for Italy indicate the existence of a link between economic dynamics – in particular that of GDP and public spending – and the fact that the judiciary (or media) are able to detect economic and political crimes and, in particular, corruption.

Economic cycles seem to have an influence on the opening and the course of the investigation, but not on the commission of crimes (in positive phases of economic cycles these crimes still occur, but are discovered with greater difficulty). This is probably due to an increase in conflict between the parties involved in economic (and, more generally, *white collar*) crimes: in particular, one can assume that a decline in GDP (and growth) weakens political power and, particularly, its hold on public opinion and, therefore, its ability to react to the discovery of cases of corruption. In addition, the decline in public spending may increase the signs of dissension within cartels of undertakings who use corruption as a primary tool for the award of public procurements. This creates the possibility of wedging into the illicit agreements for the investigators, getting collaboration more easily by those subject to investigation and witnesses.[9] In fact, due to the lack of reports of crimes, the difficulty of initiating a criminal proceeding starts to characterize the crimes at issue: for corruption the number of complaints is very low compared with what has emerged in the context of certain proceedings and, in any case, with what can be induced from the substantial financial resources of public officials in the face of their relatively modest incomes. This is mainly explained by the "conspiracy of silence" which is nearly a defining feature of the crime: in cases of corruption and illegal financing there is a plain and convergent interest in silence on the part of both the active and passive offenders, with a view to avoiding the criminal and non-criminal consequences of the crime (e.g. respectively, convictions, imprisonment, fines, on the one hand annulment of administrative acts, administrative and civil liability suspension and disqualification from public offices, on the other).

The struggle to collect reports of crime and gather evidence also stems from the significant number (real or perceived) of officers involved in these practices, resulting in fear of retaliation against those who have filed complaints or who have cooperated with the authorities in any investigation of such crimes.

It should be kept in mind that corruption crimes, at least in certain sectors, are featured by the seriality and wide dissemination. As for the seriality, the consideration of common sense according to which those who commit these crimes and get used to having far greater financial resources than those lawfully earned, hardly cease the unlawful conduct, has been supported by the findings of the proceedings. The same holds true for those who, working in relation with the public administration, are used to resolving the dispute or to win competition not on the basis of professional training, management skills or other requirements, but on the basis of preferential relationships with officials or politicians.[10] The diffusion of the crime, should rather be highlighted in two ways: on

---

9 Arnone and Davigo (2005) argue that mafia cases may appear to be an exception. Such cases seem to follow an autonomous cycle according to the following pattern: striking anti-mafia action – repression – restoring balance. However, they argue that outstanding actions by the mafia represent a reaction to noncompliance with (tacit or explicit) agreements by economic and political powers, which could be the result of the weakening of such powers due to an economic crisis and, therefore, a reduction in available resources or to a lower grip on public opinion: this leads to difficulties on the part of politicians or administrators who collude in the legislative or administrative measures designed to ease pressure on criminal organizations.

10 Several confessions were gathered, finding criminal relations which lasted ten or even twenty years.

the one hand, the large number of infidel officials in some sectors of the public administration with surprising massive deviations; on the other, the participation of persons in the crime. In the elementary hypotheses corruption requires an active and a passive side. However, it was frequently found that the illicit agreements involve a large number of people, both on the active and the passive side, (or acting as intermediaries) in a context of such pervasiveness that honest officials were isolated or removed.

The usual "conspiracy of silence" that surrounds these crimes can be broken when at least one such crime is discovered, but success requires the cooperation of at least some of the perpetrators, apart from the rare cases where documentary evidence is found.

The beginning of investigations into corruption crimes can cause a strong reaction by interest groups. Such a reaction can be weakened during economic downturns. There seems indeed to be an empirical relationship between success in investigating and economic cycles in the sense that in times of crisis there is a reduction in the ability of interest groups lapped by the investigations to prevent their development. This course can also depend on the need for political authorities to respond to the pressing demands of public opinion towards the political class, instances that seem more pronounced in times of recession, because social needs become more substantial in the face of scarcer resources.

To sum up, on the one hand, economic crises seem to lead to greater responsiveness from the public against attempts to conceal cases of corruption. On the other, leading to a reduction in public expenditure, they accentuate crises and conflicts between companies that exclusively or predominantly deal with the public administration. This tends to generate tensions that eventually lead to collaborative behavior with the investigating authorities or, at least, makes agreements on what to keep hidden more difficult to be reached and sustained.

The figures presented in Arnone and Davigo (2007) are quite telling. Their first figure presents the most important events in political, administrative or economic malfeasance in light of GDP dynamics. The second figure presents the same events in the light of variations in public spending. Except for a very limited number of cases, they support the thesis that economic recessions facilitate the emergence of corruption. Downturns in the economic cycle may be those in which supervisory and regulatory authorities, as well as the judiciary, find it less difficult to pursue more successfully their institutional goals in terms of both prevention and repression of anti-competitive behavior and corruption.

3.8 CORRUPTION AND PERSISTENCE

So far in our analysis we have more than once mentioned that corruption is highly persistent. This means that domestic corruption is stable over time and does not vary significantly on a year-to-year basis. Persistence is due to the fact that corruption is the fruit of multiple coexisting factors, many of which are of an environmental nature, and is not significantly subject to influence from one-time, ad hoc policies with temporary effects. Economic, legal, and social policies must have permanent effects to impact socio-economic environments; once the environment has changed, the spreading of corruption is curbed by changing agents' incentives, hence driving changed behaviors of agents in the economy. Secondly, there is no limit to the number of bribes that a business might have to pay in order to do business there. Shleifer and Vishny (1993) argue, for instance, that foreigners wishing to operate in Russia often must bribe all the foreign trade offices, including the foreign investment office, the appropriate industry ministry, the finance office, the executive branch of the local government, the legislative branch, the central bank, the property right bureau, and so on. This catalog does not even include the manifold levels of officials in each organization that the foreign operators might "need" to bribe in order to operate.

Figure 3.21 shows the relationship between CPI in 2002 and in 2010,

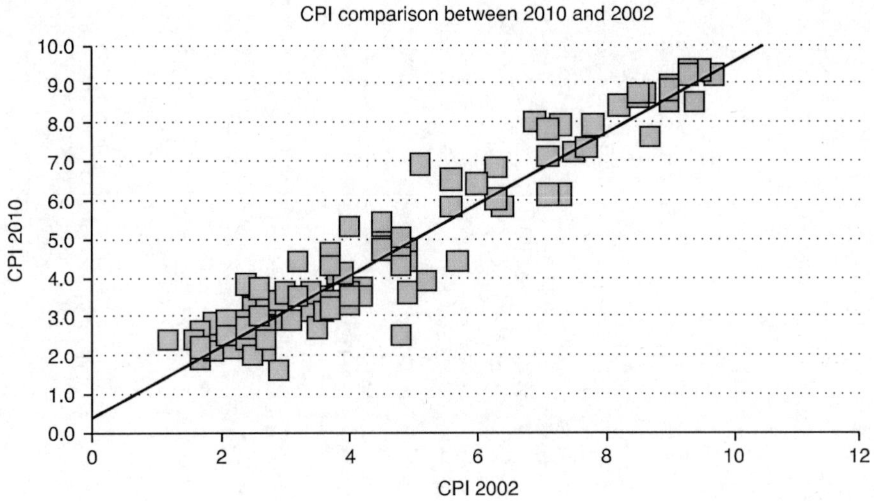

Note: CPI = 10 denotes absence of corruption while CPI = 0 denotes highest corruption level.

Source: Authors' calculations from TI data.

Figure 3.21 CPI in 2002 and 2010: a comparison

which supports our arguments above: it is very strong and the data present very low dispersion around the trend line. This means that CPI values change little on a year-to-year basis. That corruption is persistent in time allows us certain simplifications that facilitate our analysis. If no empirical evidence is available relative to the year for which CPI values are known, a comparison is nevertheless reasonable with neighboring years; over time, values change relatively little and the fundamental relationship is stable.

Section 2:

Finance

INTRODUCTION

The earlier chapters offer an analysis of the economic effects of corruption at the micro and macro level, – i.e. (a) the perverse effects of corruption on the markets, and (b) the systemic costs of corruption caused in national economies – by mapping its consequences for a sample of around 140 countries. Among the other evidence, we have shown that corruption is associated with a wide variety of social and economic problems, including lower economic growth and foreign direct investment, poor public spending, intolerable economic and social inequality, and misallocation of talents.

The impact of corruption on financial markets is arguably the least explored area of inquiry in such a multi-faceted field of study. Research on the effects of corruption in the financial markets has been sporadic and a systemic inquiry into the impact of the misuse of public powers for private gains on financial markets does not yet exist. Some of the main financial consequences of the crime must indeed be traced within purely economic studies.

As put forward by Roubini (2009), when corruption extensively penetrates public and private realms, uncertainty rises in the financial system as well, nullifying the correct functioning of the market mechanism in an inherently unstable sector with potentially destructive consequences for the whole economy. As we have shown in Chapter 2, this holds true, for instance, as regards the relationships between corruption and investment risk and interest rates, and the quality and accountability of financial market supervision, as we document in Chapter 7.

Now, we complement our earlier economic analysis with specific research on the impact of corruption on corporate finance and some specific financial markets. Hopefully, this can contribute to clarifying some of the key relationships between macroeconomic factors (such as, for instance, political stability and reliability) and the often erratic courses of financial markets.

We show that corruption can affect the performance of all types of financial markets and instruments, whether sophisticated like those in advanced economies or still in their infancy, like those in developing countries. Also, corruption affects the financial performance of firms, be they large listed corporations or relatively small microfinance institutions.

At one end of the financial spectrum we consider advanced financial markets. Chapters 4 and 5 focus on the impact of corruption on advanced financial markets in terms of how it may affect firms' financial performance, the bond and stock markets, and other financial instruments.

In Chapter 4 we assess in detail the issue of politically-connected firms in advanced economies, by first defining such entities and then identifying the types and levels of advantages they enjoy because of their contiguity to political power. The chapter focuses on the level of access to finance and costs of capital for the same group of firms. Our results are in keeping with recent studies on business-politics relationships, and show that politically-connected firms enjoy better access to finance, stronger market power, and tax benefits. We also show that, notwithstanding these advantages, these businesses perform generally worse than their competitors. Political connections constitute a case of conflict of interest, which is the foundation of any case of corruption and constitutes its breeding ground: on the one hand, politicians should act in the interest of the general community; on the other hand, by taking positions of power in large companies, they tend to act in the interest of the companies.

Chapter 5 illustrates our own elaboration of the impact of corruption on shares' returns for a sample of 1,058 listed industrial companies belonging to the eurozone countries in the period 1996–2006.

At the other end of the financial spectrum, we consider corruption with respect to development finance: specifically, microfinance. In Chapter 6 we then consider microfinance as a growing sector which has been changing the way we think about the development of cooperation programs, representing a way out from pure assistance and donations, which have often helped to keep people in perverse mechanisms of dependence on aid. Microfinance is today acknowledged as a tool that stimulates productive activities, economic development, and the dignity of individuals. Although it is not enough to put money in people's hands to trigger a productive development, and it is still a device that must be improved upon and adapted to different contexts, it has an undeniably important role in the fight against poverty. Therefore, it is important to consider the impact of macro-governance factors – specifically, corruption and political stability – on the main determinants of corporate finance performance (operational efficiency and operating costs).

Microfinance institutions (MFIs) form a relatively new set of financial institutions, still mostly unregulated. Chapter 6 extends the work of Arnone, Bellavite Pellegrini, and Messa (2010) – who recognize the importance of the strictly financial aspects of MFIs and find empirical evidence of their similarity to the world of traditional commercial banking – by providing an empirical analysis of the significance of operational efficiency for the operating costs of MFIs along with some governance factors, such as corruption and political stability. The explicit consideration of such governance factors represents a key contribution.

4. Financial markets: bonds, stocks, and politically-connected firms

Laura Pellegrini[1]

4.1 BORROWING COSTS

As emphasized by Bai and Ng (2006: 829) in their conclusive study on the issue, "asset prices are forward-looking and market-driven." They thus represent good barometers for evaluating the cost of corruption from the investors' perspective. Ng recalls a number of previous empirical studies which examine the effects of corruption on financial markets and which we recap in the following. In greater detail, Ciocchini et al. (2003) look at bond spread as a proxy for borrowing cost, whilst Fishman et al. (1991) and Lee and Ng (2006) examine stock market valuation.

When it comes to borrowing costs, Ciocchini et al. (2003) and, then, drawing heavily on that study, Ng (2006) show that corruption increases borrowing costs for governments and firms in emerging markets. They focus on the role of corruption in determining the price of emerging market bonds sold on the global bond market. Ciocchini et al. (2003) use the launch spreads of these bonds, i.e. the spread between the initial yield of these bonds and the rate commanded by a risk-free bond of the same maturity. The spread of these bonds reflects the higher default probability associated with emerging market debt. As Ng (2006: 829) remarks, "they are in effect studying the relationship between corruption and the perceived likelihood that a firm or government will default on its debt." The study thus compares the average corruption scores for developing countries that issued bonds in the 1990s, on the one hand, and the average corporate and sovereign bond spreads in these countries, on the other. The resulting regression shows that average bond spreads increase with corruption in the country. Therefore, the first preliminary finding of relevance is that a country's borrowing costs increase when corruption increases.

In order to investigate such relationships further, Ciocchini et al. (2003)

1 Research Fellow, Università Cattolica del Sacro Cuore, Italy.

add two further operations. Firstly, they control for other variables that affect bond spreads in a multivariate setup. Secondly, they take into consideration the endogenous nature of the decision to launch a bond: firms and countries that choose to issue debt will differ systematically from those that do not.

Secondly, they control for the likelihood of new issues by different classes of borrowers. Their empirical strategy consists of estimating the impact of corruption on spreads, first by ordinary least squares (OLS) and then by means of the Heckman procedure, which controls for possible sample selection problems. As to the estimation results for the spreads, the study uses a set of control variables that consists of bond characteristics and country characteristics as well as global interest rates and yield curve(s). Even after these controls, the coefficient on the corruption score is negative and significant; the same result is confirmed by different robustness checks based on OLS regression, different regions, and different time periods.

In sum, the main finding of the analysis is that global investors require a substantially greater return on debt when the issuer is a more corrupt country. This holds true even after controlling for other factors that determine default risk. Their estimation includes macroeconomic variables, such as GDP growth and external debt, as well as a credit rating score that captures political risk.

As Ng (2006: 831) puts it, "corruption plays an important role in determining default risk even apart from its impact on other types of economic performance".[2] More specifically, higher corruption increases borrowing costs on the international market for both government and firms in these countries.

According to Ciocchini et al. (2003), and Ng (2006) for government debt, the most direct impact of corruption is that officials might confiscate loaned funds or other sources of government income, limiting the government's ability to meet debt obligations. Secondly, higher levels of corruption are associated with lower tax revenue, which would in turn lower the government's ability to repay loans. In Section 1, however, we mentioned a wide variety of reasons why highly corrupt countries' economies end up with being tremendously weakened by widespread corruption with obvious consequences for governments' ability to meet their own obligations. For corporations, corruption may increase the likelihood of

---

2 The study, for instance, estimates that a decrease in the level of corruption from that of countries such as Ukraine to that of Turkey or Lithuania is associated with about a 20 percent decrease in spreads.

arbitrary management actions that, in turn, may end up reducing profits and leave the firm unable to repay loans. As extensively shown in Chapter 7, corruption is often associated with poor and unequal legal enforcement, weakened regulatory oversight and, possibly, bad corporate governance, which, among other things, may allow management to easily divert resources from the firm and make use of such resources for their own private benefits, at the expense of bondholders (and other stakeholders like workers, clients, suppliers, and stockholders).

4.2 STOCK PRICES

As suggested by the previous analysis, corruption can affect equity value drivers like a firm's long-term growth. This is further examined in Chapter 5, where, as mentioned above, we elaborate on a sample of 1,058 listed industrial companies belonging to eurozone countries in the period 1996–2006. Here, we summarize the main results of the prior literature on the subject. Even if rather limited in terms of its consideration of the geopolitical context, the first interesting study on the issue is Fishman et al. (1991), who examine the value of political connection in Indonesia by assessing the stock prices of companies that have different degrees of political connections. Fishman et al. relate the news of the former Indonesian president Suharto's health condition to the stock returns of these companies, and show that bad news on Suharto's condition led to substantially lower stock returns for companies with extensive political connections than for independent companies.

In addition to the evidence in Indonesia, there is also evidence that corruption affects stock prices in other countries. A more recent paper that explores the cost of corruption on a cross-country level is Lee and Ng (2006), who document the empirical relationship between the level of corruption within a country and the valuation of its corporations to shareholders. In greater detail, Lee and Ng (2006) use firm-level data from 43 countries to evaluate the empirical relationship between corruption and international corporate values. Lee and Ng (2004) find that firms from more corrupt countries trade at significantly lower market multiples. According to their analysis, corruption considerably reduces equity values after controlling for many other firm- and country-level control factors: firms from more corrupt countries trade at significantly lower market multiples. Therefore, corruption has significant economic consequences for shareholder value.

As confirmed by our study, one potential reason why corruption may affect stock valuation has to do with corporate governance. In order to investigate this hypothesis, Lee and Ng (2006) examine the impact of corruption on corporate governance. Their model clearly confirms that an insider has more incentives to expropriate an outsider where bribery reduces the probability that the insider will get caught. As a consequence, higher corruption is associated with worse corporate governance. When it comes to methodology, Ng and Qian use firm-level corporate governance from two different surveys (i.e. those of Credit Lyonnais Securities Asia and Standard and Poor) and assess how country-level corruption data would affect corporate governance in different firms. Their empirical analysis suggests that corruption has a significant impact on both corporate governance and a firm's valuation. The quality of corporate governance in more corrupt countries tends to be weaker, and firms are accordingly traded at lower valuation multiples.

Another reason why corruption may affect stock price has to do with the behavior of foreign investors. In Chapter 2 we showed that lower country transparency is associated with lower investment from international funds. Gelos and Wei (2005) find that, during financial crises, international funds flee non-transparent countries by a greater amount than their transparent counterparts. Given the link between secrecy and corruption mentioned earlier, it seems quite reasonable to assert that corrupt countries will receive less investment from foreign investors.

4.3 DEBT RELIEF: GOVERNANCE AND CORRUPTION IN HEAVILY INDEBTED POOR COUNTRIES

When given to corrupt governments that lack the resources and know-how to budget, monitor and account for public resources, debt relief does not provide the right incentives for the implementation of better economic policies and structural reforms (Arnone and Presbitero 2010).

Debt relief granted to irresponsible governments is at best ineffective and likely detrimental: giving resources to corrupt and undemocratic governments means weakening the rule of law (ROL) by supporting those actually responsible for breaking it; worse still, in the presence of civil tensions and/or ethnic differences (quite common features in several African countries, although not only there), indiscriminate debt relief or financial support often means that more resources could be used by the recipient group in power in order to discriminate, suppress or weaken another group in the same country. Additionally, debt relief to corrupt or undemocratic governments might also represent a lost opportunity to help better-governed countries to eradicate poverty.

Even abstracting from ethical considerations and looking exclusively at the economics of debt relief, Arnone and Presbitero (2010) argue that corruption, poor macroeconomic management and bad governance must be taken into account in the allocation process and that debt relief should be granted only to countries for which the debt burden represents an actual constraint on economic growth, following a growth diagnostic approach (Hausmann, Rodrik, and Velasco 2005, 2006). Finally, an appropriate selectivity mechanism should be used as an incentive mechanism to encourage countries to undertake structural reforms and improve their governance.

The direction of a large share of scarce resources to a limited number of countries, lacking some of the most basic infrastructures and institutions that might trigger economic growth and enable permanent exit from debt dependence, means that fewer resources are made available to assist other poor countries better equipped to profit from external assistance: as a matter of fact, there is evidence of some positive results at country level, mostly in the presence of sound policies and good institutions.

4.4 INCENTIVES AND POLITICALLY-CONNECTED FIRMS

The empirical literature takes into consideration national realities in the form of immature phases of the democratic system and low levels of industrialization. However, the problem of politically-connected firms is substantial also in modern democracies and industrialized countries. Therefore, we turn now to an analysis of this issue. We have chosen Italy for our econometric analysis, because, at least within the European Union, it represents a significant case of a highly industrialized economy, where the proximity to political powers constitutes a prominent factor in determining the prosperity or the failure of nearly all major businesses. The results of our empirical analysis are in line with those of the earlier literature and add new findings.

4.4.1 Incentives and Capture

In analyzing the latest institutional evolutions and regulatory responses to corruption (see also Chapter 7 and Part II), we highlight that some of the perverse systems of incentives and the still existing widespread situations of improper mixtures between the private and public realms (e.g. conflict of interests) have the potential to annihilate the breakthroughs made by the international community on the matter. It is noteworthy that only few of such situations can be addressed by proper regulatory measures. Most need comprehensive policy and system-wide reforms in incentives.

Also, when addressing the impact of corruption on financial markets, it should be kept in mind that one of the main neglected dimensions of corruption is "State capture" or just "capture". In this scenario, powerful companies (or individuals) bend the regulatory, policy, and legal institutions of the nation for their "private benefit" (Kaufmann 2009: 1). Kaufmann argues that this is typically done, not only through high-level bribery, but also through subtler forms of capture and "legal corruption", which, arguably, underlie the 2008–12 economic and financial crisis that started in the US.[3]

There are also cases where the element of "capture" is endemic to certain economic systems. For example, the vigorous presence in a given market of what we will refer to as politically-connected firms cannot be effectively coped with through regulatory responses, and calls for radical systemic reforms. As we show in the following, proximity to political power gives such entities decisive advantages, for example, in terms of costs of capital and access to finance. Such advantages constitute actual financial assets, which may result decisively in obtaining or maintaining a certain market. The exploitation of such favorable conditions by firms which should not benefit from them clearly represents predatory behavior: nonetheless, this rarely gives rise to an act of corruption or violates the law.

3 Some of the cases put forward by Kaufmann to show how the element of capture has contributed to the systemic failures of oversight, regulation and disclosure in the financial sector, are rather striking and worth reporting: "First, the way Freddie Mac . . . and Fannie Mae . . . spent millions of dollars lobbying some influential members of Congress in exchange for, among other things, lax capital reserve requirements for these mortgage giants. Second, how AIG's (NYSE: AIG – news – people) 'small' derivatives unit located in London managed to obscure its accounts, be governed by lax regulatory oversight, and take inordinate risks that effectively brought down AIG's empire of 100,000 employees in 130 countries, accelerating the global financial crisis. Third, how giant mortgage lenders such as Countrywide Financial switched regulators so as to fall under the lax oversight of the Office of Thrift Supervision, which was funded by fees paid by the regulated banks (and which also supervised AIG's derivative unit). Fourth, how in April 2004, during a 55-minute-long meeting at the SEC, the largest investment banks persuaded the SEC to relax its regulatory stance and allow them to take on much larger amounts of debt. Finally, Madoff's giant Ponzi scheme, some of which appears to be plain fraud, though system-wide irregularities also point to subtler forms of corruption and capture. Years ago the SEC knew that Madoff, who had served on the commission's own advisory committee, had multiple violations and was misleading it in how he managed the funds of his customers. Yet the SEC failed in unmasking the Ponzi scheme."

The purpose of the present Section 2, therefore, is to show how corruption represents an influential and distorting factor in determining the values of certain crucial financial variables (e.g. the cost of borrowing and shares' returns) and impacts on other marginal but growing financial sectors (e.g. microfinance). In order to provide a more inclusive illustration of the implied risks in economic structures characterized by intense "improper" (but not necessarily "corrupt") relationships between the private economic sectors and the public realm, we will also consider the outcomes in terms of the economic performance of firms contiguous to political powers.

In the remaining part of Chapter 4 we assess the issue of politically-connected firms, by first defining such entities and then identifying the typologies and levels of the advantages they enjoy because of their contiguity to the public powers. Finally, the chapter focuses on the level of access to finance and costs of capitals for the same category of firms. Our results confirm the empirical evidence as provided by recent studies on business-politics relations, which show that politically-connected firms enjoy better access to finance, stronger market power and tax benefits. Nevertheless, empirical evidence also shows that these businesses perform generally worse than their competitors.

4.5 POLITICALLY-CONNECTED FIRMS

Empirical evidence, as provided by studies focused on business-politics relations, confirms that access to finance is one of the key factors in determining the success of new businesses and the competitiveness of new market entrants. Far from being at odds with these findings, these studies confirm that politically connected firms enjoy better access to finance, stronger market power and tax benefits. Conversely, empirical evidence also shows that politically-connected firms generally perform worse than other businesses.

4.5.1 Politically-connected Firms in Italy: Do Political Connections Matter?

Economic theory has been paying increasing attention to the several political connections that feature in both developed and less developed economic systems. However, a proper definition of political connection is not easy. Similarly, it is quite difficult to find proxies to measure the impact and the value of political connections.

It is possible to recognize in the phenomenon of political connections an alternative way of distributing income that does not operate entirely through the market system, and represents a special sort of market failure. Political connections could partially act as a substitute for the market mechanism and the price system. Such a feature framed many totalitarian regimes[4] in Europe in the first part of the last century as well as other regimes still in existence in many parts of the world, including some European systems during the second part of the 20th century. The same thing occurred in the so-called "bureaucratic" economies of Eastern Europe after World War II, as Schumpeter (1942) underlined.

One may think that political connections should distinguish countries in which industrial capitalism[5] and the financial systems are still not well developed,[6] or countries in which the political system does not accurately balance powers among them, like poor countries, dictatorships, totalitarian regimes or poorly performing countries. However, the economic and historical evidence of political connections suggests that such a blurred relationship between business and politics includes in multiple forms a large sample of economic and historical national experiences:[7] Italy represents a telling example of an industrialized and democratic country, where the impact of political connections within the economic system is considerable.

Economic literature has progressively defined political connections as situations in which economic entities, like individuals or corporations, have some degree of market power due to an existing link of a political nature. Such connections do not necessarily originate in monetary transactions, but can take more indirect forms, like the trading of influences.

---

4 From a corporate finance perspective, a totalitarian regime represents a context where extremely large portions of private benefits can be obtained by a relatively small number of people (Shleifer and Vishny 1986, 1995; Jensen and Meckling 1976; Fama and Jensen 1983a, 1983b; Grossman and Hart 1982). Non-democratic States or dictatorships allow the government to maximize private benefits instead of GDP.

5 From this point of view political connections should be more relevant, according to Gerschenkron's famous (1962) definition, in the latecomers' countries, i.e. nations that developed their industrialization process from the second half of the 19th century, like Germany, Italy, France, and Japan. However, there is no clear empirical evidence on this.

6 There is a flourishing literature about the connections between financial development and economic growth. In this context we consider as a simple proxy for financial development the ratio between market capitalization and the gross domestic product.

7 See Donahue (1989); Carino (1986); De Soto (1989) and Depaak (1985).

4.5.2 Survey of the Literature

Only recently corporate finance studies have focused their attention on the corporate value of political connections. Despite the negative effect of corruption on aggregate economic growth, recent research shows that political connections may be beneficial for specific firms in some respects and costly in others. Anecdotal evidence in the financial press shows possible sources of advantage for politically connected firms. A number of recent papers have documented the prevalence of personal connections between politicians and firms in many countries around the world.

The earlier literature focuses on event studies, identifying an event, like the sudden death of a connected politician (Roberts 1990; Fisman 2001; Faccio and Parsley 2006), which could help identify the private benefits of the politically-connected firms. Recent literature examines the economic and financial benefits gained by connected firms, showing a new point of view from which to analyze this field.

Other important research covers some related fields, showing links and relationships among political and corporate governance institutions, and economic and financial effects (Johnson and Mitton 2003, following a previous paper by Rajan and Zingales 1998). In addition, there is some important research by Shleifer and Vishny (1993), mainly focused on a particular bargaining model between politicians and managers in order to explain the behavior of public companies. They focus their attention mainly on the behavior of firms with political interactions, noting some key political aspects. According to the authors, these "political connections" are the main cause of inefficiency in corporations owned by the government.

A growing literature documents a wide range of benefits provided by government to favored firms, such as: preferential access to credit (Chiu and Joh 2004, Khwaja and Mian 2005,[8] Cull and Xu 2005,[9] Dinç 2004; Faccio 2007), government contracts (Goldman, Rocholl, and So 2006[10]);

---

8 About the Pakistani context from 1996 to 2002.

9 Cull and Xu remark that Chinese firms show a sort of "atypical political connection" (firms that make an informal payment to government officials) and may borrow more from banks. This type of "connection" is very important even for Italy, in particular considering the economic and political situation in the past.

10 In the US context, Goldman, Rocholl, and So analyze the value impact of political connections of publicly traded companies. The sample includes all the companies in the S&P 500 from 1996 to 2000. They underline two main results. Firstly, the authors find support for the idea that political connections create value by generating future benefits for corporations. Therefore firms' value increases in anticipation of future benefits following the nomination of politically-connected

preferential treatment by government-owned firms, lighter taxation (De Soto 1989), and greater market power (Faccio 2007). In the meantime, some of these works point out that connected firms could show worse accounting performance and worse productivity than non-connected firms; hence overall financial performance of such firms is uncertain (Chen, Fan, and Wong 2004,[11] Faccio 2007).

A relevant work by Faccio (2006), unlike previous works presented here, "provides a widespread look at the corporate political connections around the globe." Using a two-boundary Tobit model, Faccio proposes a country approach using a sample of 20,202 publicly traded firms in 47 countries between 1997 and 2001. Defining a new measure of political connections and trying to quantify the added value derived from these "relationships", she finds that corporate political connections are quite common[12] but unequally distributed across countries; Faccio suggests that connections are more common in countries with higher levels of corruption, in the presence of restrictions on foreign investments, and in countries with less transparent systems. Then, following the same idea, connections are less common in the presence of more stringent regulation on political conflicts of interest. Moreover, using an event study,[13] she tests the hypothesis that if connections add value to the firm, announcements should be associated with a positive cumulative abnormal return. In her article, the author also shows that different relationships with business people and politicians have different value for the firms, asserting that stock prices and benefits in general are more relevant if the connections are related to large shareholders or prime ministers rather than top officers or members of parliament. Nevertheless, Faccio suggests that even if connections are linked with benefits for the firms, these show lower market performances than the average, with significant consequences for capital allocation, investment decisions and economic growth.[14]

Following her 2006 paper about politically-connected firms, Faccio (2007) investigates political connections across a large number of coun-

---

individuals, showing that this value is independent with respect to the specific nature of the connections. Moreover, this paper shows abnormal cumulated stock returns following the board nomination, indicating that these effects are more pronounced for large companies.

11 In a sample of 617 neo-privatized Chinese firms, listed on the Chinese Stock Exchange from 1993 to 2000.

12 Faccio finds political connections in 35 of 47 countries in the sample.

13 Around the time of an announcement that officers or large shareholders are entering politics, or that politicians are joining boards.

14 This empirical evidence is consistent with the existence of private benefits.

tries. She focuses on firms' characteristics in order to verify the presence of differences between connected and non-connected firms in terms of leverage, taxation, market power, productivity, accounting performance and market-to-book ratio. Using the data set defined in Faccio (2006) for 47 countries, she extracts a sample of 458 connected firms and 15,733 non-connected peers, in 1997. Statistical evidence shows that connected firms have higher leverage[15] (on average, 28.14 percent as against 24.19 percent for non-connected firms), lower tax rate (on average, 29.67 percent against 32.7 percent) and greater market share (on average, 18.04 percent against 9.48 percent). However, in spite of these advantages, "connected firms have poorer accounting performance than non-connected firms[16] and these differences are greater when the partner in the connection has more power, in particular when firms are connected through owners rather than directors."[17]

Finally, there are two relevant studies by Bertrand, Kramarz, Schoar, and Thesmar (2004)[18] and by Claessens, Feijen, and Laeven (2008),[19] followed by other recent works (Chen, Ding, and Kim 2006; Kroszner and Stratmann 1998; Riahi-Belkaoui 2004; Aggarwal, Meschke, and Wang

---

[15] As a proxy for access to debt financing. Faccio defines leverage as: "the ratio of long-term debt (excluding the current portion of long-term debt, pensions, deferred taxes, and minority interests) to total capital x 100." Total capital represents the total investment in the company and it is the sum of common equity, preferred stock, minority interests, long-term debt, non-equity reserves and deferred tax liability in untaxed reserves.

[16] For example, Faccio finds that the return on assets (ROA) for connected firms is significantly lower (-2.41 percent with a p-value < 0.01) than for non-connected firms, and even their market-to-book value is lower (-0.48 percent, the difference being only marginally significant).

[17] The purpose of Faccio's paper is quite similar to the purpose of our study. The main difference concerns the sample of observation (47 countries instead of one, Italy) and the period analyzed (just one year instead of 20 years). It goes without saying that the methodology of the analysis will be partially different.

[18] This study investigates a reverse perspective on the nature of the exchanges that may occur between politicians and firms. The authors consider French listed firms, from 1989 to 2002. If we focus our attention on the last part of this paper, we can remark that they note two substantial levers used by politicians to affect business: tax breaks and subsidies. They find out that CEOs of connected firms have on average a lower tax rate and receive more subsidies.

[19] They analyze the Brazilian framework during the 1998 and 2002 elections, studying the political connections that firms gain by contributing to the campaigns of election candidates and the possible channels politicians use to repay these contributions. According to the growing literature, they find that political connections may register a significant impact on firm value and access to bank finance. They further state a strong link between stock market return and contributions to firms.

2007; Cooper et al. 2010), who analyze the problem of political connections from new perspectives. Using Faccio's (2007) methodology, we study the Italian context from 1987 to 2006. Here we explicitly exclude the further issue of corruption (see Chapter 5), which is sometimes very close to the topic of political connections. We do not consider the possibility of an improper use of market power derived from a political connection being exchanged in the market for money. In our opinion economic or financial fraud[20] is a possible consequence of political connection, but we leave this issue out of consideration in this research.

4.5.3 Methodology and the Definition of Political Connection

Our work covers 20 years, divided into two different stages. The first period, 1987–92, was characterized by the strong economic role of the Italian government. We consider just the last five years of this period. The second stage, 1992–2006, is characterized by a decreasing role of State in institutions.

Several relevant criteria for defining the political connections of the firms may be identified: firstly, a "geographic" approach, i.e. politicians favor "local" firms (Faccio 2006); secondly, an "indirect" connection, i.e. if the top management of a firm is closely affiliated (relative ties, friendship, business connections) with politicians (Fisman 2001); thirdly, a "direct" connection, i.e. a member of the top management of a firm is a deputy, a governor or a minister (Faccio 2007). In keeping with the third approach, we define political connection as follows: "A company is identified as being connected with a politician if at least one of its large shareholders (anyone controlling directly or indirectly at least 10 percent of voting shares) or one of its top officers (anyone who is a member of the board of directors or a member of the audit committee) is: (a) a member of parliament, (b) a minister (including the prime minister), or (c) the president of Italy."

According to this definition of politically-connected firms in Italy, we can identify three main types of connections: the first is the connection through the board of directors or members of the audit committee; the second is the connection through large shareholders as described above; and the third typology is when a firm is connected at the same time both

---

20 Historically all over the world, the financial system has been accurately controlled by regulations both in order to protect people's savings and in order to regulate the relationships between banks and industry. In countries like Italy, in which the credit system has for a long time been owned by the State, the value of the political connections has been extremely high.

through top officers (member of the board of directors or member of the audit committee) and large shareholders (double connections are defined as "connection through both").

Testing if political connections impact on the value of industrial and holding listed companies in Italy during the period 1987–2006 requires addressing two basic challenges. The first challenge has been met by identifying an exogenous measure of political connections. The second challenge is to find a setting that would allow us to test whether they affect company value.

Firstly, we create three data sets for the empirical analysis. Our data sets combine sources of information about Italian politicians and all 414 Italian industrial and holding listed firms in Italy during the period 1987–2006, their top officers and their large shareholders. In order to define the sample of politically-connected firms, we combine three different data sets created using publicly available sources.

The first data set, named "politicians", is about all politicians, as defined above, holding office during the period 1987–2006 in Italy. Overall, data sources allow us to identify 2,945 politicians who covered 5,593 institutional offices, with a prevalence of parliamentary positions (86 percent). On average each politician covered 1.9 institutional offices.

The second data set, named "top officers", is about top officers for all Italian industrial and holding listed firms in Italy in the same period (1987–2006). We collected the names of companies' top officers by "Il Calepino dell'Azionista", published by Mediobanca. We consider the full name (first, middle and last name) of all top officers as reported by the "Il Calepino dell'Azionista" classification.[21] The full database contains 7,935 names who covered 14,107 company charges,[22] for a total of 50,659 company charges[23] over 414 listed companies in the sample. On average each politician maintains a company charge for 3.59 years (3 years in median terms). Moreover, we underline that each politician covered, on average, almost 2 company commitments (1.78).

---

21 We considered the name of all top officers as defined by "Il Calepino dell'Azionista". The professional figures we included in this data set are: "Presidente Onorario, Presidente Consiglio di Amministrazione (CDA), Vicepresidente Consiglio di Amministrazione, Amministratore Delegato (AD), Consigliere, Direttore Generale (DG), Segretario del Consiglio, Presidente Collegio Sindacale, Sindaco effettivo" and other professional figures associated with new alternative models of corporate governance.

22 Without considering the temporal aspect.

23 Considering each company commitment for each year as an individual company charge.

The third data set is about the large shareholders of the 414 Italian listed companies included in the sample,[24] constructed using "Il Calepino dell'Azionista", "Il Taccuino dell'Azionista" and the Borsa Italiana website. The full data set includes 748 names (including individuals and firms that control at least 10 percent of voting shares) for about 6.019 large shareholdings. Each "large shareholder" (individuals and/or firms) shows, on average, about 8 "large shareholdings" greater than 10 percent, indicating a concentrated ownership structure.

Then, we carried on with two types of matching. Firstly, we matched the politicians' data set with the data set about top officers; secondly, we matched the politicians' data set with the large shareholders' data set. The matching procedure is mainly as follows: firstly, a politician is matched with a top officer, if their full names (first, middle and last) match exactly.[25]

4.5.4 Empirical Analysis

We identify 79 Italian industrial and holding listed firms that are politically connected with 44 politicians from 1987 to 2006.

Leaving out banks and insurance companies, foreign companies and the market segment for small-cap firms (Expandi), but considering semi-public and State-owned firms instead, the sample includes 74 corporations (representing 20.2 percent of all 367 Italian industrial and holding firms listed on the MTA-MTAX markets; 16.4 percent in terms of market capitalization of the same markets and 13.5 percent of market capitalization in terms of the whole market) that are connected with 40 politicians in the MTA-MTAX markets[26] (who represent about 1.4 percent of all politicians with an institutional office), for a total amount of 629 "years connection" (where 61.7 percent are connections through large shareholders). Table 4.1 shows some of the evidence.

We observe that 70 percent of connected politicians are members of parliament, 15 percent are ministers. From a sectoral point of view, for

---

24 Considering direct and indirect shareholdings, as defined above.

25 It is important to notice that, given this literal matching of names, there can be a type of error: incorrect exclusion. Thus, considering this possible error in matching politicians to firms, our calculations of political connections are likely to underestimate their presence. Moreover, we eliminated those names, and then the firms, for which we could not determine the presence of people with simultaneous positions in political institutions and firms' boards. Secondly, we checked for the possible presence of homonymies, eliminating them.

26 Which represents, in median terms, 82.2 percent of the whole Italian market capitalization (banks and insurance companies included).

Table 4.1 Political connections – descriptive statistics – classification by type

	Connections by type			Total	Percent
	I) Connections through top officers	II) Connections through large shareholders	III) Connections through "both"		
No. Connected Politicians:	31 (77.5%)	4 (10%)	5 (12.5 %)	40	100
– Connections with deputies	11	1	2	14	35
– Connections with senators	12	1	1	14	35
– Connections with tenure senators	–	1	1	2	5
– Connections with ministers	6	–	–	6	15
– Connections with prime ministers	–	1	–	1	2.5
– Connections with under-secretaries	2	–	1	3	7.5

Source: Authors' calculations.

automobiles and parts the figure is 46 percent, for media 41 percent, for construction and materials 35 percent, for holding and chemicals 29 percent.

Turning to the dynamic aspects, in terms of the number of politically connected firms over the total number of 367 Italian industrial and holding firms listed at MTA-MTAX, and in terms of market capitalization, we notice a different trend across the years. Firstly, we find a high concentration of connected firms during the end of the 1980s and in the early 1990s. In particular, we observe a first trend characterized by a rise in connections from 1987 to 1994; subsequently, connections drop sharply from 1994 till the end of 2005 with an 80 percent reduction in the number of firms, and there is a drop of 20 percent in market capitalization from 1994 to 1996.

We analyze the difference between connected and non-connected corporations in order to find out if connected firms show greater market power but poorer performances, in keeping with the literature. The statistics in Table 4.2 seem to confirm this hypothesis.

Table 4.2 Descriptive statistics – Politically-connected firms and whole sample

Balance sheet items	Connected		State controlled		Non- connected		Whole sample	
	Mean	Median	Mean	Median	Mean	Median	Mean	Median
No. total employees	23,477	4,232	19,640	5,221	3,930	1,067	8,534	1,269
Turnover (€'000)	3,430,000	520,817	4,499,178	800,542	787,753	163,168	1,600,118	197,645
Total assets (€'000)	5,352,496	1,072,744	8,454,503	1,628,340	1,226,702	258,793	2,673,046	339,741
Leverage	0.27	0.21	0.25	0.16	0.23	0.17	0.24	0.17
Total asset turnover	0.67	0.66	0.50	0.44	0.73	0.73	0.69	0.68
Return on assets (%)	3.39	3.30	3.47	3.40	2.99	3.76	3.12	3.66
Mkt capitalization (€'000)	1,164,291	349,964	4,983,058	584,961	612,628	119,487	1,226,977	150,220
Market share (%)	0.74	0.25	1.45	0.35	0.21	0.05	0.43	0.07
Price/book value	1.48	1.19	2.07	1.52	2.09	1.32	2.01	1.33

Source: Authors' calculations.

We are aware that several other characteristics may affect the relationship between political connections and the variables described above. Politically-connected firms – and State-controlled ones (connected by definition) – show in median terms greater size in terms of: number of employees, turnover, total assets, and market capitalization, compared with non-connected firms (Table 4.2). In addition, we find poorer efficiency and poorer accounting performance for connected and State-controlled firms than for other listed companies. Market share and market capitalization weight are substantial for connected and State-controlled firms as opposed to non-connected firms.

After this brief descriptive analysis, we implemented: (1) a pooled model, (2) a fixed effect over least squares dummy variable (FE/LSDV) model, and (3) a random effect (RE) model, on a panel of 367 Italian industrial and holding listed firms during 1987–2006. The variables we focused on are: (a) return on assets (as a proxy for accounting performance); (b) total asset turnover (as a proxy for efficiency, in productivity terms); (c) market share (as a proxy for market power). The models are structured as follows:

$$\textit{Return on Assets}_{it} = \alpha + \beta_1 \textit{ Connected}_{it} + \beta_2 \textit{ State controlled}_{it}$$

$$+ \beta_3 \textit{ Size}_{it} + \Sigma_1^c \delta_c \textit{ Sector}_c + \Sigma_1^k \gamma_k \textit{ Year}_k + \varepsilon_{it}$$

Tables 4.3 and 4.4 show the empirical findings.

According with Faccio (2007), we find that politically-connected firms and State-controlled firms show an inverse correlation with ROA. Therefore, this first result seems to reflect the evidence that politically-connected firms and State-controlled firms perform poorly in comparison with non-connected ones. One might expect connected firms to be characterized by better performance because of the benefits gained from connections. We consider two main reasons to explain this evidence: firstly, the relationships between politicians and firms have a value (Shleifer and Vishny 1993); secondly, the possibility that companies try to establish connections to address their problems. From this point of view, poor performance could reflect ex ante performances.

If we focus on efficiency indices, we get the same results. Table 4.4 summarizes the empirical findings.

Are connected firms more or less efficient than their non-connected peers? Table 4.4 shows again that political connection has a negative correlation with total asset turnover. In other words and in keeping with the literature, politically-connected firms appear less efficient than non-connected ones, and the same result occurs for State-controlled and large firms.

Table 4.3 Politically connected firms – ROA

	Pooled (OLS) Robust		Fixed Effects (FE)/LSDV		Random Effects (RE)	
	Coeff.	t-stat.	Coeff.	t-stat.	Coeff.	z
Connected	−1.158***	−3.75	−1.363***	−2.56	−1.308	−2.63
	(.309)		*(.534)*		*(.497)*	
State controlled	−1.538***	−4.20	2.564	0.41	−.461	−0.39
	(.366)		*(6.317)*		*(1.189)*	
Size	.736***	6.75	.130	0.78	.504***	3.84
	(.109)		*(.167)*		*(.131)*	
Sectorial dummies	Yes		Yes		Yes	
Temporal dummies	Yes		Yes		Yes	
Constant	−2.338	−1.55	4.317*	1.69	0.571	0.27
	(1.505)		*(2.560)*		*(2.121)*	
R-square adj.	0.15		R-sq Within	0.104	R-sq Within	0.102
			R-sq Between	0.172	R-sq Between	0.236
			R-sq Overall	0.175	R-sq Overall	0.138
N. obs.	3,012		3,012	332 groups	3,012	332 groups
F(37,2,974)	F stat on â	10.866***	F stat on ì (i)	5.44***	Wald chi2(37)	=396.86***

Notes:
* significant at 10% level; ** significant at 5% level; *** significant at 1% level.
LM: $chi^2(1)$ = 524.59 - Prob. > chi^2 = 0.0000.
Hausman test: $chi^2(25)$= 56.58 Prob>chi^2 = 0.0003.

Source: Authors' calculations using Stata 9.0.

Table 4.4 Politically-connected firms – total asset turnover

	Pooled (OLS) Robust		Fixed Effects (FE)/ LSDV		Random Effects (RE)	
	Coeff.	t-stat.	Coeff.	t-stat.	Coeff.	z
Connected	−.078***	−4.63	−.019	−1.38	−.024*	−1.72
	(.017)				*(.014)*	
State Controlled	−.236***	−8.51	−.789***	−3.08	−.287***	−4.55
	(.027)		*(.256)*		*(.063)*	
Size	.068***	18.63	.123***	28.53	.117***	28.72
	(.004)		*(.004)*		*(.004)*	
Sectoral dummies	Yes		Yes		Yes	
Temporal dummies	Yes		Yes		Yes	
Constant	−.342***	−6.31	−.755***	−11.51	−.880***	−11.09
	(.054)		*(.065)*		*(.079)*	
R-squared adj.	0.338		R-sq. Within	0.254	R-sq. Within	0.252
			R-sq. Between	0.051	R-sq. Between	0.293
			R-sq. Overall	0.073	R-sq. Overall	0.283
N. obs.	3,128		3,128	333 groups	3,128	333 groups
F (37,3,090)	F stat on â	67.72***	F stat on Ì (i)	32.19***	Wald chi2(37) = 1,060***	

Notes:
* significant at 10%; ** significant at 5%; *** significant at 1%.
LM: $chi^2(1)$ = 6682.24 - Prob. > chi^2 = 0.0000 - Hausman test: n.a.

Source: Authors' calculations using Stata 9.0.

If we look at the market share, the picture is rather different. Two observations are in order: firstly, oligopolistic and monopolistic conditions can reasonably influence market power; therefore, a company could be motivated to gain in connections to protect its dominant position. Secondly, firms with greater size may find connections to be more valuable and, therefore, be more likely to establish them.

The evidence indicates the presence of a positive correlation between connections and market share in both connected firms and State controlled ones, statistically significant at the 1 percent level. These results confirm the hypothesis that connections are associated with greater market power.

4.5.5 Concluding Remarks

The statistical analysis we propose underlines the presence of a relationship between politicians and business in the Italian stock exchange during the period 1987–2006. We notice that politically-connected firms differ significantly from their non-connected peers in terms of size, performance, efficiency, and market power. In particular, we find, in median terms, that size is greater in connected firms. Connected firms also show greater market power, but poorer accounting performance and efficiency, than non-connected ones. These results are generally consistent for all presented models. According with the existing literature, we argue that firms with political connections gain financial benefits in terms of greater market power, but show poorer performance and efficiency than non-connected firms, maybe because of the presence of private benefits that could exceed the cost of obtaining a connection.

5. The impact of corruption on shares' returns of euro-area listed industrial firms[1]

Carlo Bellavite Pellegrini and Laura Pellegrini

5.1 INTRODUCTION

This chapter illustrates an empirical analysis of the impact of corruption on the return of shares for a sample of 1,058 listed industrial companies belonging to the eurozone countries between 1996 and 2006.

Bellavite Pellegrini (2008) uses an innovative method to measure the relevance of the impact of control variables on returns of European stocks since the introduction of the euro. This study shows that control variables like governance and productivity have a clear connection with the determinants of stock returns, even though they represent a second-best condition with respect to the importance of the state variables according to the Fama and French analysis (Arnone, Bellavite Pellegrini and Graziadei 2006).

Moreover, the division of the sample into different portfolios, according to different levels of capitalization, highlights that control variables are definitely more important in portfolios with low-capitalization companies than in portfolios with highly-capitalized companies. The study suggests similar evidence for both productivity and governance. Low-capitalization companies' managers may influence aggregate productivity more intensively than managers of highly-capitalized companies.

Indeed, the main (when not the only) element on which the growth of the former companies is based is strictly connected with the dynamics of productivity, whereas the high-capitalization companies are also characterized by other growth factors, such as market power or political

[1] This chapter was jointly written by Carlo Bellavite Pellegrini and Laura Pellegrini. Sections 5.1 and 5.4 were written by Carlo Bellavite Pellegrini; Section 5.2 was written by Laura Pellegrini and Section 5.3 was jointly written by Carlo Bellavite Pellegrini and Laura Pellegrini.

connections. The skills of such companies' management are far closer to political than to pure managerial virtues.

Similar evidence seems to characterize macroeconomic governance. Low-capitalization companies benefit more significantly in terms of stock returns from a well-structured and developed system of macroeconomic governance, while highly-capitalized ones probably have other means at their disposal in order to influence stocks' performance, such as market power or cross-country fiscal arbitrage, which, in turn, makes a good system of macroeconomic governance less relevant. The resulting scenario is composed of two types of euro-area industrial listed companies: a small number of highly-capitalized ones and a more consistent number with low capitalization.

This research contributes to the identification of a control variable affecting stock performance: namely, corruption. Our aim is to investigate the connections between European industrial stocks returns, on the one hand, and a macroeconomic index of corruption, on the other, in order to assess the impact of corruption on the performance of listed European industrial companies.[2] In greater detail, we present the data and the methodology. Subsequently, we present an econometric exercise to assess the impact of the control variable of corruption on listed euro-area industrial companies.

5.2 DATA AND METHODOLOGY

The database includes the complete population of 1,058 listed industrial companies belonging to 11 euro-area[3] countries.[4] In terms of market capitalization, we obtain the following results:

The relative weight of capitalization for Germany and the Netherlands drops significantly, Belgium and Portugal have stable capitalization weights, and all the remaining nations exhibit substantial growth in their relative percentages. The euro is likely to have improved the relative performance of small nations. Table 5.2 describes the dynamic of the capitalization of the market. The table is organized in the following way.

---

2 The research does not take into consideration 169 banks, financial and insurance companies because of the peculiarities of their balance sheet and because of poor comparability with industrial companies' indexes. The research considers only companies with a statutory provision of "one share-one vote" (Harris and Raviv 1988).

3 Companies' balance sheets are published in euros since 1996.

4 The sample includes Austria, Belgium, Finland, France, Germany, Greece, Ireland, Italy, the Netherlands, Portugal, and Spain. It does not include Luxembourg because of its limited significance in terms of GDP and market capitalization in the whole sample.

Table 5.1 Percentage of the relative weight of market capitalization for each year and each nation

Country	1996	1997	1998	1999	2000	2001	2002	2003	2004	2005	2006	Mean
Austria	1.37	1.07	0.95	0.76	0.52	0.61	0.78	1.05	1.51	1.96	2.22	1.16
Belgium	4.52	4.25	4.78	3.56	3.05	3.53	3.85	3.73	4.48	4.56	4.25	4.05
Finland	2.30	2.51	2.68	4.75	6.97	3.56	3.80	3.65	3.04	3.34	3.32	3.63
France	23.60	21.22	22.55	23.36	26.19	28.29	27.41	28.02	27.70	27.96	29.64	25.99
Germany	26.79	28.82	26.46	26.38	23.36	22.91	22.96	21.03	21.36	20.45	20.20	23.70
Greece	0.88	0.99	1.36	2.12	1.68	1.25	1.72	1.84	1.80	1.97	2.17	1.62
Ireland	1.44	1.42	1.55	1.68	1.45	1.94	1.70	1.69	1.86	1.87	1.87	1.68
Italy	11.55	10.14	12.81	12.81	14.53	14.14	13.51	14.73	13.82	13.34	13.73	13.19
Netherlands	18.37	19.64	16.36	15.70	13.81	14.19	13.59	12.23	11.72	11.63	9.13	14.22
Portugal	1.27	1.77	2.02	1.43	1.44	1.23	1.36	1.35	1.51	1.18	1.37	1.45
Spain	7.91	8.17	8.48	7.45	7.00	8.35	9.32	10.68	11.20	11.74	12.10	9.31
Total	100	100	100	100	100	100	100	100	100	100	100	–

Source: Authors' calculations from Eurostat data.

Table 5.2 Relative weight of the different samples' capitalization in total market capitalization (million euros as of end December)

Year	Total market capitalization	Capitalization of 1,227 companies "Sample 1"	Weight of "Sample 1" in total market capitalization	Capitalization of 1,058 industrial companies – "Sample 2"	Weight of "Sample 2" in total market capitalization
1996	1,393,952.00	1,254,018.74	89.96%	977,165.62	70.10%
1997	2,383,987.00	1,786,052.70	74.92%	1,301,240.81	54.58%
1998	3,710,022.00	2,302,694.51	62.07%	1,579,315.04	42.57%
1999	4,016,236.00	3,307,709.86	82.36%	2,410,544.16	60.02%
2000	5,603,740.00	3,564,701.40	63.61%	2,509,656.44	44.79%
2001	4,501,959.00	3,068,215.73	68.15%	2,191,570.76	48.68%
2002	3,549,293.00	2,110,178.47	59.45%	1,553,706.55	43.78%
2003	3,224,704.00	2,487,319.47	77.13%	1,792,965.17	55.60%
2004	3,602,792.00	2,793,223.44	77.53%	2,000,873.67	55.54%
2005	4,462,800.00	3,570,253.18	80.00%	2,496,527.96	55.94%
2006	4,908,905.00	4,326,571.54	88.14%	2,991,760.05	60.95%
Mean	*3,759,853.64*	*2,779,176.28*	*74.85%*	*1,982,302.38*	*53.87%*

Source: Authors' calculations on Eurostat data.

Table 5.3 Real average yearly variation of Sample 1 and Sample 2 market capitalization

Period	Average real yearly variation of market capitalization (in percent)	Average real yearly variation of Sample 1 (in percent)	Average real yearly variation of Sample 2 (in percent)
1997–1999	43	36.51	33.94
2000–2002	−2.65	−14.42	−14.52
2003–2006	6.81	17.27	15.42

Source: Authors' calculations based on Thomson Financial Datastream data.

The first column describes market capitalization at the end of December of each year. The second column presents the capitalization of all the listed companies without any interruption since the beginning of the period. The third column highlights the relationship between column 2 and column 1. The fourth column presents the capitalization of industrial companies which have been listed without any interruption since the beginning. The last column highlights the relationship between column 4 and column 1.

The medium weights of Sample 1 and Sample 2 in total market capitalization are 74.85 percent and 53.87 percent, respectively. The medium weight of the difference between the two samples, i.e. the capitalization of the 169 financial companies that are listed without interruption for the whole period is roughly 20 percent of market capitalization. Our analysis takes into consideration the industrial companies belonging to Sample 2 which represent a consistent percentage of market capitalization in the period examined above. Table 5.3 describes the average real variation of total market capitalization and of the two samples of European companies examined above. To some extent the results of Table 5.3 could approximate stock performance.

Table 5.4 shows the geographic distribution of 1,058 listed euro-zone companies in the sample, with specific regard to market capitalization.

Some nations, such as Austria, Germany, and Italy, register a similar grouping in both number and capitalization, while other nations, such as Greece or Portugal, have a heavier weight in number of listed companies than in capitalization. Table 5.5 divides the 1,058 companies into five portfolios according to their capitalization, with a different number of companies in each portfolio.

In the second approach the companies are divided into five different portfolios according to their number, i.e. each portfolio has more or less the same number of companies. This second approach is illustrated in

Table 5.4 Number of companies for each nation and percentage of the total number and of capitalization as of January 1996

Country	Number of companies	Percentage of the total of the sample	Percentage of capitalization
Austria	40	3.78	4.53
Belgium	52	4.91	2.09
Finland	51	4.82	2.89
France	272	25.71	28.99
Germany	243	22.97	21.87
Greece	112	10.59	0.50
Ireland	22	2.08	0.95
Italy	74	6.99	5.92
Netherlands	84	7.94	22.69
Portugal	44	4.16	0.96
Spain	64	6.05	8.61
Total	*1058*	*100*	*100*

Source: Authors' elaborations on Thomson Financial Datastream data.

Table 5.6. Each portfolio has the same number of listed companies, i.e. 211–12. Having the same number of companies means there is a relevant difference in the weight of the market capitalization of each portfolio. The first methodology prefers taking into consideration portfolios with similar market capitalization weight notwithstanding the different significance in terms of number of companies, while the second methodology completes this perspective by taking into consideration more appropriate and representative portfolios in terms of number of observations.

The variables considered as regressors in our empirical exercise are the market risk premium, market capitalization, the productivity index, the level of perceived corruption in each country, and the average of a series of country governance indices. The dependent variable in our model is the total annual investment return of each company. The total annual investment return represents the annual return index of a public traded company: it tracks the capital gains of the stock over time, and assumes that any cash distributions, such as dividends, are reinvested in the company. We use the following as independent variables in our model: (a) market capitalization: it represents the total market value of all of a company's outstanding shares. It is calculated by multiplying a company's shares outstanding by the current market price of one share; (b) market risk premium, that is, the difference between the return on a market portfolio and the risk-free rate. Because of the difficulty in finding common data for the euro-area stock

Table 5.5 Division of companies by market capitalization quintiles,[5] for each year

Year	Large Cap (5th quintile)		Large-Middle Cap (4th quintile)		Middle Cap (3rd quintile)		Middle-Small Cap (2nd quintile)		Small Cap (1st quintile)	
	% value	no. of companies	% value	no. of companies	% value	no. of companies	% value	no. of companies	% value	no. of companies
1996	21.17	6	20.60	11	20.01	22	20.06	66	18.16	953
1997	21.83	6	20.63	12	20.32	22	20.11	68	17.11	950
1998	20.21	6	20.78	12	20.36	19	20.03	56	18.62	965
1999	21.32	4	19.49	9	20.56	17	20.12	47	18.51	981
2000	22.43	4	21.56	9	20.65	17	20.09	51	15.27	977
2001	20.14	4	20.51	8	20.21	15	20.08	42	19.06	989
2002	20.20	4	20.21	8	20.64	19	20.19	50	18.76	977
2003	20.41	5	20.26	9	20.02	19	20.02	54	19.29	971
2004	20.70	5	20.46	10	20.59	23	20.02	63	18.23	957
2005	20.29	5	20.75	11	20.21	24	20.01	64	18.74	954
2006	22.00	7	20.42	14	20.13	29	20.06	70	17.39	938
Mean	*20.97*	*5*	*20.52*	*10*	*20.34*	*21*	*20.07*	*57*	*18.10*	*965*

Source: Authors' calculations based on Thomson Financial Datastream data.

5 Each portfolio represents 20 percent of the total market capitalization.

Table 5.6 Capitalization divided into quintiles[6] of equal number of companies, for individual years

Year	Large Cap (5th quintile), in percent	Large-Middle Cap (4th quintile), in percent	Middle Cap (3rd quintile), in percent	Middle-Small Cap (2nd quintile), in percent	Small Cap (1st quintile), in percent
1996	91.99	5.70	1.63	0.53	0.15
1997	92.12	5.69	1.59	0.48	0.12
1998	92.81	5.19	1.45	0.45	0.10
1999	93.68	4.46	1.37	0.41	0.08
2000	94.73	3.82	1.05	0.33	0.07
2001	94.54	4.01	1.04	0.34	0.07
2002	93.51	4.78	1.24	0.39	0.08
2003	93.03	5.14	1.37	0.39	0.07
2004	92.52	5.62	1.43	0.36	0.07
2005	92.15	5.94	1.48	0.36	0.07
2006	91.53	6.42	1.59	0.39	0.07
Mean	*92.96*	*5.16*	*1.39*	*0.40*	*0.09*

Source: Authors' calculations based on Thomson Financial Datastream data.

markets before 2000, the market risk premium for the period 1996–9 has been calculated each year as the difference between the return on the country's market portfolio and the ten-year government bond return of every single nation. This difference has then been weighted by the average weight of the percentage weight of GDP over the percentage weight of the total market capitalization of the countries in our sample (it is a ratio of ratios: [(GDPi/GDPtot)/(Capi/Captot)]%). For the period 2000–06 the market risk premium has been calculated as the difference between the Morgan Stanley Capital International Euro Index (MSCI EMU)[7] and the European Central Bank (ECB) interest rate; (c) a productivity index, which represents the ability of the companies to generate revenues from fixed assets, calculated as the ratio between annual revenues and total fixed assets, in logs; (d) as an indicator of the level of corruption we use the CPI; (e) we use a governance index, represented by the Index of Economic Freedom.

6 The full sample of 1,058 companies has been divided into five portfolios, each of 211–12 companies.

7 It measures the performance of the stocks of 11 euro-area developed markets: Austria, Belgium, Finland, France, Germany, Greece, Ireland, Italy, the Netherlands, Portugal and Spain. The index includes almost 300 stocks and represents about 85 percent of market capitalization in these countries.

5.3 EMPIRICAL RESULTS

Having defined the different variables considered as regressors, we now describe the regression model used to explain the annual investment return of each company included in the sample. The regression model is specified as follows: $y_{it} = \alpha + x'_{it}\beta + \varepsilon_{it}$.

As summarized in Table 5.7, the full sample provides quite a low explained variance. However, the independent variables influence the total investment return as all the variables are statistically significant. The measure of the coefficient is quite small, with the exception of the market premium. We focus our attention on the perceived corruption variable. In particular, the perceived corruption index shows a 0.12 positively correlated and statistically significant coefficient. A lower level of perceived corruption positively affects the total annual investment return. If we divide the sample into five different portfolios according to market capitalization, we obtain a more articulated variety of results. Low-capitalization companies, i.e. the 965 companies belonging to the first portfolio, show quite similar results to that of the full sample: a 0.14 positive and statistically significant coefficient. Total annual investment returns of low capitalization companies gain a little, but significantly, benefit from a lower level of perceived corruption. The four other portfolios present a negative relationship between the total investment return and the variable. The coefficients of perceived corruption of the second and third portfolios are small and not statistically significant, while the coefficients of the fourth and fifth portfolios are bigger, but only the coefficient of the fourth portfolio is statistically significant, although at the 10 percent level. Even though the fourth portfolio includes 20 companies, the result is interesting because it suggests the idea that the highest capitalization companies are likely to obtain bigger benefits from a higher level of corruption (this portfolio registers a negative and significant coefficient). This result is confirmed by the coefficient of the governance index. Only companies belonging to the first and second portfolios are likely to receive benefit in terms of total annual investment return. Their perceived corruption coefficient is small, but statistically significant. Higher capitalization companies register a very small and not meaningful coefficient. They are likely to receive substantial gain from factors other than macro governance indexes.

If we divide the sample into five different portfolios, each with the same number of companies, we have similar evidence. Table 5.8 illustrates this.

The companies of the first, second, third, and fourth portfolios show a positive relationship between the two variables. The coefficients range from 0.06 for the second portfolio to 0.24 for the third portfolio. All of

Table 5.7 Total annual investment return for companies divided into five portfolios of equal market capitalization

	Full sample	5th quintile	4th quintile	3rd quintile	2nd quintile	1st quintile
Market Capitalization	0.00000888***	0.00000948**	0.0000666	0.00004325	0.00044005	0.00808988***
	(3.23)	(2.88)	(1.57)	(0.55)	(0.96)	(2.98)
Market premium	1.00843456***	1.61971258**	1.31970606***	1.01589890***	1.05677401***	0.99848280***
	(12.96)	(2.27)	(4.45)	(7.61)	(8.42)	(11.62)
Productivity Index	0.04516757***	0.0064617	−0.14559077	0.04742918	0.07287435***	0.04618008***
	(3.35)	(0.07)	(−1.26)	(132)	(3.21)	(3.18)
Corruption Perception Index	0.12048293***	−0.44376503	−0.37278229*	−0.08099484	−0.09692919	0.14533516***
	(4.58)	(−1.79)	(−2.04)	(−1.12)	(−1.65)	(5.05)
Governance Index	0.03901593***	0.00527009	0.01980828	0.02614193	0.02410477**	0.04321053***
	(5.95)	(0.19)	(0.72)	(1.62)	(2.28)	(5.53)
Austria	−0.95044406***				0.58661395**	−1.04950268***
	(−5.59)				(2.23)	(−5.89)
Belgium	−0.79826203***				0.17441195	−0.86070008***
	(−5.70)				(1.43)	(−5.94)
Finland	−1.19139742***	2.57365331*		−0.80938052***	0.50848575	−1.34314367***
	(−5.32)	(2.09)		(−11.73)	(1.56)	(−5.60)
France	−1.55875865***	0.83410966	−1.14545318	−1.66465226***	−0.24295242	−1.71301172***
	(−6.37)	(1.07)	(−1.25)	(−4.13)	(−1.13)	(−6.27)

Germany	−1.47191682***	1.41531228	−0.78222291	−1.29240465***	−0.02472234	−1.62024504***
	(6.59)	(1.76)	(−1.24)	(−5.45)	(−0.11)	(−6.63)
Ireland	−0.88190047***			−1.04403239***	0.44479858*	−0.98630715***
	(−5.14)			(−11.07)	(1.73)	(−5.47)
Italy	−0.69546424***		−1.77330556*	−1.46639038***	0.05701704	−0.73187643***
	(−5.65)		(−1.77)	(−4.41)	(0.29)	(−5.73)
Netherlands	−1.54592938***	1.63020815	−0.18853737	−1.29035797***	0.07829661	−1.71615847***
	(−6.29)	(1.57)	(−0.43)	(−6.30)	(0.30)	(−6.38)
Spain	−0.89543322***	1.04611342*	−1.3132255	−1.19296375***	0.20520453	−0.98861759***
	(−5.39)	(2.05)	(−1.52)	(−5.91)	(1.35)	(−5.57)
Portugal	−0.79874647***			−0.83012909***	0.21917273	−0.86283329***
	(−5.63)			(−5.29)	(1.57)	(−5.87)
Intercept	0.01714399	2.12948056*	3.44168573*	1.71237838***	0.49270777**	−0.09751157
	(0.17)	(1.85)	(1.99)	(2.84)	(1.99)	(−0.89)
Number of obs.	8557	51	106	215	598	7587
R-squared	0.0472	0.4842	0.3294	0.3727	0.1847	0.046

Notes:
* p-value < 0.1, ** p-value < 0.05, *** p-value < 0.01.
Figures in parentheses represent the t-statistics for the estimated coefficient.

Source: Authors' calculations using Stata 9.0.

Table 5.8 Total annual investment return for companies divided into five portfolios with an equal number of firms

	Full sample	5th quintile	4th quintile	3rd quintile	2nd quintile	1st quintile
Market Capitalisation	0.00000888***	0.00000692**	−0.00867652	2.84474579	20.81162717	314.64431188*
	(3.23)	(1.9)	(−0.21)	(1.4)	(1.00)	(1.76)
Market pretmim	1.00843456***	0.93350761***	1.40901126***	1.45845933***	0.55497825***	0.25239429***
	(12.96)	(14.80)	(7.47)	(5.39)	(6.52)	(3.23)
Productivity Index	0.04516757***	0.02818285**	0.07115397*	0.07380661	0.03024411	−0.01814841
	(3.35)	(2.19)	(1.95)	(1.46)	(1.59)	(−0.92)
Corruption Perception Index	0.12048293***	−0.03787289	0.17685504**	0.24800752***	0.06919496	0.19275748***
	(4.58)	(−1.18)	(2.54)	(3.14)	(1.28)	(3.24)
Governance Index	0.03901593***	0.01752401***	0.03225859***	0.06251869***	0.02493481**	0.03312359***
	(5.95)	(2.89)	(2.67)	(3.43)	(2.16)	(2.89)
Austria	−0.95044406***	−0.5401003	−2.08536837***	−1.81938214***	−0.15271481	−0.53739521***
	(−5.59)	(−1.36)	(−3.96)	(−3.23)	(−0.73)	(−2.70)
Belgium	−0.79826203***	−0.73197324*	−1.76094180***	−1.47846027***	−0.09878678	−0.32190219**
	(−5.70)	(−19.2)	(−3.88)	(−3.24)	(−0.79)	(−2.46)
Finland	−1.19139742***	−0.48380251	−2.48886469***	−2.04957586***	−0.31881911	−0.90354256***
	(−5.32)	(−1.16)	(−3.84)	(−2.72)	(−103)	(−2.88)
France	−1.55875865***	−0.97482220**	−2.51701286***	−2.71697082***	−0.55499771**	−0.88790568***
	(−6.37)	(−2.39)	(−4.06)	(−3.55)	(−1.98)	(−3.56)

Germany	−1.47191682***	−0.84585597**	−2.47229442***	−2.59430237***	−0.58418600**	−0.91535348***
	(−6.59)	(−2.10)	(−4.08)	(−3.61)	(−2.35)	(−3.89)
Ireland	−0.88190047***	−0.55268617	−2.00235818***	−1.75350760***	−0.35473702	−0.58379035***
	(−5.14)	(−1.40)	(−3.81)	(−3.12)	(−1.37)	(−2.72)
Italy	−0.69546424***	−0.71144773*	−1.57530300***	−1.28426616***	−0.17064439	−0.04178188
	(−5.65)	(−1.87)	(−3.91)	(−3.35)	(−1.40)	(−0.45)
Spagna	−0.89543322***	−0.67681544*	−1.84598785***	−1.76609016***	−0.21383293	−0.04320476
	(−5.39)	(−1.74)	(−3.71)	(−3.29)	(−1.18)	(−0.16)
Portogalko	−0.79874647***	−0.63645530*	−1.76262087***	−1.55458256***	−0.03832936	−0.24273012
	(−5.63)	(−1.66)	(−3.96)	(−3.46)	(−0.24)	(−1.40)
Olanda	−1.54592938***	−0.83214614**	−2.62855177***	−2.77265289***	−0.62192781**	−1.10359652***
	(−6.29)	(−2.02)	(−3.96)	(−3.51)	(−2.10)	(−3.80)
Intercept	0.01714399	1.01034162**	0.67947676**	−029513052	−0.3389443	−1.05987671 •**
	(0.17)	(2.56)	(1.97)	(−1.19)	(−1.41)	(−3.87)
Number of obs	8557	2087	1965	1877	1575	1053
R-squared	0.04724307	0.16793643	0.11713518	0.05457517	0.03935931	0.05884725

Notes:
* p-value < 0.1, ** p-value < 0.05, *** p-value < 0.01.
Figures in parentheses represent the t-statistics for the estimated coefficient.

Source: Authors' calculations using Stata 9.0.

them are statistically significant, with the exception of those for the second portfolio. Companies belonging to the fifth portfolio show a negative relationship with a small but not statistically significant coefficient. Dividing the sample into portfolios, according to the number of companies, provides complementary evidence. High-capitalization companies do not benefit from a lower level of corruption. Table 5.8 provides the same evidence for the governance index. This index is positive and statistically significant in all portfolios, with a coefficient ranging from 0.017 for the fifth portfolio to 0.062 for the third portfolio. In all the portfolios companies (according to the number) benefit from better macroeconomic governance, but its effect is higher in small-capitalization companies' quintiles.

5.4 CONCLUSIONS

This research has taken into consideration the impact of a specific control variable, the perceived corruption index, on total annual investment return. The perceived corruption index clearly affects the performance of the total annual investment return of the sample, with a 0.12 positive and statistically significant coefficient. Euro-area listed industrial companies clearly benefit from a lower level of perceived corruption. If we divide the sample into five different portfolios, according to their market capitalization and ensuring an equal number of companies, we have clear evidence that for lower capitalization companies, this benefit is more consistent. Higher capitalization companies show a negative and not statistically significant relationship. This evidence confirms the intuition that higher capitalization companies have other tools, like market power or political relevance, with which to influence total annual returns.

6. Operational efficiency, corruption, and political stability in microfinance

Carlo Bellavite Pellegrini[1]

6.1 INTRODUCTION

In recent decades, rapid growth and great diversity has emerged in the market for microfinance, with microfinance institutions (MFIs) – increasingly engaged in finding the right balance between profit and social commitment – becoming, within a short time, a "vast network of institutions" (Zacharias 2008). Hence, for these companies there arises the need for increasing financial development and self-sufficiency, indispensable ingredients to achieve a good level of maturity.

Starting from this premise, Arnone, Bellavite Pellegrini, and Messa (hereafter ABPM) (2010) examined and assessed the relevance of financial variables with respect to the level of efficiency of MFIs.

The difficult situation facing microfinance institutions in Africa is clear to all and, in this regard, it is important to note that these intermediaries have extremely high operating costs. This aspect has contributed, maybe decisively, to severely limit their development (mainly because of very low, or completely absent, profit margins), negatively affecting the quality of services offered and the number of clients. In other continents, such as Asia, MFIs have achieved much lower costs, above all thanks to higher efficiency levels which have impacted positively on the development of microfinance in this region.

It is clear that achieving a high level of efficiency is a priority, not only to foster the development of the sector, but also for a wider dissemination of the product. Therefore, ABPM (2010) addressed the issue of operational efficiency as a proxy for the different links that exist between the traditional banking system and microfinance institutions, highlighting how the common ground between the two sectors is so important that

1 Associate Professor, Università Cattolica del Sacro Cuore, Italy.

it impels MFIs to care more for the strictly financial aspects, without neglecting the pursuit of their social mission.

The study of these aspects related to the world of microfinance traces its origins from a comparatively recent and expanding literature, driven by increased awareness of the importance of this set of instruments. Financial information on MFIs has reached a reasonable level of richness. It is no accident that Brau and Woller (2004) have summarized many different studies on microfinance in a single major study. The relative absence of reliable data had previously limited the development of extensive statistical analysis, which initially relied on anecdotal evidence and/or economic theory (Morduch 1999a).

It is especially through the creation and development of the Microfinance Information Exchange (MIX) database in 2002 that one begins to get reliable and practical data on the firms engaged in the sector. Since then, new studies have been conducted with the aim of examining the efficiency of MFIs (Baumann 2004). The information gap compared with normal commercial institutions was indeed partly filled. Other examples are the seminal studies by Cull, Demirguc-Kunt, and Morduch (2007) and Gutierrez-Nieto, Serrano-Cinca, and Mar Molinero (2007), which were of considerable importance in the analysis of the sector and a source of inspiration for many subsequent studies.

Zacharias (2008)[2] benefited substantially from the increased data availability for his investigations on economies of scale in microfinance, emphasizing the importance of the size of MFIs with respect to their efficiency: this finding represents an important connection between microfinance and the traditional commercial banking sector, and inspired ABPM (2010), which carried out two econometric exercises (based on different time horizons) providing interesting results in several aspects.

Building on ABPM (2010), which highlights the centrality of financial aspects in the management of MFIs, in the present chapter we introduce some important governance variables: namely, corruption and political stability. The latter aims at assessing the weight of those factors that are external to MFIs, traditionally committed to operating in developing and emerging market countries.

Against this background, we conducted an econometric analysis of the efficiency of MFIs with a cross-sectional regression for the year 2007. The same results hold for a balanced panel data approach, built on data related to the period 2002–07, but not presented here (ABPM 2010).

---

2 In his analysis, the author indicated a significantly R^2 with a value of 58.77 percent.

6.2 THE BALANCED PANEL DATA ANALYSIS

6.2.1 Methodology

Panel (or longitudinal) data refers to a cross-section repeatedly sampled over time, but where the same economic agent has been followed throughout the period of the sample. Its use allows several advantages over a simple cross-sectional analysis because it considers both the space and the time dimension of data, favoring increased precision of the regression estimates and allowing a study of the dynamics of change with a short time series. The spatial dimension pertains to a set of cross-sectional units of observations represented by the data of MFIs. The temporal dimension, instead, concerns periodic observations of the same set of variables, featuring these cross-sectional units over a time span of six years, from 2002 to 2007.

The data set is called a *balanced panel* because each firm is observed every year, and this homogeneity helps increase the depth of the analysis.

Our analysis makes use of two different approaches:[3]

- a fixed effects (FE) model;
- a random effects (RA) model (with and without dummies).

6.2.2 Data

Data on the MFIs were obtained from the MIX. In this case, however, the time range is much longer, reducing the availability of MFIs with complete data. Thus, the number of MFIs is reduced to 700, but considered over an extended time horizon (five years instead of six because of a lagged independent variable) for the three continents: in Asia there are 200 observations for 40 different companies, in Latin America there are 265 from 53 MFIs and in Africa there are 235 observations pertaining to 47 institutions.

6.2.3 Selected Variables

The dependent variable in the model is "operating costs", while independent variables are size, profitability, macroeconomic indicators, governance indicators, and dummies. Given that the purpose of our analysis is to

---

[3] To evaluate the difference between the two models we make use of the Hausman specification test.

evaluate the operational efficiency of the selected institutions, we use the average operating costs, expressed by the operating expenses divided by the gross loan portfolio, converted to a log scale.

Regarding the independent variables, the category *size* is composed of:

1) gross loan portfolio (GLP);
2) average loan size;
3) both in logs.

The category *profitability* consists of:

1) return on assets (ROA);
2) operational self-sufficiency.

In the category *macroeconomic indicators* we make use of:

1) GDP lagged one year;
2) GDP growth;
3) inflation.

The category *governance indicators* consists of:

1) control of corruption;
2) political stability.

The *dummies* included in the analysis are:

1) regions;
2) emerging markets.

6.2.4 Empirical Findings

Africa[4]

We begin our study by assessing the situation in Africa. We applied to each continent three different models. Starting from the evaluation of the FE and RE models without dummies, we observe a value of the explained variable (R^2 overall) that is similar in both cases: 29.64 percent for the

---

4 This area includes Benin, Burkina Faso, Cameroon, Ethiopia, Ghana, Kenya, Madagascar, Mali, Mozambique, Nigeria, Senegal, South Africa, Swaziland, Tanzania, Togo, Uganda.

FE and 33.06 percent for the RE. The same levels of significance for the existing variables in the categories "size" and "profitability" are generally good. Considering the value of the Hausman test and turning to the RE model improved with the dummies, we obtain a value for the explained variable equal to 69.08 percent, quite a surprising level for a continent where information is normally less accurate.

Looking at the signs of the independent variables, economies of scale are confirmed: an increase in size corresponds to a reduction in costs and, therefore, greater efficiency. In particular, if we look at the last and most comprehensive used model, an increase in the value of the gross loan portfolio leads to a decrease in operating costs and the value of the coefficient is equal to 0.1006. Thus, an increase in average loan size also leads to a decrease in operating costs, marking a coefficient of 0.1431.

Regarding "profitability", Africa retains negative signs for both the independent variables used in the long-term analysis. Unlike what we notice in Latin America, here the sign of the ROA is not changed, which means that its increase is related to a decrease in costs. This result applies only to Africa and it might seem counterintuitive. It could be explained by the fact that the MFIs of this continent, compared with those of Asia and Latin America (which both show an inverse relationship), operate in a less favorable environment at both macro and micro level.

Even operational self-sufficiency continues to be inversely linked to operational costs in all models.

Finally, observing the two dummies, if it is true that the one relating to "emerging markets" is not so very significant, the dummy "regions", instead, confirms the presence of higher costs related to the companies of Southern Africa, which are likely to be less efficient than those in the top part of the continent.

Asia[5]

In Asia, a comparison between the first two models (FE and RE1) shows significant differences only in the variables related to macroeconomic indicators, particularly in the inherent value of GDP lagged, which, for the latter, changes sign and becomes much more significant.

As for the explained variable (R^2 overall), even in this case the RE (1) performs better, reaching a level of 44.46 percent (for the FE it was 28.49 percent). The significance levels for the four variables related to the

---

[5] This area includes Armenia, Bangladesh, Cambodia, China, Georgia, Kazakhstan, Kyrgyzstan, India, Mongolia, Nepal, the Philippines, Tajikistan, Vietnam.

Table 6.1 Balanced panel data – Africa

Africa						
Operating Costs[1]	FE Model		RE Model (1)		RE Model (2)	
	Coefficients	$p>\|t\|$	Coefficients	$p>\|z\|$	Coefficients	$p>\|z\|$
Size						
GLP [1]	−0.1185	*0.000*	−0.096	*0.000*	−0.1006	*0.000*
Average Loan Size [1]	−0.1155	*0.006*	−0.125	*0.001*	−0.1431	*0.000*
Profitability						
Return on Assets	−0.3997	*0.065*	−0.3713	*0.091*	−0.3112	*0.152*
Op. Self-Sufficiency	−0.1087	*0.024*	−0.126	*0.009*	−0.1405	*0.003*
Macro ind.						
GDP (US$) [2]	0.0616	*0.265*	0.0899	*0.053*	0.1467	*0.002*
GDP growth	−0.5898	*0.011*	−0.5959	*0.008*	−0.6283	*0.004*
Inflation	−0.2901	*0.034*	−0.2922	*0.033*	−0.3895	*0.004*
Governance ind.						
Control of Corruption	0.1046	*0.055*	0.0614	*0.212*	0.0188	*0.677*
Political Stability	0.0603	*0.049*	0.0562	*0.036*	0.0589	*0.014*
Dummies						
Regions	–	–	–	–	0.3502	*0.000*
Emerging Markets	–	–	–	–	−0.253	*0.110*

Constant	0.7427	*0.000*	0.5998	*0.000*	0.5487	*0.000*
R^2 Within	0.5169		0.5111		0.4967	
R^2 Between	0.2651		0.3030		0.7218	
R^2 Overall	**0.2964**		**0.3306**		**0.6908**	
Corr (μit ; Xit)	–0.1517		0 (assumed)		0 (assumed)	
Σμ	0.2215		0.1789		0.1062	
Σε	0.0811		0.0811		0.0811	
P	0.8858		0.8296		0.6318	
Overall significance	F: 21.28	*0.0000*	Wald: 198.35	*0.0000*	Wald: 315.11	*0.0000*
Hausman Test	$chi^2 = 149.13$; *Prob>chi*^{2} = *0.0000*				–	
Regions: 2	*Observations: 235*		*No. of groups: 47*		*Obs. per group: 5*	

Note: [1] on a logarithmic scale; [2] this variable has a lag of one year.

Source: Authors' calculations using Stata.

Table 6.2 The Balanced Panel Data – Asia

Asia						
Operating Costs[1]	FE Model		RE Model (1)		RE Model (2)	
	Coefficients	$p>\|t\|$	Coefficients	$p>\|z\|$	Coefficients	$p>\|z\|$
Size						
Gross Loan Portfolio[1]	−0.1287	*0.000*	−0.1037	*0.000*	−0.0477	*0.027*
Average Loan Size[1]	−0.1411	*0.005*	−0.1262	*0.002*	−0.2422	*0.000*
Profitability						
Return on Assets	0.765	*0.001*	0.8919	*0.000*	0.8159	*0.001*
Op. Self-Sufficiency	−0.3951	*0.000*	−0.4118	*0.000*	−0.4003	*0.000*
Macro ind.						
GDP (US$)[2]	0.0036	*0.590*	−0.0116	*0.023*	−0.0168	*0.001*
GDP growth	0.4669	*0.289*	0.7057	*0.104*	0.7505	*0.075*
Inflation	−0.2852	*0.190*	−0.3992	*0.067*	−0.4092	*0.056*
Governance ind.						
Control of Corruption	−0.0962	*0.049*	−0.0721	*0.102*	−0.1033	*0.024*
Political Stability	0.036	*0.336*	0.0241	*0.430*	0.0154	*0.606*
Dummies						
Regions (south)	–	–	–	–	−0.4388	*0.000*
Regions (east)	–	–	–	–	−0.2158	*0.000*
Emerging Markets	–	–	–	–	0.1421	*0.010*

Constant	0.9	*0.000*	0.7343	*0.000*	0.7709	*0.000*
R^2 Within	0.6523		0.6378		0.6222	
R^2 Between	0.2140		0.4057		0.7739	
R^2 Overall	**0.2849**		**0.4446**		**0.7433**	
Corr (µit ; Xit)	−0.1544		0 (assumed)		0 (assumed)	
Σµ	0.2115		0.1579		0.1038	
Σε	0.0723		0.0723		0.0723	
P	0.8953		0.8265		0.673	
Overall significance	F: 31.47	*0.0000*	Wald: 284.71	*0.0000*	Wald: 365.54	*0.0000*
Hausman Test	$chi^2 = 21.03$; $Prob > chi^2 = 0.0125$				–	
Regions: 3	*Observations: 200*		*No. of groups: 40*		*Obs. per group: 5*	

Notes: [1] on a logarithmic scale. [2] this variable has a lag of one year.

Source: Authors' calculations using Stata.

quality of firms are good in both cases: they are always below the level of 1 percent. After evaluating the differences between the two models using the Hausman test, the RE was improved by adding the category "dummies". The new explained variable inherent in the RE model (2) is now much more significant: 74.33 percent.

As regards the variables, analyzing the component "size", we can read that the value of GLP has a negative sign and a coefficient of 0.0477. This means that, even in this situation, an increase in the gross loan portfolio leads to a decrease in operating costs, with a quite similar value to that observed in the cross-section analysis. Regarding the value of the average loan size, which is extremely significant, the sign is negative and the coefficient is equal to 0.2422. Hence, an increase in the average loan leads to a decrease in costs, with intensity similar to that highlighted in 2007 alone.

From the analysis of the relationship between size and efficiency, the presence of economies of scale, which noted a gain in efficiency in the case of an increase in the size of the firm, was thus confirmed.

As regards the category "profitability", there are no particular differences compared with cross-sectional analysis. The ROA and operational self-sufficiency once again have opposite signs (the first is negative and the second is positive). An increase in the return on assets thus leads to higher costs, for a value of 0.8159, as in the short term, but with a slightly lesser intensity. The same goes for an increase in self-sufficiency, which leads to reduced operational costs and thus to an increase in efficiency with a value of 0.4003; this is once again negative, but with slightly less intensity than occurred on average in Asia for 2007 alone.

Considering the dummies and starting from the one specific to emerging markets, it is confirmed that these countries are associated with higher costs. Even more significant are the two dummies related to geographic location. This category confirms that the MFIs in West/Central Asia are linked to higher costs than in the East and especially in South Asia, which has lower expenses and therefore greater efficiency.

Latin America[6]

As for Asia, in this case too we start to analyze the two different models (FE and RE) without the use of dummies, which are only applied later. There are no great differences between the two cases. The explained variable (R^2 overall) is pleasing for both (52.40 percent for FE and 61.71 percent for the RE), the levels of significance for the variables "size" and

---

6 This area includes Bolivia, Colombia, Costa Rica, Ecuador, El Salvador, Haiti, Mexico, Nicaragua, Paraguay, Peru.

"profitability" are similar (for the RE all the levels are contained within 1 percent) and there are no differences in the signs.

As in the past, after analyzing the value of the Hausman test, we have expanded the RE model through the introduction of the two dummies "regions" and "emerging markets", further improving the explained variable, which reached a value of 66.29 percent. The significance levels are below 1 percent for both categories of variables related to MFIs.

Observing the relationship between the size and operational efficiency of microfinance institutions, the gross loan portfolio again has a negative sign, but with a greater intensity (0.1295) compared with that observed in the cross-section analysis. An increase of the GLP is therefore linked to an even stronger decrease in operating costs. No differences are to be found by looking at the sign of the average loan size, which again shows an inverse relationship to operating costs for a value of 0.2146, thus slightly less than that observed in 2007. It is also confirmed that an increase in size improves operational efficiency.

Looking at profitability, there is no news regarding operational self-sufficiency, whose increase leads to a decrease in operating costs with intensity even higher over the long term (0.5002). What changes is the sign of the ROA. In the cross-sectional analysis, in fact, this value showed a negative sign (like Africa, but unlike Asia); now the return on assets is found to have a positive impact on costs. In contrast to what happened for 2007 alone, the panel data show an opposite relationship between this variable and operational efficiency. Hence, an increase in the ROA leads to increased operating costs, with a very high intensity (the coefficient is equal to 1.1737).

Examination of the two dummies is not very revealing. The geographic variable "regions" is not very significant and has a negative value similar to that already observed in the cross-sectional analysis. Also according to the panel data, the MFIs in South America are linked to reduced costs and a greater efficiency. As for the "emerging markets" dummy, the positive sign is confirmed, and therefore the presence of higher costs in more developed countries.

World[7]

In Table 6.4 we present the situation for our regression worldwide. As we may see, the explained variable for the regression is good if we think about the enormous breadth and diversity of the sample. Indeed, for the FE model, the significance level of the explained variable is 33.60 percent,

---

7 This area includes all the nations present in Africa, Asia and Latin America.

Table 6.3 Balanced panel data – Latin America

Latin America						
Operating Costs[1]	FE Model		RE Model (1)		RE Model (2)	
	Coefficients	$p>\|t\|$	Coefficients	$p>\|z\|$	Coefficients	$p>\|z\|$
Size						
GLP[1]	−0.1692	*0.000*	−0.1244	*0.000*	−0.1295	*0.000*
Average Loan Size[1]	−0.103	*0.096*	−0.2352	*0.000*	−0.2146	*0.000*
Profitability						
Return on Assets	1.067	*0.000*	1.1437	*0.000*	1.1737	*0.000*
Op. Self-Sufficiency	−0.4569	*0.000*	−0.4858	*0.000*	−0.5002	*0.000*
Macro ind.						
GDP (US$)[2]	0.034	*0.182*	0.0449	*0.004*	0.0325	*0.036*
GDP growth	0.4189	*0.132*	0.2897	*0.283*	0.3728	*0.170*
Inflation	0.312	*0.029*	0.2489	*0.072*	0.2436	*0.080*
Governance ind.						
Control of Corruption	−0.0542	*0.119*	−0.0498	*0.102*	−0.0692	*0.024*
Political Stability	0.0018	*0.951*	0.0155	*0.500*	0.0008	*0.972*
Dummies						
Regions	–	–	–	–	−0.075	*0.122*
Emerging Markets	–	–	–	–	0.1565	*0.004*

Constant	1.2264	*0.000*	1.3286	*0.000*	1.3269	*0.000*
R^2 Within	0.4586		0.4461		0.4497	
R^2 Between	0.5298		0.6329		0.6826	
R^2 Overall	**0.5240**		**0.6171**		**0.6629**	
Corr (μit ; Xit)	0.0683		0 (assumed)		0 (assumed)	
Σμ	0.1661		0.1395		0.1312	
Σε	0.0592		0.0592		0.0592	
P	0.8871		0.8473		0.8306	
Overall significance	F: 19.10	*0.0000*	Wald: 251.93	*0.0000*	Wald: 272.94	*0.0000*
Hausman Test	$chi^2 = 33.13$; *Prob > chi² = 0.0001*				–	
Regions: 2	*Observations: 265*		*No. of groups: 53*		*Obs. per group: 5*	

Notes: [1] on a logarithmic scale. [2] this variable has a lag of one year.

Source: Authors' calculations using Stata.

Table 6.4 Balanced panel data – World

World						
Operating Costs[1]	FE Model		RE Model (1)		RE Model (2)	
	Coefficients	$p>\|t\|$	Coefficients	$p>\|z\|$	Coefficients	$p>\|z\|$
Size						
GLP[1]	−0.1289	*0.000*	−0.1064	*0.000*	−0.1062	*0.000*
Average Loan Size[1]	−0.1249	*0.000*	−0.136	*0.000*	−0.1442	*0.000*
Profitability						
Return on Assets	0.3815	*0.002*	0.4459	*0.000*	0.4401	*0.000*
Op. Self-Sufficiency	−0.293	*0.000*	−0.3088	*0.000*	−0.3065	*0.000*
Macro ind.						
GDP (US$)[2]	0.0069	*0.273*	−0.0059	*0.226*	−0.0071	*0.161*
GDP growth	−0.171	*0.264*	−0.2231	*0.133*	−0.1812	*0.227*
Inflation	−0.144	*0.093*	−0.1612	*0.055*	−0.1511	*0.073*
Governance ind.						
Control of Corruption	−0.0046	*0.859*	0.0014	*0.952*	−0.0145	*0.547*
Political Stability	0.0344	*0.062*	0.0392	*0.011*	0.0436	*0.005*
Dummies						
Africa	–	–	–	–	0.0768	*0.086*
Latin America	–	–	–	–	0.1007	*0.020*
Emerging Markets	–	–	–	–	0.083	*0.084*

Constant	0.9157	*0.000*	0.8278	*0.000*	1.3152	*0.000*
R^2 Within	0.4918		0.4869		0.4861	
R^2 Between	0.3154		0.3675		0.4013	
R^2 Overall	**0.3360**		**0.3820**		**0.4116**	
Corr (μit ; Xit)	−0.0980		0 (assumed)		0 (assumed)	
Σμ	0.2078		0.1886		0.1842	
Σε	0.0745		0.0745		0.0745	
P	0.886		0.8649		0.8592	
Overall significance	F: 59.24	*0.0000*	Wald: 600.88	*0.0000*	Wald: 609.88	*0.0000*
Hausman Test	$chi^2 = 29.32$; *Prob > $chi^2 = 0.0006$*				–	
Regions: 3	*Observations: 700*		*No. of groups: 140*		*Obs. per group: 5*	

Notes: [1] on a logarithmic scale. [2] this variable has a lag of one year.

Source: Authors' calculations using Stata.

which becomes 38.20 percent in the case of the RE model without dummies. After analyzing the value given by the Hausman test, this value rises to 41.16 percent, using the RE model (2).

As regards the variables, analyzing the component "size", we can read that the value of GLP has a negative sign and a coefficient of 0.1062, stressing that an increase in the gross loan portfolio leads to a decrease in operating costs. Regarding the value of the average loan size, the sign is negative and the coefficient is equal to 0.1442. Hence, an increase in the average loan leads again to a decrease in costs, confirming, even in this global panel data analysis, the presence of economies of scale, which noted a gain in efficiency in the case of an increase in the size of the firm.

As regards profitability, there weren't any particular surprises. The ROA and operational self-sufficiency once again have opposite signs (the first is negative and the second is positive). An increase in the return on assets thus leads to higher costs, with a value of 0.4401. An increase in self-sufficiency, instead, leads to reduced operational costs and thus to an increase in efficiency with a value of 0.3065.

Regarding the dummies and starting with the one for emerging markets, it is confirmed that these countries are associated with higher costs. Instead, the two dummies related to geographic location confirm that the MFIs operating in Asia are linked to lower costs than those in Africa and Latin America, emphasizing the improved efficiency of the oriental continent.

Macroeconomic indicators

As with the cross-sectional analysis, the macroeconomic indicators are viewed separately, because they follow different dynamics than those related to the other independent variables.

At first glance, we immediately notice that the level of significance of the variables generally improves by using the two RE models. Indeed, using the FE model, the value of GDP (with a lag of one year) has a positive sign in each continent, but is never significant. Using one of the two other models, however, this variable always has a good significance level (rarely above 5 percent), and changes its sign in Asia. In fact this latter is the only continent where costs are inversely related to a higher level of GDP. In Latin America and Africa, however, a higher GDP is linked with an increase in costs in the next year. This result is consistent with basic macroeconomic models.

As regards growth, the variable has a positive sign for both Asia and Latin America, but for the latter it is not significant whichever model is adopted. In Africa, however, this variable is very significant and favorable growth in GDP brings lower costs.

Table 6.5 Macroeconomic indicators

Macroeconomic Ind.	FE Model		RE Model (1)		RE Model (2)	
	Coeff.	$p>\|t\|$	Coeff.	$p>\|z\|$	Coeff.	$p>\|z\|$
Africa						
GDP (US$)[1]	0.0616	*0.265*	0.0899	*0.053*	0.1467	*0.002*
GDP growth	−0.5898	*0.011*	−0.5959	*0.008*	−0.6283	*0.004*
Inflation	−0.2901	*0.034*	−0.2922	*0.033*	−0.3895	*0.004*
Asia						
GDP (US$)[1]	0.0036	*0.590*	−0.0116	*0.023*	−0.0168	*0.001*
GDP growth	0.4669	*0.289*	0.7057	*0.104*	0.7505	*0.075*
Inflation	−0.2852	*0.190*	−0.3992	*0.067*	−0.4092	*0.056*
Latin America						
GDP (US$)[1]	0.034	*0.182*	0.0449	*0.004*	0.0325	*0.036*
GDP growth	0.4189	*0.132*	0.2897	*0.283*	0.3728	*0.170*
Inflation	0.312	*0.029*	0.2489	*0.072*	0.2436	*0.080*
World						
GDP (US$)[1]	0.0069	*0.273*	−0.0059	*0.226*	−0.0071	*0.161*
GDP growth	−0.171	*0.264*	−0.2231	*0.133*	−0.1812	*0.227*
Inflation	−0.144	*0.093*	−0.1612	*0.055*	−0.1511	*0.073*

Note: [1] this variable has a lag of one year.

Source: Author's estimations.

Inflation has a negative value in both Asia and Africa, where an increase in the inflation rate leads to lower costs. In America, by contrast, the variable has a positive sign and is therefore linked to an increase in costs.

Finally, looking at these indicators worldwide, we can see that inflation is the only significant factor (the others are insignificant because there are vast differences from region to region), and shows a negative sign in all the models analyzed.

Hence, as previously with cross-sectional analysis, we can see how each continent follows a singular story with regard to the macroeconomic aspects, and this evidence is verified even in our balanced panel data.

Governance indicators

Looking at the governance indicators we can highlight some differences between regions and different models of panel data used. Hence, the clear situation presented in the cross-sectional analysis is now characterized, in the long term, by a panorama of more complex interpretation, in particular for the variable "control of corruption".

Starting with this indicator, we can highlight how significant it is,

Table 6.6 Governance indicators

Governance Ind.	FE Model		RE Model (1)		RE Model (2)	
	Coeff.	*p*>|*t*|	Coeff.	*p*>|*z*|	Coeff.	*p*>|*z*|
Africa						
Control of Corruption	0.1046	*0.055*	0.0614	*0.212*	0.0188	*0.677*
Political Stability	0.0603	*0.049*	0.0562	*0.036*	0.0589	*0.014*
Asia						
Control of Corruption	−0.0962	*0.049*	−0.0721	*0.102*	−0.1033	*0.024*
Political Stability	0.036	*0.336*	0.0241	*0.430*	0.0154	*0.606*
Latin America						
Control of Corruption	−0.0542	*0.119*	−0.0498	*0.102*	−0.0692	*0.024*
Political Stability	0.0018	*0.951*	0.0155	*0.500*	0.0008	*0.972*
World						
Control of Corruption	−0.0046	*0.859*	0.0014	*0.952*	−0.0145	*0.547*
Political Stability	0.0344	*0.062*	0.0392	*0.011*	0.0436	*0.005*

Source: Authors' calculations using Stata.

especially in Asia and Latin America, where it has a negative sign. Here, an increase in the controls on corruption reduces costs and increases the level of efficiency of MFIs. This relationship is reversed, however, in the case of Africa, where it is significant only in the first model (FE). Instead, in the worldwide analysis, this variable is never significant in the long period if we examine all three continents simultaneously. But, if we analyze the situation for this variable in Asia and Latin America together, coefficients change decisively, and the variable becomes highly significant.

Regarding the variable "political stability", the positive sign of the relationship is clearly confirmed in every situation. It appears, however,

Table 6.7 Governance indicators – control of corruption in Asia and Latin America

Governance Ind.	FE Model		RE Model (1)		RE Model (2)	
	Coeff.	*p*>|*t*|	Coeff.	*p*>|*t*|	Coeff.	*p*>|*t*|
Asia & Latin America						
Control of Corruption	−0.0813	*0.003*	−0.0576	*0.021*	−0.083	*0.001*

Source: Authors' calculations using Stata.

especially significant in Africa and in the world, while the values are not significant in Asia and Latin America.

6.3 CONCLUDING REMARKS

Confirming the results of Zacharias (2008), a first important finding is the presence of economies of scale in the microfinance market. This can be seen in both the cross-sectional and the panel data analyses. Indeed, an increase in the size of firms leads to improvements in the efficiency of MFIs. The evidence is clear in any used model. In particular, in every continent and examined time period, an increase in the value of the gross loan portfolio is always an important determinant of the decrease in costs.

There is also evidence linking an increase in the value of the average loan to a cost reduction. This situation, as we have repeatedly emphasized, is a small paradox since the loans granted by MFIs consist of very small amounts. Reading, instead, the results for both the cross-section and the panel data analysis, it is clear that efficiency improves with an increase in the value of the average loan granted. This does not inevitably mean that MFIs improve when they move away from the original idea of microfinance, but stresses the importance of finding a balance between profit, stability and the pursuit of their social mission. In this sense, therefore, the size component leads to better efficiency, and cannot be overlooked by institutions, which must be necessarily attentive to this aspect.

The empirical evidence shows that the relationship between gross loan portfolio and costs is even stronger when we consider a time span of several years, while the ratio between the value of the average loan and operating costs is more relevant in the cross-sectional analysis for 2007 alone.

With regard to profitability, however, we observed some very peculiar dynamics with regard to the influence of ROA on costs. In the cross-section exercise, only the Asian regions highlight a direct connection (with a positive sign) between these two variables. The situation changes if one uses the panel data approach, which shows that an inverse relationship, leading to lower costs when the level of ROA increases, remains only in Africa. However, since Africa is a market influenced by other external factors, the long-term investigation leads us to notice that there is generally a direct relationship between rising costs and an increase in the level of ROA.

The link between operational self-sufficiency and efficiency is clearly more straightforward since, in every instance analyzed, an increase in self-sufficiency is connected with lower operational costs. Hence, improved stability of the examined firms always leads to better efficiency. The fact that this holds true also in the long-term analysis strengthens the evidence for such a relationship.

Regarding the connection between the internal efficiency of MFIs and the various macroeconomic indicators, we have already seen how the relationships change in different contexts. This evidence, which at first glance may seem surprising, can be explained by the fact that, in our analysis, many different environments have been taken into consideration, and every continent/region follows distinct macroeconomic dynamics. Consequently, changes in the results of both the long-term and the cross-sectional analysis are not surprising.

The most important novelty in our work is the assessment of the impact of factors of governance on the efficiency and development of microfinance institutions. The first variable considered is the "control of corruption". This indicator is especially significant in Asia and its growth is usually linked to lower costs that mean an improvement in the efficiency level, stressing the importance of a good level of control and macroeconomic governance to limit the phenomenon of such a serious and negative impact. The second governance indicator analysed is "political stability", which is especially significant in Africa, a continent where this component has always been a very sensitive factor. Its sign (positive) has the same explanation as for the emerging markets dummy, pointing to improved well-being, increased productivity, and hence cost-dynamics having the highest absolute value in those countries that have achieved better political stability.

Moreover, as to the analysis of the two dummies, the emerging markets dummy (though sometimes not very significant) constantly emphasizes the presence of higher costs in emerging market countries than in developing ones. That statement does not, however, indicate a lower efficiency on the part of the former. A different relationship with costs, which are higher where there are more possibilities and a better economic situation, is certainly to be expected at different stages of economic and financial development.

The results highlighted by the dummy "regions" are indeed very interesting, stressing the importance of geographic location in the management of costs. In Latin America, the higher efficiency of institutions in the South is very clear (especially in the short term). In Africa, the northern regions can obtain smaller expenses; while in Asia the South is the region with the lowest costs, followed by East Asia, while the least efficient institutions are in Central/West Asia. Therefore, the evidence confirms that the reference context is able to greatly affect the efficiency of MFIs.

To recap, our investigation leads us to recognize the key role, relative to the level of efficiency, of the dimensional and operational aspects of institutions themselves, the importance of the geographic and economic context, and the strong influence of factors related to various conditions of governance in the countries examined, among which control of corruption stands among the most influential. Accordingly, in addition to strictly financial factors, macroeconomic governance factors are also influential in fostering the growth and development of increasingly efficient MFIs, helping them to reduce their operating costs still further.

Those involved in microfinance have too often overlooked such observations, which appear to be obvious for the financial institutes of the traditional sector. The need to strike a correct balance between research on the social mission and the level of financial development appears, instead, to be confirmed in order to ensure proper stability and better development of these institutions. Doing this in future, while remaining faithful to the ethical social mission of this product, could well lead to a further spread of the instrument, improving the lives of many people with services and instruments that are more precise and appropriate to different contexts.

Section 3:

Governance

7. Governance, corruption, and effects on institutions[1]

7.1 INTRODUCTION

Corruption is capable of endangering political and social stability and security, undermining the values of democracy and the rule of law (ROL), jeopardizing social, economic and political development. The political and social costs it can provoke may differ greatly. However, it is no secret that it can irremediably damage the openness and equity of any human society. The present section aims to illustrate the effects of corruption in terms of the erosion of the ROL and democratic society. It has to be noted at the outset that the social and economic consequences of corruption may significantly overlap. However, we attempt to isolate the institutional and social effects from the economic costs which were assessed in the two previous sections.

Corruption has an impact on social organizations within both the public and private sectors. When it affects a public-private sphere, corruption may appear as an obstacle to the implementation of individual choices – hence, of individual freedoms, as we pointed out in Section 1. In this case corruption affects bureaucracy and finds fertile ground in the discretion that public officials may enjoy. Corruption may also appear in the form of State capture or grand corruption and hinder the decision-making process of government and regulatory agencies. Distortions resulting in corrupt political and administrative systems have a strong adverse impact on the effectiveness of government policies and are a burden for society as a whole. If, on the one hand, bad governance is at the roots of the development of corruption (Pellegrini and Gerlagh 2004, Arnone and Iliopulos 2005), on the other hand, corruption has an adverse impact on the quality of governance. In Section 1 we also highlighted that, in the relationship between governance and corruption, the main causal direction goes from the former to the latter, but the *feedback* effects from corruption to governance should not be underestimated.

---

1 This chapter was written by Marco Arnone; Leonardo Borlini co-authored Section 7.4.1.2.

Good quality of institutions is reflected in efficient controls that may prevent vital State organizations from malfunctioning. If governmental agencies are held accountable for what they do, this limits the discretion of public officials, and therefore the development of episodes of corruption finds substantial obstacles. However, very often, institutions can avoid being held accountable for their performance by hiding behind a system of rules not transparent to citizens: complexity of regulations may reflect low transparency. Difficulties in evaluating the performance of policymakers enable self-interested public officials to pursue their individual ends.

In a system where corruption is pervasive and public officials pursue their individual interests, regulations governing society reflect bad governance. In these circumstances the laws appear not to oppose corruption and low-quality institutions. Vicious circles could only be interrupted through difficult and wide-ranging reforms. Sometimes reforms may not take place and institutions experience decline. In other cases, attempts at reforms affect only limited areas of public life and produce effects that are only temporary and partial.

These arguments highlight the importance of supervisory agencies. Complex institutional apparatuses are often difficult for the general public to comprehend. Supervisors may be established with the explicit objective of preventing degeneration and power abuse by an élite of insiders to whom the "rules of the game" are known. Financial supervision must ensure that the behavior of financial and economic actors is correct and that competitive market rules are implemented. For this, it is necessary that external influence from political or economic power be eliminated or minimized. Supervision must hence conform to such principles as independence, autonomy and competence: it is only through independence and autonomy that supervisors may make decisions that are the fruit of clear criteria and without political influence. Autonomy must include sufficient financial resources to enable high quality structures and staff in support of supervision. Also, autonomy must include instruments of control and repression to enable effective supervision, prevention and punishment of deviant behavior. Finally, supervisory authorities whose members are "of a high and recognized professional profile"[2] can perform their duties under no external influence. Should such conditions not be enforced, the quality and authoritativeness of supervisory authorities is compromised (Forti 2005).

Our analysis in this chapter aims primarily at highlighting the relation-

---

2 This is required by Italian law for the appointment of members to the Antitrust Authority.

ship between perceived corruption and market supervision and regulation; later in the chapter, we will further broaden our focus to an analysis of the relationship between corruption and public-governance-related variables.

7.2 SUPERVISION AND REGULATION

The market consists of a set of rules, institutions and agents that interact mutually to achieve efficiency in the management of resources. In Chapter 2 we emphasized how free demand and supply interaction is not a sufficient condition for perfect competition; market failures and anti-competitive behavior are a serious threat to market functioning. Correctly functioning market dynamics depend upon existing efficient regulations and correct supervision. These conditions are both of the utmost importance, together with the existence of a specific authority to ensure that regulatory and supervisory duties are performed in an efficient manner.

This section is designed to assess further the relationship between a country's domestic corruption and the quality of regulation and supervision. As we discussed earlier, quality of market regulation may significantly impact a country's domestic corruption at the same time that corrupt regulators show a general propensity to establish inefficient regulations that tend to favor abuse of power. The same logic applies to the quality of supervision.

7.2.1 Regulatory Quality

Low quality institutions tend to establish laws that reflect their quality. Bad, i.e. unclear and not transparent, regulations favor dynamics that are at the basis of widespread corruption. To quantify regulatory quality in a cross-country analysis, we use a World Bank (WB) governance index (Kaufmann, Kraay, and Mastruzzi 2010). The regulatory quality indicator not only reflects market regulatory quality, but also provides a broader focus on the general domestic regulatory environment as a proxy for market regulatory quality.

We show both the CPI and the regulatory quality index to identify the relationship, if any, between corruption and regulatory quality. The evidence in Figure 7.1 shows that, in a worldwide sample, good regulatory quality is associated with low corruption (high CPI levels). Supporting the robustness of this correlation, the data present very low dispersion around the trend line.

Like many other governance variables, regulatory quality shows strong path-dependence, i.e. it tends to remain stable over time. This is due to the

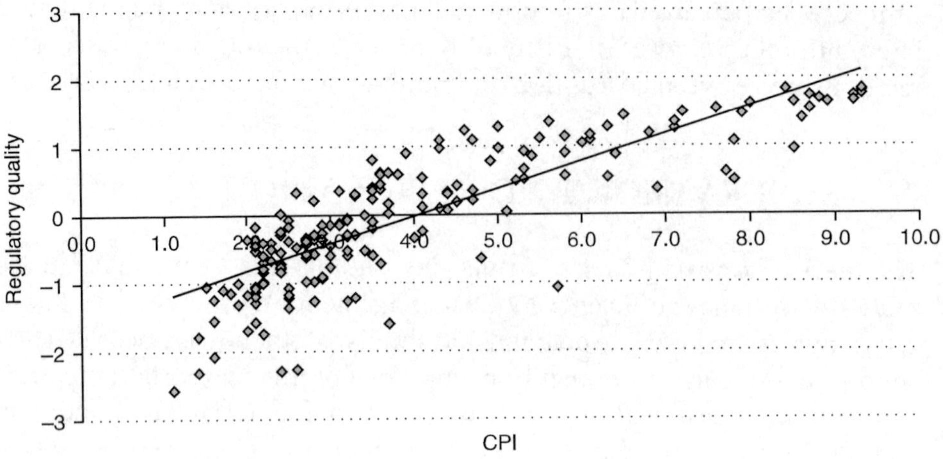

Note: CPI = 10 denotes absence of corruption while CPI = 0 denotes highest corruption level.

Source: Authors' calculations from TI data, and Kaufmann, Kraay, and Mastruzzi (2010).

Figure 7.1 Regulatory quality and corruption, 2009

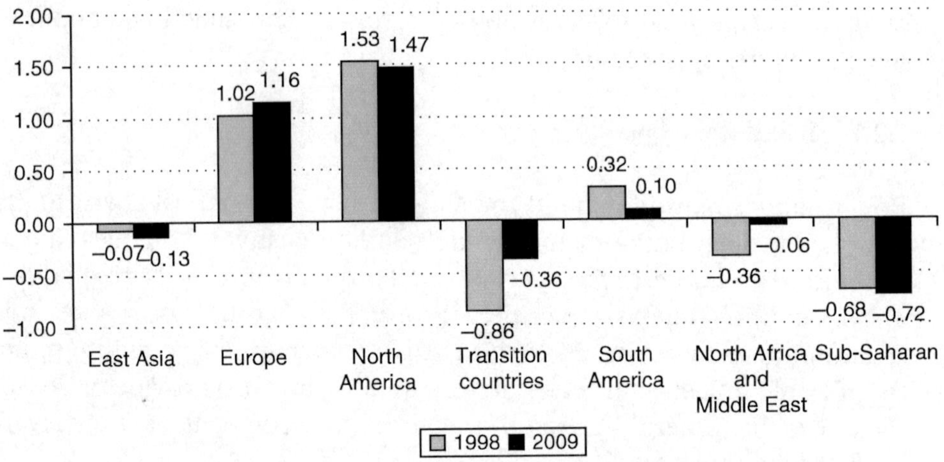

Source: Authors' calculations from Kaufmann, Kraay, and Mastruzzi (2010).

Figure 7.2 Regulatory quality over time, 1998–2009

fact that governance variables depend on environmental and institutional factors that evolve slowly. Changes have a limited material impact in the short term even in connection with reforms that are radical and sudden.

In Figure 7.2 we show the regulatory quality indicator in the period

1998–2009, based on a geographic breakdown for an analysis of the dynamics of this variable over time. We may note that countries in Western Europe, North America and transition economies experienced a widespread, material improvement in regulatory quality for the period presented. There was no regulatory quality improvement in Latin America, Asia-Pacific and Sub-Saharan Africa.

7.2.2 Quality and Quantity of Regulation

Legal systems characterized by a large number of laws and regulations may prove inefficient. If, on the one hand, there is a need for laws that are binding for institutional and individual behavior and their relationships, on the other hand constraints on actors should not be too many. Too many constraints are reflected in an overburdened bureaucracy and cause slower procedures and reduce the freedom of agents. Excess regulation may indeed conceal the fact that a system is incapable of meeting citizens' needs. Systems that are unable to address complex issues tend to address specific matters with ad hoc rules. Necessary institutional reforms and adaptation to new problems slow down in this context.

In Chapter 2 we emphasized how highly complex regulatory systems may impose high costs on firms, representing a significant impediment to the development of their business. In Figure 7.3 we show the relationship between regulatory quality and quantity of regulation. The data show

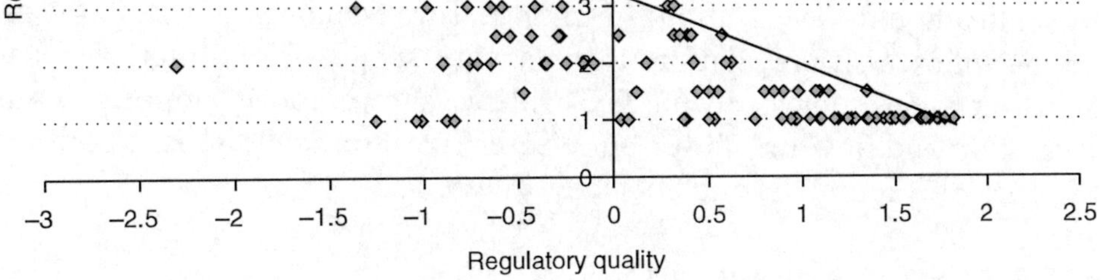

Source: Authors' calculations from Kaufmann, Kraay, and Mastruzzi (2010) and Freedom House.

Figure 7.3 Quality and quantity of regulations, 2009

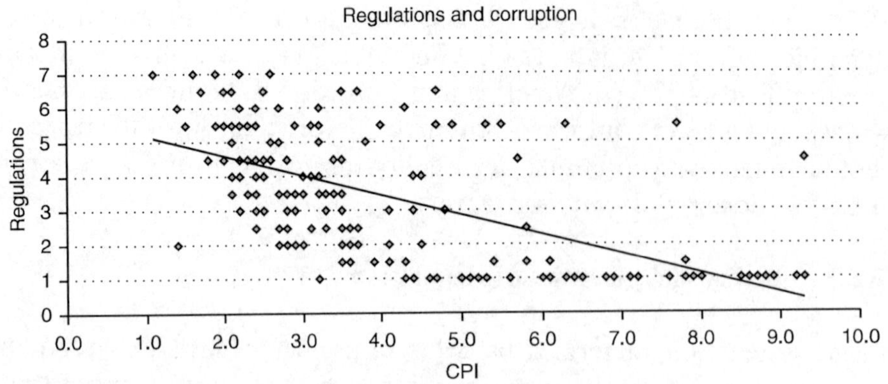

Note: CPI = 10 denotes absence of corruption while CPI = 0 denotes highest corruption level.

Source: Authors' calculations from TI and Freedom House data.

Figure 7.4 Regulation and corruption, 2009

that, in general, regulatory quality and quantity of regulation are negatively correlated. The regulation variable used is a Freedom House index of civil and economic freedom.

Figure 7.3 also shows that the higher the quantity of legislation (the higher our regulation variable) the lower the regulatory quality. Despite the fact that the regulation indicator shows very little variability and the data assume discrete values from 1 to 5, the negative relationship of this index with regulatory quality is evident. Hence, it is reasonable to think that a negative relationship exists between perceived corruption and quantity of regulation, consistent with the relationship between perceived corruption and quality of regulation. Empirical evidence from a very large sample confirms this (Figure 7.4).

Figure 7.4 shows that high CPI (low corruption) is associated with a small amount of legislation. In Chapter 1 we emphasized that, in the presence of excessive regulation, there is wider scope for self-interested actors to get round some of them. The evidence shown above supports this suggestion and how the 'fewer but clearer rules' principle proves both more efficient (Figure 7.3) and effective (Figure 7.4).

7.2.3 Supervisory Agencies

The role of supervisory agencies is to ensure general compliance with the rules governing social activities. To perform their duties supervisors must act in conformity with established quality standards to ensure that they remain independent of the interests of individual operators.[3] Autonomy (or independence) and competence are necessary features of supervisory authorities, given the critical role of these agencies.

One important distinction is between goal and instrumental autonomy. Supervisors may choose their goals, and/or the instruments needed to achieve such goals, depending on the laws establishing them. But these characteristics do not prove sufficient to ensure efficient supervision: to prevent supervision from being thwarted by possible external conditioning it is key that supervisory authorities should also be financially independent and that staff be competent in the specific area under supervision. If these conditions are not all met, the quality of supervision cannot be guaranteed.

Once established as independent (control) institutions, the supervisors must conform their behavior to the principles of accountability and transparency: they should act in such a way that they can be held responsible for their actions, and their actions should be transparent to the markets, the agents, and the general public. These are minimal requirements for non-elected, public (control) institutions in a democratic society.

7.2.4 Financial Supervision

In sectors like banking, insurance, securities and pension funds, international organizations are increasingly setting the standards and monitoring compliance (Arnone and Padoan 2008). To define quality levels for the supervisory authorities means assessing the conformity of their actions with respect to established parameters; to enable international comparison, these parameters must achieve international recognition. Different markets have different types of supervision/regulation based on diverse sectorial needs. It is evident that markets open to cross-border exchanges must be regulated on the basis of internationally compatible rules; enforcement of standards and the quality of the supervisors must be measured accordingly. Market globalization has favored international agreements that establish fundamental principles for market governance. Accordingly, these principles have enabled the definition of criteria to evaluate supervision. An illustration of new indicators based on internationally accepted standards, as assessed by the IMF and the WB, follows below.

---

3 A recent (and fortunately rare) case where these quality standards were patently violated involved the then governor of the Bank of Italy, Antonio Fazio, who later resigned but only after months of widespread pressure from domestic and international institutions, public opinion, and judicial investigations.

7.2.4.1 Banking supervision

Because of their importance for domestic and international finance, banking markets are closely scrutinized by the IMF and country authorities. Since 1997 the IMF has been committed to assessing compliance with the Basel core principles (BCP) for banking supervision in banking systems around the world. We present here a numerical indicator with overall country scores as in Arnone, Darbar, and Gambini (2007), and Arnone and Gambini (2006a and 2006b).

Given the strategic importance of banking markets to the economy, it is useful to verify whether our argument on the relationship between supervision and corruption may be reflected in an empirical relationship between the quality of a country's banking supervision and domestic corruption. Any such relationship, if it exists, would corroborate our arguments as discussed above.

In Figure 7.5 we show the relationship between a country's compliance with the BCP (which is a good proxy for a country's quality of banking supervision) and the CPI. Corruption and compliance with the BCP are negatively correlated: countries with high quality banking supervision experience lower corruption.

An indicator for transparency of the banking supervisor may also be identified: transparency is a proxy for good governance in banking supervision (Arnone, Darbar, and Gambini 2007; Arnone and Gambini

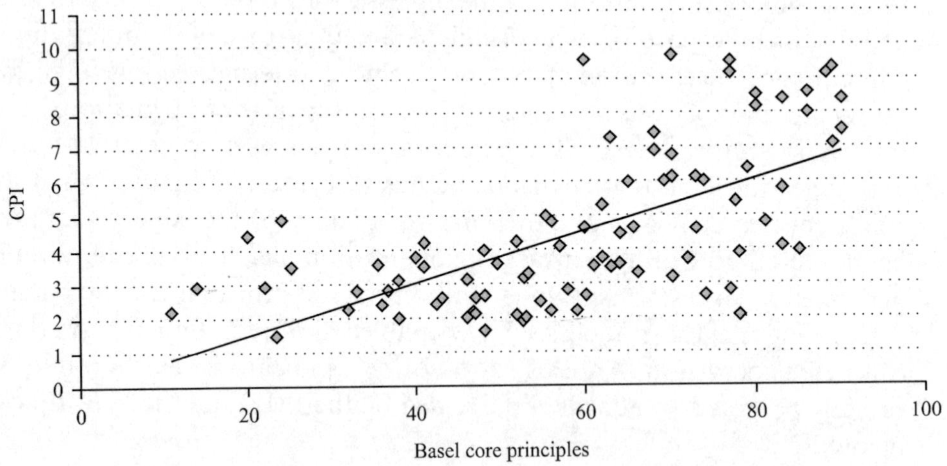

Note: CPI = 10 denotes absence of corruption while CPI = 0 denotes highest corruption level.

Source: Authors' calculations from TI and IMF–WB data.

Figure 7.5 Banking supervision and perceived corruption, 2004

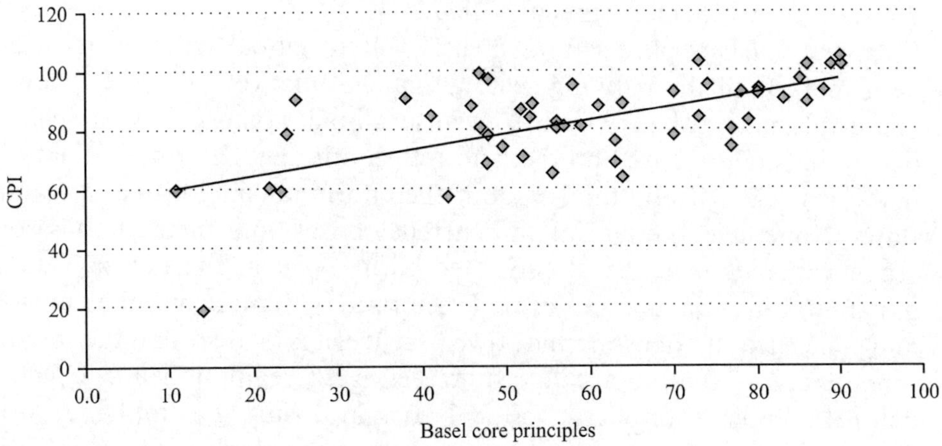

Source: Authors' calculations from IMF–WB data.

Figure 7.6 Transparency in banking supervision and conformity with Basel core principles, 2004 (transparency in banking supervision on vertical axis = y)

2006b). This indicator is very important in the context of this book because, as we have emphasized many times, corruption finds fertile ground in environments dominated by secrecy and low transparency. If it were possible to identify a connection between the quality of supervision and compliance of supervisors with transparency practices (and therefore with good governance), the economic policy implications would be clear. In this case, corruption would be negatively correlated with the quality and transparency of supervision; hence, transparency-based reforms of supervision would be useful in achieving multiple objectives (better institutional governance, better supervision and lower corruption).

In Figure 7.6 we show the relationship between transparency of banking supervision and conformity with the BCP for a worldwide sample. The correlation between transparency and regulatory quality is very strong: high transparency is generally associated with a high degree of conformity with regulatory quality standards. Hence, it is possible to deduce that domestic corruption and transparent banking supervision are negatively correlated: high corruption levels are associated with non-transparent banking supervision. Given the significant implications, this empirical evidence makes a statement in favor of transparency (and good governance) and emphasizes how important it is that the actions of the supervisory authorities should comply with the principle and practices of transparency.

7.2.4.2 Securities markets supervision

Financial markets play a fundamental role in global wealth allocation; even more than the banking sector, financial markets are to be viewed in an international perspective because global savings move to where demand is higher, based on risk and return criteria. The role of financial markets is clear if one thinks about the enormous magnitude of capital flows. Nonetheless, financial and currency crises, and their ruinous consequences, make the risks associated with financial market operations apparent. Financial markets are characterized by significant inherent risks and concentration of economic power. Hence, it is evident that the smooth functioning of these markets requires efficient regulation and effective controls. Supervision has a critical role in ensuring compliance with market rules and in protecting smaller agents from operators with larger capital and strong market power. The negative consequences of financial market failures provided the incentive for the creation of supervisory/regulatory standards that are binding not only for the agents but also for supervisors themselves.

Based on the Basel Committee model, the International Organization of Securities Commissions (IOSCO), a committee of securities markets supervisors, has established quality standards for securities markets supervision since 2000, while the IMF and the WB have assessed conformity with respect to these standards. We processed this information into new indicators of quality and transparency of securities supervision. Given the importance of securities markets in the worldwide economy and the strong capital concentration that characterizes these markets, it is possible that the general relationship between supervision and corruption is reflected in securities market supervision.

In Figure 7.7 we show the relationship between an indicator of the quality of securities markets supervision and perceived corruption. We use a quality indicator based on principles established by the IOSCO. This index reflects the conformity of securities markets supervision with these standards. Figure 7.7 clearly shows that high corruption is associated with very low quality of securities markets supervision.

By analogy with other segments of the financial markets, we show the relationship between the quality and transparency of securities market supervision (Figure 7.8). This information is particularly useful in its implications for corruption: transparent financial supervision is associated with high quality supervision and, hence, with low corruption levels.

7.2.4.3 Insurance markets supervision

Good supervision of insurance markets protects operators in their risk management choices; given this broad perspective, supervision may

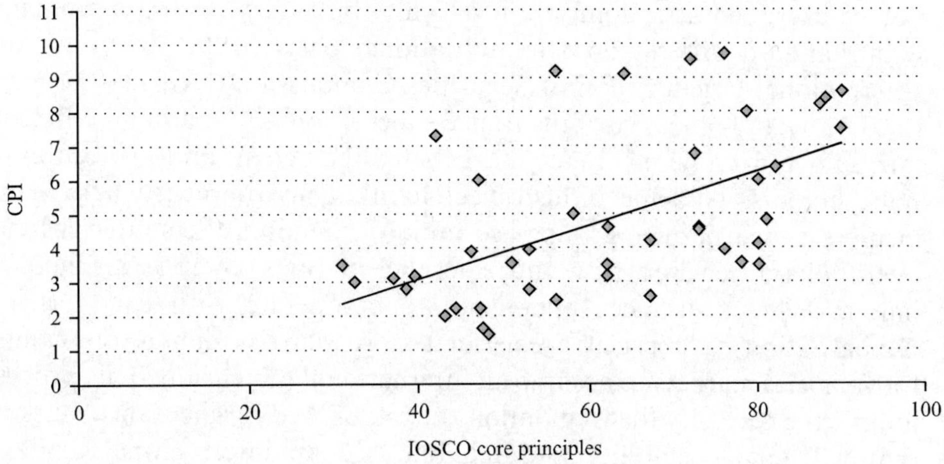

Note: CPI = 10 denotes absence of corruption while CPI = 0 denotes highest corruption level.

Source: Authors' calculations from IMF–WB data.

Figure 7.7 *Corruption and quality of securities markets supervision, 2004*

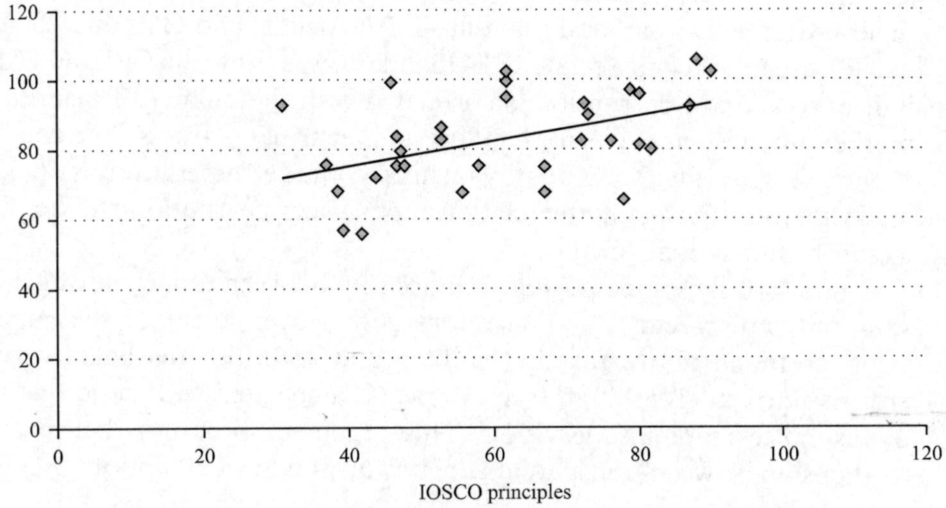

Source: Authors' calculations from IMF–WB data.

Figure 7.8 *Quality and transparency of supervision in securities markets, 2004 (transparency of securities market supervisors/regulators on vertical axis = y)*

not be exercised at a domestic level only, but must ensure compliance with standard criteria on an international basis (IAIS 1999). As the International Organization of Securities Commission (IAIS) (1999) puts it: "The overall objective of insurance supervision is to maintain efficient, fair, safe and stable insurance markets for the benefit and protection of policyholders. To achieve this objective in an environment where many insurers and insurance groups are rapidly extending their international operations, often into new and emerging markets, there is an increasing need for insurance supervisors to co-operate with each other." Globalization has recently accelerated a broader risk dimension, calling for financial markets to assume an international dimension. This process implies the necessity that regulations be established for insurance markets that will enable stability and reliability in an international context. Insurance markets are critical to prevent losses that may trigger chain reactions. For this reason, supervision of compliance with regulations to protect insurance markets strengthens both national and global financial stability.

In the mid-1990s the IAIS established quality standards for insurance supervision. Compliance with these standards is assessed under the financial sector assessment program (FSAP) established by the IMF and the WB. These evaluations, which we present in a new numerical index (Arnone, Darbar, and Gambini 2007; Arnone and Gambini 2006a, 2006b), are reflected in a related "IAIS index". We show the CPI and IAIS indices to verify if corruption is correlated with the quality of insurance market supervision, as it is for banking and securities markets. The data in Figure 7.9 show that good quality insurance market supervision is associated with low CPI; again, the relationship between corruption and quality of supervision is confirmed.

Figure 7.10 shows the positive relationship between quality of supervision and transparency (and therefore good governance) of the supervisor, as found above for the banking and securities markets: in our cross-country analysis, high transparency is associated with good quality of insurance market supervision. This argument supports the general relationship between transparent supervision and low corruption.

7.3 MONETARY POLICY AND TRANSPARENCY

In the same vein as fiscal policy, monetary policy aims at preventing monetary variables from developing according to trajectories that may have an adverse impact on the economy. In Chapter 3 we emphasized how one key objective of monetary policy consists of price stability, as it is

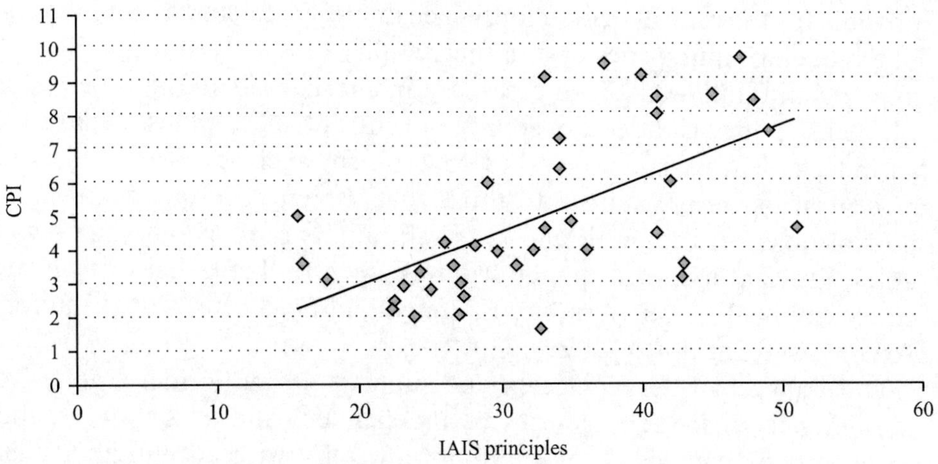

Note: CPI = 10 denotes absence of corruption while CPI = 0 denotes highest corruption level.

Source: Authors' calculations from TI and IMF–WB data.

Figure 7.9 Corruption and insurance markets supervision, 2004

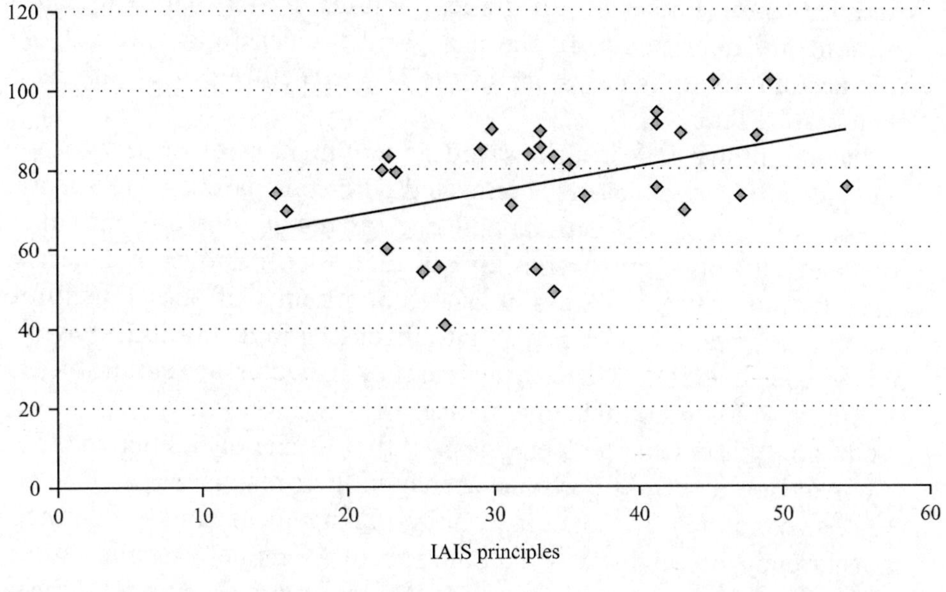

Source: Authors' calculations from IMF–WB data.

Figure 7.10 Quality and transparency of insurance markets supervision, 2004 (transparency of supervisor/regulator in insurance markets on vertical axis = y)

possible for the central bank to influence interest rates and affect inflation. The monetary authorities ensure the stability of money and the financial markets and, in a number of cases, are in charge of banking supervision. Monetary policy is the responsibility of central banks, and is managed on an independent basis unlike other government agencies. If the objectives of central banks are subject to those of national governments, it is not possible to ensure domestic and external stability of monetary macro variables. Efficient monetary policy requires a central bank that is independent of political power (Arnone, Laurens, and Segalotto 2006a; Laurens, Arnone, and Segalotto 2009).

Our analysis of the regulatory and supervisory authorities emphasized the necessity that such agencies be independent and autonomous: their staff must be competent and act in conformity with accountability and transparency principles. As an agency with monetary policy authority, it must be held accountable for, and transparent with respect to, its actions before citizens, markets and institutions, at both domestic and international level.

Public sector accountability is a key condition to ensure that established objectives and measures are effectively implemented and comply with public institutions' good governance framework. Accountability must be extended to all spheres of government actions, rather than being limited to monetary policy only. In the paragraphs which follow we will show how accountability is necessary in the very structure of institutions in a democratic State.

Accountability of institutions and governments with respect to policy management is a goal closely connected with transparency; lack of transparency in government actions and unclear regulations prevent supervisors and citizens from exercising adequate control over the decisions taken by policymakers. To establish accountability of public institutions and bureaucrats, it is necessary that citizens be in a position to evaluate policymakers' actions. Hence, transparency is a necessary condition at the foundation of good public governance.

Our analysis in Chapter 3 emphasized that fiscal policies may be subject to corruption if there is no transparency in their management. This argument also applies to monetary policy management. In the absence of transparency, broad discretion on the part of the monetary policy authorities leaves scope for possible conflicts of interest and the pursuit of private benefits or personal interests.

Empirical evidence supports our earlier arguments and shows how, in an analysis of a 60-country data set, high corruption (low CPI) is associated with low transparency in monetary policy. Furthermore, by combining our evidence in Chapter 3 with our evidence here, we can assert that

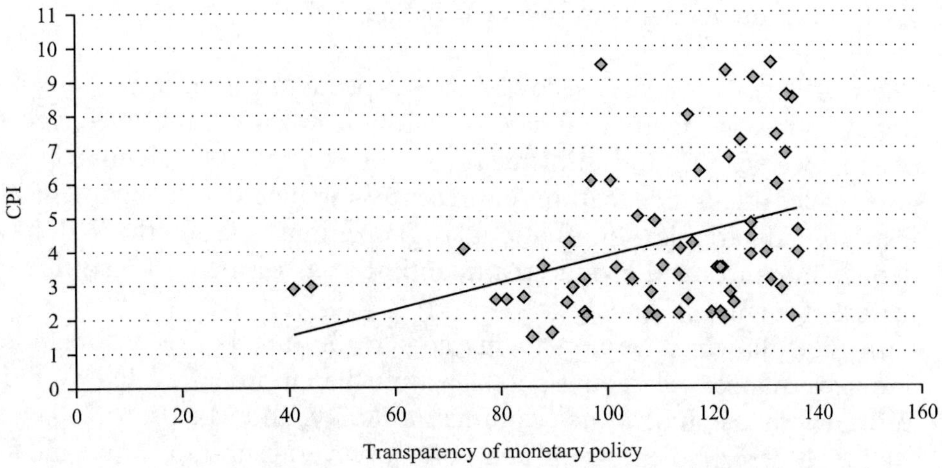

Note: CPI = 10 denotes absence of corruption while CPI = 0 denotes highest corruption level.

Source: Authors' calculations from TI and IMF data.

Figure 7.11 Transparency of monetary policy, 2004

high transparency in monetary policy is associated with high transparency in fiscal policy, as an indication of a complementary role between aspects of monetary and fiscal policy. This result confirms (Figure 7.11) that low quality of individual institutions has negative spill-over effects on other institutions, hence favoring the preconditions for the development of corruption.

7.4 CORRUPTION AND GOVERNANCE

The above analysis has focused on those features of governance which directly affect the functioning of markets; however, as already mentioned, corruption is a manifold phenomenon and does not affect only markets. Corruption is an endogenous outcome deriving from the fundamentals of a society; in turn, its effects reach several dimensions of society. In this section we concentrate our attention on the dynamics that link corruption to the institutional-political dimension of countries. Here we analyze the transmission channels that link corruption with governance indicators. We first consider the legal-political dimension of governance; then, we focus on institutional variables. Finally, we will focus on indicators of democracy.

7.4.1 Institutions and Governance Indicators

The quality of a country's governance depends on a variety of institutional and social factors, and has a strong impact on the effectiveness of the specification and implementation of policies. The significance of governance qualitative features has recently stimulated a strong interest in institutional variables. International organizations, such as the WB, have defined measures and produced a quantitative assessment of institutional features for empirical analysis.

In the following, we aim to investigate the link between corruption and governance; our analysis is based on the empirical evidence of the WB Governance Indicators (Kaufmann, Kraay, and Mastruzzi 2004 and 2005). These six indicators are composed of several sub-indicators and are the starting point for the empirical evidence on governance features. They focus on the processes by which governments are selected, monitored and replaced; the capacity of governments to effectively formulate and implement sound policies; the respect of citizens and government for the institutions that govern economic and social interactions among them.

With respect to the process by which those in authority are selected and replaced, the indicator of *voice and accountability* includes a number of sub-indicators measuring many aspects of the political process, civil liberties and political rights. It measures the extent to which citizens of a country are able to participate in the selection of governments. Kaufmann, Kraay, and Mastruzzi also include in this category indicators measuring the independence of the media. The indicator of *political stability and absence of violence* reflects the idea that the quality of governance in a country is compromised by the likelihood of turbulent changes in government. This would not only have a direct effect on the continuity of policies, but also at a deeper level would undermine the ability of all citizens to peacefully select and replace those in power. The indicator of *ROL* includes several sub-indicators measuring the extent to which agents have confidence in, and abide by, the rules of society. It is composed of several sub-indices related to perceptions of the incidence of crime, the effectiveness and predictability of the judiciary, and the enforceability of contracts. The indicator of *control of corruption* concerns perceptions of domestic bribery and is an alternative proxy for the CPI. Finally, the indicators of *government effectiveness* and *regulatory quality* focus on the ability of the government to formulate and implement sound policies. The indicator of government effectiveness combines measures of the quality of public services, quality of the bureaucracy, competence of civil servants, its independence from political pressures, and the credibility of the government's commitment to policies. The indicator of regulatory quality evaluates policies and includes measures of the incidence of market-unfriendly policies such as price controls or inadequate bank supervision, as well as perceptions of the burdens imposed by excessive regulation in areas such as foreign trade and business development.

7.4.1.1 Accountability

When institutions are accountable to their citizens or towards supervisory authorities there is a strong incentive in favor of meritocratic selective processes. Discretionary choices can no longer be managed arbitrarily and *objective* criteria are needed. It is thus clear that accountable institutions should tolerate neither abuses of power nor the pursuit of private interest.

Both transparency and accountability significantly affect the quality of institutions and the possibility that degenerative dynamics could hinder the attainment of public welfare. These considerations are supported by the following empirical evidence relating to more than 140 countries. High degrees of accountability are associated with high levels of CPI (i.e. low levels of corruption). See Figure 7.12.

Among all governance indicators, the indicator of accountability is the one that probably presents the highest degree of persistence. This is due to the fact that the degree of institutional accountability is deeply rooted in the structure and culture of institutions. It is thus possible to significantly affect the accountability of a country only through a process of wide-ranging reform of government organizations. In the period considered,

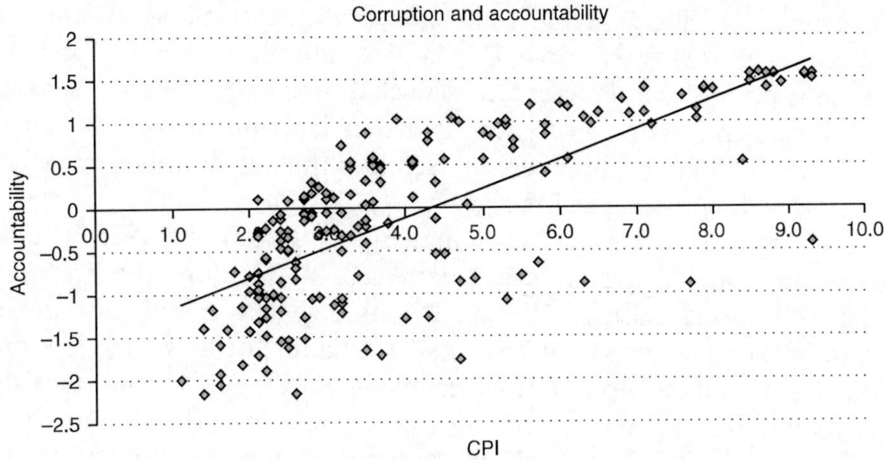

Note: CPI ranges between 10 (highly clean) and 0 (highly corrupt).

Source: Authors' calculations from TI data and Kaufmann, Kraay, and Mastruzzi (2010).

Figure 7.12 Corruption and accountability, 2009

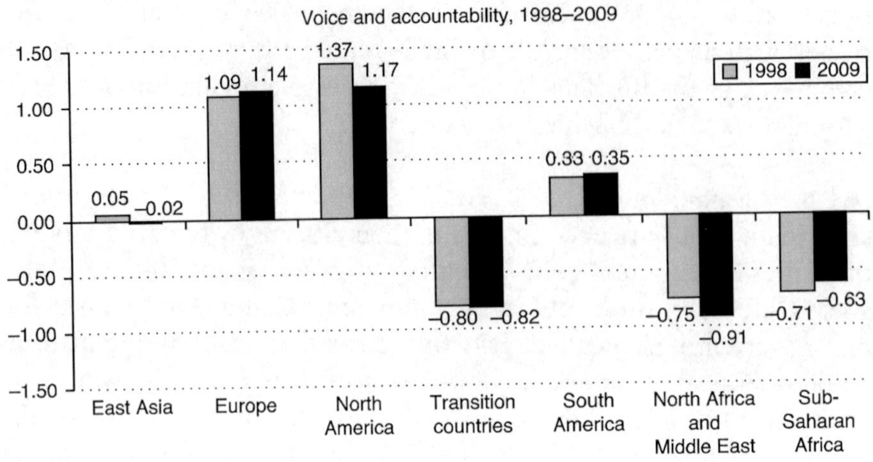

Source: Authors' calculations from TI data and Kaufmann, Kraay, and Mastruzzi (2010).

Figure 7.13 Accountability over time, 1998–2009

data for Western European and transition countries and Latin America show a positive trend. In the same period, North America experienced only minimal deterioration, while the rest of the world shows a significant decrease in accountability (Figure 7.13).

7.4.1.2 Rule of law

Corruption is likely the most effective challenge to the ROL and democratic society. Massive corrupt dynamics, indeed, weaken the basic foundations both of the representative mechanisms underlying the separation of powers and of human rights. As the Italian Constitutional Court held in 1988, corruption ultimately undermines the possibility of every citizen exercising her/his own rights consciously.

Let us start by considering human rights: Lucchini (1995: 21) defined corruption as "*l'envers de droits de l'homme*". Notably, the Preamble of the 1789 Declaration of Human Rights depicts an etiological relationship between ignorance, neglect and contempt for human rights on the one hand, and corruption of governments on the other. Since corruption generates discrimination and inequality, this relationship, in the first place, bears on civil and political rights. For instance, it strengthens the misappropriation of property in violation of legal rights. Again, as already shown, it likely leads to the rise of monopolies which either wipe out or gravely vitiate freedom to trade. Corruption strikes at economic and social rights as well: the commissioning by a public entity of useless or overpriced goods or services, and the choice of poorly performing undertakings through perverted public procurement mechanisms are mere examples of how corruption can endanger the second generation of human rights.

The relationship between fundamental human rights and corruption could not be expressed more vividly than in the words of the UN High Commissioner for Human Rights, Navy Pillay: "Let us be clear. Corruption Kills. The money stolen is enough to feed the world's hungry every night, many of them children; corruption denies them their right to food, and in some cases, their right to life. A human right-based approach to anti-corruption responds to the people's resounding call for social, political and economic order that delivers on the promises of 'freedom from fear and want.'[4] A human right-based approach to development has recently become the subject of an inquiry by the United Nations Development Program (UNDP). The UNDP has recently worked out an accurate human rights-based approach (HRBA) to development against which to weigh inter alia the effect of corruption, especially in developing countries (Pilapitiya 2004). According to the UN High Commissioner for Human Rights, an HRBA is a conceptual framework for the process of human development that is normatively based on international human rights standards and operationally directed toward promoting and protecting human rights.[5] The departure point and organizational principle of the 2004 UNDP's analyst study is that "Corruption affects the poor disproportionately, due to their powerlessness to change the status quo and inability to pay bribes, creating inequalities that violate their human rights. The HRBA with its main elements of Express Linkages to Rights, Accountability, Empowerment, Participation and Attention to Disadvantaged Groups, has been developed specifically to address these inequalities and to ensure that the poor and disadvantaged are also equal partners in development" (Pilapitiya 2004: 2).

Yet, by creating and crystallizing fundamental inequalities in the poor's access to justice and development services, the results envisaged by the HRBA are seriously endangered, if not impossible to achieve. Pilapitiya argues that this provides a strong case for adding the main elements of the HRBA to anti-corruption programs.

---

4 United Nations Human Rights. Office of the High Commissioner (2013), p.3.

5 UN High Commissioner for Human Rights, at www.unhchr.ch/development/approaches.html. See also United Nations Human Rights. Office of the High Commissioner (2013), pp.5–7. The main core principles of human rights-based approach to anti-corruption are crystallized in the Human Rights Council, Resolution 7/11. The role of good governance in the promotion and protection of human rights and in the Human Rights Council Resolution 23/9. The negative impact of corruption on the enjoyment of human rights.

As to the menace posed by corruption to democratic legitimacy, one could go so far as to state that it annihilates the trust upon which the mechanism of representation is grounded. To illustrate this specific issue, eminent voices in legal doctrine have referred to the dichotomy between laws that have failed to be enforced by a negligent monarch, on the one hand, and a corrupt government, on the other, as noted by Montesquieu: "The monarch who, through bad advice or negligence, fails to enforce the law, can easily repair the damage. But when the laws have ceased to be enforced in a people's government, as can only occur through the corruption of the Republic, the State is already lost." The political antinomy between corruption and democracy was thus already revealed by Montesquieu in the 18th century: "the autonomy extends into the judicial fields, since law presupposes order based on distinctions, as between the public and the private, and separations such as between the legislature, the executive, and the judiciary", but corruption inevitably obscures and muddles such distinctions. It is almost pleonastic to stress that where corruption strikes the major public institutions, it simultaneously affects legality and the guarantee of justice, reducing them to mere fictions. The consequences of corruption in less stable societies can indeed be dramatic. Pope (1995: 142) of TI suggests that "to any observer, it is clear that a quantum shift has taken place. Whereas in former times the people of a country crippled by corruption would have looked to the army to topple the tyrants, today, in many parts of the world, they march to do it for themselves." In a similar line of reasoning, according to Carrington (2007: 111), the under-enforcement of law caused by corruption, unless somehow corrected, can eventually result in a *failing* and then a *failed* State.

The human and social costs of corruption may also be more subtle, although not less noxious. Its impact on wealth distribution is a good example. Corruption distorts the distributive role of the State, by facilitating fraud, breeding tax evasion, leading to poor tax administration, and exemptions that disproportionately favor the well-connected and wealthy population groups. Since it reduces government revenue by reducing the tax base, it places a progressively heavier burden on a steadily falling number of taxpayers. As a result the progressive regime of the tax system is undermined, likely leading to increased income inequality. In turn, this increases the incentive to turn to the informal sector and, as a mediate consequence, to start a vicious circle.

Secondly, corruption and rent-seeking can have a negative impact on growth when they create incentives for highly talented individuals to go toward rent-seeking and other under-productive activities rather than toward productive activities. The human cost in terms of waste of talent, and, hence, growth may be enormous. Again, corruption might affect the targeting of social programs for the truly needed. Government-funded programs can be misused to be extended to relatively wealthy population groups and public funds siphoned off from poverty alleviation projects to well-connected individuals. Moreover, corruption of the enforcement apparatus is likely to bring about a harmful side-effect in terms of a rise in organized criminal predatory activities in the private sector.

Finally, the freedom and independence of the media is seriously menaced in highly corrupted societies. In other words, the value of the freedom of the press, which clearly stands as an essential safeguard against authoritarian aberrations and is preserved by several constitutional regimes, can be seriously imperilled.

The indicator of ROL of a country reflects the efficiency and effectiveness of the set of rules that govern it. If laws and regulations are not respected, society is pervaded by a high degree of uncertainty and the set of rights and duties established by the legal system is not granted. In Chapter 2 we remarked that for enterprises the cost of uncertainty can be significant indeed as it can cause several inefficiencies. The same considerations apply to society at large when compliance with the rules cannot be taken for granted.

A low degree of ROL creates a breeding ground for the diffusion of episodes of corruption. The latter spreads in an environment where it is possible to violate laws with a low probability of being caught and punished accordingly. Therefore, there is space to obtain illegal extra-profits.

Figure 7.14 shows the existence of a correlation between the indicator of ROL and the CPI. The data show that there is a significant positive relationship between the two indicators. In more than 143 countries, a strong ROL is associated with low degrees of corruption.

We now show the trends for the indicator of ROL, comparing 1998 and 2009 (Figure 7.15). The data show an improvement in the indicator for Western European countries and transition economies. The indicator is stable in North America, the Middle East and Sub-Saharan Africa. Finally, it shows a deterioration in Latin America, Asia-Pacific, and the Caribbean.

7.4.1.3 Control of corruption

The above analysis has been based on extensive economic literature and some new indicators; it shows the relationships that link corruption to many diverse variables. Also, we have provided rich empirical evidence that confirms our deliberations. Our empirical analysis is based on trends in the CPI. However, alternative proxies for corruption can be found. One of these is the WB governance indicator of control

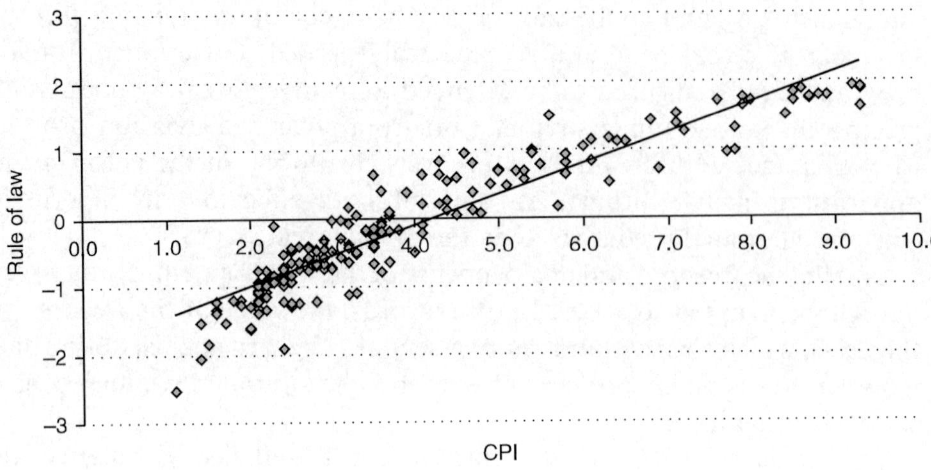

Note: CPI ranges between 10 (highly clean) and 0 (highly corrupt).

Source: Authors' calculations from TI data and Kaufmann, Kraay, and Mastruzzi (2010).

Figure 7.14 Corruption and the ROL, 2009

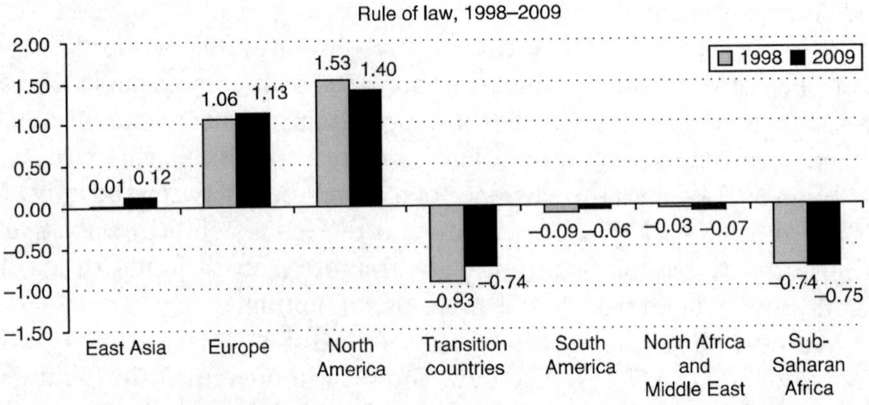

Source: Authors' calculations from TI data and Kaufmann, Kraay, and Mastruzzi (2005).

Figure 7.15 ROL over time, 1998–2009

of corruption: it reflects the perceptions of individuals concerning the frequency of episodes of bribery, estimates of episodes of State capture, and political corruption. The main difference between the CPI and the indicator of control of corruption lies in the methodology involved in collecting data and weighting the sub-indices. However, the two indicators present a very high degree of correlation (Kaufmann, Kraay, and Mastruzzi 2004).

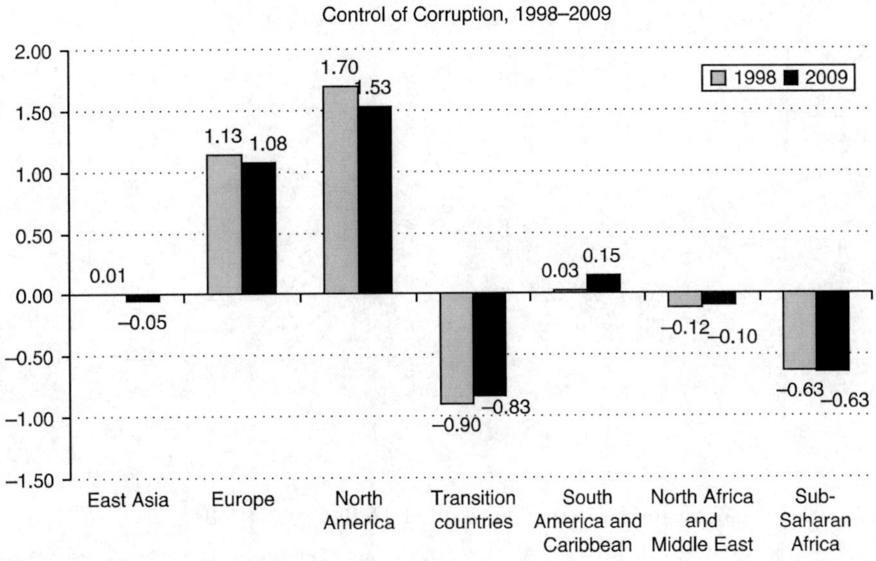

Source: Authors' calculations from TI data and Kaufmann, Kraay, and Mastruzzi (2010).

Figure 7.16 Control of corruption over time, 1998–2009

Figure 7.16 shows the evolution of control of corruption from 1998 to 2009. Notice that the index shows clear improvements in Western Europe, North America and the Middle East. In contrast, it has tended to deteriorate in Asia-Pacific, Sub-Saharan Africa and the Caribbean. The index is stable in Latin America and the transition countries.

7.4.1.4 Government effectiveness

The indicator of government effectiveness reflects the ability of the government bureaucracy to produce and implement good policies and deliver public goods – consistently with its mandate. Clearly, the degree of effectiveness is also reflected in government's normative ability and in its ability to manage public goods. It is thus not surprising that high levels of CPI (low degrees of corruption) are associated with good levels of government effectiveness. Indeed, the ability of the governance structure to help the government pursue public welfare – without being affected by those private interests that corrode public bureaucracies through secret and illegal channels – is negatively correlated with the degree of domestic corruption.

The correlation between government effectiveness and the CPI in Figure 7.17 is significant and the data present a very low degree of dispersion around the regression line. The data in Figure 7.20 show that this indicator has recently experienced an improvement in Western Europe,

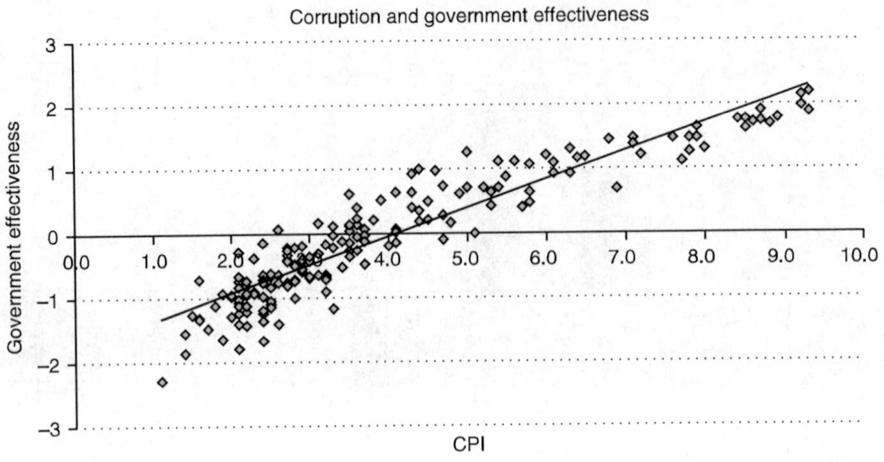

Note: CPI ranges between 10 (highly clean) and 0 (highly corrupt).

Source: Authors' calculations from TI data and Kaufmann, Kraay, and Mastruzzi (2005).

Figure 7.17 Government effectiveness and domestic corruption

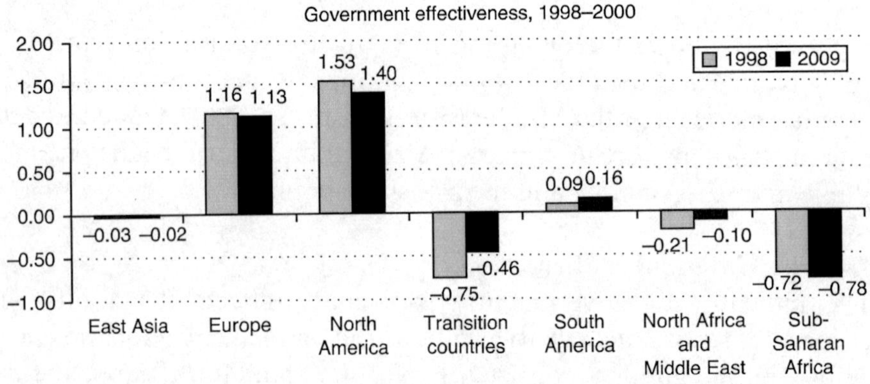

Source: Authors' calculations from TI data and Kaufmann, Kraay, and Mastruzzi (2010).

Figure 7.18 Government effectiveness and persistence over time, 1998–2009

North America, the transition economies, and the Caribbean. In contrast, Latin America, Asia-Pacific, and Sub-Saharan Africa experienced a deterioration in their trends of government effectiveness. Finally, trends have remained stable in the Middle East and North Africa.

PART II

Birth and evolution of a global anti-corruption legal standard

TRANSNATIONAL CORRUPTION AND EFFECTIVE REGULATION

The fall of the Soviet Union and the end of the Cold War, the diffusion of democracy, globalization, and the development of the internet and ICT (information and communication technology) has made possible an incredible flow of information, goods, and money. We are witnessing an extreme contraction of the two dimensions in which human activity typically occurs: space-time. One of the most noticeable effects of this development is that a specific human action, no matter where it originates, can directly widen its scope from one side of the world to the other.

At the same time transnational crime has been emerging as one of the defining issues of the 21st century for policymakers, business, and the general public. The menace it poses for the economy and society has been dealt with in the previous part of the present work.

The offspring of the progression of international developments in communication technology, rapid money movements, increasing mobility of individuals, financial interdependence, and decreasing importance of national boundaries – in short, the globalization of economic and financial activities – has also been benefiting public and private institutions (including corrupt governments and firms, especially large corporations, and global banks) and criminal organizations, endowed today with unprecedented opportunities.

In the case of corruption, evidence for the process under discussion is represented by the countless means exploitable for carrying out instantaneous collusive communications and transfer of capital flows across borders.

By contrast, the same dynamics have increased difficulties for public authorities, equipped almost only with nationwide repressive powers, to limit the growth of illegal financial activities internationally and transnational corrupt conduct.

In the last 20 years there has been a fundamental shift in social, political, and business attitudes towards corruption. Several factors have contributed to increased public awareness with regard to illegal international activities. The internationalization of a common regulatory paradigm against national and transnational bribery was initially promoted by American business interests in reaction to compulsory domestic rules against transnational bribery. Also, a decisive factor is the protection and enhancement of free and fair trading conditions for all participants in today's liberalized markets.

As a consequence, the multilateral institutions and international financial institutions (IFIs) played a catalytic role in enhancing public and institutional awareness: they promoted multilateral initiatives to fight corruption and money laundering, contributed to making public the negative impact of these activities, stimulated governments to take a more proactive role in this fight. In addition to the key role of the IMF and the WB (and non-governmental, business-oriented organizations like TI), among the most sensitive institutions are the UN, regional organizations like the African Union (AU), the Council of Europe (COE), the World Customs Organization, the EU, the League of Arab States, the OECD, and the Organization of American States (OAS).

In Part I of this book we highlighted that the task of combating corruption is a daunting one with no simple answers. The establishment and the constant repowering of an international legal regime is (but) one essential component that drives the process forward.

The socio-economic analysis shows that this is a continuous evolution requiring an incessant dialogue between the main intergovernmental institutions and the single States, with a view to setting and progressively fine-tuning a comprehensive and effective institutional and legal strategy. In essence, the interaction between international and national legal systems makes substantive progress only when the identification of the shortcomings in the regulatory apparatus is treated in international fora as a necessary input for rethinking and amending existing domestic law.

This process rests on truly functioning international specialized supervising mechanisms, which, unfortunately, are not always operative within the framework of the main international organizations. Some of the central elements of an effective regulation (e.g., raising the efficacy of the criminal apparatus, bridging the gaps opened by the transnational dynamics of the crime, and complementing criminal law with civil remedies) may be exemplified by analyzing a sample of recent case studies.

Before proceeding to assess the international legal apparatus against corruption (Chapters 10 to 17), we consider a selection of practical cases (Chapter 8) with the aim of providing a good picture of the multiple threats posed by corruption to States and international organizations, in line with the main doctrinal literature. The same elements find their archetypical expression in the US Foreign Corrupt Practices Act (FCPA) 1977, so we then turn our attention to its salient features (Chapter 9).

Section 4:

Cases of transnational corruption: description and legal issues

8. How corruption affects the economic and institutional textures of States: three case examples

The impact of corruption on economies provides the strongest case for the ever-growing commitments of States and international institutions in preventing and tackling such crime. However, the illustration of some recent cases of "grand" national and transnational corruption is even more explicative in showing its pernicious and pervasive effects. Sadly enough, the number of suitable cases for this purpose appears uncountable.[1] Nevertheless, some of them may also serve the scope of

---

[1] At time of the final submission of this manuscript (January 2014) the *Wall Street Journal* reported that in 1989, Alcoa World Alumina began using a consultant who arranged bribe payments to Bahrain's royal family through a series of shell companies, according to the U.S. Department of Justice's charging documents. Then in 1997, as the company ramped up its sales to Aluminum Bahrain, a lawyer asked questions about these arrangements. See http://blogs.wsj.com/riskandcompliance/2014/01/09/alcoa-unit-attorneys-raised-bribery-concerns-in-1997/?KEYWORDS=alcoa+bribe. Also, our assertion in the main text is plainly confirmed by the numerous cases of "grand corruption" reported by two invaluable sources on the matter: 1) the StAR's thorough analysis of cases of corruption also involving international asset recovery, which are contained in the database this body has prepared and kept on updating over the last 7 years. Cases are ordered according to the jurisdictions involved, number and type of vehicle companies misused, occurred/alleged violations of relevant international provisions, status of the criminal proceeding if existing. To the best of our knowledge there is no comparable database in terms of comprehensiveness and ease of access. The database is available at: http://star.worldbank.org/corruption-cases/assetrecovery/?f[0]=bundle%3Apuppet_masters. For further information on the Stolen Asset Recovery Initiative, see http://www1.worldbank.org/finance/star_site/. For a first assessment of the initiative we refer to Chapter 17 of this work and bibliography referred therein. 2) The annual Progress Report, published by Transparency international (TI). See Transparency International (2013). TI annual progress report on foreign bribery enforcement presents an independent assessment on the status of enforcement in all of the 40 Parties to the OECD Convention against transnational bribery, including Russia and Colombia, where the Convention entered into force in 2012 and 2013, respectively – available at: http://www.transparency.org/whatwedo/pub/exporting_corruption_progress_report_2013_

testifying the relevance of the international initiatives against corruption – especially in furthering the criminalization of transnational corruption and international cooperation – and at the same time, pointing out some of the open issues still to be dealt with. Similarly, other cases demonstrate how problematic an effective enforcement of criminal provisions can be, even where the statutory law seems *prima facie* to adhere to the international standards. Accordingly, we report three cases we deem particularly indicative of the above-mentioned issues. In the *Oil for food*, and the *TSKJ Consortium*, cases the transnational element is self-evident: the corruptors bribed foreign/international public officials: the absence of national provisions criminalizing corruption of the foreign or international public agents could have impeded the very exercise of the criminal action. On the other hand, in the *Fininvest* case, aside from the crucial importance of the sector involved, the most relevant element from a legal viewpoint is represented by the gap between the statutory law and the effectiveness of the enforcement of criminal provisions. This gap was partly bridged by the Italian Civil Courts issuing a rather debated ruling.[2]

8.1 THE ABUSE OF THE OIL-FOR-FOOD PROGRAMME

8.1.1 Description and Inquiries

The Oil-for-Food Programme (in short, the Programme) was established in 1995 under UN Security Council Resolution 986 and terminated in late 2003. Its stated intent was to allow Iraq to sell oil on the world market in exchange for food, medicines, and other humanitarian needs for ordinary Iraqi citizens without allowing Iraq to further its military capability. The Programme was meant as a response to arguments that ordinary Iraqi citizens were very badly affected by the international economic sanctions aimed at the demilitarization of Saddam Hussein's Iraq, imposed in

---

assessing_enforcement_of_the_oecd#sthash.43lDieSg.dpuf. See also Vlasic and Cooper (2011).

[2] The cases under discussion are technically rather complex – which represent a further motive of the interest they raise. Furthermore, the offspring of the *Oil-for-Food* and the *TSKJ* cases are still subject to criminal proceedings in some national jurisdictions. Thus, in the present context our attempt is to chronicle their factual background, and, thereafter, highlight how the international standards and the national implementing pieces of legislation would have allowed/allow the competent authorities to deal with their underlying corrupt schemes.

the wake of the First Gulf War. The sanctions were discontinued on 21 November 2003 after the US invasion of Iraq, and the humanitarian functions handed over to the Coalition Provisional Authority.[3] Originally conceived as a temporary program, the Oil-for-Food Programme lasted seven years with more than $100 billion in transactions. Under the Programme, the Government of Iraq sold $64.2 billion of oil to 248 companies. In turn, 3,614 companies sold $34.5 billion of humanitarian goods to Iraq (mainly, food and medicines).[4] The Programme was terminated shortly before the US and British forces invaded Iraq: UN Secretary-General Kofi Annan suspended it and evacuated more than 300 workers monitoring the distribution of supplies. On 28 March 2003, Secretary-General Annan, the United States, and Britain asked the Security Council to ensure that nearly US$10 billion in goods that Iraq had ordered and that had already been approved, including US$2.4 billion for food, could enter the country when conditions allowed. As is widely known, on 22 May 2003, UN Security Council Resolution 1483 granted authority to the Coalition Provisional Authority to use Iraq's oil revenue. The Programme's remaining funds of $10 billion were transferred over a six month winding-up period to the Development Fund for Iraq under the Coalition Provisional Authority's control; this represented 14 percent of the Programme's total income over five years. The Programme was formally terminated on 21 November 2003 and its major functions were handed over to the Coalition Provisional Authority.

As soon as the Programme elapsed, there were revelations of corruption involving the funds.[5]

---

[3] See the Independent Inquiry Committee into the Oil-For-Food Programme's Report on the Impact of the UN Oil-for-Food Programme on the Iraqi people, issued 7 September 2005, available at: http://www.iic-offp.org. For an effective overview of the impact of the Programme within Iraq's international trade patterns, see also the US Congressional Research Service Report for Congress, Iraq's Trade with the World: Data and Analysis, updated 23 September 2004 (received through the CSR Web).

[4] For more detailed financial figures see the Independent Inquiry Committee into the UN Oil-For-Food Programme's Report on the Management of the Oil-for-Food Programme, issued on 7 September 2005, available at: http://www.iic-offp.org. Here it suffices to recall that over US$65 billion worth of Iraqi oil was sold on the world market. About US$46 billion were intended to provide for the humanitarian needs of the Iraqi people such as food and medicine in the context of international economic sanctions. A considerable amount was spent on Gulf War reparations through a compensation fund (25 percent since December 2000), UN administrative and operational costs of the Programme (2.2 percent) and costs of the weapons inspection program.

[5] One of the earliest allegations of wrongdoing in the Programme surfaced

In April 2004, UN Secretary-General Kofi Annan appointed an independent, high-level IIC (Independent Inquiry Committee) to investigate the administration and management of the Programme in Iraq.[6] Following this, the United Nations Security Council unanimously adopted Resolution 1538 (2004), which endorsed the inquiry and called for full cooperation in the investigation by all UN officials and personnel, the Coalition Provisional Authority, Iraq, and all other Member States, including their national regulatory authorities.

According to the IIC's fifth and final (2005) report, nearly half of the 4,500 participating companies were accused of paying kickbacks and illegal surcharges to win lucrative contracts, allowing Saddam Hussein to pocket $1.8 billion. Similar figures are evidenced also by the a 2004 CIA investigation: Saddam Hussein managed to exploit the program, earning some $1.7 billion through kickbacks and surcharges, and $10.9 billion through illegal oil smuggling; large-scale mismanagement and unethical conduct on the part of some UN employees also plagued the program, according to the UN Independent Inquiry Committee.

The IIC Report on Programme Manipulation complements the IIC report on the adequacy of the Programme's management by the United Nations:[7] serious vulnerabilities in the Programme and its management

---

on 25 January 2004, when *al Mada*, a daily newspaper in Iraq, published a list of individuals and organizations alleged to have received oil sales contracts via the UN's Oil-for-Food Programme. The list came from over 15,000 documents which were reportedly found in the state-owned Iraqi oil corporation, which had close links with the Iraqi Oil Ministry. Named in the list of beneficiaries were British MP George Galloway and his charity, the Mariam Fund; former French Interior Minister Charles Pasqua; and Shaker al-Kaffaji, an Iraqi-American businessman. India's foreign minister, Natwar Singh, was removed from office because of his role in the scandal. Many prominent Russian firms and individuals were also included on the *al Mada* list. Even the Russian Orthodox Church was supposedly involved in illegal oil trading. The former assistant to the Vatican secretary of state, Rev. Jean-Marie Benjamin, is said to have received rights to sell 4.5 million barrels (720,000 m^3). George Galloway subsequently won two libel actions against the *Christian Science Monitor* and the *Daily Telegraph*, which reported the allegations. Noticeably, the *al Mada* list does not discuss bribes paid to Iraq – it denounces bribes paid to individuals so that they would support Iraq.

6 http://www.iic-offp.org/story27oct05.htm. The appointed IIC was chaired by Paul Volcker, former Chairman of the United States Federal Reserve. Committee Members included Mark Pieth of Switzerland, an eminent expert on corruption and money-laundering and President of the Working Group on Bribery of the Organisation for Economic Co-operation and Development (OECD), and Richard Goldstone of South Africa, former Prosecutor of the International Criminal Tribunals for the former Yugoslavia and Rwanda.

7 Note that the IIC also issued three preceding interim reports and two

were exploited by some within the UN and several outside it, including the Iraqi regime, seriously damaging the reputation and credibility of the organization itself (Borlini 2005). In the words of the IIC Chair Paul A. Volcker: "The results of the Committee's investigation into corrupt and illicit activity by many buyers of oil and sellers of humanitarian goods reinforce the Committee's central conclusion of failures in UN oversight and management. The need for stronger executive leadership, thorough going administrative reform, and more reliable controls and auditing within the UN is underscored" (IIC 2005: 2).

The IIC's Report on Programme Manipulation chronicles in detail the perversion of the Programme by Saddam Hussein's regime in Iraq and provides a selection of examples of oil buyers and humanitarian goods sellers many of whom paid, directly or through intermediaries, illicit oil surcharge or kickbacks on humanitarian goods contracts through a variety of devices. Along with the careful assessment of the conduct of the role of the Banque Nationale de Paris (BNP) – the bank selected to hold and service the escrow account where all Programme proceeds were deposited and from which all suppliers were paid – these case studies are the centerpieces of the Report. It then concludes by addressing the activity of oil and goods inspection companies and the conduct of two humanitarian coordinators.

---

briefing papers. A September report faults UN Secretary-General Kofi Annan, his deputy, and the UN Security Council for allowing Saddam Hussein to graft over $1 billion from the humanitarian operation. The Volcker committee has issued four interim reports since it began its work in April 2004. These reports found there is no evidence of corruption on the part of UN Secretary-General Kofi Annan in administering the program. However, it finds that his son, Kojo, inappropriately concealed his business relationship with a major Oil-for-Food contractor. Kojo Annan, who was not a UN employee, received some $400,000 from Swiss-based Cotecna Inspections SA between 1995 and 2004. Kojo Annan formally stopped working for Cotecna in 1998, leaving just before the company won its $10-million a year UN contract. But he continued to receive monthly payments from the firm until 2004, as part of an unusual arrangement in which he was paid thousands of dollars a month to refrain from joining a competing firm. The committee's January briefing paper alleged that UN management of the Oil-for-Food Programme "operated in an ineffective, wasteful, and unsatisfactory manner", leading to some $5 million in documented contractor overpayments, and "undoubtedly much higher" losses not discovered by the limited UN audits. The February interim report found the Programme's procurement office did not follow established rules "designed to assure fairness and accountability." It also accused the former head of the Programme, Benon Sevan, of an "irreconcilable conflict of interest" because he helped a company owned by a friend obtain valuable contracts to sell Iraqi oil. Other allegations against Sevan are also being investigated. Sevan retired from the United Nations in 2004 and has denied any wrongdoing.

In conjunction with such assessment, the ICC proposed several changes they believe should be enacted within a year, but experts say that is unlikely to happen. Among the Report's recommendations: (i) the UN Security Council should be clearer about UN operations' purposes and criteria; (ii) a Chief Operating Officer should be nominated by the Security Council to provide a needed focus for the Secretariat's administrative responsibilities; (iii) an Independent Auditing Board should be established to fully review UN programs and hiring; (iv) tasks should be coordinated more effectively between UN agencies; (v) further personnel policy reforms to redress the appearance and possibility of conflict of interests along with rigorous enforcement of the organization's existing ethical standards for senior-level officials.

For our purposes it is of particular interest to consider the main findings of the IIC's final report which uncovered the regime's complex and lucrative schemes to earn illicit funds. As mentioned above, under the Program, the UN was supposed to monitor and approve all of Iraq's oil sales. All profits went into special escrow accounts that the UN controlled. Because the purpose of the program was to help feed and provide for the basic needs of the Iraqi people, Iraq was not permitted to buy military equipment or so-called dual-use items – items that could potentially be used in banned weapons programs – with its oil proceeds. Yet, Iraq was given wide latitude to determine to whom it sold its oil, and was also permitted to select the vendors from which the UN would purchase goods with Iraqi oil profits. Saddam Hussein skimmed billions from the program by controlling these decisions. In a particularly egregious abuse, Saddam was found to be using secret "oil vouchers" worth millions of dollars to reward individuals and companies for helping Iraq subvert sanctions.

Companies and other individuals and entities which paid the illicit kickbacks were from some 66 Member States, while those paying illicit surcharges on oil purchases came from, or were registered in, around 40 Member States. The IIC collected a very substantial amount of data to support this area of investigations, which are detailed in both the interim reports and the report on the manipulation of the Programme. The Programme was just under three years old when the Iraqi regime began openly to demand illicit payments from its customers. This could happen because, under the Programme, Iraq could sign final oil contracts only with a set number of approved "lifting" companies – major oil companies that could transport the oil.[8]

---

[8] Although the sale of crude oil was monitored and approved by the Security Council's sanctions committee (known as the "661 Committee"), the Iraqi

However, as also documented by the CIA report, Saddam Hussein developed a complex internal system – officially unreported to the UN – that moved the oil through middlemen before it got to the final buyer. The initial oil sale, the CIA report said, was generally to a company or individual whom Saddam wanted to influence or favor. Senior Iraqi leaders, such as former deputy prime minister Tariq Aziz and Iraqi ambassadors, could nominate an individual or company to receive secret oil vouchers – guarantees from the regime that the holder of the voucher could buy a certain amount of oil at a set price. Iraq priced this oil below market value, so that the holder of the voucher could make a significant profit when s/he sold it on to another middleman or international oil company. Saddam Hussein personally approved all the names on the voucher recipient lists, the report states. Of course, a voucher holder's earnings depended on the price of the oil, although the CIA report say that voucher holders could earn from 10 to 35 cents per barrel beyond the regular market profit. The same report contains a list of more than 1,300 oil vouchers that Saddam Hussein gave to more than a hundred corporations, foreign officials, individuals, and political parties around the world. This information came from lists found at Iraq's state oil company and interviews with captured regime officials.

According to investigators from the House International Relations Committee, to take a voucher could be illegal in that, if individuals and companies knowingly received profits from oil sales not approved within the Programme, they broke the rules and violated the terms of UN Security Resolutions that established the program and the sanctions against Iraq. In the case of UN employees, accepting bribes would also violate the rules of that body. However, whether individuals on the list will be prosecuted, it would be in most cases the decision of their own governments and subject to the domestic laws of each nation. In the US, as in some other nations, the sanctions became part of domestic law.

Another key question in the US context would be whether these vouchers truly served as bribes that caused individuals to work on Saddam Hussein's behalf to modify US policy. A series of laws, including the 1977 Foreign Corrupt Practices Act (FCPA), regulates the overseas business practices of American citizens. In addition, US firms could be prosecuted if they failed to receive the required approval from the US Treasury to

Ministry of Oil and its marketing arm, the SOMO, were given significant leeway in choosing customers and the amount of oil to be sold to each customer. Initially, SOMO contracted with oil companies without regard to the nationality of the owner and its corporate base.

purchase Iraqi oil. It is noteworthy that, at the time of the perpetration of the first illicit manipulation of the Programme few of the other States involved had established in their own domestic legal system the corruption of foreign or international public officials as a criminal offence.

According to the ICC Report, Saddam earned his illicit funds by exploiting his political influence over world leaders and companies, but it didn't bring in much cash to the regime. As early as phase II of the Programme its politicization was already manifest, the Iraqi government began directing oil allocations to particular countries and individuals, clearly favoring countries friendly to Iraq and individuals perceived as being able to influence public opinion in favor of Iraq. In phase IV of the Programme, Iraqi leaders decided to deny American, British, and Japanese companies direct oil allocations due to the opposition of these countries to the lifting of the sanctions. At the same time, Iraq leaders gave preferential treatment to France, Russia, and China, as these countries were permanent members of the Security Council and perceived as more sympathetic towards Iraq and more favorable to the lifting of sanctions. In the early fall of 2010, the Iraqi government ordered that surcharges be imposed on every barrel of oil sold under the Programme. The surcharge scheme on the selling of crude oil, implemented by the Ministry of Oil and the State Oil Marketing Organization (SOMO), lasted for over two years from the middle of phase VIII through the middle of phase XII when it was effectively stopped with the advent of retroactive pricing. Along with kickbacks on the provision of humanitarian goods, this represented the source of illicit earnings for the Iraqi regime and the companies involved. In phase IX of the Programme beginning in December 2000, the imposition of mandatory surcharges on the selling of crude oil by the Iraqi regime created a crisis in the domestic oil industry, particularly when established buyers refused to pay the higher surcharge. The Ministry of Oil and SOMO moved quickly to find new customers willing to pay the surcharges. Oil sales increasingly resembled contracts with front companies, backed financially and technically by several international trading companies, willing to ease surcharge payments. The collection of the surcharges is reflected in the SOMO database, where they are organized by beneficiary and contracting company. The database recorded the amount of the surcharge paid, how it was paid, and the name of the individual or entity making the payment. Most surcharges were paid through deposits to designated SOMO bank accounts in Jordan and Lebanon or through cash payments made at Iraqi embassies abroad.

Turning to humanitarian imports, which represent the other main element in the Programme, the Report showed in detail that Iraq's largest source of illicit income came from kickbacks paid by companies that it selected to receive contracts for humanitarian goods. Such payments were disguised through different subterfuges (e.g. by collecting them as transportation fees or after-sale-service fees) and were not reported to the UN by Iraq or the participating contractors. As set forth in the IIC Programme Management Report, the available evidence indicates that Iraq derived more than $1.5 billion from these kickbacks. Furthermore, as with its selection of oil purchasers, political considerations influenced Iraq's selection of humanitarian vendors. The kickback policy began in mid-1999 with Iraq's efforts to collect the "cost" of transporting goods to inland destinations after their arrival by sea at the Persian Gulf port of Umm Qasr. These side payments were unauthorized. Moreover, it was easy for Iraq to impose "inland transportation" fees that far exceeded the actual transportation costs. By mid-2000, Iraq instituted an even broader policy to impose in general a 10 percent kickback requirement on all humanitarian contractors in addition to the requirement for the contractors to pay inland transport fees. Iraq described its more general kickback requirement as an "after-sale-service" fee. After-sales-service fee provisions were often incorporated into contracts as a way of inflating prices and permitting contractors to recover from the UN escrow account amounts that they had paid secretly to Iraq in the form of kickbacks. Many companies, if not willing to go along openly with Iraq's schemes, would make payments to third parties or agents without examining or admitting to the likely purpose of these payments. The Committee calculates that more than 2,200 companies worldwide paid kickbacks to Iraq in the form of inland transportation fees, after-sales-service fees or both.[9]

Finally, the Report considers the role of the BNP: in 1996 the UN selected the BNP to serve as the escrow bank to receive and disburse funds from transactions under the Programme. According to the Report on the Management of the Programme, the BNP's tasks under the contract were threefold:

(i) establishing and managing an escrow account to deposit proceeds from the sale of Iraqi oil and to disburse amounts for Iraq's purchase of humanitarian goods;
(ii) confirming letters of credit issued by banks retained by companies buying oil from Iraq;
(iii) issuing letters of credit (LCs) for the purchase of humanitarian goods.

---

9 The Report examines the individual roles of a sample of 23 companies that participated in the payment of kickbacks for humanitarian contracts. The companies fall roughly into four groups: (1) Iraqi front companies; (2) major foodstuff providers; (3) major trading companies; (4) major industrial and manufacturing companies.

Over the course of the Programme, BNP confirmed LCs for the purchase of oil and maintained an account into which $64.2 billion in oil proceeds was ultimately deposited, either directly or through one of its affiliates – it also issued letters of credit for all humanitarian purchasers for the south and central governors of Iraq and for approximately three-fourths of all LCs for oil transactions. These amount to about $34.5 billion. As highlighted by the IIC Report on the Manipulation of the Programme, BNP was not forbidden from issuing such LCs in its contract with the UN. However, its dual role and responsibility, the duty of secrecy to a private contracting or financing party (claimed by BNP's Geneva affiliate) was potentially in conflict with the interest of full disclosure to BNP's primary customer – the UN – of the true financial arrangements underlying transactions run under the Programme. Most importantly, according to the Report, whilst some elements of the BNP's relationship with the UN remain in dispute, BNP was clearly inhibited from disclosing fully the firsthand knowledge it got of the actual financial relationships that fostered the payment of illicit surcharges. The IIC Report, describing the way in which the potential conflict of interest was resolved by the bank, raises broad questions of fiduciary responsibility and the relevance of the international efforts to deal with money-laundering and corporate corruption.

The involvement of the UN itself in the scandal began in February 2004 after the name of Benon Sevan, executive director of the Programme, appeared on the Iraqi Oil Ministry's documents as the beneficiary of vouchers for a substantial quantity of oil.

The CIA's Report states that as Sevan was administering the UN program, he accepted Iraqi oil vouchers through various companies that he recommended to the Iraqi government. An investigation by the now-defunct Iraqi Governing Council uncovered a letter linking Sevan to a Panamanian-registered company called the African Middle East Petroleum Company, which set up an oil deal on his behalf, the report states. Some 7.3 million barrels were allegedly sold by Sevan before 2003, which could have netted him between $730,000 and $2 million, depending on market conditions. While heading the Programme, Sevan claimed that it had only a 2.2 percent administrative cost and that it was subject to more than 100 audits (internal and external), blaming restrictions by the Security Council for making the situation difficult. He also claimed that 90 percent of the Iraqi population relied on the Programme for its monthly food basket.

While Sevan was in charge of the Programme, he stonewalled efforts to review and investigate it. In 2000, Dileep Nair, the UN corruption watchdog, wanted to determine the Programme level of vulnerability. Sevan, along with UN deputy Secretary-General, Louise Frechette, rejected any such investigation, claiming that it would be too expensive to be worthwhile. According to an interim report released on 3 February 2005 by the IIC, much of the food aid supplied under the Programme "was unfit for human consumption". The Report concluded that Sevan had accepted nearly $150,000 in bribes over the course of the Programme, and in 2005 he was suspended from his position at the UN as a result of the investigation of fraud in the Programme.

The IIC closed its office effective from 31 December 2006. The Office of the Independent Inquiry Committee has continued to process requests from UN Member States for information relating to IIC investigations, in accord with the Secretary-General's bulletin ST/SGB/2006/16 (22 December 2006).[10]

8.1.2 Legal Issues

Overall, from a strictly legal viewpoint, the main legal issues posed by the manipulation of the Programme, may be summarized as follows:

A) Individuals and organizations sympathetic to the Iraqi regime, or those just easily bribed, were offered oil contracts through the Programme. These contracts for Iraqi oil could then be sold on the open world market and the seller was allowed to keep a transaction fee, said to be between $0.15 and $0.50 per barrel (0.94 and 3.14 $\$/m^3$) of oil sold. As already stressed in our economic analysis (Chapter 2), corruption and distortion of competition go hand in hand.

B) The seller was then to refund the Iraqi government a certain percentage of the commission. Such a practice irremediably perverted the Programme and its institutional aim, by allowing the Iraqi regime to collect bribes which could be used for the most variegated (including not permitted) purposes.

C) Similar considerations may be advanced as to the contracts to sell Iraq humanitarian goods. Such contracts were given to companies and individuals based on their willingness to kick back a certain percentage of the contract profits to the Iraqi regime. Companies that sold commodities via the Programme were overcharging by up to 10 percent, with part of the overcharged amount being diverted into private bank accounts for Saddam Hussein and other regime officials, and the other part being kept by the supplier. Once again,

10 See http://www.iic-offp.org/closing.htm.

such manipulations of the Programme distorted its institutional aim and showed all its vulnerabilities.

D) Not only does the fact that UN officials were involved have a considerable symbolic relevance for the image of the entire Programme, and, supposedly, for the UN's policy in Iraq, but it also had a strictly legal bearing, when one considers that only in 1997 the OECD had adopted the first international instruments requiring the State Parties to establish as a criminal offense the corruption of foreign (including international) public officials in the context of transnational business transactions.[11] The same holds true with respect to the corruption of Iraqi officials: before the elaboration and entry into force of the national implementing pieces of legislation following the first relevant anti-corruption international treaties, no domestic national law but the 1977 US FCPA had established corruption of foreign public officials and officials of international public organizations as criminal offenses. Thus, for several jurisdictions, the penal relevance of such conduct, on the part of both natural and legal persons, was *nihil*.[12]

E) The circumstance that individuals and companies registered or operating in several different jurisdictions took advantage of the manipulation of the Programme has emphasized the need for accurate mechanisms of international legal cooperation, which, at this point in time, is still at an embryonic stage.

---

11 Convention on Combating Bribery of Foreign Public Officials in International Business Transactions, text available at: http://www.oecd.org/dataoecd/4/18/38028044.pdf, accessed on 10 October 2010. The Convention entered into force on 15 February 1999. As of October 2013, the 34 OECD member countries and six non-member countries – Argentina, Brazil, Bulgaria, Colombia, Russia, and South Africa – have adopted this Convention. For details of ratification and implementation status see http://www.OECD.org/daf/nocorruption. Note, however, that some of the G20 states (namely, China, India, Indonesia and Saudi Arabia) have not ratified the OCED Convention yet, in spite of the Group's repeated recommendations to do so. Also other States, which play a growing role in international business, are not parties of the Convention yet: Hong Kong, Malaysia, Singapore and Thailand are some notable examples.

12 Indeed, when the misuse of the Programme was discovered, 'transnational' bribery was not criminalized in several of the relevant jurisdictions. As a matter of fact, criminal prosecution was only possible for the segments of the corrupt conduct which could be proved to be committed after the entry into force of national laws criminalizing the corruption of foreign/international public officials. This is due to the fundamental principle of several advanced criminal legal systems (irrespective of either of the common law or the civil law tradition) according to which nobody can be prosecuted and, eventually, convicted for a conduct that did not constitute an offence at the time of its commission.

F) The role of BNP confirms the crucial importance of; i) effective due diligence on the part of financial intermediaries, ii) serious sanctions in case they fail to guarantee the proper functioning and full transparency of the operations they are supposed to monitor and filter.

8.2 THE TSKJ CONSORTIUM CASE

The TSKJ consortium provides us with a telling example of a "global cartel", which successfully competed for an extremely profitable market by means of bribery of members of the Nigerian government. The international legal framework and, in particular, the 1997 OECD Anti-bribery Convention have constituted important tools to prosecute and punish such an illicit pact, and to send a clear message to the international business community as to the way to do business in developing countries.[13] Nevertheless, oil, gas and other resources companies still have a high risk of corruption,[14] and specific safeguards and rules should be introduced in this sector, especially when companies operate in developing countries. On the other side, it is crucial to improve coordination between judicial authorities in order to carry out effective investigations, imposing dissuasive sanctions and guaranteeing legal certainty for the companies involved.

8.2.1 Factual Background and Basic Figures

At the heart of this case there is the international "TSKJ" Consortium, a private limited liability company registered in Madeira, Portugal, whose members were Kellogg Brown Root Inc. (KBR Inc. of the US, a Halliburton subsidiary); Technip SA (of France), Snamprogetti Netherlands BV (a former unit of ENI SpA of Italy, now part of Saipem SpA), and JGC Corp. (formerly Japanese Gasoline Corporation of

---

13 In the sense that the TSKJ case may "incentivize voluntary extractive industry corruption reform" see Spahn (2012).

14 The natural resource extractive industries have been identified by NGOs such as Transparency International and Global Witness for their corrupt exploitation of nations rich in resources but with weak governance structures. Cf. Transparency International (2011a). Global Witness calls this phenomenon the 'Resource Curse' or 'Paradox of Plenty', describing it as a situation "whereby countries that are rich in natural resources such as oil, gas or minerals, end up poorer and more unequal than countries without them. This can be because of corruption, a decline in the competitiveness of other economic sectors, and volatility on commodity markets. Countries that have successfully escaped the resource curse include Botswana and Norway."

Japan), each of which had an approximate 25 percent interest in the venture. TSKJ entered into various contracts worth $6 billion to build and expand the liquefied natural gas project for Nigeria LNG Limited, which is owned by the Nigerian National Petroleum Corporation, Shell Gas BV, Cleag Limited (an affiliate of Total), and Agip International BV (an affiliate of ENI SpA of Italy).

The main allegation concerns claimed payments by TSKJ of a total of US$180 million in bribes to Nigerian government officials between 1994 and 2004 in connection with the LNG project. Additional allegations reportedly relate to payments made to a political party in connection with the project by employees of the Nigerian company Julius Berger Nigeria, minority held by Bilfinger Berger Nigeria, which is wholly owned by the German construction company Bilfinger Berger.

8.2.2 Operation of the Scheme in a Nutshell

Before analyzing the findings and the outcomes of an investigation carried out in multiple jurisdictions and which first started in France in 2003,[15] it is important to recall the most important dates and facts concerning the TSKJ consortium and the award of the contracts through a corrupt scheme.[16]

In September 1994 the newly formed TSKJ Consortium submitted a bid to Nigeria LNG to build a natural gas plant in Nigeria owned by the Nigerian government. The first $2 billion contract was awarded only in December 1995, after the consortium hired a British solicitor and legal advisor to KBR, Mr Tesler, as agent (March 2005). The employment contract provided that Mr Tesler would be paid $60 million if Nigeria awarded the construction contract to TSKJ. In 1999 the TSKJ partners, with KBR acting as the lead partner, agreed to appoint Mr. Tesler as its agent, despite the fact that the representative from the French partner wanted a different agent. The same year the Nigerian government

---

15 The bribery first came to the attention of the French authorities in 2002, when a Paris prosecutor received information from an official of Technip about a Nigerian "slush fund". The case was then transferred to French magistrates Renaud Van Ruymbeke and Eva Joly, who began investigations in 2003 and discovered evidence during their investigation of the French oil company (at that time called Elf-Aquitaine), eventually referring the matter to the US authorities. On the French investigation see Zagaris (2004) and Clark (2004).

16 See also George and Lacey (2006). For an exhaustive and detailed timeline of events see also 'Halliburton and Nigeria: A Chronology of Key Events in the Unfolding Bribery Scandal', available at http://www.halliburtonwatch.org/about_hal/nigeria_timeline.html.

awarded a $1.2 billion contract to TSKJ to expand construction of the natural gas plant from two to three trains in order to increase the plant's capacity by 50 percent. Finally in 2003 a preliminary investigation carried out by the *Police Judiciaire* of France began to reveal the bribery scheme, according to which the consortium's company 'LNG Servicos e Gestao de Projectos' based in Madeira made payments of $132 million at periods of time that roughly coincided with the award of contracts (Landers and Whittle 2004). In particular, the payments went to a Gibraltar-based company Tri-Star Investments Ltd, controlled by Mr Tesler, and then to a Swiss bank account that was later closed at the request of the bank. The rest of the money provided by TSKJ to bribe Nigerian officials (more than $50 million) was paid to a Japanese trading company.[17]

8.2.3 Findings and Outcomes of Investigations

Despite TSKJ never having been tried as a single legal entity, after more than ten years of investigations and proceedings taking place in the US, the UK, Italy, France, Germany and Nigeria, the consortium is almost universally considered responsible for bribing the Nigerian government in exchange for the award of contracts in the liquefied natural gas sector.[18] Here is a summary of the outcomes of TSKJ-related proceedings in different countries:[19]

- In the US the Department of Justice and the Securities and Exchange Commission have obtained more than $1.7 billion in penalties and forfeiture orders from the prosecution of four joint

---

17 The reconstruction of events is mostly based on documents from the US Department of Justice (www.justice.gov) and the US Securities and Exchange Commission (www.sec.gov); further information is provided by the FCPA blog (www.fcpablog.com) and by the following newspaper articles which appeared when the scandal first came out: *Financial Times*, London, 16 September 2004; *Wall Street Journal*, 29 September 2004; *Dallas Morning News*, 25 January 2004.

18 According to the reconstruction of the investigation by George and Lacey (2006: 507), "Handwritten notes have been discovered covering conversations, which occurred from 1993 to1998, among representatives of the consortium discussing the possibility of bribes for Nigerian officials to win bids for construction of the $12 billion Nigeria Liquefied Natural Gas Project."

19 Although the bribery scheme is now clear, proceedings are still ongoing in some of these countries. For a comprehensive overview of TSKJ proceedings and their updates around the world see StAR (2013) and Transparency International (2012). Available at: http://www.transparency.org/whatwedo/pub/exporting_corruption_country_enforcement_of_the_oecd_anti_bribery_convention.

venture partners, two third-party intermediaries, and other culpable individuals for breaches of the Foreign Corruption Practice Act (FCPA). In particular, KBR paid fines and penalties of $579 million, Italy's Snamprogetti $365 million, France's Technip $338 million, and Japan's JGC $218.8 million. In addition, the first intermediary Jeffrey Tesler paid $149 million as part of his plea deal, and was given 21 months of prison,[20] while Marubeni Corporation, the second (Japanese) intermediary, agreed to enter into a deferred prosecution agreement with the Department of Justice (DOJ) and to pay $54.6 million.[21] Finally, chairman and CEO of Houston-based Kellogg Brown & Root (now known as KBR), Mr Stanley, pleaded guilty in 2008 and was recently sentenced to 30 months in prison and three years' probation following his release.[22]

- In the UK, after a civil settlement in February 2011, a subsidiary of KBR, MW Kellogg (MWKL) was ordered by the UK High Court to pay over £7 million (US$11 million) in connection with the TSKJ case.[23]
- In Italy a criminal action was brought against the Italian company Snamprogetti (now part of Saipem SpA), a subsidiary of Eni SpA, as well as against five former managers. Due to the expiry of the statute of limitations in February 2012, the case against the managers was dismissed, while the case against the company continues.[24]
- As in Italy, in France and Switzerland the outcomes of investigations are still unknown at the time of writing.
- In Germany, an investigation by the Wiesbaden public prosecutor of the engineering and construction company Bilfinger Berger relating to the activities of its Nigerian subsidiary Julius Berger

---

20 See http://www.fcpablog.com/blog/2012/2/23/tesler-gets-21-months.html.

21 See https://www.boardmember.com/Article_Details.aspx?id=8152.

22 See http://www.fcpablog.com/blog/2012/2/23/stanley-jailed-for-30-months.html.

23 See http://www.sfo.gov.uk/press-room/latest-press-releases/press-releases-2011/mw-kellogg-ltd-to-pay-7-million-in-sfo-high-court-action.aspx. Noticeably, across the globe there is an increased use of settlement to enforce foreign bribery law. This trend is taking place in jurisdictions irrespective of either common or civil law tradition and in both developed and developing countries. For the limited purposes of our analysis we take the same definition the StAR (2013: 17) uses for settlement, as 'any procedure short of a full trial'. We refer to the same document for an updated and comprehensive overview of settlements practice by civil and common law countries that have been active in the fight against bribery.

24 See http://www.corriere.it/notizie-ultima-ora/Economia/Saipem-tribunale-prescrizione-manager-tangenti-Nigeria/05–04–2012/1-A_001371533.shtml.

dating to 2006 was reportedly ended in 2008 and handed over to the Frankfurt Public Prosecutor's Central Anti-Corruption Office in 2010. In March 2011 the Frankfurt office was reported to be examining allegations that the subsidiary had made payments to a political party in connection with the Bonny Island project.

- In Nigeria, besides the investigations of the House of Representatives (2004)[25] and of the Senate (2009), the Economic and Financial Crimes Commission (EFCC) arrested in 2010 23 executives, including ten employees of Halliburton Energy Services Nigeria Limited in Lagos and two employees from Saipem Contracting Nigeria (a subsidiary of an ENI subsidiary) and Technip Offshore Nigeria.[26] From December 2010, the federal government of Nigeria began settlement negotiations with TSKJ consortium's partners: Snamprogetti entered into a settlement and non-prosecution agreement, agreeing to a criminal penalty of US$32.5 million;[27] JGC Corp reached a settlement of US$28.5 million;[28] charges against Halliburton Co were dropped after an agreement was reached for a settlement of US$35 million.[29]

8.2.4 Systemic and Legal Issues

Crimes involving corruption schemes like the one at stake, if committed systemically (a sort of "kleptocracy"), drain a population of its national income thereby impeding the necessary investment in health, education and basic infrastructure. According to conservative estimates, every year through corruption between $20 billion and $40 billion is diverted from developing countries and finds safe haven in foreign jurisdictions.[30]

Typically, the foreign debt of such developing countries increases dramatically. In countries like Nigeria, the abundance of funds at the disposal of the ruling class stands in stark contrast to the poverty of up to 95 percent of the rest of the population.

---

25 Nigerian House of Representatives Petition Commission (2004); see Ogbu (2004).

26 See http://uk.reuters.com/article/2010/11/27/uk-nigeria-halliburton-idUKTRE6AQ1TA20101127.

27 See http://www.saipem.com/site/Home/Press/Corporate/articolo6034.html.

28 See http://www.templars-law.com/pages/posts/jgc-corp-reaches-us-28-million-settlement-112.php.

29 See http://www.iol.co.za/news/africa/halliburton-will-pay-nigeria-in-graft-case-1.1003951#.UAbejJFv2Ao.

30 See UNODC and World Bank (2007: 1).

Public looting often goes hand in hand with serious violation of human rights, including the illegitimate expropriation of assets belonging to political opponents or activists (the case of "Papa" or "Baby Doc" of Haiti).

In Bonny island the construction of the LNG facilities, devoid of any control by the national authorities, has brought about grave natural disasters with permanent consequences to the detriment of the local population.

Finally, it must be taken into account that poor nations often lack both the resources and a sufficient legal tradition to guarantee the independence of judges and other civil servants responsible for law enforcement. Under-enforcement of the law may therefore be chronic and often grave in such countries. In light of this consideration it is encouraging to point out that Nigeria is currently considered one of the developing countries which is most active in prosecuting domestic bribery by foreign companies.[31]

Coming to the main legal questions raised by cases such as the one just described:

A) With regard to the crucial issue concerning the enforcement of the 1997 Anti-bribery Convention (and the other international conventions against corruption) in different jurisdictions, given the increasingly transnational nature of contemporary corruption cases, the more countries implement and enforce the latter Convention, the more the "multiplicity of jurisdiction issue" will be relevant.

B) In this context, the complexity of the jurisdiction issue may be enhanced by additional factors, such as that the corruption scheme (i) operates through legal entities, which (ii) are formed by subsidiaries whose parent companies have multiple nationality, and which (iii) are established in tax havens to elude controls and better pursue the illicit scheme.

C) For these reasons, despite the US Department of Justice stating that "significant assistance was provided by authorities in France, Italy, Switzerland and the United Kingdom",[32] cooperation among enforcement authorities needs further support to ameliorate. Not only could prosecutorial resources and expertise be better focused and directed depending on the circumstances of the case at issue, but the whole system and all the actors – companies especially –

---

31 For an overview of recent cases and investigations by law enforcement authorities in Nigeria see Transparency International (2011b), pp. 73 ff.

32 As of June 2012, the most recent TSKJ settlement (January 2012), whose text is available at http://www.justice.gov/opa/pr/2012/January/12-crm-060.html.

could be guaranteed the fundamental principle of legal certainty. Furthermore, once greater cooperation is established, countries would have smaller room to exercise prosecutorial discretion (in the *TSKJ* case Japan and the Netherlands are notably absent from the list of jurisdictions which took action), and would thus be obliged to cooperate more actively with other Parties to the Convention. Finally, cooperation could facilitate the introduction of mechanisms to distribute monetary penalties collected from bribing companies to countries where enforcement is weak but the damages (social, environmental, economic) are greatest.

D) Considering that currently bribery is 'an international problem, but the law doesn't have an international solution for it', in carrying out investigations into companies, the conduct of which may be legally relevant in multiple jurisdictions,[33] a sound and effective coordination of the different national public prosecutors should be, thus, established, and the utmost respect for the international legal principle *ne bis in idem* should not be in question.

E) In this context the OECD Anti-bribery Convention (Article 4(3)) considers prosecutorial coordination and provides the following mechanism to implement it, despite it having never been invoked so far: When more than one party has jurisdiction over an alleged offense described in this convention, the parties involved shall, at the request of one of them, consult with a view to determining the most appropriate jurisdiction for prosecution.

F) If Parties to Anti-bribery Conventions will not improve the level of enforcement coordination, their effectiveness may be endangered: the phenomenon of "forum shopping" may neutralize the efforts of countries complying or trying to comply with Conventions.

G) The successful results of the subsequent prosecutions in different jurisdictions seem to provide a negative answer to the question of whether the principle of double jeopardy (as it is known in the common law countries) – or the *ne bis in idem* doctrine (as it is known,

---

[33] For instance under the US FCPA, companies the stocks of which are listed in the US Stock Exchange are also criminally liable. This is why the Italian *Snamprogetti* was prosecuted also in the US. The trend towards a growing transnational dimension of corruption seems not to slow down: a first reading of the last three TI's annual progress report on exporting corruption constitutes an impressive anecdotal evidence of such a trend: cases of transnational bribery in business transactions are reported for nearly every country which is part of the OECD Convention. See Transparency International (2011b), Transparency International (2012), Transparency International (2013).

in the civil law tradition)[34] – does substantiate a significant impediment to multiple prosecutions in different jurisdictions for offenses that are transnational in nature. Unless a fully international treaty is in force[35] or limitations in this sense exist as a consequence of countries' specific voluntary commitments codified in their domestic legislation or deriving from their basic legal principles, multiple prosecutions for transnational offenses are possible. There seems not to exist, indeed, 'any jurisprudence applying the principles in cases where prosecutions were pursued in multiple jurisdictions' (StaR, 2013: 59). Moreover, 'from a technical-legal perspective, the principle usually bars only subsequent criminal prosecutions, not subsequent civil or administrative sanctions' (ID.). In other words, in cases where a country pursues foreign bribery through the enforcement of administrative or civil sanctions, that activity falls outside the boundaries of the double jeopardy principle as understood in most jurisdictions.[36]

H) Finally, the United Nations Convention against Corruption's (UNCAC's)[37] provision on technical assistance to developing countries[38] has the potential to substantially improve the capability of

---

34 According to the principle at issue, in most legal systems, subjecting a suspect to criminal prosecution more than once for the same misconduct or offence is considered contrary to the principles of fairness and proportionality.

35 This is the case of the provisions contained in Articles 54–58 of the Convention implementing the Schengen Agreement, which require parties to refrain from multiple prosecutions for the same acts.

36 See StAR (2013: 59), adding: 'There are examples of subsequent prosecutions of the same companies in different jurisdictions for closely related offenses, including . . . the cases of BAE, Innospec, Siemens and Stanoil . . .'

37 United Nations Convention against Corruption (UNCAC), Doc. A/58/422, in 43 ILM 37 (entered into force on 14 December 2005). The Convention was adopted by the General Assembly of the United Nations on 31 October 2003 at the United Nations Headquarters in New York. It was open to all States for signature from 9 to 11 December 2003 in Merida, Mexico, and thereafter at the United Nations Headquarters in New York until 9 December 2005, in accordance with Article 67(1) of the Convention. As of November 2013, the Convention has been ratified by 168 States Parties. Countries that have ratified the Convention include Brazil, China, Egypt, France, Indonesia, Mexico, the Netherlands, Nigeria, Russia, South Africa, the United Kingdom, and the United States. Yet, it is a matter of serious concern that two major world economies, Germany and Japan, have failed to do so. For details of ratification and implementation status see http://www.unodc.org/unodc/crime_signatures_corruption.html. The text of the Convention is also available at: http://untreaty.un.org/english/notpubl/corruption_e.pdf.

38 Article 60(2) of the UNCAC reads: "States Parties shall, according to their capacity, consider affording one another the widest measure of technical assist-

dealing with such cases (on both the supply and the demand side of the corrupt operation, also at domestic level).

8.2.5 Lessons Learned

Paying bribes in doing business abroad has become a crime only recently in most countries of the world, and the current international legal framework would have been unexpected a decade ago. In this sense the odds that a company would be penalized for bribery violations in one country were slim; the odds that a company, or its executives, would be sanctioned by more than one country were even slimmer.

The TSKJ Consortium case represents one of the clearest examples of the current international capacity to prosecute international corruption: four out of the six largest FCPA monetary penalties have arisen out of this one matter (Cassin 2012). Notably, nine of the ten largest FCPA penalties assessed by the US government to date involve non-US companies.

Despite the necessary improvements in cooperation among prosecuting countries, the scenario arising from the TSKJ case seems to indirectly prove the accuracy of anti-corruption international treaties. In domestic jurisdictions, where transnational bribery has been established as a criminal offense for a long time, deterrence is high and, in all likelihood, judicial bodies and public prosecution are better equipped to cope with the crime.

From the perspective of developing countries which are not Parties of the OECD Anti-bribery Convention, asset recovery from grand corruption bribery would be a highly desirable tool: the UNCAC and World Bank Stolen Asset Recovery (StAR) mechanism might be, thus, coordinated with OECD Convention Working Group efforts to increase their effectiveness, although prosecuting corruption still relies heavily on national sovereignty and political will.

Finally, the international efforts against corruption may indirectly contribute to the creation of a widespread cultural patrimony and good practice in running international business. Such an ambitious target should be reached also through non-criminal sanctions, as required by international treaties. For instance, disqualification of future public procurement foreseen by most of the relevant national legal systems, or the

---

ance, especially for the benefit of developing countries, in their respective plans and programs to combat corruption, including material support and training in the areas referred to in paragraph 1 of this article, and training and assistance and the mutual exchange of relevant experience and specialized knowledge, which will facilitate international cooperation between States Parties in the areas of extradition and mutual legal assistance."

independent corporate monitor mechanism set up by US law (which, basically, limits and supervises future participation in international projects) can lead the companies involved to settle the case and cooperate with public prosecutors.

8.3 *CIR V. FININVEST* POLITICALLY INTERCONNECTED FIRMS (TAKING OVER THE MEDIA): THE ROLE OF CIVIL REMEDIES

Graft is not restricted to developing countries, even if impacts are felt far more acutely there. In the developed countries of the North, to say the least, debatable practices aimed at gaining control of key industries, or embezzlement of public funds, are also commonplace.

The motivation is often not so much personal gain, as the wish to generate covert means by which to buy the allegiance of political friends, or replenish empty party coffers. Even more dangerous for the virtuous functioning of modern democracies, taking control of key economic industries is a means of manipulating public opinion and building an artificial political consensus.

The case we are about to illustrate concerns the latter dynamics.

8.3.1 Factual Background

In the 1980s in Italy the head of the Mondadori publishing group was a holding company named AMEF, the principal shareholders of which were the CIR and Formenton Family (hereinafter: F).

In 1988 CIR and F, as principal shareholders of the holding company, signed a shareholder control agreement transferring F'S AMEF shares (27.75 percent) to CIR, which already owned 27.71 percent of the capital stock. The agreement included an arbitration clause.

After a corporate raid from Fininvest, which owned a minority of the shares in the holding company (8.28 percent), F sought to rescind the shareholder agreement with Ajax.

CIR initiated an arbitral proceeding according to the arbitration clause contained in the shareholder agreement and the arbitration panel ruled that there had been a breach of contract by F; thus the arbitral award ordered F to sell its stocks to CIR, according to the contract.

However, F appealed the arbitral award to the Rome Court of Appeal claiming that the award was null and void. The Court of Appeal ruled that the arbitral award, which ordered F to sell its stock to CIR, was contrary to the national public policy. As a result, Fininvest got control of AMEF.

Over the following years, Mondadori group kept on growing and took control of a substantial part of the national media.

The case was widely covered by the media because of the individuals involved – Fininvest belonged to the family of the prime minister of the national government – and the economic impact of the decision.

More than ten years after those events, a national criminal court convicted a number of persons involved in the Mondadori affair of the corruption of a Judge-Rapporteur of the Chamber of the Rome Court of Appeal that declared null and void the arbitral award. The criminal court found the judge guilty of having accepted a bribe in order to issue a decision that was favourable to F, and, indirectly, to the bribing parties.

For our purposes, we must note that not every person involved from the outset has been convicted for his act of corruption. In particular, the director of Fininvest was not tried after the end of the investigation, since the court had dismissed the case against him due to the expiry of the time limit of the relevant offence (Mariani 2013).

It is noteworthy that the national government, claiming to aim at stimulating more effective and faster criminal proceedings (according to the best practices promoted by international organizations) adopted a Bill which substantially reduced the statutes of limitation for several economic crimes, among them private to public corruption.

The net result was a substantial failure of the criminal response. Notably, the fact that international supervisory bodies in charge of monitoring the follow-up of the OECD Convention and the Council of Europe (COE) Treaties against corruption harshly criticized Italy for reducing the statutes of limitations of corruption offences has not substantially changed the criminal national legal framework thus far.

8.3.2 Civil Remedies

It is therefore worth considering the possibility of complementing the criminal enforcing mechanism with civil remedies, as required by the COE Civil Conventionon Corruption[39] and by the UNCAC. The final aim should be to design an optimal combined enforcing mechanism.

Turning back to the case at hand, it is no surprise that, given the above-mentioned deficiency of the criminal apparatus, in the aftermath of the criminal proceeding, CIR commenced a civil action to recover the damages resulting from the corruption of the judge.

---

39 Council of Europe Civil Law Convention on Corruption, April, 1999, EUROP. T.S. 127 (entered into force November 2003).

The resulting civil ruling stated some fundamental principles, which, as Mariani (2013) argues, suggest possible solutions to three of the critical legal issues standing in the way of the development of private enforcement:

1. The civil liability of the accused person found not guilty due to the expiry of the time limit.
2. The use of evidence collected in the criminal proceedings.
3. The quantification of corruption damages. According to the ruling the estimate of comprehensive monetary damage as a result of corruption takes into account the loss of profit: the compensation may cover material damages, loss of profits and non-pecuniary loss including the "loss of the opportunity" to benefit from a favorable judgment. The quantification of the latter fraction seems the most problematic issue, which may arguably be determined on a case by case basis, according to the civil principle inspiring the quantification of damages within the legal system at issue.

Section 5:

Horizontal assessment of international hard law instruments

9. The US FCPA as the archetype of supranational anti-bribery regulation

The emergence of the international framework regulating transnational bribery starts in the US with the 1977 Foreign Corrupt Practices Act (FCPA). Its key provisions criminalize the act of bribing foreign officials, and require that corporations keep fair and accurate books and records, and put in place an effective system of internal controls.

The FCPA represents the foundation upon which the subsequent international anti-corruption framework has been built, providing an original way of dealing with bribery across national boundaries and, hence, playing a pivotal role in shaping the corresponding international rules. It is beyond the scope of the present work to provide a comprehensive illustration of the FCPA. However, understanding the main features of the US FCPA (along with the case law which further delineated its contours) means understanding the underpinnings of the larger international anti-bribery scheme.

HISTORICAL BACKGROUND

The FCPA marked the end of a political (and moral) crisis triggered by the famed break-in at the US Democratic Party's National Committee offices on 17 June 1972 that led to the Watergate scandal.

The then Director of Enforcement at the Securities and Exchange Committee (SEC) initiated an investigation of undisclosed payments to domestic and foreign governments and politicians (Zarin 2012), while raising questions about how illegal political contributions made to President Nixon's re-election campaign were recorded by a publicly traded company. Further investigations revealed unreported campaign contributions. Under a voluntary disclosure program, over 400 corporations made disclosures of questionable or illegal payments of bribes and political contributions. Over 200 corporations, mostly Fortune 500 companies, admitted making questionable foreign payments, in total exceeding $300 million (Zarin 2012: § 1–1).[1]

A report by the SEC disclosed disconcerting levels of corruption, slush payments, and bribes paid by corporations to foreign public officials.[2] Lowell Brown (2003) and Makinwa (2007) stress that the position of SEC officials was that, since bribery is generally considered a crime, it would be virtually untenable for a corporation to admit in writing that it was engaging in such activities. In their view, exposing the situation would strategically stamp it out, and requiring the disclosure of all bribes paid would in effect foreclose the activity. This reasoning set the stage for the birth of the FCPA. The overwhelming moral outrage felt by the American public was echoed in the indignation felt by millions, especially in developing countries who lived in penury brought about in no small measure by the consequences of corruption, including transnational bribery.

LEGAL ASPECTS

The FCPA establishes criminal and civil penalties for illicit payments made to foreign officials by US corporations and individuals. It includes certain accounting requirements applicable to companies that have registered securities or that are required to file periodic reports with the SEC.

We now describe the features of the FCPA that have become the cornerstone of the international anti-bribery scheme, namely: (1) its scope of application, (2) the subjects which may be prosecuted under the Act, (3) the jurisdictional criteria, (4) the application of the Act to parent companies of foreign subsidiaries, and (5) the existence of a private right of action for those harmed by the violation of its provisions.

1) Firstly, there is a clear commercial context for the application of FCPA rules. The FCPA makes it unlawful for a person to whom it

---

1 Foreign Corrupt Practices and Domestic Foreign Investment Disclosure: Hearings on S. 305 Before the Senate Commission on Banking, Housing, and Urban Affairs, 95th Cong., 1st Sess. 116–18 (1977) (statement of Roderick M. Hills, Chairman of the SEC); Unlawful Corporate Payments Act of 1977: Hearings Before the Subcommission on Consumer Protection and Finance of the House Commission on Interstate and Foreign Commerce, 95th Cong., 1st Sess. 1 (1977) (hereinafter: "1977 House Hearing").

2 Report of the Securities and Exchange Commission on Questionable and Illegal Corporate Payments and Practices, 12 May, reprinted in Sec. Reg L. Rep. (BNA), No. 353, Special Supp. (19 May 1876) (hereinafter "1976 SEC Report").

applies to seek to give a bribe with the intent of inducing a person to do or omit to do an act or to use his or her influence with a foreign government to influence any act or decision of such government so as to assist such a person "in obtaining or retaining business".[3] The FCPA applies only to transactions that fall within this scope. The somewhat ambiguous language of the FCPA prohibition has led to some debate. Narrowly interpreted, the FCPA would apply only to payments that are made in order to obtain a foreign official's approval of a bid for a new government contract or the renewal of an existing government contract. The wider interpretation is that the FCPA covers payments that indirectly help the person offering the bribe to obtain or retain foreign business. The recent ruling of the US Appeals Courts in *United States v. David Kay and Douglas Murphy* definitely opts for a wider interpretation.[4]

The former chief executive officer of American Rice Inc. was charged with violating the FCPA by paying bribes to Haitian customs officials to accept false bills of lading and other importation documents so as to obtain lower custom duties. The question was whether these payments to foreign officials in order to reduce the custom duties and sales taxes a company owed the Haitian government were payments to "assist" the company in "obtaining or retaining business" within the meaning of the FCPA. The Court of Appeal held that "Congress meant to prohibit a range of payments *wider than only those that directly influence the acquisition or retention of government contracts* or similar commercial or industrial arrangements" (p. 22, emphasis added). The Court also maintained that "Congress intended that the FCPA prohibit *all* illicit payments that are intended to influence non-trivial official foreign action in an effort to aid in obtaining or retaining business" (p. 5). According to this position, any act that assists directly or indirectly in the obtaining or retaining of business will come within the purview of the FCPA. This broad standard effectively covers any inducement that affects the decision-making process regarding a business opportunity in favor of the person offering the inducement.

Secondly, not all payments to foreign officials qualify as bribes (Zarin 2012: § 4–1). The FCPA focuses essentially on transnational bribes that represent a significant attempt to influence the outcome

---

3 15 USCA §§ 78dd–1(a); 78dd–2(a); 78dd–3(a).

4 See *United States v. David Kay and Douglas Murphy S.D. Tex.* 2001, available at: http://www.usdoj.gov/criminal/fraud/fcpa/cta5opn.pdf.

of a business transaction. What matters is not the sum of the bribe but rather its purpose: that is, whether the bribe is given to influence the decision-making process regarding a business opportunity or not. Salbu (1997) argues that this reading seems consistent to a certain degree with the distinction between petty and grand corruption, which may also to some extent coincide with the distinction in the FCPA between facilitating payments and bribes. Therefore, in general it can be said that the FCPA rules apply to *grand as opposed to petty corruption*. The FCPA thus exempts from its application any facilitating payment by a person (to whom the Act applies) to a foreign official, political party, and party official to expedite or secure the performance of a routine governmental action. Thus, such "grease" or "facilitating" payments to expedite or secure non-discretionary routine government action by a foreign official do not fall within the category of unlawful payments.[5] The FCPA also excludes payments that are "lawful under the written laws and regulations of the foreign official's, political party's, party official's or candidate's country".[6] A third group of excepted payments are those reasonable bona fide expenditures, such as travel and lodging expenses incurred on behalf of a foreign official. To avoid transnational bribes disguised as reasonable expenditure, such expenses must truly be "reasonable". Excessive travel and lodging expenses, for example, may trigger an FCPA violation. In sum, the FCPA provides for an exception (related to facilitating and expediting payment to a foreign official, political party, etc.) to the general rule and establishes two affirmative defenses (i.e. for payment, gift, or promise of anything of value: (i) the payment made was lawful under the written laws and regulations of the foreign official's, political party's, or candidate's country; and (ii) provided that such payments are a reasonable and bona fide expenditure such as travel and lodging.)

---

5 15 USCA §§ 78dd–1(b), 78dd–2(b)), 78dd–3(b). With reference to § 78dd–1(b), the term "routine governmental action" is defined as: an action which is ordinarily and commonly performed by a foreign official in – (i) obtaining permits, licenses, or other documents to qualify a person to do business in a foreign country; (ii) processing government papers, such as visas and work orders; (iii) providing police protection, mail pick-up and delivery, or scheduling inspections associated with contract performance, or inspections related to transit of goods across country; (iv) providing phone services, power and water supply, loading and unloading cargo, or protecting perishable products or commodities from deterioration; or (v) actions of a similar nature.

6 15 USCA §§ 78dd–1I(1), 78 dd–2I(1), 78 dd–3I(1).

2) As to the subjective scope of application, when the FCPA was first passed it applied to US issuers or persons. In 1998, amendments to the FCPA extended its provisions to "any person" that committed an act of transnational bribery while on US territory.[7] The 2002 case of *US v. Syncor Taiwan* demonstrates how this "any person" provision can be used to extend FCPA rules to foreign subsidiaries. The SEC alleged that Syncor International's foreign subsidiaries in Taiwan, Mexico, Belgium, Luxembourg, and France gave about $600,000 in bribes to doctors employed by hospitals controlled by foreign authorities so as to use these illicit payments to influence the doctors' decisions in favor of business opportunities for Syncor. The SEC alleged that cash payments were found to have been authorized by the chairman of the board of Syncor Taiwan while he was traveling in the US. By using the 1998 amendments, the SEC founded jurisdiction on the new section 78dd-3 of the FCPA. Syncor Taiwan pleaded guilty to the charge and agreed to pay a $2 million criminal fine.[8] Noticeably, US nationals and any individual who engages in an act of transnational bribery while on US territory comes within the scope of application of the FCPA. For instance, in a recent case four former ABB employees were accused of offering, approving, and paying bribes to Nigerian officials. They were suspected of using wire transfers in the US to help secure a $180 million contract to provide equipment for an oil drilling project in Nigeria's offshore Bonga Oil Field. The former employees agreed to settle the charges without admitting or denying the allegation.[9]
3) The goal of tackling effectively transnational corruption largely relies on a wide jurisdictional basis. The FCPA properly serves the scope by extending the reach of domestic anti-corruption laws beyond national borders. In 1998, amendments to the Act provided jurisdiction based on nationality. These amendments are of primary importance, as they make unnecessary any territorial link between the act violating

---

7 Foreign Corrupt Practices Act of 1977, 15 USC, as amended by the International Anti-Bribery and Fair Competition Act of 1998, Pub. L. No. 105–366, signed on 10 November 1998. This Act added a new § 78dd – 3 to Title I of the Foreign Corrupt Practices Act of 1977. For a comprehensive illustration of the main issues related to the enforcement of the FCPA we refer the reader to Criminal Division of the U.S. DOJ and Enforcement Division of the U.S. SEC (2012).

8 *US v. Syncor Taiwan, Inc.* No. 02-CR-1244-ALL (C.D. Cal.)

9 *SEC v. John Samson, John G. A. Munro, Ian N. Campbell, and John H. Whelan*, Civil Action No. 06 CV 01217(D.D.C.) available at: http://sec.gov/litigation/complaints/2006/comp19754.pdf.

the FCPA and the US, meaning that any US national involved in transnational bribery anywhere would be subject to the penalties of the FCPA regardless of the country in which the act took place.

4) Under the FCPA, no less important is the liability of the parent company of foreign subsidiaries through which a transnational corrupt operation is perpetrated. The manifest rationale of this provision lies in the circumstance that many corporations operate through subsidiaries abroad. According to the Act, the foreign subsidiary of an "issuer" will not come within the purview of the FCPA when the act on furtherance of a bribe does not take place on US soil. However, the parent company may well be liable for the acts of the subsidiary when it can be established that the parent company or its employees authorized, directed, or controlled the activity in question. It is noteworthy that the FCPA also holds parent companies responsible for ensuring that the accounting books and records of foreign subsidiaries comply with FCPA requirements.[10] In the 2003 case of *SEC v. Schering–Plough Corporation*,[11] for example, the corporation was found liable for violations of the FCPA books and records and internal controls provisions resulting from the actions of its Polish subsidiary. The SEC alleged that the internal controls of the parent company had been inadequate to prevent or detect the payment of donations to a charity headed by a government official. Those donations were allegedly made to induce this government official to purchase Schering–Plough pharmaceutical products for his constituency's health fund. Schering-Plough did not admit or deny its liability but agreed to pay a $500,000 civil penalty in settling the claim.[12]

5) Coming to *private enforcement*, which may demonstrably play a key role in contrasting corruption, prior to 1991 it was unclear whether a private right of action could be implied from the substantive provisions of the FCPA. The basis of the controversy was an implication doctrine that the Supreme Court announced in 1916 in *Texas & Pacific Railway v. Rigsby*.[13] On this occasion the US Supreme Court held that a private right of action was implied in a statute designed to protect a certain class of persons where the violation harms such persons.[14]

---

10 USCA Title 15. Section 78m(b)(2).

11 *SEC v. Schering-Plough Corporation*, Case No. 1:04CV00945 (PLF) (D.D.C.) (9 June 2004). Available at: http://www.sec.gov/litigation/complaints/comp18330.htm.

12 SEC Litigation Release No. 18740 (9 June 2004).

13 Case *Texas & Pacific Railway v. Rigsby*, 241 US 33 (1916).

14 *Texas & Pacific Railway v. Rigsby* at 39–40.

> Eventually, however, the Court modified this proposition. By the time the issue of private rights of action was raised under the FCPA, Congressional intent was looked at as the most significant factor in determining whether a private right of action was implied by a statute.[15] Since they had been unable to find a Congressional intent to grant a private right of action, US courts of appeals consistently held that the FCPA did not give rise to such a right.[16] The Supreme Court denied *certiorari* on this issue, thereby effectively settling the law.[17]

Regarding FCPA *sanctions*, it is worth remarking that the legal and commercial consequences of a violation of the FCPA can be serious. For example, an indictment under the FCPA can result in the immediate suspension of export licensing privileges for military defense items (Aronoff 1994), or suspension from the award of US government procurement. Of course, these sanctions do not exclude the application of serious criminal fines or penalties resulting from settlements. In 2008 Siemens AG agreed to pay a total criminal fine of $450 million to the DOJ and $350 million to the SEC, for a combined record fine of $800 million. Other recent enforcement actions imposing relevant penalties include the agreement by Kellog Brown & Root LLC to pay $579 million in penalties and fines to the DOJ and the SEC for bribes paid through the TSKJ consortium to Nigerian government officials for a procurement contract.

To conclude on the US legislation, we would like to stress the potential of the new *whistleblower* provision contained in the Wall Street Reform and Consumer Protection Act, which was signed into law by President Obama on 23 July 2010.[18] Under the new law, a whistleblower who provides information to the SEC regarding a violation of the anti-bribery, books and records, or internal control provisions of the FCPA by a public company will receive an award of between 10 and 30 percent of the amount of the monetary penalty imposed by the SEC and the DOJ that results in monetary sanctions exceeding $1 million. As Zarin (2012: § 1–9)

---

15 This position was held, for instance, in *Cannon v. University of Chicago*, 441 US 677, 688–709 (1979); *Touche Ross & Co. v. Redington*, 422 US 560, 578 (1979).

16 See e.g. *Lamb v. Philip Morris*, Inc., 915 F.2d 1024, 1028–9 (6th Cir. 1990); *McLean v. Int'l Harvester Co.*, 817 F.2d 1214 (5th Cir. 1987).

17 *Lamb v. Philip Morris*, 498 US 1086 (1991). We owe the core of this meticulous case law report to Makinwa (2007).

18 Dodd-Frank Wall Street Reform and Consumer Protection Act, Pub. L. No. 111–203, § 922 (2010). Note that the whistleblower provision applies broadly to violations of the securities law by public companies.

points out, "this new provision increases the likelihood that information regarding improper payments will come to the attention of the SEC".

With the enactment of the FCPA, the United States became the first country to criminalize supply-side corruption. The international context of the Act meant that this standard would have to exist within the dynamics of multi-jurisdictional transactions.

The imposition of this standard on American companies gave them a clear handicap compared with competing companies to whom no such standard applied. For about 25 years, the FCPA stood alone. The standards it proclaimed applied only to American companies. The fact that only the US had rules prohibiting transnational bribery on its books arguably placed it at a competitive disadvantage in the global marketplace. Undersecretary of State Stuart Eizenstat is reported to have stated that US businesses lost contracts worth $30 billion from mid-1997 to mid-1998 because of corruption. The question was ultimately whether this American standard would become a universal standard or whether, in the face of business practice realities, the Americans would reconsider their standards to conform with those in the marketplace. Other countries had no rules against the bribery of foreign officials and, in several countries, Millet-Eindinber (2000) claims that quite astonishingly bribery of foreign public officials was in fact a tax-deductible expense.

With these trade concerns, the US started an international effort to redress the situation, consulted its usual allies and proposed to take coordinated, international action against international bribery. Initially, Germany, France, and other countries fervently opposed outlawing international bribery. After the adoption of the FCPA, the Reagan and Bush senior's administrations engaged in stimulating international *hard law* instruments against corruption, but the objections of some European governments seemed to persist. It was not until President Clinton took office in 1993 that the issue became a priority of the executive branch. The Departments of State, Commerce, and Treasury joined efforts to persuade the governments of European countries and Japan to support the proposals of US diplomats in several international organizations and institutions. These first efforts were supported by the newly organized Transparency International and by the press and public opinion in the wake of new corruption scandals in Europe.

10. The emergence of an international framework: regional, international, and multilateral treaties and initiatives

10.1 GENERAL OBSTACLES TO HARMONIZATION

Approximately a quarter of century after the adoption of the FCPA, there now exists a substantial and evolving array of international conventions to combat bribery.[1] The emergence of common international legal standards stands as one of the essential pillars for a long-term anti-corruption policy. In this respect, the Chief of Crime Conventions Section of the United Nations Office on Drugs and Crime (UNODC) maintains that:

> the gradual understanding of both the scope and seriousness of the problem of corruption can be seen in the evolution of international action against it, which has progressed from general consideration and declarative statements, to the formulation of practical advice, and then to the development of binding legal obligations and the emergence of numerous cases in which countries have sought assistance from other countries in investigating and prosecuting corruption and in tracing, freezing, confiscating and recovering proceeds of corruption offences. (Vlassis, 2007: 17)

The cases illustrated in Chapter 8, along with dozens of recent ones that have emerged worldwide, clearly testify to the need for the coordinated

---

1 See also Passas (2007: 10): "Corruption is neither a new phenomenon nor confined to particular international determination to act effectively against this scourge, which undermines political stability, sabotages development, distorts competition, violates the rule of law, maintains structures of inequality and poverty, and adds to other sources of insecurity, unfairness and injustice. In the last two decades, the world has witnessed many initiatives against corruption and its negative effects on governments, businesses and society at large. The growing anti-corruption momentum is supported by strong popular feelings, the recognition that corruption is connected with other important issues of public policy and a denser globalization process, whereby actions in one part of the planet have both local and international effects."

international action against corruption just sketched out. The call for such efforts plainly constitutes the basic assumption of the present part of our work.

A word of caution: an international common standard does not imply immediate and harmonized developments in national laws. The obstacles to such harmonization should be explained before entering into an analysis of the contents of any treaties. First, the anti-bribery conventions constitute the minimum common denominator and States can go and have gone further when adapting the offenses to their domestic reality. Once implemented in the diverse national contexts their inherent goal of harmonizing/approximating domestic pieces of legislation may happen to clash with the legal and institutional tradition of each State, especially when substantial changes to realms of which States are traditionally jealous (e.g. criminal law) come into play. This is the reason why we deem that accurate systems of follow-up are central to the actual implementation of such instruments. Furthermore, as aptly remarked by Schroth (2005a), some elements of the international apparatus against corruption might happen to cause an interface of long-term rights and short-term objectives in the context of accession and, subsequently, implementation of the international agreements. This is because the process of *constitutionalization* and political development of each State is somewhat unique. In the area of anti-corruption legislation it is hardly possible to prescribe a fixed order between long-term and short-term objectives – essentially, the aggressive use of criminal law to eradicate corruption on one side of the pendulum, and, on the other, a certain safeguarding of primary freedoms, human rights (e.g. the presumption of innocence), which were crystallized in the constitutional law of many countries long ago, but in many others are still in the need of firm establishment through the uncompleted process of development of democracy and constitutional law. Thus, the international stimulus ends up having dissimilar effects within national jurisdictions because of a central obstacle to constitutionalism (to be intended as in Schroth (2005: 1–2) as "the practical entrenchment of fundamental rights and freedoms, which are characteristically for the short term, in the context of functional democracy, which is characteristically for the long term"): the asynchrony of political developments. This may not infrequently result in fairly fruitless pieces of national legislation. Also, accepting that constitutionalism is inherently an open-ended process, the different stages of its life within single States should have been better taken into account when drafting some of the international anti-corruption treaties. To us, this is why some regional anti-bribery treaties, although more limited in scope, have performed relatively better (at least over the short run) in mending national legal systems' critical deficiencies.[2]

10.2 TREATIES AND OTHER INITIATIVES

(1) The trend towards international binding treaties began with a Latin American regional convention in 1996;
(2) encompassed the major capital-exporting countries with the OECD Convention of 1997;
(3) grew in regional extent with the adoption of one Convention promoted by the EU and two Conventions under the auspices of the Council of Europe: the EU Convention in the late 1990s and the Council of Europe Criminal Law and Civil Law Convention in the early 2000s.
(4) Continued with the AU Convention in 2003. Although rapid and important, regional developments have remained a patchwork;
(5) on the heels of the United Nations Convention against Transnational Organized Crime (UNCTOC),[3] which includes a number of anti-corruption provisions;
(6) in late 2000 the UN commenced negotiations for a global convention focused predominantly on the issue of corruption. After the conclusion of the preparatory work in 2001, negotiations started in early 2002, and the United Nations Convention against Corruption (UNCAC) was signed by 95 States at the conference of Merida, Mexico, in December 2003. At the time of finalizing the present work, the UNCAC celebrates its 10th anniversary. It now counts 168

---

[2] It is not by chance that the evolution of the international action against corruption has "(. . .) progressed from regional instruments developed by groups of relatively like-minded countries such as the Organization of American States, the African Union (. . .), the OECD, and the Council of Europe to the global United Nations Convention?" (Vlassis, 2007: 17–18).

[3] The United Nations Convention against Transnational Organized Crime, adopted by the General Assembly in its resolution 55/25 of 15 November 2000 and opened for signature in Palermo, Italy, from 12 to 15 December 2000, in 40 ILM 353 (entered into force 29 September 2003). As of Thursday 31 July 2008 the Convention has been ratified by 144 countries, including China, the European Community, France, Germany, the Netherlands, Nigeria, Russia, South Africa, the United Kingdom and the United States. Notable exceptions are India, Indonesia, Ireland, Japan, Pakistan, Singapore and Switzerland. For details of ratification and implementation status see http://www.unodc.org/unodc/crime_cicp_signatures_convention.html.

State Parties with two notable absences: Germany and Japan. They are the only G20 countries that have not yet followed the G20 commitment[4] to ratify the UNCAC;

(7) initiatives of the IFIs.

10.2.1 Descriptions and Issues

(1) OAS Convention

The first of these treaties was the Inter-American Convention against Corruption of the Organization of American States (OAS Convention).[5] Nineteen years after the FCPA, it was the first binding international convention aimed at combating corruption. On 29 March 1996, a specialized conference of 34 Member States of the OAS adopted the OAS Convention, which entered into force on 6 March 1997. As of October 2013, it counts 33 ratifications and, according to its Article XXIII, is open also to countries which are not OAS members.

The initiative for the Convention came from a group of Latin American governments led by Venezuela, and was strongly supported by the US. With the deposit of Brazil's instrument of notification on 24 July 2002, the OAS Convention covered the US, Canada, and all the major economies in South America. A distinctive features of the OAS Convention is that it includes developed countries, some countries "in the middle range", and some poor developing countries.

Notably, the OAS Convention does not make accession conditional on any particular requirements and it is the only anti-corruption instrument, which expressly links corruption with the proceeds of illicit narcotics trafficking.

The Treaty was designed with three major objectives: (1) preventing corrupt practices, (2) criminalizing and punishing corrupt practices, and (3) ensuring international cooperation in enforcement efforts.

Its scope is rather broad. In contrast to an earlier draft, it goes beyond

---

4 See www.g20.org/load/781360452.

5 Inter-American Convention Against Corruption (OAS Convention), 29 March 1996, 35 ILM (1996) 724. Adopted at Caracas, Venezuela. Entered into force on 6 March 1997. As of August 2008, 33 countries have ratified or accessed the Convention. These are Argentina, Antigua and Barbuda, Bahamas, Belize, Bolivia, Brazil, Canada, Chile, Colombia, Costa Rica, Dominica, Dominican Republic, Ecuador, El Salvador, Grenada, Guatemala, Guyana, Haiti, Honduras, Jamaica, Mexico, Nicaragua, Panama, Paraguay, Peru, St. Kitts and Nevis, St. Lucia, Saint Vincent and Grenadines, Suriname, Trinidad and Tobago, United States, Uruguay and Venezuela. For details of ratification and implementation status see http://www.oas.org/juridico/english/Sigs/b-58.html.

a mere multilateral treaty on extradition and mutual legal assistance. This seems to be the result of "a compromise" between the Latin American interest in mutual legal assistance and the North American agenda on criminalizing active transnational bribery (Pieth 1997).

It also applies a broad notion of bribery: in addition to addressing the supply side of corruption, it calls for the State Parties to address the demand side of corruption. A fair appraisal of such instruments cannot leave out the wide scope for making reservations allowed to Contracting Parties. Article XXIV provides Contracting Parties, at the time of adoption, signature, or ratification with the possibility of making reservations to the Convention, provided that, consistent with the general law regulating reservations, each reservation concerns one or more specific provisions and is not incompatible with the object and purpose of the Convention.

(2) OECD Convention

The momentum then moved to the industrialized West. Following several years of work on transnational corruption issues by various OECD bodies, on 17 December 1997, 28 Member States of the OECD and five non-Member States with the status of observers to its Working Group on Bribery (WGB)[6] in International Business Transactions (Argentina, Brazil, Bulgaria, Chile, and the Slovak Republic) signed the Convention on Combating Bribery of Foreign Public Officials in International Business Transactions (OECD Convention).

Institutionally, the OECD approach is grounded on the following documents. First of all, the Revised Recommendation of the Council against Bribery of May 1997,[7] a soft law instrument containing both repressive and preventive measures which defined the steps to be taken by the State Parties in such a concrete manner that some members felt the most sensitive issues (criminal law and book-keeping rules) needed to be incorporated into a legally hard law (and thus legally binding) instruments. The approach – which had already characterized the three Recommendations of 1994 and 1997, which paved the way for the multilateral treaty under

---

6 Note that The OECD and the Working Group on Bribery (WGB) – as of June 2013, made up of the 34 OECD Member countries plus Argentina, Brazil, Bulgaria and South Africa – have made significant efforts over the past year in reaching out to emerging economies that are not Parties to the Anti-Bribery Convention.

7 Organisation for Economic Co-operation and Development, Revised Recommendation of the Council on Combating Bribery in International Business Transactions, adopted by the Council on 23 May 1997, available at: www.oecd.org, accessed on 10 October 2007.

discussion – is explicitly supply-side oriented, intending to materially reduce the inflow of corruption payments into relevant markets by sanctioning active bribers and their accomplices. This approach is unilateral – or collectively unilateral as classified by Pieth (2007) – since it depends on another action being taken on the demand side at national level; hence, it allows the OECD not to encroach on other countries' sovereignty, being the behavior of foreign public officials outside the scope of the Convention. Nonetheless, the progress it represents has been an innovative step ahead for the development of international action against commercial and business corruption since the main industrialized countries, home to most multinational firms, bound themselves to prevent and repress bribery by their companies, by criminalizing active bribery of other countries' public agents, whether those countries are signatories of the Convention or not.

It is noteworthy that the signatories of the Convention have agreed to put in place new measures that will reinforce their efforts to prevent, detect and investigate foreign bribery with the adoption of the 2009 OECD Recommendation for Further Combating Bribery of Foreign Public Officials in International Business Transactions.[8] The new Recommendation includes also Good Practice Guidance on Internal Controls, Ethics and Compliance, calling on businesses to:

- adopt a clear and visible anti-bribery policy that is strongly supported by senior management;
- instill a sense of responsibility for compliance with the policy at all levels of the company, as well as independent compliance structures;
- keep up regular communication and training on foreign bribery for all employees, as well as with business partners; and
- encourage observance of anti-bribery compliance measures, and disciplinary procedures to address their violations.

The OECD Convention is plainly influenced by the fair trade approach adopted by the US. One of the prevailing aims is to assure a "level playing field", that is to say common rules for companies of different origins in international markets, as stated in its Preamble. As its name implies, this Convention addresses exclusively the issue of transnational bribery (*recte*: bribery of foreign or international public officials in transnational business transactions).

---

8 See http://www.oecd.org/document/13/0,3746,en_2649_34859_39884109_1_1_1_1,00.html.

The text of the OECD Convention is short and synthetic, a distinguishing feature if compared to the other multilateral conventions on the matter. It consists of only 17 articles covering the offenses of transnational bribery, ancillary or related offenses, jurisdiction and penalties, international cooperation in the investigation and prosecution of transnational bribery, a process for monitoring implementation, and entry into force, reservations and implementation.

It is accompanied by official Commentaries that expand on the text. As to the legal nature of the Commentaries, they do not form part of the OECD Convention and have not been signed. Moreover, they do not have an organic structure as do, for instance, the Explanatory Reports of the Council of Europe Criminal Law Convention on Corruption, and they are related only to certain articles and/or single clauses of the OECD Convention. Thus, the weight of the Commentaries is debatable. We deem they are not to be considered as preparatory work and, hence, supplementary means of interpretation to which "recourse may be had . . . in order to confirm the meaning resulting from the application of . . ." the general rules of interpretation "or to determine the meaning when the interpretation according to those rules: (a) leaves the meaning ambiguous or obscure; or (b) leads to a result which is manifestly absurd or unreasonable" (*ex* Article 32 of the 1969 Vienna Convention on the Law of the Treaties ('VCLT'). which codified customary law in this area).[9]

Rather, they should be looked at as elements of the context of the Convention, which have to be considered "for the purpose of the interpretation of a treaty . . . in addition to the text . . . upon the conclusion of the Treaty", *ex* Article 31(2) of the above-mentioned Vienna Convention. Thus, in our opinion the interpretative weight of the Commentaries is to be found in Article 31(2)(b) of the VCLT. They present the necessary element of connection with the OECD Convention. In addition, their implicit prominence has always been accepted by both the WGB and the State Parties of the OECD Convention. The Commentaries, thus, belong to those additional means for the interpretation of the treaty "which are defined as part of the context", serve together with means of para.1 of the same Article of the VCLT "to establish the meaning of a particular treaty term", and ". . . can only be invoked if all the parties to the treaty have been involved in the interpretation of a particular meaning of the treaty

---

9 United Nations, Vienna Convention on the Law of the Treaties, done at Vienna on 23 May 1969. Entered into force on 27 January 1980. United Nations, Treaty Series, vol. 1155, 331.

term by means of an agreement (. . .); or if one or more parties have been invoked by means of an instrument (. . .) or subsequent practice (. . .) to which the other parties have agreed" (Villinger, 2009: 429).[10]

The OECD Convention follows the classical model of penal law conventions, such as those of the Council of Europe, in that it defines the offenses (Articles 1 and 7), the jurisdictional basis (Article 4), the secondary rules and the means of mutual cooperation between the Contracting States in matters of assistance and extradition (respectively, Arts. 9 and 10).

Nonetheless, the OECD Convention distances itself from this model in other respects. First, the most relevant of its norms are not self-executing. For instance, the provision providing the criminalization of the corruption of foreign public officials (Article 1) generally requires reformulation for introduction into the criminal legal systems of the State Parties. Similarly, provisions on the extent and kind of sanctions (Article 3), jurisdictional bases (Article 4), and statutes of limitations (Article 6) receive no exhaustive formulation, but rather designate the minimal contents for the implementing national laws.

The method used by the Negotiated Conference, stated in the Preamble, and then, more specifically in Official Commentary 2, is termed "functional equivalence". This method was borrowed from comparative law and developed further. Firstly, the signatories are allowed to fulfill their obligations by having recourse to different measures depending on their legislative structures and principles, on the strict condition that they satisfactorily attain the prescribed result. This approach posits that each legal system has its own logic, which does not result necessarily in formal legal statutes: Pieth (2007) asserts that only a comprehensive appraisal of the law in operation including informal rules and practices as well as functions assumed by other legal institutions, allows the WGB to assess whether the overall legal effects produced by a country's legal system adequately meet the requirements of the Convention. Secondly, the Convention also includes non-criminal provisions, aiming at both transparency and prevention, in that they specify requirements for corporate accounting and

---

10 Subparagraph 2(b) of Art.31 of the VCLT refers, in particular, as a further means of interpretation to any instrument which was made by one or more parties in connection with the conclusion of the treaty. As a particular condition, the other parties must have accepted the instrument as an instrument related to the treaty. "Final acts of a conference and explanatory reports would fall to be considered under subparagraph 2(b) if prepared by governmental experts would fall to be considered under subpara. 2(b), if prepared by governmental experts", (Villinger, 2009: 430), which appears clearly the case of the OECD Convention Commentaries.

auditing. Thirdly, Article 12 confers a multilateral supervisory role on the WGB, which replaces the dispute settlement procedures frequently envisaged by multilateral penal treaties. Against this background, the WGB is called on to promote and monitor full implementation of the Convention through periodic examinations of the measures adopted by parties and their concrete and effective applications.

The (semi-)openness of the OECD Convention is problematic and requires some detailed comments. Bonucci (2007b) argues that Article 13 on Signature and Accession is one of the most peculiar provisions as, in conjunction with Official Commentary 37, it sets out a pretty unique mechanism in international law. We add that, despite the apparent clarity of the provision, this mechanism is deeply influenced by the membership requirements of accession to the OECD and might happen to challenge wide participation in the Convention and hinder its funding economic rationale. Paragraphs 1 and 2 of Article 2 address two distinct factual situations in a rather similar fashion. Paragraph 1 regulates the accession to the Convention of a country prior to the entry into force of the Convention, whereas Paragraph 2 deals with the accession of a country once the Convention has entered into force. The criteria set out by both paragraphs are the same: in order to accede to the Convention the requesting State either has to be an OECD member or a "full participant" in the WGB. This provision should be read in conjunction with Article 12(c) of the Convention establishing the OECD in 1960, which indicates that the Organization may invite non-member governments or organizations to participate in activities of the Organization. Article 13 of the 1997 OECD Convention mirrors the hybrid character of the Convention: formally detached from the OECD but, actually, intrinsically linked to it. It is thus an expression of the semi-open nature of the Convention. On the one hand, any country is in principle entitled to become a Party to the Convention, whereas, on the other hand, this is not really the case. The provisions under discussion established rather strict requirements in order to become a Party to the Convention. Even though the OECD Convention remains a fully-fledged international treaty, the close link to the OECD is, however, acknowledged by providing that any OECD member can become party to the Convention and establishing precise requirements for non-members of the OECD willing to adhere to the Treaty, and, consequently, get full participation to the WGB. These requirements generally aim at ensuring a certain homogeneity of economic features and inclinations. Naturally, according to the customary principle of sovereignty of States, no OECD member is bound to become a State Party.

In order to detail the peculiar regime involved in becoming part of the OECD Convention, Bonucci (2007b) distinguishes between the position of existing members, future members, and non-members. All current OECD members, except for Slovakia – which was, however, a full participant in the WGB – were already members at the time of the entry into force of the Convention. Thus, they were all entitled to become parties to the Convention. This was also a logical step given that only a few months before the adoption of the Convention, the same countries had adopted the 1997 Revised Recommendation, which included a directive to open negotiation promptly on an international convention to criminalize bribery. Whereas there was no legal obligation to do so, all OECD members felt compelled to become parties to the Convention. As to the position of future OECD members, Article 13 does not distinguish between current and future members of the OECD. Therefore, any country which joins the Organization is entitled, irrespective of its size and share of world exports, to adhere to the Anti-bribery Convention.

Notwithstanding the above, there could be a material difference in the position of current and future members as an indirect result of the OECD Council policy regarding future accession. In contrast to other international governmental organizations, accession to the OECD is not direct upon request. Pursuant to Article 16 of the Convention establishing the OECD, accessions to the organization require unanimous agreement of all OECD members. Moreover, negotiation for accession can begin only once the OECD Council issues a formal invitation to this effect and takes place upon the terms and conditions set out by the Council. The latter point is central, bestowing on the Council complete discretion in deciding on the substantive commitments a candidate must make in order to access to the OECD. Once negotiations on future membership are launched, the OECD Council might, thus, decide that the accession to the Convention against bribery is part of the "OECD *acquis*" and that, to become an OECD member, the candidate country must also become a party to the Convention. Were the Council to follow this course of action, future members would not have the option of not adhering to the Convention. As a consequence, any enlargement of the OECD would have an impact on the Convention, especially where the membership is conditioned upon participation in the Convention.

It can also be asserted that participation in the Convention may in turn have some consequences for OECD membership: the very fact of being a full participant in the WGB might favor deeper cooperation with participants and/or signatories of the Convention which presently are not OECD members. For instance, some of the State Parties to the Convention but non-members of the Organization, namely Chile, Estonia, and Slovenia, have lately been invited to open discussions with a view to join the OECD.

This latter remark leads us finally to address the enlargement of the

Convention to non-OECD members. The issue is far from simple. We recall that the OECD Convention (along with its vigorous and thorough peer-review monitoring system) is restricted to the contractual relationship between the current 39 States parties to the Convention. This has created a sort of two-tier system where some international players have an organized framework within which to engage in the fight against corruption, whilst major emerging economies, committed to such a fight, remain without any effective support and coordination system. If the effectiveness of some existing anti-corruption domestic laws among the main emerging economies is arguably debatable, OECD members that have ratified the Convention have a manifest interest in widening the participation of emerging economies to the Convention. The same fair trade rationale of the OECD Convention is doomed to be an empty spot without the active engagement of those major emerging economies, which are still not part of the OECD Convention. [11]

Therefore, enhancing the interplay between such countries and OECD members is now a top priority of the WGB. This is confirmed by the fact that South Africa was recently invited to become a State Party and is in the process of ratifying the Convention. Moreover, the interaction between

---

[11] As the Russian Federation has already requested since February 2009 to join the Convention, the WGB focused its efforts on China, India and Indonesia, which the Group has targeted for accession to the Convention. All three countries participate in WGB activities and have received representatives in their capitals to discuss the Convention. The Secretariat organized a technical seminar in China in October 2010 and has been requested by the Chinese government to organize a second technical seminar in the near future. In February 2011, China adopted legislation criminalizing foreign bribery. In Latin America, a conference, entitled "Latin America Conference on Corporate Responsibility for Promoting Integrity and Fighting Corruption", was organized in Brazil in July 2010 with attendance by over 500 participants from the public and private sectors and civil society from 29 different countries. In May 2011, the Indonesian government hosted an international conference on foreign bribery in Bali, back-to-back with a meeting of the G20 Anti-Corruption Working Group, co-chaired by the French and Indonesian governments. Notably, India introduced a foreign bribery offense, the "Prevention of Bribery of Foreign Public Officials and Officials of Public International Organisations Bill," to its lower house (Lok Sabha) on 25 March 2011. As of 21 November 2011, the Bill results were still pending (cfr. http://www.prsindia.org/billtrack/the-prevention-of-bribery-of-foreign-public-officials-and-officials-of-public-international-organisations-bill-2011–1601/). The Indian government also hosted the 11th Regional Seminar of the OECD/Asian Development Bank Anti-Corruption Initiative for Asia and the Pacific in September 2011, while in June, the Federation of Indian Chambers of Commerce (FICCI) will co-host a series of private- sector seminars on foreign bribery. For further information we refer to the website: www.oecd.org.

OECD members, current and prospective parties to the Convention, and non-members is further accentuated in the group of States with which the OECD has been committed to a richer engagement process (e.g. Brazil, South Africa, and more recently, China).

Official Commentary 37 states that:

> full participation by non-members in this Working Group is encouraged and arranged under simple procedures. Accordingly, the requirement of full participation in the Working Group, which follows from the relationship of the Convention to other aspects of the fight against bribery in international business, should not be seen as an obstacle by countries wishing to participate in that fight.

If weighed against the restricted number of States Parties which have acceded so far, the fairly open and welcoming phraseology of Commentary 37 appears somewhat contradictory.

This contradiction may be understood by considering the framework established by the Council for participation in the OECD and in WGB practice. As to the first point, it was only in 1992 that the OECD Council established a general framework for participation in OECD subsidiary bodies and activities. This framework was amended first in 1996, a second time in 2000 and, more recently, in 2004. According to the 1992 Resolution, the process was to be retroactive in nature. It would be initiated by a non-member which would ask to become part of one or more subsidiary bodies. Such a request would be examined by the OECD Council, which could decide whether or not to refer it to the body or bodies concerned for a technical opinion. In an affirmative case, the technical opinion was transmitted to the OECD Council a second time for a final decision. (Arguably, the Resolution used the term "technical" in order to stress that it was not for the subsidiary body to assess the political aspects of the issue, which remained a prerogative of the Council.) The technical opinion had mainly to be based upon two criteria: (1) assessment of whether a non-member was a "major player" in the field of activity covered by the OECD body; and (2) whether there was a "mutual benefit" in participation by the non-member. This process raised some concern about the effective participation of OECD non-members in the Convention as a consequence of the first criterion: it could end up excluding countries where corruption is endemic, which are able and willing to combat bribery, but which, nonetheless, do not enjoy the relevant economic position. There is at least a prima facie contradiction between this latter criterion and the openness pursued by Article 13, as further stressed by Official Commentary 37. The 2004 Resolution introduced several significant changes, including two of particular interest for the WGB and for future accessions to the Anti-bribery Convention. Firstly, the 2004 Resolution requires OECD bodies to devise a proactive strategy so that the process for extending participation by non-members would be undertaken on the initiative of the OECD and not upon the request of the non-member. This proactive strategy is to be developed by each OECD body. Secondly, the major player and mutual benefit criteria no longer appear explicitly.

Turning to the WGB's practice, a pragmatic compromise was recently achieved, whereby new requests for accession would be weighed and carefully assessed against the "willing and able" and the "mutual benefit" criteria. Thus, under this approach the "major player" criterion would no longer retain an independent value. In order to reinforce the principle of openness in line with Article 13 and Official Commentary 37 of the Convention, the WGB would then incorporate under the "mutual benefit" requirement certain elements, presumably including economic factors, considered relevant as new candidates were evaluated.

The pragmatic solution achieved by the WGB aims specifically at assessing a non-member's existing legal framework for combating bribery on a domestic level; its ability to meet the standards laid down by the 1997 Revised Recommendation (especially those contained in sections IV, V, and VII); the non-member's enforcement capacity, particularly for investigation and prosecution of bribery cases; the promptness in submitting the same rigorous monitoring mechanism as other State Parties to the Convention; whether its companies engaged in international business were involved in transactions where solicitation of bribes by/for foreign public officials could occur; its economic relevance in the geographic region or sub-region, or in particularly sensitive economic sectors; the share of GDP derived from international trade and investment activities.

To conclude, such developments seem somehow to mitigate the inherent tension between the general framework applicable within the OECD and the openness encouraged by the opening clause of Official Commentary 37. However, despite these provisions, it remains to be seen whether the State Parties to a Convention, focused on the supply side of corruption and containing quite a sophisticated and time-consuming mechanism of supervision, have a material interest in expanding participation.

(3) EU

The historical roots and the increasing competences of the EU are just two of the elements which make it an international organization of unique nature. For this reason, before giving an overview of the EU policy and instruments against corruption, one should stress the peculiar features which distinguish it from the other international organizations also in the present context. As we illustrate in the following paragraphs, despite resistance of the Member States, the EU has reached an advanced level of integration in criminal matters. Furthermore, forms of enhanced integration such as the institution of the "European Public Prosecutor's Office" are currently under discussion. Finally, emphasis should be laid on the legal instruments which deal with corruption at the EU level, the specific nature of which mirrors the reluctant but steady transfer of criminal competences to the EU level. In this context one should recall, in particular, that the treaties mentioned hereafter are to be distinguished from the other ones described in this chapter. Conventions were in fact one of the instruments provided for by Article K. 3 of the Treaty of Maastricht of 1992 to build a closer judicial cooperation in criminal matters. Accordingly, the treaty-making process followed the special rules established therein in relation to the power of initiative (the Member States or the Commission depending on the subject-matter); the competence of drafting (the Council); and the role of supervision (i.e. interpretation and resolution of dispute), which could be optionally attributed by each Convention to the Court of Justice "in accordance with such arrangements as they may lay down." "Europeanization of criminal law", further fostered by the Action Plan on the Stockholm Program which set priorities for the EU area regarding justice, freedom and security for the period 2010–14 (COM(2010) 171 final and 2010/C 115/01), is clearly beyond the scope of the present work. However, some of its aspects concerning both substantial and procedural law have a noticeable impact on the specific area of corruption. More generally, the following remarks are not intended to be exhaustive but just to provide a feel for the main profiles of the EU policy against corruption.

The 1997 Action Program on organized crime calls for a comprehensive anti-corruption policy based on preventive measures. The first communication on an EU anti-corruption policy suggested banning the tax deductibility of bribes and introducing rules on public procurement procedures, accounting and auditing standards, and measures relating to external aid and assistance. The Council's 1998 Vienna Action Plan and the Tampere European Council in 1999 also indicated corruption as a particularly important area where action on the part of the EU Member States and European institutions was needed. The Millennium Strategy on the Prevention and Control of Organized Crime reiterated the need for harmonization of national legislation and to develop multidisciplinary EU policy. Besides, it urged Member States to ratify the EU and Council of Europe anti-corruption instruments concerning the issue of corruption. 1999 saw the setting up of the European Anti-Fraud Office (OLAF), which has inter-institutional investigative powers. Also, the Council of the EU introduced the European Arrest Warrant (EAW) on 13 June 2002. As we better explore in Chapter 14, the Framework Decision on the EAW and the surrender procedures between Member States of the EU is based on the principle of mutual recognition of judicial decisions and represents a cornerstone of the judicial cooperation in criminal matters within the EU.

The EU has also established its own binding instruments to curb corruption. First, the protection of financial interests through criminal law has been emphasized as a high priority for the European Community since the middle of the 1970s. The first concrete and legal instrument adopted for this purpose was the Convention on the Protection of the European Communities' Financial Interests of 26.7.1995 (hereinafter: the PFI Convention). The PFI Convention was supplemented by two Protocols agreed in 1996 and 1997: the (first) Protocol of 27.9.1996 and the second Protocol of 19.6.1997.[12] All were adopted according to Title VI of the EU Treaty. Although the PFI instruments are intergovernmental and therefore placed under the third pillar, they pursue aims stipulated by Article 280 of the EC Treaty as well. According to the PFI Convention, all Member States shall take the necessary measures in order to (i) ensure that the conduct referred to above – including participation, instigation, or attempt – is punishable by effective, proportionate, and dissuasive criminal penalties; (ii) allow heads of businesses or any persons having the power to take decisions or exercise control within a business, to be declared criminally liable in accordance with the principles defined by national law in cases of fraud affecting the European Community's financial interests; and (iii) establish jurisdiction over the above-mentioned offenses. The PFI Convention therefore presumes the Member States shall compare, essentially, texts containing criminal law definitions of fraud according to national law with the PFI Convention text and change domestic law, where necessary. For the purposes of the protection of the financial interests of the European Communities (EC), the PFI Convention defines fraud as it affects the European Communities' financial interests. Article 1 of the Convention deals with acts designed as "fraud affecting the European Communities' financial interests". Accordingly, members undertake in principle to make such conduct a domestic criminal offense and to provide for criminal penalties which – pursuant to what has become a stereotype formula within both the EU and other international organizations' framework – are "effective, proportionate and dissuasive". It also calls for specific individual

---

12 The text of the PFI Convention and of its two Protocols is available at: http://europa.eu/legislation_summaries/fight_against_fraud/protecting_european_communitys_financial_interests/l33019_en.htm.

criminal liability for the heads of business in cases where the business commits a fraud. The remaining articles deal with issues of jurisdiction, extradition, and closer judicial cooperation between Member States in criminal matters, notably in cases of transnational fraud. Article 10 sets out a system for communicating information between Member States and the Commission. The first Protocol to the PFI Convention includes the following obligations for the EC and Member States. In order for the relevant provisions of the Convention to be made applicable to the criminal conduct covered by this Protocol, the PFI States have agreed on (1) common definitions of the Community or national "Officials" (Article 1), and (2) passive and active corruption each Member State shall take the necessary measures to ensure that, in its criminal law, the descriptions of the offenses constituting conduct of the type referred to in Article 1 of the Convention, committed by its national officials in the exercise of their functions, apply similarly in cases where such offenses are committed by Community officials in the exercise of their duties. The targeted conduct is the corruption committed by enumerated officials in the exercise of their functions – Government Ministers, elected members of its parliamentary chambers, the members of its highest Courts, or the members of its Court of Auditors. The relevant provisions need to be applied similarly in cases where such offenses are committed by or against members of the Commission of the European Communities, the European Parliament, the Court of Justice, and the Court of Auditors of the European Communities. Thus, corruption is here considered within the limited ambit of the protection of the Communities' financial interests. The Second Protocol calls on Member States to take measures and exchange information with the Commission, in order to make legal entities liable for fraud, corruption and money laundering. Since the protection of financial interests is a priority also in the TFEU (Articles 310(6), 325, 85 and 86), we should bear in mind the recent Commission Proposal for a directive on the fight against fraud relating to the Union's financial interests by means of criminal law (COM(2012) 363 /2 of July 2012), which follows a Commission Communication of May 2011 on the same matter (COM(2011) 293). For our purposes, it is enough to stress the fact that Article 4 of the proposal, when providing for a definition of corruption, contrary to the PFI Convention, does not require that the conduct is "in breach of official duties" to be covered by the provision.

Secondly, on 26 May 1997 the Council of the European Union took measures to tackle corruption amongst European Community officials. Even though it does not explicitly deal with transnational bribery, the Convention on the Fight against Corruption involving Officials of the European Communities or Member States of the European Union or

Officials of the State Members (hereinafter: "EU Convention"),[13] defines as punishable offenses the act of giving or receiving bribes across Member States and other corrupt activity by European Union officials.

Thirdly, there have been some initiatives of the EU on corruption in the private sector. A Joint Action on combating corruption in the private sector was agreed in late 1998, and this was repealed and replaced by a new instrument, a Council Framework Decision on combating corruption in the private sector, in 2003.

Fourthly, the Commission has officially expressed its approval regarding accession to a number of instruments originating with other international bodies. While negotiating in international organizations on measures to combat fraud, the Member States signed the Council of Europe Criminal Law Convention on Corruption and the Convention on

---

13 Convention on the Fight against Corruption involving Officials of the European Communities or Officials of the EU Member States, Council Act 97/C OJ 1997 C 195/01, in 37 ILM, 1998, 15. The Convention entered into force on 28 September 2005. It is open to accession by any State that becomes a member of the EU (hereinafter referred to as the EU Convention). Other EU-related acts worth mentioning are: (1) Council Decision of 8 November 2007 concerning the accession of Bulgaria and Romania to the Convention drawn up on the basis of Article K.3(2)(c) of the Treaty on European Union on the Fight against Corruption involving Officials of the European Communities or Officials of Member States of the European Union (OJ L 304 of 22 November 2007). By this decision, Bulgaria and Romania accede to the Convention against Corruption involving Officials. (2). Council Decision 2008/201/EC of 25 September 2008 on the conclusion, on behalf of the European Community, of the United Nations Convention against Corruption [Official Journal L 287 of 29.10.2008]. With this Decision, the United Nations Convention against Corruption was approved on behalf of the European Community. The Decision authorizes the President of the Council to designate the person(s) who shall be empowered to deposit the Community's instrument of formal confirmation. This instrument is binding on the Community. It consists of a declaration of the Community's competence regarding matters that are governed by the Convention (Annex II) and of a statement concerning dispute settlement on the interpretation or application of the Convention (Annex III).. (3) Council Decision 2003/642/JHA of 22 July 2003 concerning the application to Gibraltar of the Convention on the fight against corruption involving officials of the European Communities or officials of Member States of the European Union (OJ L 226 of 10 September 2003). No provision was made in the Convention on corruption regarding its application to Gibraltar, whose international relations are the responsibility of the United Kingdom. This Decision extends application of the Convention to Gibraltar. For an official explanation of the provisions of the EU Convention see the Explanatory Report of the Convention on the Fight against Corruption involving Officials of the European Communities or Member States of the European Union or Officials of the State Members (OJ C 29, 15 December 1998, p. 1 *et seq.*).

Combating Bribery of Foreign Public Officials in International Business Transactions of the OECD. With this common position the Council of the European Union was seeking to avoid unnecessary duplication between the two international instruments drawn up in the Council of Europe and the OECD and to ensure compatibility with the work carried out in the European Union. On 13 November 1997 the Council adopted a second joint position (97/783/JHA). The latter clarified the position of the Member States in the deliberations in the Council of Europe and the OECD on the draft OECD convention on the fight against corruption. The Member States' position concerns the scope of the draft OECD convention; the definition of "foreign public official" in the draft OECD convention; the inclusion of the concept of influence peddling in the future Council of Europe convention; the introduction in the two conventions of rules on jurisdiction ensuring an equivalent level of commitment for all State Parties in the suppression of acts of active corruption; the establishment of an effective monitoring mechanism within the framework of the two conventions. Lastly, in 2008 a Council Decision authorized the President of the Council to designate the persons empowered to sign the United Nations Convention against Corruption (UNCAC) on behalf of the European Community (Council Decision 2008/201/EC of 25 September 2008). The latter Convention is, in fact, open for signature by regional economic integration organizations, provided that at least one Member State of such an organization has signed it. Overall, the EU has been attempting to construct a rather comprehensive anti-corruption policy which, in principle, should not compete with those of other intergovernmental organizations. The EU approach, on the one hand, aims at promoting closer cooperation among its members consistent with the fundamental goals of the Union. On the other hand, the EU activity should be integrated within a wider framework encompassing the policies undertaken by the COE, OECD, and UN, and, hence, avoid, as far as possible, wasting and consuming cases of intra-specific competition. The EU has also adopted instruments addressing corruption which are not linked to the specific issue of the protection of the financial interests of the Union. There has been some work within the EU on corruption in the private sector. As mentioned above, a Joint Action on combating corruption in the private sector was agreed in 1998, but repealed and replaced by a Council Framework Decision on combating corruption in the private sector in 2003. The key provision requires Member States to take the necessary measures to ensure that specified intentional conduct constitutes a criminal offense when it is carried out in the course of business activities. The prohibited forms of conduct are (i) promising, offering or giving directly or through an intermediary to a person who in any capacity directs or works for a private sector entity, an undue advantage of any kind, for that person or for a third party in order that that person should perform or refrain from performing any act in breach of that person's duties; and (ii) directly or through an intermediary, demanding an undue advantage: a person requests or receives, directly or through an intermediary, an undue advantage of any kind, or accepts the promise of such an advantage, for him or herself or for a third party, while in any capacity directing or working for a private sector entity, in order to perform or refrain from performing any act in breach of one's duties. Thus, the Framework Directive requires the Member States to penalize both the active and passive side of corruption in the private sector. Nonetheless, the strength of this provision is weakened by Article 2(3), which allows a Member State to declare that it will limit the scope of the offenses to such conduct as involves, or could involve, a distortion of competition in relation to the purchase of goods or commercial services.

The aim of this Framework Decision is to involve the liability not only of natural persons in the capacity of employees but also of legal persons such as firms. As to the liability of natural persons, Member States must ensure that those committing the acts referred to are liable to a maximum penalty of at least one to three years' imprisonment. The right to engage in business activities may be temporarily suspended. Instigation to commit one of the acts set out above or aiding or abetting such conduct is also an offense. Legal persons may be held liable for offenses involving corruption if they are committed for their benefit by any natural person acting individually or who has a leading position within a legal person based on: (i) a power of representation of the legal person; (ii) an authority to take decisions on behalf of the legal person; (iii) an authority to exercise control within the legal person. Penalties for legal persons may include criminal or non-criminal fines. Moreover, Member States may consider exclusion from entitlement to public benefits or aid, temporary or permanent disqualification from the practice of commercial activities, and so forth.

By adopting the Council Act of 26 May 1997 drawing up the Convention made on the basis of Article K.3(2)(c) of the Treaty on European Union, on the fight against corruption involving officials of the European Communities or officials of Member States of the European Union (1997 EU Convention), the Council strengthens judicial cooperation between the Member States in the fight against corruption involving European officials or officials of Member States of the European Union. By extending the scope of the offenses irrespective of their actual or potential influence on the Communities' financial resources, the EU Convention aims at remedying the systematic inconsistency of the PFI Convention. The text is synthetic and consists only of 16 articles. Although the Convention addresses both the supply and the demand side of corruption – and thus does not bring about the fragmentation of the typical bilateral offense as is done by the OECD Convention – its scope and approach are narrow in that it does not include extra-criminal measures. On the basis of this Convention, each Member State must take the necessary measures to ensure that conduct constituting an act of passive corruption or active corruption by officials is a punishable criminal offense. The Convention also provides that Member States must ensure that conduct constituting an act of passive or active corruption, as well as participating in and instigating these acts, is punishable by (effective, proportionate, and dissuasive) criminal penalties. On a side note, the criminalization of participation and instigation in Article 5 seems *ictu oculi* inaccurate. It would probably be preferable to insert such conduct within the text of Articles 2 and 3.

According to the so-called "principle of assimilation", the national provisions which criminalize (active and passive) corruption of officials of the European Communities or other Member States shall "apply similarly" in cases where corrupt offenses are committed against or by its own high officials. Article 4 is designed to widen and strengthen the scope of the anti-corruption measures introduced by the Convention, by requiring that each Member State's criminal law be adjusted to accommodate certain offenses committed by individuals occupying specific posts in the Community institutions. As with the first protocol of the PFI Convention, the principle of assimilation is introduced whereby Member States will be bound to apply to members of the Community institutions the same descriptions of corruption offenses as apply to individuals occupying similar posts within their own institutions. The principle of assimilation, as introduced by Article 4 of the Convention, does not require special offenses necessarily to apply in respect of the officials addressed by the Convention in a Member State. In other words, where a Member State already applies the same provisions to the corruption of ministers, members of parliament or members of the judiciary as it applies to the corruption of officials, then it will merely be required in addition to criminalize corruption of members of the Community institutions using those general provisions. Interestingly enough, in case of a dispute between Member States over the interpretation or application of the Convention, and in the absence of a bilateral resolution, the case must be examined by the Council in accordance with the procedure set out in Title VI of the EU Treaty. If the Council has not found a solution within six months, one of the parties to the dispute may refer the matter to the Court of Justice of the European Communities. The ECJ also has jurisdiction in disputes between a Member State and the European Commission. The preliminary ruling mechanism, which characterizes the jurisdiction of the ECJ and which has been significantly contributing to the development of the law of the European Union, may be resorted to by any court in a Member State on a matter concerning the interpretation of the main provisions of the Convention (namely: Articles 1 to 4 and 12 to 16) "raised in a case pending before it and involving members or officials of Community institutions or bodies set up in accordance with the Treaties establishing the European Communities, acting in the exercise of their functions, if it considers that a decision on that matter is necessary to enable it to give judgment."

Neither the original EU Convention nor its first Protocol dealt, at least indirectly, with asset recovery. The EU reached asset recovery in the Second Protocol to the Convention on the protection of the European Communities' financial interests. The focus of the Protocol is money-laundering, not corruption, but Article 5 requires each Member State to "take the necessary measures to enable the seizure, without prejudice to the rights of bona fide third parties, the confiscation or removal of the instruments and proceeds of fraud, active and passive corruption and money laundering, or property the value of which corresponds to such proceeds." The context – as made clear in the Explanatory Report on the Second Protocol – was organized crime, rather than abusive prosecution by corrupt officials. Accordingly, it is contested that the requirement of proof that third parties are bona fide "could be seen only as a reaction to concern that criminals might hide illicit assets with third parties they controlled". The EU Convention entered into force on 28 September 2005. It is open to accession by any State that becomes a member of the EU. From the perspective of the EU fight against corruption, in a Communication of June 2011 (COM(2011) 308 final), the Commission, besides calling for the implementation of existing instruments and for greater integration of anti-corruption policies both internally and towards third States (candidate and potential candidates for EU accession; in the Neighbourhood Policy and within the cooperation and development policies), has significantly announced the setting up of a European evaluation and monitoring mechanism, the "Anti-Corruption Report".

In particular the Commission, "in order to support the implementation of a comprehensive anti-corruption policy in the Union"[14] has released an instrument[15] which established the publication – every two years – of the EU Anti-corruption Report (EU Report) which should comprise a thematic section, one dedicated to the analysis and recommendations for each Member State, and a final part which draws the trends at EU level. Since

---

14 Article 1 of Commission Decision of 6 June 2011, COM(2011) 3673 final.
15 Ibid.

the latter mechanism was supposed to start in 2013 but is now expected to produce its first results only in early 2014,[16] at the moment it is just possible to mention its objectives as stated in Article 2 of the Decision and which are: (i) the periodic assessment of the situation in the Union regarding the fight against corruption; (ii) the identification of trends and weaknesses; (iii) the formulation of tailor-made recommendations; (iv) the exchange of best practices. As for the methodology, the EU Report is managed by the European Commission, which relies on existing sources of information (other international monitoring mechanisms, OLAF and EU agencies such as Europol, Eurojust and CEPOL) and which is assisted by an expert group coming from a wide range of backgrounds and by a network of research correspondents consisting of representatives of civil society and academia. Finally, emphasis should be laid on the relationship between the EU Report and the other supervising mechanisms: while Article 5 of the Decision draws a limit in this sense, establishing that the former "shall be without prejudice to participation of Member States in regional and/ or global monitoring mechanisms, or the obligations undertaken by the Member States within those mechanisms", Article 6 properly underlines the importance of cooperating "with other networks and monitoring and evaluation mechanisms". In our view the level of synergy which the EU Report will establish with the existing monitoring mechanisms constitutes a crucial element to assess its potential impact at the EU level: while a mere recognition of the Member States' efforts within other international organizations would lead to create a weak instrument which would duplicate the review made by such organizations, the EU Report should take advantage of the unique level of integration among the EU Members' legal systems and form the fertile ground upon which the EU could develop a harmonized response to corruption as provided for by Article 83 TFEU.

Fifthly, with the entry into force of the Lisbon Treaty on 1 December 2009, the EU has recently increased its capacity to tackle corruption through the new provisions regarding cooperation in criminal matters. Despite a European criminal code not having been introduced – because of the well-known reluctance of Member States to transfer further competences in a such legal realm to the Union – the EU Institutions, through

16 The delay of the first EU Report has been confirmed by representatives of the European Commission during a Conference held in Brussels on 3 December 2013 on anti-fraud and anti-corruption measures in relation to the use of European Structural and Investment Funds. For more information about the outcome of the latter Conference see TI Europe's report of the conference at http://www.transparencyinternational.eu/2013/12/eu-anti-corruption-report-update-will-anyone-be-satisfied/.

the EU secondary law (Regulations and Directives) can now influence national criminal law systems by establishing "minimum rules concerning the definition of criminal offences and sanctions" (Article 83(1) of the Treaty on the Functioning of the EU (TFEU)). The objective of such a competence is to intervene in "the areas of particularly serious crime with a cross-border dimension resulting from the nature or impact of such offences or from a special need to combat them on a common basis" (Article 83(1) TFEU).[17] In this context corruption is explicitly listed in the text of the Treaty as one of these areas of "Euro crimes", along with nine more serious crimes (terrorism, trafficking in human beings and sexual exploitation of women and children, illicit drug trafficking, illicit arms trafficking, money laundering, counterfeiting of means of payment, computer crime and organized crime). To summarize, the entry into force of the Lisbon Treaties marks an important step in furthering the potentials of the EU to tackle corruption. Corruption belongs to those criminal offences that may potentially be subject to the procedure for harmonization of the constituent elements, as set out in Article 83(1) of the Treaty on the Functioning of the European Union (TFEU). Art. 83(1) TFEU features such crimes as "particularly serious" and "having a cross-border dimension resulting from the nature or impact of such offences or from a special need to combat them on a common basis." It is worth emphasizing that some authors contend that the rationale behind the Union intervention in such different areas, as those potentially endangered by the offences cited in Art. 83(1), lies in their peculiar transnational nature and seriousness. Chaves (2009) argues that, odious though several of those crimes may be, it can hardly be maintained that they have prominent and transnational dimensions, which distinguish them from other crimes. Instead, she puts forward that the Union is moving toward new forms of "Euro-crimes" centered on a vague notion of organized crime.[18] On the contrary, the common and distinguishing feature of such offences is that, in order to commit them, a common enterprise and prior infrastructure

---

17 As noted elsewhere, with reference to the EU legislative process towards an harmonization of the substantive criminal law aspect of the so called 'Euro crimes', "the domain of EU criminal law reveals . . . the enduring truth that the Commission not always get all that it had hoped for, as determined by its initial proposal" (Craig and De Bùrca, 2011: 955). See also Mitsilegas (2009). Herlin-Karnell (2012) provides us with an insightful account of the several uncertainties characterizing the exact meaning of harmonization 'when necessary for the effective implementation of a Union policy' pursuant to Art. 83 TFEU, as well as the actual possibilities of harmonizing outside Art. 83 TFEU.

18 On the malleable notion of "organized crime" in the EU legal system see Calderoni (2008).

would be required.[19] To conclude the point, as rightly remarked by Chalmers et al. (2011: 614), the EU has begun to focus on a very peculiar sort of criminality, "which could be serious, potentially transnational and which usually required the use of infrastructure and collective action", of which ML is a paradigmatic case. The harmonization here seeks "to create those definitions which act as a starting point for Member States to take criminal offences further" (2011: p. 615). However, such development of EU criminal law – based on the premise that it ought to facilitate the mutual recognition of judicial decisions and other forms of mutual legal assistance – cannot be looked at as a general and definite process: "extensive harmonization in this sensitive area (. . .) ends up in the fire of constitutional objections and political obstacles to further development of this policy in practice" (Peers, 2011: 297). Indeed, Malmström, the Commissioner for Home Affairs, recently stated that: "for the time being, the Commission does not . . . intend to propose new legislation on the definition of corruption or approximation of statutes of limitations of corruption offences or protections of whistleblowers".[20] To us, this testifies that, even in the most advanced and integrated supranational legal system, the "territorial element" of criminal law is so extraordinary that it is still able to resist the contemporary vigorous force towards harmonization of domestic pieces of legislation.

Sixthly, the EU has also introduced tools to strengthen judicial cooperation in criminal matters, inspired by the principle of mutual recognition rather than governed by traditional mutual legal assistance mechanisms. Besides *ad hoc* institutions such as Eurojust and the European judicial network in criminal matters (EJN), established to facilitate mutual assistance and support cooperation between judicial authorities, the EU has enacted a series of instruments intended to replace the slow and complex procedure of the "rogatory letter". Although they do not have strong binding effects and, thus, not all EU countries are complying with the provisions therein, for the purpose of fighting corruption the following should be mentioned:

- Council Framework Decision 2002/584/JHA, which introduced the European Arrest Warrant to improve and simplify judicial procedures designed to surrender people for the purpose of conducting

---

19 For example, the laundering of profits of crime rely on necessary infrastructures such as particular businesses or the misuse of the financial system in general through which money can be moved and laundered.

20 Cfr, http://www.europarl.europa.eu/ep-live/en/plenary/video?debate=1382446871858.

a criminal prosecution or executing a custodial sentence or spell in detention;

- Council Framework Decision 2008/909/JHA, which established a system for transferring convicted prisoners back to their EU country of nationality, habitual residence or another EU country with which they have close ties;
- Council Framework Decision 2008/978/JHA, which applies the principle of mutual recognition for judicial decisions when it comes to obtaining evidence for use in criminal proceedings;
- Council Framework Decisions 2003/577/JHA and 2006/783/JHA to apply freezing or confiscation orders within the territory of a different EU country where illegal goods have been placed or where a person is residing.

Seventhly, on the premise that in times of economic crisis and budgetary restriction, it is more important than ever to investigate, prosecute and bring to justice those who commit criminal offences affecting the Union's financial interests, the EU Commission proposed a regulation on the establishment of a European Public Prosecutor's Office (EPPO) based on Art. 86 of TFEU.[21] When and if established,[22] the EPPO will be an independent Union body with the authority to investigate and prosecute EU-fraud and other crimes, including corruption, insofar as (and within the limits) they affect the Union's financial interests. The establishment of the EPPO will bring about substantial changes in the way the Union's financial interests are protected. Through a system which appears to resemble the current mechanism of the EU Competition Law's enforcement, it will combine European and national law-enforcement efforts in a unified, seamless and efficient approach to counter EU-fraud.[23]

---

21 Proposal for a Council Regulation on the establishment of the European Public Prosecutor's Office/* COM/2013/0534 final - 2013/0255 (APP) */available at: http://eurlex.europa.eu/LexUriServ/LexUriServ.do?uri=CELEX:52013PC0534:en:NOT.

22 Noteworthy, national parliaments opposed to creating an EU-wide prosecutor want the European Commission to rework its flagship proposal, even though EU officials maintain that it is likely to go ahead. Chambers in 11 national parliaments got enough votes to trigger a so-called "yellow card" procedure when they filed their complaints to Brussels earlier in October 2013. They are against the creation of a new European Public Prosecutor's Office (EPPO), saying that national authorities or existing EU bodies, such as the Olaf anti-fraud agency or the joint judicial office, Eurojust, are sufficient. (The yellow card has only been triggered once before, on postal workers' rights). See: http://euobserver.com/justice/121959.

23 Currently, only national authorities can investigate and prosecute EU-fraud.

Finally, it is worth stressing that one method the EU has chosen to address corruption is by a provision in its procurement directives[24] requiring Member States to exclude persons convicted of corruption and other offences from gaining access to public contracts. Public procurement in the EU is harmonized by a legislative framework, which is constantly reformed and adapted to the needs of the consolidation of the internal market. At the same time this sector of public expenditure is frequently victim to corruption, organized crime and irregularities. Noteworthy, a wide-ranging existing EU legislation framework provides rules and laws in order to prevent corruption crime within the EU Member States in the context of public procurement. On the one hand, the EU treaties provide general principles applicable to public procurement law: Article 34 TFEU guarantees the free movement of goods within the EU; Article 49 TFEU guarantees the right of establishment in another Member State; Article 56 TFEU guarantees the right to provide services in another Member State and finally Article 18 TFEU prohibits all forms of discrimination on grounds of nationality. On the other hand, two EU directives are dedicated to public procurement issues: Directive 2004/18/EC on the coordination of procedures for the award of public works contracts, public supply contracts and public service contracts (hereinafter referred to as the public sector directive) and Directive 2004/17/EC coordinating the procurement procedures of entities operating in the water, energy, transport and postal services sectors (hereinafter: the utilities directive). The Directives cover the fundamental principles of procurement process and transparency and countries are required to apply these fundamental principle when awarding public contracts, particularly concerning non-discrimination, equal treatment, competition and transparency. Arguably, the EU Directives establish the most developed public procurement system encompassing different countries worldwide. Their main purpose is to remove barriers to trade within the internal market: such a goal, in the context of public procurement, requires the elimination of any restrictive access to public contracts within the EU. This is assumed to guarantee the opening up of procurement to competition. Moreover, the directives aim to guarantee free and non-discriminatory access of all European undertakings to public

As widely known, their competences stop at their national borders. Existing Union-bodies (such as OLAF, Eurojust and Europol) do not have and cannot be given the mandate to conduct criminal investigations. The EPPO will fill this institutional gap, being endowed with an exclusive and EU-wide jurisdiction to deal with suspicions of criminal behavior falling within its remit.

24 See European Union, EU Public Procurement Directives, available at: http://ec.europa.eu/internal_market/publicprocurement/index_en.htm.

contracts. The legal regime, as established by the EU Directives, is rather complex and under current revision.[25] For the limited purposes of our study, it suffices to emphasize that it is built upon different grounding principles, further developed by the Union's Court over the years. As said, among these principles, transparency and fair competition, as well as non-discrimination and equal treatment stand as the most important. Coming to the exclusion provision it is contained in Article 45 of the public sector directive.[26] On the contrary, the utilities directive does not expressly contain a similar provision; it incorporates the requirement by reference to the public sector directive where the procuring entity is a "contracting authority".[27] On a final note, corruption crime relating to public procurement occurs in varying forms. For instance, according to the UNCAC, procurement related corruption can take the following forms: i) Corrupt practice, i.e. offering, giving, receiving, or soliciting, directly or indirectly, anything of value to influence the action of a public official in the selection process or in contract execution; ii) Fraudulent practice, i.e. a misrepresentation or omission of facts in order to influence a selection process or the execution of a contract; iii) Collusive practices, i.e. a scheme or arrangement between two or more respondents with or

---

25 In December 2011, as announced in the Single Market Act, the Commission adopted its proposals on public procurement. The reform of the EU public procurement legislation is one of the twelve priority areas set out in the Single Market Act. To replace the current public procurement regime the Commission published the Proposal for a Directive of the European Parliament and the Council on Public Procurement (COM(2011)896) and the Proposal for Directive of the European Parliament and the Council on procurement by entities operating in water, energy, transport and postal sectors (COM(2011)895). Furthermore, the Commission introduced a new Directive on concession contracts (COM(2011)897), which were until now only partly regulated at EU level. These proposals are part of an overall programme aiming at an in-depth modernization of public procurement in the European Union.

26 The adopted version of the provision as set out in Article 45 of the consolidated public sector directive states as follows: "Any candidate or tenderer who has been the subject of a conviction by final judgment of which the contracting authority is aware for one or more of the reasons listed below shall be excluded from participation in a public contract: (b) corruption, as defined in Article 3 of the Council Act of 26 May 1997 (21) and Article 3 of Council Joint Action 98/742/JHA (22) respectively . . . Member states shall specify, in accordance with their national laws and having regard for Community law, the implementing conditions for this paragraph. They may provide for a derogation from the requirement referred to in the first subparagraph for overriding requirements in the general interest."

27 See Art.54(4) of the Directive 2004/17/EC coordinating the procurement procedures of entities operating in the water, energy, transport and postal services sectors.

without the knowledge of the procuring entity, designed to establish prices at artificial, non-competitive levels; iv) Coercive practices means harming or threatening to harm, directly or indirectly, persons or their property to influence their participation in a procurement process, or affect the execution of a contract.

(4) CoECLCC

January 1999 saw the adoption of the Council of Europe Criminal Law Convention on Corruption (CoECLCC).[28] At their 19th Conference held in Valletta in 1994, the European Ministers of Justice considered that corruption was a serious threat to democracy, to the rule of law and to human rights. The COE, being the pre-eminent European institution defending these fundamental values, was called upon to respond to that threat. The Ministers were convinced that the fight against corruption should take a multidisciplinary approach and that it was necessary to adopt appropriate legislation in this area as soon as possible. They expressed the belief that an effective fight against corruption required increased cross-border cooperation between States, as well as between States and international institutions, through the promotion of coordinated measures at European level and beyond, which in turn implied involving States which were not members of the COE. The Ministers of Justice recommended to the Committee of Ministers the setting up of a Multidisciplinary Group on Corruption (GMC), under the responsibility of the European Committee on Crime Problems (CDPC) and the European Committee on Legal Co-operation (CDCJ), with the task of examining what measures might be suitable to be included in a program of action at international level as well as examining the possibility of drafting model laws or codes of conduct, including international conventions, on this subject. The Ministers expressly referred to the importance of elaborating a follow-up mechanism to implement the undertakings contained in such instruments. On the basis of these recommendations, the Committee of Ministers set

---

28 Council of Europe Criminal Law Convention on Corruption, January 1999, EUROP.T.S. No. 173 (entered into force 7 January 2002). As of December 2013, 44 of the 47 Member States of the Council of Europe have ratified the Convention. Germany, Liechtenstein, San Marino, are yet to ratify the convention. Non-Member States of the Council of Europe that have signed the Convention are Belarus, Mexico and the United States. The text of the Convention is available at: http://conventions.coe.int/treaty/en/Treaties/Word/173.doc. The CoECLCC is provided with an organic and official Explanatory Report. See Explanatory Report to the Criminal Law Convention on Corruption, available at: http://conventions.coe.int/Treaty/en/Reports/Html/173.htm, first accessed on 4 July 2008.

up, in September 1994, the GMC and gave it terms of reference to examine what measures might be suitable to be included in an international program of action against corruption. The GMC was set up as a result of the 19th Conference of the European Ministers of Justice, held in Malta in 1994. The GMC was also invited to make proposals to the Committee of Ministers before the end of 1995 as to appropriate priorities and working structures, taking due account of the work of other international organizations. It was furthermore invited to examine the possibility of drafting model laws or codes of conduct in selected areas, including the elaboration of an international convention on this subject, as well as the elaboration of a follow-up mechanism to implement undertakings contained in such instruments. The GMC commenced its works in March 1995 and prepared a draft Program of Action against Corruption, an ambitious document covering all aspects of the international fight against this phenomenon. This draft Program was submitted to the Committee of Ministers, which, in January 1996, took note of it, invited the CDPC and the CDCJ to express their opinions thereon and, in the meantime, gave interim terms of reference to the GMC, authorizing it to start some of the actions contained in the said Program, such as work on one or several international instruments. The Committee of Ministers finally adopted the Program of Action in November 1996 and instructed the GMC to implement it before 31 December 2000. The Committee of Ministers welcomed in particular the GMC's purpose to elaborate, as a matter of priority, one or more international Conventions to combat corruption and a follow-up mechanism to implement undertakings contained in such instruments or any other legal instrument in this area. According to the terms of reference given to the GMC, the CDPC and CDCJ were to be consulted on any draft legal text relating to corruption and their views taken into account. The Ministers participating in the 21st Conference of European Ministers of Justice, held in Prague in June 1997, expressed their concern about the new trends in modern criminality and, in particular, regarding the organized, sophisticated and transnational character of certain criminal activities. At their Second Summit, held in Strasbourg on 10–11 October 1997, the Heads of State and Government of the Member States of the COE decided to seek common responses to the challenges posed by the growth in corruption and organized crime. At its Session on 6 November 1997 the Committee of Ministers of the COE adopted with its resolution (97) 24 of November 1997 the Twenty Guiding Principles for the Fight against Corruption. Firmly resolved to fight corruption by joining their countries' efforts, the Ministers agreed, inter alia, to ensure coordinated criminalization of national and international corruption (Principle 2), to ensure that those in charge of prevention, investigation, prosecution and adjudication of corruption offenses enjoy the independence and autonomy appropriate to their functions, are free from improper influence and have effective means for gathering evidence, protecting the persons who help the authorities in combating corruption and preserving the confidentiality of investigations (Principle 3), to provide appropriate measures for the seizure and deprivation of the proceeds of corruption offenses (Principle 4), to prevent legal persons being used to shield corruption offenses (Principle 5), to promote the specialization of persons or bodies in charge of fighting corruption and to provide them with appropriate means and training to perform their tasks (Principle 7) and to develop to the widest extent possible international cooperation in all areas of the fight against corruption (Principle 20). The CoECLCC criminalizes active and passive corruption, although it is of wider application. It applies not only to the Contracting parties' officials but also, as explicitly stated in Article 5, to any other State. It envisages a wide array of conduct, which delineates a rather fluid and comprehensive notion of corruption. The CoECLCC, supplemented by an Additional Protocol signed on 15 May 2003, entered into force on 1 February 2005.[29] This Protocol extends the scope of the Convention to arbitrators in commercial, civil and other matters, as well as to jurors, thus complementing the Convention's provisions aimed at protecting judicial authorities from corruption. Countries which ratify this instrument will have to adopt the necessary measures to establish, as criminal offenses, the active and passive bribery of domestic and foreign arbitrators and jurors.

CoECivLCC Quite importantly, the COE's approach is not limited to criminalization. Rather it follows different patterns of regulation. In 1999 the COE also adopted the Civil Law Convention on Corruption (CoECivLCC). This Convention contains a very broad definition of corruption and applies to every type of corrupt activity including transnational bribery. The CoECivLCC is the first attempt to define common international rules in the field of civil law and corruption. It is innovative in addressing the possibility of civil litigation in corrupt practices. Its aim is to require each party to the Convention to provide in its internal law effective remedies for persons who have suffered damage as a result of corruption, in order to enable them to defend their rights and interests, including the possibility of obtaining compensation for damage. We explore the main advantages of a complementary civil law approach in responding to corruption in Chapter 15.

---

29 The Additional Protocol is, in its turn, commented on by an Explanatory Report, available at: http://conventions.coe.int/treaty/en/reports/html/191.htm.

(5) AU Convention

The African Union Convention on Preventing and Combating Corruption[30] is the most recent of all of the international treaties dealing with transnational corruption. The AU was established in 2000 as the successor to the Organization of African Unity (OAU). The succession between the two African organizations has mirrored the change of priorities for the African continent. The OAU was born out of the struggle for independence of the 1950s and the early 1960s and officially established in 1963 in Ethiopia. The OAU's focus was mainly on removing the vestiges of colonization and apartheid. By contrast, the African Union aims to expedite the process of political and economic integration in the region. In the post-World War II atmosphere of ideological bi-polarization between East and West, some African leaders opted for non-alignment, whereas others took sides. While African countries were being wooed by the superpowers, issues such as the rule of law, public participation in decision-making, human rights, were downgraded on the political agenda. As pointed out by Muna (2004), African dictatorial regimes were mostly tolerated by Cold War superpowers that regularly fought wars by proxy throughout the continent. Mobutu Sese Seko, for instance, was one such dictator. He plundered the resource-rich Zaire (now the Democratic Republic of Congo) for more than 30 years, arguably with the tacit approval of some of his backers in Western capitals. Dictatorial regimes gradually replaced the leaders who had been a strong force in the struggle for independence (for example, Kwame Nkrumah in Ghana and Julius Nyerere in Tanzania), successful multi-party systems and powerful trade unions. During this period, anti-corruption initiatives were on no one's political agenda. After the fall of the Berlin Wall, the leadership vacuum in many countries became exposed to populations that increasingly demanded democracy, human rights and public participation. As soon as international financial institutions and bilateral donors began applying pressure for good governance and the rule of law, African states recognized that it was necessary to strike a balance between the State, private sector, civil society, and the media. Furthermore, international organizations like Amnesty International

---

30 African Union Convention on Preventing and Combating Corruption and Related Offences, in 43 ILM, p. 1 *et seq*. The AU Corruption Convention entered into force on 5 August 2006, upon the ratification of the 15th African nation. As of 2010, 31 nations have ratified the AU Corruption Convention. They are: Algeria, Benin, Burkina Faso, Burundi, Comoros, Congo, Ethiopia, Gabon, Gambia, Ghana, Kenya, Libya, Lesotho, Madagascar, Mali, Malawi, Mozambique, Namibia, Niger, Nigeria, Rwanda, Senegal, Seychelles, Sierra Leone, South Africa, Tanzania, Togo, Uganda, Zambia, and Zimbabwe.

mounted an incessant campaign against human rights violations, but the OAU only reacted in the early 1980s. The African Charter on Human and Peoples' Rights came into force in 1986.[31] The 1990s saw a return to the multi-party system. Pressure from civil society, the media, and political parties quickly pushed corruption and governance issues to the fore. According to the Chairman of Transparency International Cameroon, Akere Tabeng Muna (2004), "this trend produced ambiguous results, since it not only entrenched calls for more accountable governance, but also created mistrust of the good governance agenda . . . It was against this backdrop that the OAU, predecessor of the new AU, was to seek a continental approach to a problem that had taken on a magnitude similar to that of the human rights issue in the 1980s."[32] The fight against corruption was specifically introduced at the regional level only in June 1998, during a session of the Assembly of Heads of State and Government in Ouagadougou, Burkina Faso. The Assembly passed a resolution inviting the Secretary-General to convene a high-level meeting of experts in cooperation with the African Commission on Human and Peoples' Rights.[33] The process leading to the drafting and adoption of the Anti-Corruption Convention included two "experts" meetings in Addis Ababa, Ethiopia during the periods 26–9 November 2001 and 16–17 September 2002. The experts were called upon to consider ways of removing obstacles to the

---

31 African Charter on Human and Peoples' Rights Text available at: http://www.achpr.org/english/_info/charter_en.html, accessed on 21 October 2008. The African Charter on Human and Peoples' Rights (also known as the Banjul Charter) is a fundamental international human rights instrument that purports to promote and protect human rights and people and basic freedoms on the African continent. For a thorough analysis of its institutional and normative features see e.g. Evans and Murray (2008); Kindiki (2003).

32 Muna (2004), p. 117.

33 The African Commission on Human and Peoples' Rights, in existence since 1986, is established under the African Charter on Human and Peoples' Rights (the African Charter) rather than the Constitutive Act of the African Union. It is the premier African human rights body, with responsibility for monitoring and promoting compliance with the African Charter. The African Court on Human and Peoples' Rights was established in 2006 to supplement the work of the Commission, following the entry into force of a protocol to the African Charter providing for its creation. The African Commission possesses great promise in terms of clarifying and developing the standards that might be applied to ensure compliance with its foundational instrument, the African Charter. Similarly, the Commission is capable of assessing the degree to which State Parties are in reality acting in conformity with their obligations under the Charter. It is planned that the African Court on Human and Peoples' Rights will be merged with the African Court of Justice.

enjoyment of economic, social and cultural rights – in particular through the fight against corruption and impunity – and to propose appropriate legislative and other measures for reform. Mr Adama Dieng, who had been the Secretary General of the OAU, was entrusted with the task of studying the legal, political, and economic implications of corruption in Africa. He concluded in his 2004 report that corruption and impunity are antithetical to the enjoyment of economic, social, and cultural rights, and enemies of the principle of good governance. The experts should also consider ways of removing obstacles to the enjoyment of economic, social, and cultural rights – such as through the fight against corruption and impunity – and propose appropriate legislative and other measures for reform. It is noteworthy that, throughout the drafting process, civil society groups, including TI, pushed for the inclusion of innovative provisions concerning asset recovery, political party financing, access to information, and whistle blower protection. The Draft African Union Convention on Preventing and Combating Corruption was approved by the Ministerial Conference on the Draft African Union Convention on Preventing and Combating Corruption, held in Addis Ababa on 18–19 September 2002. Following the approval in March 2003 by the Executive Council of the AU meeting in N'djamena, Chad, the text of the Anti-Corruption Convention was finally completed, and recommended to the AU Assembly for adoption. The AU finally adopted the Convention on Preventing and Combating Corruption Maputo on 11 July 2003.

The 28-article AU pact started out as the Convention on Preventing and Combating Corruption, but definitional issues and discrepancies in the contracting parties' legal systems led the drafting committee to add the words "and Related Offences". It is noteworthy that countries that have adopted, but not ratified, the agreement may spontaneously decide to enact selected provisions of the convention into national law, instead of proceeding with the ratification process. The overall structure of the Anti-Corruption Convention is similar to that of the OAS Convention.

The Preamble clearly places the Convention in the context of the Constitutive Act of the AU,[34] the African Charter and the Plan of Action Against Impunity adopted by the 19th ordinary session of the African Commission on Human and Peoples' Rights (hereinafter: the African Commission). It recalls the human rights obligations imposed on States by these instruments; recognizes the necessity of promoting and protecting

34 Constitutive Act of the AU, 11 July 2000, OAU Doc. CAB/LEG/23 15 (entered into force 26 May 2001), available at: http://www.africa-union.org/About AU/Constitutive_Act.htm.

human rights, including economic, social, and cultural rights, noting that freedom, equality, justice, peace, good governance, and dignity are essential objectives for the achievement of the legitimate aspiration of the African peoples. Among its primary goals is promoting development through preventing, detecting, and punishing acts of corruption. The *good governance approach* is one of the distinguishing areas of emphasis of the Convention under discussion. Although the UNCAC, OAS, and AU Conventions generally share similar features, differences in emphasis can be noted. For instance, the stated purposes of the OAS Convention and the UNCAC do not directly link the challenge of corruption to development and good governance. By contrast, the AU Convention treats development and good governance as fundamental premises. By no means unique as far as its framework is concerned – compared with other international *hard law* instruments dealing with prevention and repression of corruption – the very adoption and entry into force of the AU Corruption Convention is a significant stage when considering the development of the African political scene as briefly sketched out above. Nonetheless, its real impact will depend on several crucial considerations, including the clarity of the substantive obligations imposed, proper municipal implementation of these norms, good governance, and, more crucially, proper and functioning monitoring, coupled with robust international and national enforcement. Although relatively brief, the AU Convention engages with tackling the most important aspects of transnational and national corruption which, in 2004, was reported to cost Africa approximately $148 billion annually. From the outset, it lays out the fundamental principles that underscore the obligations that State Parties assume. These principles are stated in Article 3 in part as "respect for democratic principles and institutions, popular participation, the rule of law and good governance . . ."; ". . . respect for human and peoples' rights in accordance with the African Charter on Human and Peoples' Rights and other relevant human rights instruments . . . Transparency and accountability in the management of public affairs . . . Promotion of social justice to ensure balanced socio-economic development . . . Condemnation and rejection of acts of corruption, related offences and impunity." Neither the UNCAC nor the other international anti-bribery treaties contains a parallel provision. State Parties to the AU Convention seem to believe that any attempt to combat corruption in Africa without applying these fundamental principles would be vain. This is why State Parties to the AU Convention have pledged to create and maintain accountability in government and private affairs. The overall structure of the Anti-Corruption Convention is similar to that of the Inter-American Convention against Corruption.

The AU Treaty focuses on four main approaches to counteracting corruption, namely: prevention, punishment, cooperation and education. Firstly, it aims at strengthening the municipal laws on corruption by listing offenses that should be punishable by domestic legislation. Secondly, it outlines measures to be undertaken to enable the detection and investigation of corruption offenses. Thirdly, it points to mechanisms for the confiscation and forfeiture of the proceeds of corruption and related offenses; it determines the jurisdiction of State Parties; it organizes mutual assistance in relation to corruption and related offenses. Finally, it encourages the education and promotion of public awareness of the evils of corruption, and it establishes a framework for the monitoring and supervision of enforcement of the Convention. Provisions for this monitoring process also make reference to the involvement of civil society.

Some further remarks. A starting point for discussion is its great emphasis on the negative impact of corruption on human rights. Whereas the Anti-Corruption Convention brings some salient novelties to international efforts against corruption, by distinctively linking corruption and human rights, it does not explain the precise content of this relationship, nor reflect a coherent framework of remedies for individuals or groups whose human rights are violated as a result of corruption. For its part, the AU Convention focuses merely on criminal punishment, and leaves out victims, especially vulnerable and excluded individuals or groups, thus denying them direct access to remedies, such as compensation and restitution. It remains the case that the remedies the AU Convention prescribes are similar to those pre-existing instruments that mainly adopted a crime control approach without setting forth civil remedies. The lack of clear provisions on compensation is likely one of the major flaws of the AU pact, as soon as one considers that the large-scale diversion of Africa's resources and wealth to safe havens abroad by those entrusted with their control and management has seriously affected governments' ability to fulfill their human rights obligations, locking individuals and groups into cycles of dependency and despondency. Although the issue is emphasized both in the Preamble and in Article 2, the underlying approach seems to presume the adequacy and effectiveness of the accountability institutions and the systems designed to protect human rights. As critically observed by Olaniyan (2004a), it seems to be simplistically assumed that the State interest and those of individuals or groups are the same, and will always coincide. In reality this is rarely the case.

Notwithstanding the problematic nature of the consideration of human rights within the AU Convention, Snider and Kidane (2007) emphasize that the AU Convention's attention to rights is one of its unique features: the AU Convention characterizes corruption as a phenomenon that deprives people of the enjoyment of not only their socio-economic rights but their human rights in general. The *human rights-based approach* of the AU Convention is not exhausted by the explicit consideration of the eradication of corruption as a *sine qua non* condition to allow the enjoyment of human rights by African people. Another feature that makes the AU Corruption Convention unique is its emphasis on the treatment of the accused, which seems to protect a higher value than the substantive provisions themselves. Under the title "Minimum Guarantees of a Fair Trial", Article 14 of the AU Convention guarantees to any person alleged to have committed acts of corruption and related offenses as defined by the Convention a fair trial in criminal proceedings in accordance with the minimum guarantees contained in the African Charter on Human and Peoples' Rights and any other relevant international human rights instrument recognized by the concerned State Parties.

The underlying reading seems to be the following: any law enforcement attempt that disregards the fundamental rights of the accused can cause more harm than good to society. According to Schroth (2005a) and Snider and Kidane (2007), this holds particularly true in several parts of Africa where law enforcement institutions and the judiciary in general can best be characterized as fragile. Despite the display of the theme of human rights within the AU Convention, the present authors' view is in line with that of Olaniyan (2004a), who, in an insightful analysis of the AU Convention, criticizes the way the AU Convention deals with human rights. In concluding his work, he indicates as one of several defects noticeable in the Anti-Corruption Convention the circumstance that it is devoid of human rights content, rendering it almost entirely a toothless tiger. He firstly highlights that aside from a general reference to economic, social, and cultural rights in its Preamble, the Anti-Corruption Convention does not characterize corruption as a massive and direct violation of human rights. It therefore fails to comprehensively address the critical link between corruption, especially large-scale corruption, and those rights. Secondly, the Anti-Corruption Convention, like the African Charter, suffers from excessive use of claw-back clauses which tend to limit or undermine some of its innovative provisions. The possibility of making a reservation in relation to the Convention – providing only the general requirement that each reservation concerns one or more specific provisions and is not incompatible with the object and purposes of this Convention – weakens even further the structure and potential impact of the agreement under discussion. Thirdly, the Convention lacks any serious and effective mechanism for holding States accountable for the obligations they assume under it, or for resolving disputes among State Parties, including a potential claim by one party that another is failing to properly carry out its obligations. Finally, as already said, the main flaw concerning the safeguarding of human rights menaced by massive corruption is that the Convention effectively excludes the concrete possibility of remedies for victims of official corruption. In this sense, the drafters of the Convention missed an important chance to develop international binding instruments, such as the COE Civil Law Convention on Corruption, in this area. Olaniyan (2004a) argues that the overall effectiveness of the AU Convention depends in the main on the possibility of its being firmly placed within the framework of the African Charter on Human and Peoples' Rights and its implementation mechanisms. According to this reading, the conversion of the Anti-Corruption Convention into a coherent and consistent body of international human rights law to address corruption, especially large-scale corruption, would be crucial to achieve its desired end. To give content and effect to its principles, therefore, the AU Convention should be amended in order to place it firmly within the framework of the African Charter. In Olaniyan's view this task could easily be accomplished by strengthening the Convention in the light of the Charter's main content, and adding it as a protocol to the Charter. In this way, the provisions of the Anti-Corruption Convention would be renovated into a coherent and workable body of human rights law, making up for some of the main shortcomings brought about by the very formulation, contents of the Convention, and the weakness of the monitoring mechanism it sets forth. As to the precise content of such a protocol to the African Charter, the two more critical issues relate to a clear statement of principles addressing the human rights dimension of corruption and providing victims of corruption with effective civil remedies. The latter would grant the Anti-Corruption Convention added significance and enforceability with respect to its progressive provisions. It is to be noted that the African Charter would additionally offer an established – although (still) not optimal – mechanism by which to monitor, file complaints, and report on States' efforts to remove human rights violations arising from acts of corruption.

To conclude, commentators' appreciation of the AU Convention varies significantly. Schroth (2005a), for instance, advances several reasons for revising this Convention, rather than ratifying it in its current form. He considers that the AU Convention would suffer from numerous inconsistencies as a result of inorganic amendments to the draft in 2002 and serious errors of translation in the English, Arabic, and Portuguese texts. What is more, the AU Convention's bizarre designation of mere theft, by any person and of property owned by anyone, as a crime of corruption, along with the criminalization of illicit enrichment as defined by Article 4(1), would cause several and serious consequences from the viewpoint of the safeguarding of primary human rights. According to Webb (2005), whereas the AU Convention is rather comprehensive on paper, its expansiveness might end up by deterring countries from ratifying it. Besides, the lack of a well-structured and effective follow-up mechanism is likely to cause signatories to delay or even avoid implementation. For his part, Olaniyan (2004a) criticizes the excessive use of claw-back clauses, but, on the other hand, suggests that with the effectiveness of the Convention and its consistency the human rights law would be substantially improved, were the AU Convention amended as a Protocol of the African Charter on Human and People's Rights. A more positive view on the effective and symbolic role of the Treaty at hand is taken by Muna (2004), who emphasizes some of the main benefits of the AU Convention, namely the fact that it covers: the supply and demand sides of corruption, private and public sector corruption, a broad range of criminal offenses; its prescribed requirements relating to public sector internal accounting and auditing systems (Article 5) and those related to whistle blower and witness protection (Article 5); the restrictions on immunity for public officials (Article 7); even if too narrowly drawn, the requirement for transparency in political party funding (Article 10); its broad jurisdictional provisions (Article 13); restrictions on use of banking secrecy (Article 17); it is the only anti-corruption Treaty to have mandatory provisions on other preventive measures calling for education and awareness-raising (Article 5), as well as access to information for the media and involvement of private sector and civil society in the prevention of corruption (Article 12).

(6) UNCTOC

The international regulation of transnational bribery continued with the adoption on 15 November 2000 of the UNCTOC. It signals a transition from regional to global initiatives in this field. The UNCTOC arose in response to international calls to address *global organized crime* by closing major loopholes that severely hamper international enforcement efforts and allow organized crime to flourish. It focuses on the activities of "organized criminal groups", but recognizes that corruption is often an instrument or effect of organized crime and includes several provisions to address it.

As all of its corruption-related provisions have been subsequently transferred to the United Nations Convention against Corruption (UNCAC), we only observe that the UNCTOC has inaugurated a method which weakens the effectiveness of both instruments, in providing an escape hatch by asserting that each party shall take measures that are appropriate and consistent with its legal system in many of its provisions. This means that States can avoid enforcement on constitutional grounds, claim a domestic conflict, or rely on a lack of devices for implementation. Other sections of the UNCTOC on money-laundering and the tracing, seizure and forfeiture of the proceeds of crime may be useful in specific corruption cases. It is noteworthy that the application of the provisions on international law enforcement cooperation will only apply to corruption cases if they involve an "organized criminal group" and are "transnational in nature" as defined by the Organized Crime Convention.

(7) UNCAC

On the heels of the UNCTOC, in late 2000 the UN decided to pursue the negotiation of a *global* convention focused solely on the issue of corruption. As a first step, an Intergovernmental Open-Ended Expert Group was asked to prepare draft terms of reference for the negotiation of the Convention. These terms of reference were set out in a further General Assembly resolution which requested the Ad Hoc Committee to adopt a comprehensive and multidisciplinary approach and to consider some specific elements, namely: definitions; scope; protection of sovereignty; preventive measures; criminalization; sanctions and remedies; confiscation and seizure; jurisdiction; liability of legal persons; protection of witnesses and victims; promoting and strengthening international cooperation; preventing and combating the transfer of funds of illicit origin derived from acts of corruption, including the laundering of funds, and returning such funds; technical assistance; collection, exchange and analysis of information; and mechanisms for monitoring implementation. After preparatory work in 2001, negotiations began in 2002 through an Ad Hoc Committee constituted for such purpose, the first treaty on the subject to have a universal intent. The committee held seven negotiating sessions, the last of which was in October 2003. The United States and the members of the EU participated actively in all sessions, and maintained materially diverging positions.[35] The year 2003 finally saw the adoption of the UNCAC. A report of the negotiations was submitted to the UN General Assembly shortly thereafter, and the Convention and accompanying resolution were adopted by the General Assembly. Upon the Convention's opening for signature in December 2003, the United States, most of the members of the EU, and many emerging countries immediately opted to sign.

Various devices were used in an effort to ease the process of negotiation, among which was the adoption of an Interpretative Note.[36] Seventy-five of such notes were agreed. Such Notes provide a gloss upon phrases and

---

35 For an authoritative and vivid reconstruction of the negotiation process we refer to Vlassis (2007: 21–23).

36 United Nations A/58/422/Add.1. Report of the Ad Hoc Committee for the Negotiation of a Convention against Corruption on the work of its first to seventh sessions. Addendum. Interpretative notes for the official records (*travaux*

whole paragraphs in particular Articles. The legal value of the Legislative Guide is that they show the reasoning that led the negotiators to adopt a particular approach and so make for a uniform interpretation of the text. This assumes, of course, that the Notes are read, although the text of the UNCAC makes no reference to the existence of such Notes. In so confirming the ambiguity of many provisions of the UNCAC, the UN Office on Drugs and Crime (UNODC) has developed a Legislative Guide for the Implementation of the United Nations Conventions against Corruption (hereinafter: Legislative Guide). The objective of the Legislative Guide is to assist States seeking to ratify and implement the Convention by identifying legislative requirements, issues arising from those requirements and various options available to States as they develop and draft the necessary legislation. The Legislative Guide is not intended to provide definitive legal interpretation of the Articles of the UNCAC Convention. Its content is not compulsory and, in assessing each specific requirement, the actual language of the provisions should be consulted. As to its membership, the State Parties to the UNCAC include significant international players that are not parties to any other international anti-corruption treaty. Most notably in this regard is the People's Republic of China. The Convention has already attracted adherents from virtually every region of the globe.

In commenting on its universal aspiration, some authors have been rather optimistic. According to Low (2008) and Murphy (2004), for instance, the UNCAC's rapid acceptance by a considerable (and increasing) number of countries testifies to its potential to create truly international standards, alongside worldwide infrastructure for international cooperation by governments in the prosecution of corruption cases. It is unquestionable that the very adoption of a universal treaty against corruption represents a main achievement in its own right. Rajesh Babu (2006) goes even further and argues that the capacity for universality makes the Convention capable of playing a role that no other international anti-corruption convention can play. However, as we explain below, the general structure of such a convention is affected by some shortcomings which challenge its actual universal potential as a global common standard. The Ad Hoc Committee certainly met the request for a comprehensive and multidisciplinary approach by drafting a Convention with 71 long and detailed Articles grouped into eight Chapters: Chapter, I General Provisions (Articles 1–4); Chapter II, Preventive Measures (Articles 5–14); Chapter III, Criminalization and Law Enforcement (Articles

---

préparatoires) of the negotiation of the United Nations Convention against Corruption, available at: www.unodc.org, accessed on 29 September 2008.

15–42); Chapter IV, International Cooperation (Articles 43–50); Chapter V, Asset Recovery (Articles 50–9); Chapter VI, Technical Assistance and Information Exchange (Articles 60–2); Chapter VII, Mechanisms for Implementation (Articles 63–4), and Chapter VIII, Final Provisions (Articles 65–71).

The agreement presents several important innovations with respect to existing international anti-corruption conventions; there are nevertheless a number of constants, starting with the consideration that international corruption is a socio-political and economic phenomenon, which acquires an extraordinarily aggressive impact, by extending its reach beyond the frontiers of individual States.

As to the *scope* of the UNCAC, it attempts to cover most of the areas which might prevent, curb, or control domestic and transnational corrupt activities. Not only does it deal with the full gamut of topics – from prevention to civil and criminal enforcement – but it also encompasses a wide range of criminal offenses, which only *lato sensu* may be classified as corruption. In addition, the UNCAC addresses a wide range of preventive measures, international cooperation, and technical assistance.

One of the most original features of the Convention is its provisions on asset recovery (in its Chapter V) which is expressly recognized in its Article 51 as "a fundamental principle of the Convention". The provisions on asset recovery have been hailed as ground-breaking by some, but this overstates their effective impact and probably overlooks the main issues tackled by these provisions. Notwithstanding, its explicit qualification as "a fundamental principle" of the UNCAC, the *travaux préparatoires* indicate that this wording has no legal consequences for the other provisions of the chapter. Several provisions specify the forms of cooperation and assistance: for example, embezzled public funds that have been confiscated must be returned to the requesting State.

Despite its sweeping reach, the approach taken is generally similar to that found in other anti-corruption conventions: many of its provisions are not self-executing. In other words, these provisions require implementation through the national laws of participating countries, as well as national enforcement. This is generally true with respect to preventive measures, criminalization, and a number of the asset recovery provisions as well. In contrast, some of the central provisions of the international cooperation chapter – as is the case with other conventions – are mainly self-executing. It is noteworthy that even these provisions do not operate in a *vacuum*, but work together with existing conventions in the areas of extradition and mutual legal assistance as well as national laws. With regard to all these matters, the way in which Contracting States implement and enforce these provisions will become the key issues in assessing the UN Convention's impact and effectiveness.

A first important remark on the UNCAC concerns the text: due to its length, the frequency of cross-references, and an excessive use of claw-back clauses which sometimes operate even in tandem in the same provision, the formulation of many provisions is barely intelligible without careful and time-consuming analysis. This clearly emerges when comparing the UNCAC with other Conventions, such as, for instance, the OECD Convention.

On paper, the UNCAC is by far the most comprehensive and ambitious of all the international anti-corruption conventions to date: it takes a holistic approach, covering three major aspects of fighting corruption: prevention, criminalization, and international cooperation. At the same time, the UNCAC enters territory previously almost unexplored by other conventions, including asset recovery, and provisions on collateral consequences. What is more – thus coming to one of its central problems – the UNCAC has a substantial number of non-mandatory provisions and, as stressed by Low (2005), no fewer than a dozen different levels of implementation obligations, which results in creating for States Parties a range of obligations from hard (mandatory requirements) to very soft.

Legal doctrine has highlighted this aspect, recognizing, that, on the one hand, a certain degree of flexibility is needed to take account of the different legal traditions and contingent conditions of the various participating countries, ease of implementation by States Parties and to facilitate activities required by the Convention. On the other hand, in this field there is a strong need for consistency and a degree of harmonization *at the international level.* In our view, the drafters of the UNCAC gave (some argue) 'too' high a priority to flexibility with the purpose of accommodating an agreement meeting the various contracting parties' positions. More decisively, Schroth (2005b) points to the main principles guiding the work of the Ad Hoc Committee for the Negotiation of UNCAC and highlights that it appears to have achieved consensus and to have finished on time. In supporting its case, Schroth makes us note that the Ad Hoc Committee received its mandate in General Assembly Resolution 55/61 of 4 December 2000 and General Assembly Resolution 56/260 of 31 January 2002, with the latter Resolution suggesting that the conference for signing the new Convention be convened before the end of 2003. This overwhelming aim would have resulted in radically reducing the consistency and effectiveness of the Convention as a result. Some commentators go even further: Webb (2005) wonders if the UNCAC results in a missed opportunity or in another example of *lex simulata* without legal teeth. In this spirit, Schroth has titled his analytical essay "The United Nations Convention Against

Doing Anything Serious About Corruption. Termites in the House: A Polemic", which could have hardly better expressed his harsh criticism. Yet, it must be acknowledged that the UNCAC has a enormous symbolic significance and substantive potentials:

> Only a few years ago, speaking of the possibility of such an instrument, and saying it would be negotiated in such a short time, would have brought ironic smiles to the faces of most people (. . .) Negotiating the Convention was not an easy undertaking. There were many complex issues and concerns from different quarters that the negotiators had to tackle. It was a formidable challenge to maintain the quality of the new instrument while making sure that all of these concerns were properly reflected in the final text. Very often compromise was not easy and all countries made concessions. (Vlassis, 2007: 32)

We now venture to analyze the UNCAC's formulation and structure which has given rise to such criticism. As hinted above, the most immediate feature of the Convention is its comprehensiveness. The UNCAC obligates Member States to undertake certain obligations and set forth common standards, which need to be implemented or incorporated into their respective domestic legal systems, in the widest area of action. Most of the obligations require State Parties to enact new laws or incorporate/amend existing laws. To achieve this, the Convention attempts to set certain minimum standards, which could be used by the States within their domestic legal systems and in international cooperation. These provisions are clearly non-self-executing because, of their very nature, they need municipal legislation to implement and complete them. This framework is quite in the natural course of international treaties and their negotiations. Nor does it constitute a substantial deviation from other anti-bribery treaties. By contrast, several provisions of the UNCAC *permit* but *do not require* Contracting Parties to implement them in their own municipal legal systems. Still others just call for countries to "consider" taking certain steps. Others apparently impose requirements but then establish permissive escape hatches. Such provisions are still not self- executing, but for the very fact they establish mere options. As a consequence, the UN Convention might end up bringing about only quite limited changes in the national law, because so many of its provisions are optional, either explicitly or not, while others mainly restate the existing obligations of many countries.

Schroth (2005b) characterizes these provisions as "termites" to convey the sense that such words eat away at the substance of treaty clauses by making plain obligations no obligations at all. He identifies three picturesque sub-species of termites which allegedly erode the substance of the UNCAC, namely: ordinary workers; venomous warriors; and a (seemingly weak) queen. "Ordinary worker" termites grind down the substance of a treaty provision, leaving an empty shell. No lawyer would have much difficulty constructing an argument that "in accordance with the fundamental principles of its domestic law" or "to the extent consistent with the fundamental principles of its legal system" – two of the many formulations used by the drafters of the UNCAC, corresponding to the many varieties of protective coloration of the worker termites in the Convention – or any other similar formulations, giving priority over the Convention's provision to a competing provision of national law.

The "venomous warrior termites" directly damage the legal systems of prone States Parties. We may epitomise such type of "eroding parasite" with the illicit enrichment provision of the OAS Convention (Chapter 11) as reproduced quite faithfully by the AU Convention. Schroth argues that it was Article IX of the OAS Convention that first harboured a venomous warrior termite. As he put it, its effect is to protect the constitutionalism of countries with an entrenched presumption of innocence, while permitting countries that fail to recognize the presumption of innocence to base their denial of this human right on a treaty obligation. The same spirit seems to animate the UNCAC provision on illicit enrichment. The Article dealing with such crime was controversial since in its original formulation as it is witnessed in the Ad Hoc Committee's deliberations. Suffice it here to recall that in the May 2003 draft of the UNCAC Convention, that Article is accompanied by the note submitted by the delegations of the Russian Federation, the Member States of the European Union, and others expressing their strong wish to delete this Article. However, as happened in relation to other provisions, the disagreement concerning illicit enrichment was worked out by making the controversial provisions optional. In the final version of Article 20, State Parties that recognize the presumption of innocence are protected not only by the Convention's most powerful termite "Subject to its constitution and the fundamental principles of its legal system," – a formulation which Schroth (2005b) notes is used nowhere else in the Convention – but also by making that Article entirely optional through the paradigmatic clause "each State Party shall consider adopting . . .". Thus, Article 20 of the UNCAC mirrors a clear compromise between the acknowledgement of Parties that recognize the effectiveness of criminalising illicit enrichment, on the one hand, and, on the other, the concerns expressed by other States that such offence may conflict with the fundamental rights of the accused. The net result is that the criminalization of illicit enrichment is remitted to the will of national legislators. The pros and cons of the offence at issue (which are at the very heart of the final formulation of Art. 20) deserve some further thoughts.

BOX 10.1 CRIMINALIZATION OF ILLICIT ENRICHMENT: A LAST RESORT MEASURE?

The offence of possession of unexplained wealth, most commonly known as illicit enrichment, penalizes 'public officials for possessing wealth disproportionate to their known lawful sources of income if they cannot provide a satisfactory explanation for this' (Perdriel-Vaissiere, 2012: 2). Illicit enrichment can serve to reduce the possibly 'burdensome procedural and evidential requirements associated with other corruption offenses, helping with identification of illicit funds and triggering of asset recovery efforts' (Muzila *et al.*, 2012: 254). The primary potential benefits of such offence lies in the fact that prosecuting authorities have to establish the public official's legitimate sources of income, the extent of assets under his or her control and the discrepancy between the two. In so doing, "once such a *prima facie* case for illicit enrichment is made, the defendant can reverse the presumption by making a reasonable cases from legitimate sources." (Perdriel-Vaissiere, 2012: 2) Having such an offence established by law can ease the work of the prosecution since it avoids the requirement to establish guilt for a specific criminal offence: those States which sponsored the introduction of a duty to criminalize such an offence in the UNCAC considered it a proportionate response to the practical difficulties faced by the prosecutors when pursuing corruption. However, since the offence establishes a presumption of liability upon proof of excessive wealth, it may infringe on the right of the persons charged with criminal offence to the presumption of innocence, until proved guilty. Rather notably, the United Nations Human Rights Committee states: 'the burden of proof of the charge is on the prosecution and the accused has the benefit of doubt. No guilt can be presumed until the charge has been proved beyond any legitimate doubt' (United Nations Office of the High Commissioner for Human Rights 1984, 124, para. 7). Notwithstanding the above, the principle of presumption of innocence does not prevent legislatures from creating criminal offenses containing a presumption by law as long as the principles of reasonableness and proportionality are duly respected (Muzila *et al.*, 2012). The ECHR's jurisprudence on the issue is crystal clear: resorts to presumptions are compatible with the presumption of innocence subject to the following two conditions: i) the primary responsibility for proving matters of criminal relevance against the accused rests with the prosecution (i.e. there is no reversal of the burden of proof onto the defendant; ii) the presumptions are rebuttable (*Salabiaku v. France*, ECHR, 1988, Application no.10519/83). The legislative Guide to the UNCAC (UNODC, 2006) states also that the offence established in Art. 20 of the Convention should not be seen as contrary to the presumption of innocence. Some commentators share this standing (Muzila et al., 2012; Jayawickrama, Pope, and Stolpe 2002; De Speville 1997), whilst Wilsher (2006) and Snider and Kidane (2007) argue that the offence of illicit enrichment infringes on the rights of the accused since no act needs to be proven for the crime to be presumed (i.e. the constituent elements of the offence – being a public official with excessive and unexplained wealth – do not themselves constitute criminal activity. Furthermore, as rightly remarked by Perdriel-Vaissiere (2012), this raises a further issue with reference to another fundamental principle we already mentioned in the book: the principle of legality, which requires that offences be clearly defined under the law so that "the individual can know from the wording of the relevant provision what acts and omissions will make him liable" (*Kokkinakis v. Greece*, ECHR, 1993). The fact that the above referred constituent elements of the illicit enrichment offence do not require an explicit connection between excessive wealth and criminal activities (corruption, embezzlement, and so on) may prevent public officials from having clear criteria enabling them to avoid engaging in prohibited conduct, thus infringing the fundamental principle of legality. In light of the above, we do believe that the compromise of which Art. 20 of the UNCAC is the result was the only viable option for the negotiators: criminalization of illicit enrichment represents an effective *and* proportionate response to the impossibility (or extreme difficulty) for the prosecution to pursue corruption offences only to the limited extent that the above referred principles – codified in several constitutional systems of the States Parties – are not cut down.

This explains why the offence of illicit enrichment is seen as an *extrema ratio* resort, which must be accompanied by sufficient guarantees: first, its use must be proportionate in the sense of strictly necessary – i.e. "when enforcement authorities can pursue cases by prosecuting regular corruption offences, the illicit enrichment offence, with its implied limitations of defendant's rights, should not be considered a proportionate response" (Perdriel-Vaissiere 2012:3). Secondly, resort to what substantially is a presumption must not infringe the principle of the presumption of innocence: the two conditions set out by the ECHR in *Salabiaku v. France* cannot tolerate any minimal derogation. Finally, by resorting to the offence of illicit enrichment, public prosecutors are not preempted from presenting whatever evidence is available that the unexplained possession of wealth is likely to result from conduct punishable under criminal law. To conclude the point, when such safeguards are in place, criminalization of illegal enrichment could be possible while the rights of the accused are not compressed: by easing the work of prosecutors and confiscation of unexplained wealth the offence of illicit enrichment as established in the UNCAC can alter the balancing of "risk versus reward" in several corruption cases (Jayawickrama, Pope, and Stolpe 2002), (i.e. the more likely the prosecution becomes and the more frequent the confiscation of assets, the less public officials' temptation to engage in corruption should result. On the other hand, "it is also essential to ensure the final administration of justice" both for pragmatic and legal reasons: "the more defendant's rights are respected, the less likely it is that the final decision will be challenged, and the more likely it is that a confiscation order will be enforced." (Perdriel-Vaissiere 2012:4). It is finally worth stressing that, though the criminalization of illicit enrichment is meant to alleviate the difficulties in prosecuting corruption cases by requiring public prosecutors to simply prove the existence of unexplained wealth, there remain significant operational hurdles, the most significant of which is probably the collection of evidence. "For example, in many countries there are not up to date, searchable databases that can be used to identify assets. The same impediments arise for the identification of bank accounts. (. . .) In addition, financial investigations are particularly difficult in countries where there is a substantial clash economy". Furthermore, "preparation of financial profile is further complicated by the use of third parties, front entities and straw men to disguise ownership of assets" (Muzila et al., 2012: 252). Such hurdles explain why the utility of illicit enrichment in the prosecution of corruption and in the confiscation process depends largely on its integration into a wider anti-corruption policy and on the existence of systems in place to ease the identification of potential cases and produce the relevant information to support the investigations.

Schroth goes even further in illustrating cases of UNCAC provisions which would limit the entire effectiveness of the Treaty itself. The "queen termite" is found in Article 65 of the UNCAC, which rules the entire implementation of the Convention's provision, and reads as follows:

1. Each State Party shall take the necessary measures, including legislative and administrative measures, in accordance with fundamental principles of its domestic law, to ensure the implementation of its obligations under this Convention.
2. Each State Party may adopt more strict or severe measures than those provided for by this Convention for preventing and combating corruption.

If the purpose of Article 65 (especially, paragraph 1) is to ensure that municipal legislators act to implement the provisions of the UNCAC in conformity with the fundamental principles of their legal system – as would seem to be the case from a reading of the Legislative Guide to the UNCAC, at paragraph 18 – and, consequently, to ease the implementation of the Convention, the provision at issue read in its entirety is not crystal clear. Indeed, it leaves open two possible interpretations. As Schroth (2005b) and Borlini and Magrini (2007) note, the clause in Article 65(1) could first be understood as requiring each State Party to do everything necessary to carry out its obligations set forth in the rest of the Convention, with the "in accordance" wording merely about the manner in which it is to be done; in the end little more than a make-up clause. In the alternative interpretation, one might argue that the clause must be read as a fundamental general provision qualifying each obligation of a State Party set forth anywhere in the UNCAC by the limitation that it needs to comply only to the extent that in so doing it acts in accordance with the fundamental principles of its domestic law. It is plain that the two readings lead to rather diverging outcomes as to the actual strength of the UNCAC with respect to municipal jurisdictions. For this reason, a decision on the point by the ICJ would have been more than welcome. Coming to Article 65(2), it brings less substantial problems: "strict or severe measures" is a vague formula, open to interpretation. However, it seems beyond reasonable doubt that its drafters meant only that the Convention sets minimum standards.

Overall, all the variant and qualifications provided by the several Articles of the UNCAC increase the complexity so much that any analysis of the Convention and its potential impact must be considered carefully, also (if not above all) by the Member States when implementing it.

The status of implementation is rather advanced; unfortunately, too advanced to give us any hope of decisive amendments by the State Parties or, with reference to Article 65(1), for a key interpretation by the ICJ. Thus, it is now the responsibility of each Member to vigorously enact the innovative provisions of the UNCAC: its setting of a floor for national measures without prescribing the precise approach to be taken in adopting such measures leaves States with the freedom to adopt measures that may or may not be consistent with the measures adopted by other States. According to Low (2005), this does not only affect the whole efficacy of the international anti-corruption system, but, from a business compliance standpoint, the UNCAC seems to complicate unnecessarily what is already a considerably more complex picture than existed before the emergence of the first international anti-corruption agreements. We believe that this minimal outcome should have been foreseen and accurately prevented; the entire international anti-corruption apparatus would have greatly benefited from mandatory basic provisions. In support of the same thesis, Low (2005) provides other interesting examples: those obligations, which, in the case of a few provisions, are dependent on a country's economic means; the fact that, for some measures, two or more of the above-mentioned qualifiers operate in tandem, and the circumstance that in several places the UNCAC appears to give overarching deference to national sovereignty (e.g. Article 4) and domestic policy decisions. This intricacy arises even before turning to the question of the possible reservations countries may take (not specifically addressed in the Convention), the mechanisms for implementation, and the aptitude of countries to implement its obligations. This lack of simplicity also increases the likelihood that the Convention, despite its goal of universality, will not harmonize international standards. Rather, it will produce an even more diverse array of national obligations than already exists.

To conclude, it is worth reporting the evocative comment of the late Ambassador Héctor Charry Samper at the Third Session of the Ad Hoc Committee which now seems prophetic:

> The Chairman also expressed his concern at the repeated reference in the draft text of the convention to the conformity of its provisions with domestic law. In his view, such references should be the exception rather than the norm, because international law was not meant to be a mere reflection of national law. Further, the Chairman expressed the view that the Ad Hoc Committee had to work earnestly to avoid the perception that some proposals might [reduce]

> the scope of the new convention. In that connection, the Chairman recalled General Assembly resolution 56/260, in which the Assembly had requested the Ad Hoc Committee to develop a broad and effective convention, following a comprehensive and multi-disciplinary approach.[37]

The ambitious design of the UN text has a *second fundamental shortcoming* highlighted specifically by commentators who give serious consideration to the needs of developing countries. Freeman (2005) voices the criticism towards one of the main issues overlooked by the text: the need for adequate resources so that developing countries are put in a position to be able to fully comply and reap benefit from it. Since adequate resources are a *sine qua non* condition of real progress, no State can operate at the UNCAC's required level of sophistication unless it has the necessary legal, administrative, educational, and professional infrastructures, coupled with the political will. Before concluding this general outline of the UNCAC, we reflect on its two innovative chapters.

In what several observers consider a major breakthrough, States have agreed on asset recovery. This is potentially a particularly relevant innovation for many developing countries where high-level corruption has plundered national wealth and where resources are badly needed for reconstruction and the rehabilitation of society under a new government. The negotiating process of the UNCAC reveals the objective of recovering the public assets stolen through *lato sensu* corrupt practices, by despots like Alberto Fujimori in Peru, Mobuto Sese Seko in Zaire, Mohamed Suharto in Indonesia, and Robert Mugabe in Zimbabwe. Reaching agreement on this chapter of the Convention involved intensive negotiation, as the needs of States seeking such illicit assets had to be reconciled with the legal and procedural safeguards of the States whose assistance was sought.

Article 54(1)(a)–(b), 54(2)(a)–(c), Article 55 in its entirety, and Articles 56 and 59 specify how cooperation and assistance are to be rendered. In particular, in the case of the embezzlement of public funds, the confiscated property is to be returned to the State requesting it (Article 55(1)(a)–(b)). On the other hand, in the case of the proceeds of any other offense covered by the Convention, the property is to be returned, providing there is proof of ownership or recognition of the damage caused to a requesting State (Article 55(2) and 57(3)(a)–(b)). In all other cases, priority consideration is to be given to the return of confiscated property to the requesting

37 Report of the Ad Hoc Committee for the Negotiation of a Convention against Corruption on the work of its first to seventh sessions, para. 49, available at: http://www.unodc.org/unodc/en/treaties/CAC/background/adhoc-committee.html, accessed on 27 March 2006.

State, to the return of such property to the prior legitimate owners or to compensation of the victims. Effective provisions on asset recovery should support the efforts of States to redress some of the worst economic effects of corruption while, at the same time, sending a message to corrupt officials that there is scant possibility of hiding their illicit assets. To what extent the panoply of instruments the UNCAC envisages can accomplish such an ambitious aim is still an open issue which can be addressed only in light of the future results of cooperation between States which effectively implement the UNCAC. However, it should be stressed that there is no unanimity as regards the effective potential of the mechanisms set forth by the UNCAC: disappointment as to the issue has been advanced by authoritative voices. Notably, Webb (2005) and Schroth (2005b) argue that it is not as revolutionary as many comments tend to portray it because many of the provisions of these Articles are either qualified or entirely optional. However, the opinions just referred to mirror the main school of thought that emerged right after the adoption of the UNCAC. In our view, the very fact that Chapter V of the UNCAC provides the necessary legal framework to enable countries to prevent the transfer of proceeds of corruption and detect, trace, freeze, forfeit and return funds obtained through corrupt activities and move across jurisdictions (in some, for the operation of the StAR initiative)[38] represents a strong case for appreciating what has been defined as the main "selling point" of the Treaty at issue.

Like Article XIV(2) of the OAS Convention, Articles 60 and 62 of the Convention deal with training and technical assistance. Article 60 requires countries to develop or improve training for personnel to the extent necessary and suggests areas where such training should occur. It also obligates States Parties, although within their capacity, to provide technical assistance in training to developing countries, both bilaterally and through international organizations and agreements. Article 60 concludes by recommending that countries share the names of asset forfeiture experts, use conferences and seminars to promote cooperation, establish voluntary mechanisms to contribute financially to developing countries' efforts, and voluntarily contribute to the UN Office on Drugs and Crime to foster programs and projects in developing countries.[39] Article 62 obligates parties to make concrete efforts to enhance cooperation with developing countries, including financial and material assistance and technical assistance, and to "endeavor" to contribute to the UN funding mechanism, including through forfeited assets. Article 62 also encourages countries to persuade

---

38 See Chapter 17 of the present work.

39 UNCAC, Article 60(5)–(6).

other States and financial institutions to join in these efforts. The latter provisions are very welcome as the need for adequate resources to develop legal, administrative, educational, and professional infrastructures – at the moment missing in several States – is a *sine qua non* to allow developing countries to be able to fully comply with the UNCAC and reap material benefit from it. This issue has been correctly identified by Freeman (2005) and Borlini and Magrini (2007) as one of the main challenges to the implementation of the UNCAC.

Article 61 of the Convention suggests, but does not require, that each State Party analyze corruption trends and circumstances within its territory and share statistics, expertise, and other information in order to develop common definitions, standards, and best practices. It also suggests that countries monitor anti-corruption efforts and assess their effectiveness and efficiency.[40]

In light of the extensive prevention and enforcement measures of the UNCAC, many of the Contracting Parties will require substantial support to take the necessary steps to implement it. In our opinion, were it actually implemented, this part of the Convention would send a strong signal to the development community that assistance to curb corruption is a priority of as much importance as prevention and repression. More optimistically, Rooke (2003) suggests that the mere existence of technical assistance provisions properly emphasizes the relevance of development coordinated activities. It seems to us that the potential for such innovation relies to a significant extent on the political will of Member States to endeavor in such assisting commitments, even though appreciable in principle, as with the rest of the UN text. During the first Conference of the States Parties to the United Nations Convention against Corruption (held in Vienna, Austria, in October–December 2007), the Working Group on technical assistance has emphasized the need to coordinate "needs assessments and gap analyses" conducted by multilateral and bilateral institutions with a view to enhancing the impact of technical assistance. Finally, the provisions on technical assistance and information exchange confirm once more the need for a holistic approach to combating both traditional and new forms of corruption. Anechiarico and Jacobs (1996) aptly argued more than ten years ago that searching for effective solutions to the corruption problem, meant that States should look beyond the traditional strategies of monitoring, control, and punishment, since laws, rules, and threat would never result in a public administration to be proud of. On the contrary, the danger they emphasized was that such a one-dimensional

40 UNCAC, Article 61.

approach would create a self-fulfilling prophecy; having been placed continuously under suspicion, treated like quasi-criminals or probationers, public employees would behave accordingly as a result.

The last two chapters of the UN Convention provide for implementation, including a conference of States Parties; establishment of a secretariat; domestic implementation; dispute settlement; and entry into force, amendment, denunciation, and depositary information.

The Convention leaves partially open the issue of a monitoring mechanism (which, we discuss in detail in chapter 16). From the very text of the UNCAC, it emerges that it calls for a robust mechanism of implementation in the form of a Conference of States Parties (COSP) and with a secretariat that would be charged to assist it in the performance of its functions. These provisions are plainly inspired by the UNCTOC, 'but go considerably beyond that instrument, both in terms of scope and detail. The Secretary General is called upon to convene the first meeting of the Conference within one year of the entry of the Convention into force, and the Ad Hoc Committee which produced the Convention is preserved and called upon to meet one final time to prepare draft rules of procedure for adoption by the Conference, "well before" its first meeting' (Vlassis, 2007: 30). Eventually, the decision on a mechanism for review of implementation of the UNCAC was taken at the Third COSP in Doha, Qatar, in November 2009. The States Parties decided to set up a multi-staged peer review mechanism involving the review of each State Party by two peers. In mid 2010 the first 35 countries were drawn as well as their reviewing counterparts. The review process is supposed to take no more than six months for any given country at any given stage of the process. To cover all countries, the process will be divided into a five-year cycle. Compliance with Chapters III and IV is assessed during the ongoing first cycle, whereas Chapters II and V will be assessed during the second. The review process consists of a desk review based on the self-assessment report of the reviewed party but only intends country visits if requested by the reviewed country. External scrutiny by other actors (for example civil society or academic experts) is not required, though each State Party is free to choose such additional measures. Only the executive summaries of the country review reports is to be published, unless a reviewed country chooses otherwise.[41]

Article 66, Settlement of Disputes, provides for negotiation, arbitration, and ultimately the jurisdiction of the ICJ in resolving disputes. The Article also provides that any State may reserve to this provision. In greater

41 See Chapter 16 for a critical appraisal of such mechanism.

detail, paragraph 1 provides that where disputes arise concerning the interpretation and the application of the Treaty, State Parties are required to ("*shall*") attempt to solve them through negotiation. Paragraph 2 provides that any dispute that cannot be settled within a reasonable time by means of negotiation shall, at the request of any disputing State Party, be submitted to arbitration. Absent agreement on any other forum, the dispute is to be referred to the ICJ. Nevertheless, under paragraph 3, any State Party may, at the time of signature, ratification, acceptance, approval, or accession to the UNCAC, opt out by declaring itself not to be bound by paragraph 2. In other words, as far as the Convention itself is concerned, States may opt out of compulsory third party dispute resolution altogether.

It is somewhat debatable that a developing country would benefit from opting out. Firstly, paragraph 3 establishes that States which have opted out cannot take any other State to compulsory dispute resolution under paragraph 2. Secondly, it is possible (if not likely) that a developing country may come under various sorts of political and commercial pressure to accept the compulsory jurisdiction if disputes arise and cannot be set by negotiation. On the other hand, justice from an international jurisdiction is never free of incidental and costly legal and other expenses. Thus, it sounds sensible, as some commentators maintain, that the UN should provide marginal and weaker countries with assistance, training programs, and financial support.

Finally, it is worth stressing that Article 67(4) explicitly states the open nature of the Convention and Article 67(3) makes it possible also for international governmental organizations to become a party to the UNCAC, provided that at least one of the Member States of the international organization at issue is part of the Convention. The rationale for this provision is manifestly to ease and encourage direct contact among the different organizations dealing with the fight against corruption. The EU became part of the UNCAC on 2 March 2006.

(8) IFIs' initiatives

An important contribution by multilateral and international organizations in the fight against corruption can be summarized in the creation of a set of rules/incentives finalized to direct and constrain economic agents' behavior.

Multilateral financial organizations, the WTO and supervisory/regulatory institutions have invested a considerable amount of resources in the definition of international transparency standards and codes of conduct. This regulatory activity has been twinned with intense surveillance effort in Member States. Even the disbursement of funds has, in some cases, been linked to the introduction of anti-corruption or 'law-enhancing' rules; by constraining agents to virtuous behavior, many elements at the root of corruption have been removed. Moreover, by forcing governments to adopt more transparent data, consistent with international standards, the surveillance activity of the multilateral organization has indirectly favored a more transparent management of economic policies. The IFIs have taken new initiatives to avoid financing actual or potentially corrupt activity and to enhance the quality of public institutions. After years of disregarding the impediments to development caused by corruption, in the 1990s the regional development bank, including the European Bank for Reconstruction and Development (EBRD), the African Development Bank (AfDB), the Asian Development Bank (ADB), and the Inter-American Development Bank (IDB) began to firmly address the issue of corruption and its relationship with development.

(8.1) The World Bank's Governance and Anticorruption Strategy As known far and wide, the WB[42] provides low-interest loans, interest-free credits, and grants to developing countries for a wide array of purposes that include investments in education, health, public administration, infrastructure, financial and private sector development, agriculture, and environmental and natural resource management, with aggregate new lending commitments of approximately $60 billion and aggregate outstanding loans and credits of $230 billion in Fiscal Year 2010. With the financial support provided by the Bank, borrowers implement projects and programs, including the procurement of goods, works, and services necessary to carry out the project or program activities. Poverty reduction is the main mission of the Bank's work. With much evidence demonstrating the link between governance and poverty reduction, and between corruption, governance, and aid effectiveness, enhancing governance and fighting corruption are key to achieving this mission. Thus, the WB supports strengthening governance and addressing corruption through

---

42 The World Bank is a term used to refer collectively to two institutions, the International Bank for Reconstruction and Development (IBRD) and the International Development Association (IDA). IBRD began operations in 1947, with the purpose of providing loans to developing countries, while IDA was founded much later, in 1960, to provide financing on concessional terms to the poorest and least creditworthy developing countries. The World Bank is part of the World Bank Group, a constellation of institutions including, in addition to IBRD and IDA, the International Finance Corporation (IFC), the Multilateral Investment Guarantee Agency (MIGA) and the International Center for Settlement of Investment Disputes (ICSID).

projects and programs that improve transparency in public financial management; strengthen tax and customs administration; enhance civil service performance; support legal and judicial reform; combat corruption; and enable local and central governments to deliver services and regulate the economy more effectively. The WB commitment against illegal activities, and specifically corruption, is extremely important for both the amount of resources deployed and the number of countries involved: according to Arnone and Iliopulos (2005), from 1996 to 2004 it developed more than 600 initiatives involving around 100 countries. It has lent on average more than $5 billion per year to help member countries build efficient and transparent institutions. A vast amount of WB resources are devoted to the creation of a governance system in its member countries in line with international standards of good conduct. Governance-enhancing and anti-corruption initiatives are usually adopted jointly, in the context of a medium-term Country Assistance Strategy aimed at public expenditure management, fighting corruption, public services and judiciary reforms, tax and administration policies, decentralization, and the supply of public services. WB activity against corruption has made clear that it is necessary to focus on four objectives: assistance to countries willing to fight corruption, introduction of anti-corruption policies as an evaluation criterion for financial aid, support for anti-corruption initiatives, and financing initiatives to prevent corruption.

In March 2007, following extensive consultations, the World Bank Group's Board of Directors approved a strategy to scale up technical assistance to improve good governance and tackle corruption in member countries, known as the Governance and Anticorruption Strategy (GAC Strategy) in the service of its development mandate.[43] In order to increase development effectiveness and poverty reduction, the World Bank has made significant progress in its governance and anti-corruption work: the adoption of the 2007 GAC strategy, has made GAC an integral part of Bank operations across sectors and countries. An updated strategy, endorsed by the Bank's Board in March 2012, will take this type of work even further. The GAC Strategy is far-ranging, calling for actions at the global, national, and project levels. Overall, it is based on a three-pronged program (Recanatini, 2013):

- First, helping countries build capable, transparent, and accountable institutions (enhancement of public institutions and capacity building).

---

43 Cfr. *generally* World Bank (2007). For more on WB Group anti-corruption efforts visit www.worldbank.org/integrity.

- Second, expanding partnerships with multilateral and bilateral development institutions, civil society, the private sector, and other actors in joint initiatives to address corruption, by focusing also on prevention (collective action and prevention).
- Third, minimizing corruption in World Bank-funded projects by assessing corruption risk in projects upstream, actively investigating allegations of fraud and corruption, and strengthening project oversight and supervision (monitoring, investigation and use of administrative sanctions against firms and individuals that have engaged in fraud and corruption in WB-financed projects).

The promotion of good governance and enhancement of public institutions, the introduction of anti-corruption policies as diagnostic criterion for financial aid constitutes one of the most effective tools to stimulate high regulatory standards and their actual enforcement within countries which benefit from lending operations. As we will see, taken to its extreme, this tool can lead the WB to decide to suspend or even to cancel a loan. Furthermore, incorporating Governance and Anticorruption into the Bank's activity across Countries, Sectors, and Regions now represents a crucial element of many projects and country programs, which integrate political economy assessments, risk identification and mitigation measures, and stronger controls and oversight mechanisms.[44] The implementation of the so-called Operational Risk Management Framework ("ORAF"), which was introduced in all projects in Fiscal Year 2011, has been further enabling the Bank and the assisted countries addressing risks related to poor governance and corruption, as part of the risk framework.[45] Noticeably, in fiscal year 2011, the Bank announced that it will not lend directly to finance budgets in countries that do not publish their budgets, though will in exceptional cases where countries at least commit to publish their budgets within twelve months. In addition, in sectors, the implementation of the GAC strategy has examined how to re-orient investment lending to foster institution-building and results-orientation.[46]

---

44 "A range of innovative governance projects in 18 countries is now being implemented with the assistance of the Governance Partnership Facility", World Bank (2012a: 2).

45 There exist ". . . good examples of political economy analysis for countries, sectors, projects across all regions of the Bank that are disseminated and shared with country teams. Some good examples of these include India's Power Sector; Mauritania Utility Service Reform; West Bank & Gaza Water and Sanitation; and Yemen Water Sector" (ID).

46 *Id.*, 2: "An example is how Bank support for Brazil's flagship conditional

Prevention, the second prong of the GAC Strategy is theoretically clearly distinguishable by the other two. However, in practice, it is frequently one of the key elements or one of the outcomes of the other two prongs. Prevention has lately become a major core of the WB Integrity Vice Presidency (INT)'s work.[47] Developing preventive tools is the first step in enhancing the Bank Group's daily operations. To this end, the INT has established a Preventive Services Unit (PSU) composed of specialists in operations from across the Bank with different backgrounds and expertise in various sectors, including legal and judicial reform, infrastructure, and social sectors.[48] The PSU's mandate includes a review, analysis and publication of fraud and corruption risks in Bank-supported operations, based on lessons learned from INT's investigative work, allegations trends, and other INT information. The PSU uses such information and knowledge to provide just in time advice to operational colleagues as regards the mitigation of integrity risks in Bank's operations at the design and implementation phases. In addition, the PSU also transfers this knowledge into various preventive tools (including, for example, the Fraud and Corruption Awareness Handbook, and the Red Flags tools brochure) and practical training and capacity-building materials utilized to raise awareness of fraud and corruption risks and appropriate preventive measures with colleagues inside and outside the Bank. The range of preventive measures recommended includes technical audits to avoid substandard quality; inserting representation and warranty clauses into certain contracts; the posting of hotline phone numbers in front of buildings to allow concerned citizens to file complaints; mapping of individuals with access to procurement information;

---

cash transfer program, Bolsa Familia, has improved accountability and reduced fraud and errors in the program".

47 INT was created as a Unit of the WB Group in 2001 and acquired the Vice Presidency status in 2008. Its mandate stems directly from the Bank's Articles of Agreement and, essentially, consists of investigating allegations of fraud and corruption involving Bank-financed projects or Bank Group funds and Trust Funds. INT is endowed with full operational independence.

48 Cfr, World Bank (2010a: 14–16); World Bank (2011a: 14–20). In 2012, INT's preventive services unit delivered 178 advisory engagements, providing both Bank staff and external stakeholders with ideas about how to strengthen the design of projects, address potential fraud and corruption issues in ongoing projects, and tighten policies at the sector, country or institutional level. INT helped build precautions against fraud and corruption into 84 high-risk projects that have a combined lending volume of USD 21.2 billion. See World Bank (2012b: 26–32). INT has also undertaken assessments of the risks and lessons learned about preventive measures at the sectoral level such as the Global Roads Review.

and asset and income disclosure for project implementation unit officials handling Bank funds.

The third prong, consisting mainly of the Bank's sanctions procedures, plays a dual role within the strategy: sanctions "protect Bank projects, but they also have a broader objective at the global level. While Bank sanctions can only be a relatively small part of the picture, the Bank aims to leverage its sanctions in order to help create an overall global disincentive structure for corrupt behavior" (Leroy, and Fariello: 2012, 1). The WB sanction regime is a peculiar instance of legal and institutional evolution (within the Bank) exemplifying a more remarkable contemporary trend: "an important and expanding body of law and practice is generated as a result of the internal administrative processes of international organizations" (*ib.* 1).[49] As widely acknowledged, a distinguishing element of contemporary international law is that an important and expanding body of law and practice is generated as a result of the internal administrative processes of international organizations' (Leroy and Fariello, 2012: 2).[50] An analytical illustration of the WB Sanction Regime, thus, allows us

49 The role of international organizations as key agents in creating and shaping new norms is a phenomenon of increasing relevance within the international community and, consequently, a growing field of study. See generally Alvarez (2005). Over the past two decades, international lawyers have voiced both enthusiasm and concern regarding the proliferation of international courts and tribunals, as well as a widely noted "turn to legislation" by the United Nations (UN) Security Council. For an authoritative analysis of such positions we refer to the in-depth analysis of Szasz (2002); Talmon (2005); Buergenthal (2001); Koskenniemi and Päivi Leino (2002).

50 This body of law and practice has been traditionally considered as the proper subject matter of international institutional law. However, it "has more recently been reconceptualised in terms of global constitutionalism . . . the exercise of international public authority . . . and the emergence of a new global administrative law . . ." (Leroy and Fariello, 2012:9). As to the first position see generally Bogdandy, Dann, and Goldmann, (2008:1377) who maintain that: "the legal framework of governance activities of international institutions should be conceived of as international institutional law, and enriched by a public law perspective, i.e. with constitutional sensibility and openness for comparative insights from administrative legal thinking." The second stand is eminently expressed by Kingsbury, Krisch, and Stewart, (2005:17) defining global administrative law "as comprising the mechanisms, principles, practices, and supporting social understandings that promote or otherwise affect the accountability of global administrative bodies, in particular by ensuring they meet adequate standards of transparency, participation, reasoned decision, and legality, and by providing effective review of the rules and decisions they make". Noteworthy, at least one participant in the World Bank's sanctions process has advocated basing its further development on global administrative law principles; see, Dubois and Nowlan (2010).

to extract more general features that further, and normative considerations that shape, law-making by international organizations. Due to its unique nature and complex articulation some dedicated considerations are appropriate.[51]

(8.1.1) THE WORLD BANK'S SANCTIONING REGIME[52] The World Bank's Articles of Agreement require the institution to make arrangements to ensure that the proceeds of Bank financing are used for their intended purposes and with due attention to economy and efficiency. This core requirement is usually referred to as the "fiduciary duty",[53] which shapes the legal and policy basis for much of the Bank's fiduciary framework for its operations, including its project-level anti-corruption efforts. Accordingly, since the WB has a fiduciary responsibility to its stakeholders to ensure that development funds are used for the intended purpose of promoting development and reducing poverty, and are not jeopardized by corruption, the sanctions regime must be looked at as an integral part of the GAC strategy: the diversion of funds from development projects through corruption impairs the ability of governments, donors and the WB to achieve the twin goals of reducing poverty and boosting shared prosperity. Thus, to accomplish its mandate, the WB Group has developed, among other things, a comprehensive series of procedures for the imposition of sanc-

---

51 Please note that we deal with such procedure in the context of the present chapter for plain systemic reasons. However, the illustration of the WB sanctions regime also completes the analysis of the sanctioning provisions of the anti-bribery international treaties as formulated in Chapter 12 of the present work.

52 We owe most of the material we collected and a clarifying and insightful illustration of the comprehensive WB Sanctions Procedures together with their salient elements (to mention a few: the precise definition of the different phases of the process, their possible outcomes thereof and the conditions they depend on, the interrelation between the different bodies involved, the national offspring of the Bank's investigations, the Voluntary Disclosure Program's goal and practical effects) to Ms. Pascale Hélène Dubois, Chief Suspension and Debarment Officer (SDO), Office of Suspension and Debarment (OSD). Dr. Leonardo Borlini met Ms. Dubois at the premises of the World Bank's OSD in Washington DC, on 2 June 2011 and on 25 January 2014. The views expressed in this section are those of the author alone and should not be attributed to Ms. Dubois. Another fundamental source for our reconstruction is the study of Leroy and Fariello (2012), who, without adopting any of the specific perspectives on the WB sanctions regime's nature (international institutional law; global constitutionalism; exercise of international public authority; emergence of new global administrative law) over the others, provide us with an in-depth analysis of the evolution of such a regime.

53 Such a duty is clearly crystallized in the IBRD and IDA's Agreements. See IBRD Articles of Agreement, Article III, Section 5 (b), IDA Articles of Agreement, Article V, Section 6. See also World Bank (2012c), Art. 1, section 1.01 (a).

tions, which has been evolving over the last 18 years.[54] The Bank has had a formal sanctions regime since 1996: the establishment of the system coincided with an increased focus and growing perception on corruption as a development issue. To be clear, whereas the sanctions system is an internal administrative process intended to address fraud and corruption committed by contractors and other third-party firms and individuals,[55] the Bank has also developed more extensive anti-corruption tools aimed at borrowers and other recipients of loan proceeds. In order to fully understand the WB comprehensive sanctions regime it is, thus, appropriate to distinguish between the aforementioned two levels of actions, i.e. the "sanctions regime *lato sensu*" and the "sanctions administrative procedures *stricto sensu*," or, in other words, between the broader operational side and the narrower administrative part of the regime.

On the operational side, the Bank Group has developed anti-corruption provisions in its legal agreements with borrowers and other recipients of Bank Group funds, as well as practices and procedures aimed at reducing the risk of, or detecting and addressing, potential fraud and corruption in Bank Group-financed operations and certain practices and procedures, particularly in the area of procurement, aimed at reducing the risk of, or detecting and addressing, potential fraud and corruption in Bank-financed operation.

These include the following elements:

a) The Procurement and Consultant Guidelines laid down within the WB, IDA and the IBRD for procurement under IBRD loans and IDA credits, as well as for resort to consultants by borrowers, including anti-corruption provisions.[56] Such provisions establish as Bank policy the requirement that borrowers and loan beneficiaries, as well as bidders, suppliers, contractors and consultants, maintain the 'highest standards of ethics' and, to this end, further provide for Bank sanctions as well as contractual remedies in the event that certain defined forms of fraud and corruption occur in connection with the procurement/selection or execution of Bank financed contracts.[57] The

---

54 For a thorough reconstruction of the evolution of the World Bank Sanction regime we refer to Leroy and Fariello (2012) and World Bank (2010b),

55 The rules governing the administrative sanctions procedures are set forth in World Bank (2012c).

56 World Bank (2011b); World Bank (2011c); World Bank (2006).

57 Cfr. Section 1.14 of the Procurement Guidelines and Section 1.22 of the Consultant Guidelines. The scope of the policy has been so expanded that the current versions of these provisions cover bidders, suppliers, and contractors and

procurement guidelines set forth serious consequences for violations. Upon discovery of corrupt or fraudulent conduct by a bidder or, once financing has been granted to a borrower, the guidelines establish that the WB will reject the bidder's proposals for awards, cancel the remaining portions of loans already granted to the borrower, and exclude the borrower from future WB financing, either for a specified time period or indefinitely. To support WB officials in policing possible corrupt or fraudulent activities, the guidelines give the WB the right to inspect the books and records of any suppliers and contractors involved in the execution of a Bank-financed contract,[58] and to submit the records to outside auditors appointed by the WB.

b) The WB is also endowed with remedies under the IBRD and IDA General Conditions that allow the Bank to cancel an amount of the loan equivalent to any Bank financed contract if it had been tainted by corruption[59] and to suspend disbursements, in whole or in part, in the event that fraud and corruption occurs without timely and appropriate action being taken to address the situation.[60] In this respect – though, as yet, rather isolated – the Bank's decision of June 29, 2012 to annul a USD 1.2 billion loan to Bangladesh because of the government's "inadequate response" to substantial allegations of corruption is momentous and represents a vigorous signal to the entire international community.[61] It is 'a case of international institutions deciding *not* to turn a blind eye to the passive side of corruption' (Bonucci: 2012, 68).

c) Furthermore, the so-called "Anti-Corruption Guidelines", like the Procurement and Consultant Guidelines, are incorporated by reference into the Bank's legal agreements.[62] The Anti-Corruption

---

their agents (whether declared or not), personnel, subcontractors, sub-consultants, service providers or suppliers.

58 See the Procurement Guidelines Section 1.14 (e), and the Consultant Guidelines 1.22 (e).

59 See the IBRD General Conditions for Loans 7.03 (c) (as amended 2006).

60 *Ibidem*, at 7.02 (c).

61 See the WB's press release published on that occasion, available at: www.worldbank.org/en/news2012/06/29world-bankstatement-padma-bridge.

62 Pursuant to World Bank (2012c), Art. I Section 1.02: '"Anti-Corruption Guidelines" means (i) the "Guidelines on Preventing and Combating Fraud and Corruption in Projects Financed by IBRD Loans and IDA Credits and Grants" dated as of October 15, 2006, as the same may be amended, supplemented or otherwise revised from time to time, (ii) the "Guidelines on Preventing and Combating Fraud and Corruption in Program-for-Results Financing," dated February 1, 2012, or (iii) any similar instrument which may replace said Guidelines under

Guidelines establish the harmonized definitions of Sanctionable Practices,[63] as well as a set of undertakings by the Borrower and other recipients of Bank funds aimed at preventing and combating fraud and corruption in connection with the use of such funds. These provisions also set out the Bank's right to sanction firms and individuals found to have engaged in any fraud and corruption in connection with the use of loan proceeds, not only in connection with procurement.

d) The sanctions system applies not only to cases relating to IBRD/IDA (World Bank), but also to IFC, MIGA and investment projects guaranteed by the World Bank (known as partial risk guarantees or "PRGs"), with adjustments appropriate to their different business models. IFC, MIGA and PRG operations form an integral part of the World Bank Group sanctions regime, and parties in these operations may be sanctioned for corrupt, fraudulent, collusive, coercive, or obstructive practices, in addition to being subject to contractual remedies for these same offenses.[64]

e) Other legal tools used by the WB in order to curb corruption include the so-called "smart project design", whereby "anti-corruption mechanisms – including the direct participation of clients in selecting and implementing projects, public disclosure requirements, and improved supervision through community-based project facilitators who are linked to national networks – are embedded within the projects and programs the Bank supports" (Leroy and Fariello, 2012: 31).

f) Finally, in addition to the legal tools outlined above, the Bank has recently developed a number of non-legal tools to help in its anti-corruption efforts. Perhaps the most notable of these tools is the Company Risk Profile Database (CRPD), a database of firms and individuals under investigation by INT. The CRPD is intended to

---

which a case may be brought in accordance with these Procedures.' Thus, such Guidelines include IBRD Loan and Project Agreements, and IDA Financing and Project Agreements, as well as Grant Agreements financed by IBRD or IDA administrated Recipient-Executed Trust Funds.

63 See *infra* the specific definitions provided in the present paragraph.

64 IFC, MIGA, and the World Bank's staff working on PRG have operationalized the sanctions regime through the inclusion of appropriate provisions in their financing/guarantee documents, technical assistance agreements and other documentation. Each entity has adopted Anti-Corruption Guidelines, attached to their legal agreements, which further explain the definitions and provide examples relevant to private sector operations. The IFC also discloses the sanctions process to prospective partners through its "mandate letter," which defines the scope and basic terms of IFC's investment.

> assist the Bank's operational staff in assessing whether a company or an individual being considered for a tender award poses a fiduciary risk. Noteworthy, the database is not a basis for objecting to a contract recommendation, but a tool to focus further inquiries.[65]

On the administrative side, the WB has established a formal two-tier process for sanctioning firms and individuals that have been found to have engaged in fraud and corruption in Bank Group-financed projects, primarily by declaring them ineligible to be awarded Bank Group-financed contracts or otherwise participate in Bank Group financed activities, a step commonly known as "debarment". The sanctions procedures have been lastly revised in 2011, and adopted on 15 April 2012. Also, in 2010, the Bank concluded a major agreement with other Multilateral Development Banks (MDBs) on "cross debarment".[66] The Executive Directors of the Bank further approved, as of 28 October 2010, the expansion of the sanctions regime to include cases involving fraud and corruption in connection with the Bank's corporate procurement. The aforementioned reforms are embodied in the 2012 version of the World Bank Sanctions Procedures (hereafter, "Procedures"). Taking a general perspective, the Bank Group's sanctions process has been reformed towards an increasingly quasi-judicial model. As we detail in the following, the main aspects of such evolution include, besides the creation of the two-tier review process involving both the SDO and an independent Sanctions Board, "the introduction of concepts like early temporary suspension and settlements, the publication of cases and the consequent development of Sanctions Board 'jurisprudence', and the like" (Leroy and Fariello, 2012: 28). As also established by the current Art. 1, Section 1.01 (b) of the Procedures: "the Executive Directors of the Bank approved, on 9 July 2004 and 1 August 2006, certain recommendations pertaining to the reform of the World Bank sanctions

---

65 Access to the database is provided to IFC and incorporated into its own due diligence processes. The WB's staff have had access to the CRPD since June 2009. In November 2009, OPCS issued guidance to operational staff on the use of the database encouraging use of the database prior to issuing no objection letters to Borrowers' recommendations for contract awards, pre-qualifications and short listing of consultants. According to the Bank, usage of the database substantially increased following the issuance of the guidance, from 20 queries a month to over 320 a month by January 2010. See also the World Bank Press Release No. 2012/059/INT, available at http://web.worldbank.org/WBSITE/EXTERNAL/NEWS/0,,contentMDK:22990073~pagePK:64257043~piPK:437376~theSitePK:4607,00.html.

66 See *infra* para. 10.7.1.3.

regime, including the adoption of a two-tier sanctions process conducted by a Suspension and Debarment Officer and the World Bank Group Sanctions Board".[67] The Executive Directors also endorsed, on August 1, 2006, the establishment of a Voluntary Disclosure Program (VDP): in order to further engage the private sector, INT also operates the VDP on behalf of the World Bank Group. Similar to programs in use around the world, the VDP is a mechanism by which firms cease misconduct, undertake internal investigations, voluntarily and fully disclose their Bank-related misconduct for the past five years to INT, implement suitable compliance programs, and engage a Compliance Monitor (for five years). In exchange for full cooperation, firms remain anonymous (confidentiality), avoid the reputational damage of public debarment, and may continue to compete for Bank Group-financed contracts (no debarment). Over the medium–long period the very fact that firms enter the VDP Program[68] may trigger a virtuous circle whereby INT is better informed, which, in turn, may lead to more Banks' sanctioning of higher risks for non-VDP-Firms. The different kinds of sanction established by the current regime, and the very fashion in which the process is structured, aims at supporting the Group's fiduciary duty by excluding corrupt actors from access to Bank financing, while functioning as a deterrent both for the sanctioned firm and for others, and, at the same time, incentivizing rehabilitation.[69] Even though after the most recent round of reforms the sanctions process has moved closer to a judicial model, (e.g. involving a two-tier review process by independent bodies, the publication of decisions, and development of a sanctions "jurisprudence"), such a regime remains essentially a formal administrative process designed to protect the funds entrusted to the World Bank, while offering the accused party basic due process before deciding whether

---

[67] For a prompt visualization of the aforementioned two-tier process see Table 10.1.

[68] The program allows the private sector to cooperate with INT, especially those firms that have inherited problems, for example, as a result of an acquisition. For further information regarding the VDP and its development, please go to www.worldbank.org/vdp, and see Integrity Vice Presidency, 2010, at 9; Integrity Vice Presidency, 2011, at 25, Integrity Vice Presidency, 2012, at 16.

[69] Overall, the World Bank's two-tier sanctions process (conducted by the Suspension and Debarment Officer and the Sanctions Board) is a key element of the activity being done within the World Bank, its member countries and its partners to curb corruption and further good governance. The use of administrative sanctions helps to protect the funds entrusted to the World Bank by increasing the costs to firms and individuals that engage in fraud and corruption on World Bank-financed projects.

the party will be sanctioned, and if so, what sanction will be imposed. The system, therefore, is intended to balance substantial considerations relating to the rule of law (including principles of due process and natural justice),[70] on the one hand, and standards of good governance, as well as efficiency and effectiveness in pursuing the Bank development mandate, on the other. It provides the competent bodies with precise and effective powers of investigations and deterring sanctions applicable to firms and individuals accused of corrupt, fraudulent, collusive, and coercive practices related to projects financed or guaranteed by the WB Group. Moreover, it set outs different outcomes depending among other things on the eventual cooperation by the accused party – known as the "Respondent" also in light of the conduct of its "Affiliates"[71] – during the process. The Bank's Procedures seek to guarantee, to the extent possible and practicable, that the provisions guiding each stage of the sanctions process are consistent with the highest expressions of legality in these various traditions. The system's essence is closer to that of a sanctions regime under national administrative law although it also borrows elements from civil and criminal law processes. First, though essentially administrative in nature,[72]

> the Bank's sanctions process is not identical with any single corresponding administrative or judicial process in domestic or national law. Thus, for example, the Bank's sanctions process is considerably more elaborate than most administrative schemes, vesting as it does a quasi-investigative function in INT, placing the "burden of proof" on INT (rather than requiring Respondents

---

[70] To this end, Leroy and Fariello (2012: 7) further note: "the Bank has similarly sought to apply certain procedural principles of the rule of law, such as the conduct of hearings by an impartial tribunal that provides reasons for its decisions; and the rights of Respondents to representation, to present evidence on their own behalf, and to appeal. (. . .) These latter principles are also understood to comprise the basic requirements of due process, and have been enshrined as rights in the constitutional law of some countries and in international human rights instruments. (. . .) The same principles are frequently considered by international lawyers as being among the "general principles of law."

[71] Pursuant to the Procedures, Art. I Section 1.01, (a) '"Affiliate" means any legal or natural person that controls, is controlled by, or is under common control with, the Respondent, as determined by the Bank.'

[72] As an "essentially administrative process that does not purport to 'punish' or find Respondents criminally liable, the sanctions process is not required to uphold the strictest standards of due process, such as may be found in criminal court proceedings: accordingly, formal rules of evidence are excluded and an explicit *mens rea* requirement is omitted from most of the definitions of fraudulent and corrupt practices." (Leroy and Fariello, 2012:8). For a further assessment of the administrative nature of the process see Dubois and Nowlan (2010).

> to demonstrate that they are "presently responsible"), and conferring quasi-judicial functions upon the SDO and Sanctions Board. (Leroy and Fariello, 2012:8)

Secondly

> the fact that it is concerned with activities that are criminal in most countries also inevitably colors the way in which the Bank, Respondents, and stakeholders alike view the sanctions process. For these reasons, internal reviews and audits of the sanctions process have tended to benchmark it, among other things, against criminal law systems. (ID.)

Thirdly

> from yet another perspective, the sanctions process may be described as being based on a quasi-contractual model. The Bank's jurisdiction and the legal standards that apply under the Sanctions Procedures are established contractually, by one of the Procurement, Consultant, or Anti-Corruption Guidelines being incorporated into an agreement between the Bank and the relevant borrower. Tort law concepts are also relevant to the Bank's determination of what level of knowledge and intent should be necessary under the various definitions of sanctionable practices. (ID.)

Finally, looking beyond national law regimes, it is worth emphasizing that the Bank's sanctions regime has evolved along with the practices and norms of other international bodies: as noted elsewhere,

> there is a significant, ongoing process of harmonization and coordination between all MDBs on this issue. Among other things, in formulating its own policies and practices in the sanctions space, the Bank considers the sanctions regimes established by other MDBs such as the Asian Development Bank . . . the Inter-American Development Bank . . ., the European Bank for Reconstruction and Development . . . and the African Development Bank . . ., the sanctions practices instituted by various UN bodies and specialized agencies, as well as the standards, guidelines, and best practice models promulgated by other international organizations such the . . . OECD . . . (Leroy and Fariello, 2012:8)[73]

The main elements of the WB (*i.e.* IBDR and IDA) Sanctions Procedures may be outlined as follows:

---

73 See, for instance, World Bank (2012d) which are intended to set common standards for treatment of corporate groups.

a) Starting from the relevant conduct, the WB has agreed with other MDBs that certain forms of fraud and corruption should be sanctionable. These agreed-upon "Sanctionable Practices" include corrupt, fraudulent, collusive, and coercive practices.[74] Such definitions apply across the WB Group and are not limited to the procurement context anymore. Quite remarkably the definitions of fraudulent, corrupt, collusive and coercive practices have also been harmonized with other MDBs. Furthermore, the World Bank, together with the AfDB and the IDB, may also sanction a firm or individual for having engaged in obstructive practices in connection with an INT's investigation[75] (World Bank Group, 2011).
b) As to delimitation of the cases subject to the sanctions regime, the Procedures set out the process to be followed in cases involving Sanctionable Practices:
   (i) in connection with projects and programs financed by the Bank and governed by the Bank's Procurement Guidelines,[76]

---

[74] Cfr, Art. I Section 1.01, (a). These definitions may be found in Annex A to the Sanctions Procedures; paragraph 7 of the World Bank Anti-Corruption Guidelines (2006); and Section 1.14 of the Guidelines Procurement Under IBRD Loans And IDA Credits (May 2004, as revised October 1, 2006 and May 1, 2010); and Section 1.22 of Guidelines: Selection and Appointment of Consultant by World Bank Borrowers (May 2004, as revised 1 October 2006 and 1 May 2010). According to the attachment to the Procedures dealing with the Sanctionable Practice, '"Coercive practice" is impairing or harming, or threatening to impair or harm, directly or indirectly, any party or the property of the party to influence improperly the actions of a party; (. . .) "Collusive practice" is an arrangement between two or more parties designed to achieve an improper purpose, including to influence improperly the actions of another party; (. . .) "Corrupt practice" is the offering, giving, receiving or soliciting, directly or indirectly, of anything of value to influence improperly the actions of another party; (. . .) "Fraudulent practice" is any act or omission, including a misrepresentation, that knowingly or recklessly misleads, or attempts to mislead, a party to obtain a financial or other benefit or to avoid an obligation; (. . .)'

[75] ID.: "Obstructive practice" is (i) deliberately destroying, falsifying, altering or concealing of evidence material to the investigation or making false statements to investigators in order to materially impede a Bank investigation into allegations of a corrupt, fraudulent, coercive or collusive practice; and/or threatening, harassing or intimidating any party to prevent it from disclosing its knowledge of matters relevant to the investigation or from pursuing the investigation, or (ii) acts intended to materially impede the exercise of the Bank's contractual rights of audit or access to information.

[76] "Procurement Guidelines" as defined by Art. 1 Section 1.01, (a) of the Procedures "means the January 1995 or May 2004 edition of the document entitled 'Guidelines: Procurement under IBRD Loans and IDA Credits', or the document entitled 'Guidelines: Procurement of Goods, Works and Non-Consulting

Consultant Guidelines[77] or Anti-Corruption Guidelines[78] (such projects and programs being referred to, collectively, as "Bank-Financed Projects");

(ii) on the basis of which the Director, General Service Department (GSD) has determined, in accordance with the World Bank Vendor Eligibility Policy, that the Respondent is non-responsible;

(iii) arising from the violation of a Material Term of the Terms & Conditions of the VDP program; and

(iv) arising from violations of Section 13.06 the same Procedures, that is the cases the Respondent (or any Affiliate thereof) violates their duty not to disclose to, or to discuss with, any third party any part of the record or information relating thereto except for those specifically indicated in the same provision.[79]

Services under IBRD Loans and IDA Credits and Grants' dated January 2011, as the case may be, as amended, supplemented or revised from time to time, or any later edition or similar instrument which may replace said Guidelines under which a case may be brought in accordance with these Procedures." Cfr. *supra* note 57.

77 Art. 1 Section 1.01, (a) of the Procedures defines "Consultant Guidelines" as "the January 1997, May 2002 or May 2004 edition of the document entitled 'Guidelines: Selection and Employment of Consultants by World Bank Borrowers', or the document entitled 'Guidelines: Selection and Employment of Consultants under IBRD Loans and IDA Credits and Grants' dated January 2011, as the case may be, as amended, supplemented or otherwise revised from time to time, or any later edition or similar instrument which may replace said Guidelines under which a case may be brought in accordance with these Procedures". See *supra* note 57.

78 As defined by Art. I, section 1.02 (a) of the Procedures. Cfr. *supra* note 63.

79 Cfr. World Bank 2012, Art. I, Section 1.01, (c) and Art. 13.06. Note that the Bank also provides financing in the form of Development Policy Loans (DPLs), under which it provides budget support and other unlinked financing against achievement of defined policy measures rather than to finance specific expenditures. The Bank's sanctions regime does not extend to DPLs, since it is not possible to trace the use of loan proceeds. This approach (or the lack of one) has come under increasing criticism. See, e.g., Leroy and Fariello (2012) and the literature referred to therein.

c) As also visible in Table 10.1, the bodies responsible of the procedure are the INT; the SDO[80]);[81] and the WB Sanction Board.[82] The sanctions process *stricto sensu* start with the conclusion of the investigations by the INT and, as already introduced, is characterized as a two-tier sanctions process.
d) The process starts with investigations on allegations that a firm or individual has engaged in a Sanctionable Practice by the INT. The INT is charged with, among other things, investigating allegations and other indications that sanctionable practices have occurred in connection with Bank Group financing. In the context of the sanctioning process the INT is, thus, to be regarded as a mere fact finder, which seeks and presents both exculpatory and inculpatory evidence. When, after the conclusion of its investigation, INT deems that there is sufficient evidence to support a finding that the firm or individual has engaged in a Sanctionable Practice, INT submits a Statement of Accusations and Evidence ("SAE") to the SDO – the first tier of the World Bank's two-tier administrative sanctions process (Table 10.1). The results of the INT's external investigations of World Bank-financed projects are also issued to the interested Governments in the form of a Referral Report, in order to let them prompt their own

---

80 Arguably one of the major steps for shaping the current sanctions regime was the establishment of the INT with a mandate to investigate allegations of fraud and corruption in Bank-financed projects and present its findings to the Sanctions Committee. INT was also charged with investigating allegations of misconduct by Bank staff; this function (except with respect to misconduct amounting to significant fraud or corruption) has been transferred to the Office of Ethics and Business Conduct (EBC). Prior to INT's establishment, allegations had been investigated by a variety of means, including by outside law firms, IAD auditors, and a Corruption and Fraud Investigations Unit (CFIU). A review by a panel led by former UN Under-Secretary General and US Attorney General, Mr. Dick Thornburgh, in 2000 found that the Bank's anti-corruption efforts would be better served by consolidating the Bank's investigatory responsibility within a single department.

81 Cfr. World Bank (2011d). The WB Group has indeed four SDOs, including one for each of (i) IBRD/IDA (World Bank), (ii) IFC, (iii) MIGA, and (iv) PRGs. Thus, the Suspension and Debarment Officer appointed by the President of the Bank for cases governed by the Procedures under exam. The terms "IFC Evaluation Officer", "MIGA Evaluation Officer" and "Bank Guarantees Evaluation Officer" mean the Suspension and Debarment Officers for cases governed by the IFC, MIGA or Bank Guarantee Sanctions Procedures, respectively.

82 This is a body composed of three Bank staff appointed by the president and four non-Bank staff appointed by the Directors, all serving renewable 3-year terms. The Sanction Board Chair is external and can only serve one term as Chair. The Board convenes 3–4 times/year for hearings (at party's request) and deliberations. Cfr. World Bank (2010c).

investigations, suspend and eventually punish the corrupt officials, and review the project.[83]

e) Sufficient evidence "means evidence sufficient to support reasonable belief, taking into consideration all relevant factors and circumstances, that is more than likely than not that the Respondent has engaged in a Sanctionable practice."[84] Noticeably, "any kind of evidence may form the basis of arguments presented in a sanctions proceeding and conclusions reached by the Evaluation Officer or the Sanctions Board."[85] It is up to the SDO and the Sanctions Board shall have discretion to determine the relevance, materiality, weight, and sufficiency of all evidence offered.[86] The right of defense is safeguarded in that: "Communication between an attorney, or a person acting at the direction of an attorney, and a client for the purpose of providing or receiving legal advice and writings reflecting the mental impressions, opinions, conclusions or legal theories of an attorney in connection with a legal representation shall be privileged and exempt from disclosure."[87]

f) The WB is endowed with a protective mechanism for suspending firms and individuals from eligibility during the early investigation phase (so called, "*Early Temporary Suspension*").[88] The SDO, upon specific request by INT Limited in exceptional cases, may impose a temporary suspension on the subject of an INT investigation prior to the commencement of formal sanctions proceedings. This possibility is conditioned on the finding by the SDO that there exists already sufficient evidence that the subject has engaged in at least one sanctionable practice. Firms provide rebutting evidence and petition the SDO to lift the suspension. Early temporary suspension is a new feature of the Bank Group's sanctions process.[89]

---

[83] INT also publishes a redacted report, which adds further transparency to its investigations. See Dubois and Nowlan (2010).

[84] Procedures, Art. I Section 1.02, (a).

[85] See Procedures, Art. VII, Section 7.01.

[86] *Ibidem*, adding: 'Hearsay evidence or documentary evidence shall be given the weight deemed appropriate by the Evaluation Officer or the Sanctions Board. Without limiting the generality of the foregoing, the Evaluation Officer and the Sanctions Board shall have the discretion to infer purpose, intent and/or knowledge on the part of the Respondent, or any other party, from circumstantial evidence. Formal rules of evidence shall not apply.'

[87] Procedures, Art. VII, Section 7.02.

[88] See Procedures, Art. II. See also Dubois and Nowlan (2010).

[89] For further comments on the mechanism we refer to the study of Leroy and Fariello (2012). Suffice here to remind that to impose a temporary suspension, "the SDO is required to determine that there is 'sufficient evidence' that the firm

g) The heart of the process lies in formal sanctions proceedings, which consist of the following two tiers:
   i) As shown by Table 10.1, a first tier review of the SAE by the SDO for sufficiency of the evidence. The SDO, thus, evaluates evidence issued by INT. If the SDO finds that the accusations are supported by sufficient evidence, he/she issues a Notice of Sanctions Proceedings to the Respondent, appending the Statement of Accusations and Evidence and recommending an appropriate sanction and temporarily suspending the Respondent from eligibility for Bank-financed contracts. Therefore, the Respondent is temporarily suspended from eligibility to be awarded Bank financed contracts upon issuance of the Notice. At this point of the process, the Respondent has two paths ahead. First, he/she may appeal either or both the INT's accusations and the EO's recommended sanction by filing an Explanation with the SDO within 30 days after the delivery of the Notice seeking either dismissal of the case or a reduction in the recommended sanction. In this case, within 30 days after the receipt of such explanation, the SDO may either confirm or withdraw the Notice or revise the recommended sanction. Alternatively, the Respondent may decide not to contest the SDO's final determination. In this latter

---

or individual in question has engaged in a sanctionable practice for which the SDO would recommend a debarment for a period not less than two years. The minimum two-year period is intended to help ensure that the eventual period of debarment is not less than the period of temporary suspension, thereby preserving the principle of proportionality. This period assumes a maximum of one year for the investigation and a further maximum of one year for the sanctions proceedings. The 'sufficient evidence' standard of proof is the same standard as currently applies to Notices of Sanctions Proceedings, but when applied to early temporary suspension other factors must be considered to take into account the uncertainty inherent in a case when the investigation is not yet complete. Whether there is 'sufficient evidence' in a particular case depends on a number of factors, such as the strength, amount, and completeness of the evidence under the circumstances, including the existence or absence of corroborating evidence, and the inferences that may reasonably be drawn from the evidence. The evidence should be either reasonably complete (e.g., most or all known and available witnesses have been interviewed) as to the particular allegation that forms the basis for the Notice of Temporary Suspension, or, though fragmentary, sufficiently compelling to justify the presumption that additional evidence is unlikely to significantly alter the inferences that may be drawn from it (e.g., proof positive of a forgery, admission by the Respondent). As a general rule, the earlier in the investigation a temporary suspension is requested, the stronger the evidence required would be" (Leroy and Fariello, 2012: 13).

case, the recommended sanction (if any) is then imposed on the Respondent and both the information about the sanction imposed and the SDO's determination (if the Notice was issued by the SDO on or after January 1, 2011), are made public on the World Bank's public sanctions website.[90]

ii) When the Respondent contests the INT's accusations and/or the SDO's final determination, it triggers a (hence, only potential) second tier review by filing a Response with the Sanctions Board. This latter body must consider the case *de novo* and takes the final decision on an appropriate sanction (if any), not being bound by the SDO's recommendations. This phase of the proceedings may include hearings if either the Respondent or INT requests them.[91] The name(s) of the sanctioned party/parties) and the sanction/sanctions imposed are made public. In order to guarantee even more transparency than under the precious sanctions process, as of 15 January 2011, the Bank Group adopted a new procedure whereby the Sanctions Board will publish the full text of its decisions in sanctions cases. The procedures require the Board to issue fully reasoned decisions, including both the basic facts of the case as well as the legal reasoning underpinning their decision.[92] Similarly, also the SDO's determinations are published. Under the new procedures, the Sanctions Board also issues and plans to periodically update a digest of the legal holdings contained in Sanctions Board decisions. The digest is posted on the Bank Group's external website and contains brief discussions of the principal

---

90 Cfr. Procedures, Art. III and Art. IV and Table 10.1 of the present chapter. See also World Bank (2010d) and, for the list of SDO's Determinations in Uncontested Proceedings, http://web.worldbank.org/WEBSITE/EXTERNAL/EXTABOUTUS/ORGANIZATION/ORGUNITS/EXTOFFEVASUS/0,,contentMDK:22911816~menuPK:7926949~pagePK:64168445~piPK:64168309~theSitePK:3601046,00.html.

91 Cfr. Procedures, Art. VIII and Art. VI. The same basic procedures apply to cases relating to IFC, MIGA and Bank Guarantee operations, with adjustments appropriate to their different business models, in particular separate SDOs with more expansive standards of review and the appointment of alternate members of the Sanctions Board to hear cases relating to private sector operations. See WB Group, 2010 and Table 10.1 of the present chapter.

92 See, generally, WB Sanctioning Procedures, Art. X. Sections 10.01. For a balanced assessment of the pros and cons of such greater transparency we refer to the considerations put forward by Leroy and Fariello (2012).

Table 10.1 The World Bank Sanctions two-tier process

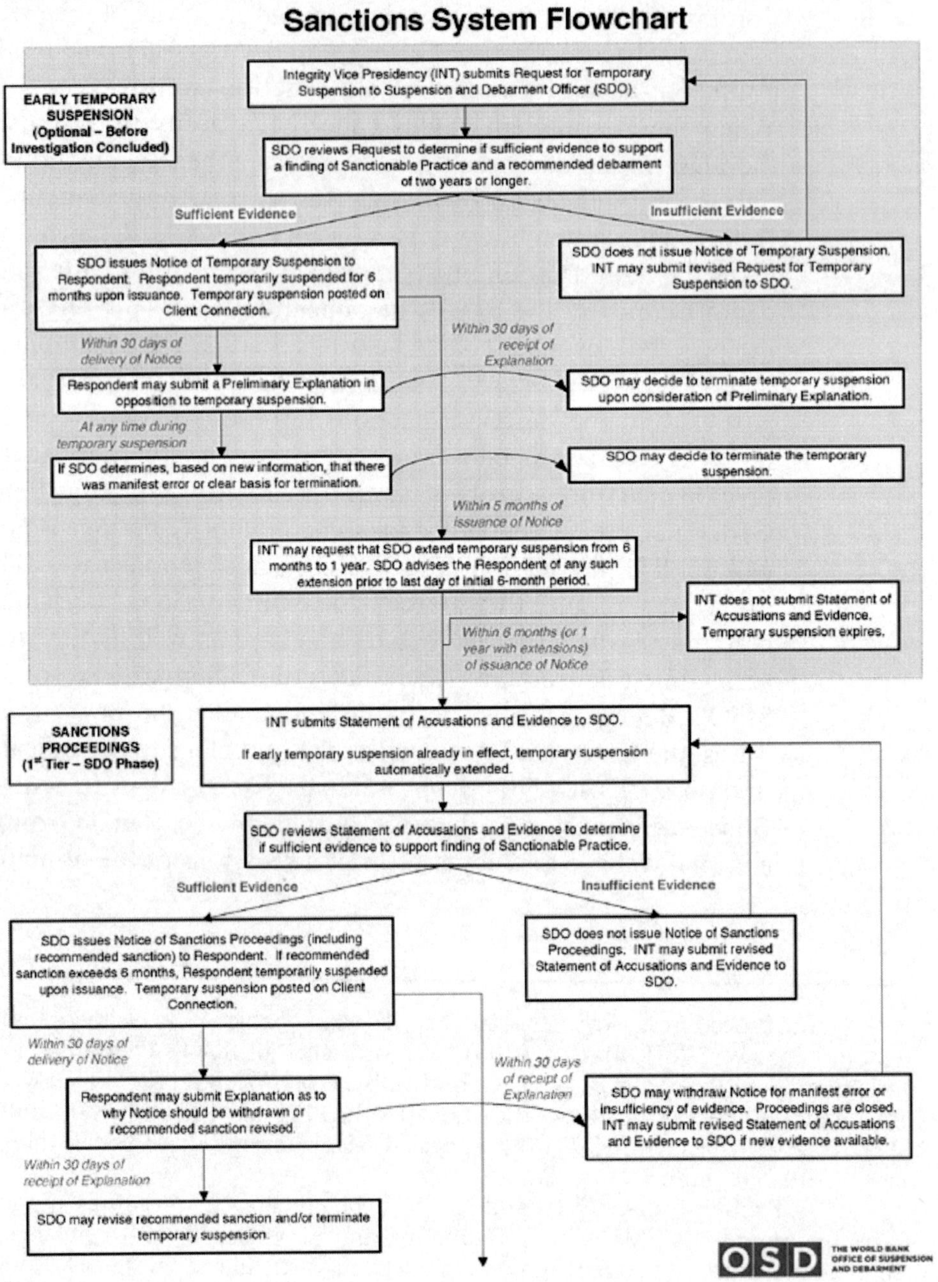

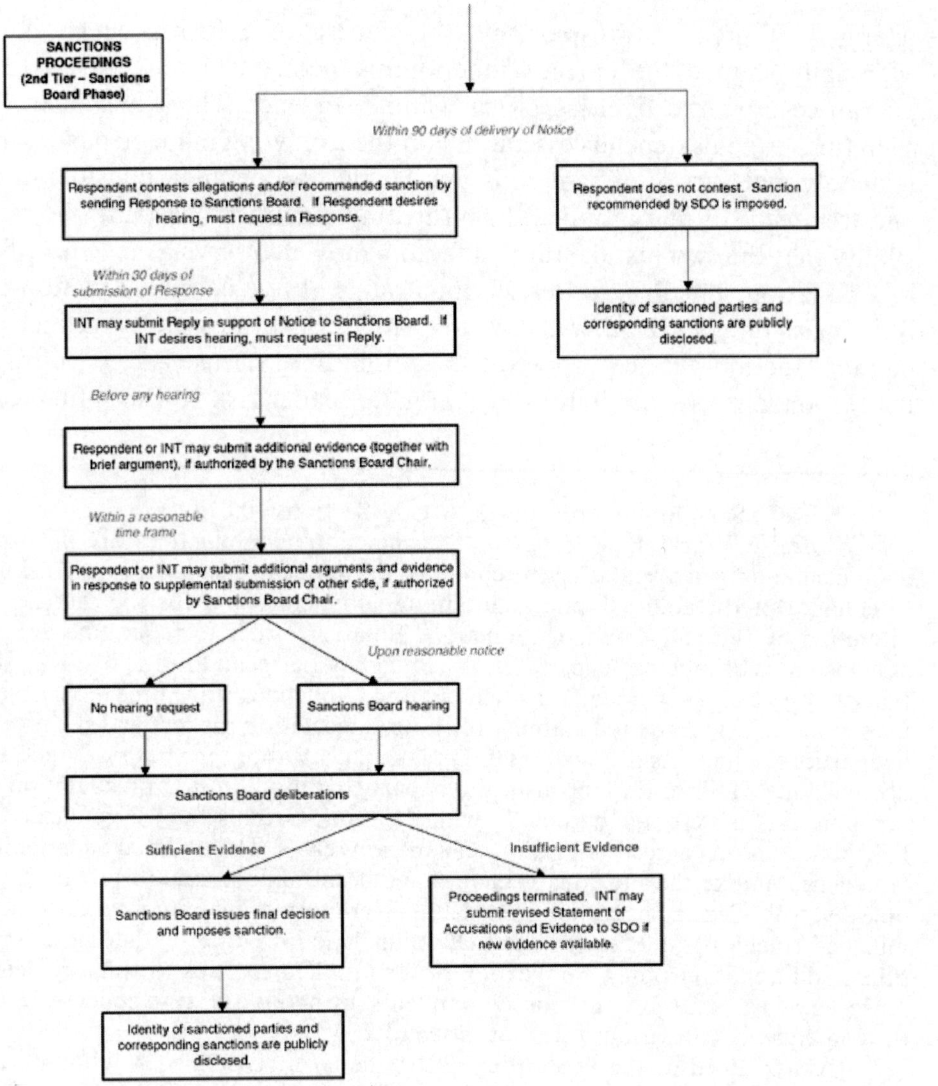

Source: World Bank Sanctions Regime, available at: www.worldbank.org/sanctions.

legal holdings in each case, together with factual background relevant to an understanding of the holding.[93]

Along with greater transparency, the course of reforms which have eventually shaped the current sanctioning mechanism are intended to guarantee more effectiveness, efficacy and deterrence. The achievement of such further goals depends essentially on the following main elements: the relatively wide array of sanctions applicable, the detailed consideration and treatment of mitigating and aggravating circumstances, and the possibility that the two just mentioned factors may also serve as incentive for rehabilitation. The Procedures set out a range of five possible sanctions:[94] i) *Debarment with Conditional Release*, which constitutes the "baseline" or default sanction.[95] The purpose of the conditional release is to encourage the respondent's rehabilitation, to mitigate further risk to Bank-financed

---

93 See WB Sanctioning Procedures, Art. X. Sections 10.01 (c).

94 See also World Bank (2011e). The Sanctioning Guidelines are a public document aiming at orientating the choice of the applicable sanctions and seeking to enhance predictability, while maintaining sufficient room for the exercise of discretion by the SDOs and the Sanctions Board in order to reflect the unique circumstances of each particular case. As argued by Leroy and Fariello (2012), the Bank Group has lastly updated its Sanctioning Guidelines with three main objectives in mind: (a) more predictability for both the decision makers and the potential parties to sanctions proceedings; (2) greater clarity about the basis of sanctions decisions to MDBs and other institutions participating in mutual recognition of sanctions (a.k.a. "cross-debarment") with the Bank Group; and (3) guidance for INT in negotiating agreed resolutions of sanctions cases. The updated Sanctioning Guidelines, unlike the previous version, have been made public to further these objectives. While the Sanctioning Guidelines were formerly an internal document intended solely as guidance to the SDO and Sanctions Board, they now serve other, additional purposes. Publication of the Guidelines helps to enhance deterrence, as well as legal certainty for Respondents, by making clear in concrete terms the consequences of various forms of misconduct.

95 As explained by the WB Group, 2010, the term "baseline" sanction means the sanction that would normally be imposed for a sanctionable practice before giving effect to any aggravating or mitigating factors. Note that "Under the sanctioning guidelines adopted by the Bank Group in 2006, the 'baseline' sanction to be imposed for any sanctionable practice was debarment for a stated period of time. Under this sanction, the Bank Group has no discretion as to whether sanctioned firms may become eligible again for Bank Group-financed contracts once they 'serve their time', and often no way of determining whether they have actually been rehabilitated or will simply continue to engage in fraud and corruption. This left the Bank Group and Borrowers alike with considerable residual fiduciary and reputational risk when a debarment expired. This vulnerability led Bank Group to examine ways to increase the effectiveness of the sanctions process in achieving its primary purpose – safeguarding Bank Group funds – by devising a mechanism to

activities. After the sanctioned party has completed its period of debarment, the latter may be released provided that it has complied with certain defined conditions. Such conditions normally include the debarred party putting in place, and implementing for an adequate period, an integrity compliance program which is fully satisfactory to the World Bank Group.

In this respect, Respondents should find relevant orientation in the recent publication of the Bank Group's Integrity Compliance Guideline. Like similar documents published by other international institutions, such Guidelines aim at giving the system greater transparency and consistency, by drawing standard business integrity models, though permitting a certain flexibility in order to be adapted to different business environments:[96]

> . . . the guidance recognizes the need for flexibility in applying fundamental principles to the particular circumstances of sanctioned parties, particularly small- and medium-sized enterprises, which play a major role in the Bank Group-financed operations in developing countries, for which a full-blown compliance program may be unnecessary or prohibitively expensive . . . Program elements will need to be tailored to the party taking into account such criteria as its size, business sector, and particularly its risk areas, as well as the legal environment(s) in which the party operates. (Leroy and Fariello, 2012: 16)

It is also worth remarking that the purpose of the change in the baseline sanction that occurred with 2010 reform is not to debar the sanctioned firms for a longer period of time or indefinitely, but to place greater stress on rehabilitation, encouraging companies to improve corporate governance by adopting adequate, effective policies and measures that make it less likely that they will engage in such misconduct again. Respondents may not be released prior to the defined debarment period, even if they meet the conditions prior to the period's lapse, but if so specified, compliance with certain conditions such as cooperation or remedial measures may lead to a reduction in the debarment period. In order to be released, respondents must expressly apply to that purpose and provide evidence that they have met the conditions for release.[97] Management, acting

---

provide the Bank Group with better assurance of rehabilitation before firms are let back into the system" (Leroy and Fariello, 2012:14).

96 World Bank (2010e). The Bank Group staff engaged in intensive negations with both public and private sector stakeholders and analyzed international best practice models including OECD (2010) in order to develop the integrity compliance guidelines for the World Bank Group against which the compliance programs of sanctioned parties would be assessed For another more recent and similar model see UNODC (2013).

97 See also World Bank (2011e).

through an Integrity Compliance Officer (ICO)[98] makes the initial determination as to whether the conditions for release have been met. In more detail, the ICO contacts and advises the sanctioned party of the general requirements and procedures for meeting the conditions. This is followed by a baseline evaluation of whatever program the party presently may have (or put in place at the time) with suggestions for improvements where appropriate. The ICO monitors the implementation of the program, including reviewing periodic reports, changes in the program, remedial actions taken in response to the sanctioned misconduct as well as other misconduct subsequently detected, and the like. After the program has been operational, normally for a period of at least one year, the party would be entitled to submit an Application setting forth arguments for and evidence of its compliance. If the decision is negative, the Respondent has the right to appeal the decision to the Sanctions Board. This appeal would not second-guess the ICO's judgment (e.g., as to the adequacy of a compliance program) but is rather meant to ensure that the ICO has not abused his/her discretion (i.e., if the ICO's determination lacks an observable basis or is otherwise arbitrary, is based on disregard of a material fact or a material mistake of fact, or was taken in material violation of the Sanctions Procedures). ii) The so-called *"Plain Vanilla" Debarment*, (also referred to as "*Debarment*"). In cases where no appreciable cause would be served by imposing conditions for release, sanctioned parties may be debarred for a defined period of time, after which they are automatically released from debarment.[99] iii) *Conditional Non-Debarment*: the Bank normally applies this sanction, consistent with the Bank's fiduciary obligations and the goals of specific and general deterrence, either to Respondents that have demonstrated that they have taken comprehensive voluntary corrective measures and that such other mitigating factors otherwise indicated so as to justify non-debarment or to sanctioned parties affiliated (parents and other affiliates) with the Respondent which are not directly engaged in the Sanctionable Practice but which bear some responsibility thereof, through, for example, a systemic lack of oversight which

98 Note that the ICO's decision is subject to the no objection of the Integrity Vice President and the Bank Group General Counsel.

99 According to World Bank (2011e: 2) "This would occur, for example, in cases where a sanctioned firm has already in place a robust corporate compliance program, the sanctionable practice involved the isolated acts of an employee or employees who have already been terminated, and the proposed debarment is for a relative short period of time (e.g., one year or less)." At the opposite extreme, in exceptional cases where there is no realistic prospect that the Respondent can be rehabilitated, it may also be sanctioned permanently. Cfr. World Bank (2010d).

made the misconduct possible. Under this sanction, the sanctioned party is not debarred provided the party complies with certain defined conditions within a set time frame. If the conditions are not met, the party is debarred for a defined period of time. The conditions imposed will likely be similar to those imposed under debarment with conditional release.[100] In the event that the sanctioned party fails to demonstrate compliance with the conditions within the time periods established by the Sanctions Board, a debarment would automatically become effective for a period of time established by the SDO and/or Sanctions Board. iv) *Letter of Reprimand*: In cases where debarment or even conditional non-debarment may be disproportionate to the offense, the Bank issues a letter of reprimand to the sanctioned party.[101] v) *Restitution*: in appropriate cases, the sanctioned party may be required to make restitution to the Borrower or to any other party or take actions to remedy the harm done by its misconduct.[102]

The choice of the appropriate sanction by the SDO or the Sanctions Board is guided by Sanctioning Guideline.[103] This non-binding document deals in detail with aggravating and mitigating factors, with indicative ranges for increases (in the case of aggravating factors) and reductions (in the case of mitigating factors). Except when permanent debarment is imposed, parties debarred for a minimum period in excess of 10 years

---

100 Compliance with conditions for non-debarment is determined by the ICO and subject to the same procedure as for conditions for release from debarment.

101 See World Bank (2010d: 4): "Examples include cases where an affiliate of the Respondent has been found to have some shared responsibility for the misconduct because of an isolated lapse in supervision, but the affiliate was not in any way complicit in the misconduct."

102 ID.: "Appropriate cases may include those where the damage caused by the misconduct is clear and quantifiable. Restitution has not been imposed to date, largely due to lack of clear criteria to how to calculate the quantum to be restituted and how to determine the appropriate recipient".

103 World Bank (2011e) indicates the following aggravating factors: severity of the misconduct (repeated pattern of conduct; sophisticated means; central role in misconduct; management's role in misconduct; involvement of public official or WB staff); harm caused by the misconduct (harm to public safety/welfare; degree of harm to project); interference with investigation (interference with investigative process; intimidation/payment of a witness); past history of adjudicated misconduct. Mitigating factors are grouped as follows: minor role in misconduct; voluntary corrective action taken (cessation of misconduct; internal action against responsible individual; effective compliance program; restitution or financial remedy) cooperation with investigation (assistance and/or ongoing cooperation; internal investigation; admission/acceptance of guilt/responsibility; voluntary restraint). See generally Sanctions Procedures, Art. IX Section 9.02.

may petition for a reduction of the minimum period of debarment after 10 years have elapsed.

As already hinted, the Sanctions Procedures establishes that affiliates of Respondents may also be sanctioned, and that sanctions may be applied to the successors and assigns of sanctioned parties.[104] This is a circumvention of Bank Group sanctions through the use of affiliates or changes in corporate forms. The Sanctions Procedures had included the ability to sanction certain affiliates of the Respondent (i.e., those controlling and those controlled by the Respondent) since 2001, but the relevant guidance was relatively sparse, leading to uncertainty, in particular in relation to the appropriate application of sanctions to large corporate groups or after a complex corporate restructuring. As part of 2010 reforms, the Bank's management developed a specific and far more comprehensive guidance for Bank Group staff, the SDOs, and the Sanctions Board, as well as corporate restructurings which may occur after a firm is sanctioned. The new guidance sets flexible principles for the application of sanctions to affiliates of the Respondent(s) and successors and assigns. The most relevant improvement is that the guidance eventually provides a definition of "control", which sets the parameters for the application of sanction, to wit: the ability to direct or cause the direction of the policies or operations of another entity. Such definition provides a list of non-exclusive signs of control that the Bank may apply in determining control, including interlocking equity ownership or management, overlapping employees, sharing of facilities, and the like.[105] Furthermore, the guidance allows targeted

---

104 See Sanctions Procedures, Art. IX Section 9.04 (b), (c).

105 To this purpose, the guidance indicates four rebuttable presumptions when applying sanctions to corporate groups: (1) sanctions apply to the entire corporate entity unless the Respondent can show that the sanctionable practice was limited to a particular unit or division; (2) sanctions are applied to all subsidiaries (i.e., entities controlled by the Respondent) unless the Respondent can show that application would be disproportionate and not reasonably necessary to avoid circumvention; (3) sanctions are not applied to parents (entities controlling the Respondent) and 'sister' firms (entities under common control with the Respondent) unless INT can show some degree of either culpability (i.e., direct involvement in the wrongdoing) or responsibility (i.e., failure to supervise or maintain adequate controls) or that application is necessary to avoid circumvention; and (4) when INT has made a prima facie case that a firm is the successor or assign of a sanctioned entity, the sanction will apply to the putative successor or assign unless it can rebut INT's case or otherwise show that such application would be inconsistent with the spirit of the guiding principles. As for successors and assigns, the general rule (subject to the presumption afore referred) is that the sanction will follow the business line of the original sanctioned party, so that if, for example, a controlling interest in a sanctioned firm is acquired by another firm and

sanctions in cases where the sanctionable practice is shown to have been limited to a particular division within a firm, and, conversely, makes it clear that affiliates under common control with the Respondent may be sanctioned.[106] The Sanctions Procedures afford parent or "sister" entities the principles of due process already established for the Respondent. In so doing parents and other affiliates, may defend themselves against charges of culpability or responsibility for the Respondent's wrongdoing, with substantially the same procedural rights as Respondents themselves.

A further remarkable element of the 2010 reforms of the Sanctioned Procedures is the introduction of the current formal mechanism for the negotiated resolution of sanctions cases, which was also introduced in 2010. Negotiated resolutions such as plea bargaining or settlement agreements are a near universal feature of civil, administrative and criminal procedure across legal systems as a useful means to enhance efficiency by resolving disputes using less time and fewer resources while providing certainty of outcome for the parties, but were missing as a formal part of the Bank Group sanctions process. Beginning in 2009,[107] the Bank

---

the sanctioned firm becomes its subsidiary, only the subsidiary would normally continue to be sanctioned. Notwithstanding the above, the guidance recognizes that there may be cases where the business of the predecessor and successor firms are so intertwined, or where the business of the predecessor constitutes such a large portion of that of the successor, that drawing a distinction would be impractical or pose an undue reputational risk for the Bank Group. In such cases, the sanction would apply to the successor in its entirety. See also Leroy and Fariello (2012).

106 As remarked by Leroy and Fariello (2012: 17), another relevant improvement of the new guidance is that it 'draws an important distinction between "responsibility" and "culpability", in an effort to provide a more nuanced, and therefore fair, approach to sanctions. Culpability means, first and foremost, direct involvement in the wrongdoing, such as through participation or instruction. "Responsibility", on the other hand, may arise simply from a failure to supervise or to maintain adequate controls or ethical culture within the corporate group such that the wrongdoing is made possible. Responsibility does not normally lead to debarment, but rather either conditional non-debarment (with the conditions including amelioration of internal controls, etc.) where the issues are systemic or, in cases involving an isolated incident of a failure to supervise, a letter of reprimand. However, egregious forms of responsibility, in particular "willful blindness" to a sanctionable practice by a controlling entity or manager, may lead to sanctions comparable to those imposed for culpability.'

107 The case referred is the "Macmillan" settlement. On April 30, 2010, the Bank Group debarred UK publisher Macmillan Limited for six years. The debarment was part of a negotiated resolution that followed Macmillan's admission that it had paid bribes in an attempt to win a contract in Southern Sudan. Macmillan has been a major supplier of educational materials for Bank Group-financed projects, winning more than $35 million in contracts since 1999. This particular

Group began using negotiated resolutions as a means of quickly resolving cases, removing corrupt firms from Bank-supported projects, and encouraging other firms to acknowledge misconduct sooner. Building on the initial success the Bank Group had in negotiating these settlements of investigations, it incorporated and formalized this mechanism as part of its sanctions regime. In appropriate circumstances, sanctions may also be imposed on a Respondent through a negotiated resolution of the case. Like VDPs, settlements are a means to encourage proactive involvement of the private sectors and robust corporate governance (compliance program, codes of conducts, etc): instituting corporate compliance programs as a condition of settlement is one way the Bank Group is encouraging the private sector to take responsibility for curbing fraud and corruption.[108] Under such mechanism, sanctions cases may be resolved by negotiations at any stage of the sanctions process up to the

---

education project included a multimillion dollar contract to print primary school text books. Acting upon information it received, INT's investigation uncovered evidence that Macmillan made a series of corrupt payments in an effort to influence the procurement process, and Macmillan was not awarded the contract. INT collaborated with national authorities, which expedited resolution of INT's investigation, as well as underscored the World Bank's commitment to working closely with governments to pursue corruption. Under the terms of the agreement, Macmillan has agreed to cooperate with the World Bank's efforts to combat fraud and corruption in World Bank Group-financed projects. Macmillan will also implement a compliance program that will be monitored by a third-party to ensure its adequacy. In recognition of Macmillan's early acknowledgement of its corrupt conduct, the Bank Group agreed to a reduced debarment of six years. (INT, 2011: 9–10).

108 Cfr. also Leroy and Fariello (2012: 22) who aptly point out the main reasons why the Bank may find it appropriate to engage in a settlement. First, "settlement is most appropriate in cases where there are significant mitigating factors, including in particular in cases where the Respondent has cooperated or is likely to cooperate in the future in a significant way with the investigation, has taken corrective measures or otherwise has shown that it no longer presents a significant fiduciary risk to the Bank Group. In such cases, conditional non-debarment or debarment with conditional release may be appropriate agreed sanctions". Second, "settlement may also be used as a tool to save Bank resources in cases where a Respondent is willing to agree to admit culpability and/or provide valuable information about its own or others' malfeasance in exchange for a reduced period of debarment or other lesser sanction within the parameters of the Sanctions Procedures and the Sanctioning Guidelines". Third, negotiated resolutions may also be convenient when "the Respondent may not be willing to admit culpability, but is nevertheless open to resolving the case expeditiously through settlement. In such cases, settlement is most appropriate where significant resources can be saved (e.g., because in the absence of a settlement the Respondent is expected to prolong proceedings or significant INT resources would be required to complete the investigation) or where the outcome of the case may be in doubt".

issuance of a decision by the Sanctions Board, or during the investigation stage prior to the commencement of sanctions proceedings.[109] Settlements may take two basic forms:

1) *Negotiated Resolution Agreements*: Such agreements do end – or, for settlements reached prior to their commencement, replace – sanctions proceedings in respect of the case with an agreed sanction which may (or may not) include compliance by the Respondent with certain conditions. As for debarment with conditional release, conditions will normally include the introduction or improvement of an integrity compliance program and/or remedial measures such as disciplinary action against the wrongdoers and, in exceptional cases, restitution. Cooperation with ongoing or future Bank investigations may also be a part of the terms of such a resolution.
2) *Deferral Agreements*, which "freeze" sanctions proceedings for a period of time pending compliance by the Respondent with certain conditions, upon compliance of which the case is then settled. The parties will jointly petition the SDO for a deferral of proceedings for a stated period of time not exceeding five years, conditioned on the performance of the obligations by the Respondent set out in an agreement. Obligations on the Respondents normally resemble those for negotiated settlement agreements. Upon the lapse of the deferral period, in cases where the Respondent has fully performed its obligations under the deferral agreement, the Notice is deemed withdrawn with prejudice and all accusations against the Respondent therein are rendered null and void. On the other contrary, when the Respondent at any time during the deferral period breaches its obligations under the settlement agreement, the sanctions proceedings, upon request by INT, are recommenced.

Among other things, the Bank Group General Counsel clears all settlement agreements, in agreement with the General Counsel of IFC or MIGA in cases involving IFC or MIGA projects. Settlements are also subject to review by the relevant SDO to confirm that: (a) the agreement was entered into voluntarily and without duress and (b) the agreed sanction, if any, does not manifestly violate the Sanctioning Guidelines. The sanction recommended in the settlement then goes into effect.[110]

---

109 See generally WB Sanctions Procedures, Art. XI, Sections 11.01–04.

110 See ID.; for a detailed assessment of the settlement procedures see, among others, Leroy and Fariello (2012).

To conclude such overview of the Bank's Sanctioning regime, it seems to us that, taken as a whole, the recent reforms have considerably enhanced the deterrence, efficiency, effectiveness, and transparency of the system.[111] Borrowing two senior officials of the Bank's thesis: "Some of the major components of the reforms, notably early temporary suspension and debarment with conditional release, were intended to strengthen the system by addressing vulnerabilities and closing 'loopholes' in the system. The adoption of new, publicly available Sanctioning Guidelines and the publication of Sanctions Board decisions and SDO determinations will . . . enhance the deterrent impact of sanctions" (Leroy and Fariello, 2012: 27). Furthermore, the new guidance on corporate groups extends the reach of sanctions to all affiliates of Respondents, and has been re-shaped in order to allow targeted sanctions and provide the primary tool to avoid, to the possible extent, circumvention of the Bank's sanctions through corporate schemes and operations. Again, through the latest reforms, the WB has built a "bridge" between the Bank Group's corporate and operational sanctions systems. Though the elements just recalled go above all in the direction of intensifying the deterrence and the effectiveness of sanctions, "private sector stakeholders should find significant comfort in these reforms, in particular those – such as the publication of the Bank Group's Sanctioning Guidelines and of Sanctions Board decisions – that increase the transparency and accountability of the system and legal certainty." (Id.). In addition, settlements represent an advantageous path for both Parties in that they provide potential Respondents and the Bank with an efficient alternative means to resolve sanctions cases, characterised by certainty of outcome. In the same spirit, the adoption of model standards of compliance, particularly to strengthen corporate governance, gives Respondents a clear idea of the Bank's customary requirements for application to the VDPs, release from debarment, access to settlement.[112]

---

111 This holds even truer when considering the cross-debarment mechanism. See *infra* para. 10.7.1.3.

112 Similar considerations are eminently voiced by others, such as Leroy and Fariello (2012: 27), who add: "the reforms also illustrate the way in which the Bank creates new law and legal policy. While the Bank, as an international organization, is not bound by any national law, it carefully considers broad rule of law values and principles, as evidenced by a benchmarking of major civil and common law legal systems, as well as international best practices, to inform its policy making. Where appropriate, the Bank consults with external stakeholders before policies are adopted and ensures that its new policies are widely promulgated afterwards. These global standards are then adapted to the Bank Group's particular needs and business model, but every effort is made to ensure that the Bank Group standards fall within the ambit of international best practice."

The last wave of reforms to the WB sanctions procedures can also be appreciated considering some figures. As a result of such reforms, the INT has ramped up its investigative, preventive and forensic resources to reduce the risk of fraud and corruption in Bank-financed projects. Below are some highlights of INT's efforts in 2010–2013.

In fiscal year 2013, the WB has debarred 47 firms, individuals, and non-governmental organizations (and their affiliates), preventing them from participating in future Bank-financed projects. To give a sense of the concrete effect a sanction can have, the SNC-Lavalin debarment also rendered 196 affiliates ineligible to do business with the World Bank.[113] The same FY, INT substantiated 49 cases (of which, 18 involved misconduct by internationally based entities and the remaining 31 by locally based entities). Previous outcomes are equally worth reporting: in FY 2010, the Bank debarred 45 firms, individuals and non-governmental organizations (INT, 2010). In FY 2011, INT closed 83 cases, managing a caseload that stemmed from 460 allegations and complaints, of which 369 involved a Bank Group-supported activity. Allegations related to 97 countries and 367 projects. As a result of INT investigations, the WB debarred 32 individuals, firms, and non-governmental organizations, preventing them from participating in future Bank Group-financed projects for varying periods of time (INT, 2011). In FY 2012, in a continued effort to finalize more cases and sanction more entities allegedly culpable of fraudulent or corrupt conduct related to Bank-financed projects, the WB sanctioned 83 entities (i.e. 144 percent more than in FY11). INT also closed 90 cases the same fiscal year, substantiating allegations in 52 percent of the cases. As a matter of policy, INT prioritizes cases that have the potential for maximizing their deterrent effect, that involve significant fraud or corruption, and that pose more severe reputational risks to the Bank Group.

(8.1.2) Mutual recognition of sanctions (a.k.a. "cross-debarment") As already hinted, on 19 March 2010, in a major breakthrough for the international collective strategy to fight corruption, the World Bank Group, together with four other MDBs – the AfDB, the AsDB, the EBRD, and the IDB – signed the Agreement for Mutual Enforcement of Debarment Decisions.[114] Under such Agreement, each participating MDB informs the others of any debarments it has imposed of more than

113 See World Bank (2013).

114 World Bank (2010d) For a first assessment of "cross-debarment" see Zimmerman and Fariello (2012).

one year in length. Subject to an "opt out" provision – allowing exceptional decisions by each MDB based on legal or policy considerations – all participating MDBs enforce each debarment thus notified to them as a matter of course, that is without subjecting them to a further sanctions process (so called, "cross-debarment"). The agreement at issue sends a clear and strong message: "cheat or steal from one of us, and you will be punished by all" (INT, 2010: iii). Over the decade preceding the adoption of the agreement, MDBs have collectively debarred more than 1,100 fraudulent and corrupt entities. The accord significantly increases their ability to jointly crack down on fraud and corruption. In addition, it provides an incentive to companies to clean up their operations and "underscores to donor and recipient countries that every development dollar must be spent as intended: to overcome poverty" (ID). The WB continues to cooperate with other signatory MDBs to advance the enforcement of the Cross-Debarment Agreement signed in April 2010. In 2011 following the implementation of the cross-debarment agreement, MDBs have jointly recognized the debarments of 37 entities. The full potential of 2010's cross-debarment agreement became readily apparent in FY 2012 and 2013. In 2012, the five MDBs jointly recognized 122 debarments. In FY 2013, thanks to the same agreement, 295 entities were jointly declared ineligible.[115]

(8.1.3) SUPPORTING COLLECTIVE ACTION ON GLOBAL GOVERNANCE The new WB Sanctions Procedures provide for the sharing of pleadings and materials submitted in connection with sanctions proceedings, on a confidential basis, with other MDBs and international organizations, as well as national authorities, if disclosure is determined to be in the best interests of the Bank Group. The decision on information sharing would be taken on a case-by-case basis by INT, in consultation with the Bank Group General Counsel. Though it does not occur with any regularity, from time to time the Bank receives requests for pleadings, for example to inform the decision of an international or national authority whether it would "cross-debar" Bank debarment decisions.[116] To this purpose, the INT has developed an internal protocol setting out the procedures and criteria for sharing information with third parties. What is more, in deciding cases governed by the IFC or MIGA Sanctions Procedures, the Bank Group

115 See World Bank (2011a); World Bank (2012b); World Bank (2013).

116 As argued elsewhere: "This has now become moot for most MDBs in light of the recent agreement on mutual recognition of debarment decisions, but such requests could still come from international organizations not party to the MDB agreement as well as from national authorities" (World Bank 2010d: 8).

General Counsel would consult with the IFC or MIGA General Counsel, as appropriate.

In December 2010, the World Bank launched the International Corruption Hunters Alliance, a network of 286 anti-corruption officials from 134 countries that aims to strengthen global anticorruption efforts through parallel investigations, facilitating access to investigative information and enforcement jurisdictions that can advance national-level prosecutions of wrongdoers. The World Bank has also supported programs such as the StAR – as introduced in the present chapter and analysed in Chapter 17 of the present book – a joint initiative of the Bank and the UNODC, and the Extractive Industries Transparency Initiative (EITI), among others.

(8.2) The IMF activities Also, the prominence given to corruption control is linked directly to the activities within the scope of the IMF's mandate: corruption can influence a country's economic performance so that the traditional duties of the Fund – macroeconomic surveillance, financial support to countries in a financial/balance of payment crisis, and technical assistance – are affected. As Siegel (2007: 47) points out, the Fund's "work in the area of anti-corruption and governance does not fit neatly into a single box. Instead, the IMF's contribution permeates its work in a number of fields within its mandate". Historically, the IMF was not significantly engaged in anti-corruption initiatives. As evidenced in our book, there exists a strong relationship of governance issues with economic growth and macro-economic stability. This connection began to be recognized in the 1990s and is explicitly acknowledged in IMF (1997). The Guiding Note articulates a role for the IMF in the area of anti-corruption and governance and sets out the boundaries for that role. According to the Guidance Note and the later developments of the IMF activity in the area of anti-corruption and governance issues, we may summarize the Fund's role in curbing corruption as follows:

i. As explicitly recognized by the Guidance Note, the Fund does not hold a specific mandate to fight corruption in member countries. "Rather, the IMF's purposes relate to collaboration on international monetary problems, promoting exchange stability, assisting in the establishment of a multilateral system of payments for current international transactions and in the elimination of foreign exchange restrictions, assisting members in correcting balance of payments maladjustments, and facilitating the expansion and balanced growth of international trade" (Siegel: 48). In developing and carrying out its work in the governance and anti-corruption area, the IMF and its staff must work within the scope of its mandate as defined in the IMF Articles of Agreement.[117] In cases of countries where economic performance had been negatively affected by corruption, the Fund requested the implementation of anti-corruption reforms.

ii. Within these areas of competences, there is an opportunity for the IMF to promote sound governance reforms in several important areas. "Such areas include public resource management with a focus on fiscal transparency, financial sector soundness, tax administration, central bank safeguards, as well as anti-money laundering and measures to counter the financing of terrorism (AML/CFT)." (Siegel, 2007: 49).

iii. Unlike the multilateral development banks, the IMF does not provide project financing. As widely known, the Fund provides financial assistance to support Members in addressing issues in their balance of payments. The IMF's financing is usually provided in support of economic reform programs of the member supposed to overcome the problems that led to the balance of payments difficulties. It is provided in a specific arrangement under which the IMF commits resources to a member State and sets up conditions for the release of those resources that are drawn directly from the member's economic reform program. A central issue arises in this context: "(. . .) to what extent the IMF can make country strategies on anti-corruption conditions for financing" (Siegel: 50). The "IMF's Guidelines on Conditionality prescribe the extent to which the IMF can make country strategies on anti-corruption a condition for financing. A criterion for establishing any condition is that it is of 'critical importance for achieving the goals of the member's program'(. . .)". Measures that are outside of the IMF's core areas of responsibility may be established as conditions, but require more detailed explanation of their critical importance. Thus, structural measures related to fighting corruption may be established as conditions, if this standard is met (ID.).

iv. The Fund also advises on anti-corruption issues addressed in the UNCAC and other international conventions against corruption as they arise in appropriate cases. According to Siegel, the advice on anti-corruption matters to date has been focused mainly on the legal frameworks and institutions necessary to promote good economic governance, such as dedicated anti-corruption commissions and asset/wealth declarations. In matters such as those covered by the

---

117 IMF (1944).

UNCAC, the IMF advice focuses not only on transparency, but also on the development of sound legal frameworks and institutions to prevent and fight corruption. Siegel (2007:52) testifies that the "IMF staff have advised several countries on the development of anticorruption regimes. As many countries have chosen to create a dedicated anticorruption commission or establish a regime for the declaration of wealth by public officials, IMF staff have been asked to comment on laws and regulations that address these matters."

v. As part of a drive to meet large demand from its members for practical, on-the-ground help – termed technical assistance – the IMF has set up donor-supported funds to boost capacity building. The funds are dedicated to specific capacity-building activities. Topical trust funds support global IMF technical assistance on specialized thematic areas and complement the work of the IMF's regional technical assistance centers and other IMF technical assistance. They incorporate international best practice and are closely aligned with recipients' development strategies. Donors are actively engaged in the governance of the topical trust funds. Insofar as they support the IMF technical assistance in building robust, sound and fair tax administration systems, efficient and transparent systems for managing natural resources and effective systems to tackle ML, the topical trust fund may significantly contribute in promoting good governance at the local level.[118]

vi. What is more, the Fund works together with the FATF,[119] the organization funded in 1989 by the G7 to define a common strategy and actions against ML. More specifically, the IMF is an observer in the FATF. It goes clearly beyond the scope of the present work to illustrate the AML international regime.[120] Here, it suffices to note that

---

118 The newest trust funds – Managing Natural Resource Wealth and Tax Policy and Administration – are currently budgeted at $25 million and $30 million respectively over the next five years and will begin operating in May 2011. The IMF's first trust fund – Anti-Money Laundering/Combating the Financing of Terrorism – was launched in 2009. For further information on their functioning and the different areas of relevance see http://www.imf.org/external/np/exr/key/ttf.htm.

119 The FATF is a Paris-based organization founded in 1989, which, initially, consisted of developed countries but now includes strategically important developing countries as well. It can be rightly considered as the world's anti-money standard setter and enforcer. The FATF's standards are applied by over 180 countries through a global network of regional bodies affiliated to the FATF.

120 For a pithy historical account of money laundering regulation see Unger (2013). For an updated illustration of the current international and EU AML's

combating ML is a cornerstone of a broader agenda to fight organized crime and other serious crimes including corruption, by depriving criminals – and in the case of corruption both corrupt public officials and corruptors – of ill-gotten gains and by prosecuting those who assist in the laundering of such ill-gotten gains (FATF, 2010). ML, indeed, can be looked at as the necessary means through which criminal activity lives on and proliferates: the reasoning is plain and well-known. Let us focus on the case of bribery as a telling example. Corruption generates illicit proceeds that need to be laundered. Such proceeds often flow through the financial system. This is why private sector entities and, particularly, financial institutions are subject to international standards – which – by means of the States' implementing pieces of legislation – require them to put in place adequate and effective measures to prevent ML. In explaining what he considers nearly an "incestuous relation", Esposito (2013: 99), adds a further layer of complexity to the interconnection between the two crimes at hand: on the one hand, the illicit proceeds generated by corruption breed the ML financial flows; whilst, on the other, ML is often made possible by resorting to different forms of corruption. Noticeably, in February 2012 the FATF Standards[121] were revised to strengthen global safeguards and further protect the integrity of the financial system by providing governments with stronger tools to take action against financial crime. At the same time, these new standards address new priority areas such as corruption and tax crimes. Furthermore, a requirement to ratify the UNCAC has been included in the new Recommendations. In essence, the revision of the Recommendations aims at achieving a balance: first, the requirements have been specifically strengthened in areas which are higher risk or where implementation could be enhanced. They have been expanded to deal with new threats such as the financing of proliferation of weapons of mass destruction, and to be clearer on transparency and tougher on

main features see Costanzo (2013); Vervaele (2013); Borlini (2013) and bibliography referred therein. For a preliminary assessment of such regime let us refer to Arnone and Padoan (2008), and Arnone and Borlini (2010). The FATF Recommendations are the basis on which Member Countries should meet the shared objective of tackling money laundering, terrorist financing and – since February 2012 – the financing of proliferation. The FATF calls upon all countries to effectively implement these measures in their national systems: they are applied by over 180 countries through a global network of regional bodies affiliated to the FATF.

[121] FATF (2012). Note, however, that at the time of this writing the IMF Board has not endorsed the new AML/CFT recommendations.

corruption. Secondly, they are also better targeted – there is more flexibility for simplified measures to be applied in low risk areas. This risk-based approach will allow financial institutions and other designated sectors to apply their resources to higher risk areas. Among the key changes to the 2003 version of the FATF Recommendations, it is worth stressing that, with the adoption of the new Standard, the FATF now addresses new and aggravated threats responding to the priorities set out by the international community. Corruption and politically exposed persons stand among the key issues addressed. The FATF Recommendations strengthen the requirements on financial institutions to identify politically exposed persons (PEPs) – who may represent a higher risk of corruption by virtue of the positions they hold. The existing requirement to apply enhanced due diligence to PEPs has been extended from foreign PEPs, with new risk-based requirements applied to domestic PEPs and PEPs from international organizations, and to the family and close associates of all PEPs – reflecting the methods used by corrupt officials and kleptocrats to launder the proceeds of corruption. Overall, another important IMF-endorsed standard for the promotion of good governance takes the form of the FATF Recommendations. The IMF plays a pivotal role in monitoring the follow-up of the FATF AML/CFT Standards. The Fund's assessments of countries' compliance with this standard are based on a methodology of about 250 criteria which the IMF has developed in conjunction with the FATF. "IMF staff conduct about six to eight assessments a year. For these assessments, Fund staff coordinate with the World Bank, the FATF and FATF-like regional bodies" (Siegel, 2007: 52). What is more, the IMF staff offer extensive technical assistance on implementation of AML/CFT standards concerning two complementary key levels: i) the legal framework and ii) the practical aspects of implementation. For instance, the Fund staff may advise on a needs assessment, provide for regional or country specific workshops, build the capacity of Financial Intelligence Units, and substantially contribute to the legislative drafting.

vii. Countries characterized by a weak financial sector – likely targets for illegal financial activities – are assisted by the Fund in the context of the FSAP (in cooperation with the WB) through the utilization of standards and codes. The surveillance activity has been progressively extended: today it covers the financial sector, institutional aspects (including the creation of international codes and standards), and the evaluation of risks and weaknesses deriving from capital market volatility.

As rightly stressed by Siegel (2007) and Arnone and Iliopulos (2005), some main features characterizing the IMF's work on governance and anti-corruption emerge. To recap, the IMF advice cannot extend to investigations into the actions of targeted individuals or enforcement of particular criminal prosecutions. "Such involvement would be outside the scope of the IMF's mandate and be seen as prejudicing proceedings launched by national authorities against particular individuals charged with corruption-related offenses" (Siegel, 2007: 48). Second, the stress is plainly on prevention, focusing on measures to promote transparency, foster good administrative practices and thereby limit the scope for corruption. Third, the main tools in furthering such objectives consist of improving the legal and institutional frameworks for addressing governance and anti-corruption issues. Fourth, the IMF strong commitment in fostering and monitoring the enforcement of the AML international apparatus is another indirect, though extremely important, device to contrast the possibility that corruptors and corrupt officials worldwide are able to benefit from the proceeds of the predicate corruption crimes.

(8.3) The WTO and the revised GPA In 2012 the Members of the WTO revised the plurilateral Agreement on Government Procurement ('GPA') and, for the first time within the WTO system, issues of corruption prevention have been explicitly mentioned. Although the GPA is still not binding, the revised Agreement will enter into force when it is ratified by two thirds of the 15 parties. To date, seven parties have ratified: Liechtenstein, Norway, Canada, Chinese Taipei, the United States, Hong Kong–China and the European Union. The Agreement is a plurilateral treaty that commits members to certain core disciplines regarding competition, non-discrimination and, most importantly for our purpose, transparency and good governance in the procurement sector. It covers the procurement of goods, services and capital infrastructure by public authorities. Even though its practical consequences cannot be assessed at this point in time, in our opinion the symbolic significance of a WTO's first concrete step in dealing with corruption should not be ignored, at least once it is shown, as we do in our book, that corruption is a grave impediment to economic development and a major obstacle for truly competitive markets.

10.3 AN ASSESSMENT

The net effect of the international anti-corruption agreements and the IFIs anti-corruption policies is that there now exists a sort of "hyper norm", or, in other words, a global standard repudiating corruption that transcends national boundaries and forms a global consensus on the criminalization of transnational bribery.

As shown by exploring the IMF and WB activities, their work in the area of anti-corruption and good governance simply does not fit neatly into a single box. On the contrary, such issues permeate their activities and work in a number of fields within their respective mandates. Furthermore, the IFI's overall impact on States' activities in the matters of anti-corruption and good governance is remarkable due to their undeniable and growing importance within the international scenario, particularly the leverage they have on the assisted countries.

Coming to international anti-bribery treaties, it is worth remarking that most of the provisions of the international anti-bribery conventions are not self-executing. As with most international agreements, a process of implementation has to follow signature and ratification. Member States are asked to implement the rules regarding transnational bribery by adopting domestic laws to this effect.

Borlini and Magrini (2007) assert that there is a difference in (a) the level of flexibility that exists about whether or not to adopt the rules, and (b) the degree to which domestic laws may stray from the guidelines set down by the international agreement. One approach suggests a mandatory method of implementation, whereas the other implies a more elastic approach that defers to the States Parties as to the way non self-executing provisions must be implemented. The two approaches, in turn, flow into two models of international regulation which Makinwa (2007) identifies as follows: a strict mandatory model and a more liberal one.

This funding difference in approach is substantial. The strict model of regulation is epitomized by the OECD Convention. It is phrased in mandatory language and emphasizes the need for a minimum standard of compliance. Members are expected not to derogate from this minimum in their domestication of the rules. The mandatory strict model provides the strongest basis for uniform application of rules regarding transnational bribery. Its narrow scope also allows easier adoption and implementation.

The liberal model is characterized by a certain degree of flexibility and discretion allotted to States Parties. Having said that all anti-corruption treaties contain a minimum core of mandatory commitments, subjecting certain rules regarding the anti-corruption international strategy to national laws and the principle of sovereignty – as is done, for example, by the UNCAC – establishes the States' faculty to decide how and to what extent their international obligations are translated into domestic law. Although more encompassing in formulation, the opting out potential of these instruments may lead to a more uncertain environment for the regulation of bribery. This is why we argue that the time has come for effective implementation. Looking at UNCAC, two issues arise in this context. First, as noted, UNCAC still needs to be ratified by some prominent G20 countries: leading by example starts from there. Second, as we maintain in Chapter 16, the UNCAC monitoring mechanism should be strengthened – for example on the GRECO or WGB model – despite some States Parties reluctance.

To conclude, the answer to the explicit question posed by some scholars regarding the actual achievement of a global common standard in fighting corruption cannot be clear-cut: whilst some may argue that there exists a plethora of treaties and other tools, this has also achieved a minimum standard in the international rules for several of the main elements of the current international anti-corruption strategy (e.g. prevention, criminalization of domestic and international corruption, liability of legal persons, international cooperation, private sector cooperation, asset recovery). More remarkably, the adoption of such treaties along with the initiatives of the IFI's testifies the gradual understanding of both the scope and seriousness of the corruption issue and the acknowledgment by the international community that corruption cannot be considered as a domestic issue any longer, and the necessity to develop and agree on a common "global" strategy.

11. Criminalization of the offense

11.1 INTRODUCTION

For the most part, the anti-bribery conventions are not self-executing, which means that they require enabling acts before they can function inside a country and bind domestic courts. As mentioned above, the anti-corruption conventions set forth *minimum* standards that national implementing pieces of legislation must meet. State Parties must firstly identify where and how their own pieces of legislation fall below the standards of the conventions or where a domestic act is needed in order to implement specific treaties' provisions. Then, they must comply with the international obligation set forth by the convention at hand, by adopting appropriate pieces of legislation. For instance, deficiencies might occur in case domestic law does not criminalize certain types of conduct (such as the bribery of foreign public officials). They may also arise when an element of an offense is narrower than the corresponding element in the international conventions (e.g. in cases where the definition of a bribe does not include non-pecuniary advantages). More generally, in most constitutional systems a specific domestic law is required in order to introduce a new offense.

As with most international criminal conventions, each of the anti-bribery treaties seeks to work out its own way to balance prima facie contrasting aims: on the one hand, to ease the adoption of a legally binding text and, thereafter, its implementation; on the other hand, to ease the harmonization of Contracting States' penal legislation. Whereas the first goal necessitates that States be granted a certain degree of flexibility, harmonization of substantial criminal law calls for clear and quite strict obligations.

How do the Conventions under discussion balance these two aims? Are their criminal provisions sufficiently precise to promote and ease an effective harmonization within the penal law of Contracting States? Are they always mandatory? What are their defective aspects?

In order to answer these questions, we start by analyzing the conduct the States Parties of the Convention are required to criminalize. We adopt a horizontal approach. The focus is on the conduct typically defined as corruption *stricto sensu* in most domestic jurisdictions and to which the legal literature unanimously refers. In a specifically legal sense, indeed, (public) corruption denotes two specific and symmetric criminal offenses. Firstly, "active corruption", that is to say the intentional offer, promise or giving of any undue monetary or other advantage, whether directly or through intermediaries, by an (*extraneus*) person to a public official, for that official or for a third party, in order that the official act or refrain from acting in relation to the performance of official duties, in order to obtain a private gain; and, symmetrically, "passive corruption", that is to say the act of an (*intraneus*) public official who intentionally acts or refrains from acting according to the performance of the official duties in order to obtain any undue pecuniary or other advantage. Please note, that the same pattern can be proposed, *mutatis mutandis*, for private corruption: in this case the qualification of *intraneus* is taken by a member of the executive body, a director or any other employee of a private entity.

A side note: although some anti-bribery treaties require State Parties to criminalize or consider criminalizing other offenses, which are related to the notion of corruption just outlined in various forms, consistently with the subject of this book, we choose to ground our analysis on corruption *stricto sensu*. Besides, corruption is also the main object of the international anti-bribery treaties so that when other crimes are considered it is usually in order to strengthen its prevention and repression.[1]

---

1 For instance, as seen in Chapter 10, Art IX of the OAS Convention requires that "subject to its Constitution and the fundamental principles of its legal system, each State Party that has not yet done so shall take the necessary measures to establish under its laws as an offense" illicit enrichment. Similarly, the AU Convention contains provisions requiring State Parties to take the necessary steps to establish as criminal offences the laundering of proceeds of corruption, and, subject to the principles of their domestic laws, illicit enrichment. On its part, the CoECLCC requires State Parties to criminalise trading in influence, although such an obligation is subject to the possibility of reservations. Again, according to art. 13 of the same Treaty, States Parties must also criminilise money laundering of proceeds from corruption offences, and, pursuant to Art. 14, establish – "to the extent the Party has not made a reservation or a declaration" – as offenses liable to criminal or other sanctions the following accounted offences when committed intentionally, in order to commit, conceal or disguise the offences of corruption or trading in influence: "a) creating or using an invoice or any other accounting document or record containing false or incomplete information; b) unlawfully omitting to make a record of a payment. Interestingly, the UNCAC does not define corruption as such. It rather defines specific acts of corruptions that should be considered in every jurisdiction covered by the Convention. These include bribery and embezzlement, but also illicit enrichment, ML, concealment, and obstruction of justice. More specifically, on the one hand, States Parties are obliged to crimi-

We then explore the provisions concerning the sanctioning standard and liability of legal persons by following the same horizontal pattern. As a result, a clear portrait of the international standards concerning substantial criminal law should emerge.

Our analysis also attempts to draw attention to differences in the anti-corruption treaties' scope *ratione materiae*. Where remarkable, such differences might end up by postponing and/or affecting the implementation of the national criminal law and, as a mediate consequence, the consistency and efficacy of the whole anti-corruption apparatus. Prima facie duplications characterized by tiny variations may have the same effect. In addition, one should consider the frequent adoption of non-mandatory provisions and the vagueness which characterizes some of the norms under discussion.

A substantial lack of homogeneous international standards, indeed, can raise difficulties for countries which are about to implement two or more anti-bribery treaties. The coexistence of different international standards can sometimes cause a harmful intra-specific competition which might challenge the task of national parliaments and governments. In contrast, where the drafters of the different international conventions choose the same or a similar paradigm – as, for example, in the case of legal persons' liability regime – the duties incumbent upon the national parliaments and governments have resulted in clear (minimum) standards, the implementation (or the non-implementation) of which can be easily assessed.

Finally, another aspect to be noted is the clarity (or otherwise) of texts under discussion. The interpretive issues raised by certain formulations are sometimes substantial and demand noticeable exegetic efforts. It is therefore crucial that all the elements encompassed within the definitions provided for by the relevant provisions are meticulously spelled out.

---

nalise bribery (both the giving of an undue advantage to a national, international or foreign public official and the acceptance of an undue advantage by a national public official) as well as embezzlement of public funds. Other offenses that States Parties are required to criminalize are, conversion or transfer of criminal proceeds; misappropriation or other diversion of property by a public official; money laundering, and obstruction of justice. Sanctions extend to those who participate in or attempt to commit corruption offences. On the other hand, "in recognition of the fact that there may be other criminal offences which some countries may have already established in their domestic law, or may find their establishment useful in fighting corruption" (Vlassis, 2007: 24) the UNCAC includes a number of provisions asking States Parties to consider establishing as criminal offenses other conduct. Acts States are encouraged – but not required – to criminalize include, among others, such forms of conduct as trading in influence, concealment, abuse of functions, illicit enrichment, or bribery in the private sector.

BOX 11.1 DEFINING CORRUPTION: THE NEED FOR A PRECISE LEGAL STANDARD

Ordinary concepts like corruption are difficult to define, because of their frequent use in so many overlapping contexts. Corruption, in fact, can be approached from different complementary angles. References to corruption as an illicit and immoral phenomenon can be found in the most ancient and different cultures. In one of his essays on the matter, Osborne (1998) reports the references contained in the Holy Bible (*The Exodus*, Chapter 18, versicles 21–22; Deuteronomius versicle 19; Samuel, Chapter 8, versicles 3–5); Law of Manu (Chapter 7, sections 123–4); Confucius and Buddha's doctrines; Plato's dialogue on the Law; Christian doctrine (Luke, Chapter 3, versicles 12–15); and the Koran (sura II, 188–9). Political philosophers typically envisaged corruption as a significantly wide phenomenon, which encompassed the degeneration of a whole political system. Plato and Aristotle illustrated the three possible pure forms of government – monarchy, aristocracy, and constitutional government – vis-à-vis their perverted forms, respectively: tyranny, oligarchy, and democracy. Machiavelli maintained that corruption was a process of such gradual decadence of citizens' virtues, that the rise and intervention of a heroic leader became necessary, able to transfer into the entire population his/her own virtue. In *Grandeur des Romains et de leur décadence*, Montesquieu (1734), described corruption of the public virtues and the annihilation of the constitutional order which follow to the extension from the *urbs* to the *orbs*. In his *Du contrat social*, Rousseau deeply perceived that his time was an extremely corrupted era, and took it as one of his missions to make his contemporary civilians acknowledge the perils and menaces of the phenomenon. Incidentally, it is not pleonastic to highlight that Rousseau also proposed a kind of Spartan solution. Turning to the Anglo-Saxon tradition, in the *Leviathan* Thomas Hobbes considered corruption as an autonomous and grave sort of illicit act, having the effect of making judgements ineffective. More than one century later, and in a more precise fashion, Jeremy Bentham (1862), after distinguishing the offence of *active bribery* (or *bribe-giving*) and *passive bribery* (or *bribe-receiving*) – characterised the complex dynamic of *bribery* by focusing on the activities of giving and receiving a certain advantage. Moreover, in Bentham's view, the latter symmetrical activities could also create a seductive means to induce a trustee to violate the duties that derive from his/her title. One of the latest editions of the *Oxford Dictionary of English* (2006: 389) defines "corruption" as a "dishonest or fraudulent conduct by those in power, typically involving bribery", and, consequently, "bribery" as "the giving or the offering of a bribe", where bribe is to be intended to "dishonestly persuade (someone) to act in one's favour by a gift of money or other inducement" (2006: 212). According to this definition, the notion of bribery has a derivative nature, being, in the specific context of a corrupt conduct, the payment for a corrupt act. Thus, the wrongfulness of the payment depends on the forbidden nature of the consideration for the bribe. Notably, the difference between the two concepts at hand is mirrored also in other languages: *Korruption* and *Bestechung* in German, *corruption* and *cohecho* in Spanish, *corruzione* e *baratteria*, in Italian. Despite the prominent sources mentioned above and the insights the reported definitions provide, defining corruption in view of the purposes of our work necessitates less opaque contours. As Senior (2006:18), aptly points out, ". . .there are likely to be wide variations, between countries, regions, ethnic group both now and through time about what constitutes corruption and the extent to which the law must punish it". Clearly, only once a clear definition of corruption is provided, conduct of individuals and institutions, including companies, can be judged as corrupt or incorrupt, because a sufficiently accepted standard can be applied. In the following, we thus assess various attempts to define the crime under discussion and address the most remarkable questions arising when considering the various proposals by the economic, sociological and legal doctrine. In the end, we first show the reasons why legal standards are to be preferred, at least in the context of the second part of our work, and, then, confine the notion of corruption to a precise definition, to which I refer throughout this thesis. We start from proposal of definitions for economic studies. In 1976, Williams (1976:22) stated: ". . .there are nearly as many definitions of corruption as there are species of tropical plants and they vary as much in their appearance, character and resilience. The point is that the search for the true definition of corruption is, like the pursuit of the Holy Grail, endless, exhausting and ultimately futile". Senior (2006) argues that Williams's contention represents an academic hyperbole, being far from truth.

What is more it impedes any attempt to discuss economics of corruption before such a discussion could take place. According to the British economist, it is possible to work out a suitable definition in order to investigate the causes, consequences and cures of corruption under an economic perspective. Senior proceeds in his research by first exploring and assessing some of the main definitions proposed in the socio-political and economic literature. He starts considering the classical definitions of Waterbury (1973: 533), according to whom corruption is "the abuse of public power and influence for private ends" and the earlier and commonly quoted definition of Nye (1917: 419), which shares the same framework, but is far more detailed: "corruption is behaviour which deviates from the formal duties of a public role because of private-regarding (personal, close family, private clique) pecuniary or status gains; or violates rules against the exercise of certain types of private-regarding influence". These definitions are, thus, grounded on two main constitutive elements: 1) the violation of a deontological duty, that is to say the intentional violation of a formal duty or an abuse of official powers; 2) a subjective element: that is the reason underlying the will to obtain some sort of direct or indirect personal advantages. Senior maintains that all the definitions which follow Nye and Waterbury's pattern present significant flaws. The main shortcoming of the Nye-type definitions is that they confine corruption to the *public* sector for *private* aims. Whereas the latter dynamic is probably the most frequent, it cannot exclude that corruption occurs within the private sector and non-governmental sector as well. Let us suppose that the employee of a large company who is responsible for awarding contracts may take a bribe as readily as a government functionary. In this case, it is evident that the public sphere is completely excluded. The second flaw of the Nye-type definitions is that they refer to rules which prevail *at the time*. Senior's take is that the extreme variability of laws, regulations and rules among the different countries, and within particular countries and from time to time, does not constitute a safety anchor to which any economic study can be affixed. Alam (1989: 483) proposed a definition based on the relationship between principals and their agents, pursuant to the related traditional management theory. He asserts: "corruption may be defined as (1) the sacrifice of the principal's interest for their agent's, or (2) the violation of norms defining the agent's behaviour". This approach is questionable at least under two main aspects: First, since it is directly related to the relationship between principals and their agents, the very concept of corruption would be equally applicable to an agent who simply went to sleep during the afternoon. . .thus sacrificing his principal's interests and violating norms defining the agent's behaviour. Yet, nobody would argue that this idleness substantiates a form of corruption. Second and more remarkably, the assimilation of the problems of corruption within the public sector to those of the model principal-agent seems even more debatable in that it does not take into due consideration the peculiarities of the two realms. Indeed, in private firms the principal's aim is clear and clearly defined, that is to say to make profit (*recte*: to respect its contractual duties designed to permit the principal to make profit). Accordingly, the agents' behaviour is constantly assessed and monitored in light of this criterion. Moreover, to monitor a private firm's management constitutes always a costly cooperative and organizational issue. On the contrary, a similar general aim, susceptible of being constantly monitored lacks in the case of the activities of the highest members of the government. Senior (2006: 22) attempts to overcome the various flaws above highlighted by proposing his own definition which is grounded on five conditions that "*must all be satisfied simultaneously*. Corruption occurs when a corruptor (1) *covertly* gives (2) *a favour* to a corruptee or to a nominee to influence (3) *action(s)* that (4) *benefit* the corrupter or a nominee, and for which the corruptee has (5) *authority*". The British economist argues that the definition he puts forward has many advantages. It is succinct and transparent. It distinguishes corruption from crime in general and from fraud and theft in particular. It is applicable to actions that take place at any level in any institution within any sector – public, private, voluntary and charitable. It is independent of time. We consider Senior's definition a good parameter for economic researches in that it avoids many of the flaws the above-referred study present. However, Senior's contention that it is necessary to work out a notion of corruption that is not dependent on the possible legal definition does not suit the purposes of our work. When addressing the required constitutive elements of corruption as defined by the international anti-bribery conventions, one of the main aims of such treaties is to harmonise the notion of corruption between the contracting parties in order to enhance the possibilities of effectively prosecuting the offenders and, moreover, the facilitation of the international criminal cooperation mechanisms. A suitable definition of corruption therefore cannot leave out a consideration of legal standard. What is more, Senior's definition neither hints to the necessary bilateral nature of the crime at hand, nor considers the difference between, respectively, the wide and the broad concepts of corruption, which draw the contours of the notion we take. However, the extreme difficulties of defining corruption are testified also by recent attempts which, instead of proposing a closed formula, provide a list of forms that corruption can take, which should capture the main manifestations of the phenomenon under discussion. A first example is the list proposed by Johnson and Sharma (2004), including: bribery and graft; kleptocracy; misappropriation; non-performance of duties; influence-peddling; acceptance of improper gifts; protecting maladministration; abuse of power; electoral malpractice; manipulation of regulations; rent-seeking; clientelism and patronage and illegal campaign contributions. A similar approach is used in the recent insightful study published by Della Porta and Vannucci (2007), who attempt to define corruption by using a broad network of "hidden deals" where they include an extreme variety of illicit, illegal, and improper deals. Another rather comprehensive definition is that provided by the United Nations Development Programme (UNDP) in its Anti-Corruption Practice: corruption is defined as "the misuse of public power, office or authority for private benefit – through bribery, extortion, influence peddling, nepotism, fraud, speed money or embezzlement". According to the AsDB "Corruption involves behaviour on the part of officials in the public and private sectors, in which they improperly and unlawfully enrich themselves and/or those close to them, or induce others to do so, by misusing the position in which they are placed". A final definition worth considering is proposed by the non-governmental organization Transparency International (hereinafter: TI) which defines corruption as "the misuse of entrusted power for private gain". (2007: xxi). According to TI "both financial or material gain and non-material gain, such as the furtherance of political or professional ambitions" (ID.). The definitions just mentioned, though rather comprehensive, do not include forms of corruption which are also worth mentioning (such as, for instance corruption in the private sector) or address the main defining issues of a notion being used for legal purposes and studies. It is, therefore, necessary to explain a better-targeted definition of corruption for the legal analysis of the main international anti-corruption treaties. In their analytical comparative study Zimring and Johnson (2007) explain why a legal approach is a criterion to be preferred over other standards put forward by the socio-political sciences. Assuming that all the analysts agree that corruption involves a deviation from certain *standards* of behaviour, the key question, therefore, and the pivot around which the conflict revolves, is what criteria to use to establish those standards. The two authors weigh an approach based on a legal standard against two other paradigms grounded, respectively, on public interest and public opinion. According to Zimring and Johnson (2007: 459) "the *legal approach* defines corruption in terms of the criteria established by official statutes and judicial interpretation". Therefore, an act of corruption occurs when it is prohibited by laws, and, conversely, in case it is not illegal, it does not corrupt even though unethical or abusive. Quite the opposite, the *public interest approach* is centred "on the effects of an act, rather than its legal status." (ID.) Accordingly, if a conduct is harmful to the public interest it substantiates corruption, even though legal. On the contrary, if a certain conduct benefits the public interest it is not corrupt even if illegal. It goes without saying that the vague contours of the notion of "public interest", whereby the corrupt conduct could be seen as too broad and too restrictive, cannot satisfy any analysis of the phenomenon which needs precise and certain contents. The *public opinion approach* posits that a conduct is corrupt if some of the public defines it as such. Since public opinion may vary considerably, analysts of this school classify corruption in the following three classes, *black*, *grey*, and *white* corruption. Black corruption occurs when a majority of both elite and mass opinion indicates that a certain conduct is to be condemned and punished. On the other hand, grey corruption indicates that some observers, usually elites, want to see the action punished, while others do not, being the ambivalent majority. Finally, white corruption signifies that the majority of both elite and mass opinion tolerates a certain activity and does not want the conduct to be punished. Once again, the inherent uncertainty of this classification can ground neither legal nor economic analysis of the phenomenon, not to mention that, as maintained by Senior (2006: 24): '(i)t is hard to imagine a less workable set of definitions in which public opinion has to be polled on whether punishment is warranted into "elite" and "mass" opinion.' Therefore, our take is that only a legal standard can provide a definition of corruption that qualifies analytically both the conduct of the corrupter and the conduct of the corrupted subject as specific crimes and allows to compare and distinguish the offenses of corruption from other crimes like, for example, those of fraud, abuse of power, and embezzlement. The dichotomy which shapes the legal notion of corruption – set out by most of the criminal legal systems and the international instruments under exam – and which orientates the present part of our work is focused on two concepts of corruption: i) the "broad" notion of corruption (referred to also as corruption *lato sensu*); and ii) the "restricted" notion of corruption (referred to as corruption *stricto senso*). The last part of the present box deals with such dichotomy in order to demarcate the definition of corruption representing the *theoretical basis* upon which each of the relevant notions set out by the international anti-bribery conventions can be subsumed. The word "corruption" suffers from an essential semantic ambiguity in the (political-) legal language due to the circumstance that it is used in order to indicate two rather different concepts. On the one hand, the concept of corruption generally identifies the abuse of powers (or the violation of duties) in order to obtain a private gain, referred to as corruption *lato sensu*. As to the contents of this notion, it evidently encompasses certain forms of offenses which find a specific collocation within the statutes and case-law of the national penal systems (*e.g.* abuse of functions; embezzlement). Therefore, the notion under discussion does not suit the purposes of the present work in the sense that it cannot satisfy the necessary principles of determination and certainty of the legal definition of an offense, which every penal system must respect. On the other hand, in a more technical and legal connotation, corruption (referred to as corruption *stricto sensu*) normally denotes two specific criminal offences: 1) active corruption, that is to say the intentional offer, promise or giving of any undue monetary or other advantage, whether directly or through intermediaries, by an (*extraneus*) person to a public official, for that official or for a third party, in order that the official act or refrain from acting in relation to the performance of official duties, in order to obtain a private gain; and, symmetrically, 2) passive corruption, that is to say the act of an (*intraneus*, public/private) official who intentionally acts or refrains from acting according to the performance of the official duties in order to obtain any undue pecuniary or other advantage. We make use of such a notion of corruption *stricto sensu* as a parameter to investigate the constitutive elements of the corrupt offences as defined by the anti-bribery conventions, since it better reflects the requirements of determination and precision which any "criminal offense" definition must comply with. On the contrary, the notion of corruption *lato sensu* is similar to most of the definitions put forward by the economic and socio-political sciences, being characterised by similar vagueness and flaws.

11.2 OBJECTIVE ELEMENTS OF THE CORRUPTION OFFENSES

11.2.1 The Offender: Any Person

For active corruption *stricto sensu* –of both national and foreign public officials, all the anti-bribery treaties do not require any peculiar qualification for the offender. Aside from Article VIII(1) of the OAS Convention – according to which the offender is to be a national, a person having his/her habitual residence in the territory, and businesses domiciled in the territory of the State Party subject to the obligation of criminalizing the conduct under discussion – in none of the other criminalizing provisions is there any required qualification. The wording of the relevant provisions is clear in stating that the offender can be "any person". As aptly remarked by Zerbes (2007), while commenting on Article 1 of the OECD Convention, and Borlini and Magrini (2007) with reference to the UNCAC, two consequences stem from this. Firstly, the array of the potential offender is unlimited, active corruption not being a "special offence" that can be committed solely by certain categories of subjects (e.g. a company's executive). Secondly, liability for acts of active corruption rests not only with natural persons, but also with legal persons.

On the contrary, when passive corruption is being criminalized, the offender must be a (national or foreign) public official according to the definition provided by the Conventions. Note that even though the offender can be anyone, the recipient must be a public official also when active public bribery is concerned.

11.2.2 Actus Reus: Offering, Promising or Giving a Bribe to a National Public Official

The OAS, EU, COE, AU, and the UN Conventions all require (in mandatory terms) their signatories to criminalize the "offering", "promising" and "giving", or "offering" and "granting" a bribe. This normative choice reflects the attitude of the international community that all three types of conduct represent corrosive behavior that should be prohibited and punished. As already mentioned, the only agreement which covers neither the active nor the passive corruption of national public officials is the OECD Convention.

It is worth stressing that there are noticeable differences between "offering", "promising" and "giving" a bribe.

"*Offering*" occurs when a briber indicates that s/he is ready to provide a bribe. In greater detail, offer is to be intended as a declaration by the bribe-giver, on his/her own initiative, indicating his/her *readiness* to *pay* the public official to act or refrain from acting in the exercise of his or her functions. In this case, the danger exists and commences as the public official can recognize or count on an "undue" advantage.

"*Promising*" is when a briber who agrees with an official to provide a bribe (e.g. where the briber agrees to a solicitation from the public official). By promising to do so, the offender makes a *definitive commitment*. The anti-bribery treaties do not require that the offer and promise be explicit. Arguably they can be tacit, and this extensive interpretation accords better with both literal and systematic interpretative criteria and with a teleological exegesis.

"*Giving*" occurs when the briber actually transfers the undue advantage to the control of the recipient. How that process occurs depends on the nature of the advantage. For instance, whereas funds can be electronically transferred to a bank account, a physical object obviously requires the handing over of possession. In the case of giving, the peril exists because the advantage is materially available.

Finally, as the OAS and AU Conventions use the word "granting" in parallel with "offering", our take is that the former expression means to include both the promise and the giving of a bribe: by making a definitive commitment or materially transferring the advantage to the control of another person, the offender *grants* this person the advantage at stake. As noted by Snider and Kidane (2007) under Article 4(1)(b) of the AU Corruption on active bribery of national public officials, the prohibition extends to an offer, an actual grant, or a promise, but does not apply to authorizations, and this peculiar omission is common to the OAS Convention (Article VI) and the UNCAC (Article 27).

On these authors' interpretation, we can extend to all the treaties at hand Zerbes's (2007) reading with reference to the OECD Convention that neither "offering" nor "giving" a bribe requires an actual agreement between the briber and the public official. In other words, offering and giving do not need the public official to *accept* the offer or gift, or, in the case of giving, that s/he has received the gift (e.g. where the offer or gift is intercepted, for instance by the law enforcement authorities, before it is delivered to the public official). Firstly, this interpretation plainly stems from the ordinary meaning of the words "promise" and "offer", which do not entail whatsoever active attitude by the recipient. Secondly, by resorting to teleological interpretive criteria, this interpretation is confirmed: assuming the aim of effectively contrasting corruption as the guiding principle of the international conventions, one cannot consistently claim that acceptance and/or the material reception of the bribe on the part of the national public official is to be proven in any case. At least, such a higher standard of proof can hardly be set forth at the international level. On the other hand, when the evidence of the so-called *pactum sceleris* can be given, this naturally renders the proof of a pre-existing autonomous offer or giving by the corrupter pointless. In this sense the limit posed by the international conventions is a minimum standard.

To recap, the three means of committing the offense just described – offer, promise, and giving of the bribes – cover every sort of pressure and compulsion implied by the agreement between the offender and the recipient, as well as its fulfillment.

The comprehensiveness of the pattern adopted by the anti-bribery treaties is completed by requesting State Parties to criminalize inchoate offenses[2] and participation. The OAS Convention expressly establishes the crimes of participation, conspiracy, and attempt as part of the general definition of the underlying crimes. This pattern (virtually the same as adopted by the OECD and AU Conventions) seems to be the clearest model. With an original option, the EU Convention refers only to participation in and instigation of the corrupt offenses considered therein within Article 5(1), which deals with penalties and not with the conduct being criminalized.

On the basis of Article 1(2) of the OECD Convention, complicity, in the

---

2 An inchoate offense or inchoate crime is the crime of preparing for or seeking to commit another crime. The most common example of an inchoate offense is conspiracy (Gaines and Miller 2006). "Inchoate offense" has been defined as "Conduct deemed criminal without actual harm being done, provided that the harm that would have occurred is one the law tries to prevent" (McCord and McCord 2006).

form of incitement, aiding and abetting, and authorization of a foreign bribery official in the context of transnational businesses transactions, must constitute penal offenses as well. Similarly, the same provisions require State Parties to criminalize the *attempt* and the *conspiracy* to transnational corruption, in the same way that they criminalize the attempt or conspiracy of a national public official. Thus, as far as conspiracy and attempt are concerned, the OECD Convention aims at the assimilation of transnational bribery with domestic law.

Given the noticeable divergences and the inherent complexity of the national legal regimes concerning instigation, complicity and attempt, the further specifications contained in the Official Commentary 11 to the OECD Convention appears rather accurate: accordingly, such offenses "are understood in terms of their normal content in national legal systems", meaning that "if authorization, incitement, or one of the other listed acts, which does not lead to further action, is not itself punishable under a Party's legal system, then the Party would not be required to make it punishable with respect to bribery of a foreign public official".

The CoECLCC mandates only the criminalization of participatory acts, particularly *aiding or abetting* the commission of any of the criminal offenses envisaged by the Convention itself.

As to AU Convention, in a rather comprehensive formulation, Article 4(1)(i) lists: "participation as a principal, co-principal, agent, instigator, accomplice or accessory or after the fact, or any other manner in the commission or attempted commission of, in any collaboration or conspiracy to commit, any of the acts" referred to in the same Article which defines the scope of application of the Convention at issue.

The UNCAC establishes inchoate offenses and offenses of complicity, including preparation, participation, and attempt, in a general provision (Article 27) which refers to all the offenses considered in the framework of the Convention. Although Article 27(1)–(2) of the UNCAC makes use of mandatory language for the establishment of criminal responsibility for participation as an accomplice, assistant, or instigator, State Parties are only required to *consider* the criminalization and punishment of attempt and preparation. Besides, the repeated use of the expression "*in accordance with its domestic law*" leaves the Contracting States some flexibility even where the provision appears mandatory. In the end, the provision is not well-formulated and leaves open the door to contrasting interpretations. What is more, Article 27 allows different ways of implementation: legal certainty and harmonization of domestic law might be endangered.

Finally, even though the UNCAC includes a separate provision outlawing preparation and attempt and mandates the very controversial criminal offense of preparation to commit the underlying offenses, it inexplicably omits conspiracy as a criminal offense.

Five additional remarks. Firstly, let us stress that all these methods of committing the crime are to be covered by the national criminal law. Whilst normally all the signatories of the international anti-corruption treaties criminalize the giving, some of these countries criminalize "preparing" or "attempting" to bribe, which may cover some, but not necessarily all, instances of offering and promising a bribe.[3]

Secondly, only the OECD Convention, following the FCPA, expressly addresses "authorization" in Article 1(2). The AU Convention's provision extends in relevant part the duty of criminalization part to "participation, as a principal, co-principal agent, instigator, accomplice or accessory after the fact, or in any other manner in the commission or attempted commission . . .". Only an extensive interpretation of the expression "in any other manner" allows the prohibition to extend to authorizations. The omission is also characteristic of the OAS and EU Conventions, the CoECLCC, and the UNCAC. The significance of authorization responsibility relates to the chain of command in multilateral enterprises, which often operate through agents and subsidiaries. The practical effect of this omission is even more significant when officials of multinationals who are not subject either to the FCPA or to other national laws which criminalize authorization carry out the authorization.

Thirdly, all of the conventions cover direct and indirect forms of bribery. Indirect bribery occurs when a briber gives, offers or promises a bribe to an official through an intermediary. It also includes cases when an official solicits or receives a bribe through an intermediary. An intermediary can be anyone and does not have to be someone who is connected with the briber or the public official. For example, indirect bribery may occur when a briber uses an agent, a financial institution or a company to transmit an offer, promise or gift to an official on his/her behalf. The same principle applies irrespective of whether the recipient of the undue advantage is the official. This holds true irrespective of the active/passive, public/private, national/transnational nature of the corrupt conduct. Thus, there is no need to repeat this remark when dealing with the other corrupt offenses in the remaining sections of the present chapter.

---

3 According to the OECD, Corruption: A Glossary of of International Criminal Standards, 2007, available at: www.oecd.org/dataoecd/1/9/39532693.pdf (hereinafter: OECD Glossary), p. 22: "For example, the courts of some countries may consider that an oral offer of a bribe does not constitute attempted bribery; the briber must take further steps before the offence is complete, *e.g.* withdrawing the bribe money from a bank."

Fourthly, the anti-bribery treaties cover bribes given in order that an official act or refrain from acting in the exercise of his/her official duties or functions. In other words, both acts and omissions by an official are included. The conventions do not, however, require that the official's act or omission be illegal or in breach of duties. It may still be an offense where an official accepts a bribe or an offer to perform an act or omission that does not contravene the law per se, or even an act that complies with his or her duties. For instance, as said by Commentary 4 to the OECD Convention, an offense is committed whether or not the company concerned was the best qualified bidder or was otherwise a company which could properly have been awarded the business. Commentary 3 makes it clear that this reflects a general standard of the OECD Conventions. Zerbes (2007) and Borlini and Magrini (2007) argue that the rationale underlying this standard is intrinsically related to the concept of impartiality: this is the public official's fundamental and inalienable obligation, to act impartially. The OECD Convention established that the duty is not subject to alteration by national legislation. We refer again to Commentary 3 to the same Convention in support of this reading, where it states: "provided that it was understood that every public official had a duty to exercise judgment or discretion impartially and this was an 'autonomous' definition not requiring proof of the law of the particular official's country". Obviously, insofar as the OECD Convention is concerned, the act of the public official is subject to all the limits of the Convention: it must be the duty of a *foreign* public official, in the context of transnational corrupt conduct within the framework of a transnational business transaction and the further limitations to business advantage. However, as is made clear by paragraph 39 of its Explanatory Report, the same principles explicitly inspire the CoECLCC, and are to be maintained also with regard to all the other conventions: inclusion of legal acts is important because tolerance of this kind of corruption would undermine the integrity of and public confidence in the civil service. In particular, a bribe for the purpose of obtaining an impartial exercise of judgment or discretion by a public official must be covered, regardless of whether this is considered an illegal act or in breach of duties. As a consequence, countries which only prohibit bribes in order that an official perform an act that is illegal or against the interest of the public service should consider removing this requirement, or make illegality of the acts of a bribed official only an aggravating factor of the offense. As to the required elements of the act of a public official, the legislative choice just illustrated should arguably be interpreted as inherent in all of the *stricto sensu* corrupt offenses defined by international instruments. The conventions also require that the bribe be paid in order that the official acts or refrains from acting in the exercise of his/her duties.

Thus, there must be an etiological link between the bribe and the official's actions or omissions. This entails that an offer or request for a bribe must take place before the official acts or refrains from acting in the exercise of his/her duties. The actual acceptance or receipt of the bribe, however, could take place after.

Finally, the general attitude to setting forth a wide definition of the objective element of offense is also confirmed by the unanimous choice by all the anti-bribery conventions to criminalize corrupt conduct irrespective of the fact that the undue advantage offered, given or promised by the offender, and/or solicited, requested or accepted by a public official, benefits that official or a third party. Incidentally, this normative policy reflects the traditional position of most national criminal systems. Again, since this holds true irrespective of the transnational/national, passive/active, public/private nature of the offense, we will not take up the matter again when addressing other *stricto sensu* corrupt offenses.

11.2.3 Actus Reus: Requesting, Soliciting, Receiving, or Accepting a Bribe by a National Public Official

Bribery offenses against national public officials fall into two general categories: (i) when an official "requests" or "solicits" a bribe, and (ii) when an official "receives" or "accepts" a bribe. The only treaty which does not cover the offense at issue is the OECD Convention.

Requesting or soliciting a bribe occurs when an official indicates to another person that the latter must pay a bribe in order that the official act or refrain from acting in the exercise of his or her official duties. As with "offering", "promising" and "giving", the *iter criminis* is completed once the official requests or solicits the bribe. Thus, there need not be an actual agreement between the briber and the official. Furthermore, the person solicited need not be aware of nor have received the solicitations (for instance, the solicitation is intercepted by the law enforcement authorities before it is delivered). By contrast, receiving or accepting a bribe occurs only when the official actually takes the bribe.

11.2.4 Actus Reus: Bribery of Foreign Public Officials and Officials of International Public Organizations

The definition of (active) bribery of a foreign public official usually follows faithfully that of bribery of a national public official. In other words, the offenses of offering, promising or giving a bribe to national and foreign public officials have the same essential elements. The only notable differences are that (a) one obviously applies to national public officials while the other applies to foreign public officials, and (b) under the OECD Convention and the UNCAC, bribery of foreign public officials is an offense exclusively when the bribe is paid in order to obtain or retain business or other undue advantages in relation to the conduct of international business. The international conventions do not define this element, but the Legislative Guide for the Implementation of the UN Convention states that international business includes the provision of international aid. Otherwise, all required elements of the offense (promise, offer, giving), the nature of the undue advantage and the subjective elements are defined in the same way in the two Conventions at issue.

As to the OECD Convention, the limitation to business advantage sounds definitely consistent with the object and the spirit of the instrument at stake. It is no secret that the essence and the spirit of the Convention is to prevent bribery being used as a means of advancing one's economic interests on the global market. In detail, Article 1 of the OECD Convention is limited to the use of bribery "in order to obtain or retain a business or other improper advantage in the conduct of international business". As spelled out by Commentary 4 to the OECD Convention, this approach requires that all would-be bidders for a contract should be punished for bribery, even the bidder who might have won without resorting to illegal methods, that is to say the best bidder as well as those less qualified. Accordingly, it is neither the economic advantage which may accrue to the country concerned from a viable contract nor the feasibility of the offer that is to be assessed. It would not be reasonable to expect a judicial body to test (comparatively scarce, or insufficient) the quality of a bid or to prove a negative. As Zerbes (2007) aptly stresses, under the OECD Convention, it is always bribery for a foreign public official to be paid in return for granting a business, without regard to the economic benefit which the transaction might bring to the foreign State concerned.

Notably, under such an agreement the bribery of a foreign public official is not restricted to obtaining or retaining of "business", but covers, according to the Official Commentary 5, "every other improper advantage". The same Commentary states that "(e)very other improper advantage" refers "to something to which the company concerned was not clearly entitled, for example, an operating permit for a factory which fails to meet the statutory requirements", and, hence, further broadens the scope of the provisions. Such other advantages could stem from official decisions concerning the day-to-day operation of the business rather than the obtaining and retaining of (public) contracts (e.g. official authorizations of all sorts; possible grant of subsidies or grants relating to business operations, the relaxing of certain environmental or working regulatory standards, tax breaks, and so forth.) As to the adjective "improper", it is intended to mean that the undertaking is not entitled to, nor has any claim upon, it. In detail, the proper or improper nature of the advantage is to be determined on a case-by-case basis: whether in a specific case a business advantage can be regarded as legitimate, and therefore as proper, can be determined only in the context of the underlying official act from which it derives or accrues. In other words, the advantage represents the outcome, the intended outcome, of the official decision induced by the offer, promise, giving of the bribe. A legitimate business advantage, accordingly, must be based on a legitimate official's decision, meaning one taken in conformity with official duties. Finally, as noted by Sacerdoti (2000), whereas neither the Convention nor the Commentaries define "international business transactions", the latter expression is intended to refer not only to exports, transboundary investments and procurements, but also to related contracts and business even if subsequent to the main operation.

The final clause of Article 16(1) of the UNCAC is somewhat surprising. In limiting the (active) bribery of foreign public officials to conduct committed "in order to retain or obtain a business or other undue advantage in relation to the conduct of international business", the fundamental meaning of corruption as offense related to *primary public (and often constitutional) values* still remains marginal. If this normative choice is consistent with the general approach of the OECD Convention, our belief is that this can hardly be argued with reference to the UNCAC. At least in the Preamble, the UNCAC seems to give serious consideration to the public dimension of the crime under discussion. As regards *national* public officials such a limitation does not exist. We think that, as occurred in many other cases, this provision was the result of intensive negotiations to reach a compromise. In this case, the position of countries which already had domestic law prohibiting corruption of foreign public official only in the case of transnational business and were not willing to substantially amend their law, has probably prevailed.

The OAS Convention's provisions on the matter are not crystal clear. On the one hand Article VI(a) and (b) require State Parties to criminalize in mandatory terms corruption of a "government official or of a person who performs public functions", without making it clear whether the public official is to be intended as only national or foreign as well. However, Article VIII deals specifically with transnational bribery. According to a systematic interpretation, we would argue that Article VI (a)–(b) is limited to corruption of national public officials, and the transnational parallel offense is addressed only by Article VIII. Yet, the opening clause of Article VIII(1) ("subject to its Constitution and the fundamental principles of its legal system") in the end makes criminalization for States Parties optional. What is more, Article VIII(1) requires State Parties to criminalize transnational bribery only "in connection with any economic or transnational transaction". The double qualification enshrined in Article VIII(1) leaves no room for doubt: assuming that it is such a provision that deals with transnational bribery, then State Parties of the OAS Convention are not obliged to introduce such an offense in their domestic criminal systems.

As to the EU Convention, the obligation of criminalizing corruption of public officials of the Community (as defined by Article 1(a) and further detailed by Article 4) and officials of other Member States is in line with the duty of assimilation and delimits the relevant notion of foreign public official to those of the EU and other Members.

The corresponding offense – referred to in Articles 2 and 3, when involving a public official of any other State – in the Council of Europe Criminal Law Convention does not include the limitation to business and is therefore broader than the OECD and UNCAC's paradigms.

The offenses of soliciting or receiving a bribe by foreign public officials (passive transnational corruption), which are not covered by the OECD and the OAS Conventions, are also largely similar to their counterparts for national public officials under the Article 2.4; 2 and 16(2) of the COE, and UN Conventions, respectively. However, the provisions under the UNCAC are (1) optional, i.e. States Parties only have to "consider adopting" such an offense, and (2) not limited to bribes paid in relation to the conduct of international business. Article 16(2) thus constitutes a telling example of permissive provision: State Parties shall only "*consider*" establishing the solicitation or acceptance of an undue advantage by foreign public officials as a criminal offense. This normative choice is generally justifiable for a number of reasons. *In primis*, criminalization of public officials of a foreign State would have incurred serious jurisdictional problems. Secondly, had a State criminalized the conduct of foreign public officials, it would have violated the principle of sovereign equality and non-intervention in the domestic affairs of other States, which, incidentally, also found explicit expression in Article 4 of the UNCAC. Finally, at least insofar as the relationship among State Parties is concerned, passive bribery of the foreign public official is covered by Article 15 requiring criminalization of national public officials. However, this excludes the mandatory obligation to work out a satisfactory solution for officials of international public organizations, whose position has been commented on above. Interestingly, even though criminalization of foreign public officials for conduct of passive corruption is optional, there is no reference to international economic and/or commercial operations. The absence of such specification makes the UNCAC drafters' choice concerning the limitation to business of active corruption of foreign public officials appear even more unusual.

As to the AU Convention, unless accepting an extensive interpretation of the notion of "public official" as defined in Article 1 which also includes officials of third States and international governmental organizations, it is to be concluded that neither passive nor active bribery of foreign public officials is addressed by the Convention at issue.

11.2.5 A Central Notion: Definition of a Public Official

The notion of "public official" is plainly central to each of the anti-bribery treaties. First, in case of active corruption of a (national or foreign) public official, whereas the perpetrator of the crime can be "any person", the recipient must always exercise a public function. Secondly, where the Conventions cover also the demand side of corruption, the offender must be a public official or a person exercising *de iure* or de facto a public function.

The notion of public official entailed in each of the instruments at issue is, therefore, central to the very definition of the conduct being criminalized at the national level. Even though most of the agreements under discussion attempt to broaden the categories of subjects covered by such a notion, there is no homogeneity in the essential paradigm they choose to anchor the definition of public official.

We will start with the OECD Convention, by illustrating the wide notion of "foreign public official" it implies, and attempt to distill some remarks which are of use also for the definition contained by the other Conventions. Secondly, when dealing with the other anti-bribery instruments, we highlight the main differences with the OECD Convention.

In accordance with Article 1(4) of the OECD Convention, a foreign public official is on the receiving end of the corrupt conduct. Since each State has its own notion of who is to be regarded as a public official, how should a multilateral treaty deal with the matter? Since the initiatives against corruption demand that countries adopt a definition of foreign public official which is as uniform as possible, the OECD Convention set forth an autonomous definition. Zerbes (2007) argues that in so doing the Convention succeeded in removing the "national law variable", which can result in a distortion of competition caused by different national laws. In the end, punishment and sanctions will not depend upon the varieties of national laws on the matter: given the decision to impose an autonomous definition, the national law of the victim State applies only to determine the *actual field of activity* of the official (e.g. it determines whether the foreign public official is a member of the Government, the Parliament or a judge of the "victim" State). Zerbes goes on to state that the goal of homogeneous application of the Convention could not be achieved if the definition of "public official" was left to the law of his or her home State (victim State). To provide an example, at the conclusion of the First Phase of the monitoring process, Belgian and Mexican implementing legislations were for this reason considered inadequate.

Article 1.4 (a) defines *foreign public officials* as any person in a foreign country who holds a legislative, administrative or judicial office, or who exercises (also *de facto*), a public function, including a public agency or enterprise, and any official of an international organization. Notably, this wide definition combines subjective and formalistic qualifications with objective and functional criteria (e.g. the objective exercise of a public function) in a manner similar to that of many State Parties' regulations. The underlying rationale is to take into due account the mutable framework within which the State directly exercises economic functions. What is more, it aims at adequately considering that the recent trend towards privatization which has characterized the last two decades has entrusted the private sector with primary public functions. In the end, the adoption by national laws of a special definition of foreign public official in line with that provided by Article 1(4) of the OECD Convention (widely integrated by the Official Commentaries) should serve the purpose of safeguarding legal clarity and certainty.

It is of primary importance to note that, as in the case of the OAS, CoECLCC, AU, and the UNCAC, the foreign public officials must necessarily be of a Contracting State. There is no need to resort to a teleological interpretation: the locution "any other States", or the absence of an explicit qualification "of a State Party", suffices to make it clear that the anti-bribery provisions also cover officials of a third State.

Some further comments are in order.

Firstly, as hinted above, the functional understanding of the notion at hand is the basic principle underlying the OECD approach and is expressed in the phrase "exercising a public function for a foreign country," contained in Article 1(4)(a) of Convention. Rather than being determined by the (formal or informal) allocation to the executive, legislative, or judiciary organs of a State, this status is determined by the objective exercise of a public function for another country. This principle has plenty of consequences. Official Commentary 12 expands upon the definition of Article 1(4)(a) as follows: "'(p)ublic function' includes any activity in the public interest, delegated by a foreign country . . .". Therefore, two elements are implied: on the one hand, the act of delegation by the foreign country concerned; on the other, the existence of a nexus between the delegated activity and the public interest. Official Commentary 12 provides us with a leading example of this form of delegation by a foreign country ". . . the performance of a task delegated by it in connection with public procurement". A State which signs a contract for tender usually delegates an array of diverse functions. In commenting on this Commentary, Zerbes argues that all the persons engaged to assist with the tender procedure should be considered as public officials in the functional sense" (e.g. from technical workers, such as engineers, financial experts, IT experts, down to reporters assessing the tenders received). As to the act of delegation, it should be noted that it is carried out by the foreign country, and, according to the general trend to give an extensive interpretation to Article 1(4) of the OECD Convention, it does not need to take any particular form. Furthermore, Commentaries 13–16 make it clear that an activity is always to be considered in the public interest where the authority of the State stands behind it. To sum up, every activity carried out following an act of delegation of State powers by a foreign State implies the exercise of a public function within the meaning of the Convention. Thus, the person delegated with such powers is a "public official" (at least) in the functional sense. Sacerdoti (2000) and Zerbes (2007) provide us with an example that illustrates the concept at hand: a physician entrusted with the giving of an opinion on the admission of specific medicine to the market under public authorization procedures would perform an activity in the public interest. Equally an historian engaged by an administrative agency to issue a report on a building in order to assess its suitability for protection as part of national heritage would qualify as a public official. By the same token, a lawyer who is called to comment on a legislative proposal for a Ministry of Justice is considered a public official.

Secondly, the further specification of the bodies who may be engaged to carry out a public activity contributes to widening the notion of "foreign public official" even further. According to Article 1(4)(a) combined with Official Commentaries 13–16, an activity in the public interest may be delegated to:

1) bodies enjoying the status conferred by public and administrative law, that is to say exercising a public function including a public agency;
2) under private law provisions, in particular public enterprises exercising a public function, including for a public enterprise. On a side note, Sacerdoti (2000) remarks that the extension to the behavior of executives of private enterprises controlled by the State gave rise to considerable discussion and it was not possible to insert supplemental specifications in the text. Further explanations, therefore, are provided by the Commentaries. According to the Official Commentary 14, a company is to be deemed "public" when the State is capable of exercising a dominant influence on it, no matter through which specific means. In other words, it is the *de facto dominance* or *influence* exercised by the

State, which lends to the activities of the public enterprise the quality of public functions. Secondly, the Official Commentary 15 clarifies that the responsible person in such a company would not exercise a public function, only if the company operates as a private company, on a normal commercial basis and without any sort of State support (e.g. preferential subsidies). In addition, it indicates that it is to be presumed that the person responsible for a public enterprise does exercise a public function;

3) without a specific legal authorization but in the exercise of a de facto state power. Official Commentary 16 explains that "in special circumstances, public authority may in fact be held by persons (e.g., political party officials in single party states) not formally designated as public officials. Such persons, through their de facto performance of a public function, may, under the legal principles of some countries, be considered to be foreign public officials."

Thirdly, the OECD Convention goes a step further when not bounding the definition of public official to statehood in the narrow sense. Firstly, according to Article 18, the offense of bribery under Article 1 also applies to officials acting in the name of an ". . . organized foreign area or entity". This term would be intended to catch all bodies which, despite the fact that they do not possess sovereignty over territory and population, have established a de facto governmental authority in terms of their territorial and/or personal rule, such as an autonomous territory or a separate customs territory. As to the first case, the vague term "autonomous territory" seems to address the rulers of such territory which are in occupation of and subject to a certain degree of control by a (completely sovereign) State. However, they also usually exercise sovereignty autonomously. Thus, the office holders in such a territory should be regarded as public officials. Notably, they should be considered "foreign" vis-à-vis the State to whose partial control they are subject as well. An "organized foreign area or entity" within the meaning of Article 1(4) of the Convention may exist when the issue of sovereignty over the area in question is disputed. For example, Northern Cyprus is regarded only by Turkey as an independent State. It is, however, hardly contestable that, as a matter of fact, an autonomous government operates there.

Fourthly, the anti-bribery rules of the OECD Convention also addressed public international organizations, to be intended, as stated by the Official Commentary 17, as "any international organization formed by states, governments, or other public international organizations, whatever the form of organization and scope of competence, including, for example, a regional economic integration organization such as the European

Communities". In so doing, the OECD Convention helps to fill the gap left by many national legal systems. In order to highlight the relevance of such a provision, it suffices to mention the activities of the main economic intergovernmental public organizations (e.g. IMF, WB, EBRD, AsDB, AfDB, IDB), the officials of which may be the recipients of offers, promises, and/or the giving of bribes. The protected legal interest seems twofold in the case of this offense: the transparency and fairness of the decision-making process of foreign public administrations – traditionally considered a domestic affair, globalization has made this consideration highly debatable – and the protection of fair competition for businesses. As to non-governmental organizations (NGOs), in principle they do not fall under the definition of the Convention. Nor are their activities covered when the members of their staff participate in the sovereign tasks of states or international public organizations. However, such an extensive interpretation is not accepted among commentators or even by the WGB.

Under the OAS Convention, criminalization is to be extended to any "public official", "governmental official" or "public servant". These terms are used equivalently, all meaning "any official or employee of the State and its agencies, including those who have been selected, appointed, or elected to perform activities or functions in the name of the State or in the service of the State, at any level of its hierarchy," as a combined reading of Article I, Article VI and Article VIII makes plain. Furthermore, according to Article I, the scope of the OAS Convention extends to any person who performs a "public function", meaning ". . . any temporary or permanent, paid or honorary activity, performed by a natural person in the name of the State or in the service of the State, at any level of its hierarchy". In respect of transnational bribery, the OAS Convention is comparable to the OECD Convention: both the instruments aspire to an extreme coverage with their notion of foreign public official, set forth by using an autonomous and functional definition. On a side note, the OECD Convention is more precise than the OAS Convention in that, through the Official Commentaries, its drafters have been able to further specify the notion under discussion. Noteworthy is the fact that the OAS Convention does not cover officials of international governmental organizations. Such an exclusion does not appear sensible in light of the relevant economic commitments of some international organizations in the Americas (especially in South America), such as, for instance, projects funded by the WB. Note that, as a general rule, within such organizations only internal statutes concerning personnel allow disciplinary measures to be taken against corrupted officials. However, such statutes are usually broad and, thus, not suitable to curb corruption or to make good any possible damage to its victims.

Turning to the EU Convention, its definition comprises national and Community officials, without resorting to an autonomous notion of "public official": Article 1(b) and (c) explain that national public officials are defined by the (criminal) domestic law of the Member State in question, whilst, according to Article 1(a), Community officials are defined by EC law. Thus, under the EU Convention, an overreaching common definition is not required. Accordingly, when national public officials are at issue, the functional understanding which characterizes the OECD and the OAS Conventions depends on the domestic legislation of the Member State concerned: where its criminal law comprises also persons who de facto exercise a public function, then Article 1(c) of the EU Convention is to be intended to include also this category within the implied notion of public official. On the contrary, since being a "Community official" is defined in a formalistic way by Article 1(a) (". . . an official or other contracted employee within the meaning of the Staff Regulations of officials of the European Communities or the Conditions of Employment of other servants of the European Communities"), we tend to exclude the functional reading.

The drafters of the CoECLCC wanted to cover all possible categories of public officials in order to avoid, as much as possible, loopholes in the criminalization of public sector bribery. Similarly to the EU Convention. However, they noted that this does not necessarily mean that States have to redefine their concept of "public official" in general. With reference to the "national law" it was the intention of the drafters that Contracting Parties assume obligations under the CoECLCC only to the extent consistent with their Constitution and the fundamental principles of their legal system, including, where appropriate, the principles of federalism. This is explicitly made clear by paragraph 27 of the Explanatory Report to the CoECLCC. As a consequence, similarly to the EU Convention, Article 1(a) of the CoECLCC defines the term "public official" – used in Articles 2 and 3 as well as in Article 5 – in terms of an official or public officer, a mayor, a minister or judge as defined in the national law of the State, for the purposes of its own criminal law. In order to ease the fulfillment of the requisite for dual criminality, the criminal law definition is thus given priority: where a public official of the prosecuting State is involved, this means that its national definition is applicable. Since, in many countries, mayors and ministers are assimilated to public officials for the purpose of criminal offenses committed in the exercise of their powers, the term "public official" explicitly includes "mayor" and "minister". In order to avoid any leeway that could have left such important public figures outside the scope of the present Convention, express reference is made to them in Article 1(a). The term "public official" includes "*judges*" as well, who are defined in *littera* (b) as prosecutors and holders of judicial office. According to paragraph 29 of the Explanatory Report, "this notion is to be interpreted to the widest extent possible: the decisive element being the functions performed by the person, which should be of a judicial nature, rather than his or her official title". Bribery of officials of international organizations is specifically covered by Article 9.1. Finally, Articles 2–6 of the Additional Protocol to the CoECLCC extend the scope of the Convention to arbitrators in commercial, civil and other matters, as well as to jurors, thus complementing the Convention's provisions aimed at protecting judicial authorities from corruption. Countries which ratify this instrument will have to adopt the necessary measures to establish, as criminal offenses, the active and passive bribery of domestic and foreign arbitrators and jurors.[4]

The scope of the AU Corruption Convention extends to public officials and to "any other person", including members of the private sector. Tracing the corresponding provision of the OAS Convention, a public official is defined as "any official or employee of the State or its agencies including those who have been selected, appointed or elected to perform activities or functions in the name of the State or in the service of the State at any level of its hierarchy". Like the OECD and OAS Convention, the AU thus resorts to an autonomous definition and relies on functional criteria to identify the subject at issue. The AU Convention does not define "any other person" and, as such, its ordinary meaning is presumably retained. In light of this wide application, the emphasis seems to be on the corrupt act that is committed rather than on the accountability of officials.

The UNCAC probably contains a more encompassing and detailed notion of "public official" and "foreign public official". Paragraph (a) of Article 2 defines a "public official" as:

---

4 See Additional Protocol to the Criminal Law Convention on Corruption, Article 1, which provides a definition of jurors and arbitrators. Accordingly, "(t)he term 'arbitrator' shall be understood by reference to the national law of the States Parties to this Protocol, but shall in any case include a person who by virtue of an arbitration agreement is called upon to render a legally binding decision in a dispute submitted to him/her by the parties to the agreement", whereas ". . . (t)he term 'juror' shall be understood by reference to the national law of the States Parties to this Protocol but shall in any case include a lay person acting as a member of a collegial body which has the responsibility of deciding on the guilt of an accused person in the framework of a trial." Note that, in accordance with the general pattern of the CoECLCC, in the case of corruption involving a foreign arbitrator or juror, the definition is not autonomous, as ". . . the prosecuting State may apply the definition of arbitrator or juror only in so far as that definition is compatible with its national law."

(i) any person holding a legislative, executive, administrative or judicial office of a State Party, whether appointed or elected, whether permanent or temporary, whether paid or unpaid, irrespective of that person's seniority;
(ii) any other person who performs a public function, including for a public agency or public enterprise, or provides a public service, as defined in the domestic law of the State Party and as applied in the pertinent area of law of that State Party;
(iii) any other person defined as a "public official" in the domestic law of a State Party. However, for the purpose of some specific measures contained in chapter II of this Convention, "public official" may mean any person who performs a public function or provides a public service as defined in the domestic law of the State Party and as applied in the pertinent area of law of that State Party.

Thus, many of the specifications which are contained in the Official Commentary of the OECD Convention, or that may be inferred by the broad formulation adopted, for example, by the OAS and AU Conventions, are expressly contained in the very text of the UNCAC. The provision at hand gives maximum relevance to both the functional approach and the formalistic criterion referring to the legal system of the home/victim State. Borlini and Magrini (2007) argue that the final clause, which does not entail an autonomous definition, is to be read as aiming at completing possible interpretative issues. In any case, it also seems to refer to the fact that the domestic law of the (home) State applies to determining the actual field of activity of the official.

More to the point, the UNCAC considers three different elements in determining who is the subject of its terms for public officials. One is a semi-autonomous definition that is grounded on traditional considerations as to whether an individual holds a legislative, executive, administrative or judicial office of a party. A second element consists of a semi-autonomous and plainly functional standard associated with determining whether an individual performs a public function (also de facto), including for a public agency or enterprise. Deming (2005) qualifies these two definitions as *semi*-autonomous because what constitutes a public function or public service is defined by the domestic law of a State party. According to the third (residual) definition, a public official is any individual who is otherwise defined as holding a public office in the legal system of the State Party concerned. The definition of foreign public official is largely similar. Under Article 2(b) of the UNCAC, a foreign public official means ". . . any person holding a legislative, executive, administrative or judicial office of a foreign country, whether appointed or elected; and any person exercising a public function for a foreign country, including for a public agency or enterprise." The following paragraph (c) of Article 2(c) provides a definition of "official of a public international organization" in line with those set forth by the other anti-bribery treaties.

11.2.6 The Bribe: Any Undue Pecuniary or Other Advantages

All the international conventions describe a bribe as an undue advantage. In other words, not all advantages are prohibited; only those that are "undue". Even though the wording of the different conventions may vary slightly in this respect, the qualification "undue", owing to its broadness, opens the door to what is "due" under different legislations. What constitutes "undue" advantage will be of central importance in the transposition of the Convention into national law. We might reconstruct some further elements by turning to the text, along with the official commentaries, interpretative notes, and explanatory reports issued by the various international organizations which promoted the adoption of the instruments under discussion. For instance, under the OECD Convention, Official Commentary 8 states that there is no offense if the advantage was permitted or required by the written law or regulation of the country of the foreign public official, including case law. In addition, Commentary 7 to the OECD Convention confirms that an offense is committed irrespective of, among other things, the value of the advantage, its results, perception of local custom, the tolerance of such payments by local authorities, or the alleged necessity of the payment in order to obtain or retain business or other improper advantage. According to paragraph 38 of the Explanatory Report to the CoECLCC, "undue" "should be interpreted as something that the recipient is not lawfully entitled to accept or receive". Furthermore, as witnessed by paragraph 37 of the same Explanatory Report, for the drafters of the Convention, "the adjective 'undue' aims at *excluding* advantages permitted by the law or by administrative rules as well as minimum gifts, gifts of very low value or socially acceptable gifts". An undue advantage may be of a pecuniary or non-pecuniary nature. It may also be tangible or intangible. Again, in light of the provisions which establish that the offer and promise suffice to meet the objective elements of the offenses, it might be safely argued that the undue advantage does not have to be given immediately to a public official of the State concerned. Moreover, the various treaties are clear in stating that the advantage may be given only indirectly to the officers, by means of intermediaries.

An undue advantage may be money, a loan, shares in a company, a holiday, food and drink, sex, enrollment in a school for an official's child, or a promotion and other forms of professional advancement, as long as it places the official (or a third person and/or entity) in a better position than he/she was before the commission of the offense. However, in widening the category of "undue advantage" beyond the tangible/material benefits, the certainty and objectivity of criminal law must be always guaranteed.

Therefore, the advantage must be susceptible to being evaluated: without any sort of *measurement* it would not be possible to say that an advantage has occurred. How far does the necessity of preserving certainty and objectivity of criminal law restrict the notion of undue advantage? As observed by Zerbes (2007) in commenting on Article 1.1 of the OECD Convention in light of the horizontal comparison among the implementing laws of State Parties made possible by the evaluation reports of the WGB, insofar as it is possible to give a monetary value to an immaterial benefit, it may be stated that an "undue advantage" has occurred.

Accordingly, mere ingratiation or simple polite approaches should be excluded by the scope of the anti-bribery treaties, for, without more, they cannot be objectively evaluated. *Mutatis mutandis* this holds true for the other anti-corruption conventions as well.

On the other hand, professional promotion, more leisure time, a larger office, enrollment in school for an official's child can be measured in monetary terms. Note that, if the bribe at stake consists of new contacts, of a personal or also sexual nature, there is a market for this, which enables the price to be approximately calculated.

This approach squarely reflects the paradigm drawn up by many national provisions which refers also to immaterial benefits explicitly and with precision. To limit our survey to OECD countries, this is the case with the provisions addressing bribery of foreign public officials of Argentina, Australia, Canada, Bulgaria, Denmark, Iceland, Italy, Japan, Mexico, the Netherlands, New Zealand, and the United Kingdom.[5]

To conclude, under none of the anti-corruption criminal treaties can the consideration of a due advantage be an illegal action of the public official. In other words, only advantages which are specifically and explicitly authorized by law or the jurisprudence of the State concerned should not be criminalized.

---

[5] See respectively, Article 258 *bis* of the Argentine Criminal Code; Section 70.1 of the Australian Criminal Code; Article 3(1) of the Canadian Corruption of Foreign Public Officials Act 1998; Article 304 of the Bulgarian Criminal Code; Denmark Phase 1 Evaluation Report, at p. 3; Section 109 of the Icelandic Criminal Code; Article 322 *bis* of the Italian Criminal Code; Article 10 *bis* (1) Japanese Unfair Competition Prevention Law; Article 222 *bis* Mexican Federal Criminal Code; Articles 177, 177a, 178 of the Dutch Criminal Code; UK Phase 1 Evaluation Report, at p. 5.

11.3 SUBJECTIVE ELEMENT OF THE CORRUPTION OFFENSES

11.3.1 Mens Rea: Intention

The mental element of the corruption offenses demands legislative decision-making and poses some relevant criminal issues as well. Even though the latter are less numerous than those raised by the definition of *actus reus*, they highlight an inherent trade-off between the overall effectiveness of the anti-bribery criminal measures, elaborated at the international level, and the full observance of general principles of criminal justice (e.g. legal certainty and presumption of innocence). On the one hand, a truly effective enforcing action would demand the easing of the standard of proof with respect to the mental element of such offenses in order to overcome obstacles in the production of evidence, which, in the case of transnational operations, have been becoming more and more substantial. On the other hand, at the national level, an excessively wide and/or vague notion of *mens rea* is highly controversial owing to the necessity to respect the constitutional principles of legal certainty, presumption of innocence, and above all, the tenet *nullo crimen sine lege*. Some premises must be taken. First, the precise identification of *mens rea* is not simple, since its borders are not capable of being clearly and accurately drawn by international provisions. As the latter are to be implemented in national legal systems, doubt exists as to whether it is suitable to scrutinize international texts with respect to *mens rea*.

However, some relevant indications emerge from the international anti-bribery texts and, thus, should be considered. International instruments against corruption present the following framework: the OECD and EU Conventions, the CoECLCC, and the UNCAC expressly incorporate an intent requirement. All the corrupt offenses established by those treaties must be committed "intentionally".[6] In other words, they are intentional offenses. The adverb "intentionally" is explicitly used by the OECD, COE, and the UN Conventions. Articles 2 and 3 of the EU Convention describe the criminalization of corrupt conduct as "deliberate". By contrast, the criminalization provisions of the OAS and AU Conventions consistently and completely omit any reference to the subjective element requirement. Presumably left to the State Parties' own decisions in their domestic jurisdictions, this could result in inconsistent application of the criminalization

---

6 OECD Convention, Article 1.1; EU Convention Articles 2, 3; CoECLCC, Articles 2, 3, 5; UNCAC Articles 15(a); 15(b); 16.

provisions of such Conventions and may have a profound effect on the actual content of the assumed obligations.

The respective legal traditions of the Contracting States of the first group of Conventions will eventually establish the concrete elements of the Conventions' standards of intentional corruption. English laws and systems derived from, or related to, it use the term "*mens rea*" to describe the various sorts of mental requirements for the commission of a crime. *Mens rea* can consist in intention or knowledge, in recklessness, or in negligence. Under the legal regime of most Continental legal systems, a further distinction between intention, on the one hand, and negligence and recklessness, on the other, is also drawn. Intention conveys the idea of a certain degree of volition, which distinguishes it clearly from negligence and recklessness. Within the array of definitions of intention which one can find in the various national criminal systems, two elements are usually present. Firstly, a certain degree of *knowledge*, at least in the form of the existence of the various elements of the offense, which goes beyond carelessness. Secondly, a certain degree of *conscious choice* or *volition*, at least in the form of an acceptance of the crime (element of volition).

In light of the above, we can now address more closely the treaties which explicitly incorporate the subjective element of corrupt offenses. In the end, what exactly falls under "intentionally/deliberate" in their respective contexts, and what other elements may be included in the definition of corruption offenses, are not laid down by the Conventions at issue, or are laid down only in a very general fashion. However, by resting on ordinary means of interpretation, it might be argued that, for active bribery offenses, the briber must offer, promise or give the bribe with the intention that the bribed official acts or refrains from acting in the exercise of his/her functions or duties, etc. As to the passive side of the conduct (when criminalized), it is to be maintained that the mental element is only that of intending to solicit, request, or accept the undue advantage for the purpose of altering one's conduct in the performance/course of official duties. However, under the international agreements, this does not mean that the intended result must in fact have occurred. This interpretation fairly accords with most of the domestic criminal systems, where the bribery offenses require proof that the briber intended to influence the actions of the bribed official (or that the recipient intended to solicit, accept etc. the bribe with a view to disregarding his/her official duties), without requiring proof that the official did, in fact, alter his/her conduct. The standard required seems thus to be the so-called *dolus eventualis*.

Arguably, some link must be established between the offer, promise or giving of the advantage and inducing the official to act or refrain from acting in the exercise of his/her functions or duties. Given the fact that the conduct covers cases of merely offering a bribe, comprising cases where it is not accepted or where it could not have affected the conduct in another fashion, the link must be that the accused briber intended not only to offer the bribe, but also to influence the conduct of the recipient, regardless of whether or not this actually took place. Where, as in the case of Articles 1 of the OECD Convention and 16(1) of the UNCAC, active bribery of foreign public officials and officials of international organizations constitutes a criminal offense insofar as it is committed to retain or maintain a business or other undue advantage in relation to the conduct of international business, it is to be argued that the intentional element comprises this latter element as well. The specific intentional element is thus explicated in two directions: (a) in relation to the illicit conduct of the recipient, *and* (b) in relation to the further aim of obtaining/maintaining a commercial/economic advantage. In other words, the above-mentioned link must be that the accused briber intended not only to offer the bribe, but also to influence the conduct of the recipient in order to obtain a commercial/economic advantage, regardless of whether or not this actually took place (i.e. *dolus eventualis*).

Article 28 of the UNCAC goes a step further in expressly allowing intent to be inferred from circumstances. The rationale of the provision seems to lie in the recognition that proving the requisite intention is not always an easy task since direct evidence (e.g. a confession) is often unavailable. As a matter of fact, corruption can be difficult to detect and prove due to its covert nature, and because neither party to the transaction wants the offense exposed. The offender's mental state thus may have to be inferred from objective factual circumstances. For example, a supplier tenders a bid for a contract. Soon after, he provides an expensive car as a gift to the public official who will choose the winning bid. It may then be inferred that the supplier intended to influence the official's decision in the choice of the bid. There is no doubt that if rules of evidence in criminal procedural codes permitted this form of proof, public prosecutors and judicial bodies' activities would be extremely facilitated. It remains to be established to what extent the commitment implied under this provision is stringent. In our opinion the signal given by Article 28 has the merit of stressing the importance of the issue, but it should not be overstated. Whereas there is no weakening parenthetical clause, by stating that "knowledge, intent, or purpose required as element" of a corrupt offense "may be inferred from objective factual circumstances", the issue of what objective factual circumstances may be considered is inevitably left to the national law. It could hardly have been otherwise, given that the standard of inferred proof is a highly controversial question even within each legal system.

To recap, with reference to active bribery, by using the adverb "intentionally" (or the adjective "deliberate") the provisions under discussion prohibit the offense in the presence of two central conditions, that is to say: on the one hand, knowledge (*nihil volitum nisi precognitum*) and intentionality of the conduct, and, on the other, knowledge and intention directed also to the illicit conduct of the recipient as well as, where relevant, the maintenance/gain of an undue economic/business advantage, as specified above. Therefore, the relevant international provisions require the standard of intent (or intention, arguably in the form of *dolus eventualis*). As a corollary, it is not permitted to limit the offense with knowledge: firstly, this would leave too much room for abuse, owing to the fact that lack of knowledge is not easily disproved; secondly, it would not be consistent with the international anti-bribery standards for a State Party to set a *stricter* standard of intention than *dolus eventualis* as its starting point for criminal liability. Of course, *higher* forms of intention will be caught by the more moderate kind. Nonetheless, the OECD, EU, COE, and UN Conventions leave it to the Parties whether or not to include other sorts of mental element like recklessness or negligence in their definitions. Secondly, as far as passive bribery is concerned, the mental element is only that of intending to solicit, request, or accept the undue advantage for the purpose of altering one's conduct in the performance/course of official duties. Finally, in line with previous treaties patronized by the UN, like the 1988 UN Convention against drug trafficking and the UNCTOC, the UNCAC explicitly establishes that these requirements may be inferred from objective factual circumstances.

11.4 AN OPEN ISSUE: FINANCING OF POLITICAL PARTIES

One of the main shortcomings affecting the international criminal apparatus against corruption regards the treatment of the financing of political parties. Some of the offenses envisaged by the anti-corruption treaties may indirectly cover illicit funding of political parties. However, except for these provisions and, despite the efforts of some delegations in the negotiating proceedings, the resulting scenario is still unsatisfactory.

Despite the strong pressure they exercised during the negotiations for the OECD Convention, the US did not succeed in obtaining the extension of the criminalizing provisions to illicit financing of foreign political parties. In all likelihood, the US position did not prevail because the other Contracting States preferred not to intervene in a topic, the legal regime of which may vary dramatically from country to country. This stance finds further confirmation in Official Commentary 10 to the Convention. On the one hand, it is recognized that "under the legal system of some countries, an advantage promised or given to any person, in anticipation of his or her becoming a foreign public official, falls within the scope of the offences" covered by the Convention. On the other, it is stated that "under the legal system of many countries, it is considered technically distinct from the offenses covered by the present Convention", to conclude by stressing "a commonly shared concern and intent to address this phenomenon through further work." To the current authors' knowledge, no material results have followed the intention proclaimed *in fine* of Commentary 10. On a side note, the circumstance that financing of political parties has found only a soft consideration in the Commentaries, rather than in the very text of the Convention, bears testimony to the sensitiveness of the issue and the substantial disagreement between the Contracting States.

It is however to be stressed that the scope of the OECD Convention covers certain specific cases, namely:

i) the case where the official of the political party or the political party itself is the vehicle (e.g. intermediary) of the bribery operation; where the political party is the third beneficiary of the undue advantage offered, promised or given to the foreign public official *ex* Article 1.1 of the Convention;
ii) when the officials of the political party participate along with the corrupter relating to the bribery in one of the forms described by Article 1.2 of the Convention;
iii) the bribery of political party officials in single party states, where, in special circumstances, public authority may be held by persons who are not formally designated as public officials. Under the legal principles of the country concerned, in fact, the officials of the unique party through their de facto performance of a public function may be considered to be foreign public officials.

We now turn to regional anti-corruption agreements. The OAS Convention does not cover illicit funding of either national or foreign political parties, except where the political party (or its officials) is the third entity to eventually benefit from the undue advantage granted/given to or solicited/accepted by the public officials; where the same subjects are the intermediaries of the corrupt offenses; and where they participate in those offenses in one of the manners described by Article VI(1)(a)–(b), (e) of the OAS Convention.

Mutatis mudandis, the same holds true with regard to the EU Convention. Apart from the hypotheses just sketched out, Article 12 of the CoECLCC indirectly targets illicit funding of political parties by criminalizing trading in influence. In so doing, the CoECLCC seeks also to reach the close circle of the political party to which the official belongs and to tackle the corrupt behavior of those persons who are in the neighborhood of power and try to obtain advantages from their situation, contributing to the atmosphere of corruption.

Article 10 of the AU Convention expressly addresses the issue. However, under sub-paragraph (a) of such provision, State Parties are only required to prohibit (it being unclear whether by means of criminal, civil, or administrative provisions) "the use of funds acquired through illegal and corrupt practices to finance political parties". However, illicit funding of political parties where funds to come from legal sources (e.g. the use of funds raised legally but which goes beyond the possible limits proscribed by national laws; the disguised/concealed financing by using legal funds) remain outside the scope of the provision. It is to be stressed that also the AU Convention requires State Parties to criminalize *trading in influence* under Article 4(1)(f). Thus, similarly to the CoECLCC, an indirect coverage of illicit financing of political parties through the criminalization of such conduct is possible. The obligation to incorporate the principle of transparency into funding of political parties *ex* Article 10(b) appears just little more than window-dressing.

For its part, the UNCAC does not criminalize illicit funding of political parties because the officials of political parties do not fall under the wide definition of *public official* and *foreign public official* provided by Article 2(a)–(b).

Noticeable indications, however, can be found by scrutinizing the preparatory works: Webb (2005) remarks that the most intense debate during the negotiation of the Convention was reserved for the provision on the financing of political parties. According to the same commentator, there are two dynamics underlying this controversy. Firstly, and more generally, corruption in *elections* is of universal concern. Systemic corruption in the political process is one of the most important issues. It causes a lack of trust in political parties which, in turn, undermines their legitimacy and can encourage a culture of corruption throughout public administration and the public sector. The second, more specific, dynamic is the issue of *campaign financing*. As Offe (2004) observes, party competition, which is an integral part of democratic government, generates an insatiable appetite for campaign funds. The costs of this competition are increasing in a media society where opportunities for communicating must be purchased. This flow of campaign finance generates two problems. Firstly, when large amounts of money reach a politician, there is a temptation to divert the funds for personal use. Secondly, even if the donations are not diverted, they can be used, in effect, to "purchase" an elected official's support or vote on legislation.

The negotiations in the Ad Hoc Committee centered around Article 10 on the funding of political parties proposed by Austria, France, and the Netherlands.[7]

At the fourth session of the negotiations, the Article read:

> 1. Each State Party shall adopt, maintain and strengthen measures and regulations concerning the funding of political parties. Such measures and regulations shall serve:
>   (a) To prevent conflicts of interest;
>   (b) To preserve the integrity of democratic political structures and processes;
>   (c) To proscribe the use of funds acquired through illegal and corrupt practices to finance political parties; and
>   (d) To incorporate the concept of transparency into funding of political parties by requiring declaration of donations exceeding a specified limit.
> 2. Each State Party shall take measures to avoid as far as possible conflicts of interest owing to simultaneous holding of elective office and responsibilities in the private sector.[8]

The Article's legally mandatory language and broad scope elicited a negative reaction from several delegations. The US, which had been very concerned about corruption in political parties during the negotiating process for the OECD Conventions, rather ironically refused to endorse the UNCAC if it included that Article and called for its deletion.[9] Within the OECD framework, the US delegates believed that excluding political party officials would create a huge loophole for foreign countries, which could then channel illicit payments to party officials rather than government officials.

The US ultimately triumphed in the negotiations and Article 10 was deleted during the penultimate session of the Ad Hoc Committee, as

---

7 Proposals and Contributions Received from Governments: Austria, France and The Netherlands, UN Doc. A/AC.261/L.21 (2002).

8 Revised Draft United Nations Convention Against Corruption, at 18, UN Doc. A/AC.261/3/Rev. 2 (2002).

9 See Transparency International, Zambia President Dr. Chanda Criticizes US' Unilateralism, *Africa News,* 15 August 2003. See also, Transparency International Press Release, US Weakens UN Convention by Blocking Measures Tackling Political Corruption, 11 August 2003, available at http://www.transparency.org/pressreleases_archive/2003/2003.08.11.us_blocking_measures.html, cited by Webb (2005: 217, note 205).

the deadline for completion quickly approached.[10] The current Article 7 plainly represents a substantial compromise. The binding language of Article 10 is watered down by two non-mandatory clauses in Article 7(2) and (3) which, respectively, ask States to "consider" adopting measures to "prescribe candidature for and election to public office" and to "enhance transparency in the funding of candidatures . . . and, where applicable, the funding of political parties". Rooke (2003) argues that this was the most dramatic fault line to emerge in the negotiations.

Some final remarks to conclude. Firstly, the intense debate during the negotiations and the outcome itself confirm that the relationship between money and politics is complex and hard to constrain without creating incentives for illegality. The Ad Hoc Committee ultimately recognized the crucial role of political parties within the democratic systems of numerous countries.

Secondly, considering the peculiar role played by political parties within the electoral system of several States, it is not surprisingly that the Committee in the end was not willing to adopt binding and stringent provisions on the matter, susceptible of conflicting with a crucial aspect of States' political life. Several delegations to the Ad Hoc Committee questioned whether the negotiation of such a provision was practical given the enormous variations in political systems.

Thirdly, having highlighted the intimate and thin relationship between financing of political parties and formation of democratic governments, it remains to be seen whether the final solution worked out by the UNCAC suitably addresses the intimate and thin relationship between illicit financing of political parties and corruption crimes.

Our stance is that the UNCAC has not filled the gap left open by the other international agreements on the matter: that is to say the legitimacy of "purchasing" who is not a public official, but could become one, and, in any case, by virtue of the parties' network, may likely be in the position to exercise a strong influence upon those who *are* public officials.

---

10 It is noteworthy that, following the decision, the representatives of Benin, Burkina Faso, Cameroon and Senegal expressed their wish that the report of the Ad Hoc Committee "reflect their preference for a separate binding Art. on the financing of political parties; however, because of their willingness to accommodate the concerns of other delegations and to ensure the successful finalization of the draft convention, they felt compelled to join the consensus on the deletion of Art. 10 and the incorporation of a new paragraph in Art. 6". See Report of the Ad Hoc Committee for the Negotiation of a Convention Against Corruption on its sixth session, held in Vienna from 21 July to 8 August 2003, UN Doc. A/AC.261/22, 23 August 2003, p. 10.

Fourthly, the negotiations for the OECD agreement and UNCAC suggest that the issue under examination is not likely to find a satisfactory solution at the international level. No agreement has been achieved within the OECD. Nor has the ambitious project of the UN arrived at more than a compromise. We even wonder if, as a matter of perspective, the stronger legal and political co-operation achieved by States in regional contexts like the UE and the COE may represent a likely avenue to follow.

12. Sanctions and corporate liability

12.1 INTRODUCTION

In Chapter 9 we highlighted the primary importance of increasing the effectiveness and deterrence of criminal sanctions against corruption. Here we detail the international conventions' provisions on this point with the aim of assessing their capacity to concretely enhance national standards.

Most of the anti-bribery agreements call for Parties to punish corruption by "effective, proportionate and dissuasive" criminal sanctions. This is a quasi-stereotyped formula within the landscape of cooperation in criminal matters. However, this standard may be further spelled out. By dismantling the three-pronged test with reference to the agreements under discussion, we likely obtain some indications as to the nature and severity of the sanctions required. In addition, effectiveness, proportionality, and deterrence are not the only requirements which (some of) the treaties envisage as regards the sanctioning standards. The conventions under analysis call upon State Parties to take the necessary measures to confiscate bribes, the proceeds and instrumentalities of bribery, the converted proceeds and, in a provision which presents innovative features for many national criminal systems, the equivalent value.

Having regard to the subject allegedly responsible for the crime, the empirical evidence shows that most grand corruption cases are perpetrated through the scheme or in the interest of companies. In light of the above, when exploring the sanctioning standards drawn up by the international anti-corruption countries we also address the issue of corporate liability.

The present chapter is thus divided into three main parts. Firstly, we analyze the sanctioning requirements for natural persons of the anti-bribery conventions which explicitly address the issue. Secondly, since the agreements under discussion frequently envisage confiscation of the bribe and/or the proceeds of the bribe, we spell out the contents of the related provisions. Finally, the legal regime for crime committed through or in the interest of legal persons is explored.

12.2 SANCTIONING STANDARDS: NATURE AND SEVERITY

Unlike the OAS and AU Conventions, which are silent on the matter, the OECD, EU, COE and UN Conventions establish minimum standards for the sanctioning of the offenses they consider.

Under Article 3.1 of the OECD Convention, "the bribery of a foreign public official shall be punishable by effective, proportionate and dissuasive criminal penalties. The range of penalties shall be comparable to that applicable to the bribery of the Party's own public officials and shall, in the case of natural persons, include deprivation of liberty sufficient to enable effective mutual legal assistance and extradition." Article 3.4 requires State Parties to ". . . consider the imposition of additional civil or administrative sanctions upon a person subject to sanctions for the bribery of a foreign public official".

"Effective, proportionate and dissuasive criminal penalties" are also required by Article 5(1) of the EU Convention. Such sanctions should include "at least in serious cases, penalties involving deprivation of liberty which can give rise to extradition".

As to the CoECLCC, Article 19.1 mandates State Parties to provide, in respect of those criminal offenses established in accordance with the same Treaty, "effective, proportionate and dissuasive sanctions and measures, including, when committed by natural persons, penalties involving deprivation of liberty which can give rise to extradition".

The relevant provisions of the UNCAC are somewhat more controversial. The usual mantra "effective, dissuasive and proportionate" may, at best, be only implied by an extensive interpretation of Article 30(1), which reads as follows: "Each party shall make the commission of an offence established in accordance with this Convention liable to sanctions that take into account the gravity of that offence".[1] Also the term "sanction" is used in its extensive meaning (i.e. including both criminal sanctions *strictu sensu* and "ancillary" sanctions). This is to say that it encompasses both criminal and non-criminal administrative or civil sanctions. However, "in the cases in which the Convention requires establishing certain conduct 'as a criminal offence' non-criminal sanctions may accompany criminal sanctions but cannot substitute them" (UNODC, 2009: 83).

---

[1] From a systemic perspective, one may recall that "States Parties may also wish to consider the sentencing guidance of article 26 (4) which (for legal persons) speaks of *effective, proportionate* and *dissuasive* sanctions" (UNODC, 2009: 84; emphasis added).

Similarly in Article 11(1) of the UNCTOC, this provision follows the model deriving from the 1988 Vienna Convention Against Drug Trafficking: Article 30(1) of the UNCTAC is virtually identical to Article 3(4)a of the 1988 Vienna Convention, which, nonetheless, ends with examples of appropriate sanctions, "such as imprisonment or other forms of deprivation of liberty, pecuniary sanctions, and confiscation". Borlini and Magrini (2007) and McClean (2007: 60–62) argue that, as with Article 11(1) of the UNCTOC, the Ad Hoc Committee likely deemed that such examples added very little to the text and, in the end, saw no reason to include them. The severity of the punishment for the offenses established in accordance with the Convention is therefore left to the States Parties, which must take into account the gravity of the offense.[2] The primacy of national law in this respect is affirmed, whilst it is not clear whether a more specific obligation to draw up criminal sanctions which are effective, proportionate and dissuasive can be inferred from consideration of the gravity of the offense. In general, it seems fair to assert that "to provide for sanctions that take into account the gravity of the offence, criminal sanctions for corruption offences established in accordance with the Convention should not fall short of the sanctions for comparable economic crimes" (UNODC, 2009: 83). Moreover:

> for transborder corruption, in which mutual legal assistance and extradition play a major role, it is important that the range of penalties are sufficient to enable effective mutual legal assistance and extradition. For some States Parties, this might require that the offences provide for a certain length of custodial sentence so as to comply with dual criminality demands (ID.).

On the whole, Article 30 is a rather intricate provision which, sanctions aside, addresses also prosecution and adjudications. Note that paragraph 2 requires States Parties to establish or maintain, in accordance with their legal system and constitutional principles, an appropriate balance between any immunities or jurisdictional privileges accorded to their public officials for the performance of their functions and the possibility,

---

2 This is confirmed by the Technical Guide to the UNCAC, which reads as follows:

> The Convention does not specify the severity of sanctions. Since penalties reflect diverging national traditions and policies, the Convention acknowledges that penalties for similar crimes may diverge across jurisdictions. In fact, sanctions for corruption offences have to be in line with the national legal tradition and suit the general framework of penalties provided for by the criminal law of States Parties (UNODC, 2009: 83)

when necessary, of effectively investigating, prosecuting and adjudicating offenses established in accordance with the Convention. The idea under Article 30(2) is to eliminate or prevent as much as possible cases where corrupt public officials shield themselves from accountability and investigation or prosecution for serious offenses. An interpretative note explains that the appropriate balance referred to in Article 30(2) would be established or maintained in law and in practice.[3] However, this provision is somewhat troublesome in that it seems to give State Parties virtually unfettered discretion regarding the proper balance between immunities and effective investigation, prosecution, and adjudication of public officials allegedly involved in corrupt operations. It is worth stressing that the provision under examination follows a "functional" notion of immunities or jurisdictional privileges. To rephrase it, immunities or jurisdictional privileges attach to the office, not the office holder. This has an immediate impact on the assessment States Parties have to carry out in order to maintain the afore mentioned balance between legitimate immunities and other privileges, on the one hand, and the possibility of effective investigations and prosecutions, on the other: as a result, immunities and other privileges must be strictly restricted to those which constitute necessary means to safeguard the functioning of institutions of the State.[4]

---

[3] See A/58/422/Add.1, para. 34. See also Legislative Guide for the Implementation to the UNCAC, paras. 387–8, at 182.

[4] According to such a reading, States Parties may consider a number of elements: First, they:

> may wish to draw attention to the list of persons enjoying immunities or other privileges and consider if the balance may require a restricted list of privileged public offices and public functions. In general, States Parties may wish to take into account that immunities and jurisdictional privileges are designed to allow the office holder to act without fear of legal consequence. In this case, they may wish to follow those States which grant a limited immunity which does not cover corrupt or otherwise criminal behaviour whether conducted in a private or official capacity. Thus, States Parties may consider applying an immunity rule or a jurisdictional privilege by evaluating whether the granting of immunity or a jurisdictional privilege is essential to assure the execution of the public office or function in question (UNODC, 2009: 85).

In addition:

> (a)ccording to the functional notion of immunities or privileges, States Parties may consider applying immunities and jurisdictional privileges only with regard to acts committed in the performance of the public official's duties, and only where the official has performed the roles and responsibilities of that

Two further (non-mandatory) indications are provided for in paragraphs 7 and 10. According to Article 30.7: "where warranted by the gravity of the offence, each State Party, to the extent consistent with the fundamental principles of its legal system, shall consider establishing procedures for the disqualification, by court order or any other appropriate means, for a period of time determined by its domestic law, of persons convicted of offences established in accordance with this Convention

---

office under the law. Moreover, States Parties may consider that immunities or jurisdictional privileges should only be granted during the time a public office or a public function is performed. Consequently, immunities and jurisdictional privileges should not extend to acts or omissions committed after the public official has left office or has stopped performing public functions. Correspondingly, immunities and jurisdictional privileges are not in an appropriate balance with the necessity of law enforcement when former office holders enjoy privileges in proceedings that take place after the person has left office. Even in cases in which such proceedings relate to deeds committed during the time of holding office, the person should face equal rights and duties like any other citizen (UNODC, 2009: 86).

Furthermore:

States Parties may wish to consider laws or legal guidelines which specify the necessary conditions and procedures of when and how to lift immunities. With regard to these laws or guidelines, States Parties may wish to take into account the following aspects and models: Laws and guidelines to specify the grounds to waive immunities must not allow for politically motivated discretion. States Parties may wish to consider specifying that the commission of corruption offences would constitute a legal reason for the lifting of immunities or privileges. States Parties may bear in mind that proceedings to determine whether immunities would be lifted should be designed in a way that enables expeditious decisions in order to prevent the suspect from escaping or obstructing the investigations. States Parties should consider avoiding possible conflicts of interests in the decision-making to waive immunity. In circumstances where it is not possible to lift the immunity or privilege States Parties may consider liaising with foreign jurisdictions who may be in a position to undertake some level of criminal or civil action against the individuals for possible offences committed in that jurisdiction. States Parties may wish to consider appropriate rules that enable prosecution and adjudication subsequent to the tenure of office. Most importantly, States Parties may consider suspension of the lapse of time set for statutory limitations during any tenure of office. States Parties that do not provide for a lifting of immunities during the time of holding office may consider this as an appropriate way to meet the balance required by article 30. Finally, States Parties may take into consideration that immunities or jurisdictional privileges applying to one person do not frustrate prosecution and adjudication of cases involving other persons implicated in corruption (UNODC, 2009: 86 *et seq.*).

from: (a) Holding public office; and (b) Holding office in an enterprise owned in whole or in part by the State".

On the other hand, Article 30(10) of the Convention recognizes that reintegration into the society of persons convicted of corrupt offenses is an important goal of control systems and, consequently, requires Contracting States to promote such an aim.

In summary, three orientating criteria seem to emerge from the provisions just illustrated.

Firstly, the international conventions require their signatories to impose effective, proportionate and dissuasive sanctions or sanctions that take into account the gravity of the offense. The obligation to make corruption offenses punishable under criminal law would of course lose much of its effect if it was not supplemented by an obligation to provide for adequately severe sanctions. When prescribing that imprisonment and pecuniary sanctions should be the sanctions that can be imposed for the relevant offenses, the standard set forth by the Treaties leaves open the possibility that other sanctions reflecting the seriousness of the offenses are provided for. As a matter of fact, the relevant provisions do not mean that a prison sentence must be imposed every time that a person is found guilty of having committed a corruption offense established in accordance with those Conventions, but that national criminal laws should provide for the possibility of imposing prison sentences of a certain level in such cases.

Secondly, to be effective, proportionate and dissuasive, sanctions for corruption frequently need not be limited to criminal penalties such as fines and imprisonment. Civil and administrative sanctions can also be applied. Sanctions for bribers, therefore, may include exclusion from entitlement to public benefits, disqualification from participation in public procurement or privatization, or from the practice of other commercial activities. Corrupt officials could be sanctioned through disciplinary penalties, and removal or suspension from office. Again, with regard to Article 8 of the OECD Convention dealing with accounting standards, civil sanctions for accounting violations may include: monetary fines; orders prohibiting offending natural persons from managing a corporation; and joint and several liability of company administrators and managers when the accounting offenses cause damage to third parties.

Thirdly, sanctions for corruption must be sufficiently severe to allow for extradition and mutual legal assistance. Since most countries can seek and provide extradition and mutual legal assistance only for crimes that are punishable by sufficiently severe sanctions, Parties to the conventions at issue should ensure that the sanctions for their corruption offenses meet this threshold.

Coming closer to the three-pronged test elaborated by the OECD, EU, and COE Conventions, sanctions must be sufficiently severe to deter or dissuade the offender and others from committing the offense, but not so heavy as to be disproportionate to the gravity of the offense. These standards are the only orientating parameters for national pieces of legislation. A wide range of factors should be considered in determining whether sanctions for corruption are effective, proportionate and dissuasive. One consideration is whether sanctions for bribers and corrupt officials are comparable, since the EU and COE Conventions make no distinction between sanctions for the two types of individuals. Whether sanctions are effective, proportionate and dissuasive may also depend on whether they are comparable to those in other countries. In many OECD countries, the maximum penalty for foreign bribery is five years' imprisonment. Another element may be whether the same sanctions apply to different modes of committing bribery (i.e. offering, promising and giving an undue advantage) since the international conventions do not distinguish between them. As has been said, other fundamental factors to consider are whether the sanctions are sufficient to enable effective mutual legal assistance and extradition, as well as whether the statute of limitations (which is usually based on the level of sanctions) is long enough to ensure the effective investigation and prosecution of the offense.

By seeking to give an autonomous meaning to each of the three methodological indications expressed by the adjectives *effective, proportionate*, and *dissuasive*, Manacorda (1999) and Borlini and Magrini (2007) argue that proportionality and dissuasion qualified the sanctioning burden and the techniques for designing national offenses. From this perspective they introduce, respectively, a lower and an upper limit for national legislators, when the latter subjects are to set forth the political-criminal response to corrupt offenses. On the other hand, the effectiveness principle seems to characterize the executing phase of the sanction rather than its design.

More recently, Cullen (2007) has tried to further qualify the formula "effective, dissuasive, and proportionate sanctions". In spite of the three-pronged requirement, it may be argued the Conventions' standards are measured by effectiveness and proportionality alone. Although the phrase "effective, proportionate, dissuasive" is, in the end, always applied to Parties' sanctions as a joint test, sometimes sounding almost mantra-like, Cullen (2007) argues that the elements "effective" and "dissuasive" appear to form a synonymous couple. *The Oxford English Dictionary* defines "dissuade" as a verb meaning "to persuade not to take a particular course of action". Criminal sanctions complying with such a standard are, for instance, imprisonment of the natural persons responsible for the violation, fines applied to them (or the legal entity on the behalf or in favor of which accounting offenses are committed).

When addressing proportionality in the context of the sanctioning standards contained in the OECD Convention, Cullen (2007) points out that, as a matter of fact, the WGB treats proportionality as part of the "effective, dissuasive, proportionate" mantra, with the emphasis "invariably on the lack of effective and dissuasive sanctions".[5] He further remarks that *proportionality* is unified together with concepts suggesting that, if the sanction is not effective, then, equally, the proportionality standard is not met. He goes on to remark that, in the absence of a clear analysis of the definition by means of the WGB's monitoring procedure, it is very difficult to extrapolate a clear understanding of the requirement at issue in the context of the OECD Convention.

However, it might well be surmised that the severity of *penalties* should be determined with reference to the *seriousness* of crimes. For one thing, this is one of the basic assumptions of criminological sentencing theory. Secondly, in the context of international criminal conventions, an analogy with the EU instruments is advanced by Cullen himself. In *SA Buitoni v. Fonds d'orientation et de régulation des marches agricoles* (1979), the European Court of Justice, in analyzing sanctions for conduct affecting an EC interest, opined that "they must not be disproportionate to the gravity of the infringement" and that the "penalty must not exceed what is appropriate and necessary to attain the objective sought".[6] Thirdly, such interpretation has been lately confirmed also by the UNODC (2009: 83), in maintaining that "(w)hile not stipulating any particular form of sanctions, the Convention emphasizes that there should be appropriate measures in place to ensure that, whether through fines, imprisonment or other penalties, the punishment reflects the level of the offence (. . .)" and indicating among the elements to be considered in order to determine the gravity of the offence not only ". . . the value of, for example, an undue advantage" but also ". . . other factors, such as the seniority of those involved, the sphere in which the offences occur, the level of trust attached to the public official and so on".

5 Cullen (2007: 22).

6 The case at issue regarded a non-criminal sanction (forfeiture of a security) imposed under Community law. See Case 122/78 *SA Buitoni v. Fonds d'orientation et de régulation des marches agricoles* (1979) ECR 677, para. 16. "As regards the problem of proportionality, it should be examined whether the penalty laid down by the (EC Regulation) for failure to comply with the period of presentation of the proofs proscribed by that provision exceeds what is appropriate and necessary to attain the objective sought."

Overall, the conventions under examination do not establish their own sanctioning regime. They pursue instead a minimum degree of harmonization based upon these rather general standards. The underlying thinking is plain. Since the anti-corruption conventions are oriented towards national systems of criminal justice, the sanctioning requirements they set can be met with full respect to national autonomy, traditions, and peculiar substantive and procedural features. It is then up to the monitoring systems, operating within the international organizations which have promoted the adoption of the anti-bribery agreements, to assess whether or not the national peculiarities have been accommodated within the scope of compliance with criminalization and effective sanctioning of the corrupt offenses established in accordance with the same treaties.

In conclusion, it is only in the EU context that a wider notion of *effectiveness* has been elaborated. As aptly pointed out by Craufurd Smith (1999) and Tobler (2005), this has led the ECJ to prescribe in more detail how national judicial bodies or other authorities should sanction breaches of Community law. First, this approach has led the ECJ to support criminalization of conduct which is gravely detrimental to a fundamental Community interest. On the other hand, the ECJ has further developed the *proportionality* principle to moderate the stringent effect of national criminal law on the exercise of Community rights.

Accordingly, national sanctions are susceptible to being overridden by Community law, in cases where they prove too onerous in terms of the effect on Community rights of freedom. In addition, they must not be used in a discriminatory manner against persons from other Member States.[7] *Effectiveness* and *proportionality* have been interpreted on a case-by-case basis, in a rather flexible way, and with due regard to the sanctioning court (or other authority) being allowed a certain margin of appreciation.

12.3 CONFISCATION

12.3.1 Confiscation of the Bribe, and Proceeds and Instrumentalities of Bribery

Virtually all international anti-bribery treaties require their signatories to be able to confiscate either the bribe (*intrumenta sceleris*) or the proceeds of bribery (*producta sceleris*) or both. The EU Convention does not

---

7 Case C-348/96 Criminal Proceedings against *Donatella Calfa* (1999) ECR I-11.

explicitly provide for confiscation. However, this flaw is compensated to the extent active and passive corruption of officials of the European Communities or of other Member States thereof damages or may damage the European Communities' financial interests, by Article 5 of the Second Protocol of the PFI Convention which requires Member States to: "take the necessary measures to enable the seizure and, without prejudice to the rights of bona fide third parties, the confiscation or removal of the instruments and proceeds of fraud, active and passive corruption and money laundering, or property the value of which corresponds to such proceeds. Any instruments, proceeds or other property seized or confiscated shall be dealt with by the Member State in accordance with its national law."

All the other Conventions dedicate specific provisions to forfeiture and confiscation. Article XV of the OAS Convention obligation is limited to the duty upon State Parties to: "provide each other the broadest possible measure of assistance in the identification, tracing, freezing, seizure and forfeiture of property or proceeds obtained, derived from or used in the commission of offences established in accordance with this Convention."

Compared with the OAS provision, the OECD text targets confiscation in mandatory terms and more precisely. Article 3.3 reads as follows: "Each Party shall take such measures as may be necessary to provide that the bribe and the proceeds of the bribery of a foreign public official, or property the value of which corresponds to that of such proceeds, are subject to seizure and confiscation or that monetary sanctions of comparable effect are applicable."

By the same token, under Article 19(3) of the CoECLCC, Contracting States are required to: ". . . adopt such legislative and other measures as may be necessary to enable" them "to confiscate or otherwise deprive the instrumentalities and proceeds of criminal offences established in accordance with this Convention, or property the value of which corresponds to such proceeds." It is to be noted, however, that State Parties to the CoECLCC are under no specific obligation to provide for the criminal confiscation of substitute assets because the words "otherwise deprive" permit their civil forfeiture as well. This is probably because confiscation in civil proceedings is often more expedient because it usually requires a lower standard of proof and the conviction of the perpetrator is not necessary.

To the same effect, Article 16 of the AU Convention mandates State Parties to adopt such measures as may be necessary to enable: (a) their competent authorities "to search, identify, trace, administer and freeze or seize the instrumentalities and proceeds of corruption" when "pending a final judgment;" "(b) confiscation of proceeds or property, the value of which corresponds to that of such proceeds, derived, from offences established in accordance with this convention;" "(c) repatriation of proceeds of corruption." Paragraphs 2–4 of the same Article set forth the discipline and the conditions of the more general issue of cooperation between Parties in the form of the seizure or remittance of any object which may be required as evidence of the offense in question, or which has been acquired as a result or for which extradition is requested, and which, at the time of arrest, is found in the possession of the persons claimed or is discovered subsequently.

Article 31 of the UNCAC – which is part of Chapter III on criminalization and law enforcement – starts by requiring each State Party to provide for the confiscation of proceeds or equivalently valued property, or instrumentalities and things that were "destined for use" in defined offenses. The *travaux préparatoires* indicate that the term "instrumentalities" should not be interpreted in an overly broad manner.[8] By the same token, "destined", in this context, should be interpreted as "intended", although the word might be considered ill-chosen. In emphasizing its potential and problematic pervasiveness, Schroth (2005b) compares Article 31(1)(b) to the "precogs" in Philip K. Dick's tale "The Minority Report". However, he concludes that such a provision must be strictly interpreted as requiring conviction of a crime as a condition of final confiscation, which seems to be the only reading of the Chinese text and possibly confirmed by almost all the dictionaries consulted for the other five languages. Above all, this interpretation seems to be confirmed by the fact that it is the only reading consistent with the provisions of Articles 53 and 54 and with the acknowledgment, in the Preamble to the UNCAC, of "the fundamental principles of due process of law in criminal proceedings and in civil or administrative proceedings to adjudicate property rights".

Whereas other provisions in the UNCAC provide for civil forfeiture or recovery of assets, Article 31 specifically addresses identification, tracing, freezing, seizure and confiscation which apply solely to criminal proceeds, property equivalent to the value of criminal proceeds, and instrumentalities used or destined for use in offenses. Paragraphs 31(2) and (3) require States Parties to take the measures necessary to find and to hold the assets for final confiscation or release. Paragraphs 31(4), (5) and (6) include transformed and converted assets, criminal assets intermingled with innocent assets, and the income or other benefits proceeding from

---

8 Report of the Ad Hoc Committee for the Negotiation of a Convention Against Corruption on the work of its first to seventh sessions, Addendum, Interpretive notes for the official records of the negotiation of the United Nations Convention against Corruption, UN Doc. A/58/422/Add.1, at para. 63.

the criminally gained assets. Paragraph 31(7) requires States Parties to grant the appropriate authorities the power to subpoena or seize bank, financial and commercial records, and to lift any barrier of bank secrecy to actions under Article 31 and commercial records, and to lift any barrier of bank secrecy to actions under Articles 31 (and 55). In emphasizing its pervasiveness, Articles 31(9) and (10), respectively, protect the rights of *bona fide* third parties and, like many other provisions of the UNCAC, deprive the entire provision of legally binding effects, by subjecting Article 31 obligations to the undefined domestic law of the States Parties.

On the whole, the international legal instruments against corruption provide for a rather detailed discipline of confiscation which addresses many of the problematic aspects of such measures in a balanced approach, susceptible of having a deep impact on national legal systems. This reflects the empirical evidence shown by the inquiries of criminologists and data provided by public prosecutors on the efficiency of such measures in the fight against corruption. On the other hand, some issues (e.g. how to regulate confiscation from third parties) are necessarily left to national implementing laws on the sole binding condition of assuring effective compliance with international standards. In the following, we explore the international regime, by illustrating the problematic aspect of the criminal measure at hand.

As pertinently recalled by Daams (2003) and Pieth (2007), interestingly enough, when dealing with confiscation little (if any) attention is paid to the fact that national and international legislation revitalizes a pretty old sanction, frequently abused in the past, and abolished after harsh battles some 200 years ago. Confiscation lived on merely as a safety measure in respect of a dangerous object. However, the wider concept of confiscation was reintroduced in the context of growing concern about the increase in illicit drug-trafficking in the 1970s and the 1980s. As stressed by McClean (2007), the 1988 UN Convention Against Illicit Trafficking in Narcotic Drugs and Psychotropic Substances made the confiscation of proceeds a worldwide standard for effective anti-drug law enforcement.

After that, such measures gained increasing acceptance at the regional and national level. Since the adoption of the UN Convention Against Drug Trafficking the standard has been broadened to other types of economic and organized crimes. The relevant provisions in the anti-bribery criminal treaties are a telling example of the progressive increase in the use of such sanctions in multilateral criminal treaties.

However, there exist some notable differences between the international legal regime of confiscation in the context, respectively, of the fight against illicit drug-trafficking and organized crime, on the one hand, and corruption on the other.

Firstly, as noted by Pieth (2007), whereas in drug-trafficking the basic contract is illegal and the goods themselves are *extra commercium*, in the case of corruption the underlying contract is typically a licit exchange of goods and service for remuneration. Even though, from a civil law perspective, also at the international level the view has lately been gaining ground that the illegal corruption contract (*pactum sceleris*) also makes void the underlying contractual relationship or license, according to prominent commentators, one should seriously consider the causal link between the bribe and the underlying contractual relationship, that is to say, whether or not the bribe was actually the determining factor behind the conclusion of the contract, decision on the license, and so on. In light of the above, it is not surprising that, whether explicitly or not, all the anti-bribery treaties reserve the rights of the victims. Moreover, as regards the standards for the protection of the defendant or the owner of the assets, the legal regime they set forth is subject to the constitutional standards and all the pertinent international human rights instruments, such as the European Convention on Human Rights.[9]

Secondly, whereas most countries would demand forfeiture of the whole investment in the illicit-drug case, confiscation of proceeds of a bribe should not go beyond the net profits, for the basic contract is licit. This adds a further layer of complexity because of the difficulties the prosecuting or adjudicating authorities might stumble into when attempting to determine the part of the benefit stemming from the licit contractual relationship constituting the proceeds of the bribe. The evaluation reports of Phase 2 of the monitoring process of the OECD Convention bears stark testimony to such problems. The solution chosen by some countries to allow the court discretion to determine the amount to be confiscated is not without its shortcomings: Pieth (2007) argues that, even if practical, it might end up introducing legal uncertainty by eschewing the development of clear criteria.

In order to indicate permanent expropriation in relation to a criminal offense, States use different terms: in legal systems of the Anglo-Saxon tradition, forfeiture is usually the term applied to the power of the State's competent authority to take instruments of the crime (*instrumenta sceleris*), whereas confiscation applies more particularly to the proceeds of the crime (*producta sceleris*). As the terms are, however, used interchangeably, the international conventions under discussion address both with no substantial difference.

---

9 See Council of Europe, European Convention for the Protection of Human Rights and Fundamental Freedoms (ETS No. 5, 4 November 1950), esp. Article 6(1) and (2).

In the framework of the anti-bribery treaties, proceeds include any economic advantage or assets as well as any savings by means of reduced expenditure derived from such an offense. They may be a physical object, such as an asset that the briber purchased as a result of a contract awarded by the bribed official. They may also be intangible, such as shares in a company, movable or immovable objects, directly or indirectly obtained. Under the OECD, COE, AU and UN Conventions, to the extent possible under their legal systems, signatories should take measures to enable confiscation of property, equipment or other instrumentalities that were used or were intended to be used in the commission of an offense. The same holds true with respect to the OAS Convention, although the obligation upon States under Article XV is less demanding. This concept is prima facie fairly broad and may cover a wide range of property. For example, if a briber calls an official on his/her mobile phone and offers a bribe, then that phone could be subject to confiscation. At the other extreme, if a briber takes his/her private jet to meet an official and delivers the bribe, then the jet might also be subject to confiscation.

Note that Articles XV of the OAS Convention, 3(3) of the OECD Convention, 5 of the Second Protocol of the EU PFI Convention, 16 of the AU Convention and 31 of the UNCAC extend the obligation set forth therein to "seizure". Seizure is to be considered an umbrella term which covers all sorts of temporary/provisional retaining orders, issued in a pre-trial phase in order to secure movable or immovable property deemed to be the instruments or proceeds of the crime. Seizure may serve different objectives: "probatory seizure" is intended to secure evidence for the court hearing; "preventive seizure" is meant to secure ultimate confiscation.

12.3.2 Fines and Confiscation of Equivalent Value

In many cases, the bribe and the proceeds of bribery may not be available for confiscation. For example, they may have been hidden away or already spent, or they may be in the possession of a bona fide third party. Article 3(3) of the OECD Convention, Article 5 of the Second Protocol to the PFI Convention, Article 19(3) of the CoECLCC, Article 16 of the AU Convention, and Article 31(4)(5) of the UNCAC thus require that Parties either confiscate the bribe and the proceeds of bribery, or property of an equivalent value. Article 3(3) of the OECD Convention provides the further option of monetary sanctions with a comparable effect.

In spite of the prevalent use and meaning of confiscation as a crime-contrasting measure, its rationale varies considerably from State to State. Pieth (2007) comments on a comparative framework including all OECD States. The President of the Working Group on Bribery maintains that in some countries the aspect of additional deterrence (the so-called punitive effect) is foremost. By contrast, other countries place their emphasis on restitution, be it to victims, or, more generally, by siphoning off illicit gains. This is the case, for example, in the Dutch Legislation where the motto is: "crime shall not pay". Another model places the prevention of further (organized) crimes at the very center of policy efforts. The underlying idea, which is, for instance, the primary goal of Swiss legislation, is that the accumulation of capital and financial resources is deemed menacing in itself, for it allows criminal organizations to survive and proliferate. Significant variation exists in the methods and approaches employed by different legal systems to deal with cases where the proceedings of instrumentalities are not available for confiscation.

Some States opt for a purely property-based system, that is a system which allows only confiscation of property found to be proceeds or instrumentalities of crime. This model focuses on "tainted property". In Canada, for example, the sentencing judge may order the confiscation of property that constitutes the proceeds of crime where the offense for which the conviction was obtained was committed in relation to those proceeds. Even if not satisfied that the property relates to the specific offense, the court may also order forfeiture of property if satisfied beyond reasonable doubt that the property is the proceeds of crime. Because this system is specific to property, if the property cannot be located, has been transferred to a third party, is outside the country, has been substantially diminished in value or commingled with other property, the court may order a fine instead. Other States provide for a value-based system, while still others combine the two.

The second system allows the determination of the value of proceeds and instrumentalities of crime and the confiscation of an equivalent value. The value-based confiscation system originated in the United Kingdom. Under this system, the court can calculate the "benefit" to the convicted offender for a particular offense. Having determined the accrued benefit, the court may then assess the defendant's ability to pay (i.e. the value of the amount that might be realizable from the defendant's assets). On the basis of these calculations, the court would make a "confiscation" order, in the amount of the benefit or the realizable assets, whichever is lower. It is noteworthy that, in order to implement Article 3(3) of the OECD Convention, the Italian legislator introduced a new form of confiscation to the equivalent value for corruption offenses (Article 322 *ter* of the Italian Criminal Code), which presents several remarkable differences from the general regime of criminal confiscation provided for by Article 240 of the Italian Criminal Code. As recalled also in the Legislative Guide to the UNCAC, some countries (e.g. Australia) employ a combined system, which allows for orders relating to the "benefits" and the confiscation of tainted property. In other States, there is limited provision for confiscation without conviction if the accused person has died or absconded.

Increasingly, however, States have adopted separate regimes independent of criminal conviction-based confiscation, which allow for assets to be confiscated through civil proceedings aimed at the property itself, where no person needs to be convicted of an offense (e.g. Colombia, Germany, South Africa, and the United States). In other jurisdictions a discretionary power to reverse the burden of proof is provided. In those cases the offenders have to demonstrate the legal source of the property (for example, Hong Kong Special Administrative Region of China).

As hinted above, confiscation for equivalent property has been provided for by most of the anti-bribery criminal conventions. The OECD treaty even goes a step further: by applying the principle of functional equivalence, Article 3(3) of the OECD Convention seeks to bridge the gaps, and provides for the alternative of introducing proper confiscation or providing "that monetary sanctions of comparable effect are applicable". Even though the text may create the impression that fines and confiscation are interchangeable, from a legal perspective this is not the case. Sanctions are, in fact, based on, and calibrated according to, culpability, whereas the rationale of confiscation is based on the origin of the funds derived from crime.

To conclude the point, it is important to remark the role that confiscation for equivalent property may play in cases where the offender succeeds in concealing the proceeds within a corporate vehicle or a legal entity. Given that the offender will no longer be technically in possession, the criminal confiscation of the object/proceed of the offense might end up proving technically impossible in those legal systems where corporate criminal liability is narrow or even non-existent. Such difficulties might be overcome through value confiscation systems. A prime reason is that value confiscation systems can be enforced against money or assets that may not be directly connected in any way with criminal activity, but rather acquired with the criminal proceeds. Thus, "there is no need to trace the exact assets obtained through the offence but rather to determine what value may have been gained and confiscate that value from any available asset belonging to the offender or over which the offender exercises control" (UNODC, 2009: 94). Furthermore, unlike object confiscation systems, when using "value confiscation systems there is no need to be concerned with direct or indirect proceeds, or with intermingled legal and illegal assets. Once the value to be confiscated is determined, the origin of the property against which it is enforced does not matter" (ID.). Finally, "as value confiscation only operates against property owned by the offender – operating in personam – it will never affect rights acquired after the offence by bona fide third parties" (ID.).[10]

12.3.3 Confiscation of Converted Proceeds and Benefits Deriving from Proceeds

Criminals often do not leave the proceeds of their crimes in the original form. Instead, they may transform or convert the proceeds into other asset for their benefits (e.g. by buying a house) or to hide the origin of the proceeds (i.e. money laundering). To be effective, legislation should therefore allow for the confiscation of proceeds that have been transformed or converted, in part or in full, into other property. This is a commonly accepted standard of several national criminal systems and is also expressed by most of the international anti-corruption conventions, expressly established under Article 3(3) of the OECD Convention; Article 5 of the Second Protocol to the PFI Convention, Article 19(3) of the CoECLCC, Article 16 of the AU Convention; UNCAC, Article 31(4)–(5).

12.3.4 Confiscation from Third Persons

Treatment of confiscation from third parties demands some premises. Confiscation should not impede victims' right. On the contrary, where victims have a right to proceeds, they should be restored to them, not confiscated. On the other hand, in all likelihood the most problematic issue in the area of confiscation is how to prevent the defendant from simply evading confiscation by using third party recipients, while at the same time protecting the rights of bona fide third parties, which means third parties who are both innocent and not in league with the accused party.

The third party in possession of the asset may have been complicit in the crime or is aware that the asset is the proceeds of crime. Legislation should allow for confiscation of the property from such third parties. By contrast, a third party may have no connection with the offender and have acted in good faith, for example, when a briber sells an asset that s/he had obtained from a corrupt transaction, and the purchaser has no knowledge

---

10 In this respect, the UNODC consider also the obvious drawback of the system which occurs "in cases where the offender has transferred all of his/her property to other natural or legal persons and has no property under his/her own name. It can be argued, however, that any person acquiring such property is likely to be committing a money-laundering offence, the proceeds of which are subject to confiscation as proposed in article 23. Therefore, the property could still be confiscated under a value-based system" (UNODC: 2009: 94 *et seq.*).

of the crime. In principle, confiscation of the property against such a third party would not be justified. Instead, alternative sanctions (such as confiscation of an equivalent value or a fine) should be imposed against the briber. However, solutions which exclude confiscation from third parties altogether clearly invite circumvention of the rules set forth by the international legal apparatus. Even though these orientating indications are rather broad, international conventions against corruption do not provide for further requirements.

To recap, it is not up to the conventions to draw up minimal standards for the protection of third parties: as argued also by Pieth (2007), in this area constitutional principles and standards set up by the international human rights instruments prevail and (should) inspire the different and balanced solutions adopted by domestic criminal law.

12.4 LIABILITY OF LEGAL PERSONS

12.4.1 Introductory Remarks

In 1821 William Hazlitt hauntingly portrays the crucial problems we meet when considering corporate crime: "corporate bodies are more corrupt and profligate than individuals, because they have more power to mischief, and are less amenable to disgrace and or punishment. They neither feel shame, remorse, gratitude nor goodwill".[11]

Two central dynamics are captured in the excerpt just quoted. Firstly, Hazlitt seems to suggest the reason for crime perpetrated by corporations or legal entities in that they have considerable (economic and/or political) power. Secondly, he clearly addresses the dilemma about any (attempt at) punishment of such entities, that is, the extremely problematic issue of identifying effective sanctions applicable to legal persons.

The problem of attributing criminal liability to legal persons represents one of the most fascinating challenges for any penal scholar and has been one of the leading penal-political debates in the field of economic criminal law in recent decades.

The primary importance of the issue may be properly appreciated by taking into consideration the following aspects: *in primis*, criminal law was traditionally created to deal with individual acts and individual offenders who shape criminal acts; secondly, as noted, the modern models of corporate governance seem to have been undergoing fresh scrutiny in the last

---

11 Hazlitt (1901: 359).

decade with uncertain results. Another element of interest is represented by the various solutions observable in a comparative perspective. Although several countries in the Anglo-American context have traditionally been ahead in recognizing that the liability of legal persons is needed to address corporate conduct that falls beyond the responsibility and knowledge of any individual,[12] many European jurisdictions have become more active in shaping such a responsibility with results that vary considerably from one country to another.

There is no doubt that one of the most controversial issues related to the repression of corruption offenses nowadays concerns the imposition of liability on legal persons. Therefore, the debate as to whether and how to punish legal entities is parallel to our subject and deserves a specific analytical study.

In the remaining part of this section, we first examine the solutions adopted by the international criminal apparatus against corruption. Thereafter, we advance some brief considerations regarding a certain *vis attractiva* of the international treaties under discussion in promoting reforms within national legal systems traditionally reluctant to recognize liability of legal persons for the commission of crime. Before focusing on the situation at the supranational level, we briefly introduce the various models used for imputing responsibility to corporations.

12.4.2 Models of Corporate Liability

A premise: there exists no universal theory of legal persons' liability. Firstly, the range of solutions, both actual and potential, to the problem of attributing responsibility to a corporation varies according to the area of law concerned. Secondly, in relation to criminal law, diversity of approaches depends on the specific jurisdiction at hand.

Two reports published by the OECD in 2000 argue that in general three different theories for the attribution of liability to corporations compete

---

12 For an insightful and critical study, see Wells (1993). When criminal liability of legal persons is at issue, our thoughts automatically turn to the common law systems: it is here that this principle was born; and here it has been developing in the theory in order to be rooted in the legislation thereafter. Yet, even in these systems its evolution has been intermittent and not undisputed. Suffice it to recall the formula "No soul to damn, no body to kick", whereby the English courts continued to deny the validity of the principle of the liability of legal persons in the 18th century. For a comprehensive analysis of the birth, theoretical framework, and limits of corporate criminal liability see Coffee (1983), Beck and O'Brien (2000); Clark and Drew (2005); Gobert and Punch (2003).

for attention.[13] According to the traditional version of the first theory, a company is liable for the wrongful acts of a limited layer of senior officers thereof, identified as its *brains*. The second model aims to activate the regulatory forces of the entity to shape their future activities safely, regardless of the actual commission of transgressions by its employees. The third model places corporate blame on the procedures, operating mechanisms or culture of the company. It is noteworthy that, despite the specific model applied, some countries limit corporate liability to a restricted list of offenses. In addition, the boundaries between the models outlined above might happen to be very thin. Overall, the three theories at issue cover a broad spectrum in which different levels of corporate liability are shaped.

The central thesis of the first model, the so-called Identification or Alter Ego Theory, which originates from English criminal law, is the following. As a consequence of the essential equation of individual with collective responsibility, the corporation is held responsible for external as well as for internal offenses committed by some of its employees. In his landmark study, Wells (1993) remarks that it was not until the 1940s that English law envisaged a kind of corporate liability which could apply to serious offenses marked by the relevance of the mental element of intention, recklessness or negligence. Courts developed the Alter Ego Theory, whereby certain key personnel are said to act *as* the company (rather than on *behalf of* it, as in the case of so-called *vicarious* liability, which, under the English binary scheme, represents the other form of responsibility for corporates and applies to certain regulatory offenses only). The idea behind this theory is that a distinction may be made between employees who act as *hands* and those who represent the *brains* of the company. Considered in the leading case of *Tesco Supermarkets Ltd v. Natrass*,[14] this theory reflects an anthropomorphic conception of the corporation: the offense eventually committed by the key officers is *automatically* imputed to the corporation, with no need to trigger any further translating or ascertaining mechanism. There is a wide range of variations as to the circle of personnel covered by the principle. In English case law this circle is restricted to leading employees, namely persons who control or manage the affairs of the company. Other regimes have broadened the circle of offenders to all persons who exercise a control function, even down to a level below middle management. According to the OECD (2000b), in France, Germany and Sweden, for instance, violation of supervisory duties is sufficient, even at lower levels of management, whereas legislation in

13 See OECD (2000a, 2000b).
14 *Tesco Supermarkets Ltd v. Natrass*, 1972, AC, pp. 153 ff.

Denmark, and Belgium envisages liability for offenses committed by any employee if the corporation profits from this act. The Identification Theory has attracted criticism since, as illustrated by Wells (1993), it seems refractory in taking into due account the multiversity of legal persons which differ from one another as to dimension, legal statute, and organization. Moreover, whilst this model may be accurate in relatively simple situations, where subjects are well identified and identifiable, and act with full determination, being absolutely aware of the consequences of their behavior (as in traditional fraud offenses), it may prove insufficient to characterize more complex situations, where the liability of the individual does not emerge with clearness owing to the fact that the harm/danger is caused by a series of managing mistakes or omitted controls due to flaws in the organization.

The Faulty Corporate Organization Theory no longer requires individual offenses to be imputed to legal persons. Rather, the central assumption is the idea of original responsibility on the part of the corporate entity. Representatives of this model are, for instance, the US and the Netherlands. The notion of supervisory liability (*respondeat superior*) is at the core of the theory at hand: it is the defective organization of the corporate entity which has led to the offense. The standard of diligence for running a corporation is no longer measured with respect to managers' behavior; rather the leading parameter is constituted of indicators such as the corporation's size, market share, economic activity, and organizational model. This approach is not without its drawbacks: the precise definition of the criteria which characterize faulty organizations may be significantly troublesome for both courts and legislators.

According to the Strict Liability Model (Causation Principle), evidence of actual deficits in corporate organizations causing or facilitating offenses is completely dispensed with. The essence of this theory is that the creation of an entity with complex operational structures carrying out an intrinsically dangerous process is rather deemed to be per se sufficient to impute dangerous consequences to the corporation whose business activities are the source. The inquiry led by the OECD (2000b) tells us that in Europe this "holistic" approach was traditionally limited to technical law and non-compliance with administrative standards (quasi-criminal law in Poland, Portugal, and Sweden), whilst the same approach was also found in some US regulatory offenses.

12.4.3 Anti-corruption Law and Liability of Legal Persons

Coming to the relationship between corruption and corporate liability, although with a variety of intonations, several studies stress the frequent involvement of corporate entities in the perpetration of this crime.[15] The underlying argument is quite plain: to an even wider extent than individuals, legal persons manage their activities within an international scenario. Unlike the former, the latter can be operative in more than one country simultaneously. Legal persons may thus be tempted to exploit their subsidiaries located in havens of secrecy as channels for laundering activities. Symmetrically, as stated in the recent UN Commentary on the 1988 Vienna Convention: 'a sanction imposed on the institution, rather than on the individual, can act as a catalyst for the reorganisation of the management and supervisory structures to ensure that conduct is deterred'.[16]

Over time the view has been gaining ground that the only way to remove the shield for serious crime represented by "the corporate veil" is to introduce liability for legal entities. However, the 1988 Vienna Convention contains no provision on such responsibility, although, as noted, its Commentary acknowledges the benefits of adopting a system of liability for legal persons, as separate from natural persons. As to the anti-corruption treaties, the issue is directly addressed by Articles 2 and 3(2) of the OECD Convention, Articles 1(d), 18 and 19 of CoECLCC, Article 10 of the UNCTOC, and Article 26 of the UNCAC, whereas Article 6 of the EU Convention, reproducing verbatim Article 3 of the PFI Convention, requires State Parties to take the necessary measures "to allow heads of business or any other persons having power to take decisions or exercise control within a business to be declared criminally liable". The same regime for legal persons is also envisaged in Article 5 of the 2003 EU Framework Decision on Combating Corruption in the Private Sector. For the sake of comprehensiveness, we must add that Article 3(2) of the Second Protocol of the PFI Convention provides for the liability of legal persons, where lack of supervision or control by a person having power of representation, authority to take decisions or to exercise control within the legal person has made possible the commission of an act of

---

15 For an analytical survey on these aspects see also e.g. OECD (2001) and FATF (2006).

16 See UN Commentary on the United Nation Convention against Illicit Traffic in Narcotic Drugs and Psychotropic Substances, paragraph 3.54. For further analytical comments see United Nations, *Legislative Guide for the Implementation of the United Nations Convention against Corruption*, New York, 2006 (hereinafter: The Legislative Guide to the UNCAC), paragraphs 315–24. Incidentally, the imposition of liability on legal persons for a series of offenses mirrors also the proposals made in the *Corpus Juris*, a study prepared on the request of the European Parliament and under the aegis of the Commission, reflecting the views of researchers from the Association of European Lawyers for the Protection of Financial Interests of the EC. See Delmas-Marty (1997a), esp. Article 14.

fraud, active corruption or money-laundering for the benefit of that legal person, a person under its authority. It is thus to be maintained that, *in* case of actual or possible damage to EC financial interests, liability of legal persons must be established for active corruption offenses.

Rather appropriately, the language of the different instruments leaves the door open to a wide notion of legal persons. They may take a variety of forms: to be effective, a scheme for liability must cover a wide array of entities. The relevant definition of a legal person should therefore include any entity having such status under the applicable national law, including criminal and company laws. More specifically, it should include corporations (whether or not they are listed on a stock exchange), partnerships, societies, associations, foundations, and not-for-profit bodies.

Only Article 1(d) of the CoECLCC explicitly provides for a definition of "legal person", including "any entity having such status under the applicable national law, except for States or other public bodies in the exercise of State authority and for public international organizations". The CoECLCC provides also an exception to the definition of legal persons for states or other public bodies in the exercise of state authority and public international organizations. According to the Explanatory Report on the Council of Europe Convention, parties are not required to impose liability against ministries and bodies that exercise public powers at national, regional, state and local levels of government. Nonetheless, and this is a crucial point, according to the same Explanatory Report, the exception for state and public bodies should not be extended to state-owned or state-controlled enterprises.

The wording of the OECD Convention, the CoECLCC, and the UNCAC provisions presents some differences. Nevertheless, all these provisions share notable common features. Firstly, all of these instruments require that liability for offenses be established both for natural persons and for legal persons. Particularly, they call for States Parties to take the necessary steps, in accordance with their fundamental legal principles, to provide for liability of legal persons.

Secondly, this liability can be criminal, civil or administrative, thus accommodating the various legal systems and approaches.

At the same time, they provide for the criteria that shall lead the national legislators to establish (criminal and non-criminal; monetary or other) sanctions to be imposed on the legal persons liable for the relevant offenses, namely, effectiveness, proportionality and deterrence. Official Commentary 24 of the OECD Convention makes it clear that States may also wish to consider sanctions such as temporary or permanent exclusion from contracting with the government (e.g. public procurement, aid procurement and export credit financing), forfeiture or confiscation of proceeds of crime, restitution, disentitlement to public benefits or aid, disqualification from the practice of commercial activities, placement under judicial supervision, winding up of the legal person, publication of the judgment, the appointment of a trustee, the requirement to establish an effective internal compliance program and the direct regulation of corporate structures. We find a similar indication at paragraph 338 of the Legislative Guide for the Implementation of the UNCAC Convention.

Again, the imposition of liability on legal persons does not exclude criminal proceedings against natural persons who are perpetrators, instigators or accessories in corruption offenses. The liability of natural persons who perpetrated the acts, therefore, is *in addition* to corporate liability (whatever its form), and must not be affected in any way by the latter. The CoECLCC goes even further, by distilling in Article 18(1) the criteria which constitute the basis for imposing such liability: the existence of a connection between the legal person and the offense, since the latter must have been committed for the former's benefit; along with the existence of a link between the physical offender and the legal person, normally a leading position ascertained through a series of formal and substantial criteria (e.g. power of representation of the legal person; authority to take decisions on behalf thereof, or authority to exercise control within, the legal person).

In addition, Article 18(2) of the same agreement extends liability to cover cases where offenses are committed by an individual subordinate to the person in a leading position. Liability is thus imposed on the legal person when corruption has been possible because of a lack of supervision and control of the subject in leading positions (so called *culpa in vigilando*). Our view is that the latter provisions do not necessarily imply an objective responsibility on the part of legal persons, at least because this model of liability is not consistent with the constitutional systems of several State Parties, especially regarding the principle of culpability. Indeed, such an interpretation could undermine the effectiveness of the provisions of the instrument at issue, in contrast with the principle of effectiveness.[17] Rather, they might be interpreted as being restricted where legal persons

---

17 On the relevance of the principle see *ex multis* Shaw (2008: 842), who remarks that this principle "will be used . . . in order to give effect to provisions in accordance with the intentions of the parties . . . and the rules of international law". See the International Court of Justice in the *Fisheries Jurisdiction* (*Spain v. Canada*) case stated that the principle of effectiveness "has an important role in the law of the Treaties". See the *Fisheries Jurisdiction* (*Spain v. Canada*) case, ICJ Reports, 1999, pp. 432 ff., especially p. 455 and the International Court of Justice

as such may be blamed for culpable behavior of persons acting on their behalf.

Some final considerations.

The question of the liability of legal persons is extremely delicate; definitive solutions are not taken at the international level and probably never will be, in view of the problems it still raises: particularly, its imposition on soulless entities with the potential to undermine the principle of moral culpability and blame, and the extension of punishment of legal entities in cases where employees commit offenses in breach of their duties or company guidelines.

Even within the single domestic legal system the issue is still disputed: the design and adoption of paradigms of effective and deterrent *ex crimine* liability of legal persons is to be coordinated with the general principles of substantial and procedural criminal law: a task far from being easily accomplished by national legislators. Furthermore, in most legal systems, the gravity of sanctions (no matter if criminal, administrative or civil in nature) concretely apply to legal persons depend on the comprehensiveness and effectiveness of internal preventive and compliance systems designed to prevent and control the "corruption-risk". In sum, the company's compliance with the legal prohibition and the related internal controls, ethics, and compliance programs or measures is the duty of the individuals at all levels of the company (OECD Rec 2009, Annex II A).3. Guidance). In several legal systems, a proved "*in abstactro* effective" compliance system may represent an important mitigating factor or even a defense for the legal entity involved in a corruption case. As already hinted, it appears that over the last five years a substantial consensus on the relevance and the main elements of such corporate governance systems has emerged among the main international organizations with competence on the manner (the WB, the OECD, the UNODC, to name a few). As a matter of fact, most of the models promoted by different international organizations share common founding features: they foster anti-corruption preventive and monitoring functions in the private sector through serious risk-assessment; active involvement and commitment of the management (so called "tone from the top"); clear definition and transparent application of substantive rules and procedures on due diligence and on contracting with business partners; accounting and auditing standards; adequate communication and training of the personnel; establishment of discreet channels of notifications; regular reviews of the entire system against a

---

in *Fisheries Jurisdiction* (*Spain v. Canada*), ICJ Reports, 1999, pp. 432 ff., especially p. 455.

changing risk or regulatory environment; and, where appropriate, introduce disciplinary sanctions for non-compliance on the part of employees, consultants and agents.[18] Though a detailed assessment of such approach is clearly beyond the scope of the present work, in light of its growing relevance within the international scenario we would like to provide some words of caution. First, it must be stressed that the net effect of such systems is irremeably dependent on the actual will of the single company to design, update and enforce a concretely effective and strong system aimed at preventing, monitoring and reducing the "corruption risk". For instance, implementation of a code that follows the "develop and file" approach is more than frequently completely inadequate. This involves codes that are developed but then filed away in an induction manual, or are prepared without staff involvement and periodical tests and reassessment of the risks. This approach risks the possibility of staff becoming cynical about the codes and models' usefulness or even regarding it as irrelevant because staff may feel it was imposed on them, or, even worse, the entire model becomes outdated and therefore useless for its intended scope. Secondly, a too optimistic (or naïve) reliance on such models runs the risk that, as Rossi (2003) puts it, the "ethics of business" becomes a "business of ethics". Rossi argues that it is hardly questionable that the implementation of the various ethical codes and compliance programs is less than a making-up operation.[19] Even without necessarily taking such a strong stance and assuming that compliance measures are more than window-dressing a policy issue remains to be carefully assessed. Although effective anti-corruption compliance systems supposedly prevent future crimes, domestic legislators should still consider whether or not the future deterrent value of sanctioning a company still outweighs the prophylactic benefits of imposing internal compliance.

On the positive side, the remarkable fact being highlighted is that the international instruments have exercised a discernible *vis attractiva* with respect to various reforms occurring at national level. Particularly, by adopting a *flexible approach* to recognizing that the *criminal* response does not represent the only possible model, they have inspired national

---

[18] For a more in-depth illustration of the different elements of such programs as indicated by the international best practices see, among the others, Pieth (2012), at 47ff.

[19] More recently, in commenting on Milton Friedman's article 'The Social Responsibility of Business Is to Increase Its Profits', published in *The New York Times Magazine* on September 13th, 1970, Rossi (2008) argued that the various models of corporate social responsibility are just pretense because they are not capable of creating and regulating anything.

legislators to adopt alternative/hybrid solutions, even in States traditionally disinclined to punish legal persons. This has been the case in Italy, where anti-corruption conventions have led the Parliament and the Government (officially delegated for this purpose) to introduce a new paradigm of liability for legal persons where certain offenses are committed "in the interest or for the benefit" – this being the wording of the Italian Law 300/2000 and Legislative Bill 231/2001 (as subsequently amended) – of these organizations, regardless of the particular *nomen juris* of such liability. Other Continental legal systems, where the tenet *societas delinquere non potest* has long been defended, have introduced frankly criminal models of liability for legal persons. This is the case with the 1994 French reform, which saw the amendment of the French Penal Code through the inclusion of Articles 121–2, which introduced general criminal liability for *personnes morales*, where this was expressly provided for in the relevant legislation. Similar changes have occurred in Belgium as a result of the Law of 4 May 1999 *introduisant la responsabilité pénale des personnes morales*.

Another telling example is given by the adoption of the UK Bribery Act in 2010. Before the enactment of the new law, "the OECD Working Group on Bribery criticised the UK harshly at various instances"[20] (Pieth, 2012: 33) for not having adequately fought international bribery. In 2008, the WGB went as far in its criticism as to ask the UK to report every quarter of a year on legislative progress and stressed that: ". . . failing to enact effective and comprehensive legislation undermines the credibility of the UK's legal framework and potentially triggers the need for increased due diligence over UK companies by their commercial partners or Multilateral Development Banks".[21]

---

[20] OECD UK-Ph1, 1999, 25; OECD UK-Ph1bis 2003; OECD UK-Ph1ter 2010; OECD UK-Ph2 2005; OECD UK-Ph2bis 2008.

[21] OECD UK-Ph2bis 2008, 70 et seq.

13. Jurisdictional issues

13.1 INTRODUCTION

The primary criminal issues generally covered by the anti-bribery treaties deal with the offenses being criminalized by the Contracting Parties; typology and level of sanctions; liability of legal persons; jurisdictional criteria; statute of limitations and provisions on international (criminal) cooperation.

After having addressed the provisions regarding offenses, sanctions, liability of legal persons – that is to say the main *substantive* criminal issues – we now attempt to conduct a horizontal examination of the different conventions' provisions with reference to competence *ratione loci* and the mechanisms of judicial cooperation foreseen by the instruments under analysis.

13.2 INTERNATIONALIZATION OF CRIME AND TRADITIONAL JURISDICTIONAL REGIMES

The increasing challenges posed by the internationalization of crime to traditional jurisdictional regimes are effectively depicted by the stark contrast between two eminent British jurists' statements. In 1891, Lord Halsbury LC could straightforwardly declare: "All crime is local. The jurisdiction over crime belongs to the country where the crime is committed".[1] Exactly a century later, Lord Griffiths observed: "unfortunately in this century crime has ceased to be largely local in origin and effect. Crime is now established on an international scale".[2] As pointed out also by Rosi (2008), in the context of economic globalization offenders habitually try to elude municipal regimes by moving between States or engaging in acts within the territories of more than one State. As argued throughout this

1 *Mcleod v. Attorney-General for New South Wales*, 1891, AC, pp. 455 ff., at p. 458, cited *ex multis* by Cockyane (2005); Hirst (2003: 29).

2 *Somchai Liangsiriprasert v. US Government*, 1991, 1, AC, pp. 225 ff., at p. 241.

BOX 13.1 JURISDICTION AND THE *DUMEZ NIGERIA LTD* CASE

The vital role of the jurisdictional provisions as to corruption activities may be illustrated by referring to a case recalled by Jean Ziegler (2003) in his *Les nouveaux maîtres du monde et ceux qui leur résistent*: in February 2000 a French judge dismissed a case against the CEO of *Dumez Nigeria Ltd*. He was suspected of diverting $60 million via shell companies with a substantial part of the money being paid to public figures (generals and high public officials) in Nigeria. The public prosecutor submitted that Dumez Nigeria Ltd belonged to the "consolidation basis" of Dumez France. Since France was a Party to the OECD Anti-bribery Convention, he held that the bribes paid by the CEO of Dumez Nigeria Ltd would have been illegal under French legislation implementing the OECD instrument. However, as Hatchard et al. (2004) remark, it was not possible to prove the "dependence" and the case was dropped by the trial judge because, in legal terms, the Nigerian subsidiary was an independent and separate entity from the parent company in France and was incorporated in a country which was not party to the Convention.

book, the problem of corruption does not confine itself neatly to discrete regions or countries.

Corrupt practices are characterized by a "race to the bottom" – that is, a search by those participating in them for those jurisdictions that offer the most forgiving rules, the least transparency and accountability, the greatest ease of "no questions" operation. This is particularly accurate in the case of serious corruption activities, where perpetrators might be significantly powerful, organized, and mobile, and the resort to transnational schemes constitutes a frequent practice.

The cluster of anti-corruption treaties we are analyzing is a clear indicator that the international community aims at ensuring that no serious crime goes unpunished and that all parts of the crime are punished wherever they occur. In short, jurisdictional gaps that facilitate fugitives finding safe havens should be reduced or eliminated. Similarly, in cases where a criminal organization is active in several States which may have jurisdiction over the conduct of the organization, there should be a *corpus* accessible to those States in order to facilitate coordination of their efforts. On the other hand, where the organization is represented by corporate entities serious problems may arise over punishing its conduct.

Rules establishing the criminal jurisdiction *ratione loci* constitute the necessary *trait d'union* between criminalization and sanctioning of corruption activities, or, more accurately, the basic condition to criminalize this conduct and, secondly, to allow judicial cooperation between States to the extent this is necessary in order to repress the same conduct.

In the remaining part of the present chapter, firstly, we examine the solutions adopted by the international instruments against corruption as to criminal jurisdiction. Overall, our exegesis of the relevant provisions shows that, regardless of the possibility to assume binding obligations as to the adoption of criteria allowing wide scope to prescribe extra-territorial criminal jurisdiction, the States Parties seem to have preferred to preserve the margin of discretion permitted by international customary law in this respect. Secondly, we question the aptness of this solution in view of the increasingly transnational dynamics of corruption practices and the eventual deployment of corporate entities in perpetrating these crimes. In particular, we seek to investigate this latter issue by examining possible answers that are consonant with the conventional provisions which have been proposed in doctrinal writings. Finally, we explore the different mechanisms of judicial cooperation provided by international anti-corruption treaties.

13.3 GENERAL REMARKS

Some premises. Jurisdiction is concerned with "the State's right of *regulation*, or, in the incomparably pithy language of Mr Justice Holmes, with the right *to apply the law to the acts of men*".[3]

It should be stressed from the outset that, in the present context, with the term *jurisdiction* we usually refer to *jurisdiction to prescribe* or *prescriptive jurisdiction*. For the purposes of our work we assume, according to the thesis submitted by O'Keefe (2004), that jurisdiction is *not* a unitary concept; it encompasses, within the criminal context, two different notions, namely *prescriptive jurisdiction* and *enforcement jurisdiction* or *jurisdiction to enforce*. Whereas the latter refers to "a State's authority under international law actually to apply its criminal law, through police and other executive action, and through the courts; prescriptive jurisdiction refers, in the criminal context, to a state's authority under

---

[3] Mann (1964: 111 ff.); emphasis added. See also Akehurst (1972–3), Lowe (2003: 329 ff.), Jennings and Watts (1992), Oxman (1997); Giuliano (1956), Treves (1973).

international law to assert the applicability of its criminal law to given conduct", or, more simply, "to a state's authority to criminalise a given conduct".[4] As particularly regards prescriptive jurisdiction, O'Keefe (2004) and Gaeta (2005) argue that State practice discloses a number of definitely accepted criteria or *heads of jurisdiction*, according to which, as a matter of international law, States can assert the applicability of their criminal law since each of these heads is thought to evidence a sufficient link between the impugned conduct and the interests of the prescribing State. To put it another way, according to general international law, to assert jurisdiction allowed by international law is ultimately a matter for individual States. Therefore, within the borders drawn by two fundamental principles of general international law (i.e. sovereignty of the State and equality of States), each national legal system is free to determine the ambit of its criminal law.

As explained in the landmark study by Mann (1964), there is no general international rule which imposes a precise jurisdictional criterion. This principle was explicitly acknowledged by the Permanent Court of International Justice in the *Lotus* case.[5] In examining the general principles governing criminal jurisdiction under international law, the Court concluded that each State enjoys considerable freedom to delimit the territorial and extraterritorial ambit of its own laws. Such freedom also covers the possibility for groups of States to sign multilateral treaties in order to establish certain *binding* jurisdictional criteria upon which to assert and, eventually, exercise their criminal jurisdiction in relation to given conduct. The latter practice has constantly increased over the years in view of the various problems posed by transnational and international crimes. As first clarified by the pioneering Harvard Law School Research in International Law (1935) on jurisdiction with respect to crime, in order to meet the increasing opportunities for committing crimes, the constituent elements of which take place in more than one State, the jurisdiction of crime has been expanded in several ways. As specifically concerns corruption, the frequent atomization of its constituent elements within the soil of different States requires the reach of criminal law to be extended beyond the territorial boundaries of individual States.

---

4 O'Keefe (2004: 737). As to the so-called *jurisdiction to adjudicate* or *judicial* or *curial* jurisdiction, we embrace the thesis of O'Keefe (2004) and Berman (2003), who deem that "in criminal law legislative jurisdiction and judicial jurisdiction are one and the same", the latter being "the exercise or actualisation of prescription".

5 *France v. Turkey*, 1928, PCIJ Report, Series A, No. 1.

13.4 PROVISIONS ON JURISDICTION

Coming to the international legal texts, we now examine the jurisdictional provisions of the UN Conventions, leaving room for some consideration of the discipline envisaged by the other treaties in the second place.

13.4.1 The UNCTOC and the UNCAC Provisions

Indeed, Article 15, and Article 42, respectively, of the UNCTOC and UNCAC seem more articulated and share a common framework. Moreover, most of the conclusions achievable for them might be enlarged to the latter. It should be preliminarily noticed that, regardless of the different scope *ratione materiae* of the two treaties at issue, the provisions on jurisdiction are extremely similar in terms of structure and contents.

Our aim is to answer the following questions: (1) what heads of jurisdiction do they provide for in order to allow State Parties to criminalize the corruption offenses to be established in accordance with them, and are the related provisions always mandatory? (2) Does the treaty-based mechanism satisfactorily serve the aim of solving the jurisdictional problems raised by the transnational dynamics of corruption activities?

Here we address the first point. The UN Conventions establish both mandatory *requirements* (i.e., the obligation to take legislative or other measures) and *optional measures* (i.e. measures which Parties may wish to consider).

Regarding mandatory provisions, under Articles 15(1) and 42(1) respectively of the UNTOC and the UNCAC, States Parties are required to establish jurisdiction where the offense in question is actually committed in their territory, aboard vessels flying their flag or aircraft registered under their laws at the *tempus commissi delicti*. In other words, these provisions require that States Parties assert jurisdiction on the usual basis of the territorial principle. That is, according to the unsurpassed Harvard Research's formula, a State has jurisdiction with respect to any crime committed in whole or in part within its territory. As confirmed inter alia by an interpretative note to the UNCAC, the offense might be committed in whole or in part in the territory of the State Party.[6] As a corollary, it follows that States Parties, whose penal jurisdiction does not currently extend to all of the offenses established in accordance with the Conventions committed in their territory or on board the above-described ships or aircraft, will need to supplement their existing jurisdiction regime.

6 UN A/58/422/Add.1, paragraph 41.

Secondly, both Conventions require States Parties to be able to assert jurisdiction over the envisaged offenses committed outside their territory by their own nationals, when extradition is denied on grounds of nationality of the offender, that is the principle of *active nationality – rei publicae interest bonos subditos habere*.

Under Articles 16, paragraph 10, and 44, paragraph 11 of UNCTOC, and UNCAC, respectively, they must also be able to apply the principle of *aut dedere aut prosecui*. It follows that States may already have jurisdiction over the specified conduct, but they must ensure that they have jurisdiction for conduct committed both inside and outside their territory by one of their nationals.

Furthermore, the UNCTOC and the UNCAC contain specific obligations with respect to the coordination of efforts when more than one State Party investigates a particular offense. They require States Parties that become aware that other Parties are investigating or prosecuting the same offense to consult with those States, where appropriate, to coordinate their actions. These provisions are expressions of the far-reaching aim of the Conventions to promote cooperation to prevent and repress corruption more effectively.

More interesting for our purposes appear to be the *optional criteria*. These leave room for an application of jurisdictional bases which might have the potential to extend criminal jurisdiction over extraterritorial conduct. However, it must be stressed, the Conventions *only encourage* States Parties to consider establishing jurisdiction in additional instances. The Treaties adopted under the auspices of the UN set forth a number of further bases for jurisdiction that States parties *may* assume when:

1) the offense is committed against one of their nationals (the so-called offender's or passive nationality principle);
2) the offense is committed by one of their nationals or by a stateless habitual resident in their territory;
3) the offense is linked to money-laundering *planned* to be committed in their territory;
4) the offense is committed against the State Party (the so-called protective principle or *compétence réelle*).

In case State Parties decide to adopt the second of the latter *optional* criteria as a base for jurisdiction and consider including legal persons in the concept of "national", few additional considerations may be added. As illustrated in UNODC (2009: 135), two models of implementations could be envisaged in order to hold responsible a national legal person for a corruption offence: in the first one, States may exercise jurisdiction over corporations which have been founded according to its national law or which reside in the territory. Alternatively, a legal person may be regarded as national if the acting natural person within the corporate structure is a citizen of that State. Besides noting that the former model is considered majoritarian in this context, it is the latter one which may cause enforcement gaps because in assessing corporate liability, investigations frequently face substantial hurdles when it comes to identifying with reasonable certainty those who instigate or perpetrate the conduct.

Furthermore, the Treaties provide an additional non-mandatory basis for jurisdiction that States Parties may wish to consider. In contrast to the mandatory establishment of jurisdiction addressed above to enable domestic prosecution in lieu of extradition of its nationals, these provisions allow the establishment of jurisdiction over persons whom the requested State Party does not extradite for other reasons.

Finally, the Conventions make clear that the listing of these bases for jurisdiction is not exhaustive. States Parties can establish additional bases of jurisdiction without prejudice to the norms of general international law and in accordance with the principles of their domestic law.

13.4.2 The Other Treaties' Provisions

Turning to the remaining anti-bribery Conventions: the jurisdictional criteria set forth by the OAS Convention are consistent with those established in the UN treaties. While under Article V(1)–(2) certain jurisdictional bases are mandatory (namely: territoriality, along with the case of the alleged criminal present in the territory of the concerned State Party, when this party does not extradite such person to another country on the basis of his/her nationality), under paragraph 3 of the same Article, others are optional (nationality, and habitual residence). Paragraph 4 of Article V allows the Parties to establish, in conformity with their national law, other types of jurisdiction as well.

Article 4 of the OECD Convention requires Parties to prosecute the offense by applying the traditional jurisdictional criteria of their own systems. In more detail, Article 4(1) requires jurisdiction to be established over the bribery of foreign public official when the offense is committed in whole or in part in the territory of the State Party concerned.[7] Official Commentary 25 provides us with a key interpretative note by adding that:

---

7 OECD Convention, Article 4(1). Official Commentary 25 adds: "the territorial basis for jurisdiction should be interpreted broadly so that an extensive physical connection to the bribery act is not required".

"(t)he territorial basis for jurisdiction should be interpreted broadly so that an extensive physical connection to the bribery act is not required".

On the other hand, Article 4(2) requires only State Parties which already prosecute their nationals for offenses committed abroad to do the same in respect of bribery of foreign public officials. In addition, paragraph 4 of the same Article invites State Parties to review whether their current bases for jurisdiction are "effective in the fight against foreign bribery of foreign public officials and, if not" to "take remedial steps". In commenting on this Article the current President of the OECD WGB, Pieth (2007) admits that this approach to jurisdiction is rather timid and likely to become obsolete. He further remarks that, as a result of the continuous review of the effectiveness of the basis of jurisdiction envisaged by Article 4(4), active nationality will likely soon be part of the standard of all State Parties.

Turning to the EU text, under EU Article 7(1)(a)–(c) both territoriality and nationality seems prima facie mandatory. Again, Member States shall establish jurisdiction based on nationality when the offender is an official of the EC institutions as listed in Article 4(1) of the same treaties. In addition, according to Article 7(1)(d), jurisdiction shall be established when "the offender is a Community official working for a European Community institution or a body set up in accordance with the Treaties establishing the European Communities which has its headquarters in the Member State in question." However, the mandatory language of Article 7(1)(a)–(d) is watered down by the following Article 7(2) according to which "each Member State may declare" – when giving the notification to the Secretary-General of the Council of the European Union of the completion of the procedures laid down by its constitutional requirements for adopting the Convention – "that it will not apply or will apply only in specific cases or conditions one or more of the jurisdiction rules laid down in paragraph 1 (b), (c) and (d)". To put it in more simple words, Member States are left with the option of not modifying their respective traditional regimes dealing with criminal jurisdiction.

Article 17(1)(a) of the CoECLCC lays down the principle of territoriality. As it is not subject to reservation, this criterion is the only one to be always mandatory. It does not require that a corruption offense as a whole be committed exclusively on the territory of a State to enable it to establish jurisdiction. Paragraph 1(b) sets out the principle of active nationality, whereas paragraph 1(c) is also based on the principle of protection (of national interests). The difference with the previous paragraph is that here jurisdiction is based on the bribed person's status: either s/he is a public official or a member of a domestic public assembly of the Party (therefore not necessarily a national) or s/he is a national who is at the same time an official of an international organization, a member of an international parliamentary assembly, a judge, or an official of an international court. Article 17(2) allows States to enter a reservation to the jurisdiction grounds laid down in paragraph 1, (b) and (c). According to the Explanatory Report to the CoECLCC, in such cases, however, it stems from the principle of *aut dedere aut iudicare* set forth in paragraph 3 that there is an obligation for the Contracting Party to establish jurisdiction over cases where extradition of the alleged offender was refused on the basis of his nationality and the offender is present on its territory. In light of the recognition that in the field of corruption the territoriality and nationality principles may not always suffice to exercise jurisdiction, for example over cases occurring outside the territory of a Party, not involving its nationals, but still affecting its interests, paragraph 4 of this Article allows the Parties to establish, in conformity with their national law, other types of jurisdiction.

The AU Corruption Convention follows typical jurisdictional grounds for investigation and prosecution: the place of commission of the offense, the nationality and residence of the offender, and the presence of the offender in a given territory. In what might be considered a slight deviation from the traditional jurisdictional grounds, Article 13(d) of the AU Corruption Convention also permits a State Party to exercise its authority based on a consequences-or-effects test, which is satisfied "when the offence, although committed outside its jurisdiction, affects, in the view of the State concerned, its vital interests or the deleterious or harmful consequences or effects of such offences impact on the State Party." The coverage may potentially be extremely broad. Particularly worthwhile is the "deleterious and harmful consequences" grounds for jurisdiction. This provision presents at least two serious problems. First, the assessment of such consequences is left entirely to the subjective determination of the given State Party. Secondly, as pointed out by Snider and Kidane (2007), it is very likely that this provision will face serious challenges in being implemented by some State Parties endowed with mature constitutional systems.

13.5 THE TREATY-BASED MECHANISMS: AN EFFECTIVE AND COMPREHENSIVE SOLUTION?

The answer cannot be plain and univocal. To the extent that offenses under the Convention, and particularly the offense of transnational bribery, are complex and capable of commission in more than one jurisdiction, the application of the requirements illustrated above, if strictly followed by States Parties to establish only one place where an offense can be committed, may limit jurisdiction. In this regard, the jurisdictional provisions may not prove to be adequately developed. Overall, despite the opportunity to adopt binding obligations as to additional heads of jurisdiction (besides territoriality), the instruments at issue maintain the relative freedom left to States by customary international law on this matter. In contrast, the fact that the principle of territoriality has been increasingly challenged by transnational crimes is widely and indisputably recognized. The anti-corruption treaties seem to lay down a heteronymous mechanism which in principle could properly address the challenges posed by the transnational nature of the crime. However, a deeper analysis of the provisions at issue leads to controversial results. Some choices reveal a consistent and effective design, whereas other solutions are open to question.

First, by interpreting the Convention pursuant to the general rules of treaty interpretation (especially, the teleological approach and principle of effectiveness), it could be maintained that there is no need for an extensive physical connection to the criminal conduct in order to assert jurisdiction on the basis of territoriality, which, as highlighted, is the most common head of jurisdiction by far. A simple email/call from a certain state territory, which authorizes a foreign bank to transfer money to another foreign bank, might suffice as part of the relevant offense. In the same vein, even extraterritorial attempts intended to have effects on the territory could suffice if the relevant national legal system adheres to the subjectivist theory of attempt (i.e. the intent to commit an offense is punishable per se, with no need to be supported by outward behavior): in this case, the State on whose territory the offense was planned to be carried out could claim jurisdiction, even though the plan had not resulted in any external act.

Secondly, the imposition of territoriality as the only compulsory jurisdictional basis – as well as the specific obligations with respect to the coordination of efforts when more than one national investigation occurs reflects the Parties' concerns about the maintenance of their discretion on the matter, and, at the same time, the aim of getting the most out of the coordination of actions of those States which can assert their criminal jurisdiction in the relevant case.

Finally, the clear (although non-mandatory) indication of comprehensive and alternative approaches implies at least a *political* commitment to considering additional criteria, and answers the echo of those who maintain the need for a more far-reaching system.

This is confirmed inter alia by some of the official documents which are supposed to orientate the implementation of the international anti-corruption conventions. So far so good.

Yet, the treaty solutions leave some noticeable open questions. Indeed, whilst alternative heads of jurisdiction are expressly mentioned, their non-mandatory nature does not appear apt at properly addressing certain challenges posed by the transnational nature of corrupt crimes. For one thing, as illustrated by Mann in 1964, "in view of the steadily increasing reluctance to *localize* facts, events, or relationship", territorial principles' ability to cope with borderline situations has to be reconsidered.[8] Aside from *passive nationality* (since victims of corruption are frequently hardly identifiable) and with some reluctance to resort to the *protective principle*, other jurisdiction criteria (especially, *active nationality*) are needed to address *pure* extraterritorial offenses, also because the assertion of criminal jurisdiction over extraterritorial conduct of aliens on the basis of the *effects* doctrine remains controversial, if apparently not objectionable in all cases. In order to understand why it could be problematic to assert criminal jurisdiction on the basis of territoriality over corruption conduct where the transnational hook is merely represented by the *effect* it should suffice to highlight that corruption is almost invariably considered to be a conduct offense and not a result offense. The result of corruption is thus not a constituent element of the offense: as such, under international law, it does not suffice to justify the assumption of legislative jurisdiction.

Notwithstanding the above, there is a discernible trend that several national legal systems are increasingly adopting nationality as head of criminal jurisdiction. Arguably, by inviting the Parties to consider adopting it (along with other alternative criteria), the Conventions would drive the remaining States to extend their criminal jurisdiction on this basis, respecting, at the same time, their autonomy. This viewpoint sounds reasonable.

Alas, the related solution does not bridge the jurisdictional gaps permitted by the deployment of corporate entities in corruption operations: "a test developed . . . at a time when corporations did not yet play a predominant role in international life is unlikely to satisfy a generation which is suspicious of rigidity and, indeed, of principles".[9] On the other hand, the lack of precise obligations in this respect appears somewhat inconsistent with the relevant role played by the Conventions at issue in promoting new paradigms for sanctioning legal entities.

Regardless of the particular model of liability of legal persons at issue, the application of nationality seems an indispensable path towards the

---

8 Mann (1964: 27–8). see also Viscount Simonds in *Metliss v. National Bank of Greece*, 1958, AC, pp. 509 ff., p. 524.

9 Mann (1964: 28).

prevention and punishment of corruption where committed through foreign subsidiaries of complex corporate entities. The latter, indeed, may use their branches in secret havens as channels for the payment of the bribes. States where the head office of the corporate entity is located may have an obvious interest in sanctioning this conduct, as the chances that these offenses will be punished in such secret havens are, to say the least, low.

However, even a general application of the active nationality head of jurisdiction is not plain in these cases. Pieth (2007) rightly argues that the application of nationality to foreign corporate crimes requires solving a preliminary primary issue, namely determining the nationality of a corporation. The possibility that crimes committed by foreign subsidiaries go unpunished has been pointed even outside academia.[10]

We wonder whether, in the particular area of the jurisdictional issues raised by corrupt offenses committed through corporate entities, the various treaties could have dared more. *Binding* commitments, which set up a mechanism to establish ex ante the jurisdiction of the country where the parent is established/incorporated over extraterritorial crimes of the foreign subsidiaries (or their officers/employees), represent a solution worthy of further consideration in all its possible elements of complexity (e.g. the clear establishment of the nature/intensity of the link between the parent companies and its subsidiaries sufficient to trigger the legal liability of the former). Of course, such a path is not without hurdles: it is impossible to imagine its adoption, unless in the context of wider legislative reforms in domestic legal systems. Such reforms should be shared by a common will of many States: without such a common design, intergovernmental organizations' initiatives will hardly succeed, for they are likely be perceived as excessive concessions to international fora in the field of criminal law. We think that as to this matter the testimony of public prosecutors who frequently strive in the hard task of investigating transnational corruption cases is particularly meaningful: for instance, Rosi (2007), who expresses the stance of a public prosecutor often involved in transnational corrupt cases, opines that the absence of concrete and functional domestic regulations as to the modalities for consultation and coordination among States, which may assert jurisdiction over transnational crime, does not raise optimism in this respect.

By the same token, unilateral actions by single States are likely to be fiercely criticized. Moreover, it appears that, at a national level, a general theory of group liability has not yet reached the stage to defeat the general

---

10 See, for instance, the survey titled The Short Arm of the Law (2002).

rule of corporate separateness. Again, *soft law* appears manifestly inadequate for such an aim.

A political step toward establishing greater transparency of legal persons through coordinated efforts is taken by the Resolution 5/4 adopted at the fifth session of the Conference of the States Parties to the UNCAC (25–29 November 2013), which encourages States "to exchange best practices in the identification of beneficial owners of legal structures used to commit crimes of corruption or to hide or transfer their proceeds". Although constituting an important appeal for governments to take action, the latter Resolution presents some problems, not only for its non-binding character, but also because of the undefined contours of the concept of "beneficial ownership", which does not have an unequivocal legal meaning. To better address the latter notion, StAR (2011a: 3), in its analysis of the links between large-scale corruption and the concealment of stolen assets through opaque corporate structures, has stressed the significance of embracing a substantive approach which focuses both on the exercise of control and on the benefit derived.

More generally, StAR (2011a) constitutes an insightful tool which provides practical guidance to States in order for them to meet international standards designed to tackle the misuse of legal entities within grand corruption schemes. It is thus relevant to briefly recall the other outcomes and recommendations of the report.

Broadly speaking StAR (2011a) aims at enhancing the transparency in the ownership, control and benefit of corporate vehicles, and calls on governments to elaborate a detailed policy which fills up the gaps existing between the compliance on paper and in practice. For this reason the following five issues are considered crucial to address:

1) Firstly, the information available at company registries should be improved and made more easily accessible.
2) Since company registries have serious limitations in practice, the latter source of information can only be a starting point which has to be complemented. Hence another crucial actor in this context, i.e. service providers,[11] should collect ownership information and allow access to

---

[11] StAR (2011: 267) defines Trust and Company Service Providers as:

> [A]ny person or business that provides any of the following services to third parties: acting as a formation agent of legal persons; acting as (or arranging for another person to act as) a director or secretary of a company, a partner of a partnership, or a similar position in relation to other legal persons; providing a registered office, business address or accommodation, or correspondence or administrative address for a company, a partnership, or any other legal person

it. The key role of some corporate service providers as facilitators of corruption through the setting up of shell companies is also pointed out by Sharman (2013: 3–4),[12] who deems such companies "the most common mechanism by which the proceeds of corruption are transferred and laundered". In his view, governments should focus on practical matters and intervene with effective means like licensing corporate service providers and imposing on them a duty to establish the true identity of their customers. In this regard, development agencies could play an important role by ensuring the adoption of the latter duties in developing countries, where international financial centers are emerging. At the same time, the highly liberalized financial markets of OECD countries constitute fertile grounds for shell companies to be incorporated and therefore policy coherence should also be established among government agencies and within relevant international organizations. Finally, as shown through the Seychelles example, Sharman (2013: 3) contends that best practices could be learned from non-OECD countries which, as a result of international pressure, have elaborated comparatively robust regulatory and implementation regimes.

3) Considering that both service providers and registries have a vital role for law enforcement to access beneficial ownership information and

---

or arrangements; acting as (or arranging for another person to act as) a trustee of an express trust; or acting as (or arranging for another person to act as) a nominee shareholder for another person.

12

Untraceable shell companies are the most common means of facilitating grand corruption. . . . They are just legal personalities; they do not produce any goods or services. They are identities that can be created or annulled by a legal fiat within days at a cost of between few hundred and few thousands dollars. The majority of shell companies are used for legitimate purpose . . . Yet the combination of legal personality, intangibility, and disposability means that the shell company becomes a very useful mechanism to those who seek to conceal criminal funds, including the proceeds of corruption. In particular, where transactions are booked or assets held in name of a shell company, rather than in the criminal's own name, this obscures the trail from a given crime to the funds that result (Sharman, 2012: 1).

As the non-governmental organization Global Witness (2012:4) points out: "Shell companies . . . are the key to the outflow of corrupt money that keeps poor countries poor. Those who loot state funds to corrupt or deprive the state of revenues through tax evasion need more than a bank: they need to hide their identity behind a corporate front." Thus it is of capital importance to remove the "corporate veil" represented by companies that cannot be traced and, thus, be able to link shell company with the real owner.

that relevant information about corporate vehicles may be dispersed across different jurisdictions, countries should ensure that a resident person maintains beneficial ownership information on any entity incorporated under its laws. To achieve such requirement, StAR (2011a: 8) proposes, for example, to impose the latter obligation on a resident director or other corporate officer, or on a resident registered agent or a service provider;

4) Another problematic issue to be tackled with regard to the transparency of ownership and the control of corporate vehicles is represented by companies that have issued bearer shares and bearer-share warrants: for such legal entities it is in fact difficult to know who owns the shares at any given point in time. The solution put forward as fourth point is either to immobilize these shares (effectively rendering them registered shares) or to abolish them;
5) The fifth issue to be addressed relates to the skills and capacity of investigators on the use of corporate vehicles. In light of the disparity of knowledge, expertise, technology and resources across jurisdictions, StAR (2011a: 9) considers it a priority to make the existing gaps narrower through "greater education, development, and training of investigators". This last recommendation becomes particularly meaningful considering that corruption schemes are often transnational and investigators from different jurisdictions should be able to receive assistance from each other in an "adequate and timely manner".

The need to better put into practice the formal commitments taken by governments which emerges from StAR (2011a) is also stressed by Sharman (2012: 3–4), who highlights the key role of shell companies in grand corruption cases and elaborates a few remarks as to the way the latter issue should be addressed. On the one hand he argues that the issue should be given greater emphasis within policy deliberations and forums dealing with development; similarly, counterparts of development agencies should also be aware of the real impact of the issue. On the other hand the author maintains that more action by governments is needed, especially in relation to FATF Recommendation 24, which clearly and straightforwardly states that "countries should take measures to prevent the misuse of legal persons for money laundering or terrorist financing. Countries should ensure that there is adequate, accurate and timely information on the beneficial ownership and control of legal persons that can be obtained or accessed in a timely fashion by competent authorities" (FATF, 2012).

Finally, some doctrinal attempts to envisage alternative solutions in respect of the issue of jurisdiction for corporate entities bear testimony to the significant difficulties of designing a clear and effective strategy at the international level.

Sacerdoti (2003) points out that the balance between different systems could be reached through non-criminal sanctions over legal entities. That should allow leaving aside the strict territorial links necessary for asserting criminal jurisdiction, sanctioning operations committed by foreign controlled subsidiaries. This solution stands outside penal law and needs to accurately balance criminal and non-criminal answers, which seems prima facie no easy task.

Some other authors like Valenti (2003) and Pieth (2007) advocate a decisive role by the monitoring mechanism provided for by international treaties themselves. Effective supervision on the part of these mechanisms should encourage States to extend their extraterritorial jurisdiction in order to ensure the effectiveness of their conventional commitments.

Draetta (2003) indicates as a promising avenue to be explored the possibility of prosecuting the parent for crimes committed by subsidiaries *in the interest or to the benefit* of the parent, where such criminal/administrative liability of legal entities is established by the relevant national legal system. The gist of this thesis is that only very specific and minor cases could exonerate the parent company from any liability; according to Draetta, one should imagine cases of crimes committed by a foreign subsidiary totally upon the initiative of one of its officers/employees, which result in no advantage for the parent. Again, the crucial element to assess the efficiency of this strategy would be the specific national regime on corporate liability envisaged for the peculiar offenses at stake.

All of the sensible solutions just illustrated assume that prescriptive jurisdiction on the parent companies' crime is asserted on nationality. In addition, they manifestly rely to a significant extent upon the existing and/or implementing national pieces of legislation: Sacerdoti's on a proper balance between different sorts of sanctioning regimes over companies; the second strategy on the review of national legislation stimulated by the treaties' monitoring systems; the last on a sophisticated regime of liability to be assessed on a case-by-case basis. In the end, their achievements widely depend on a shared design by the States concerned, without which an international binding commitment addressing the particular issue of jurisdiction over corporate crimes could not take place.

In conclusion, since corporate entities are far more efficient at delocalizing their activities than individuals, to require the application of nationality for corruption offenses perpetrated through foreign subsidiaries stands as the necessary prerequisite for repressing transnational corruption operations involving legal entities. An obligation in this respect, along with the treaty provisions on legal persons' liability, would constitute the basis upon which States could shape suitable *coordinated* enforcement activities. As stressed by Pieth (2007), the approach just submitted would also accord with the emerging solidarity concept, portrayed as "far more concerned with the foreign public goal than the previously more introspective attitude of the traditional Nation State".[13] As seen while illustrating StAR's recommendations the strategy at issue should then be complemented with substantive initiatives at both the international and national level which focus on the exercise of control of corporate vehicles and benefit derived.

A final remark. A binding international commitment, demanding the application of nationality over legal entities for corruption offenses perpetrated through foreign subsidiaries, would not simplistically move a problem unsolved at a domestic level to the treaty-mechanism. Rather, it would entrench an even deeper connection between international and national legal systems over the mid to long period.

In other words, the solution put forward still significantly relies on devices already enshrined in the anti-corruption treaties (such as, for instance, follow-up mechanisms), but requires that States progressively accept that a de-localized and more cooperative legal strategy probably represents the most effective response to de-localized criminal phenomena.

Our concern is whether there is the political will to find a feasible framework for that strategy, given that, as witnessed by Rosi (2007), nobody, not even the smallest State, seems willing to renounce criminal jurisdiction in the name of a more effective repression of serious crimes and a common emerging solidarity.

---

13 Pieth (2007: 271), according to whom "(a)s a part of the reorientation towards a more co-operative approach" the protected legal interest has been redefined with a view to serving the purpose of protecting foreign interests. See also Cassani (1996: 237).

14. Mutual legal assistance and extradition

Another aspect which deserves particular attention has to do with the dynamic and the mutual influence amongst the various international instruments which, while different in subjective and objective scope, have continuously influenced each other. If one pays enough attention, she/he will find a common "*fil rouge*" in all these legal documents. It clearly seems that as far as certain provisions are concerned, the drafters have always been influencing each other, resulting in the step-by-step positive evolution of the international legislation and practices against corruption. In our opinion, this holds in particular with regard to the measures on mutual legal cooperation and extradition.

14.1 UNCTOC

Starting our analysis with the provisions of the UNCTOC Convention dealing with extradition and mutual legal assistance, they are similar to provisions already in place in many regional or bilateral agreements. The major significance of these provisions is that a large number of States were expected to ratify the Convention, making legal assistance and extradition available much more widely than was the case at the time of the negotiations. Such provisions are intended to set minimum standards only. States may go further in bilateral or regional arrangements and are, in fact, encouraged to do so. Under Article 16, extradition from another State Party may be sought for the specific offenses established by the Convention independently of the involvement of an organized criminal group, given that the offense itself is punishable by the domestic laws of both States.

Where extradition is refused solely on the ground that the person concerned is a national of the requested State Party, the requested State Party must, at the request of the State Party seeking extradition, submit the case without undue delay to its competent authorities for the purpose of prosecution (*aut dedere aut prosequi*, Article 16, paragraph

10).[1] States Parties may not refuse a request for extradition on the sole ground that the offense is also considered to involve fiscal matters (Article 16, paragraph 15).

Pursuant to Article 18, States Parties are to provide one another with the widest measure of mutual legal assistance for investigations, prosecutions or judicial proceedings in relation to offenses covered by the organized crime convention. The provisions of this Article can be used to obtain statements or other evidence, conduct searches or seizures, serve judicial documents, examine objects or sites, obtain original documents or certified copies, identify or trace proceeds of crime or other property, obtain bank, corporate or other relevant records, facilitate the voluntary appearance of persons in the requesting State Party or obtain any other form of assistance permitted by the laws of the required State Party (Article 18, paragraph 3). Since the range of assistance available is generally consistent with many existing agreements on legal assistance, the provisions of the Convention are of major significance in that they extend mutual legal assistance to a much greater number of States than was previously the case.

According to Article 18, paragraph 8, of the Convention, States Parties to the Convention may not decline to render such mutual legal assistance on the ground of *bank secrecy*.

In addition, the UNCTOC also provides the general basis for conducting joint investigations (Article 19), cooperation in special investigative procedures such as electronic surveillance (Article 20) and law enforcement cooperation (Article 27). The development of domestic training programs (Article 29) and the provision of technical assistance to other States in training matters (Article 30) are also encouraged.

Monitoring of the UNCTOC is carried on by means of a Conference of States Parties, which also has the power to recommend improvements. Nonetheless, no specific time frame is set: reviews need only be made "periodically" (Article 32). Moreover, there is no process for verifying country reports.[2] Only a clause in the general assembly resolution

---

1 Literally "extradite or prosecute", as in the English version of recent international agreements. This principle is the modern application of Grotius's maxim *aut dedere aut punire*. On account on the presumption of innocence, Grotius's tenet has evolved to the *aut dedere aut judicare* maxim. Currently, it is widely admitted that the obligation for the requested State is to prosecute rather than to judge, where, for example, there is no sufficient supporting evidence: hence the eventual evolution of the wording from *judicare* to *prosecui*. For a systematic study on the principle *aut dedere aut judicare* see e.g. Bassiouni (1999b: 333 ff.); Wise (1999: 15 ff.).

2 McClean (2007: 298) remarks that "(l)ittle need be said about this Art., which is descriptive of the work of the Conference of State Parties, about which more can gathered from the reports of the meetings of the Conference" For

55/25 adopting the Convention embodies the decision that the Ad Hoc Committee would complete its tasks arising from the elaboration of the Convention by holding a meeting well before the convening of the first session of the Conference of the Parties and other rules and mechanisms described in Article 32, being communicated to the Conference of the Parties at its first session for consideration and action.

A relevant breakthrough of the UNCTOC is that it "did introduce the idea of mandatory criminalization requirements at the global level and established a wide range of cooperation and technical assistance provisions" (Webb 2005: 204). What is more, its relatively rapid negotiation and entry into force demonstrated that there was a sufficient level of consensus for an international agreement on corruption and, specifically, for intensifying the mechanism for mutual legal assistance on a much wider basis.

The procedural provisions of the Convention accomplish two primary objectives: setting forth jurisdictional grounds and laying out enforcement mechanisms. As mentioned above, the provisions regarding international cooperation and mutual legal assistance play a key role within the framework of the Convention. For a long time issues of criminal justice policy were thought of in almost exclusively national terms. Given the frequent use of international financial channels to effect and hide transnational bribery, a prompt and effective mechanism of mutual legal assistance must be developed, at least, among State Parties of anti-bribery treaties in order to ease investigation and prosecution of this kind of offense.

14.2 OAS CONVENTION

Reflecting this aim, the OAS Convention requires State Parties, to the extent permitted by their national laws, to cooperate and provide mutual legal assistance (Article XIV). This obligation includes situations where transnational bribery or illicit enrichment may be involved, provided that such acts are crime under a party's national law.

Notably, the OAS Convention precludes the use of bank secrecy laws and limits the use of the political offense exception as bases for refusing to cooperate.[3]

---

a comprehensive study of the mechanisms of mutual legal assistance, see e.g. Gilmore (1995); Huet and Joering-Joulin (2005); McClean (2002), chapters 5–10 and the literature referred to therein; Bassiouni (1999b: 333 ff., esp. 347–86). With specific reference to transnational crime I refer to e.g. Prost (1998).

3 See Article XVI (Bank Secrecy) of the OAS Convention. Note that, at the same time, each requesting State is obligated not to use any information received

Extradition treaties among the Parties are, as a matter of fact, extended to encompass the criminal offenses which result by implementing the Convention. The legal basis for extradition is also provided between Parties that do not have an extradition agreement (Article XIII of the OAS Convention). The principle *aut dedere aut prosequi* finds a tenuous application in the OAS Convention: not only is it subject to the provisions of the domestic law of the requested State and its extradition treaties, but the requested State is also invited to verify that ". . . the circumstances . . . are urgent" (Article XIII(7)). Also, to ease the mutual cooperation that is decisive for prompt and effective prosecution, Article XVIII anticipates the possibility of direct notifications between the designated competent authorities of the State Parties, in lieu of diplomatic channels.[4]

Finally, as all the anti-corruption treaties provide in some way – that is to say, addressing it directly or, indirectly, by way of provisions on seizure and confiscation[5] – it addresses the issue of *recovery of asset*. The subject is dealt with in Article XV, which provides for assistance by other States Parties "in the identification, tracing, freezing, seizure and forfeiture of property or proceeds obtained, derived from or used in the commission of offenses" defined in that Convention. The formulation of such a provision seems aimed at the proceeds of criminal business, but, unlike the later EU, COE, and OECD Conventions, it may possibly be read as explicitly including stolen property. However, it does not require that States Parties enact laws allowing seizure and forfeiture, but only that they assist one another in enforcing any such laws.

---

that is protected by bank secrecy for any purpose other than the proceeding for which that information was requested, unless authorized.

4 As above, Article XVIII (Central Authorities).

5 See Schroth (2005b: 15) who points out: "Apply the hammer of penal law, rather than the tools of Property law (although there is a hint of the latter in the EU's documents, noted below). In particular, their provisions are framed in terms of confiscation of the proceeds of crimes of corruption, rather than of restitution (common law) or vindication (civil law) of state property. The historical basis of this approach is efforts against drug dealers, some of whom have amassed enormous profits from their illegal businesses. The analogy is not exact, however, because the businesses of drug dealers may be quite successful without any theft and theft of state property may be accomplished by dishonest officials without any business. That is, the 'proceeds' of crime can have two quite different senses, with possibly quite different consequences: one is the property of another that is taken unlawfully and therefore should be restored to its owner; the other is the profits of a forbidden business, such as trafficking in unlawful drugs. That said, it is difficult to find any support for the proposition that the drafters of any of the pre-2003 conventions meant to include stolen property in the concept of 'proceeds'."

14.3 OECD CONVENTION

Turning to the OECD Convention, it also contains detailed provisions on mutual legal assistance (Article 9) and extradition (Article 10). Article 9 lays down an obligation for signatory states reciprocally to provide prompt and effective legal assistance, for both criminal and non-criminal procedures. It is noteworthy that paragraph 3 of this provision forbids the refusal of assistance in criminal matters solely on the basis of bank secrecy.

The OECD Convention follows the classical model of the penal law conventions, such as those of the COE, in that it defines the offenses (Articles 1 and 7), the jurisdictional basis (Article 4), the secondary rules and the means of mutual cooperation between the Contracting States in matters of assistance and extradition (respectively, Articles 9 and 10).

In more detail, the OECD Convention's multilateral obligations consist of mandatory obligations to cooperate and assist other Parties in the investigation and prosecution of transnational bribery. Parties' obligations regarding mutual legal assistance, including grounds for refusal and bank secrecy, are set forth in Article 9 of the Convention.

In addition, the OECD Convention obliges Parties to take measures to enable the seizure and confiscation of illegal proceeds from corruption-related offenses (Article 3(3)) and sets standards for handling jurisdictional conflicts between Parties (Article 4(3)).[6] Again, unlike the OAS Convention, which is silent on the issue of penalties, the OECD Convention requires States Parties to institute a comprehensive apparatus in this field, requiring inter alia "effective, proportionate and dissuasive criminal penalties" comparable to those applicable to bribery of the Party's own domestic officials (Article 3(1)).

Moreover, as already mentioned, the OECD Convention establishes that where a Party's domestic law does not subject legal persons (e.g. corporations) to criminal responsibility, the Party shall ensure that legal persons are "subject to effective, proportionate, and dissuasive non-criminal sanctions, including monetary sanctions" (Article 3(2)).

Besides, the Convention also contains detailed provision on mutual legal assistance (Article 9) and extradition (Article 10). Article 9 lays down an obligation for signatory States to provide reciprocally prompt and effective legal assistance, for both criminal and non-criminal procedures.

---

6 See also Sacerdoti (2000); Borlini and Magrini (2007). For a detailed analysis of the mechanisms of international cooperation in the OECD Convention, I refer the reader to Harari and Berthod (2007: 407–44, esp. 409–12).

Paragraph 3 of this provision forbids the refusal of assistance in criminal matters solely on the basis of bank secrecy.

Notably, the OECD Convention requires, in Article 3(3), that Parties make "the bribe and the proceeds of the bribery of a foreign public official" subject to seizure and confiscation (or comparable monetary sanctions). However, the OECD Convention does not explicitly mean recovery of stolen property. Article 9(1) also requires assistance to other Parties "for non-criminal proceedings within the scope of this Convention brought by a Party against a legal person". As Schroth (2005b) highlights, in case anyone might doubt that the latter term excludes human individuals, it should suffice to recall that Article 5 refers to "natural or legal persons".

Turning to the obligation concerning international legal cooperation, since the State Parties to the Convention emanate from very different legal systems, the OECD Convention attempts to coordinate the different models' criminal liability for foreign public officials in order to achieve a minimum standard. On the one hand, the Convention addresses mutual legal assistance (Article 9) and extradition aspects (Article 10) of cooperation in the battle against foreign bribery, and, as with the corresponding provision of the OAS Convention, mandates Contracting States to establish proper aspects of communication to ease the implementation of Articles 9 and 10, and 4(3) (concerning the accommodation of possible overlaps of jurisdiction). On the other hand, it does not set forth a new standard, mainly referring to the pattern designed by the existing agreement. Article 9 lays down an obligation for signatory States to provide reciprocally prompt and effective legal assistance for criminal as well as non-criminal proceedings.[7] The rationale for the provision is plain: no legal jurisdiction can nowadays effectively investigate and prosecute transnational forms of crimes by means of isolated proceedings. Thus, Article 9(1) requires State Parties to keep requesting authorities informed of implementation of any demand for judicial assistance, such as searches, transmission of documents, or dispositions of witnesses. This binding

---

7 Article 9(1) of the OECD Convention which reads as follows: "Each Party shall, to the fullest extent possible under its laws and relevant treaties and arrangements, *provide prompt and effective legal assistance* to another Party for the purpose of criminal investigations and proceedings brought by a Party concerning offences within the scope of this Convention and for non-criminal proceedings within the scope of this Convention brought by a Party against a legal person. The requested Party shall inform the requesting Party, without delay, of any additional information or documents needed to support the request for assistance and, where requested, of the status and outcome of the request for assistance" (emphasis added). See, *ex multis*, Sacerdoti (2000) and Harari and Berthod (2007: 409–12).

commitment has unquestionable value for judicial authorities and prosecutions, who often complain of the lack of collaboration by other States, and, above all, when collaboration is provided, for delays in obtaining information and documents of crucial relevance for investigative and prosecuting activities. Pursuant to Article 9 the requesting authority must also be informed, if such is the case, of the need to provide additional elements and information. Also this specification should be read under the general aim of providing the most effective and complete assistance.

The obligations under discussion are further specified by the Official Commentary on Article 9, with regard to "... persons, including persons in custody, who consent to assist in investigation or participate in proceedings".[8] The Official Commentary calls on Contracting States "... upon request" to "... facilitate or encourage the presence or availability" of such subjects.[9] In addition, "Parties should take such measures to be able in appropriate cases, to transfer temporarily such a person in custody to a Party requesting it and to credit time in custody in the requesting Party to the transferred person's sentence in the requested Party. . . .".[10] The clarity of the provision and the obligations it contains do not compensate for a structural problem of the mechanism of assistance envisaged by the OECD Convention. The execution of rogatory commissions in corruption cases is frequently a lengthy procedure, likely to "get stuck" in certain countries, thus frustrating effective prosecution in the requesting country where the entire documentation, in particular banking documents, is located abroad. This can undermine the effectiveness of investigation (especially when the statute of limitations looms) and, additionally, make it problematic to guarantee individuals' rights (in light of the need to go to trial within a reasonable time).

Up to now, within the OECD context, there has been lacking a mechanism which would allow mutual legal assistance to be handled directly, i.e. without going through diplomatic channels. Such a model is now working within the context of the EU, where, pursuant to Articles 6 and 7 of the Convention on Mutual Legal Assistance among Members of the European Union of 29 May 2000, there can be spontaneous exchanges of information.

We thus subscribe to the position of the WGB members that "(s)implifying the procedures for applying the OECD Anti-Bribery Convention in this way would have the dual merits of accelerating and reinforcing relations

---

8 See the Official Commentary 31 to Article 9 of the OECD Convention.
9 Ibid.
10 Ibid.

among prosecutors, who . . . are not always interested solely in facilitating execution of international rogatory commissions".[11] Promptness and speed of assistance are factors that are by no means secondary: this is even more the case for transnational crimes in a global context. Another possible useful avenue for the OECD Convention States to explore is the possibility to require, especially in complex cases, continuous and close cooperation among the law enforcement authorities of different States, and to promote joint inter-State investigating teams. This would allow evidence to be assembled in one State in accordance with local legal requirements, but in such a way that it could be usefully exploited by the judicial authorities of the other State. Again, the paradigm for such cooperation could be that existing within the European Union context thanks to the European Convention on Mutual Legal Assistance (Article 13).

International conventions on criminal cooperation and national legal systems embody the so-called *dual criminality test*; a prerequisite of cooperation is that both the requesting and the requested Parties criminalize the conduct underlying the offense: the facts under investigation by the requesting State must be qualified as a criminal offense in the legal system of the requested State. Usually, the dual criminality test is applied *in abstracto*, i.e. the requested State does not have the obligation to ascertain the guilt or innocence of the offender or the existence of extenuating circumstances. The latter State has only the obligation to verify that the conduct constitutes an offense in both States. Article 9(2) addresses the dual criminality requirement, confirming the *in abstracto* paradigm. What is more, to tackle the impediment to international cooperation created by dual criminality, it encourages the establishment by all State Parties of the same offense of bribery of a foreign public officials. However, since the Convention does not require full uniformity, but only functional equivalence, a generous interpretation of the dual criminality requirement is required when effective mutual legal assistance is to be ensured:

> (w)here a Party makes mutual legal assistance conditional upon the existence of dual criminality, dual criminality shall be deemed to exist if the offence for which the assistance is sought is within the scope of this Convention.[12]

---

11 Pieth and Lelieur (2007: 3).

12 See OECD Convention, Article 9(2). Further details of this provision can be found in Official Commentary 32, which states: ". . . (p)arties with statutes as diverse as a statute prohibiting the bribery of agents generally and a statute directed specifically at bribery of foreign public officials should be able to cooperate fully regarding cases whose facts fall within the scope of the offences described in this Convention."

The aim of facilitating prompt and effective legal assistance also inspires Article 9(3), which excludes the refusal of assistance in criminal matters solely on the basis of bank secrecy. The latter provision mirrors a neat position of the OECD Convention drafters, and may be of crucial relevance as regards the relation among State Parties of the Convention. Like similar norms of other treaties (e.g. the OAS Convention, CoECLCC, and UNCAC),[13] the provision at hand aptly makes clear that the disclosure of bank account details is often crucial evidence in corruption cases. Nonetheless, it should not be forgotten that several offshore "heavens" are not signatories of the treaty at hand, and this circumstance materially reduces the impact of Article 9 on the effectiveness of investigations and prosecutions.

Some remarks.

Firstly, when legal assistance is requested of a State that is not a Party to the Convention, Article 9 does not apply. As a consequence, such requests must be executed in accordance with multilateral or bilateral conventions for mutual legal assistance, when they exist. This situation can give rise to several difficulties. From a strictly legal viewpoint, the main problem has to do with dual criminality. In fact, bribery (*recte*: active bribery of foreign public officials) is not necessarily a crime in all other States. Even if a request for legal assistance might be receivable for corruption in general, it could fail because the bribery of foreign public officials is not specifically a crime. Similarly, the granting of mutual legal assistance could be stymied by banking secrecy (of the Convention).

It is noteworthy that these two questions are covered by the UNCAC. Article 43.2 of the latter treaty provides that the condition of dual criminality is deemed to be fulfilled irrespective of whether the laws of the requested State classify or denominate the offense in the same way as the requesting State.[14] Article 46.8 stipulates that States may not decline to render mutual legal assistance on the ground of bank secrecy.[15] In principle, the ratification

---

13 See OAS Convention, Article XVI; CoECLCC, Article 26(3); UNCAC, Article 46(8). Note that the 1988 United Nations Convention against Drug Trafficking, Article 7(5) was the first to take this stand. See United Nations Convention against Illicit Traffic in Narcotic Drugs and Psychotropic Substances (E/Conf./82/1528, in 28 ILM, 1989, pp. 493 ff.; hereinafter: the 1988 Vienna Convention), adopted 19 December 1988. The text of this Convention is also available at: www.unodc.org/pdf/convention_1988_en.pdf, last visited 22 March 2008. The 1988 Vienna Convention, entered into force 11 November 1990, still constitutes the central instrument within international cooperation on the fight against drug trafficking.

14 See UNCAC, Article 43.2.

15 Ibid., Article 46.8.

of the UNCAC by all the Parties to the OECD Convention might represent a way out of the impasse just described. If all States were Parties to the UN Convention, whether or not they are Parties to the OECD Convention, the two problems would be circumvented, at least in legal terms. Consequently, ratification of the UN Convention could perhaps be a political priority for States party to the OECD Convention, with the WGB perhaps in future being empowered to monitor this matter. Additional consideration should also be given to seeking other solutions. From a practical viewpoint, improving cooperation between the judicial authorities of States Parties and other countries would seem to be essential.[16]

Article 10 on extradition does not contain innovative stands compared to the general regime envisaged by international treaties on criminal cooperation. Firstly, Article 10(1) seeks to set a wide basis for extradition among Parties to the Convention, by requiring that the offense being introduced according to Article 1 be an extraditable offense under their laws and extradition treaties between them.

Secondly, in order to facilitate the execution of extradition requests, Article 10(2) establishes that the Convention may be considered to form the legal basis for extradition if the extradition relations of the requested Party are conditional on the existence of an extradition treaty and no such a treaty exists between the State Parties involved.

Thirdly, Article 10(3) embodies the principle *aut dedere aut prosequi*. State Parties are required either to take appropriate measures for extradition of their nationals, or to prosecute them in respect of conduct contrary to Article 1. As observed by Harari and Berthod (2007), States have frequently considerable difficulties in trying a person outside the territorial jurisdiction of the court. As of today, the most remarkable achievements in the area of extradition have been accomplished among States which already enjoy very close relations of a political and judicial nature: for instance, the Member of the COE[17] and, even more significantly, the Member States of the EU.

---

16 In a report of 16 October 2003 entitled Overcoming Obstacles to Enforcement of the OECD Convention on Combating Bribery of Foreign Officials (available for download at: www.transparency.org), Transparency International suggests that the Working Group should organize periodic meetings attended by law enforcement officials from Convention States and from non-party States – in particular developing countries – for the purpose of improving channels of cooperation on foreign bribery cases. This idea surely merits consideration.

17 In Europe the leading role in developing cooperation in criminal law matters has traditionally been played by the CoE. Beginning with the 1957 Convention on Extradition (signed on 13 December 1957, in force since 1960), 1959 Mutual Assistance in Criminal Matter (signed on 20 April 1959, in force since 12 June 1962) and their additional protocol (COE 1975, 1978b, 1978a, 2001), the COE

Finally, under Article 10(4), the dual criminality requirement, often prescribed in the country to which an extradition request is addressed,[18] is considered to be fulfilled when the offense for which it is requested falls within the scope of the OECD Convention. Thus, implementation alone by the requesting Party should suffice as a basis for extradition. As international cooperation in criminal matters is governed by a wide range of international agreements, among which the instruments adopted within the framework of the COE and EU are the more advanced, for the Parties of whose instruments the OECD Convention only supplements their substantive legislations. Arguably, in light of the fact that more than two-thirds of the Parties to the OECD Convention are located in Europe, "the OECD Convention is therefore not in the forefront of practical innovation" (Harari and Berthod 2007: 441).

14.4 CoECLCC

In a similar vein, also the CoECLCC deals with the procedural issues related to mutual legal assistance. It provides for enhanced international cooperation in the prosecution of the corruption offenses defined therein, in particular regarding extradition, mutual judicial assistance and the exchange of spontaneous information.[19] The Convention also contains provisions concerning jurisdiction,[20] the setting up of specialized anti-corruption bodies,[21] protection of persons collaborating with the investigating or prosecuting authorities,[22] and gathering of evidence and confiscation of proceeds.[23]

As regards mutual assistance, it foresees that parties will create special designated central authorities to deal with requests in a prompt manner.[24] While mutual assistance may be refused if the request undermines the fundamental interests, national sovereignty, national security or *ordre public* of the requested party,[25] it may not be invoked on the grounds of bank secrecy.[26]

---

has made further remarkable advances in judicial cooperation by developing commonly used instruments, which mirror general concepts and are adhered to by most European States.

18 The condition of dual criminality is deeply rooted in extradition practice.
19 See, respectively, Articles 21, 27, 26 and 28.
20 Article 17.
21 Article 29.
22 Article 22.
23 Article 23.
24 Article 26(1).
25 Article 26(2).
26 Article 26(3). This provision is drafted along the lines of that of Article

Article 19(3) of the Criminal Law Convention on Corruption requires each Party to adopt the measures necessary to enable it "to confiscate or otherwise deprive [sic] the instrumentalities and proceeds of criminal offenses established in accordance with this Convention, or property the value of which corresponds to such proceeds" and Article 23 requires assistance to other Parties in the enforcement of such measures. Paragraph 93 of the Explanatory Report attached to the Criminal Law Convention ties Article 19(3)[27] to the COE's 1990 Convention on Laundering, Search Seizure and Confiscation of the Proceeds of Crime,[28] which, it reads, is "based on the idea that confiscation of the proceeds is one of the effective methods in combating crime". As already noted when commenting on the OECD Convention's provisions on international cooperation on criminal matters, the Member States of the COE enjoy privileged political and judicial relations, and the Organization itself has traditionally been at the forefront as regards international cooperation in criminal matters. Thus, the procedural provisions of the CoECLCC should be looked at within the broader framework of the number of relevant treaties addressing judicial cooperation, adopted by the COE's Member States.[29]

14.5 AU CONVENTION

As to the AU Convention, the international cooperation provisions include extradition;[30] tracing, seizure, and confiscation of proceeds of corruption;[31] and mutual legal assistance.[32] The AU Convention also

---

18, paragraph 7 of the Convention on the Laundering, Search, Seizure and Confiscation of the Proceeds of Crime (8 November 1990, ETS 141). As we have seen, a similar provision is also to be found in the OECD Convention on Combating Bribery of Foreign Public Officials (Article 9, paragraph 3). Before affording the assistance required, involving the lifting of bank secrecy, the requested Party may, if its domestic law so provides, require the authorization of a judicial authority competent in relation to criminal offenses. See Explanatory Report to the Criminal Law Convention on Corruption, paragraph 126.

[27] Explanatory Report to the Criminal Law Convention on Corruption, paragraph 93.

[28] Convention on Laundering, Search Seizure and Confiscation of the Proceeds of Crime, Strasbourg, 8 November 1990, ETS 141, text available at: http://conventions.coe.int/Treaty/EN/Treaties/Html/141.htm.

[29] The text of treaties on judicial cooperation, adopted by the CoE's Member States are available for download at: www.coe.int.

[30] See AU Convention, Article 15.

[31] Ibid., Article 16.

[32] Ibid., Article 18.

provides for the revocation of bank secrecy defenses that might be available in the course of investigations, tracing, and confiscation efforts. International cooperation also extends to collaboration with non-parties so that corrupt officials may not be able to enjoy "ill-acquired assets" in countries that are not a party to the Convention.[33] Notably, the AU Convention stresses the importance, although in non-mandatory language, of eradicating corruption in development aid,[34] even though, unfortunately, it does not mention corruption in humanitarian aid.

Finally, the AU Corruption Convention maps out two important steps with respect to international cooperation: (1) the creation or designation of a national authority for purposes of mutual legal assistance and cooperation, and (2) the establishment of an advisory board on corruption within the AU as a follow-up mechanism (Advisory Board).[35]

14.6 UNCAC

Chapter IV (International cooperation) of the UNCAC deals with mutual legal assistance and extradition as well. As with other anti-corruption conventions, the UNCAC provisions on these issues are designed to operate as independent treaties where permitted by local laws. Furthermore, they are also intended to supplement existing extradition and mutual legal assistance treaties. As in other parts of the Treaty, the provisions in each area are exceedingly meticulous, and would require many pages to fully explore.

The general approach of the UNCAC is to try to create a broad enabling framework for international cooperation in investigations and enforcement proceedings, and to eliminate impediments (such as dual criminality requirements and bank secrecy laws) that are thought to have hindered prosecutions in the past. Article 40 requires that, in cases of domestic investigations of offenses established in accordance with the Convention, States Parties have appropriate mechanisms available within their domestic legal system to overcome obstacles that may arise out of the application of bank secrecy laws. Moreover, Article 46(8) excludes bank secrecy as a ground to decline mutual legal assistance. Even if bank secrecy has begun to erode in recent years, aided by other conventions that restrict

---

33 Ibid., Article 19(8).

34 Article 19(4).

35 See Article 22. The role and limits of the Advisory Board are addressed in Chapter 16, Section 16.5, subsection titled AU Convention.

its use as a defense against criminal law enforcement, it has by no means been eliminated. Therefore, the inclusion of this provision is potentially quite important.

The presence of similar provisions in the OAS and OECD Conventions mirrors an important step in the international strategy to curb this crime. However, those treaties apply only *between* State Parties, and not towards State Parties. Given its universal vocation, were the UNCAC extensively implemented at the national level, the chance of relying on bank secrecy to deny mutual judicial cooperation would be significantly reduced.

The possible obstacle to international judicial cooperation represented by dual criminality is addressed by Article 43(2) and Article 46(9).[36] Once again, the interpreter faces exceedingly articulated provisions. However, the underlying orientations seem to be the following: firstly, Article 43(2) provides that the condition of dual criminality is deemed to be fulfilled irrespective of whether the laws of the requested State classify or denominate the offense in the same way as the requesting State;[37] secondly, it is possible for a requested State Party to decline to render assistance on the basis of the absence of dual criminality where this assistance entails coercive measures such as arrest, search or seizure,; thirdly, Parties are invited to adopt legislative measures in order to set up a wider scope of assistance in the absence of dual criminality; fourthly, the provisions mentioned above are, however, affected by parenthetical clauses that make it

---

36 Such provisions are the results of a compromise. In the context of the negotiations it emerged that:

> (a) key issue in developing the international cooperation requirements arose with respect to the scope or range of offences to which they would apply. The broad range of corruption problems faced by many countries resulted in proposals to criminalise a wide range of conduct. This in turn confronted many countries with conduct they could not criminalise (for example, the illicit enrichment offence) and which were made optional as a result. Many delegations were willing to accept that others could not criminalise specific acts of corruption for constitutional or other fundamental reasons, but still wanted to ensure that countries which did not criminalise such conduct would be obliged to cooperate with other States which had done so Vlassis (2007: 27).

As a consequence, the "dual criminality requirements were narrowed as much as possible within the fundamental legal requirements of the States which cannot criminalise some of the offences established by the Convention". (ID.)

37 As Vlassis (2007: 27) puts forward: "(t)he underlying rule, applicable to all forms of cooperation, is that where dual-criminality is required, it must be based on the fact that the relevant States Parties have criminalised the conduct underlying an offence, and not whether the actual offence provisions coincide".

highly discretionary for a State to effectively tackle the dual criminality impediment.

The relevant provisions of this Chapter are self-executing in nature. Unlike the criminalization provisions, they require that no implementing legislation be passed by countries that are party to the UNCAC. By way of example, States are bound by the Convention to render specific forms of mutual legal assistance in gathering and transferring evidence for use in court in order to extradite offenders. States are required to undertake measures to support the tracing, freezing, seizure and confiscation of proceeds of corruption as well.

In some cases such provisions will be subject to existing national laws, while in others, they will be affected by treaties. Accordingly, they do not operate in a legislative vacuum. Whether or not a criminalization of a particular offense is mandatory or permissive under Chapter III, Chapter IV applies once that offense has been implemented at the national level. The character of the cooperation obligation imposed by Chapter IV depends in some cases on whether the offense is one for which dual criminality (criminalization in both the requesting and requested State) is present. For instance, Article 44 (Extradition) applies on a mandatory basis to offenses for which there is dual criminality between the country making the extradition requests and the country where the person whose extradition is requested is present. It is almost pleonastic to stress that, without such dual criminality, the provisions contained in Article 44 apply only on a permissive (discretionary) basis with the requested country. As in other anti-corruption treaties, the underlying rationale is to create a mechanism for extradition within the treaty, without having to resort to other treaties or national laws.

The drafters have, however, recognized that some countries (such as, for instance, the US) require that an extradition treaty exists with any country to which it extradites. In order to accommodate that country's judicial system, the UNCAC, by means of a rather debatable solution, *encourages* States that do not accept the Convention as a basis for extradition to seek to conclude such treaties with other UN Convention countries to implement this Article.[38]

It is noteworthy that the grounds for refusing extradition under the UN Convention are restricted. Article 44(15) establishes that:

> Nothing in this Convention shall be interpreted as imposing an obligation to extradite if the requested State Party has substantial grounds for believing that

---

[38] UNCAC, Article 44(6)(b).

> the request has been made for the purpose of prosecuting or punishing a person on account of that person's sex, race, religion, nationality, ethnic origin or political opinions or that compliance with the request would cause prejudice to that person's position for every one of these reasons.[39]

Any grounds for refusal to extradite present in domestic law or applicable extradition treaties may be invoked as well.[40]

On the positive side, the UNCAC permits States Parties to adopt measures to further the simplification and improvement of the extradition process, including through systems of backing or recognizing foreign arrest warrants.[41]

Following a sensible approach that has already inspired the UNCTOC, the UNCAC establishes that the fact that the offense involves fiscal (tax) matters must not be a ground for refusing to extradite.[42] In earlier times, extradition was not available for fiscal offenses. This choice manifestly reflected a reluctance by States to reinforce the fiscal law of other States. Nowadays, it is clear that in the context of corrupt offenses, and offenses related to it (e.g. organized and economic crimes), criminal activity may well be associated with tax fraud. Therefore, the paragraph under discussion has obvious merits.[43]

Mutual legal assistance is required under the UN Convention for a wide collection of activities, although confidentiality requirements and limited use principles may be applied. Bank secrecy is not a basis for refusal (Article 46(8)). Nor, as noted above, is there a defense for a fiscal request. Nonetheless, States retain various grounds for refusal, including sovereignty, security, public order, and other essential interests.

As aptly remarked by Low (2008), some of these grounds are potentially

---

39 Ibid., Article 44(15), verbatim.

40 Ibid., Article 44(8).

41 As explained by UNCAC (2009: 151):

> (t)he backing of warrants schemes is a simplified form of surrender between States which represents a relatively recent stage in the evolution in extradition, marked by the mutual recognition of arrest warrants whereby an arrest warrant issued by a competent authority in one State is recognized as valid by one or more other States and is to be enforced. One of the best examples of such a scheme is the Commonwealth Scheme, which mainly applies to common-law tradition States Parties. Variants of the scheme are successfully applied between such jurisdictions as Singapore, Malaysia and Brunei; Australia and New Zealand; and the United Kingdom and certain Channel Islands.

42 Ibid., Article 44(16).

43 Note that McClean (2007) puts forward analogous comments in relation to Article 16(15) of the UNCTOC.

BOX 14.1 REFUSAL TO EXTRADITE AND BILATERAL TREATIES: THE CASE OF HENRIQUE PIZZOLATO IN THE BRAZILIAN *MENSALÃO* SCANDAL

Article 44(8) of the UNCAC may be relevant in a case involving the Italian and Brazilian jurisdictions.

The ex-director of *Banco do Brasil*, Henrique Pizzolato, was sentenced in 2012 to more than 12 years in jail for money-laundering, embezzlement and active corruption charges within the *Mensalao* (literally, "big monthly allowance") scandal together with many other Brazilian politicians, businessmen and bankers.

By the time the Supreme Court issued the arrest warrant against him in November 2013, he had already fled Brazil for Italy: according to Pizzolato's lawyer, his decision was driven by the fact that, unlike prosecutions in Brazil, Italy could offer a "media-free" trial.

The relevance of the latter case in the present context lies in the fact that Pizzolato, although Brazil has not yet submitted any request to the Italian authorities, may well benefit from the ground of refusal provided for by Article 44(8) of the UNCAC.

Because Pizzolato is not only a Brazilian but also an Italian citizen, Italy may in fact decide not to extradite him pursuant to Article 6(1) of the Treaty on Extradition between Italy and Brazil of 1989, which allows any of the two parties to refuse the extradition of its own citizens. As a consequence, the latter ground for refusal may also be a valid one pursuant to Article 44(8) of the UNCAC.

None of the other Anti-corruption Conventions may compel Italy to extradite Pizzolato to Brazil: however, an alternative option may be feasible to ensure his prosecution. According to Article 44(11) of the UNCAC but also to Article 16(10) of the UNCTOC and Article 10(3) of the OECD Convention,[44] if Brazil decides to request the extradition of Pizzolato without success, the principle of *aut dedere aut prosequi* will induce Italy to submit the case to its competent national authorities for prosecution.

---

44 Italy and Brazil are both parties not only to the UNCAC but also to the UNCTOC and to the OECD Convention.

As explained in UNODC (2009: 149), the latter obligation should be read together with Article 42(3) of the UNCAC, which requires State parties to establish the proper jurisdictional basis when the requested State "does not extradite such person solely on the ground that he or she is one of its nationals".

very broad, especially if the refusing State is permitted to define their scope, meaning that the concrete effectiveness of the UNCAC drastically depends on how States implement its non-self-executing provisions and enforce both its self-executing provisions and the national laws implementing the treaty.

More to the point, Article 47 provides for States to consider the transfer of criminal proceedings from one state to another of cases involving Convention-related offenses where such transfer "is considered to be in the interests of the proper administration of justice, in particular where several jurisdictions are involved, with a view to concentrating the prosecution".[45] According to Low (2008), this goes a step beyond other Conventions' very general, and soft, obligation in Article 42 of reciprocal consultations where multiple proceedings arise, and is potentially very useful.

Article 49 established the possibility of joint investigations,[46] and Article 48 calls for transboundary law enforcement cooperation. Like much else in the Convention, these two Articles attempt to reconcile the pressing realities of contrasting corruption effectively with State sovereignty. The wording of Article 49 is unequivocal in establishing their non-mandatory nature. Whilst mutual legal assistance can remarkably facilitate the investigation and prosecution of transnational crimes, in complex cases closer cooperation is essential.[47] Joint investigations, with personnel recruited from two or more States, may prove more effective. Notably, the municipal law of each State normally allows only the officers of that State to take action. Thus, not only does an attempt by a foreign officer to exercise those functions fail, but it also offends against State sovereignty. Joint

---

45 UNCAC, Article 47.

46 See UNCAC, Article 49. The relevance of such a form of cooperation in the investigative process within the framework of transnational crime is authoritatively highlighted by Rosi (2007). Since the author has been actively involved in several investigations concerning transnational forms of crime, we believe that Rosi brings a meaningful testimony on the potential utility of well-established mechanisms for joint investigation.

47 This is the view of many authors and practitioners. See, among others, Rosi (2007); McClean (2007: 238).

investigations reduce these issues to small practical problems, as the "local" members of the team may act on behalf of their foreign colleagues where necessary. Article 49 is limited to the investigative phase and imposes no legal obligation on State Parties, but encourages standing arrangements in bilateral form (e.g. as between two adjacent countries) or multilateral form (for instance, within the EU), or, on case-by-case arrangements.

On a side note, the EU Convention on Mutual Assistance in Criminal Matters of May 2000[48] takes this matter further, by providing a telling example of a regional multilateral arrangement. In short, it provides for the appointment as team leader of a person representing the criminal investigation authority of the State in which the team operates. A seconded member may request his or her own national authorities to take measures which are required by the team, without any further request under the Convention.[49]

Experience to date with other international conventions remaining under the patronage of the UN (two telling example are the United Nations Convention against Illicit Traffic in Narcotic Drugs and Psychotropic Substances – which might be regarded as the archetype of "universal" conventions against transnational forms of crime – and the UNCTOC) has demonstrated that the cooperation provisions are potentially the most significant tools of this sort of agreement, especially where transnational offenses are concerned. That is mainly because the evidence is almost by definition located in multiple jurisdictions. At present, international cooperation is much more developed than was the norm ten years ago.

The crucial importance of international cooperation within the framework of the UNCAC also emerges from UNODC (2009: 139), which emphasizes the need for "more effective, responsive and prompt international cooperation to combat corruption" through more confidence in foreign legal systems. At the same time UNODC (2009: 163) recalls the practical significance of implementing the measures which concern mutual legal assistance (Article 46 of the UNCAC) in light of the international mobility of the people committing corruption offenses and considering the increasing development of technology and international banking practices. In order to establish an efficient and effective level of mutual trust among national authorities, UNODC (2009: 140–141) identifies the challenges and limits which should be carefully addressed by the State parties:

---

48 See OJ C197, 12 July 2000. The Official Explanatory Report appears at OJ C379, 29 December 2000.

49 See European Union's Convention on Mutual Assistance in Criminal Matters, Article 13(3)–(7).

> (i) the absence of adequate and appropriate legal framework to help States Parties implement their treaty obligations; (ii) the existence of overly complex, cumbersome and formalistic procedures that impede the provision of assistance in an expeditious manner, as well as (iii) the lack of resources or experienced personnel and the limited institutional capacity to foster cooperation.

More recently in the field of mutual assistance and cooperation one should also take note of Resolution 5/1 adopted at the fifth session of the Conference of the States Parties to the UNCAC (25–29 November 2013). The latter Resolution, besides further encouraging cooperation among State Parties and identifying the promotion, facilitation and support of international cooperation as one of the priorities and purposes of the UNCAC, touches two points of more practical relevance. Firstly, it *recommends* that State Parties consider the conclusion of bilateral agreements and arrangements in order to better prevent, detect and prosecute natural and legal persons committing corruption offenses. Secondly, it *decides* to bring together the next intergovernmental meeting of experts on international cooperation under the UNCAC with the corresponding Working Group on International Cooperation under the UNCTOC. While the former recommendation recalls Article 46(30) of the UNCAC and seeks to incentivize forms of enhanced mutual legal assistance between two States when it is deemed necessary and consistent with the Convention, the latter decision constitutes an important step taken by the Conference of the State Parties to rationalize the resources and to avoid the duplication of efforts in the overlapping field of international cooperation between the UNCAC and the UNCTOC.

A closer international cooperation at both formal and informal level and a mutual understanding of the misuse of legal entities are identified as priorities also by StAR (2011) which inquires about the abuse of corporate vehicles to conceal the proceeds of corruption.

On the whole, the UNCAC's provisions in this regard could have a profound impact, not only because of their depth and extent, but, most importantly, because "of their potential for creating a global, possibly even universal, enforcement network" (Low 2008: 19). Obviously the more countries ratify the Convention, the more potential this network could have. On the other side – and this holds true also for the provisions of the other anti-bribery treaties – the effective relevance of provisions relating to international cooperation must not be overstated, because many of the legal instruments they aim to reinforce are traditionally conditioned upon different requirements established both by national law and international agreements. These conditions characterize the general legal regime concerning international cooperation, and mainly attempt to properly balance the different interests at stake.

The UNCAC addresses also the issues of critical confiscation and special investigation techniques, namely the clause contained in Article 31(1) and that set forth in Article 50(1). As to the former, the clause may be read "as authorizing pre-emptive confiscation of the property of one who has not yet committed, much less been convicted of, any crime, if the property is 'destined for use in offenses established in accordance with this Convention,' but only "to the greatest extent possible within its domestic legal system".[50] As to the clause in Article 50(1), it seems to permit any "appropriate" use of "special investigative techniques, such as electronic or other forms of surveillance and undercover operations, within its territory", but only "to the extent permitted by the basic principles of its domestic legal system and in accordance with the conditions prescribed by its domestic law" (if any).[51]

14.7 EU INSTRUMENTS

The EU Anti-corruption Convention establishes that, in serious cases, these could include penalties involving deprivation of liberty which can give rise to extradition. Member States must take the necessary measures to allow heads of businesses or any persons having power to take decisions or exercise control within a business to be declared criminally liable in cases of active corruption by a person under their authority acting on behalf of the business.

The provisions on jurisdiction are rather precise: each Member State must take the measures necessary to set up its jurisdiction over the offenses it has established in accordance with the obligations arising out of this Convention in the following cases: when the offense is committed in whole or in part within its territory; when the offender is one of its nationals or one of its officials; when the offense is committed against European or national officials or against a member of the EU institutions who is also one of its nationals; when the offender is a European official working for a European Community institution, agency or body that has its headquarters in the Member State in question.

Articles 8 and 9 concern, respectively, the traditional issues of extradition and prosecution, and cooperation of Member States.

The principle *Ne bis in idem* is also clearly articulated. Member States may adopt internal legal provisions which go beyond the obligations set out in the Convention.

---

50 Ibid., p. 10, and Article 30(1) of the UNCAC.

51 See Article 50(1) of the UNCAC.

Looking more closely at the judicial cooperation in criminal matters within the EU area, the EAW decision[52], referred to above, deserves some further consideration since it probably represents one of the most advanced and articulated mechanisms of judicial criminal cooperation at the supranational level, with manifest potential also in terms of furthering prosecution of those involved in corruption-related offenses, against the interest of one or more Member States of the EU. At the beginning of 2004, a new procedure started being implemented within the EU introducing the so-called EAW. Such new mechanism replaces the traditional extradition proceedings among Member States.

The Framework Decision on the EAW and the surrender procedures between Member States of the European Union (EAW – Introduced by the Council of the European Union on 13 June 2002) is based on the principle of mutual recognition of judicial decisions, which is considered to be the cornerstone of judicial cooperation in criminal matters within the EU, and apply both to judgments and other decisions of judicial authorities. The Framework Decision defines "European arrest warrant" as any judicial decision issued by a Member State with a view to the arrest or surrender of a requested person by another Member State, for the purposes of conducting a criminal prosecution or executing a custodial sentence or a detention order (Article 1(1)). The EAW may be issued for acts punishable by the law of the issuing Member State by a custodial sentence or a detention order for a maximum period of at least 12 months or, where a sentence has been passed or a detention order has been made, for sentences of at least four months (Article 2, para. 1).

The EAW process is a complete substitution for the traditional extradition procedures between ratifying EU Member States with a simplified fast-track common arrest warrant system – streamlining and accelerating surrender procedures between them, as if they were a single jurisdiction, by introducing some innovative procedures.[53]

---

52 See supra Chapter 10.3 The Council Framework Decision of 13 June 2002 on the European arrest warrant and the surrender procedures between Member States (2002/584/JHA) (Acts adopted pursuant to Title VI of the former Treaty on European Union) is published in the Official Journal of the European Communities, 18.7.2002, L 190/1 and ff.

53 The EAW process is based on the following innovative principles: i) Expeditious proceedings: The final decision on the execution of the EAW should be taken within a maximum period of 90 days after the arrest of the requested person. If that person consents to the surrender, the decision shall be taken within ten days after consent has been given (Article 17). ii) Abolition of double-criminality requirement in prescribed cases: The deeply ingrained double-criminality principle in traditional extradition law is no longer verified for a list

With effect from January 2004, the EAW also replaced existing extradition treaties and agreements between EU Member States (insofar as they relate to extradition, these included: the 1957 European Extradition Convention and its protocols; the 1978 European Convention on the Suppression of Terrorism; the 1989 Agreement between the then 12 EU Member States on simplifying the transmission of extradition requests; the relevant provisions of the 1990 Schengen Agreement; the 1995 Simplified Extradition Convention; and the 1996 Extradition Convention). However those States can still enter into bilateral or multilateral agreements to further simplify or facilitate the surrender procedures. Notwithstanding a remarkable initial delay, the EAW is now operational in most of the cases provided for. According to the UNODC (2009: 153):

---

of 32 offenses, which, according to Article 2, para. 2, of the Framework Decision, should be punishable in the issuing Member State for a maximum period of at least three years' imprisonment and defined by the law of the Member State. These offenses include, inter alia, corruption and laundering of the proceeds of crime. For offenses that are not included in this list or do not fall within the three-year threshold, the double-criminality principle still applies (Article 2, para. 4). iii) "Judicialization" of the surrender: The new surrender procedure based on the EAW is taken outside the realm of the Executive and is placed in the hands of the judiciary. Both the issuing and executing authorities are considered to be the judicial authorities which are competent to issue or execute a EAW by virtue of the law of the issuing or executing Member State (Article 6). Consequently, since the procedure for executing an EAW is primarily judicial, it abolishes the administrative stage inherent in extradition proceedings, i.e. the competence of the Executive authority to render the final decision on the surrender of the person sought to the requesting State Party. iv) Surrender of nationals: The EU Member States can no longer refuse to surrender their own nationals. The Framework Decision does not include nationality as either a mandatory or optional ground for non-execution. Furthermore, Article 5, para. 3, provides for the option of making execution conditional on a guarantee that, upon conviction, the individual is returned to his/her State of nationality to serve the sentence there. v) Abolition of the political offense exception: The political offense exception is not enumerated as a mandatory or optional ground for non-execution of an EAW. The sole remaining element of this exception is confined to the recitals in the preamble of the Framework Decision (Recital 12) and takes the form of a modernized version of a non-discrimination clause. An additional deviation from the rule of speciality: Article 27, paragraph 1, of the Framework Decision enables Member States to notify the General Secretariat of the Council that, in their relations with other Member States that have given the same notification, consent is presumed to have been given for the prosecution, sentencing or detention with a view to carrying out of a custodial sentence or detention order for an offence committed prior to surrender, other than that for which the person concerned was surrendered.

> . . . its impact is positive, since the available indicators with regard to judicial control, effectiveness and speed are favorable, while fundamental rights are basically observed. In relation to the expeditious manner in which surrenders are carried out, it is provisionally estimated that, as a result of the entry into force of the Framework Decision, the average time taken to execute a warrant has fallen from more than nine months to 43 days. This does not include those frequent cases where the person consents to his/her surrender, for which the average time taken is 13 days.

Such figures seem in line with the very rationales of the main anti-corruption international treaties' provisions on mutual legal assistance: furthering and simplifying international judicial cooperation without infringing the fundamental rights of the accused persons. The inspiring principles of the EAW process, therefore, may be looked at as elements to be considered and transplanted in other contexts where international judicial cooperation may be intensified.

15. Preventive and non-criminal-related measures

15.1 PREVENTION

While criminal measures represent the core of most of international anti-corruption treaties, they also set mechanisms to make corruption difficult and prevent this phenomenon from flourishing.

OAS Convention

For instance, the importance of such measures in the context of the OAS anti-corruption treaty seems corroborated by the circumstance that they are established at the beginning of the Convention by Article III, although it contains the "laxest" measures in the hierarchy of the Convention. These provisions are non-self-executing and non-mandatory in nature (". . . the States Parties agree to *consider* the applicability of measures . . .").[1] Nonetheless the comprehensiveness of Article III is remarkable. The measures can be grouped in four primary areas.

Firstly, States Parties agree to *consider* systems for registering the income, assets, and liabilities of certain public officials and, where appropriate, to make that information public.[2] States Parties are also required to consider measures relating to transparency and accountability in government procurement and functions. In particular, States Parties agree to consider measures relating to government procurement and government hiring processes to guarantee their "openness, equity, and efficiency", and analogous measures regarding the government revenue collection and control systems that "deter corruption".[3]

Secondly, State Parties are required to consider measures to create, maintain, and strengthen ethics rules applicable to public officials.[4]

---

1 See Article III (Preventive Measures) of the OAS Convention; emphasis added.

2 See Article III (2)–(3) of the OAS Convention.

3 Ibid., Article III (5)–(6); See also Low (2008: 23).

4 Ibid., Article III(1)–(4). For further comments we refer to Low (2008: 23–4),

Thirdly, States Parties agree to consider measures to create, maintain, and strengthen prophylactic safeguards against corrupt activities by private concerns. Of particular relevance, at least as a matter of perspective, is the agreement of States Parties to consider laws that deny favorable tax treatment for expenditures made in violation of the States Parties' anti-corruption laws.[5]

They also agree to consider mechanisms to ensure that publicly-held companies and similar institutions "maintain books and records which, in reasonable detail, accurately reflect the acquisition and disposition of assets, and have sufficient internal accounting controls to enable their officers to detect corrupt acts".[6] Notwithstanding the significant results achievable by applying strict accounting regulations, the OAS Convention makes accounting provisions for the private sector optional.

As regards bank secrecy a rather cautious approach emerges: it is established that in the event of a request for assistance and cooperation, "the Requested state shall not invoke bank secrecy as a basis for refusal to provide" such assistance.[7] However, the potential impact of such provision is tempered by the final clause of the same paragraph 1 of Article XVI, which permits each Contracting Party to strike a balance between the conflicting aims of easing criminal prosecution and protecting personal data, by applying the Article at issue, "in accordance with its domestic law, its procedural provisions, or bilateral or multilateral agreements with the requesting State".[8]

In addition, States Parties agree to consider measures to protect public servants and private citizens who report acts of corruption ("whistleblowers"), including protection of their identities, according with the basic principles of States Parties' domestic legal systems.[9] Again, Contracting

---

who adds: "In particular, these include: standards of conduct for the 'correct, honourable, and proper fulfilment of public functions'; standards to prevent conflicts of interest; standards to 'mandate the proper conservation and use of resources entrusted to government officials'; and standards to require government officials to report acts of corruption to the appropriate authorities."

5 See Article III(7) of the OAS Convention.

6 Ibid., Article III(10).

7 Ibid., Article XVI(1).

8 Ibid., Article XVI(1).

9 Ibid., Article III(8). As detailed in Chapter 16 of this book, the Implementation of the Convention is overseen by the Mechanism for Follow-Up on the Implementation of the Inter-American Convention against Corruption (MESICIC). The reports show that apart from Canada, the US and Peru, most OAS countries do not have specific whistleblower laws, but most have some protection for whistleblowers contained in criminal laws, procedural laws or

States agree to consider measures "to advance the anti-corruption effort, including anti-corruption oversight bodies, programs to encourage broader involvement in the effort" (Low 2008: 24), along with further measures that answer for the correlation between "equitable compensation and probity [honesty] in public service".[10]

OECD Instruments

Coming to the OECD instruments, it is to be stressed at the outset that the Revised Recommendation of May 1997 (Article IV): "URGES the prompt implementation by Member countries of the 1996 Recommendation which reads as follows: 'that those Member countries which do not disallow the deductibility of bribes to foreign public officials re-examine such treatment with the intention of denying this deductibility. Such action may be facilitated by the trend to treat bribes to foreign officials as illegal'".[11]

This provision thus reinforces the 1996 Recommendation of the Council of Tax Deductibility of Bribes to Foreign Public Officials. The latter instrument is the result of a detailed review of Member countries' tax legislation commenced in 1994 by the Committee on Fiscal Affairs (CFA), the main tax-policy body of the OECD, in order to identify any provisions that may indirectly encourage the bribery of foreign officials. The CFA agreed that when such provision exists and where changes would effectively discourage the corruption of foreign public officials, tax administrators should be encouraged to make them. In its review, the CFA first assessed the effects of tax deductibility and non-deductibility of bribes to foreign officials. As a consequence, the CFA examined whether a deduction for such bribes should be either disallowed or subject to conditioned disclosure. On the proposal of the CFA, in April 1996 the OECD Council adopted the

---

labor laws. There is also a smaller group of countries without regulation on the subject. Reports frequently recommend measures of protection for whistleblowers where they are considered incomplete (e.g. Argentina, Brazil, Chile, Nicaragua, and Trinidad and Tobago). The latest reports on Bolivia and Paraguay call for the implementation of whistleblower systems, which have been enacted but then left aside. The report finds that in Bolivia, at least, whistleblowers are often persecuted. On the other hand, Costa Rica argues that no whistleblower system is necessary as – surprisingly – there have never been any reprisals against whistleblowers. Notably, in 2010 the OAS agreed a model whistleblower law. This model law was updated and approved by the OAS Anti-Corruption Mechanism on 19 March 2013.

10 See Article III(9), (11)–(12) of the OAS Convention.

11 Ibid., Article IV. See Recommendation of the Council of Tax Deductibility of Bribes to Foreign Public Officials, adopted by the Council on 11 April 1996.

Recommendation on tax deductibility, which calls on Member countries that allow deductibility, if bribes are to foreign officials, to re-examine it with the intention of denying such a regime.[12] It is noteworthy that the 1996 Recommendation has been strengthened by a new soft law instrument: the 2009 Recommendation of the Council on Tax Measures for Further Combating Bribery of Foreign Public Officials in International Business Transactions,[13] confirming the relevance of the issue.

Looking more closely at the non-penal provisions, it might well be argued that Article 8, which regards company accounting,[14] characterizes the Convention as certainly having a practical and innovative approach. As hinted above, this goes far beyond the penal framework and takes on a predominantly preventive function.

In more detail, Article 8(1) of the OECD Convention requires each State Party to adopt accounting and auditing standards prohibiting ". . . the establishment of off-the-books accounts, the making of off-the-books or inadequately identified transactions, the recording of non-existent expenditures, the entry of liabilities with incorrect identification of their object, as well as the use of false documents, by companies subject to those laws and regulations, for the purpose of bribing foreign public officials or of hiding such bribery."[15]

Article 8 resembles other provisions of the Convention. Article 8(1), for instance, like Article 5 (Enforcement) requires a precise action under the Convention's general mandate, that Parties take necessary (accounting and auditing) measures to "combat bribery of foreign public officials effectively". Article 8(2), like Article 3 (Sanctions), provides "effective, proportionate and dissuasive civil, administrative or criminal penalties" for violating the related provisions.[16]

The accounting standards required by the Convention aim to facilitate the identification and prosecution of individuals and entities involved in the bribery of foreign public officials. What is more, accounting standards, and sanctions for violating those standards, usually do not require a *scienter* requirement. Thus, the role of these standards in combating transnational bribery may be enhanced further. In the framework of OECD

---

12 See Millet-Einbinder (2000) and Uckmar (1995).

13 See: http://www.oecd.org/document/21/0,3746,en_2649_34859_2017813_1_1_1_1,00.html.

14 Here the term "accounting" is used to refer to all laws and regulations relating to "the maintenance of books and records, financial statement disclosures, and accounting and auditing standards . . .". Article 8.1, verbatim.

15 Article 8(1) of the OECD Convention.

16 Article 8(2) of the OECD Convention.

Convention, Article 8 is not an ancillary provision at all. On the contrary, it assumes fundamental importance in that the existence of a system aimed at eliciting reliable financial data is imperative in combating "supply-side bribery" – bribery focused on the bribe payer as opposed to the bribe recipient. Its purpose is to reinforce the preventive function of accounting requirements that already exist in national pieces of legislation and of controls on them for "grand" corruption abroad, which appeared from investigations in various countries. In line with the Convention's guiding principle of obtaining functional equivalence, Article 8 defers to Parties' national laws regarding the maintenance of books and records, financial disclosures, and accounting and standards to provide the framework for prohibiting the establishment of disguised slush funds, off-the-books accounts and other documentation deficiencies and omissions forbidden by Article 8 itself. The obligations set out by Article 8 should result in re-examinations by competent national authorities of the effectiveness of the internal accounting and audit controls in place (Sacerdoti 2003; Borlini and Magrini 2007).

Two further elements explicitly considered in the official Commentary and related to the obligations set out by Article 8(1) and (2) are to be addressed.

Firstly, Article 8 is also relevant to the consideration of the potential liabilities under the Convention (in particular its Articles 3 and 8) in financial statements of companies which are required to issue financial statements disclosing their material contingent liabilities.[17]

Secondly, it should be recalled (as the Commentary does) that they are also relevant to the discharge of their duties by auditors.[18] To put it more bluntly, after the entry into force of the OECD Convention, auditors are to be considered liable if they have not detected corruption by properly examining a company's balance sheets and other records.

The provisions of the OECD Convention regarding accounting standards must be read jointly with Section V of the 1997 Revised Recommendation, which lists the following "adequate accounting requirements":

---

[17] See Official Commentary 29 of the OECD Convention: ". . . One immediate consequence of the implementation of this Convention by the Parties will be that companies which are required to issue financial statements disclosing their material contingent liabilities will need to take into account the full potential liabilities under this Convention, in particular its Arts. 3 and 8, as well as other losses which might flow from conviction of the company and its agents for bribery".

[18] Ibid.: "This also has implications for the execution of professional responsibilities of auditors regarding indications of bribery of foreign public officials."

i) Member countries should require companies to maintain adequate records of the sums of money received and expended by the company, identifying the matters in respect of which the receipt and expenditure takes place. Companies should be prohibited from making off-the-books transactions or keeping off-the-books accounts.

ii) Member countries should require companies to disclose in their financial statements the full range of material contingent liabilities.

iii) Member countries should adequately sanction accounting omissions, falsifications and fraud.[19]

Even though the word "adequate" is repeated in both the Convention and the Revised Recommendation, neither of the two specifies what level and/or kinds of internal accounting controls are to be considered "adequate". This may be explained by the circumstance that suitability of internal accounting controls and standards depends on a range of aspects, which are unique to each entity (e.g. organization size, complexity, ownership characteristics, business nature, number of employees).

As regards the sanctions set out in Article 8(2) for the violation of the accounting requirements and transparency standards, the OECD Convention calls again for "effective, proportionate, dissuasive" sanctions for accounting offenses. It is noteworthy that the Convention does not require State Parties to adopt criminal sanctions for accounting offenses. Thus, deterring administrative and/or sanctions can perfectly comply with the Convention. This leeway leaves certain discretion to State Parties. However, as in the case of Article 3 (Sanctions), the question of what minimum standard of effectiveness is tolerated by the Convention is to be addressed by considering the key principle of functional equivalence. In addition, it should not be forgotten that there exist, within the international scenario, a number of conventions that provide tools which could be of use in contrasting corruption such as, for example, the many regional conventions dealing with money-laundering, search, seizure and confiscation of the proceeds of crime.

Finally, though the OECD Convention does not contain any explicit provision on the issue, the OECD WGB Working Group on Bribery (WGB) explores whistleblowing in its reviews, as Section IX(iii) of the 2009 Anti-Bribery Recommendation calls for measures to protect from disciplinary or discriminatory measures any public- and private-sector

---

19 See Organisation for Economic Co-operation and Development, Revised Recommendation of the Council on Combating Bribery in International Business Transactions, adopted by the Council on 23 May 1997, available at: www.oecd.org, accessed on 10 October 2007, Section V.

employees who report suspicions of foreign bribery to competent authorities.[20]

AU Convention

Some further considerations on preventive measures of the AU Convention. These measures are set forth in scattered provisions following some criminalization provisions and are very brief. In relation to the public sector, they require that all or at least "some designated" public officials "declare their assets at the time of assumption of office during and after their term of office in the public service".[21] The provisions also call for the creation of internal bodies or committees to establish, implement, and monitor codes

---

20 Whistleblower protection is seen as a horizontal issue which confronts its Member States. In its report the WGB has engaged rather frequently with the issue. For instance:

> the Phase 3 report on the UK points out that the law does not apply to nationals working abroad on contracts made under a foreign law. The Phase 3 report on South Korea cited the enactment of the 2011 law as an important development, since the law extends protective measures to private-sector employees who report foreign bribery cases. The Phase 3 report on Japan noted the requirement for a review of its 2004 law after approximately five years. As the Act came into force in 2006, the review took place in March 2011. It was conducted by the Consumer Commission – made up of representatives from academia, the business community, the legal profession, media, etc. They concluded there was no need to amend the Act but that, due to the insufficiency of legislative information for the review, further research was recommended. The Phase 2 report on Chile notes the 2007 law establishing whistleblower protection in the public sector, encourages the authorities to expand it to state companies, and recommends that Chile enhance and promote the protection of private- and public-sector employees. According to the 2009 follow-up report of the recommendations of the Phase 2 report, this recommendation has been only partially implemented. See TI (2013: 21).

For an in-depth illustration of the OECD follow-up mechanism see *infra* Chapter 16. Noticeably, this OECD anti-corruption initiative published guidance on whistleblower protection in 2012 (OECD, CleanGovBiz, 2012). Among the other things, the document shows that "Australia, Canada, Ghana, Japan, South Korea, New Zealand, Romania, South Africa, the UK and the US are among the countries that have passed comprehensive and dedicated legislation to protect public sector whistle-blowers". It also records that legal protection for whistle-blowers grew from 44 percent to 66 percent in OECD countries between 2000 and 2009.

21 Cf. AU Convention, Article 7(1).

of conduct for public servants.[22] They also require maintenance of internal accounting, auditing, and follow-up systems.[23]

Remarkably, these provisions are stated in non-mandatory language[24] and no particular penalizing scheme can be inferred for failure to comply with these requirements.[25] The absence of deterrent measures attached to the preventive provisions makes the latter likely to be ineffective. Even though the role of the public official remains central, the AU Treaty also includes a requirement to "adopt legislative and other measures to prevent and combat acts of corruption and related offences committed in and by agents of the private sector".[26] Furthermore, they also include the "establish[ment of]mechanisms to encourage participation by the private sector in the fight against unfair competition, respect of the tender procedures and property rights".[27] As part of the preventive measures, the AU Corruption Convention calls for the involvement of civil society and the media primarily to "hold governments to the highest level of transparency and accountability in the management of public affairs".[28] Overall, in spite of the apparent emphasis on the principles and objectives of the AU Corruption Convention, the prescribed preventative measures fall short of ensuring compliance because they require no penal or deterrent scheme, in contrast, for instance, to the FCPA's superior deterrent effect. The legal scholarship inserts the provisions on protection of whistleblowers among the measures with *lato sensu* preventive aim.[29] The AU Convention requires signatories to "adopt legislative and other measures to protect informants and witnesses in corruption and related offences, including protection of their identities"[30] and to "adopt measures that ensure citizens report instances of corruption without fear of consequent reprisals".[31] However, these efforts to ensure whistleblower protection may be undermined by a

---

22 Ibid., Article 7(2).

23 As above, Article 5(4).

24 See ibid., Article 7 ("In order to combat corruption and related offences in the public service, State Parties commit themselves to . . ."), Article 11 ("State Parties undertake to . . .").

25 Ibid., Article 7.

26 Article 11.

27 Ibid., Article 11(2). The AU Corruption Convention also calls for the adoption of "other measures as may be necessary to prevent companies from paying bribes to win tenders". Ibid., Article 11(3).

28 Article 12.

29 See AU Convention, Article 2(5) and (6). See e.g. Schroth (2005a: 33–4).

30 Article 5(5). The final clause of Article 5(5) suggests awareness of possible physical damage to whistleblowers.

31 Article 5(6).

provision calling on signatories to "adopt national legislative measures in order to punish those who make false and malicious reports against innocent persons in corruption and related offences",[32] which some scholars identify as one of the original aspects of the AU Convention. Such provision, the aim of which is to prevent a misuse of the Convention itself, might paradoxically well result in a general *impasse* of the investigation. What is more, in many countries the menace of such punishment is an effective deterrent to truthful whistleblowers who expose the guilty.[33] Even truthful assertions, indeed, may be very difficult to prove, especially "if the opposition of the court has the extensive resources of the state or a large corporation" (Schroth 2005b: 34). Overall, the general impression given by Article 5 is that the provision is badly worked out, resulting in inorganic discipline. Muna (2004) advances that other forms of redress, such as civil action, should normally suffice in such situations, without the side-effects of Article 5(7), whereas Schroth (2005b) maintains the need for a more nuanced provision amending the present text of Article 5 and "protecting even those whistle-blowers whose assertions turn out to be false, provided that they are not proved to have been unreasonable in the circumstances" (Schroth 2005b: 34).

UNCAC

The UNCAC devotes an entire chapter to preventive measures, with measures directed at both the public and private sectors. The underlying idea is plain: corruption can be prosecuted after the fact, but first and foremost it requires prevention. Unlike the AU Convention, several of these provisions contain complementary deterrent measures that make them more likely to be effective. Keeping in mind that most of the provisions are non-mandatory in nature, it remains to point out that the array of measures considered is significantly wide-reaching and, were such measures implemented by State Parties, they would be rather invasive and likely to entail relevant changes within the existing national laws.

The measures envisaged by the UNCAC include model preventive policies[34] (Chapter II, Articles 5–14). The UNCAC "contains a compendium

32 As above, Article 5(7).

33 For instance Schroth and Bostan (2004) point out that laws of this sort have sometimes dissuaded even the news media from reporting corruption in Romania.

34 UNCAC, Article 5, paragraphs 34–8. For a further and extremely detailed comment see the Legislative Guide to the UNCAC, paragraphs 2–168, pp. 16–54, and Borlini and Magrini (2007).

of preventive measures which goes far beyond those of previous instruments in both scope and detail, reflecting the importance of prevention and the wide range of specific measures which have been identified by experts in recent years" (Vlassis, 2007: 25), such as the establishment of anti-corruption bodies[35] and enhanced transparency in the financing of election campaigns and political parties.[36] States must endeavor to ensure that their public services are subject to safeguards that promote efficiency, transparency, and recruitment based on merit.[37] Once recruited, public servants should be subject to codes of conduct, requirements for financial and other disclosures,[38] and appropriate disciplinary measures.[39] Accordingly, those who use public services must expect a high standard of conduct from their public servants. State Parties must also promote transparency and accountability in matters of public finance.[40] Specific requirements are established for the prevention of corruption in particularly critical areas of the public sector such as the judiciary and public procurement, which should be based on the principles of transparency, competition and objective criteria in decision-making;[41] measures to prevent corruption involving the private sector; participation of society; and measures to prevent money laundering. Preventing public corruption also requires an effort from all members of society at large, in particular from so-called "civil society".[42] For these reasons, the Convention calls on States to promote actively the involvement of NGOs and community-based organizations, as well as other elements of civil society, and to raise public awareness of corruption and what can be done about it.[43]

As to the *private sector*, by means of a complex and largely non-mandatory in nature Article, State Parties are called on, "*in accordance with the fundamental principles of its domestic law*, to prevent corruption involving the private sector, enhance accounting and auditing standards in the private sector and, where appropriate, provide effective, proportionate and dissuasive civil, administrative or criminal penalties for failure

---

35 As above, Article 6.

36 As above, Article 7(2) and (3). The most intense debate during the negotiating process of the UNCAC was reserved for the provision on the financing of political parties.

37 UNCAC, Article 7(1)(a)–(d).

38 As above, Article 10.

39 As above, Article 8.

40 As above, Articles 9(2) and 10.

41 As above, Articles 9 and 11.

42 See Article 13.

43 Ibid.

to comply with such measures".[44] Such measures are further detailed in Article 12, paragraph 2(a)–(f) – which provides a non-exhaustive list of measures such as promoting the development of codes of conduct, preventing the misuse of procedures for subsidies and licenses, and preventing conflicts of interests – and paragraph 3, which addresses national regulations about the correct and regular maintenance of books and records, financial statement disclosures, accounting and auditing standards, and requires States Parties to prohibit off-the-books accounting.

Some further considerations on the point. The recognition that private sector corruption is a serious issue has been intensifying in developing and developed countries for manifold reasons. Firstly, the private sector is larger than the public sector in many countries.

A second and related reason is that the line between the public and private sectors is being blurred with the widespread *privatization* and outsourcing processes which have been characterizing the last two decades. Not only does privatization increase the number of public-oriented activities being conducted in the private sector, but it also generates opportunities for corruption through the very process of transferring the assets of large State enterprises. Insider dealing, assurances of lenient regulatory oversight, and retention of monopoly rents are to be expected.

Thirdly, as already hinted, the huge economic influence of multinational corporations and the resulting leverage they have in relation to States, means that they represent actors that can hardly be excluded from an effective international anti-corruption strategy.

Fourthly, corruption in the private sphere undermines values like trust, confidence, or loyalty, which are necessary for the maintenance and development of social and economic relations. From this perspective, civil remedies may not be sufficient. Even in the absence of a specific pecuniary damage to the victim, private corruption causes damage to society as a whole. This requires redesigning the rules that protect the interests of the private sector and govern its relations with its employees and the public at large.

According to Webb (2005), extending the Convention to cover the private sector was one of the most contentious issues during the negotiations.[45] The EU, consistently with the measures it has promoted among its Member States, headed the drive to criminalize bribery in the private sector. It was supported by the Latin American and Caribbean States whose representative argued that, in view of the linkage between the two sectors, adopting an approach restricted to the public sector "would adversely affect the

---

44 UNCAC, Article 12(1), verbatim (emphasis added).

45 Webb (2005: 213).

implementation of the future convention".[46] Nonetheless, the US resisted intrusions on "purely private sector conduct". A US official explained that private-to-private sector bribery was not a crime in the United States, and that sort of conduct is dealt with in different way by the US legislation. The US views prevailed in the final version of the Convention which only has a non-mandatory framework for criminalizing bribery and embezzlement in the private sector,[47] whereas a slightly stronger stance is set forth on prevention.

Preventive measures are not exhausted by Chapter II of the UNCAC. Some other provisions are to be found in other parts. For instance, the provisions of Articles 32 and 33[48] (as well as Article 35) – which are contained in Chapter III – address the protection of witnesses, thereby complementing efforts regarding the prevention of public and private corruption, obstruction of justice, confiscation and recovery of criminal proceeds, as well as cooperation at the national and international levels. Even though the aim is far from easy to achieve, the underlying rationale is obvious: unless people feel free to testify and communicate their expertise, experience or knowledge to the authorities, all objectives of the Convention could be undermined.[49] Consequently, States Parties are mandated to take appropriate measures, within their means and consistent with their legal system, against potential retaliation or intimidation of witnesses, victims and experts. States are also encouraged to provide procedural and evidentiary rules strengthening those protections as well as extending some protections to persons reporting in good faith to competent authorities about corrupt acts.[50] The Legislative Guide to the UNCAC asserts that measures

---

46 See Report of the Ad Hoc Committee for the Negotiation of a Convention Against Corruption on its third session, held in Vienna from 30 September to 11 October 2002, UN Doc. A/AC.261/9 (2002), at 3.

47 Articles 21 and 22 of the UNCAC.

48 As detailed by TI (2013c: 6):

> Article 33 is not about witness protection, which is covered by Article 32. The Technical Guide explains the difference by saying Article 33 was made to cover indications of corruption that fall short of evidence. In practice, there is an overlap as some whistleblowers may possess solid evidence, and become witnesses in legal proceedings, but the main point is that Article 33 covers early stages when there may well be no question of proceedings. Indeed, the ideal situation is where a whistleblower raises concerns in time so that action can be taken to prevent any offence.

49 See Articles 31, 32, and 35 of the UNCAC and Legislative Guide to the UNCAC, paragraph 430 at 141.

50 Legislative Guide to the UNCAC, paragraph 431, at 141.

of protection may include psychological support, institutional recognition of reporting, and transferring whistleblowers within the same organization or relocating them to a different one. In addition, in its discussion of Article 8, the Legislative Guide mentions that provision of confidential in-house advice to whistleblowers is also part of an effective protection system. UNODC (2009) mentions compensation and civil damages as protective measures.

Some further considerations on protection of whistleblowers should be put forward. As maintained also by TI (2013c), recent corruption-related scandals emphasize the importance to all economies of encouraging whistleblowers in all sectors to raise concerns before corruption hollows out and shatters economic, social and political institutions. In this respect, the main problem is to find out feasible and effective tools in order not to put whistleblowers in a dangerous version of the Hirschman's dilemma "exit" or "voice".[51]

In more detail, Article 33 of the UNCAC states:

> Each State Party shall consider incorporating into its domestic legal system appropriate measures to provide protection against any unjustified treatment for any person who reports in good faith and on reasonable grounds to the competent authorities any facts concerning offences established in accordance with this Convention.

According to the UNCAC review process,[52] there exist wide variations among States Parties in whistleblower protection. UNODC's thematic report of 27 August 2012 records that overall there is "an absence of specific regulations and systems" that where protective regulations do exist they often do not apply to private-sector employees.[53]

---

51 The treatise 'Exit, Voice, and Loyalty' (1970) is considered one of the masterpieces of the economist Albert O. Hirschman. The work hinges on a conceptual ultimatum that confronts consumers in the face of deteriorating quality of goods: either "exit" or "voice". The basic thesis can be summarized as follows: any member of an organization, whether a business, a nation or any other form of human grouping, has essentially two possible responses when they perceive that the organization is demonstrating a decrease in quality or benefit to the member: they can exit (withdraw from the relationship); or, they can voice (attempt to repair or improve the relationship through communication of the complaint, grievance or proposal for change). For example, the citizens of a country may respond to increasing political repression in two ways: emigrate or protest. In case of whistleblowers the "voice" option is even more dangerous, since it may bring about serious retaliations on the part of those who are reported.

52 See *infra* Chapter 16.

53 CAC/COSP/IRG/2012/7/Add.1, available at: www.unodc.org/unodc/en/

TI (2013: 6) argues that "there are important steps states should take beyond creating obligations for reports of offences to be made, anonymous hotlines, and provisions outlawing dismissal for whistleblowing". Furthermore, "(s)ome of the reasons why such measures do not suffice have been mentioned in country reports" (ID.)[54]

UNODC (2009) indicates the general criteria that States Parties should follow when establishing how to protect reporting persons. Since these subjects:

> may be concerned that they may face a variety of unjustified treatment (. . .) the tools to thwart such treatment are manifold. In general, the measures of protection should be commensurate to the danger, although care must be taken in cases where the reporting person is unaware of the seriousness of the report or of the possibility of subsequent inquiries becoming, as the report is investigated, disproportionate to the initial allegations (UNODC, 2009: 108).

First, States Parties should "consider the feasibility of ensuring anonymity to reporting persons. . . . Where the anonymity cannot be ensured, States Parties may consider whether criminalizing threats, intimidation or retaliation would be an effective way of providing protection to reporting persons" (ID.).[55]

---

treaties/CAC/IRG-session3-resumed.html. The UNODC thematic report of 14–16 November 2011 contains a synthesis of information on whistleblowing from the country reports then completed. From its points, made in a general way, it is clear there are widespread problems, as mentioned in 1.3. This is a very important and useful finding. The report highlights specific country examples, without identifying the country involved.

54 Among the most relevant we would recall: situations where the act has not yet taken place or when the whistleblower is not sure whether the behavior is corrupt; the conflict that is likely to arise when the whistleblower's report contains material that his/her employers have classified as confidential; situations where the normal reporting channels are tainted or inactive; forms of retaliation that do not amount to dismissal; and the burden of proof issue: dismissal and other reprisals are always likely to be presented as being carried out for other reasons, so a legal presumption that whistleblowing was the cause is essential.

55 Also reported by the UNODC, in this respect there exists a relevant jurisprudence of the "ECHR according to which the maintenance of the anonymity of the witness does not entail infringement of article 6 of the Convention on fair trial 'if the handicaps under which the defence laboured were sufficiently counterbalanced by the procedures followed by the judicial authorities'." (e.g., questioning the anonymous witness in the presence of counsel by an investigating judge who was aware of the witness' identity, even if the defence was not) (see *Doorson v The Netherlands*, Judgement of 26 March 1996, Appl. No. 20524/92, Reports 1996-II, paras. 72–73).

Secondly, they should "consider implementing provisions and procedures offering appropriate legal protection to reporting persons against the loss of employment, such as the possibility of judicial enforcement of continued employment or civil damages. Moreover, States Parties may bear in mind that reporting persons may face the risk of being professionally discriminated" (ID.).

As a consequence, State Parties should consider providing for legal remedies against such forms of reprisal.[56]

However, such criteria are rather general and probably, given the broad spectrum of States Parties they address, it could not be realistically otherwise. On the bright side we find more precise indications on the critical issues undermining effective systems aimed at protecting whistleblowers when looking at the outcomes of the aforementioned UNODC's thematic report of 27 August 2012, the recent TI's study on the issue and some national pieces of legislation on the matter.

Some exegetic issues about Article 33 must be addressed (TI, 2013). First, Article 33 encourages States to provide protection against "any unjustified treatment". Therefore, its scope is not limited to physical threats or dismissal. As a matter of fact, several legal systems establish measures to cover crude forms of retaliation. Yet, "there may be a gap as regards more subtle forms, which can have equally serious consequences (e.g. by forcing resignation). It is a strength of Article 33 that it has this wide scope, as any finite list of forms of mistreatment would risk missing something" (TI, 2013: 6). Secondly, the same provision applies to "any person" who reports facts about offenses. The term "whistleblowers" is frequently used as a more convenient term, but it does not have quite the same broad scope as Article 33. "The term 'whistle-blower' is traditionally reserved for insiders – organisation members who disclose wrongdoing under the control of that organisation – and this is generally the focus of national laws" (ID.). These are indeed the subjects who are best placed to assist investigations and also those who are most exposed to risks of retaliation. However, under Article 33, the position of ordinary citizens also needs to be considered.[57] A second point is related to the behavioral standards that reporting persons should respect: not only does Article 33 require whistleblowers to have "reasonable grounds" but also "good

---

56 See UNODC (2009: 108) which adds; "Measures to protect reporting persons from unfair dismissal must be compatible with the labour laws of the State concerned. In particular, where employers are able to dismiss employees without reason, affording appropriate protection to reporting persons may require exceptions."

57 See Article 13(2). Articles 37 and 39 cover other categories of person.

faith". While, "reasonable grounds" is a sufficiently clear term – and there is general agreement on the fundamental point that, provided whistleblowers have reasonable grounds to suspect wrongdoing, their reports should be protected, even if they are mistaken – "good faith" is more vague and there is no definition of the term either in the UNCAC, or in its Legislative or Technical Guidance. Thus, we deem it necessary to have a clear take of the national implementing pieces of legislation on the point and a further consideration in the context of the UNCAC Review mechanism.[58] Thirdly, Article 33 deals with reports to "competent authorities", which are deemed to be the institutions endowed with the powers to address the wrongdoing exposed by the whistleblower (e.g. anti-corruption commissions, ombudsmen, audit bodies or the police).[59] Finally, Article 33 is about reports of misconduct concerning all offenses under the UNCAC, which, as assessed in Chapters 10 and 11 of the present book, covers a wide variety of transgressions. In practice, most of the State Parties that have developed whistleblower systems have given them a very wide scope, covering reports of all illegal acts (and sometimes misconduct that is not actually illegal) in addition to UNCAC offences. Notwithstanding the above "the view may be taken in some countries that corruption is the most serious and pressing issue, and it is an option to start with corruption and extend the scope later. This was done in South Korea" (TI, 2013: 6).

Besides the widespread and substantial problems testified to,[60] the

---

58 TI (2013c: 14) argues that:

> (i)f 'good faith' is required, but remains undefined, that opens the door to a legal tactic of questioning a whistle-blower's motives in every case. What, if anything, should be required of whistle-blowers beyond 'reasonable grounds' to suspect? Does it matter if their motives are not pure? Also, it seems illogical, in cases where there is an obligation to report, to have any requirement of good faith. If 'good faith' is to be required, it would be useful for national laws to define the term narrowly (. . .) It is also useful to provide that the whistle-blower's good faith is presumed until shown otherwise. (. . .).

59 In cases where such institutions have sufficient and effective enforcement powers and deal with the issue promptly and discreetly, it may be safely assumed that risks of retaliation against the whistleblower are fairly low. Noteworthily, Article 33 does not cover reports to the media or anonymous leaking platforms, but, according to some NGOs, national laws will be more effective if they address this issue. See TI (2013c: 13).

60 The problematic implementation of effective protection systems at the national level is shown also in the more restricted European area. The GRECO – the Council of Europe's anti-corruption body – has played a role in whistleblowing developments in Europe. In its second evaluation round GRECO made a limited examination of whistleblowing laws in its Member States as part of its monitoring

UNODC thematic report of 14–16 November 2012 on whistleblowing also highlights the substantial differences which often characterize the various national mechanisms because of the needs of complying with the founding principles of the respective legal systems. A unique recipe is thus not realistic but some ingredients are to be maintained. For instance, State Parties should carefully ponder the requirements on the standard of proof about retaliation on the whistleblower, when not considering reversing the burden of proof in favor of the reporting person: "(t)his is because it is often difficult for whistle-blowers to prove that their report was the cause of the retaliation and it is all too easy for the employer to present another reason" (TI: 2013c: 8). Further key prescriptions can be drawn upon the UNODC thematic report. Notably, State Parties should adopt laws aimed at protecting reporting persons effectively against any sort of retaliation (not only dismissal). Secondly, they should provide confidential advisers to assist staff who wish to make reports. In addition, they should clearly address in the law any possible contradiction between whistleblowing and the disclosure of confidential information.[61] Another essential ingredient of an effective system is to guarantee to whistleblowers who do not wish to

---

of codes of conduct for public officials. The interim findings were discussed in GRECO's seventh General Activity Report (2006). One important finding was that the widespread use of requirements for public officials to report corruption did not seem to have had much impact. This work was updated in 2009, at which time it was clear that much remained to be done, and that some of developments occurred were not considered satisfactory by GRECO. See Speckbacher (2009).

[61] In this respect its is worth recalling a recent ruling of the ECtHR in case *Guja v Moldovia* Case no. 14277/04, 12 February 2008. In such context, the ECtHR established relevant principles in order to determine whether an interference in a person's right to free expression could be justified. Such principles may be summarized as follows: i) the public interest in the disclosed information. ii) Whether the person had alternative channels for making the disclosure. iii) The authenticity of the disclosed information. iv) The motives of the person. v) The damage, if any, suffered by the employer and whether this outweighed the public interest. vi) The severity of the sanction imposed on the person, and its consequences. In more detail, the Strasbourg-based Court has held that "disclosure should be made in the first place to the person's superior or other competent authority. It is only where this is clearly impracticable that the information could, as a last resort, be disclosed to the public". Mr Guja was Head of the Press Department of the Prosecutor General's Office. After proceedings against some policemen for mistreating suspects were dropped, he sent the press two letters on the case, which suggested that the proceedings could have been dropped for improper motives. One of these letters was from a high-ranking official in the Parliament. For doing this he was dismissed. The ECtHR, having considered the case against the six principles above, held that Mr Guja was justified in revealing information to the press in the circumstances of his case.

be identified that their confidentiality will be respected. That means that their identity will not be disclosed outside the organization they report to without their consent. Also an accurate system of compensation may have a positive impact on whistleblowing. A strict compensation model only restores the whistleblower to where s/he was before s/he took the risk and trouble of blowing the whistle. Therefore, it seems vital that compensation should be available. Equally, the mechanism should take into account the material risks the reporting persons run: a strict compensation system may not be enough to encourage whistleblowers.[62]

As hinted above, other lessons may be learned by national best practices on the issue. The relevant provisions of the 2002 US Sarbanes-Oxley Act (SOX) represent a telling example.[63] For the limited purposes of our work suffice it to stress that, unlike most whistleblower laws, the SOX's whistleblower protection provisions are not limited to providing a legal remedy for wrongfully discharged employees. In addition to containing employment-based protections for employee whistleblowers, the law contains four other provisions directly relevant to whistleblower protection. First, the law requires that all publicly traded corporations create internal and independent "audit committees". As part of the mandated audit committee function, publicly traded corporations must also establish procedures for employees to file internal whistleblower complaints, and procedures which would protect the confidentiality of employees who file allegations with the audit committee. Second, the SOX sets out new ethical standards for attorneys who practice before the Securities and Exchange Commission (SEC). This law, and the SEC's implementing regulations, require attorneys, under certain circumstances, to blow the whistle on their employer or "client". Third, the SOX amended the Federal Obstruction of Justice Statute and criminalized retaliation against whistleblowers who provide "truthful information" to a "law enforcement officer" about

---

62 TI (213: 15) also testifies that:

> Rewards systems have been introduced in several countries [e.g. the US and South Korea]. In general they provide the whistleblower with a proportion of any funds recovered or penalties enforced as a result of the report. In this way they are self-financing and arguably focus on the underlying issue, assuming it is financial wrongdoing, better than compensation models do. It is of course important that the body tasked to deal with claims for rewards should be capable of handling the volume of claims received, or else the system will fall into disrepute.

63 Cfr. Sarbanes–Oxley Act of 2002 (Pub.L. 107–204, 116 Stat. 745, enacted July 30, 2002).

the "commission or possible commission of any Federal offense". This provision of the SOX was not limited in its application to publicly traded corporations; it covers every employer nationwide. Fourth, Section 3(b) of the SOX contains an enforcement provision concerning every clause of the SOX. This section states that "a violation by any person of this Act [i.e. the SOX] . . . shall be treated for all purposes in the same manner as a violation of the Securities Exchange Act of 1934". This section grants jurisdiction to the SEC to enforce every aspect of the SOX, including the various whistleblower-related provisions. It also provides for criminal penalties for any violation of the SOX, including the whistleblower-related provisions.[64] These four provisions of the Sarbanes-Oxley Act collectively provide a unique and comprehensive federal framework for enforcing whistleblower protections for corporate employees. In addition to them, the law contains an employee protection provision which permits whistleblowers to file a complaint before the US Department of Labor alleging unlawful retaliation. The UNCAC also requires State Parties to disallow the tax deductibility of expenses that constitute bribes,[65] an issue to which the OECD has devoted a specific but non-binding recommendation. In so doing the UN Convention strengthens the standard set by the OECD. Although the UNCAC does not take the rights approach followed by the Drafters of the AU Convention, it makes a similar provision for protecting the rights of the accused.[66]

More importantly, the UNCAC contains an independent provision dealing with corruption relating to the judiciary and prosecutorial services.[67] This is unique to the UNCAC.

15.2 CIVIL REMEDIES

The *Fininvest* case shows that deterrent civil remedies, complementary to penal sanctions, can be highly effective in big corruption cases. At the international level, the two main instruments which contain a detailed set of provisions regulating civil remedies are (1) the Council of Europe Civil Law Convention (CoECivLCC) and (2) the UNCAC.

---

64 Cfr. Kohn (2012).

65 See Article 12(4) of the UNCAC.

66 See UNCAC, Articles 30(4), 44(14).

67 As above, Article 11(1)–(2): "[T]ake measures to strengthen integrity and to prevent opportunities for corruption among members of the judiciary [and prosecution services]. Such measures may include rules with respect to the conducts of members of the judiciary [and prosecution services]."

CoECivLCC

The Convention, which applies only to bribery and similar acts, is divided into three chapters, covering: measures to be taken at national level, international cooperation and monitoring of implementations and final clauses. In ratifying the Convention, the States undertake to incorporate its principles and rules into their domestic law, taking into account their own particular situation.

The Convention deals with compensation for: damage; liability (including State liability for acts of corruption committed by public officials); contributory negligence; reduction or disallowance of compensation, depending on the circumstances; validity of contracts; protection of employees who report corruption; clarity and accuracy of accounts and audits; acquisition of evidence; court orders to preserve the assets necessary for the execution of the final judgement and for the maintenance of the status quo pending resolution of the points at issue; international cooperation.

Under the Convention, damages must not be limited to any standard payment but must be determined according to the loss sustained in the particular case.

This excludes punitive damages; however, parties whose domestic law provides for punitive damages are not required to exclude their application. The extent of the compensation is to be granted by the court, which can provide for the compensation of material damages, loss of profits and non-pecuniary loss (Article 3(2)). A striking aspect of the Convention under discussion lies here: the complete silence regarding restitution (common law) or vindication (civil law).

In order to obtain compensation, the plaintiff has to prove the occurrence of the damage, whether the defendant acted with intent or negligently and the causal link between the corrupt behavior and the damage. The main achievement in this context concerns the usually reduced evidentiary requirements necessary in civil proceedings. Each State Party shall provide in its internal law for effective remedies for the persons who have suffered damage as a result of corrupt conduct.[68] As far as unlawful and culpable behavior on the part of the defendant is concerned, it should be pointed out that those who directly and knowingly participate in the

---

68 Article 2 defines "corruption" as "requesting, offering, giving or accepting, directly, or indirectly, a bribe or any other undue advantage or prospect thereof, which distorts the proper performance of any duty or behaviour required of the recipient of the bribe, the undue advantage or the prospect thereof".

corruption are primarily liable for the damage, including the giver and the recipient of the bribe, as well as those who incited or aided the corruption or failed to take the appropriate steps, in the light of the responsibilities that rest with them, to prevent corruption.[69]

The Convention also addresses the issue of State responsibility for acts of corruption by public officials.[70] Nevertheless, the Convention does not indicate the conditions for the liability of a State Party but leaves each party free to determine in its internal law the conditions under which the Party would be liable.

As to the validity of contracts, according to the respective provision, each Party is to provide in its internal law for any contract or clause of a contract providing for corruption to be null and void.[71] Furthermore, each Party is to provide in its internal law for the possibility, for all Parties to a contract whose consent has been undermined by an act of corruption, to be able to apply to the court for the contract to be declared void, notwithstanding their right to claim for damages, in order to enable them to defend their rights and interests, including the possibility of obtaining compensation for damage.[72] In particular, those who have suffered damage as a result of corruption must be given the right to initiate an action in order to obtain full compensation for such damage, covering material damage, loss for profits, and non-pecuniary loss.[73] A failure to take reasonable steps to prevent acts of corruption on the part of the defendant, may, in some circumstances, provide a basis for liability.[74] It is noteworthy that the State itself may be required to pay compensation to persons who have suffered damage as a result of an act of corruption by its public officials in the exercise of their function.[75]

In addition, the CoECivLCC aims to protect the interests of whistleblowers by obliging States Parties to take the necessary measures to protect from being victimized employees who report in good faith and on the basis of reasonable grounds their suspicions of corrupt practices.[76]

The Convention also addresses international cooperation. Under the Convention, the parties are required to cooperate effectively on matters relating to civil proceedings in cases of corruption, especially concerning

69 Article 6 (Contributory negligence).
70 Article 7.
71 Article 8.
72 See Article 1.
73 Article 3.
74 Article 4(1).
75 Article 5.
76 Article 9.

the service of documents, obtaining evidence abroad, jurisdiction and recognition and enforcement of foreign judgments and litigation costs, in accordance with the provisions of the relevant international instruments on international cooperation in civil and commercial matters to which they are parties, as well as with their internal law.[77] The Convention allows no reservations.[78]

Of note is that the CoECivLCC also reduces the control of government agencies over the overall anti-corruption strategy, leaves out potential litigants who do not have sufficient resources or access to the courts, and could lead to conflicting civil and criminal proceedings.

The manifest advantage of the civil law approach is that it makes corruption controls partly self-enforcing by empowering victims to take action on their own initiative. The CoECivLCC requires Contracting Parties to provide in their domestic law "for effective remedies for persons who have suffered damage as a result of acts of corruption, to enable them to defend their rights and interests, including the possibility of obtaining compensation for damage" (Article 1). Damages can be recovered against anyone who has committed or authorized the act of corruption, or failed to take reasonable steps to prevent such an act, including the State itself, if a causal link between the act and the damages can be shown (Articles 4 and 5 of the Convention).

UNCAC

Turning our attention to the UNCAC, Chapter III contains highly controversial provisions relating to private rights of action and the consequences of corruption. We refer to the potentially far-reaching provisions on civil liability and collateral consequences set forth in Article 34 (Consequences of acts of corruption) and Article 35 (Compensation for damage).

As to Article 34, it breaks significant new ground among international anti-corruption conventions. It obliges States to take measures to address the consequences of corruption, including through the annulment or rescission of contracts, withdrawal of concessions, or other similar instruments that may have been tainted by corrupt practices.[79]

The provision at hand appears prima facie to be written in mandatory terms, but States are called upon to give due regard to the rights of third parties acquired in good faith – a key qualification – and, which might

---

77 See Article 13.
78 See Article 17.
79 See UNCAC, Article 34.

happen to weaken the enforcement of the provision, the obligation is subject as well to the fundamental principles of the State's domestic law. On the other side, it is not limited by its terms to those actually convicted of violations of the offenses (i.e. the offenders) prescribed by the Convention. According to Low, the absence of such a limitation may enable this Article to be applied in a wider variety of situations than its inclusion in the criminalization chapter of the Convention suggests. Accordingly, Low adduces that companies that do business abroad or at home through government contracts, concessions, licenses and permits "should be aware that this provision may prompt more widespread revocation of rights than has historically been the case" (Low 2008: 16). Interestingly, this Article does not address explicitly the issue of debarment or contracting ineligibility of the person found to have engaged in corrupt practices. It rather focuses on the property acquired through such practices. Nonetheless, since, as a general rule, the UNCAC sets minimum standards, it would not preclude debarments or declarations of ineligibility by national authorities.

Closely related to Article 34, Article 35 requires States to take such measures as may be necessary, *but* in accordance with their domestic law principles, to ensure that entities or persons who have suffered damage as a result of an act of corruption have the right to initiate legal proceedings against those responsible for that damage in order to obtain compensation.[80]

The Article thus prima facie requires States to establish private rights of action in civil proceedings for damages. However, the *travaux préparatoires* to the Convention make clear that, as to redress of corruption-related activities, Article 35's provisions are not intended to require or endorse any particular choice made by a State.[81]

Should the clear non-mandatory model followed by the drafters of Article 35 and the above-mentioned remark of the *travaux préparatoires* not suffice to highlight the mere optional nature of the provision under discussion, the Legislative Guide (paragraphs 460–01) would sweep any

---

80 See UNCAC, Article 34, and Legislative Guide to the UNCAC, paragraph 458, at 147.

81 See, Interpretive Notes, n. 8, reporting the wording of the preparatory works: ". . . this Art. is intended to establish the principle that States Parties should ensure that they have mechanisms permitting persons or entities suffering damage to initiate legal proceedings, in appropriate circumstances, against those who commit acts of corruption (for example, where the acts have a legitimate relationship to the State Party where the proceedings are to be brought). While Art. 35 does not restrict the right of each State Party to determine the circumstances under which it will make its courts available in such cases, it is also not intended to require or endorse the particular choice made by a State Party in doing so."

remaining doubt away.[82] Thus, a closer analysis of the UNCAC (particularly the *travaux préparatoires*) confirms that the Convention drafters intended to give States Parties the widest degree of leeway in how they implement Article 35.

Although the UNCAC is not the first international anti-corruption treaty to focus on this area, the broader reach of the UN Convention accelerates the recent trend for parties who claim injury from another's corrupt practices to bring civil suits. These civil liability risks, on top of the enhanced criminal liability risks, 'put an additional premium on preventive measures' (Low 2008: 18). What is more, the implementation of the UNCAC may represent a remarkable opportunity for State Parties to design a balanced combination of criminal responses, on the one hand, and civil remedies, on the other. Assuming a fairly optimistic viewpoint, it might be argued that, with specific reference to corporate crime, the issue of the *over-civilization* of the remedies, which has recently moved to an *over-criminalization* (and, hence, *under-civilization* of corporate law) of legal responses, could be addressed in the framework of a broad revision of national laws.[83]

Therefore, Articles 34 and 35 signal a resolution on the part of the negotiators of the UNCAC to unleash the potential of private civil litigation and collateral legal and administrative sanctions on persons that commit corrupt practices. Article 35, in particular, can be seen as a further step toward the privatization of law enforcement.

---

82 Legislative Guide to the UNCAC, paragraph 460, at 147, stating that: "This does not require that victims should be guaranteed compensation or restitution, but legislative or other measures must provide procedures whereby it can be sought or claimed". Ibid., paragraph 461, at pp. 147–8, merely reproduces the contents of the above-mentioned Interpretative Note. Low (2008) notes that, since the Article was written in non-self-executing terms, national legislation is required to implement it. The US Government interprets this Article as not requiring it to adopt new federal legislation establishing a cause of action for damages suffered from corruption. See Treaty Doc. No. 109–6, at 10 (noting that "the current laws and practices of the United States are in compliance with Art. 35"). The government's analysis also negates any intention that this provision create private rights of action under the US Foreign Corrupt Practices Act. Ibid. Nonetheless, it might well occur that other countries adopt measures that permit injured parties to sue for compensation for acts of corruption. As seen (Section 15.2, subsection titled CoECivLCC), measures promoting civil liability are required by the Council of Europe Civil Law Convention Against Corruption. The implementation of such a Convention might constitute the *occasio legis* for reforming regulations concerning compensation for acts of corruption in those States Parties which do not satisfactorily address the issue.

83 This problem has been recently highlighted and assessed in the context of an extremely insightful study by Hurt (2007).

This course would have pros and cons. On the one side, given the difficulties national law enforcement authorities face in prosecuting bribery offenses, some benefits may derive from encouraging possible litigation: evidence developed in such litigation may be useful in subsequent criminal prosecutions, or may alert prosecutors to situations which should be investigated. On the other hand, civil suits also increase the costs of corruption. Moreover, such remedies may be abused.

16. Follow-up procedures as specific cases of international supervision

16.1 INTRODUCTION

Whether one assumes the traditional dualistic theoretical construct, or accepts the monistic conception advocating the primacy of international law, or maintains that "international law no longer constitutes a sphere of law tightly separate and distinct (subject to one or two exceptions) from that of national law systems" (Cassese 2008: 217), the fact remains that one of the crucial issues of contemporary as well as modern international law concerns the mechanisms for monitoring and guaranteeing compliance with international rules by States to which they are addressed. International treaties against transnational crimes are no exception.

It might well be argued that one of the distinguishing features of contemporary international law is that States have gradually realized that, in many spheres, dispute settlement should be replaced by the establishment and running of mechanisms designed to *monitor compliance* with international legal standards on a permanent or quasi-permanent basis, and, thus "*prevent* or *deter* as much as possible deviation from those standards" (Cassese 2008: 283; emphasis added). The monitoring mechanisms established by *some* of the international anti-bribery treaties are a paradigmatic case of the mechanisms just sketched out.

What is more, the effective operation of such mechanisms and their relative strength or weakness represents a key disparity among the various treaties we have described. To put it differently, the fact that the monitoring mechanism envisaged by some of the Conventions at stake is (at least, up to now) relatively ineffective or in an embryonic state amounts to one of the most serious of their shortcomings. The present section questions how far each monitoring device substantially contributes (or can be expected to contribute) to the successful achievement of each anti-bribery convention. Since these monitoring mechanisms belong to the *genus* of so-called international supervision, we first delineate the contours of this institution.

16.2 INTERNATIONAL SUPERVISION VS ADJUDICATION

International supervision represents a flexible means to prevent disputes. In order to obviate to the renowned deficiencies of the international order in the resolution of conflicts and legal disputes, "a new system of inducing compliance with international rules" has gradually been pioneered for scrutinizing the behavior of States parties of specific treaties (Cassese 2008: 291).

This system essentially reflects a guarantee function of the international legal system. In turn, this function – which represents the mediate goal of the international supervision – aims at preserving the integrity of the legal values of a certain legal system from activities, conduct and facts which may result in shattering this integrity. In the case of international agreements, the above-mentioned guarantee function works through the assessment and the decision on compliance by State parties with international standards – that is, the immediate goal of international supervision. International supervision, however, is not exhausted by the compliance decision for it necessitates, firstly, the knowledge of the object under supervision, and, secondly, the production of legal effects, varying from mere declaration of either conformity or non-conformity or more penetrating interventions of the international organizations concerned.

It differs from the adjudication in many respects. Firstly, the composition of the body in charge of monitoring the implementation of international provisions is normally different from that of judicial bodies, because the supervisory body can also be made up of representatives of States instead of individuals acting in a personal capacity. Moreover, it might happen that overseeing functions are entrusted to more than one organ. In this case, the various bodies often differ in their composition, as one or more are composed of independent individuals, whilst others consist of State officials.

Secondly, as a general rule, the initiative for supervisory provision is not left to the aggrieved State. Rather, it can be taken either by the beneficiaries of the international rules (for instance, individuals, groups of individuals, or representatives of the States who directly benefit from the obligations imposed upon the aggrieved State), or even by the supervisory body acting *proprio motu*, that is to say, on its own initiative (such as in the case of anti-corruption monitoring mechanisms). At times there is no need for anybody to initiate the proceedings, for the simple reason that the procedure is a standing and automatic one, involving periodic scrutiny of the behavior of the States concerned. This is the case, for instance, with the operative monitoring proceedings set forth by the OAS, OECD, and COE Conventions.

Thirdly – as has just been remarked – whereas adjudication is triggered *after* a dispute has arisen, supervision is generally carried out with a view to *deterring* infringement of international legal standards. "In other words, normally supervision is designed to have *preventive* purposes" (Cassese 2008: 292).

Fourthly, the hearings of judicial bodies are usually public. In contrast, the debates between the contending parties either before an overseeing body or, when the procedure is not continuous in character, the investigative activities of the supervising organ, are run in camera, so as to avoid attracting publicity to possible violations committed by the State under supervision while the investigation is still under way.

Finally, as a rule, the outcome of the overseeing procedure does not consist in a binding decision. Rather, it takes various forms (such as, for instance, recommendations, reports either public or not, etc.), which, whatever their official label, mainly rely on "*besoin d'honorabilité international*", assumed to be taken into notable consideration by States. It is, in other words, a sensible diplomatic and moral pressure. The underlying idea is that internal and international pressure of public opinion on non-complying States should represent a valid spur to eventual compliance, once States' deviation from international standards is ascertained and made public.

Thus, international supervision shares only some of the features of adjudication and it stands as an essentially "*non-contentieux*" supervision or control.

Cassese (2008) identifies the reasons why international lawmakers resort to this ingenious system for impelling States to abide by international law. He suggests two closely interrelated reasons.

Firstly, in the aftermath of World War I, States began to rely on international treaties to regulate matters which until then had remained within their domestic jurisdiction. The evolving international legislation regulating these issues presents one peculiar aspect: it did not impose reciprocal duties, that is to say obligations entailing each Contracting Party being interested in abiding by the rules for fear that other Contracting State might feel free to disregard them as well. On the contrary, the international rules emerging in the aftermath of World War I belonged to that peculiar category of norms which safeguard the interests of entities other than the subjects assuming the rights and obligations at issue (such as, for instance, individuals, groups, populations subject to a mandatory system, associations of workers and employers, and so forth).

Secondly, Cassese goes on to state that in these new areas it was not at all easy to establish mechanisms and procedures for ensuring that the new international standards were faithfully observed. According to the

Italian legal scholar, resort to adjudication was not feasible on a number of grounds, mainly the circumstance that States, even though they had accepted such original and bold obligations, were reluctant to submit to judicial bodies. What is more, the unique feature of the subject matter made adjudication scarcely appropriate. The non-reciprocal character of the obligations set forth by those rules meant that the infringement of one of them could be passed over silence, in case it was only the Contracting States that had the right to demand compliance. Therefore, it was only logical to confer the right to exact respect for the rules upon the very entities for whose advantage they had been agreed upon. However, a stumbling block remained. It was, indeed, impossible for States to accept the granting of truly *locus standi* before international courts to individuals and groups. As frequently happens in political and social processes a compromise was reached. It allowed individuals or groups of individuals to appeal international bodies that were devoid of any judicial function.

In order to meet all the requirements mentioned above, ingenious monitoring systems were conceived. To make them suitable for States, it was deemed necessary to water down their possible impact on State sovereignty. That is the reason why no binding force was attached to the final assessment of supervisory bodies. Moreover, alongside organs consisting of impartial individuals acting in their own capacity, bodies composed of representatives of States were set up as well. It is almost a pleonasm to stress that the latter bodies are more sensitive to States' interests and needs, and, thus, more inclined to attenuate possible harsh evaluations. At the same time, it was also decided that the sessions and meetings of the monitoring bodies should normally occur in camera, for the manifest rationale of shielding States from public exposure.

16.3 SUPERVISORY MECHANISMS AND PROCEDURES

Supervisory mechanisms and procedures proved a reasonable and relatively effective means of impelling States to measure up to their international undertakings. Not surprisingly, certain of those systems lived on after World War II. By way of example, the ILO mechanisms for monitoring the application of international labour conventions, and the systems for scrutinizing conventions on narcotic drugs exist and are operative.

As recently remarked by Cassese, the areas in which supervision is at present most widespread are: (i) treaties and other international standards on human rights; (ii) the peaceful use of atomic energy; (iii) the environment; (iv) the Antarctic and outer space; (v) international economic law;

(vi) international and internal armed conflict. We add: (vii) international cooperation against corruption.

The expansion of supervision in such relevant areas bears testimony that it responds to State needs. Moreover, it shows that comprehensive groups of States are prone to supervision, for even those which are reluctant to accept other international means of investigation do not oppose international monitoring. Needless to add that this openness of States to such a mechanism is mainly due to its inherent flexibility and to the fact the international monitoring bodies do not put the States concerned "in the dock".

As to the modalities through which supervisory is effected, the legal scholarship is unanimous in identifying four principal means, namely:

(1) Examination of periodic reports submitted at set intervals by the State concerned.
(2) Inspection, which is far more effective and penetrating than the assessment of States' reports, where the inquiring body must confine itself to the data provided by the State concerned. Investigation on the spot permits international bodies (or, as in the case of the Treaty on Antarctica and other outer space, the other State Parties to the Treaty) to ascertain whether the State concerned respects or disregards the Treaty.
(3) Supervision carried out by means of a contentious procedure, where the Parties to a dispute, or the State under monitoring and the supervisory body, engage in contentious examination of the case.
(4) Adoption of measures aimed at preventing the possible commission of international wrongdoings by a State. According to Cassese, the most effective form of preventive supervision has been essentially established in the area of the peaceful use of atomic energy and protection of the environment. The peculiar character of the subject matter accounts for the exceptional characteristics of this international scrutiny.

16.4 INTERNATIONAL SUPERVISION AGAINST CORRUPTION

By exploring the foremost aspects of those among the monitoring mechanisms established by the anti-bribery Conventions, which are already operative and have been effectively stimulating a beneficial system of feedback between the legal orders of the State Parties and the bodies charged with the supervising function, we prove that international cooperation against corruption might be rightfully included in Cassese's list. The modalities themselves through which these monitoring systems work unambiguously confirm such a nature, and put them in the framework of modern and flexible means of monitoring compliance with international standards, which, according to Dupuy (2004), might beneficially *complete* adjudication, which, by its very nature, takes place only through sporadic and exceptional intervention, for it can be triggered only *after* an alleged violation of international law.

A good starting point is to stress that, according to Michael and Hajredini, the "UN, OECD, and COE Conventions against corruption have been relatively ineffective because these conventions, while ratified by national parliaments, are not being implemented in the government agencies most prone to corruption" (e.g. the trafficking policy, security service, customs and tax inspections). This critical remark and other questions raised by practitioners and legal scholars as to the effective implementation and enforcement of the anti-bribery treaties may be better understood if read in the context of the assessment of countries' reports carried out by the monitoring systems set forth by most of the Conventions at issue.

16.5 CONVENTIONS

OAS Convention

According to Webb (2005), the Achilles' heel of the OAS Convention lies in the mechanism for monitoring its implementation, or more precisely with its late elaboration and functioning. The text of the Agreement is silent on this matter and the creation of the follow-up mechanism appears to have been just an afterthought. This fact might be considered of only symbolic relevance. Yet, in a field like corruption, symbols are far from being immaterial signals to States, administration of justice, civil society. What is more, it was not until four years after the Convention came into force that the Conference of States Parties met to establish a follow-up mechanism.[1]

The OAS uses a *peer review* system whereby a government-appointed Committee of Experts selects countries for review, obtains information using questionnaires, and prepares a preliminary report concerning

1 See OAS General Assembly Resolution AG/RES.1784 (XXXI-O/01), 5 June 2001, and Summary of the Minutes of the Conference of States Parties, annexed, 2–4 May 2001, Buenos Aires. Hereinafter: the Document of Buenos Aires.

compliance with the international obligations by the State Parties to the Convention.

More specifically, the Follow-up Mechanism for the Implementation of the Inter-American Convention against Corruption (MESICIC) headquartered at the OAS is an intergovernmental body established within the framework of the OAS.[2] It supports the States Parties in the implementation of the provisions of the Convention through a process of reciprocal evaluation, based on conditions of equality among the States. In such a mechanism, recommendations are formulated with respect to those areas in which there are legal gaps or in which further progress is necessary. In summary, it essentially consists of a supervising mechanism that should allow the States which have ratified the OAS Convention to promote its implementation and follow-up on the commitments assumed by the States Parties and analyze the manner in which they are being implemented, thus contributing to the achievement of its purposes. In principle, it should also facilitate technical cooperation activities; the exchange of information, experience and best practice; and the harmonization of legislation. The Mechanism is guided by the purposes and principles established in the Charter of the OAS. It thus takes into account the principles of sovereignty, non-intervention, and the juridical equality of the States Parties, as well as the need to respect the Constitution and the fundamental principles of the legal system of each State Party. Impartiality, and objectivity should inspire its operation and the conclusions that it reaches; it operates on the basis of consensus and cooperation: "it neither sanctions, grades, nor classifies states, rather it facilitates cooperation between them. The MESICIC seeks to establish an adequate balance between the confidentiality and transparency in its activities. In addition, although it is inter-governmental in nature, it may receive contributions from civil society organizations."[3] In principle the aim of the mechanism is thus twofold: on the one hand, to promote the implementation of the Convention, and, on the other, to guarantee an impartial system for assessing the concrete steps taken by the Contracting Parties to comply with the international obligation established by the Convention itself. Besides these, it also aims to guarantee

---

2 States Parties to the MESICIC are: Antigua and Barbuda, Argentina, Bahamas, Belize, Bolivia, Brazil, Canada, Colombia, Costa Rica, Chile, Dominican Republic, Ecuador, El Salvador, Grenada, Guatemala, Guyana, Haiti, Honduras, Jamaica, Mexico, Nicaragua, Panama, Paraguay, Peru, Saint Kitts and Nevis, Saint Vincent and the Grenadines, Suriname, Trinidad and Tobago, United States, Uruguay and Venezuela.

3 Cfr. http://www.oas.org/juridico/english/mesicic_intro_en.htm, lastly accessed January 2014.

fair application and equal treatment among States Parties, striking an appropriate balance between the confidentiality and transparency of its activities.

Coming to the description of its structural composition, the MESICIC consists of two main bodies. The Conference of States Parties, which has the general authority and responsibility for implementing the Mechanism, lies at the heart of the Mechanism, responsible for determining the general guidelines and direction of the Mechanism within the framework of the purposes and basic principles contained in paragraphs 1 and 2 of the Document of Buenos Aires. The Committee of Experts is responsible for the technical review of the implementation of the Convention. The Conference of States Parties has the authority and overall responsibility for supervising implementation of the Mechanism and for adopting the decisions it deems appropriate to achieve its objectives, in accordance with Article 2 of its Rules of Procedure.[4]

The Committee of Experts is comprised of experts designated by each State Party. This Committee is responsible for technical analysis of the implementation of the Convention, as well as for facilitating the activities of technical cooperation within the framework of the Mechanism. Secretariat services are carried out by the Secretariat General of the OAS through the Office of Legal Cooperation of the Department of International Legal Affairs, The Conference of State Parties and the Committee of Experts and the bodies are supported by a Technical Secretariat, exercised by the General Secretariat of the OAS, through the Department of Legal Cooperation of the Secretariat for Legal Affairs.

As to its functioning, the MESICIC has developed a process of reciprocal evaluation among States that form a part of it, within the framework of successive rounds aimed at reviewing how the states are implementing the provisions of the Convention selected for each round. For such purposes, country reports are adopted, which formulate concrete recommendations to each state, in order to stress the legal gaps that have been detected; suggest how to correct the inadequacies that have been found; and have indicators in place which allow an objective determination of the results that have been achieved in relation to the implementation of those provisions. Civil society organizations participate in this process, by submitting information alongside the information submitted by the respective state. At the conclusion of a round, the Committee adopts a Hemispheric Report.[5] The preliminary reports are first reviewed by the country and

---

4 See the Document of Buenos Aires. See also Anon. (2004: 23 ff.).

5 Cfr. also the Rules of Procedure and Other Provisions of the Committee of

then a final version is submitted to the Conference of States Parties and published.[6] It is noteworthy that it was not until February 2003 that the first report – on Argentina – was adopted. It seems, however, that the pace has eventually been improved.[7] The Conference of State Parties has also agreed upon a timetable in order to accelerate the process of analysis and complete the production of final review reports (for example, for the first round, 12 per year).[8] As mentioned, the Committee can recommend

---

Experts of the MESICIC (document SG/MESICIC/doc.9/04 rev. 4) are available at: www.oas.org/juridico/eng lish/mesicic_rules.pdf; and the Methodology for Conducting On-Site Visits (document SG/MESICIC/doc.276/11 re v. 2) is available at: www.oas.org/juridico/english/met_onsite.pdf.

6 Technical Secretariat for Legal Cooperation Mechanisms, Follow-up Mechanisms for the Implementation of the Inter-American Convention against Corruption, available at: http://www.oas.org/juridico/english/followup.htm, last visited 1 May 2011. Note also that The Inter-American Juridical Committee, an OAS body, has developed a model implementing legislation for the transnational bribery provisions. See Model Legislation on Illicit Enrichment and Transnational Bribery, OEA/Ser.G, CP/doc. 3102/98, 9 September 1998. The proposed legislation tracks the language of the OAS Convention. It is accompanied by a detailed commentary, which the authors describe as a legislator's guide to the development of implementing legislation.

7 See Technical Secretariat for Legal Cooperation Mechanisms, Schedule for Accelerating the Process of Analysis within the Framework of the First Round, available at: http://www.oas.org/juridico/english/mec_sched_2005.htm, last visited 2 November 2012. See also Mechanism for Follow-up on Implementation of the Inter-American Convention against Corruption. Inter-American Program of Cooperation to Fight Corruption, OEA/Ser.L/XXIII.2.2. MESICIC/CEP-II/doc.5/06 rev. 2, 21 November 2006; and the Schedule for the third round of peer-review, Second Meeting of the Conference of States Parties, 20–21 November 2006, Washington, DC, Mechanism for Follow-up on Implementation of the Inter-American Convention Against Corruption, 12 January 2009, Fourteenth Meeting of the Committee of Experts, Washington, DC. OEA/Ser.L SG/MESICIC/doc.233/08 rev. 1.Original: Spanish 8–12 December 2008, available at: http://www.oas.org/juridico/english/mesicic_schedule_IIIround.pdf, last accessed on 10 December 2013. Finally, see the schedule for the ongoing fourth round of peer-review, Mechanism for Follow-up on Implementation of the Inter-American Convention Against Corruption, 14 September 2012, Nineteenth Meeting of the Committee of Experts, Washington, D.C., OEA/Ser.L AN SG/MESICIC/doc.299/11 rev. 2 Original: Spanish 12–16 September 2011, available at: http://www.oas.org/juridico/PDFs/schedule_IVround.pdf., last accessed on 10 December 2013.

8 See Technical Secretariat for Legal Cooperation Mechanisms, Schedule for Accelerating the Process of Analysis within the Framework of the First Round. The reports adopted thus far are available at: (i) http://www.oas.org/juridico/english/mec_ron1_rep.htm, (as to the first round of review); (ii) http://www.oas.org/juridico/english/mesicic_II_rep.htm, (as to the second round of review); (iii)

improvements but not sanctions of any kind. Thus, there are no disciplinary "penalties" the Committee or the Conference can resort to where Contracting States clearly violate the obligations of the OAS Convention. Accordingly, the Mechanism mainly relies for its effectiveness on its moral and hortatory force – along with the reputational consequences on States Parties which complies with the commitments they assumed with the ratification of the OAS Convention – as normally occurs as an outcome of international supervision proceedings. However, it should be recalled that the OAS Convention permits countries to take reservations when ratifying it, provided such reservations are not incompatible with the "object and purpose of the Convention".[9] What is more, using the Articles VIII and IX claw-back clauses, Contracting Parties may avoid enacting the transnational bribery and illicit enrichment provisions of the Convention even without taking a reservation.[10]

Again, the Convention contains no timetable within which States must implement its provisions and no provision for declarations when the escape clauses are invoked. Accordingly, implementation appears to be left *excessively* to the discretion of each State and it is legitimate to question how far the MESICIC is capable of modifying this state of affairs.

OECD Convention

Recognizing that the effectiveness of the Convention is entirely dependent on the adoption of implementing legislation and on enforcement at the national level, the OECD Convention required all States, as a condition of adherence, to join its WGB.

Thus, the OECD Convention provides in Article 12 for a mechanism of "*self* and mutual evaluation", whereby: (1) States Parties will report to the OECD on steps taken in their country to implement and enforce the Convention and the OECD's 1997 Revised Recommendation of the Council on Combating Bribery (which also urges prompt implementation of its Recommendation on Tax Deductibility of Bribes to Foreign Public Officials); and (2) other States Parties will assess the extent to which those States Parties have in fact implemented the Convention and are enforcing it effectively. The process envisaged is, thus, a peer-review process:

---

http://www.oas.org/juridico/english/mesicic_III_rep.htm, (as to the third round of review); (iv) http://www.oas.org/juridico/english/mec_ron1_rep.htm, (as to the fourth round of review).

9 OAS Convention, Article XXIV. See Chapter 10, Section 10.2.1, (1) OAS Convention, when dealing with the Convention under discussion.

10 Ibid., Article XXIV.

it has elements of both mutual and self-evaluation, and the outcome consists essentially of reports and recommendations, the value of which is essentially exhortatory. The Convention did not set out in detail how that process was to occur but left its elaboration to the Working Group.

The Working Group has established a three-stage process for monitoring implementation of the Convention. In Phase 1, monitoring focuses on the extent to which the implementing legislation enacted by a country is consistent with the requirements of the Convention.[11] In Phase 2, monitoring focuses on enforcement and the overall effectiveness of the country's systems and structures in preventing, deterring, and punishing transnational bribery.[12] Phase 3 involves a shorter and more focused evaluation than Phase 2, and concentrates on the following three pillars: progress made by Parties to the Convention on weaknesses identified in Phase 2; issues raised by changes in the domestic legislation or the institutional framework of the Parties; enforcement efforts and results, and other key group-wide cross-cutting issues. The review at each stage is conducted by two other States Parties designated as peer reviewers and by personnel from the OECD Secretariat. Thus, in each Phase, the OECD reviewers submit detailed written questions to the appropriate authorities of the country under review and receive written responses.

In line with what was established by Commentary 34 of the Convention, the main objective of Phase 1 is to assess whether the legal texts through which participants implement the OECD Convention meet the standard set by the Convention. Phase 1 also evaluates the initial actions taken to implement the 1997 Revised Convention Recommendation. Additionally, the evaluation provides an opportunity for countries to learn from the experiences and approaches of others. It is noteworthy that Phase 1 includes elements of both self- and mutual evaluation. The approach is "vertical", that is to say based on examinations country-by-country. In consultation with the country examined, two countries are chosen to lead the examination. The countries acting as lead examiners appoint the experts who take part in the preparation of the preliminary report. The entire group of countries party to the Convention evaluates each country's performance and adopts conclusions. In concrete terms, Phase 1 operates as follows:

---

[11] See OECD, Bribery Convention: Procedure of Self- and Mutual Evaluation, Phase 1, available at: http://www.oecd.org/daf/anti-bribery/antibriberyconvention/phase1countrymonitoringoftheoecdanti-briberyconvention.htm. The reports adopted after Phase 1 are available on the same webpage.

[12] See OECD, Bribery Convention: Procedure of Self- and Mutual Evaluation, Phase 2, available at: http://www.oecd.org/oecd/pages/home/displaygeneral/0,3380,EN-document-31-nodirectorate-no-3–7223–31,00.html.

(1) A questionnaire is sent to the country, soliciting information on the implementation of the Convention and the implementation of the 1997 Revised Recommendation.[13] The replies to the questionnaire must be precise and provide sufficient detail to permit an assessment of conformity of laws with the Convention and consistency of laws and practice with the 1997 Recommendation. Replies must reflect all relevant elements of the legal system (including other relevant laws, regulations, judicial precedent, other treaties, the constitution) to provide a complete picture of the legal implementation of the Convention and implementation of the Revised Recommendation. Replies to questions concerning the Convention must also take into account information in the Commentaries to the Convention. Replies to the questionnaire as well as relevant texts must be provided in one of the two official languages of the OECD: English or French.
(2) The replies are then circulated to all participants in the Working Group.
(3) The lead examiners and the OECD Secretariat examine the replies to ensure they are complete and, if necessary, request additional information from the examined country.
(4) A draft report, issued by the WGB Secretariat on the basis of the answers by the State under review to the standard questionnaire prepared by the OECD, is presented to the WGB and is discussed in plenary (around one hour of discussion on average).
(5) The report is then re-examined by the two lead examiners and the Secretariat along with the reviewed country during an informal meeting, where the reviewed country is also presented with draft conclusions prepared by the Secretariat and the lead examiners. The reviewed country can comment on the draft conclusions, including by disagreeing with some or all of them, but cannot block the submission of the draft conclusions.
(6) The draft conclusions are submitted to the WGB for adoption. The reviewed country is provided with a last chance to express its own views. However, if necessary the report which concludes Phase 1 can be adopted on the basis of consensus minus one.

The purpose of Phase 2 is to study the structures put in place to enforce the laws and rules implementing the OECD Anti-Bribery Convention and to assess their application in practice. Phase 2 broadens the focus of monitoring to encompass more fully the non-criminal law aspects of the 1997

---

13 See Bonucci (2007a) for a description of the questionnaire.

Revised Recommendation. Like the Phase 1 review, the Phase 2 review is an intergovernmental process; business groups and other non-governmental organizations are not invited to participate in the formal evaluation process, including consultations in the Working Group and the evaluation exercise. Again, Phase 2 includes elements of both self- and mutual evaluation. The approach is "vertical" or based on examinations country-by-country. In consultation with the country examined, two countries are chosen to lead the examination. The countries acting as lead examiners choose the experts who take part in on-site visits and preparation of the preliminary report. The entire group of countries party to the Convention evaluates each country's performance and adopts conclusions. The Phase 2 evaluation includes: preparation of the consultation in the WGB; the appointment of two countries to act as lead examiners; replies to an evaluation questionnaire;[14] an on-site visit to the country examined; preparation of a preliminary report on country performance; consultation in the Working Group on Bribery; and, finally, adoption by the Working Group of a report, including recommendations, on country performance (Bonucci 2007a).

Visits *in loco* represent a peculiar feature of the supervising process set forth by the OECD Convention. On-site visits, which last approximately one week, are carried out in accordance with predetermined terms of reference. During on-the-spot visits, the reviewed State is not required to disclose information that is otherwise protected by its laws and regulations. To what extent this might impede an effective assessment of the implementation and enforcement of the Convention inevitably depends on the use the State concerned makes of its laws and regulations, and ultimately on the State's authorities' willingness not to misuse the right of external non-interference, of which the laws and regulations under discussion are likely to be an expression. On-site visits by the lead examiners and OECD Secretariat present three manifest advantages. Firstly, they are an effective way to obtain information on enforcement and prosecution. Secondly, they also offer the chance to talk directly with magistrates, police, tax and other authorities responsible for applying the law (Bonucci 2007a). In addition, informal exchanges with key representatives of the private sector and civil society can contribute to determining the impact that the laws and enforcement have had on behavior, including compliance schemes.[15]

---

14 The Working Group adopted a questionnaire for Phase 2, which is sent to the country to be examined. Supplementary questions specific to the country concerned take into account the results of the Phase 1 evaluation of that country. The questionnaire elicits information concerning implementation of the Revised Recommendation. See Bonucci (2007a: 457 ff.).

15 The Phase 2 process also includes visits *in loco*, that is to say, into the

Turning to the preliminary reports assessing performance, they include an evaluation and recommendations for improvement. These reports are based on replies to questionnaires, information obtained during an on-site visit to the country being examined, and independent research carried out by the lead examiners and Secretariat. The State undergoing evaluation has an opportunity to comment on the preliminary report. The preliminary report is drafted by the lead examiners and the Secretariat. After the issuance of the preliminary report, the mutual evaluation is undertaken through a consultation in the WGB. The consultation provides an opportunity to discuss difficult issues, to listen to a country explain its legal system and approach, and to formulate the recommendations that the Group agrees to make. The examined country may bring experts to the session, including from the enforcement community, to respond to questions from the WGB. Finally, the WGB formulates recommendations concerning the reviewed country's performance, which is incorporated in the report. Discussions in the WGB and interaction between the lead examiners, the Secretariat, and the examined country ought to ensure that the evaluation reflects the fullest possible understanding of the country's approach. The examined country cannot block the WGB's decision to adopt the evaluation. However, it has the right to have its views, comments and explanations fully reflected in the report and the evaluation. Whether information submitted to the OECD in the course of a review is kept confidential is to be determined by the State Party under review. It is noteworthy that, once the final report is transmitted to the Council, it becomes public, although publication of the report can lag the actual evaluation by a significant period of time.

As to the results emerging from Phase 2, generally speaking, while bribery of foreign officials has remained rife in most of the world since 1997, very few criminal investigations have been launched and prosecutions are even rarer. The number of convictions handed down by the courts is very low. The Phase 2 country monitoring reports by the WGB and studies conducted by civil society reveal a pressing need to improve the situation.[16]

In this context, Pieth and Lelieur (2007) propose actions of three

---

country under review. The reviewers prepare a draft report, which is discussed in the OECD Working Group on Bribery. Note that informal civil society consultations during the site visit *in loco* are encouraged. This should help the examiners to assess to what extent national laws and regulations have actually restrained private actors from transnational corrupt conduct. The host country is to be consulted regarding the matter of seeking such input.

16 Cfr. the Country reports adopted in the context of Phase 2, available at:

kinds to be considered. The first involves the OECD WGB, which should keep on carrying out the mutual evaluation of signatory States' application of the Convention since it came into force. To this end, a third follow-up phase is now ongoing. On the other hand, it is essential for the WGB to maintain the "*tour de table*" process to keep track, as effectively as possible, of the way concrete cases of foreign bribery are handled.

The second kind of action depends on the States Parties themselves. As aptly remarked, "they need to persevere in raising awareness about the bribery phenomenon, in training competent personnel, and in allocating sufficient resources" (Pieth and Lelieur 2007: 2). What is more, it goes without saying that when the WGB has identified gaps in national legislation, the States Parties concerned should be expected to remedy any breaches of their international obligations immediately, if they have not already done so.

The third approach is squarely international. Given the transnational nature of the crime addressed by the OECD Convention, it is indispensable to improve international coordination of laws and national enforcement systems, and to strengthen cooperation among government authorities in the anti-bribery campaign. Moreover, one should not forget that good cooperation between countries can in some cases make up for insufficient resources.

Finally, Transparency International (TI) made constructive recommendations for strengthening the OECD monitoring process concerning Phase 3, by emphasizing the need for further on-site reviews, including more experienced prosecutors on country review teams, and encouraging civil society participation.[17] The WGB appears to have taken into consideration these suggestions for shaping Phase 3 of its monitoring process.

Indeed, it adopted a post-Phase 2 assessment mechanism in December 2009, to act as a permanent cycle of peer review, involving systematic on-site visits as a shorter and more focused assessment mechanism than for Phase 2. The aim of the mechanism is to improve the capacity of Parties to fight bribery in international business transactions by examining their undertakings in this field through a dynamic process of mutual evaluation and peer pressure. The first cycle of review under this mechanism is known as Phase 3.

---

http://www.oecd.org/daf/anti-bribery/countryreportsontheimplementationoftheoecdanti-briberyconvention.htm.

[17] Transparency International (2003: 1); Laws Fail to Halt International Business Bribery, *USAID Democracy and Governance Anti-Corruption News*, 23 August 2003, available at: http://www.usaid.gov/our_work/democracy_and_governance/ technical_areas/anti-corruption/news/403_2.html.

The purpose of Phase 3 is to maintain an up-to-date assessment of the structures put in place by Parties to the OECD Anti-Bribery Convention to enforce the laws and rules implementing the Convention and the 2009 Recommendations. As hinted above, Phase 3 involves a shorter and more focused evaluation than Phase 2, and concentrates on the following three pillars: progress made by Parties to the Convention on weaknesses identified in Phase 2; issues raised by changes in the domestic legislation or the institutional framework of the Parties; enforcement efforts and results, and other key group-wide cross-cutting issues.

As with Phases 1 and 2, the approach to Phase 3 evaluations is "vertical" (based on evaluations for each country). The Working Group on Bribery has established a schedule of Phase 3 evaluations from 2009 to 2014, which includes the designation of two countries to act as lead examiners in each evaluation. The countries acting as lead examiners choose the local/national experts who take part in on-site visits and they prepare a preliminary country report. The entire Working Group on Bribery, made up of representatives from all States Parties to the Anti-Bribery Convention, evaluates each country's performance and adopts conclusions.[18] The structural elements of the Phase 3 Evaluation are the appointment of two countries to act as lead examiners;[19] replies to an evaluation questionnaire; on-site visit to the country being evaluated;[20] preparation of a preliminary

---

[18] See http://www.oecd.org/daf/anti-bribery/anti-briberyconvention/phase3countrymonitoringoftheoecdanti-briberyconvention.htm. For further information see: http://www.oecd.org/document/61/0,3746,en_2649_34859_44684959_1_1_1_1,00.html.

[19] The questionnaire is prepared by the WGB and sent to the country to be evaluated. Supplementary questions specific to the country concerned take into account the results of the Phase 2 evaluation of that country. The questionnaire elicits information concerning implementation of the Convention and the 2009 Recommendations by the country being evaluated. The questionnaire is available at: http://www.oecd.org/daf/anti-bribery/anti-briberyconvention/44685243.pdf.

[20] On-site visits are normally conducted over a three-day period (as opposed to approximately one week in Phase 2), and are carried out in accordance with the Phase 3 procedure. During on-site visits, a country is not required to disclose information that is otherwise protected by a country's laws and regulations, and/or professional rules of conduct. On-site visits by the lead examiners and OECD Secretariat are meant to be an effective way to obtain information on enforcement and prosecution. In addition, they also offer the possibility to talk with magistrates, police, tax and other authorities responsible for applying the law. Also, informal exchanges with key representatives of the private sector and civil society can contribute to determining the impact that the laws and enforcement have had on behavior, including compliance schemes. Each country is consulted on the best manner of obtaining input from the private sector and civil society. Both Marco

report on country performance; evaluation in the Working Group on Bribery; adoption by the WGB of a final report, including recommendations, on country performance.[21] Preliminary reports include an evaluation and recommendations for improvement. Each report is based on the replies to the questionnaires, information obtained during the on-site visit to the evaluated country, and independent research carried out by the lead examiners and Secretariat. The country undergoing evaluation has an opportunity to comment on the preliminary report. The preliminary report is drafted by the lead examiners and the Secretariat. The subsequent stage includes the mutual evaluation undertaken through an evaluation by the WGB. The evaluation represents a chance to discuss troublesome issues, to listen to a country explain its legal system and approach, and to formulate the recommendations that the Group agree to make. The evaluated country may bring experts to the session, including from the enforcement community, to respond to questions from the Group. The WGB formulates recommendations concerning the country's performance, which is incorporated in the report. Discussions in the Working Group and interaction between the lead examiners, Secretariat and the country being evaluated, ensure that the evaluation reflects the fullest possible understanding of the country's approach. The evaluated country cannot block the Group's decision to adopt the evaluation and its recommendations. However, it has the right to have its views, comments and explanations fully reflected in the report and the evaluation. Like in Phase 2, evaluated countries will be asked to provide follow-up reports on the implementation of recommendations adopted by the Working Group. Oral reports will not be automatic, however. Instead, during the adoption of the Phase 3 report and recommendations, the Working Group may determine that an evaluated country should be required to report orally within 12 months on specific recommendations or follow-up issues. In all cases, the evaluated country is required to submit a written report within 24 months of the adoption of the evaluation report explaining steps taken by it concerning all Phase 3 recommendations and follow-up issues. When considering those steps taken, the Working Group may require the evaluated country to give a further oral report within a further 12 months on key outstanding recommendations.

Arnone and Leonardo Borlini took part as representatives of the civil society to the on-site visit in the context of the Phase 3 monitoring evaluation of Italy.

21 See the Phase 3 Monitoring Information Resources booklet, which contains the text of the Phase 3 procedure and questionnaire, and the Convention. Document available at: http://www.oecd.org/daf/anti-bribery/anti bribery convention/Phase3InformationResourcesManualENG.pdf.

Looking at the reports adopted thus far, it appears that while progress was made over the past years, clearer signs are necessary to show that all the Parties to the Convention are committing the political leadership and resources that effective enforcement requires.[22]

EU Convention

As regards the monitoring of the EU Convention, it appears that up to now, whereas the EU makes bold statements in non-binding instruments, it drafts narrow and specific legal initiatives. As mentioned in Chapter 10, in 2003 the European Commission adopted a Communication on a Comprehensive EU Policy against Corruption.[23] The Communication is commendable in its scope and intent. It appeals to EU leaders to undertake additional efforts to detect and punish all acts of corruption, to confiscate illicit proceeds and to reduce opportunities for corrupt practices through transparent and accountable public administrative standards. In addition, it asks member States to swiftly enact all relevant supranational and international anti-corruption instruments, particularly those of the EU, OECD and COE. Finally it also emphasizes the crucial role of monitoring and peer-review evaluation between countries participating in these initiatives. Also the launch of the "Anti-Corruption Report" to be released by the Commission every two years will play a relevant role in this framework.[24] Yet, at the end of the day, we agree with Webb who argues that "the terminology is 'should' not 'shall'; it is an exercise in communication rather than legislation."[25] More to the point, the Communication also points to the lack of a proper follow-up or evaluation mechanism comparable to GRECO, the group that monitors the implementation of the COE's anti-corruption measures. However, the Commission to date

---

22 Cfr. OECD (2012) and OECD (2013), in particular the executive summaries of the Phase 3 reports of the following countries: Bulgaria; Canada; Germany; Italy; Japan; Korea; Luxembourg; Mexico; Norway and Switzerland (2011); Australia; Austria; France; Greece; Hungary; Netherlands; Slovak Republic; Spain; Sweden; United Kingdom. Note that at the time of this writing the last report adopted in the context of phase 3 is the Phase 3 Report on Implementing the OECD Anti-bribery Convention in Ireland adopted by the OECD Working Group on Bribery, on 13 December 2013. Report available at: http://www.oecd.org/daf/anti-bribery/IrelandPhase3ReportEN.pdf.

23 See Communication on a Comprehensive EU Policy against Corruption, COM(2003) 317, adopted 28 May 2003, available at: http://europa.eu.int/eur-lex/en/com/cnc/2003/com2003_0317en01.pdf.

24 See *supra* § 10.1.2.

25 Webb (2005: 202).

does not seem in favor of setting up a separate evaluation and monitoring mechanism for the EU, in order to avoid duplication of effort. Although the COE's civil and criminal law conventions on corruption and the Statute of GRECO all contain specific accession clauses for the EU, the EU has not yet acceded to them. The Commission is indeed preparing for accession.[26] If full membership in GRECO is not regarded as a viable option, the possibility of setting up a separate EU evaluation mechanism should be considered.[27]

COE Conventions

The COE (criminal and civil) Conventions share a sophisticated monitoring system involving the GRECO, which was established in 1999 by 17 European States.[28] GRECO uses a combination of mutual evaluation and peer pressure to monitor implementation. Ad hoc teams of experts are appointed, on the basis of a list proposed by GRECO members, to evaluate each member in each evaluation round.[29] GRECO evaluation procedures involve the collection of information through questionnaire(s), on-site country visits enabling evaluation teams to solicit further information

---

[26] Cfr. European Commission, Communication from the Commission to the European Parliament, the Council and the European Economic and Social Committee. Participation of the European Union in the Council of Europe Group of States against Corruption (GRECO), Brussels, 19.10.2012 COM(2012) 604 final, available at: http://www.google.it/url?sa=t&rct=j&q=&esrc=s&source=web&cd=1&ved=0CDQQFjAA&url=http%3A%2F%2Feurlex.europa.eu%2FLexUriServ%2FLexUriServ.do%3Furi%3DCOM%3A2012%3A0604%3AFIN%3AEN%3APDF&ei=Wvb0UqymEc3Z4QTy3oHIBw&usg=AFQjCNGULGnObSS3zoWCfcPt9ej9JMXnPg&sig2=GbnMlj7yjYAix2wHfqLaGg&bvm=bv.60799247,d.bGE. Thus, the Commission intends to step up cooperation between the EU and the GRECO, following the Commission's "anti-corruption package" of 6 June 2011. The Commission envisages a two-stage approach consisting first of a "full participant" status based on Article 220 of the Treaty on the Functioning of TFEU that may, in a second stage, lead to full EU membership of GRECO. Accordingly, cooperation should increase in intensity, within a relatively sort time-frame, on the basis of full participant status and pending an analysis of how full membership, including valuation of EU institutions by GRECO, would be organized in practice.

[27] Communication on a Comprehensive EU Policy against Corruption, COM(2003) 317.

[28] See Article 24 of the COE Criminal Convention and Article 14 of the COE Civil Convention. GRECO was set up under Resolution (99)5, adopted on 1 May 1999, available at: http://www.greco.coe.int/docs/ResCM(1999)5E.htm.

[29] COE, Group of States against Corruption, http://www.greco.coe.int/ (visited 4 November 2013).

during high-level discussions with domestic key players, and drafting of evaluation reports. These reports, which are examined and adopted by GRECO, contain recommendations to the evaluated countries in order to improve their level of compliance with the provisions under consideration. Measures taken to implement recommendations are subsequently assessed by GRECO under a separate compliance procedure.[30] To date GRECO has launched four evaluation rounds.[31] The three evaluation rounds conducted between 2000 and 2011 assessed GRECO member States' compliance with selected provisions from key Council of Europe legal texts, namely Resolution (97) 24 of the Committee of Ministers on the Twenty Guiding Principles for the fight against corruption, the Criminal Law Convention on Corruption, and Recommendation (2003)4 of the Committee of Ministers on common rules against corruption in the funding of political parties and electoral campaigns, the Additional Protocol to the Criminal Law Convention on Corruption (ETS 191); the Twenty Guiding Principles for the Fight against Corruption (Resolution (97) 24); and the Recommendation on Codes of Conduct for Public Officials (Recommendation No. (2000)10).

Applying a consistent methodological approach, GRECO adopted in-depth evaluation reports in respect of each of its member States gathering information of primary import from the field, on issues, such as: (i) independence, autonomy, and powers of persons or bodies in charge of preventing, investigating, prosecuting and adjudicating corruption offences; (ii) specialisation, means and training of persons or bodies in charge of fighting corruption; (iii) extent and scope of immunities from investigation, prosecution and adjudication of corruption offences; (iv) criminalisation of corruption; (v) measures for the identification, seizure and confiscation seizure of the proceeds of corruption; (vi) corruption within public administration; (vii) measures to prevent legal persons from being used to shield corruption offences; (viii) transparency in the funding of political parties and electoral campaigns; (ix) public administration and corruption (auditing systems; conflicts of interest); (x) tax and financial legislation to counter corruption and links between corruption, organized crime and money-laundering. In more detail, GRECO's First Evaluation

---

30 See ibid. and COE, GRECO Evaluations, http://www.greco.coe.int/evaluations/Default.htm (last visited 1 November 2013). See also Articles 10 to 16 of the Statute of the GRECO (Appendix to COE Resolution (99)5) and Title II of GRECO Rules of Procedure, Doc. No. Greco (2003) 6E Final Rev (11 July 2003). See also Locati (2003: 219–22).

31 On 1 January 2012, the GRECO had officially entered into its Fourth Round of mutual evaluations.

Round (2000–2002) dealt with specific provisions of the Twenty Guiding Principles for the Fight against Corruption: independence, specialisation, means and resources of national bodies engaged in the prevention and fight against corruption, and the extent and scope of immunities enjoyed by certain categories of holders of public office and/or elected representatives in respect of the investigation, prosecution and adjudication of corruption offences. The Second Evaluation Round (2003–2006) dealt with themes based on specific provisions of the Twenty Guiding Principles and associated provisions of the Criminal and Civil Law Conventions on Corruption: identification, seizure and confiscation of corruption proceeds, anti-corruption policies and mechanisms in public administration, prevention of legal persons being used as shields for corruption, tax and financial legislation to counter corruption, links between corruption, organised crime and money laundering. GRECO's third Evaluation Round (launched in January 2007) addressed two distinct themes. First, it deals with the incriminations, and the related substantial and procedural criminal provisions provided for in the Criminal Law Convention on Corruption, its Additional Protocol and Guiding Principle 2 (namely: definition of bribery offenses; sanctions; establishment of jurisdiction; statute of limitations; special or other defences). Secondly, it addresses the highly controversial themes of the transparency of political party funding, as understood by reference to the Committee of Ministers' Recommendation on Common Rules against Corruption in the Funding of Political Parties and Electoral Campaigns;[32] the main features of national electoral systems and political parties; political party accounts funding, contributions and contributors. GRECO's current Fourth Evaluation Round, launched on 1 January 2012, deals with corruption prevention in respect of members of Parliament, judges and prosecutors. The same priority issues are addressed in respect of all persons/functions under review, namely: ethical principles, rules of conduct and conflicts of interest; prohibition or restriction of certain activities; declaration of assets, income, liabilities and interests; enforcement of the applicable rules; awareness.[33]

---

[32] See Committee of Ministers' Recommendation on Common Rules against Corruption in the Funding of Political Parties and Electoral Campaigns. (Rec(2003)4). For further information on the procedures, questionnaires, and outcomes of the three rounds of evaluations which have been carried out by GRECO see: www.coe.int.greco. GRECO's pioneering venture of looking into political financing during its ongoing Third Evaluation Round, has proved to be a most valuable and unique initiative.

[33] As regards parliamentary assemblies, the evaluation focuses on members of national Parliaments, including all chambers of Parliament and regardless of

In each of the four Phases the evaluation process proceeds as follows:

(i) A first analysis of the situation in a member State is carried out by the Secretariat on the basis of replies to the questionnaires.
(ii) An Evaluation Team, supported by a member of the Secretariat, carries out an on-site evaluation visit (up to five days) during which further information is gathered through high-level discussions with key domestic players; the visit also includes talks with representatives of civil society (NGO's, media, professional organisations, etc.).
(iii) The members of the Evaluation Team submit their individual written contributions to the draft Evaluation Report, including proposals for recommendations, and a first draft of the Evaluation Report is prepared by the Secretariat and submitted to the Evaluation Team for comments.
(iv) A second draft is then drawn up by the Secretariat and sent to the member undergoing evaluation for comments.
(v) The Secretariat consults the Evaluation Team on the comments made by the member. If the views of the evaluators differ, a solution is negotiated; if necessary, a coordination meeting between national representatives, the Evaluation Team and the Secretariat is arranged.
(vi) A third draft is then sent to all GRECO members.
(vii) Draft evaluation reports are examined by GRECO during its plenary meetings and a revised draft containing any changes required by the debate is prepared for a second reading before adoption by the plenary.
(viii) Adopted reports are published with the authorisation of the country concerned.

A key ingredient of the procedure is the so-called Situation Report prepared by the member concerned, which has to be submitted 18 months after the adoption of the relevant Evaluation Report. On the basis of the Situation Report, a Compliance Report is prepared which assesses the level of implementation of each recommendation issued by GRECO in the Evaluation Report. The assessment ends up with three possible outcomes,

---

whether the members of Parliament are appointed or elected. Concerning the judiciary and other actors in the pre-judicial and judicial process, the evaluation focuses on prosecutors and on judges, both professional and lay judges, regardless of the type of court in which they sit, who are subject to national laws and regulations.

namely that a given recommendation has been implemented satisfactorily or otherwise dealt with in a satisfactory manner; has been partly implemented; has not been implemented. Members are required to report back to GRECO on the action taken in order to address partially or non-implemented recommendations within another 18 months. The additional information submitted is appraised by GRECO and leads to the adoption of an Addendum to the relevant Compliance report. The adoption of the Addendum usually terminates the compliance procedure in respect of the country concerned. All information pertaining to evaluation and compliance procedures is confidential. However, it is standing practice for members to authorise the publication of Evaluation and Compliance Reports, usually shortly after their adoption by the plenary. The mutual evaluation process aims at pursuing utmost transparency: the reports (Evaluation reports, Compliance reports and Addenda to Compliance reports) relating to the First, Second, Third and Fourth evaluation rounds are made available on-line in the public part of GRECO's website, once authorisation to publish has been given by the member State concerned.[34]

Overall, we believe that the GRECO's monitoring mechanism (alongside that of the OECD in relation to the OECD Convention) has been proved the more effective in supervising the implementation of the various parties of the COE Conventions. The activity the GRECO has carried out is massive: in about ten years GRECO has issued a large quantity of detailed evaluation reports, which are available on the internet and raised the governments' and public attention on the main obstacles to an effective anti-corruption action. The experience gathered in the context of the GRECO mutual evaluation process suggests that, in principle, evaluations should be limited in scope, with clear decisions having been taken as to the relevance of certain topics and sub-topics. In the same vein, key questions need to be carefully phrased. Evaluations should also be based on clear and identifiable standards. One of the most meaningful lessons learned by GRECO, throughout its years of operation, is that the collection of first-hand information during on-site evaluation visits (a fundamental feature of GRECO's modus operandi) contributes significantly to the quality of evaluations.[35] On-site visits are a major asset for the credibility

---

34 COE, "GRECO Evaluations", http://www.greco.coe.int/evaluations/Default.htm (last visited 1 November 2013). See First GRECO Report, Second GRECO Report, Third GRECO Report, and Fourth GRECO Report at; http://www.coe.int/t/dghl/monitoring/greco/evaluations/.

35 On this point let us remark that both the authors of the present book took part as experts and members of the civil society to the on-site Third Mutual Evaluation of Italy in Phase 3.

of the whole process in that they enable evaluation teams to hold thorough discussions with domestic key players (including representatives of civil society), to request additional information on-the-spot, and to shed light on often blurred and contentious issues. On-site visits also have the potential of adding value to the "mere" evaluation of legislation. Just to give an example, delicate issues of interpretation of certain legal concepts, relevant to the corruption offence (e.g., "undue advantage", "breach of duty"), the ensuing jurisprudence, as well as the problems involved in properly applying the legislation under scrutiny, cannot be adequately addressed without the possibility of discussing these matters with domestic practitioners.

Moreover, the GRECO has not avoided making public the various deficiencies on the part of the Contracting States as to implementation and enforcement of both the COE Conventions on Corruption. In addition, the wide scope of the COE Criminal Convention on Corruption has allowed the GRECO to verify the actual extent of the harmonization of national criminal law. This side-effect must not be understated since a common basis concerning the constitutive elements of the corrupt offenses plays a potentially crucial role also in easing international-criminal cooperation. Most importantly, the formation of the GRECO – a group of member States, non-member States, and organizations – puts the COE Convention in a broader context.

AU Convention

Turning to the AU Convention, the Advisory Board, modelled on the African Commission on Human and Peoples' Rights, is the AU's only formal monitoring measure at the international level and at the level of the AU Commission. The follow-up mechanism provided for in Article 22 calls for an Advisory Board of 11 members elected by the AU Executive Council, serving for a period of two years, renewable once, from among a list of experts of the highest integrity and recognized competence in matters relating to preventing and combating corruption and related offenses. Board members are to "serve in their personal capacity", but the fact that they are proposed by signatories does not help to guarantee their independence.

The Board has broad responsibilities for promoting anti-corruption work, collecting information on corruption and on the behavior of multinational corporations operating in Africa, developing methodologies, advising governments, developing codes of conduct for public officials, and building partnerships. In addition, pursuant to Article 22(5) of the Convention, the main mandate of the Board is to promote and encourage the adoption of measures and actions by State Parties to prevent, detect, punish and eradicate corruption and related offences in Africa as well as to follow-up on the application of those measures. It is required to submit a report to the Executive Council on a regular basis on the progress made by each State Party in complying with the provisions of the AU Convention.[36] At the same time, States Parties are required to report to the Board on their progress in implementing the AU Convention within a year after the coming into force of the AU Convention and thereafter on an annual basis through reports by national anti-corruption authorities to the Board. States Parties are also required to ensure and provide for the participation of civil society in the monitoring process. The Board is to submit regular reports to the executive council on the progress made by each signatory in compliance with the provisions of the convention.

However, the Board lacks any powers of 'investigation' and of acting *proprio motu.* Another drawback of this system is that the AU has no means of sanctioning countries that fail to report, unlike in the reporting process for the African Charter on Human and Peoples' Rights. Overall, the Convention mechanism for holding States accountable for the obligations they assume under it is defective. As noted above, there is no system for resolving disputes among State Parties, including a potential claim by one party that another is failing to properly carry out its obligations. As already suggested, amending the Convention as a protocol to the African Charter should seriously be considered to guarantee a minimum level of effectiveness for the Convention.

UNCAC

The UNCAC leaves open the issue of the form and structure of a follow-up or mutual evaluation mechanism. Given experience with other anti-bribery and anti-corruption conventions, our stance is that a vigorous mutual evaluation mechanism, with the possible involvement of civil

---

36 The Advisory Board held its first meeting in May 2009 in Addis Ababa, Ethiopia. The Board held its second meeting held in Addis Ababa, Ethiopia, in December 2009. The Advisory Board held its third meeting in March 2010 in Addis Ababa, Ethiopia. The meeting elected its new Bureau and discussed among other things, its 2010 activities programme, and follow-up actions on the establishment of the Secretariat of the Advisory Board; strengthening of the capacity of national anti-corruption bodies and mapping of corruption in terms of its nature and scope; and the promotion of the AU Convention on Preventing and Combating Corruption. The Board remained committed to ensuring the full implementation of the AU Convention on Preventing and Combating Corruption, entered into force in August 2006, and will fulfill its mandate as defined by the decisions of the Executive Council and the Assembly of Heads of States of the African Union.

society, is vital to securing effective national implementation and enforcement. However, proposals for such a mechanism proved too controversial to resolve before the Convention was adopted. Numerous concerns were raised, including the scope of the Convention, the potential for duplication of other convention review mechanisms, differences in political systems, concerns about sovereignty, cost and lack of capacity. Therefore, unlike the OECD Convention, which established from the very outset a supervising mechanism to ensure appropriate implementation and enforcement, and similar provisions of the COE criminal and civil law conventions on corruption, the UNCAC does not prescribe such a mechanism. Rather, Article 63 establishes a Conference of States Parties (COSP) to the Convention which will meet periodically to facilitate the aim to "promote and review its implementation",[37] and to facilitate cooperation, technical assistance and training, as well as information exchange. In the end, the COSP is charged solely with establishing rules and activities necessary to secure and review implementation. Note that Chapter VI also provides for technical assistance and training, as well as information exchange.

Some of the proposals certain delegations of States made during the negotiating process are presented in Box 16.1. By comparing them with the current we attempt to show that the UNCAC missed a unique chance to design a truly innovative supervising system.[38]

According to the text of the UNCAC, the COSP may establish a mechanism to "assist in the effective implementation of the Convention", but only if "it deems it necessary".[39] The *travaux préparatoires* indicate that nothing in this section is intended to limit the discretion of the Conference of States Parties in making this decision.[40] As some commentators argue, the challenges faced by other international bodies in making their respective monitoring mechanisms effective suggest that an UNCAC monitoring mechanism would have faced even higher hurdles. Had the UNCAC established such a mechanism from the outset, it seems likely its potential for effectiveness would have been widely questioned. On the other hand, experience to date has shown that some monitoring capacity, whether

---

37 See UNCAC, Article 63, esp. paragraphs 4, 7.

38 We owe most of our analysis to the thoughtful reconstruction of Webb (2005).

39 As above, Article 63(7).

40 Report of the Ad Hoc Committee for the Negotiation of a Convention Against Corruption on the work of its first to seventh sessions, Addendum: Interpretative notes for the official records (*travaux préparatoires*) of the negotiation of the United Nations Convention against Corruption, at 12, UN Doc. A/58/422/Add.1 (2003).

BOX 16.1 UNCAC MONITORING MECHANISM: SOME PROPOSALS MADE DURING THE NEGOTIATING PROCESS

At the second session of the Ad Hoc Committee charged with drafting the future Convention, Austria and The Netherlands submitted a proposal for a monitoring mechanism[41]. They suggested the establishment of a Conference of States Parties with the objectives of facilitating training and technical assistance, exchanging information, cooperating with regional organizations and NGOs, reviewing implementation "periodically", and making recommendations to improve the Convention.[42] They also called for a Subsidiary Body of ten experts elected by the States parties which would assess reports submitted by States parties on their implementation of the Convention (thus combining mutual and self-review).[43]

The weak spot of this proposal was that reports need *only* be submitted every five years and even though the Subsidiary Body could request further information, there was no mention of on-site visits or other means of verifying the accuracy of the country reports.[44]

Subsequently, Norway submitted an amendment to this aspect of the Convention that was much more rigorous. It proposed a regional evaluation process whereby States Parties in Africa, America, Asia, Europe, and Oceania appoint a Bureau to assist the Subsidiary Body. Our view is that had this proposal been accepted, the UNCAC could have resorted to an innovative

---

41 Proposals and Contributions Received from Governments: Austria and The Netherlands: Amendments to Articles 66 to 70, UN Doc A/AC.261/L.69 (2003).

42 Article 66 in Proposals and Contributions Received from Governments: Austria and The Netherlands: Amendments to Articles 66 to 70, UN Doc A/AC.261/L.69 (2002).

43 Articles 67 and 68 in Proposals and Contributions Received from Governments: Austria and The Netherlands: Amendments to Articles 66 to 70, UN Doc A/AC.261/L.69 (2002).

44 Article 68 in Proposals and Contributions Received from Governments: Austria and The Netherlands: Amendments to Articles 66 to 70, UN Doc A/AC.261/L.69 (2002).

monitoring mechanism, which inter alia could have better coped with its universal vocation.[45]

Norway also set out a two-phase evaluation process, based on the OECD Convention. Phase 1 would focus on whether the domestic laws of each state party fulfill the requirements of the Convention. Phase 2 would study the structures put in place to enforce the laws, with provision for on-site visits.[46]

In addition, Norway's proposal set forth innovative methods for addressing non-compliance with the Convention, including positive (targeted technical assistance) and negative (suspension of the State Party from the Convention) measures. This would have manifestly gone a step further than any other previous multilateral initiative against corruption. At the end of the day, neither of these proposals secured enough support.

The Austrian and Dutch proposal for establishing a Conference of States Parties to facilitate activities and information exchange was retained.[47] Yet, the proposals on the Subsidiary Body and the regional evaluation process did not make it into the final Convention. Instead, each State party is to provide information on its implementation measures "as required by the Conference of States Parties".[48]

The role of civil society is weak: the UNCAC may consider inputs from NGOs "duly Accredited" in accordance with procedures that are yet to be decided, with no time limit specified for such a decision.[49]

challenged or not, is essential. It cannot, thus, simply be concluded that the UN are not in the proper position to effectively monitor such an all-embracing instrument. Rather, the way being followed seems to lie in crafting a mechanism that is complementary and non-duplicative of the efforts of other organizations that are judged to be effective. The resource-intensiveness of monitoring systems suggests that every effort should

---

45 Proposals and Contributions Received from Governments: Norway: Amendments to Article 68 as Submitted in the proposal by Austria and The Netherlands, UN Doc A/AC.261/L.78 (2002).

46 Ibid.

47 Article 63 of the UNCAC.

48 As above, Article 63(6).

49 Ibid.

be made to rationalize monitoring efforts among different international bodies and to avoid duplication and inefficiency. Though difficult to achieve, the UN should also promote harmonization in implementation as far as possible.

Nonetheless, the Conference of State Parties of the UNCAC has convened six times, in December 2006, January–February 2008,[50] November 2009, October 2011 and November 2013.[51] To establish an effective monitoring system has been one of the main priorities of the Conference, but progress has appeared limited for a long time, with the Contracting Parties still continuing to work on the precise framework and scope of the monitoring program. As Low (2008) aptly points out, it appears that relevant variations in terms of both degree and nature of implementation may be occurring by region, with countries in Europe and the Americas having more uniform and comprehensive implementing laws than in other regions, where prior anti-corruption conventions were not in force or entered into force only recently. In light of the above, efforts through the UNODC to provide technical assistance to parties in adapting their legal regimes to the UNCAC requirements are highly recommended. As a matter of fact, in November 2009, the third UNCAC COSP adopted a formal review mechanism for the UNCAC, including Terms of Reference for that mechanism. In short, the resolution adopting the review mechanism encouraged governments to include civil society and private sector inputs to their self-assessments and left it optional for governments to decide whether to allow a country visit and whether to involve civil society and the private sector to make inputs during the country visits. In July 2010, the Implementation Review Group (IRG) that oversees the review mechanism met for the first time in Vienna and adopted guidelines for governmental experts and the secretariat, which to our disappointment

50 The Conference of State Parties has been assisted in its efforts by the Intergovernmental Working Group on Review of the Implementation of the United Nations Convention Against Corruption. See Report on the meeting of the Open-ended Intergovernmental Working Group on Review of the Implementation of the United Nations Convention Against Corruption (12 September 2007), available at: http://css.undoc.org/pdf/crime/convention_corruption/cosp/session2/V0786745e.pdf; and Report of the Conference of State Parties to the United Nations Convention against Corruption on its second session, held in Nusa Dua, Indonesia, from 28 January to 1 February 2008. CAC/COSP/2008/15, also available for download at: www.unodc.org/unodc/en/treaties/CAC/CAC-COSP-session2.html.

51 For further information on the monitoring procedure and the reports of each session of the Conference of State Parties, see: http://www.unodc.org/unodc/en/treaties/CAC/CAC-COSP.html.

do not reference these various options.[52] The IRG also selected the countries to be reviewed in each year of the first five-year round of the review process, covering the topics of Criminalisation, Enforcement and Mutual Legal Assistance (UNCAC Chapters III and IV).[53]

In more detail, in its Resolution 3(1), entitled "Review mechanism", the Conference recalled Article 63 of the UNCAC, especially paragraph 7, according to which the Conference should establish, if it deemed necessary, any appropriate mechanism or body to assist in the effective implementation of the Convention. In the same resolution, the COSP adopted, subject to the provisions of the Resolution 3(1), the terms of reference of the Mechanism for the Review of Implementation of UNCAC, contained in the annex to the present resolution, and the draft guidelines for governmental experts and the secretariat in the conduct of country reviews and the draft blueprint for country review reports, contained in the appendix to the annex, which have been lately finalized by the Implementation Review Group at its first session. Furthermore, in its Resolution 4(1), entitled "Mechanism for the Review of Implementation of the United Nations Convention against Corruption", the COSP recalled its decision, contained in its Resolution 3(1), by which the Group was charged with following up and continuing the work undertaken previously by the Open-ended Intergovernmental Working Group on Technical Assistance, and taking into account the circumstance that, pursuant to paragraph 11 of the terms of reference, one of the goals of the Mechanism is to help States Parties to identify and substantiate specific needs for technical assistance and to promote and facilitate the provision of technical assistance. In the same resolution, the Conference recalled in particular, as laid out in its Resolution 3(4), its endorsement of country-led and country-based, integrated and coordinated technical assistance programme delivery and its encouragement to donors to accord high priority to technical assistance to implement the United Nations Convention against Corruption.[54] From a practical angle, the Mechanism for the Review of Implementation of the UNCAC, supervised by the IRG,

---

52 The IRG is an open-ended group, composed of representatives of the States Parties.

53 Cfr. http://www.unodc.org/unodc/en/treaties/CAC/IRG.html.

54 In addition, in the same resolution, the COSP endorsed Implementation Review Group Resolution 1(1), entitled "Resource requirements for the functioning of the Mechanism for the Review of Implementation of the United Nations Convention against Corruption for the biennium 2012–2013". For further specific information on the IRG Country Profiles see http://www.unodc.org/unodc/en/treaties/CAC/country-profile/index.html. Detailed information on the Sessions of the Implementation Review Group, List of Governmental Experts, Country Pairings for the Review Cycle, UNCAC Self-Assessment Checklist see the basic

combines a self-assessment with a governmental peer-review, each country being reviewed by the governmental representatives of two other countries. The review process at issue consists of the following three steps: (1) a self-assessment report is produced by the country under review by completing a comprehensive checklist; (2) the self-assessment report is assessed by experts from two reviewing countries, including a country visit if requested by the reviewed country; and (3) the reviewers produce a final country review report, which is finalised in agreement with the country under review. The Mechanism started operation in July 2010. Two review cycles of five years each will take place. As hinted above, in the first cycle (2010–2014), the implementation of UNCAC Chapter III on Criminalization and Law enforcement and Chapter IV on International cooperation will be reviewed. The second cycle (2015–2019) will cover Chapter II on Preventive measures and Chapter V on Asset recovery.

Considering the vague formulation and non-mandatory nature of several provisions of the UNCAC, alongside the relatively weak monitoring mechanism (particularly, the absence of timelines and concrete means of commitment),[55] not surprisingly, some have questioned whether this global and wide-reaching exercise might constitute a paradigmatic example of what Reisman calls a *lex simulata*,[56] that is to say "a legislative exercise that produces a statutory instrument apparently operable, but one that neither prescribers, those charged with its administration, nor the putative target audience ever intend to be applied".[57]

---

documents available at: https://www.unodc.org/unodc/en/treaties/CAC/IRG.html.

55 Most notably, no follow-up process has been established yet in order to address the implementation by national Parliaments and governments of the recommendations made in the context country reviews.

56 Webb (2005: 221), who goes on to state: "(t)his is an area where UNCAC has not shown any innovation. It follows the formula of the weakest regional conventions by giving state parties a large degree of leeway to decide if and how far to incorporate the Convention into national law. Deferring consideration of a monitoring mechanism until the Conference of States Parties is convened one year after the Convention acquires 30 ratifications and enters into force will probably result in a delay of several years. In the meantime, governments have little incentive to pass implementing laws. As imperfect as they are, the monitoring mechanisms of the OECD and COE demonstrate that peer review and mutual evaluation can produce some results such as raising public awareness and encouraging the passage of implementing laws. Moreover, the UNCAC could have taken this opportunity to propose the creation of a new international institution for review and adjudication. Rose-Ackerman suggests that tribunals in the fields of human rights, international labor standards and nuclear energy might be models."

57 Reisman (1979: 31).

If the (ambitious) aim of the UNCAC is to work as a blueprint for policy reform at a global level, it is necessary to consider not just the formal provisions, but how they will impact on societies. To this end, a functioning and effective supervisory mechanism to impel States to measure up to their international undertakings is essential. It is no secret that "Law", in the sense of a set of formal written normative documents, is largely irrelevant if the rules are not embedded in an institutional and organizational structure that permits compliance.[58] The work by Thomas and Grindle suggests an "interactive" model of reform which requires States Parties to follow through on their decision to sign and ratify the Convention. In light of the above, the UNCAC must be translated into visible, meaningful, and sustainable changes on the ground.[59] From yet another angle, the underlying idea of a working and vigorous monitoring system is to assure as far as possible the "effectiveness" of the Treaty, to be intended as effective compliance with its provisions on the part of those who are subject to these obligations, who are the same subjects who have adopted, signed and ratified it. When considering the (current) monitoring mechanism set forth by the UNCAC along with the many optional provisions about remarkable issues (e.g. criminalization of private-to-private corruption; the *vexata questio* of illicit financing to political parties; the several offenses the criminalization of which is optional; the extension of jurisdiction beyond the territorial criterion and so forth), it is still an open question whether the extremely ambitious aims of a unique "global" anti-corruption treaty are likely to be achieved.

After more than three years of operation the UNCAC IRG Mechanism seems off to a promising but unbalanced start with substantial room for improvement in a number of key aspects.

First, no follow-up process has been established yet to address the implementation by governments of the recommendations made in the country reviews. Without timely follow-up it is hardly possible to ensure that the recommendations are acted upon and the purpose of the review process is undermined. We explain the point further. After investing considerable resources[60] into running country reviews it stands to reason that there should be follow-up on the findings and recommendations. Without

---

58 Rose-Ackerman (2004).

59 See Thomas and Grindle (1990). This position is voiced also by Borlini and Magrini (2007).

60 Overall cost of the Review Mechanism is approximately USD 3,000,000 in a given year as reported to the Implementation Review Group. For the detailed budget see: www.unodc.org/documents/treaties/UNCAC/WorkingGroups/ImplementationReviewGroup/14–16November2012/V1257290e.pdf.

a clear and prompt process for follow-up, governments might simply move on to other business instead of implementing the recommendations in the country review. Therefore, in its next reunion, the COSP should require States Parties to prepare national "action plans" to respond promptly to recommendations made in the country review reports and overcome the deficiencies highlighted therein. Such plans should be submitted to UNODC, the two peer-review countries and the IRG, as well as, in order to guarantee the utmost transparency of States' commitments, published on the UNODC website. The action plans should include information on technical assistance required, where applicable. Publication of countries' action plans on the UNODC website is also recommended.

Second, as stressed by TI (2013b), the UNCAC's review procedure is significantly behind schedule with approximately 120 country reviews to be completed in less than two years remaining in the first cycle of reviews. UNODC has built up a high-quality expert staff to manage the implementation review process and to support the governments conducting peer reviews, but the delays in the review process indicates that a more responsive attitude of States Parties is needed to deal with such issue. This should help speed up the completion of lagging country reviews and possibly introduce broader, systemic steps to expedite the review process.[61]

The third issue is about transparency. Forty-five executive summaries have been completed and published on the country pages of the UNODC website as of September 2013. However, only 17 country review reports and 16 country self-assessment reports have been published.[62] Unlike the OECD and COE's procedures, publication of self-assessment reports and country review reports is not mandatory and remitted to the voluntary authorisation of some States Parties. The executive summaries published by UNODC are informative, but the low number of published country review reports remarkably restricts the possibility to assess the adequacy of the summaries and to dispose of detailed information on the shortcomings of the national implementing pieces of legislation. Furthermore, such deficiency of the UNCAC's supervisory system affects public understanding about the review process and the Convention itself.

It is, therefore, recommended to make it compulsory to publish the country review reports as well as government self-assessment reports

---

61 Note that even the Fifth COSP, which occurred in November 2013, failed to achieve such goals despite the substantial efforts made by both the UNODC Secretariat and some of the States Parties.

62 Either on the UNODC website or on national websites. See TI (2013b).

on the UNODC website and, possibly, also publish them on national websites.

Fourth, the practice of country visits has become the norm[63] and should be followed in all countries undergoing review. Accessibility and quality of information that is published about the country visit (including information about the focal point and schedule) should be increased.

Sixth, country reviews in many countries have emphasised that several governments need technical assistance to enable them to comply with the UNCAC. In spite of the fact that assistance is already being provided by UNODC and some governments, resources do not suffice, and, as a result, technical assistance is insufficient to meet the demand. To have at their disposal qualified technical assistance is a key element for implementing the UNCAC in several of the countries mostly affected by corruption. The issue should be coped with at both the national and international level. On the one hand, indeed, in order to streamline the use of resources, States Parties that have requested or will require technical assistance should include information about its delivery as part of their action plan. On the other hand, within the UNCTOD, it should be assessed whether, other inter-governmental institutions with competences on the matter and non-governmental organisations with expertise in areas covered by technical assistance should be invited to participate in the development and, where appropriate, delivery of technical assistance programmes.

Finally, it is worth remarking that, the *sine qua non* conditions for the actual success of the OECD and COE Conventions, namely: governments must prosecute bribe payers (as far as the OECD must accelerate monitoring of enforcement and close loopholes in the Convention); public awareness of the Convention must be increased; companies must be sanctioned to adopt effectively and proportionately in case of involvement in corrupt misconduct; and civil society groups must exert pressure to assure that all these steps are taken. Since these conditions are necessary for the OECD Convention – the scope of which is extremely restricted if compared with that of UNCAC – *mutatis mutandis* analogous and stricter conditions should be met also for achieving the goals of the UNCAC. Accordingly, the review mechanism must be particularly rigorous in respect of the above-referred areas and complemented with a proper follow-up process established in order to address the implementation by national Parliaments and governments of the recommendations made in the context country reviews.

---

63 According to TI (2013b), almost 90 per cent of the 60 countries surveyed, governments have agreed to permit country visits.

A final remark. The publication of detailed and rigorous evaluation reports envisaged by the monitoring systems of the OECD Convention and the COE Criminal and Civil Conventions – which, in our opinion, are the best-designed and most effective among the supervising mechanisms of the international anti-bribery treaties – might respond to those who advocate a return of an authentic *shame culture* (comparable to the Ancient Greeks' ostracism) also within the international community.

Firstly, it permits legal operators and scholars to rely on *official* documents upon which are grounded a balanced and objective assessment, not only of the implementing legislation, but also of the pieces of municipal legislation *adopted after* the implementation of the international provisions, which may happen to conflict with the latter, and the application of the implementing of national laws. In this sense, the case of the Italian legislation adopted after the implementation of the OECD Convention, between 2001 and 2003, so vividly described by Sacerdoti (2003), is most telling. Similar considerations may be advanced with reference to the UK anti-corruption law prior to the adoption of the UK Bribery Act in 2010: the OECD WGB "criticised the UK harshly at various instances"[64] (Pieth, 2011: 33), and this has played a pivotal role in stimulating the drafting of the new legislation on corruption.[65]

What is more, the data in the reports allow public officials, along with legal and economic scholars and practitioners, to engage in horizontal comparative studies of the national implementing laws, the role of which is essential for those who are willing to evaluate the impact of international *hard law* on different national legal systems and the possible feedbacks international organizations may get from the national authorities who must apply the municipal pieces of legislation. For example, after Phase 1 of the monitoring mechanism envisaged by Article 12 of the OECD Convention, Magrini submitted a meticulous study which, in light of the evaluation reports of the WGB, identifies some remarkable flaws

---

64 Cfr., e.g., OECD, United Kingdom: Review of Implementation of the Convention and 1997 Recommendation: Phase 1 bis Report, 03.03.2003; OECD, United Kingdom: Phase 2: Report on the Application of the Convention on Combating Bribery of Foreign Public Officials in International Business Transactions and the 1997 Recommendation on Combating Bribery in International Business Transactions, 17.03.2005; OECD, United Kingdom: Phase 2 bis: Report on the Application of the Convention on Combating Bribery of Foreign Public Officials in International Business Transactions and the 1997 Recommendation on Combating Bribery in International Business Transactions, 16.10.2008.

65 Cfr. Pieth (2011).

within the implementing legislation of Australia, Canada, France, and Switzerland.[66]

Secondly, public opinion (at least the part of it which is willing to understand whether and how a certain State complies with its international obligations) is energetically stimulated to realize and, eventually express its discontent towards, the conduct of a certain State. For instance, at least at the international level, notable emphasis has been placed on the fact that, during the on-site visit to Italy in the framework of the Phase 2 of the OECD follow-up procedure, the examination team was not able (*recte*: was not put into the conditions) to meet the law enforcement officials in Milan, who, inter alia, investigated, disclosed, and prosecuted the widespread systemic corrupt practices which had plagued the Italian political and economic system (the "Clean Hands" case), and carried out the investigative process in relation to other extremely complex and relevant corrupt cases.

Thirdly, one can easily note that media attention concerning the OECD and COE reports has steadily increased in recent years.[67] Staying with the Italian case, in an interview for *L'Espresso*, Drago Kos, then Chairman of the GRECO,[68] vibrantly voiced his skepticism regarding a series of actual and possible legislative reforms which might amend the Italian criminal procedural provisions as regards the investigative phase, and especially the legal regime of wire-tapping.[69]

Finally, practitioners also make use of these reports to assess national pieces of legislation, and sometimes denounce their main flaws.

---

66 See Magrini (2003).

67 See, for instance, the following reports on OECD Phase 2: with reference to Italy, Giudici Off Limits, *L'Espresso*, 26 December 2004. As to the UK, suffice it here to mention the following: Embarrassment for Blair as UK Faulted on Bribery Drive, *Financial Times*, 19 March 2005; OECD Criticises UK Bribery Fight, *BBC News*, 18 March 2005.

68 Incidentally, Italy adhered to the GRECO only in 2007. For a comprehensive assessment of the Italian anti-corruption legal framework and its compliance with COE's instruments against corruption see GRECO, Joint First and Second Evaluation Round, 2 July 2009 GRECO Eval I/II Rep (2008) 2E (particularly, the criticism expressed about the lack of a coordinated anti-corruption program, ID. p. 28); GRECO, Compliance Report on Italy, 27 May 2011, GRECO RC I/II (2011) 1E; GRECO, Third Evaluation Round, 23 March 2012, GRECO Eval. III Rep (2011) 7E.

69 See Tangenti SPA, *L'Espresso*, 2 October 2008, pp. 61–5, esp. p. 63.

17. Asset recovery

17.1 LEGAL GROUNDS AND EVOLUTION OF THE REGULATIONS REGARDING THE MECHANISMS OF INTERNATIONAL RESTITUTION OF PROCEEDS FROM ILLICIT ACTIVITY

The idea of creating a multilateral cooperation system for the recovery and restitution of assets that originate from crime is quite recent despite the fact that this phenomenon has had a significant economic and social impact, as everybody knows, especially with regard to developing countries.[1] The IMF has estimated that the money that is laundered each year is equivalent to 3–5 percent of worldwide GDP: it is a sum that fluctuates between $600 billion and $1,800 trillion, of which a considerable part originates from corruption crimes.[2] Furthermore, several cases show not only how relevant it is to recover such assets but also how difficult

---

1 According to the Nyanga Declaration on the Recovery and Repatriation of the African Wealth, for example, "an estimated US$ 20–40 billion has over the decades been illegally and corruptly appropriated from some of the world's poorest countries, most of them in Africa, by politicians, soldiers, businesspersons and other leaders, and kept abroad in the form of cash, stocks and bonds, real estate and other assets". The Nyanga Declaration was signed on 4 March 2001 by the representatives of Transparency International in Botswana, Cameroon, Ethiopia, Ghana, Kenya, Malawi, Nigeria, South Africa, Uganda, Zambia, Zimbabwe, available at: www.transparency.org.

2 See Ad Hoc Committee for the Negotiation of a Convention Against Corruption, Global Study on the Transfer of Funds of Illicit Origin, especially Funds Derived from Acts of Corruption, 4th Session, Agenda Item 3, Doc. A/AC.261/12, November 2002, p. 3. We may understand the economic impact by taking Nigeria as an example; the representative of this country in the Second Committee of the General Assembly – 57th session – declared that approximately $100 billion were transferred abroad from Nigeria: an enormous amount considering that in 2001 the external debt amounted to $28 million, with a GDP equal to $41 billion and 124 million people living on less than $1 per day. The Declaration of the Representative of Nigeria is in the UN Press Release of 14 October 2002 (GA/EF/3002), p. 8. The data is from World Bank, *World Development Indicators 2001*, pp. 45 and 65.

it is for countries to retrieve assets from an illicit source. Unfortunately, despite the recent international efforts to improve the anti-corruption legal framework and internationally-based asset recovery strategies, "money continues to get stolen", and, what is more, "get stolen at a much faster pace than it is being recovered" (Pieth, 2013: xi). Among these cases, it is worth mentioning the sums stolen by the Congolese dictator, Mobutu, by Marcos in the Philippines or Sani Abacha in Nigeria from 1993 to 1998, a period when he misappropriated a sum of between $2 and $5 billion, and, more recently, several significant cases of stolen asset emerged from the Arab Spring. For example, ex-Libyan leader Muammar Gaddafi is estimated to have looted between $30–80 billion from state coffers, whilst the former Tunisian President, Zine el-Abidine Ben Ali, is said to have stolen $3–5 billion during his term of office.[3] The estimates concerning the value of funds stolen by the former Egyptian leader Hosni Mubarak are even more undetermined, though of no less concern. Experts place the amount at anywhere between $1–70 billion.[4] Some of the mentioned cases will be examined in greater detail, if briefly, hereinafter with regard to the relative regulations provided by the UNCAC.

The first proposals regarding mandatory repatriation of the assets originating from corruption were developed by internationalist doctrine in the 1980s. Some authors advanced the idea of introducing the crime of "*spoliation indigène*", "*patrimonicide*" (Kofele Kale 1995b; Reisman 1989; Harms 2000) or "*kleptocratie*" (Hartmann 1997)[5] into the international legal system. This offense is defined as "an illegal act of depredation committed for private ends by constitutionally responsible rulers, public officials or private individuals" (Kofele Kale 1995b: 48), or as "large scale corruption committed by modern day governments . . . at the expense of the general populations of nations" (Kofele Kale 1995b: 56). According to this definition, "*spoliation indigéne*" goes beyond "simple" corruption or a mere crime against property; it is seen as a violation of human rights and, in particular, of a nation's right to freely use its own wealth and resources:[6]

---

3 See StAR Asset Recovery Watch Database, available at: http://star.worldbank.org/corruption-cases/arwcases.

4 See Dornbierer and Fenner Zinkernagel (2013). We refer to Saad, Feller *et al.*, (2013) for an effective illustration of the main obstacles met by the authorities involved in recovering the assets stolen by Mubarak, once a part of them had been partially located. According to the authors, his case, like some recent others demonstrates that there is an undeniable need for targeted internationally-based strategies to be furthered and utilised to better streamline and coordinate asset recovery processes.

5 "Kleptocracy" literally means "rule by thieves".

6 In this regard see UN Resolutions 1515 (XV) of 1960 and 1803 (XVII) of

"The right of people not to be dispossessed of their wealth and natural resources is not just any ordinary human right, but the fundamental human right, the right that transcends all others" (Hartmann 1997: 170). Enhancing efforts to recover stolen funds, thus, is an effective way to curb corruption: it impedes criminals from the benefits of their misconduct and, in the end, may reduce motivations for corruption in the future.

From the profile given above of the crime of international corruption, the obligation to return the stolen assets to the States concerned seems to be a logical consequence. Until the 1990s, the mechanisms for the restitution of goods originating from an illicit activity were provided almost exclusively by the treaties for the protection of cultural objects or traffic of drugs. We are going to briefly mention only the case regarding cultural objects since this might be a potential model for solving the matter regarding the restitution of goods stolen and taken abroad by corrupt officers. Incidentally, we would like to point out that, also in this case, some authors believe that there is actually already an international obligation to return cultural objects (Goy 1979; Frigo 2001).

The United Nations Educational, Scientific and Cultural Organization (UNESCO) Convention on the means to be adopted to prohibit and prevent the illicit import, export and transfer of cultural property[7] (1970) also deals with the restitution of those goods that are illicitly transferred and provides *in primis* a general obligation upon the competent national services, i.e. it facilitates the restitution of property[8] that has been illicitly

1962, the Declaration on the Creation of a New International Economic Order (Res. 3201) with the relevant action plan, but also the several opposing positions regarding the adoption of the Charter of Rights and Duties of States of 12 December 1974 (Res. AG 3281). See in this regard Gallagher's declaration; he was the Irish representative who admitted that the charter was adopted "against the wishes of a small but important number of States representing an indispensable component without which a new international economic order could have little real meaning" (UN Doc. A/C 2/SR 1709, pp.4–5). Ribadu (2008) provides a brilliant illustration of the challenges of and opportunities for asset recovery in a developing economy

7 Convention on the Means of Prohibiting and Preventing the Illicit Import, Export and Transfer of Ownership of Cultural Property. The UNESCO Convention of 14 November 1970 came into force on the 24 April 1972.

8 Incidentally, it is noteworthy that "the term 'cultural property' means property which, on religious or secular grounds, is specifically designated by each State as being of importance for archaeology, prehistory, history, literature, art or science and which belongs to the following categories" (Article 1 UNESCO Convention). Article 1 defines the coverage of the Convention, including all those goods that have an artistic, historical, archeological, literary and scientific importance and have been indicated as such by the State Party. Therefore the list is not

imported (Article 13, letter b). The said obligation (which indiscriminately refers to all objects that are illicitly transferred) is mitigated by the limit of the "consistency with the current national laws"; the limit is inserted in the first comma of Article 13. Furthermore, Article 13, letter c, provides that governments have to include in their own legal system an action for recovery of property with regard to the goods either lost or stolen and the same is to be exercised by the legitimate owner or by someone else who is a legitimate representative. In this case, the State Parties undertake to facilitate the restitution of the property that is classified and declared *inalienable* by the country of origin (Article 13, letter d).[9] Article 7, letter b) ii) is the most important provision related to the restitution of property, according to which the State Party undertakes to take appropriate measures to recover and return the cultural property stolen from a museum or a religious or secular public monument or similar institution to the State of origin – either a Party to this Convention or any State asking for the restitution. The condition for the restitution is that the cultural property is included in the institution's inventory, the request is through diplomatic offices and a just compensation is paid to third parties who are innocent legally rightful purchasers or a person who has a valid title to the property in question. In any case, the UNESCO Convention does not solve certain issues related to the restitution of property, such as the relation between the action *ex* Article 7 and the ordinary claim of ownership, the criteria for calculating the just compensation to innocent third parties, and deciding upon the exact content of the burden of proof upon the requesting State.

The principles included in the UNESCO Convention have been acknowledged by the International Institute for the Unification of Private Law (UNIROIT) Convention on Stolen or Illegally Exported Cultural Objects, adopted in Rome on 24 June 1995; this latter convention deals with some of the issues left unsolved by the Treaty of 1970. It is a uniform-law convention that aims to establish "common, minimal legal rules for the restitution and return of cultural objects between Contracting States, with the objective of improving the preservation and

---

complete or absolute. Moreover Article 4 describes the categories of goods that are part of the "cultural heritage" of a country, i.e. those goods that, according to the Convention, are considered part of the cultural heritage of each State Party, regardless of the designation of the State Party itself. "In this way the individual national heritages of the State Parties and a limited and identified nucleus of goods that are a common international heritage" (Frigo 2001: 7).

9 The term "Country of origin" is used to identify the place from which the goods are transferred.

protection of the cultural heritage in the interest of all" – as is written in the preamble; in other words, the aim is to obtain a larger harmonization of the international law relating to cases of "restitution" of stolen cultural objects (Article 1, letter a) and "return" of the illegally exported goods (letter b).[10] Focusing attention on the first hypothesis, according to Article 3, the possessor of a stolen object, or an object which has been unlawfully excavated or lawfully excavated but unlawfully retained, when the theft is consistent with the law of the State where the excavation took place, has to return it even if the possessor is in good faith.[11] It has to be highlighted how innovative this principle is: it is not included in several civil-law systems, which traditionally apply the "possession-equals-legal title" rule and in such cases the latter is quite difficult to apply efficaciously. Several judgments with regard to the restitution of stolen goods claimed by the legitimate owner against the possessor in good faith[12] were not, in fact, in favor of the claimant.[13] The claim for restitution has to be brought within a period of three years from the time when the claimant became aware of the location of the object and the identity of its possessor, or within 50 years from the time of the theft, if the claimant is not aware of the aforementioned information. Vice versa the action of claiming the restitution of goods from public collections or an identified archeological site does not undergo any statute of limitations (Article 3, § 4), except for the term of three years starting from the time when both the location and the possessor were known (goods of a

---

10 Article 1 of the Convention. Restitution of property illicitly exported concerns goods that were transferred "from the territory of a State Party" violating the relevant rules. With regard to the definition of cultural goods, Article 2 provides that they are "the goods that, on religious or secular grounds, are relevant for archeology, prehistory, history, literature, art or science, in particular those that belong to one of the categories listed in the annex to the present Convention". This definition, even if similar to the one given by the UNESCO Convention, differs in one key respect: definition of the "relevance" of the work is not given exclusively to the domestic law of the State Parties. Article 2 provides that the application of the Convention is directed to the goods that are included in the definition *ex* Article 1 and that belong to the categories included in the relative annexed list.

11 Dealing with a stolen object as if it were an archeological object from either lawful or unlawful excavations allows a request for restitution to be exercised also with regard to the objects that have not been included in an inventory.

12 Actually the UNIDROIT Convention talks about *due diligence*.

13 See the *Wildenstein v. Pazzaglia and others* controversy with regard to the claim of the "Danese Espagnole" painting by the artist Giovanni Boldini. The controversy was already judged by the first and the second instance courts, respectively by the Italian Court (judgment of 5 January 1995) and the Court of Appeal of Bologna (judgment of 17 July 1998).

sacred nature or of a collective importance that belong to autochthonous or aboriginal communities are considered equal to the aforementioned goods).

With regard to compensation, Article 4 provides that the possessor in good faith of stolen cultural objects, if requested to return them, is entitled to "fair compensation": the amount of which is to be calculated on the basis of the free judgment of the competent judge. The State Parties undertake[14] to provide that the person who assigned the cultural object to the possessor pays the compensation if this is consistent with the law of the State in which the claim of restitution is brought; if, on the other hand, the payment of compensation is done by the owner, the claimant can recover it from any other person involved in the crime (paragraphs 2 and 3 Article 4). In this way, those who purchase cultural objects without performing a thorough enquiry – "due diligence" – before purchasing them will be punished. According to § 4 of Article 4, the good faith of the possessor can be assessed following some objective criteria mentioned in this section: "the character of the parties, the price paid, whether the possessor consulted any reasonably accessible register of stolen cultural objects, and any other relevant information and documentation which the possessor could reasonably have obtained, and whether the possessor consulted accessible agencies or took any other step that a reasonable person would have taken in the circumstances".

Therefore, the burden of proof is upon the possessor, who has to prove his due diligence and that it was not reasonably possible to know the illicit origin of the object: the said rule definitely seems to effectively discourage illicit traffic of cultural objects.[15] Finally, Article 4.5 provides that the possessor in good faith of a cultural object, received either by inheritance or otherwise gratuitously, is not to be in a more favorable position than the person from whom he acquired the cultural object. In other words, the aim is to prevent the current possessor from taking advantage of the bad faith of the person from whom he received the object either by inheritance or gratuitously.

With regard to a claim for restitution, Article 8 provides that the action has to be brought either by the State or by a private citizen through the current legal proceedings of the State in which the object is.

---

14 Literally "reasonable efforts shall be made to have the person who transferred the cultural object to the possessor, or any prior transferor, pay the compensation where to do so would be consistent with the law of the State in which the claim is brought" Article 4(2).

15 With regard to the question of easing the burden of proof to efficaciously tackle corruption see Jayawickrama, Pope, and Stolpe (2002).

17.2 THE RECOVERY OF ASSETS THAT ORIGINATE FROM CRIME

Returning to the subject of recovering capital that originates from crime and in particular from corruption, in 2000 the first declarations in favor of international cooperation for the identification, tracking and recovery of "laundered" funds were made; this was done first in the General Assembly of the United Nations and afterwards during the G7 meeting at Okinawa.[16] In January 2000, the UN adopted a Resolution to strengthen international cooperation ". . . inter alia, through the United Nations system, in devising ways and means of preventing and addressing illegal transfer, as well as in repatriating illegal transfer of funds to their countries of origin, and calls upon other countries and entities concerned to cooperate in this regard".[17] In 2001, it was the turn of the Economic and Social Council to issue a resolution[18] for the improvement of international cooperation in order to prevent and tackle the transfer of funds of illicit origin, arising from corruption – including money-laundering – and the repatriation of these assets. In the resolution the Council asked the General Secretary to prepare a thorough related study, with innovative ideas about the most efficient procedures through which States could track funds belonging to them that were in other States and obtain their restitution; the study was intended for the Ad Hoc Committee for the Negotiation of a Convention against Corruption.[19] Finally, in January 2002, the General Assembly, in

---

16 Actions against Abuse of the Global Financial System, Report from G7 Finance Ministers to the Heads of State and Government, Okinawa, 21 July 2000: "International money laundering has often been used by government officials to assist the clandestine diversion of public assets. The vulnerability of government institutions to such crime can be especially substantial in countries with emerging democratic systems and developing or transitional economies. We agree that it would be useful if we could take stock of existing legal tools and the agencies that administer them in each of our countries that would be available to identify, trace, and seize such laundered assets, as a first step to enhancing international cooperation on this issue".

17 United Nations, General Assembly, Res. GA 54/205, 27 January 2000. Afterwards, in December of the same year, the General Assembly invited a group of experts to examine the question of the repatriation of the illegally obtained funds. Res. GA 55/188 of 20 December 2000.

18 Res. 2001/13 of 24 July 2001.

19 On 21 June 2002, during the second session of the Ad Hoc Committee, a seminar was held with regard to the recovery of the assets originating from crime. The aim was to provide the participants with the technical information about the most complex aspects related to the asset recovery issue. The workshop focused attention on the following main points: (a) transferring abroad the funds of illicit

defining the mandate of the Ad Hoc Committee for the negotiation of the Convention, provided that an interdisciplinary approach was to be used. Issues like preventing and tackling crimes and the repatriation of funds originating from the same crime, in particular from corruption activities, were examined.[20]

At this point, the issues related to the recovery of assets have become essential in the negotiation of the UN Convention against Corruption; in fact, when 58 States met in Buenos Aires in December 2001 to introduce some proposals to be used as a basis for drafting the Treaty, the United States presented a draft related only to the recovery of assets (Landmeier 2002). Over the next few years, the political consensus about this issue has increased; during the Second Session of the Ad Hoc Committee the Chairman declared that "the question of asset recovery is one of the fundamental aspects of the Convention and would also serve as an indicator of the political will to join forces in order to protect the common good".[21] The high priority given to this matter was also shown in two measures adopted by the United Nations respectively in 2000 and 2003. The first, of November 2000, is about the signature of the Convention of Palermo against transnational organized crime.[22] According to Article 14 of this Convention, the State Parties can "*envisager à titre prioritaire de restituer le produit du crime ou les biens confisqués*" to the claimant State. The second is related to the Resolution of the UN Security Council according to which the UN Member States have to freeze the foreign funds created by Saddam Hussein, transfer them to the Development Fund for Iraq and facilitate the return of Iraqi cultural objects that were illegally exported.[23]

---

origin, identifying them and confiscating them; (b) repatriating the funds or the objects of illicit origin; (c) preventing the transfer of the same funds.

20 Res. GA 56/260 of 31 January 2002.

21 Report of the Ad Hoc Committee for the Negotiation of a Convention Against Corruption on its second session, Vienna, 17–28 June 2002, UN Doc. A/AC.261/7, p. 3.

22 Convention Against Transnational Organized Crime, adopted in New York on 15 November 2000 and signed during the Palermo Conference, 12–15 December 2000. Document A/55/383 available in French at: http://www.uncjin.org/Documents/Conventions/dcatoc/final_documents/383f.pdf.

23 SC Res. 1483 (2003), UN SCOR, 4761 meeting, paragraph 23 e7, UN Doc. S/RES/1483 (2003).

17.3 THE UN CONVENTION AGAINST CORRUPTION OF 2003 AND THE ASSET RECOVERY PROCEDURE

The high point of this process was reached at the end of the negotiations for the UN Convention Against Corruption, when an entire chapter – Chapter V – was entirely dedicated to the restitution of assets originating from one of the offenses punished by the Treaty.

Article 51 provides that the restitution of the assets in question is a fundamental principle of the Convention and forces all the State Parties to provide one another with the widest measure of cooperation and assistance. For the first time at a multilateral level, the binding principle, according to which illicitly acquired assets are to be returned, has been ratified. This commitment, which is, by the way, mitigated by that mentioned hereinafter, is probably the most original contribution brought about by the Convention: the moral obligation to return the capital originating from a crime has therefore become a legal obligation.[24]

Nevertheless, it has to be pointed out that, from the outset, the preliminary works have highlighted that the definition of the "fundamental principle" of the Treaty does not have any legal consequences for the other articles of the Convention in question.[25]

What is the relevance and the legal value of this remark? The hermeneutic criteria included in Articles 31, 32 and 33 of the Vienna Convention of 1969[26] give predominant relevance to the interpretation in good faith of the Treaty. This complies with the law and the commitments undertaken.[27] In other words, we have to follow the meaning that is shown by the text itself – resulting from the logical connections between its parts (the so-called systematic interpretation). Moreover, the interpretation has to harmonize with the object and the function of the act, as inferred from the text itself (the so-called teleological interpretation).[28]

---

24 This is Tiziano Balmelli's opinion (Balmelli 2004: 63–73). Balmelli believes in the existence of a moral obligation for the restitution of confiscated assets originating from the corruption of foreign officials. He quotes a message from the Swiss Federal Council: "il serait en effet immoral dans ces cas que la Suisse conserve cet argent" (Balmelli 2004: 74, note 20).

25 A/58/422/Add.1, paragraph 48.

26 Vienna Convention on the Law of the Treaties, which was adopted on 23 May 1969 and came into force on 27 January 1980.

27 For this definition of good faith, see Basdevant (1960: 91): "esprit de loyauté, de respect de droit, de fidelité aux engagements de la part de celui dont laction est en cause".

28 In this sense, the preparatory work is a supplementary tool, a subsidiary

In Article 51 there seems to be no room for ambiguity. Furthermore Article 1(b) of the Convention mentions international cooperation and technical assistance in preventing and tackling corruption among the purposes of the Treaty, explicitly including the recovery of the assets originating from a crime, while Article 3(1), in defining the scope of the *ratione materiae* application of the Convention, mentions the freezing, seizure, confiscation and return of the proceeds of offenses established in accordance with this Convention.[29]

Therefore, it seems clear that the return of the assets illicitly obtained is included in the general scope of the Convention and that the other articles in Chapter V can be interpreted according to this view as provided by the objectivistic method acknowledged in Article 31, paragraph 1, of the Vienna Convention.[30]

---

means of interpretation of the Treaty to be adopted in case there is an ambiguous or obscure meaning in examining Article 31 or the same examination leads to a result that is patently absurd or unreasonable (Article 32 of the Vienna Convention).

29 Article 3(1).

30 Article 31(1) of the Vienna Convention: "A treaty shall be interpreted in good faith in accordance with the ordinary meaning to be given to the terms of the treaty in their context and in the light of its object and purpose." Therefore, a restrictive interpretation aimed at safeguarding sovereignty of the State Parties is not feasible; on the contrary, an interpretation that favors the widest cooperation of State Parties in this matter is required. On the other hand, those who would like to deduce from the conventional practice in the matter (and in particular from Article 51) the existence of a customary rule that provides that the assets originating from crime have to be returned, should rely on the State Parties' *opinio iuris sive necessitatis* and face strong and evident dissension on this point: during the negotiations, the developing countries wanted the return of the assets to be defined by the Convention as an inalienable right of nations, but – due to strong resistance – they finally agreed to simply include the wording "fundamental principle". This was a compromise. In order to use treaties to prove the existence of a customary law, in fact, it is necessary to prove that (1) the relative rule can generally be applied, (2) the States' behavior has complied with what is set down in the treaty, (3) it is, in particular, necessary, that *diuturnitas* is combined with necessity, i.e. the dutifulness of the behavior conducted. With regard to treaties as proof of the existence of a customary rule, see Fitzmaurice (1958). He claims that, despite the fact that treaties are generally powerless towards State third parties, these can be compelled to comply with the rules included in the treaties themselves only when the text (either totally or partially) mirrors the customary laws or when the dispositions in the treaty create a common behavior together with the *opinio juris*. In the case *Gulf of Maine* the Chamber of International Court said with regard to the Convention of 1982 about the law of the sea: "the Convention adopted at the end of the Conference [1982 Convention on the Law of the Sea UN Doc. A/CONF.62/122; 21 ILM 1261, 1982] has not yet come into force and that a number

Therefore, a restrictive interpretation aimed at safeguarding sovereignty of the State Parties is not feasible; on the contrary an interpretation that favors the widest cooperation of State Parties in this matter is required. On the other hand, those who would like to deduce from the conventional praxis in the matter (and in particular from Article 51) the existence of a customary rule that provides that the assets originating from crime have to be returned, should rely on the State Parties' *opinio iuris sive necessitatis* and face strong and evident dissension on this point: during the negotiations, developing countries wanted the return of assets to be defined by the Convention as an inalienable right of nations, but – due to strong resistance to this proposal – they finally agreed to simply include the wording "fundamental principle". This was a compromise. What remains important is that the issue has now for the first time been comprehensively addressed in a multilateral treaty (Pieth, 2008; Vlassis, 2007).

Hereinafter, the rules of the UNCAC relating to the recovery of assets originating from crime are examined. In general, the substantive provisions then set out a series of mechanisms, including both civil and criminal recovery procedures, whereby assets can be traced, frozen, seized, forfeited and returned. A further issue was the question of whether assets should be returned to requesting State Parties or directly to individual victims, if these could be identified or were pursuing claims. According to Vlassis (2007:29), the result was a series of provisions which favour return to the

---

of States do not appear inclined to ratify it. This, however, in no way detracts from the consensus reached on large portions of the instrument and, above all, cannot invalidate the observation that certain provisions of the Convention concerning the continental shelf and the exclusive economic zone . . . were adopted, without any objections . . . these provisions . . . may nevertheless be regarded as consonant at present with general international law on the question" *The Gulf of Maine* case, ICJ Reports, 1984, p. 246, at p.294; 71 ILR, pp. 74 ff., at p. 122. In 1969, again CIG said with regard to the case *North Sea Continental Shelf*, that the rules of the treaty to create customary laws "should be of a fundamentally norm-creating character such as could be regarded as forming the basis of a general rule of law", ICJ Reports, 1969, 41 ILR, p. 3, paragraph 72. Finally again CIG in the Nicaragua case [Nicaragua case (Nicaragua v. USA), (1986), ICJ Reports, 14; 76 ILR, p. 349], confirming what had already been decided in the *Continental Shelf* case, said that "for a new customary rule to be formed, not only must the acts concerned 'amount to a settled practice', but they must be accompanied by the *opinio iuris sive necessitatis*. Either the states taking such action or other states in position to react to it, must have behaved so that their conduct is 'evidence of a belief that this practice is rendered obligatory by the existence of a rule of law requiring it . . .'"; ibid., pp. 108–09; 76 ILR, pp. 442–3, citing *North Sea Continental Shelf* cases, ICJ Reports, 1969, p. 44; 41 ILR, p. 73.

requesting State Party, depending on how closely the assets were linked to it in the first place. Therefore, funds embezzled from the State are returned to it, even if subsequently laundered,[31] and proceeds of other offences covered by the UNCAC are to be returned to the requesting State if it establishes ownership or damages recognised by the requested State Party as a basis for return.[32] In other cases assets may be returned to the requesting State Party or a prior legitimate owner, or used in some way for compensating victims.[33]

We now turn to the detailed assessment of the single provisions.

Article 52 – in compliance with the mandate given to the Ad Hoc Committee – is dedicated to the prevention and detection of the transfer of the proceeds of crime. The mandate provides an interdisciplinary approach and a plurality and diversification of tools to facilitate asset recovery.

The principles of transparency and due diligence upon bank intermediaries are embedded in this rule; those intermediaries have to verify the identity of the owners of bank accounts or the beneficial owners of funds (Article 52, paragraph 1), especially if these persons are entrusted with prominent public functions. Scrutiny is to be extended also to their family members and close associates and to be designed in such a way as to ease the detection of suspicious transactions. Finally, the Article provides for the transfer of transactions performed by the persons mentioned in paragraph 1 into special archives. In other words, the "know-your-customer" policy, which had already been voluntarily adopted[34] and included in the 40 recommendations of the FAFT,[35] has been transformed into a binding international tool. The recommendations, integrated in the Eight Special Recommendations on Terrorist Financing, were acknowledged by the IMF and the WB Recommendation 6[36] is particularly relevant with

---

31 Art. 57, sub-para. 3(a).
32 Art. 57, sub-para. 3(b).
33 Art. 57, sub-para. 3(c).
34 See the Global Anti Money Laundering Guidelines for Private Banking, known as the Wolfsberg Principles, issued by Transparency International and 11 of the leading international banks in October 2000. The guidelines include procedures such as the know-your-customer procedure. www.wolfsberg-principles.com.
35 See *supra* Chapter 10 and, in particular, footnote 123.
36 The text which we refer to is that previous to the publication of the new Recommendation in 2012, which reads as follows: Recommendation 6: "Financial institutions should, in relation to politically exposed persons, in addition to performing normal due diligence measures: (a) Have appropriate risk management systems to determine whether the customer is a politically exposed person. (b) Obtain senior management approval for establishing business relationships with

regard to the know-your-customer procedures; it is about the hot topic of private banking: the preferential services provided by some financial institutions to stand-out persons who are entrusted with important public functions. The Recommendation advises continuously scrutinizing and, in establishing business relationships with such persons, involving the bank's leading figures and adopting suitable measures to verify the origin of the accounts opened. Such strict monitoring procedures are not provided by the UN Convention; this is unfortunate because, actually, these measures could hinder the deposit and transfer of illicitly originated funds between different financial institutions; they could also favor the detection just at the "*placement stage*" of the money, when it is still close to its source, i.e. the crime activity that has generated it. On the other hand, the UN Convention provides that the State Parties, in order to adopt the identification measures mentioned in paragraph 1 of Article 52, have to issue advisories[37] – in accordance with their domestic laws and the initiatives of the regional or multilateral organizations – with regard to the natural or legal person whose accounts are to be specially monitored by the financial institutions within their jurisdiction. Furthermore, the advisories have also to mention the types of accounts to be scrutinized, the transactions and the record-keeping measures. Article 52(2)(b), moreover, provides that the State Parties – again in accordance with their domestic laws and the initiatives of the regional or multilateral organizations – have to notify the financial institutions within their jurisdiction of the identity of those natural or legal persons whose transactions have to be specially monitored. Notice to the financial institutions can be carried out on the autonomous request from the State itself or at the request of another State Party of the UNCAC.

Besides the codification of the due diligence rules in the approach to clients, the Convention asks the State Parties to adopt effective measures to prevent the establishment of banks that have no physical presence in the territory and are not affiliated to a financial group (Article 52(4)). The Convention even asks the State Parties to consider the possibility of not establishing or interrupting the "correspondent banking"[38] relations with

---

such customers. (c) Take reasonable measures to establish the source of wealth and source of funds. (d) Conduct enhanced ongoing monitoring of the business relationship." www.fatf-gafi.org.

37 The UN Convention talks about *advisories* in Article 52(2)(a).

38 With regard to correspondent banking see Recommendation 7 of FATF "Financial institutions should, in relation to cross-border correspondent banking and other similar relationships, in addition to performing normal due diligence measures: (a) Gather sufficient information about a respondent institution to

such institutions. Finally, each State Party has to consider establishing, in accordance with its domestic law, effective compulsory systems (also providing sanctions for non-compliance) to disclose the financial information related to public officials[39] and to allow the sharing of this information with the competent authorities in other State Parties when necessary to investigate, claim or recover the proceeds of offenses established in accordance with this Convention (Article 51(5)).

During the study seminar about asset recovery organised by the Ad Hoc Committee in October 2002, the representatives of Japan and the Philippines highlighted the importance of prevention through the suitable management of financial intermediaries.[40] In a nutshell, the adoption of this panoply of potentially extremely effective tools, i.e. the combined and parallel use of the application of criminal law, on the one hand (related to the suppression of the crimes punished by the Convention), and a wider deterrent approach (through collaboration between the financial institutions), on the other, can really make an effective contribution to reducing the incidence of international corruption.

Cooperation will then be significantly eased by establishing a financial intelligence unit (FIU) to be responsible for receiving, analyzing and disseminating to the competent authorities reports of suspicious financial transactions (Article 58). According to the *travaux préparatories*, each State Party may consider establishing a new unit, creating a specialized branch of the financial center already in existence or more easily use an already established unit.[41] Moreover, again according to the *travaux préparatories*, Article 58 has to be interpreted in compliance with the

---

understand fully the nature of the respondent's business and to determine from publicly available information the reputation of the institution and the quality of supervision, including whether it has been subject to a money laundering or terrorist financing investigation or regulatory action. (b) Assess the respondent institution's anti-money laundering and terrorist financing controls. (c) Obtain approval from senior management before establishing new correspondent relationships. (d) Document the respective responsibilities of each institution. (e) With respect to 'payable-through accounts', be satisfied that the respondent bank has verified the identity of and performed on-going due diligence on the customers having direct access to accounts of the correspondent and that it is able to provide relevant customer identification data upon request to the correspondent bank."

39 Article 54(5) talks about effective financial disclosure systems.

40 Ad Hoc Committee for the Negotiation of a Convention Against Corruption (*Comité spécial chargé de négocier une convention contre la corruption*), *Rapport du Comité spécial chargé de négocier une convention contre la corruption sur les travaux de sa deuxième session*, A/AC.261/7, October 2002.

41 A/58/422/Add.1, pp. 11–12.

provisions of Article 14(b) with regard to cooperation and exchange of information to prevent money-laundering.

In the mid-1990s there were only a few units of this kind, which, today, have been informally united to create the Egmont Group, within which there are 101 structures that promote information sharing and contribute to integrating the competences of anti-corruption organizations all over the world. Moreover, we might even assume that the United Nations itself might establish a database with information, expertise, details of authorities to contact in order to receive judiciary support, and news to be shared with the interested State Parties. In fact, lack of coordination is one of the most frequent complaints from the State Parties involved in different recovery operations; and so is the difficulty in finding entities that are qualified and competent to carry out not only inquiries but also to prevent the committing of crimes. Again, the United Nations activities with other international organizations – through the so-called capacity-building programs – might be fundamental.[42]

In the corruption case in which Vladimiro Montesinos Torres[43] was involved, the information obtained from Swiss banks facilitated both the investigations in the home country and the recovery of large funds recycled by Montesinos himself (Brun et al. 2011). He was the chief of the powerful National Intelligence Service and an advisor to the former Peruvian president, Alberto Fujimori. The Swiss government issued very precise and strict directives[44] in order to regulate the activities of the financial intermediaries. Among other issues these directives clearly provide that the financial intermediaries must not accept funds which definitely or presumably originate from corruption or other crimes against public

---

42 For a similar opinion, see Ige (2002).

43 The inquiry carred out by the IV District Prosecutor of Zurich Canton brought to light that Montesinos's funds, which were frozen in Switzerland, originated from corruption: from 1990 Montesinos received "commissions" upon the weapons supply intended for the Peruvian government. He asked that those payoffs be deposited in his own bank accounts in Luxembourg, the United States and Switzerland. In at least 32 supply contracts, Montesinos gained payoffs equal to 18 percent of the purchase price. Also with regard to the purchase of three "MIG29" airplanes on behalf of the Peruvian airforce from the Russian national weapon factory "Rosvoorouzhenie", Montesinos took a "commission" of $10.9 million. Thanks to his position, Montesinos had some weapons dealers favored when bids were decided and received "compensation" for the same. See Jorge (2003).

44 *Directives relatives à la prévention et à la lutte contre le blanchiment des capitaux* of 26 March 1998, available at: http://www.ebk.admin.ch/f/publik/rundsch/98-1.pdf.

administration. Moreover, thanks to the recent amendments to the penal code (according to which corruption is no longer a simple offense but a real crime[45]) and also to the new Article 322 *septies* of the Swiss Penal Code (PC),[46] the financial intermediary, besides exercising the usual due diligence, has to inform the federal authority for money-laundering, about any well-founded suspicions regarding the fact that the assets in a business relationship may be the result of an offense. Therefore, as the judicial frame has changed and in compliance with the federal law against money-laundering,[47] in October 2000 the banks informed the Money-Laundering Communication Office about the deposits on the accounts belonging to Montesinos and the former Peruvian General Hermoza Rios. Later, the Communication Office transmitted this information to the IV District

---

45 On the occasion of the signature of the OCSE Convention against corruption, the Swiss Penal Code was considerably enhanced: not only was the felony of active corruption by foreign public officers introduced, as it was introduced in the other State Parties, but such felony (and also the one related to the domestic jurisdiction) is now considered a crime and no longer an offense punishable by imprisonment of up to three years. This is extremely relevant, as is mentioned in the text itself. In fact, the money-laundering crime presupposes the commitment of a prior crime. Just to understand how different the new discipline is, it is worth highlighting the difference in the two different regimes regarding fiscal fraud. The latter, being considered a crime, is not an offense like money-laundering and does not require the due diligence obligation upon the financial intermediaries, which is provided only for crimes defined by Article 9 of the PC (crimes punishable with more than three years of imprisonment).

46 Article 322 *septies* Swiss PC, introduced by the signature of the OCSE Convention: "Any person who shall offer, promise or grant any undue advantage to any person acting for a foreign State or an international organisation either as a member of a judicial or other authority, a civil servant, an expert, translator or interpreter employed by any authority, or an arbitrator or member of the military forces, for the benefit of such person or any third party, for the commission or omission of an act in relation to his official functions which is contrary to his duties or in the exercise of his discretionary powers, shall be punishable by a maximum term of five years' imprisonment".

47 Article 9 of the Federal Law on Money Laundering: "A financial intermediary must immediately file a report with the Money Laundering Reporting Office Switzerland ('the Reporting Office') as defined in Article 23 if it: a. knows or has reasonable grounds to suspect that assets involved in the business relationship: 1. are connected to an offence in terms of Article 260ter Number 1 or 305bis SCC, 2. are the proceeds of a felony, 3. are subject to the power of disposal of a criminal organisation, or 4. serve the financing of terrorism (Article 260quinquies para. 1 SCC);" Lawyers and notaries are not subject to the duty to report insofar as they are bound in their activities by professional secrecy in terms of Article 321 SCC. Article 305 *bis* punishes the crime of money laundering of which the international corruption is now the historical background. See in this regard Bernasconi (2000).

Prosecutor in the Zurich Canton. The Prosecutor froze the funds[48] and opened a criminal inquiry. The Federal Justice Office transmitted the results of the inquiry carried out in Zurich to the Peruvian Ministry of Justice, which carried out its own inquiry, asking for support from the Swiss Ministry of Justice. Finally, the indicted individual was arrested in June 2001. Meanwhile, on 20 August 2002, the bank account of the Peruvian Banco de la Nacion at Citibank in New York received a money transfer equal to $77.5 million from Switzerland as a restitution for the assets stolen by Montesinos.

Chapter V also provides mechanisms for direct recovery in civil or other proceedings (Article 53) and a comprehensive framework for international cooperation (Articles 54–55) which incorporates the more general mutual legal assistance requirements, *mutatis mutandis*: Article 53 is dedicated to measures for the direct recovery of assets;[49] in other words, it is about the available civil tools for the return of assets originating from crime. Paragraph (a) of Article 53 provides that a State Party – in accordance with its domestic law – adopts the necessary measures to allow another State Party to initiate civil action in its courts to establish ownership of property on goods acquired through the committing of an offense established in accordance with this Convention; paragraph (b) provides that, again in accordance with its domestic law, the State Parties adopt the necessary measures to permit their courts to order the offenders to pay compensation or damages to another State Party that has been harmed by the offenses established in accordance with this Convention. This rule could turn out to be particularly effective in tackling corruption: we might think, for example, about a civil lawsuit brought by the competitors that have been excluded in a bid and want to rescind or annul a contract for corruption – a hypothesis included in Article 34 of the UN Convention[50] – or ask for the payment of damages, as provided in Article 53(2) of the

---

48 The money ascribable to Montesinos amounts to $48 million in November 2000 and a further $22 million on 29 November 2000.

49 The Convention talks about "measures for direct recovery of property". The term property is defined by Article 2(d): "assets of every kind, whether corporeal or incorporeal, movable or immovable, tangible or intangible and legal documents or instruments evidencing title to or interest in such assets".

50 Article 34 of the UN Convention: "Consequences of acts of corruption. With due regard to the rights of third parties acquired in good faith, each State Party shall take measures, in accordance with the fundamental principles of its domestic law, to address consequences of corruption. In this context, States Parties may consider corruption a relevant factor in legal proceedings to annul or rescind a contract, withdraw a concession or other similar instrument or take any other remedial action".

Treaty. Obviously in this latter case, there must be a causal link between the detriment suffered and the committed crime as perfectly highlighted in Article 35 of the Convention,[51] while with regard to the request for an annulment, it is clear that, in case the implementation of the transaction implies the simultaneous committing of the crime, the validity of the contract agreed upon as a consequence of the corruption will also be affected. Actually, the UN Convention, Article 34, provides for the possibility of annulling the contract agreed on due to some acts of corruption (a similar provision is included in Article 8 of the Council of Europe Civil Law Convention (CoECivLCC)); nevertheless, it is not mentioned that the State Parties are entitled to claim this before the courts of other State Parties. Finally, according to paragraph 3 and again according to the relevant domestic laws, the necessary measures have to be implemented in order to let the national courts or the competent authorities, when having to decide on confiscation, to recognize another State Party's claim as the legitimate owner of property acquired through the committing of an offense established in accordance with the Convention. Thanks to these civil procedures, $1 billion and $180 million were recovered respectively from the Philippines and Russia, while Nigeria obtained the restitution of $1 billion thanks to a civil claim brought in the United Kingdom. In such cases, finding the competent lawyers and consultants and having the appropriate funds to pay their fees might be a significant problem. The so-called contingency fee arrangements (thanks to which professionals are paid proportionately and after the money has been recovered), ad hoc loans from international organizations, foundations or non-profit organizations and reimbursement requests to those financial institutions that haven't implemented proper checks might be among the possible solutions. Finally, if the claimant is a private person, in some State Parties he might be entitled to up to 30 percent of the assets recovered: in so-called *qui tam* actions.[52]

On the other hand, using civil claims to recover the money has the undoubted advantage of requiring a less strict burden of proof than that required in applying criminal law; nevertheless international cooperation

---

51 Article 35 of the UN Convention: "Compensation for damage. Each State Party shall take such measures as may be necessary, in accordance with principles of its domestic law, to ensure that entities or persons who have suffered damage as a result of an act of corruption have the right to initiate legal proceedings against those responsible for that damage in order to obtain compensation".

52 The term *qui tam* is an abbreviation of the sentence *qui tam pro domino rege quam pro si ipso in hac parte sequitur*. This is with reference to the United States; see Carrington (2009).

in this regard is also less developed: the UN Convention provides that the State Parties have to cooperate in criminal matters while they simply have to consider assisting each other with regard to proceedings in civil and administrative matters (Article 43).

Article 54 provides some tools to recover assets through international cooperation *ex* Article 55 of the Convention, which aims to seize the assets – one of the most efficient strategies to tackle organized crime. The properties covered by cooperation are those acquired through or involved in the committing of the offense (Article 54, paragraph 1). Article 1 of the Convention defines seizure as the permanent privation upon the order from a court or the competent authorities. Article 54(1)(a) provides that each State Party, in accordance with its domestic law, takes such measure as may be necessary to permit its competent authorities to implement an order of confiscation issued by a court of another State Party. Paragraph (b), on the other hand, provides that each State Party, according to its domestic law, adopts the necessary measures to permit its competent authorities, where they have jurisdiction, to order the confiscation of property of foreign origin, taking legal proceedings themselves against the offense of money-laundering or a crime that may be within their jurisdiction.

Paragraph (c) provides a milder commitment for State Parties: it simply exhorts (*shall*) the State Parties to consider taking measures that allow confiscation of property also without a criminal conviction in cases in which the offender cannot be prosecuted due to death (as with regard to General Abacha), absconding or absence. This provision might innovate the *in rem* or *in personam* confiscation systems of the State Parties, which usually – even though there are some significant exceptions[53] – provides, in any case, the prior issuing of a conviction, since the confiscation is still considered an accessory penalty or, in any case, a precautionary measure as in our system.

A similar level of cooperation is provided with regard to the freezing and seizure of property upon a specific order issued by a State Party or after a simple but circumstantial inquiry (Article 54(2)(a) and (b)).

International cooperation with regard to confiscation is mentioned,

---

53 For example, in both England and Wales, a confiscation order can be implemented even without a conviction judgment (1) if the indicted has been absconding for at least two years, (2) if they have tried to contact him with no results and (3) there is evidence that he took advantage of drugs trafficking. See FATF, Evaluation of Laws and Systems, in FATF, *Members Dealing with Asset Confiscation and Provisional Measures*, available at: www.fatf-gafi.org/dataoecd/32/48/34047135.pdf p. 3.

furthermore, by Article 55, according to which a State Party that has received a request from another State Party for confiscation of the goods present on its territory (which were used or destined for use in offenses), goods that are the products and the profit of an offense or the property equivalent to these proceeds according to the provisions of Article 31(1) of the Convention,[54] has to present to its competent authorities – according to its domestic law:

1) a detailed request to obtain an order of confiscation and execute it. According to both Article 55(1)(a) and Article 55(3)(a), this request has to include a description of the goods to be confiscated, the locality of the same, their estimated value and a description of the facts. New details related to the request can be inferred from Article 46(15) with regard to the requesting authority, the person involved, etc.;
2) a legally admissible copy of the order of confiscation issued by a court of the requesting State Party to be executed as provided by Article 54(a) of the Convention. Article 55(3)(b) – which has to be taken into consideration together with Article 55(1)(b) – provides that in this case there has to be a description of the facts and measures adopted to notify the third parties in good faith about the execution of the order; finally, it is provided that the order is final.

The State Party that receives this request has to adopt all the necessary measures to enable the identification, tracing and seizure of the items defined in Article 31(1). At this point, it is worth highlighting that the other objects mentioned in Article 31 (relating to confiscation) seem to be

---

[54] Article 31: "Freezing, seizure and confiscation

1. Each State Party shall take, to the greatest extent possible within its domestic legal system, such measures as may be necessary to enable confiscation of:

    (a) Proceeds of crime derived from offences established in accordance with this Convention or property the value of which corresponds to that of such proceeds;
    (b) Property, equipment or other instrumentalities used in or destined for use in offences established in accordance with this Convention."

Furthermore, it is worth highlighting that some States can seize the assets of third parties, as these parties could not have been unaware (or known or suspected) that the said assets had originated from the committing of a crime, or when the assets were still directly controlled by the indicted or if the assets were either direct or indirect gifts of the indicted.

excluded from the application of the rules about international cooperation: the objects into which the proceeds of crime have been transformed or converted or properties of legitimate origin, if the proceeds of crime have been added to these, up to no more than the estimated value of these proceeds.

All the measures of reciprocal judicial assistance already provided by Article 46 of the Convention and destined for criminal proceedings are also applied to the confiscation case, as is highlighted in paragraph 1, which provides that the support to investigations and judicial proceedings is given only with regard to the offenses covered by the Convention. The assistance *ex* Article 46(3) includes inter alia the identification, freezing and tracing of the proceeds or of the instrumentalities for evidentiary purposes and the exercise of the same actions for the proceeds of crimes according to the provisions of Chapter V of the Convention. Assistance is, then, provided in general to recover the assets in accordance with the provisions of the above-mentioned Chapter V (Article 46(3)(g), (j), (k)). We would also like to draw attention to the fact that what is provided by Article 46(21) has to be applied to the request for restitution; the Article lists the criteria according to which assistance can be refused. The list mentions lack of conformity with the provision of the article itself (letter a), non-conformity with the domestic law of the action included in the request for cooperation (letter c), contrariety to rules relating to legal assistance of the requested State Party (letter d) and, finally, the consideration that the execution of the request is likely to prejudice the sovereignty, security, *ordre public* or other essential interests of the State Party (letter b) of Article 46). Obviously reasons have to be given for the refusal (Article 46(23)). The provision, in mentioning the *ordre public*, hints at the possibility that there might be some substantial differences between the legal systems of the State Parties involved so that what is admitted in a State Party may be considered to be against the fundamental social-ethic principles of another. The Court of Justice of the European Communities – in interpreting Article 27(1) of the Convention of Brussels,[55] with regard to

---

55 Convention of Brussels regarding Jurisdictional Competence and the Implementation of the Judgments in Civil and Trade Matters of 1968 (OJ C 189 of 28 July 1990). The application of the rules of this convention was extended to the State Party members of the European Association of Free Trade (EAFT) thanks to the Lugano Convention of 16 September 1988. The application of the Convention was then extended to all the new State members of the European Union: finally, with the Convention of 29 November 1996, it was extended to Austria, Finland and Sweden (OJ C 15 of 15 January 1997). In 1998 a consolidated version of the text of the convention was published (OJ C 27 of 26 January 1998). Regulation

the lack of acknowledgment of a judgment in civil and commercial matters for *ordre public* reasons – has stated that recourse to this clause "can be envisaged only where recognition or enforcement of the judgement delivered in another Contracting State would be at variance to an unacceptable degree with the legal order of the State in which enforcement is sought inasmuch as it infringes a fundamental principle . . . the infringement would have to constitute a manifest breach of a rule of law regarded as essential in the legal order of the State in which the enforcement is sought or of a right recognised as being fundamental within that legal order".[56] Furthermore, the notion of *ordre public* includes compliance with fundamental procedure principles such as the right to a fair hearing, the impartiality of the judge, etc.; those criteria, often, cannot be complied with by the judicial systems of the developing countries that ask for assistance due to incomplete reforms or simply due to scarcity of means.

Finally, according to Article 55(7), cooperation can be refused if the evidence received by the requested State Party is not sufficient and timely or if the property is of a *de minimis* value. In this provision there is a balance between the interest to recover the funds and consideration of the technical, legal and financial difficulties the State goes through during the operation of restitution. On the other hand, from a different perspective, the countries that have suffered the most and have consistently lost money due to corruption are the ones that have to start the inquiries or long and expensive procedures to recover their assets; therefore they might decide not to proceed, if the amount of money is not significant.

Mobutu's funds, which were deposited in Switzerland, amounted to $4 million: this was too low an amount for the authorities in Kinshasa, who decided not to answer a request for clarification about the ownership of the money sent by the Swiss government (Daniel 2004).

Article 56 asks the State Parties to play an active role, exhorting them to spontaneously share information about the proceeds from crime, without a prior request from other State Parties; this might take place if a State considers that the disclosure of such information might assist another State Party in initiating or carrying out investigations or judicial proceedings or

---

44/2001 of the Council of 22 December 2000 (and following amendments) with regard to jurisdictional competence, the acknowledgment and execution of the decision in civil and trading matters (OJ L 12 of 16 January 2001) substituted the Brussels Convention. The latter continues to be applied to the State Parties that have taken part in it and are excluded by the present regulation.

[56] Court of Justice, 28 March 2000, judgment C-7/98, *Krombach v. Bamberski*, in *Rivista Diritto internazionale privato processuale*, 2000, p. 803, paragraph 21, at paragraph 37.

might lead to a request under Chapter V of the Convention. According to the study carried out by the United Nations this would significantly ease the return of funds.

The fulcrum of Chapter V is in Article 57 for the return and disposal of assets. Paragraph 1 includes the principle according to which the property confiscated by a State Party, pursuant to Articles 31 and 55, have to be disposed according to paragraph 3 of Article 57, including the restitution of these assets; the restitution has to take place in compliance with domestic laws and the provisions of the Convention. Before examining the relevant rules, two considerations must be borne in mind in light of the above-mentioned international rules. The first is that, *mutatis mutandis*, i.e. with the necessary modifications, it seems that the imperative to return the assets is similar to Article 3 of the earlier mentioned UNIDROIT Convention about "Stolen or illegally exported cultural objects". The second concerns the delocalization of the management of the confiscated assets, which is evident in comparison with the Convention of Palermo. In Article 14.1 of the latter, the confiscating State Party disposes of the assets in compliance with its domestic law; Article 57 of UN Convention, on the other hand, refers to both the provision of the Treaty itself and to the domestic laws. *A fortiori* paragraph 2 of the same Article provides that the State Parties adopt all the necessary measures – therefore not only the legal ones – that comply with their own fundamental principles and enable their competent authorities to return the assets in accordance with the Convention while taking into account the rights of bona fine third parties.

The following provisions are definitely innovative especially in terms of the improvement of the international law in this matter.

Article 57(3) provides a precise obligation upon the requested State Parties; the obligation varies if the assets derive from embezzlement of public funds or money-laundering (Article 57(3)(a)), proceeds of any other offense covered by the Convention (57(3)(b)), or all the other cases (57(3)(c)).

According to Article 57(3)(a), in case the assets are from embezzlement of funds to the detriment of the State or public money-laundering (such offenses are mentioned respectively by Articles 17 and 23 of the Treaty) and in case the confiscation was executed in accordance with Article 55 of the Convention and on the basis of a final judgment in the requesting State Party, the requested State Party has to return the confiscated property. The latter might waive the requirement of a final judgment based upon its discretion. Therefore, in case there is no final judgment in the jurisdiction from where the request comes, the requested State Party is not compelled to return the funds.

The formulation included in letter (a) of Article 57 of the Convention includes an obligation to return the public funds that were wrongly obtained in consideration of the fact that, for the serious offenses mentioned above, the State Party should not have difficulties in exercising its right of ownership on the assets in question.

This binding and automatic mechanism above mentioned is applied to the funds confiscated according to international cooperation, explicitly mentioned with reference to Article 55 and Article 46. Letters (b) and (c) of Article 57 provide a different regime for the assets that do not derive from embezzlement of public funds.

According to Article 57(3)(b), in case of proceeds from the other offenses mentioned in the Convention and in case the confiscation was performed according to Article 55 of the Convention and upon a final judgment in the requesting State Party (a requirement that can be waived by the requested State Party), the requested State Party has to return the confiscated property. Nevertheless the restitution is conditioned by two different circumstances: the requesting State Party provides reasonable evidence about its prior ownership of such confiscated property or when the requested State Party recognizes damage to the requesting State Party as a basis for returning the confiscated property.

With regard to the first of the two hypotheses provided by letter (b), the preliminary works indicate that the term "prior ownership" means the "ownership at the moment of the offence".[57] Some legal academics have objected that in case of corruption in the strict sense (Articles 15 and 16 of the Convention) or trading in influence (Article 18) it is not possible to prove that at the moment of the offense the amounts of money or the other goods unfairly received by the corrupt officer belonged to the State Party. Therefore, the effect of the first hypothesis *sub* letter (b) of Article 57 seems extremely weak ("*voir nulle*"). With regard to the second hypothesis *sub* letter (b) of Article 57 (acknowledgment of a damage suffered by the requesting State Party), we might assume that the requested State Party will want to reach a global political agreement, which also includes the provisions on the use of the funds to be returned. Therefore the automatism in the restitution mechanism is valid only for the appropriation of public funds, while in the other cases the State Parties have to proceed case by case.

In the case of Ferdinando Marcos, former president of the Philippines, the Swiss authorities negotiated a return of the assets upon the following conditions:

- a formal charge against Marcos in the requesting State Party within a year;

---

57 A/58/422/Add.1.

- a final judgment from a Philippine court confirming that the funds were stolen and had to be returned to the legitimate owner: the Philippine government;
- compliance with the proceeding guarantees fixed by the Swiss Convention and the European Convention on Human Rights during the criminal proceedings in the requesting State Party.

These conditions were obviously opposed by the Philippines and the special commission entrusted with the recovery of the funds. Finally, they agreed with the Swiss government upon an "anticipatory return", i.e. before the final judgment. At present the same is explicitly provided for Article 57(3)(b). As mentioned above, restitution of the funds was carried out in respect of a Philippine bank account controlled by the Swiss government, which finally transferred the assets after a judgment from a Philippine court; in the judgment it was proved that Marcos did not provide evidence of the lawful origin of the money.

Finally, letter (c) of the same Article, related to all other cases, asks the State Parties to give priority consideration to returning confiscated property to the requesting State Parties, to its prior legitimate owners or to compensating the victims of the crime.

Finally, the Convention provides at paragraph 5 of Article 57 that the State Parties may give consideration to concluding agreements for the final disposal of confiscated property. The Convention shows the State Parties a solution that might certainly seem difficult from the point of view of negotiations, but probably this solution is quicker than the judicial one. Furthermore, there is an undeniable advantage in allowing the requested State Party to express its interest regarding the destination of the returned assets and agree on a possible sharing of the recovered funds as an incentive to cooperate.[58] It is worth mentioning that, until May 2003, even the UN Convention provided that the State Parties might take into consideration the hypothesis of sharing the property to be returned or allocating a portion to some intergovernmental organizations dedicated to tackling corruption (Article 61 of the draft).[59] This hypothesis was erased from the text in August of the same year.[60] This

---

58 In most of the FATF State Parties there is no specific law that allows for the sharing of the confiscated assets, but, on the other hand, there is no prohibition either. Nevertheless, in most cases of sharing an agreement of mutual judicial assistance is required while some others require that assets are no less than $1.3 billion, etc. Recommendations 38 and 39 of FATF explicitly provide for the possibility of using this form of incentive.

59 See A/AC.261/3/Rev.3 and also A/AC.261/3/Rev.4.

60 A/AC.261/3/Rev.5.

form of incentive and assurance could be effective when there are some delays in returning the assets or some real refusals due to the fact that the requested State Party has real doubts about the honesty of the reasons underlying the request for the recovery of the assets; for example, State Parties might be afraid that the returned fund could be used to commit new offenses, for example in the traffic of weapons. In the case of General Abacha, the new Nigerian government (which succeeded him after his death) used a combination of sending requests for mutual assistance and lodging criminal complaints regarding money-laundering, in jurisdictions where assets of the Abacha criminal organization had been identified or were suspected to be. The strategy resulted in the freezing of about US$2 billion in ten jurisdictions, of which to date, $1.2 billion has been recovered by Nigeria through mutual assistance, forfeiture or settlements (Monfrini 2008: 41). In the case of Marcos, the money transfer from Switzerland took place through an escrow account in the name of the Philippine National Bank over which the Swiss authorities exercised detailed control. They were even able to decide the kinds of investments to be carried out with the deposited funds. In this way Switzerland "kept" the capital until they had evidence that the Philippine government was acting in the right way.[61]

To solve this problem a part of the fund, as mutually agreed, could be put aside for specific goals, such as projects for tackling corruption, reducing public debt in the country, training public officers assigned the task of preventing laundering crimes, expanding the financial intelligence unit or else the priorities in allocating the returned funds could be mutually agreed. The Convention does not give any provision in this regard, but it would be advisable to include the possibility to resort to an international and independent authority that might solve the matter *à l'amiable* taking into consideration the populations that are victims of corruption (Balmelli 2004). Also in this regard, as to the prevention measures, a different, more active role may be foreseen for the United Nations, which can now count on a Convention that has created a favorable climate for cooperation and restitution. In this way, pressure upon the requested States for assistance is even greater. Article 59 is to be read from this perspective; the Article includes a renewed exhortation to the State Parties to conclude bilateral or multilateral agreements to enhance the effectiveness of international cooperation undertaken pursuant to Chapter V of the Convention.

The identification of experts who can assist developing countries in this process is also included as a form of technical assistance (Art. 60, para. 5).

---

[61] For a thorough illustration of the case see Salvioni (2008) and Marcelo (2008).

17.3.1 Asset Recovery within the COSP to the UNCAC

As the return of the proceeds generated from corruption to its country of origin is one of the core objectives set out in Article 1(b) of the UNCAC, and considering the number of novel issues raised by the composite regulation of the asset recovery system, it is not surprising that the latter topic has been thoroughly addressed during the five sessions of the COSP to the UNCAC held so far.[62] It is not the purpose of the present chapter to enter into a detailed analysis of the content of the latter sessions:[63] however, in this paragraph it is useful to recall two sets of issues regarding the evolving attitude of State Parties toward asset recovery.

To begin with, it is remarkable that during the first session of the Conference in 2006 parties to the Convention decided to establish an interim Open-ended Intergovernmental Working Group on Asset Recovery in accordance with Article 63(4) of the UNAC and Rule 2(2) of the rules of procedure of the Conference. According to the relevant Resolution its main objective was "to advise and assist the COSP in the implementation of its mandate on the return of proceeds of corruption".[64] Significantly, the latter group has been confirmed by the following sessions of the Conference, which always accorded the extension of its mandate and the continuation of its work side-by-side to the COSP in view of building and implementing an effective system of asset recovery.[65]

Secondly, one should take note of the latest declarations made by the COSP in relation to asset recovery. Resolution 5(3), which constitutes the longest of the ones elaborated by the fifth session of the Conference,[66] has strongly called upon States to facilitate international cooperation in asset recovery. After acknowledging the difficulties and obstacles in

---

62 As to this aspect Vlassis Gottwald, and Won Park (2013 161) assert that "intense discussions in intergovernmental fora have brought about a number of resolutions and recommendations especially in the the Conference of the States Parties to the Convention . . . and its Open-ended Intergovernmental Working on Asset Recovery . . .".

63 The document reports and resolutions of the five sessions of the COSP organized up until 2013 can be found at http://www.unodc.org/unodc/en/treaties/CAC/CAC-COSP.html (last visited January 2014).

64 See Resolution 1(4) of the First session of the Conference of the States Parties to the UNCAC (Amman, 10–14 December 2006).

65 More information and documents on the work of the intergovernmental working group on asset recovery can be found at http://www.unodc.org/unodc/en/treaties/CAC/working-group2.html (last visited January 2014).

66 The fifth session of the COSP was held in Panama, from 25 to 29 of November 2013.

implementing Chapter V of the UNCAC,[67] the resolution has elaborated a number of statements which emphasize the crucial importance of intensifying the ties among State Parties. In particular, the following key points and recommendations emerge from the text of the last session of the COSP:

(i) Among State Parties there should be the widest possible cooperation and assistance in the identification, tracing, and recovery of stolen assets and proceeds of corruption and in the extradition of individuals accused of predicate offences;
(ii) The competent authorities involved in the asset recovery procedure should be afforded with independence, training and adequate resources;
(iii) The exchange of information should be developed and improved, both at the request of a State and on a spontaneous basis, but also using and promoting informal channels of communication;
(iv) Requesting States should be assisted in order to meet requested States Parties' procedural requirements for legal assistance;
(v) Techniques should be elaborated to identify, trace, freeze and confiscate the stolen assets which are hidden through the use of shell companies and other complex legal mechanisms. For this purpose it is also important that State Parties cooperate for the accessibility of reliable ownership information;
(vi) Measures should be taken so that individuals with prominent public functions, their family members and close associates do not hide their illicitly acquired assets;
(vii) Financial institutions but also non-financial services and professions should not be used to hide stolen assets;
(viii) Focal points should be appointed and the network of focal points of the Working Group on Asset Recovery should be used for the purposes of international cooperation and mutual legal assistance in asset recovery;
(ix) State Parties should take advantage of existing forms of cooperation and networks of experts like the Global Focal Point Initiative set up by INTERPOL and StAR.[68]

---

67 On this topic see also para 17.4.2 about the barriers to asset recovery from the perspective of StAR.

68 For more information about the Global Focal Point Initiative see Box 17.1 below.

The latter list reflects different kinds of challenges which State Parties are called to engage with in order to further implement the UNCAC's provisions on asset recovery. However, what seems to emerge as being the single most urgent priority to facilitate the return of proceeds generated from corruption to its country of origin, is the *political will* of States, which is considered by the above-mentioned resolution as a matter of "critical importance". Accordingly, the COSP has called States Parties, acting as both requested and requesting States, "to continue to commit the political will to act together to recover the proceeds of corruption and to work together to overcome obstacles to effective asset recovery". The need of a stronger political will, which reverberates through Resolution 5(3), echoes also in one of the most esteemed scholar's illustration of the main hurdles to overcome in order to translate the heightened awareness and understanding of the need to recover assets into true action. Such hurdles are, on the one hand, the persistent apathy of some governments to take radical actions also by hiding behind the complexity of the legislation, "using law to slow down rather than to enable the recovery of stolen assets", (Pieth, 2013: xii) and "in the massive problems with trust between the requesting and requested States, and also trust among concerned State actors, in particular in requesting states, when they come out of political turmoil" (ID.) Since asset recovery, as Davies (2013) aptly put forward, consists of an international process of engagement premised on mutual learning, expertise and constructive *dialogue*, in summary, in effective communication "even the small breakdowns in accurately transferring information can delay, or ultimately, undo the entire process" (Dornbierer and Fenner Zinkernagel, 2013: xix).[69]

17.4 STOLEN ASSET RECOVERY INITIATIVE

The International Bank for Reconstruction and Development and International Development Association (together, the "Bank") and the United Nations, represented by the United Nations Office on Drugs and Crime (UNODC), constitute the principal partners of the Stolen Asset Recovery Initiative (StAR), launched in September 2007. StAR is a collaborative arrangement whose goal is to help ensure that there are no havens for the proceeds of corruption. Firstly, we outline the purpose and management of StAR, including with respect to one or more trust funds

69 See more extensively Davies (2013).

supporting StAR (collectively, the "Trust Fund").[70] Secondly, we intend to offer a brief overview of the most crucial issues and major obstacles which StAR has identified to pursue a more effective system of asset recovery.

17.4.1 The Activities and Organization of StAR

The guiding principles of StAR are the following:

(i) The UNCAC provides the international legal framework underpinning international collaboration in anti-corruption activities and asset recovery. Activities under StAR should encourage and promote the ratification, domestication and implementation of the Convention.

(ii) StAR is focused on *international* asset recovery. Activities under StAR should have a direct or indirect effect on stemming the cross-border flow of corruptly acquired assets and facilitating countries' efforts to recover stolen assets that have been hidden in foreign jurisdictions. This may entail working on domestic issues that have international dimensions, such as national forfeiture and anti-money-laundering regimes. It will also require StAR's engagement in efforts to raise awareness about and promote the lowering of barriers to asset recovery that may exist in developed countries and financial centers.

(iii) Asset recovery is a demand-driven, country-led activity. The Trust Fund will support individual countries in their efforts to recover assets so they can build institutional capacity. StAR should only engage in countries where the government has requested StAR's assistance, and this assistance should support the government's broader governance and anti-corruption agenda.

(iv) StAR will provide assistance in the technical dimensions of asset recovery. Asset recovery can be a politically charged issue. StAR will support countries committed to good governance and to fighting corruption, taking into account the risks and benefits of engagement and the need to avoid interference in the political affairs of participating states. In providing assistance, StAR should draw on good practice, international experience and sound technical analysis to help inform the national authorities' decisions.

---

70 See StAR (2008).

The main goal of the initiative is to encourage and facilitate more systematic and timely return of assets stolen by politically exposed persons through acts of corruption. In order to meet this objective, StAR consists of a partnership between the UNODC and the WB, with the support of donors to the Trust Fund and advisory experts. The specific objectives for the Partnership and the Trust Fund are to:

(i) Promote commitment at the highest level in both recipient and sending jurisdictions to recover stolen assets and deter asset theft.
(ii) Develop knowledge products, procedures and tools that facilitate asset recovery and support their systematic, global adoption.
(iii) Promote networks of practitioners in the field of asset recovery as a means of facilitating the exchange of information, knowledge and collaboration at an operational level.
(iv) Support partner countries' efforts to build institutional capacity for asset recovery as a routine part of its anti-corruption strategy.
(v) Facilitate progress in partner countries' asset recovery efforts (StAR 2008).

StAR's activities are consistent with the aforementioned principles and objectives. These activities are grouped into three components (StAR 2008: 2). The first component mainly consists of global knowledge sharing and advocacy. Activities under this component might include:

(i) Research and consultations with stakeholders to inform the policy dialogue on UNCAC implementation, asset recovery, and related legal innovations;
(ii) Development of diagnostic tools to support and assess progress in the implementation of the UNCAC provisions on mutual legal assistance, dual criminality, and other innovative elements in the Convention related to asset recovery;
(iii) Research to expand knowledge and develop best practices in asset recovery, and disseminate this knowledge broadly;[71]
(iv) Support to international networks engaged in asset recovery, including the creation of single points of contact in each country to facilitate communication and work on asset recovery;
(v) Research and advice to identify and lower institutional and legislative obstacles to asset recovery in the major financial centers, particularly

---

[71] It is worth mentioning among the outcomes of such activities the publications by Brun et al. (2011) and StAR (2011b).

regarding their ability to respond to requests for mutual legal assistance in corruption cases.

The second component deals with building national capacity. Activities under this component will support the development of institutional capacity to undertake asset recovery activities as part of governments' anti-corruption strategies and may include:

(i) Analytical work on the asset recovery process, including legal analysis of successful and unsuccessful asset recovery cases;
(ii) Analysis of a country's overall anti-corruption institutional arrangements, capacities, and vulnerabilities in the area of asset recovery;
(iii) Advisory services to assist countries in developing coherent policies on asset recovery;
(iv) Advisory services for the design of best-fit models that integrate asset recovery into existing institutional arrangements within the judiciary, anticorruption agencies, and FIUs;
(v) Advisory services on drafting or amending the legislative and regulatory framework necessary for successful asset recovery, including anti-money laundering, asset forfeiture, and income and asset declaration laws;
(vi) Development and implementation of information systems to support investigative, legal documentation, and case management aspects of asset recovery;
(vii) Training, mentoring, and advisory services on asset recovery to enable recipient agencies to identify and handle suspicious transactions, prepare cases, as well as manage and handle mutual legal assistance requests.

The third component consists of Assistance in the recovery of stolen assets. Along these lines StAR may provide preparatory assistance aimed at collecting and sharing information to encourage the progress of a country's specific asset recovery efforts where requested to do so by national authorities. This could entail country dialogue and technical assistance, which may include:

(i) Sponsoring meetings and workshops which bring together the parties involved at a national, regional, and international level as necessary;
(ii) Advisory services to support the preparation of analytical reports, legal research, assistance with audits and financial analysis.

As to the governance structure, StAR has a two-tier decision-making structure: (i) a Management Committee, which provides strategic guidance to StAR, and (ii) the StAR Secretariat, which manages the day-to-day activities of StAR. In addition, StAR is supported by two consultative and advisory bodies: (i) the StAR Donor Consultative Group (the "Donor Group") and (ii) the Friends of StAR ("FStAR").[72]

17.4.2 Challenges and Priorities to be Addressed

After StAR has acknowledged, in one of its early reports, that "addressing the problem of stolen assets is an immense challenge" (StAR, 2007: 1), the intense research activity carried out in these years has identified a set of issues which constitute key-priorities to be tackled by State Parties to the UNCAC. Notwithstanding the fact that StAR has always stressed that asset recovery is a complex and multi-faceted issue which is to be analyzed within the contexts where it takes place, our concise exposition follows the classification used in one of StAR's most comprehensive works on asset recovery's barriers.[73] To gain a wider perspective on the current challenges in the field of asset recovery, the following paragraphs, which briefly review the most controversial matters from the StAR's perspective, should be read in close relation with the trends emerging from the latest session of the COSP[74] and with the perspectives offered by some of the most renowned experts on the current asset recovery environment.

17.4.2.1 General barriers

Political will Within the first general, or "institutional", group of barriers to the recovery of the proceeds of corruption, the lack of political will has been pointed out – as already done by the last COSP – as a "key impediment." Interestingly, StAR defines the latter concept as "a lack of a comprehensive, sustained, and concerted policy or strategy to identify asset recovery as a priority and to ensure alignment of objectives, tools, and resources to this end."[75]

Non-compliance with anti-money laundering measures Another impediment which belongs to the group of general barriers has a preventive

---

72 For a further illustration of the different roles played by such bodies we refer to StAR (2008).

73 StAR, 2011b.

74 *Supra*, para 17.3.1.

75 StAR (2011b: 2).

character: when referring to the lack of implementation of anti-money laundering measures, StAR (2011b: 2) considers them a priority for States since they constitute "means to prevent and detect the proceeds of corruption in the first place." In order to comply efficiently with anti-money laundering obligations in view of recovering assets, StAR (2009a: 21) suggested that States should coordinate their AML actions with the anti-corruption efforts, and integrate relevant agencies and bodies into "multi-agency teams" working either on specific cases or in permanent structures. Moreover, at the policy level, States should also develop guidance on the risk-assessment of the sources of the proceeds of corruption, and integrate anti-money laundering and corruption issues in their development assistance programs. In the latter regard, the international community (i.e. the UNCAC bodies and FATF, and the other intergovernmental organizations with competence on this issue) could provide appropriate supervision.

Inadequate monitoring of politically exposed persons As already mentioned, significant technical hurdles arise from the complexity and the intricacy of different ML techniques. The issue of ML legislation within the context of asset recovery assumes particular relevance in relation to politically exposed persons (PEPs), who should be given special attention by the financial institutions and their supervisor. Issues surrounding the lack of information regarding beneficial ownership continue to plague law enforcement officers in their effort to trace assets. What is manifest is that more needs to be done by the private sector to keep precise records of beneficial owners of assets, so as to disempower the money element (Shulz, 2013; Arnone and Borlini, 2010). Noting the "surprisingly low compliance with FATF requirements on PEPs, especially among FATF members",[76] StAR has undertaken a specific study on the latter issue (StAR, 2010), which rigorously illustrates the international best practices on the matter and, drawing on them, elaborates the following strategy to better address the risk that corrupt PEPs access the financial markets and launder their illicit gains:

(i) Enhanced due diligence should be applied to both foreign and domestic PEPs, despite that laws and regulations do not make such distinction;
(ii) Within due-diligence requirements, a declaration regarding the identity and details of the natural person(s) representing the ultimate

[76] According to StAR (2010: xv) "of the 124 countries assessed by FATF or by FATF-Style Regional Bodies, 61 percent were non-compliant and 23 percent were partially compliant. More than 80 percent of these jurisdictions are far behind."

beneficial owner(s) of the business relationship or transaction should be required in a written form;

(iii) Public officials should be required to provide a copy of any asset and income declaration forms filed with their authorities, as well as subsequent updates;

(iv) Customers of banking services who are also PEPs should be reviewed by senior management using a risk-based approach (at least once a year) and the results of the review should be put on the record;

(v) On top of the latter recommendations, the current international framework and requirements on PEPs should be clarified and harmonized in order to provide "helpful guidance", but also to afford "sounder and more consistent parameters" for jurisdictions and the banking sector.

Ineffective systems of income and asset disclosure A further element of key importance in relation to public officials, is to set up an effective system of income and asset disclosure, which is considered to be increasingly helpful as a tool against corruption, both at the preventive and enforcement level. In particular, it requires that public officials declare all of their income, assets, and financial interests, and it aims at preventing and detecting the use of public office for private gain. Moreover, by providing guidance about the ethical principles and behaviors to be followed while holding public office, such systems build a climate of integrity within the public administration and prevent the occurrence of conflicts of interests. Finally, for the purposes of enforcement, income and asset declarations may integrate probatory evidence and a valuable source of information for financial or corruption investigations, and may constitute key elements in situations where underlying acts of corruption may be difficult to prove. The latter are a few of the factors which have driven StAR to elaborate a specific guide on the issue of income and asset disclosure, which is not only relevant to detect bribery but it has also a broader scope insofar as it may "contribute to broader anti-corruption efforts, such as national and international financial investigations and prosecutions, international asset recovery efforts, the prosecution of illicit enrichment, and the identification of politically exposed persons."[77] Through its work, StAR has a twofold aim: firstly, to initiate a reasoned debate on the issue and, more generally, to promote interest and awareness in it. Secondly, to provide a practical tool for policymakers and practitioners which are in charge of developing systems of

77 StAR (2012: 1).

income and asset disclosure in order for them "to establish the capacities and institutional links required for this potential to be realized."[78] As for the strategy suggested to the latter addressees, the study recalls the importance of contextual choices and the considerations which should be taken into account when facing the design features and implementation challenges, such as the scope and coverage of disclosure, the verification and monitoring of mechanisms (i.e. operational issues), the enforcement of sanctions (i.e. effectiveness and credibility), and the public access to declarations of information and the role of civil society. The case of criminalization of illicit enrichment is most telling in this sense. On the one hand, illicit enrichment can serve the scope of reducing the potentially troublesome procedural and evidential requirements associated with corruption offenses, supporting the identification of illicit funds, and triggering of asset recovery. On the other, its utility in the context of the asset recovery process largely depends on a multitude of further elements: the broader context of criminalization of corruption; the monitoring regime for public officials; the specific objective to be pursued with the offence; the effective preservation of fundamental human rights when introducing and criminalizing illicit enrichment; the existence of independent and effective institutions for the administration of justice to prevent possible abuses; the possibility for investigative authorities of relying on updated and functional databases in order to alleviate the collection of evidence (Muzila *et al*, 2013).[79]

Considering that StAR (2012) finds that there is not a one-fits-all solution and that it is expressively a descriptive rather than a normative guide, it is sound to conclude by noting that the effectiveness of the system set up by each State mostly "depends on the right questions being asked and addressed at the right moment."[80]

17.4.2.2 Legal barriers

A second group of challenges in asset recovery, according to StAR (2011b), is represented by the "legal barriers and requirements that delay assistance." In this category StAR encompasses the onerous requirements which arise when States have to deal with mutual legal assistance, banking secrecy, overly burdensome procedural and evidentiary laws, and non-conviction based asset confiscation procedures. Turning our attention, in particular, to some frustrations that authorities have recently experienced in financial centers within the context of recent asset recovery cases, it

---

78 StAR (2012: 1).
79 See *supra* Chapter 10, Box 10.1.
80 StAR (2012: 1).

is worth emphasizing that, the (mis)use of the rule of law in financial hubs may end up protecting those alleged of grand corruption cases by abusing vulnerabilities and drawbacks in legal procedures. For instance, the case of Tommy Suharto (son of the former Indonesian President Haji Mohammad Suharto) that has played out in Guernsey, shows how difficult securing a favorable ruling in an offshore financial center can be. As Raffray (2013: 31 *et seq.*) brilliantly illustrates, at the heart of the problem "is the tension caused by the (proper) reliance on the rule of law by those accused of grand corruption" in financial hubs "to protect assets systemically (and laundered) through their own (apparent) lack of respect for the rule of law" in their own countries in the first place.

Issues linked to non-conviction based asset forfeitures With regards to the latter procedures, few additional considerations could be made, as StAR published a good-practice guide on this matter (StAR 2009b). Non-conviction based asset forfeiture is a legal mechanism which enables the restraint, seizure, and forfeiture of stolen assets without the need for a criminal conviction. It can be essential in successfully recovering assets when the violator is dead, a fugitive, benefits immunity, or is just too powerful to be prosecuted. As Monteith (2013) also testifies, non-conviction based forfeiture is a strategy authorities are increasingly taking to achieve asset recovery, especially when it is difficult for prosecutors to establish the criminal offences which initially generated the proceeds of corruption. For these kind of situations, Article 54(1)(c) of the UNCAC, which constitutes the only instrument containing a specific provision on this matter, urges State Parties to "consider taking such measures as may be necessary to allow confiscation (. . .) without a criminal conviction." Several sensitive issues for national jurisdictions arise in this context, ranging from the presumption of innocence, to the respect of fundamental rights. The guidance provided by StAR (2009b), not only addresses the latter challenges, but it also provides practical indications stemming from the analysis of the relevant domestic jurisprudence, and from the illustration of the ways obligations coping with national procedural impediments are implemented.

Lack of transparency in settlements of foreign bribery cases Another legal mechanism which poses several problematic issues in the recovery of the proceeds of corruption, is represented by the manner in which many cases of foreign bribery terminate, that is, through settlement which StAR defines as "any procedure short of a full trial."[81] The research conducted

81 StAR (2013: 1).

by StAR (2013) starts from the empirical observation that, considering 395 settlements cases in the period 1999–2012, out of nearly $6 billion of monetary sanctions imposed by a country different from the one of the corrupt official, only about three percent of such amount (approximately $197 million) has been returned to the State of the official.

On the one hand, one could say that the overall amount of sanctions inflicted through settlement procedures is a remarkable result and testifies to the progress made in recent years in prosecuting foreign bribery cases. On the other hand, too little of them have been recovered by States – mostly in the developing world – whose officials have been bribed. StAR (2013) acknowledges that the latter countries should make more of an effort in the investigation and prosecution of bribery by foreigners, and that all the States should pursue legal proceedings regardless of the settlement which might have taken place elsewhere. It also observes that part of the problem lies in some operational barriers among States, such as the lack of timely communication and exchange of information.

In this context, StAR (2013) finds that settlement procedure constitutes a (legal) barrier to asset recovery insofar as the countries of origin of the proceeds of corruption have not been involved and have not obtained any kind of redress.

In order to let these countries recover their assets without hampering the fulfillment of the anti-corruption commitments by other States, but also to favor dialogue and coordinated action among jurisdictions during settlements procedures, StAR (2013: 97) has elaborated some options and recommendations to address these settlement-related challenges:

(i) All States should develop a clear legal framework regulating the conditions and process of settlements;
(ii) When settlements are agreed upon, States of the respective courts should transmit information proactively to other affected States regarding basic facts of the case, in line with Articles 46 (4) and 56 of the UNCAC;
(iii) When deciding to pursue a foreign corruption case, States should mutually inform each other on the legal avenues available to participate in the investigation and to claim damages suffered as a result of the corruption;
(iv) In line with Article 53 (c) of the UNCAC, States should allow courts to recognize the claims of other affected States when deciding on confiscations in the context of settlements;
(v) States should proactively share information on concluded settlements with other potentially affected States (i.e. the terms of the settlement, the underlying facts, the content of any self-disclosure, and evidence);

(vi) The latter information could enable other States to undertake further action, such as: initiating enforcement actions, seeking mutual assistance, pursuing the recovery of assets through international cooperation in criminal matters or private civil litigation, intervening in the case in order to pursue compensation for damages, annul or rescind any public contracts that were concluded in the context of bribery cases, debarment of companies which have been found guilty as well as withdrawing them from concessions and permits which are the result of the corruption, monitoring the compliance of companies with any resolutions linked to the settlement, and obligating them to establish or reinforce their internal anti-corruption policy with respect to the operation within the affected State's jurisdiction.

In summary, StAR (2013) first underlines that in many cases the settlements' arrangements between judicial authorities and the involved parties takes place in a informal and opaque manner. In this sense it recalls that, although in some jurisdictions the outcomes of settlements are publicly available, different forms of settlements observed in the different jurisdictions (non-prosecution agreements, deferred prosecution agreements, penalty notice, or a guilty plea) have varying degrees of publicity. Moreover, most settlements provide little oversight by a judge and sometimes without any public hearing at the conclusion.

In light of the latter empirical observations, the study then calls for greater transparency in settlements, whose negotiations should be communicated to affected jurisdictions and whose outcomes should be made available to the public.

Misuse of corporate vehicles An appeal to afford greater transparency has been formulated by StAR also in relation to a further (legal) issue linked to asset recovery. That is, the ownership and control of companies, legal arrangements and foundations.[82] Considering the fact that corporate vehicles of different kinds have played a key role in many grand corruption cases, StAR has undertaken thorough research which has carefully analyzed the challenges posed by shell companies, but also the most and least effective laws and standards in this context. Finally, in its recommendations, StAR (2011a) provides some practical guidance as to the way to avoid that corrupt official successfully laundering illicit proceeds through corporate vehicles. We deal with the latter topic, when assessing the jurisdictional issues of the international anti-corruption legal

---

82 StAR (2011a).

framework. Thus, at this point we refer to that part of our work and, in particular, to the recommendations that StAR made to governments in order to fill up the gaps existing between the compliance on paper and the practice.[83]

Political Immunities The UNODC (2009), along with other sources, stressed that political immunity laws may constitute another substantial stumbling block to prosecute corruption. When, as it happens in some jurisdictions, such laws go beyond their institutional scope serve to ease corruption and prevent prosecution of criminal conduct by public officials (Marques, 2013).[84]

Major conflict of interests within the financial system Another major issue that can annihilate efforts to recover stolen assets is represented by the unfortunate case of macro-level conflicts of interests which permeate the financial systems of several countries. Just to give an example, "questions were raised by a civil society group when the Swiss Financial Market Supervisory Authority . . . failed to hold Swiss banks accountable for their relations with deposed groups and politically exposed persons . . . in the Arab Spring – raising legitimate questions with doubts regarding the level to which money laundering standards are applied to financial intermediaries when overarching political agendas and commercial considerations come into play" (Dornbierer and Fenner Zinkernagel, 2013: xix).

Toward a "clear and sound" legal framework Back to the general group of "legal barriers", StAR (2011b) sustains that States should change attitude with respect to complex legal requirements and thus to consider the adoption of some recommendations:

(i) When confronted with the issues of dual criminality and reciprocity, States should show more flexibility through a higher level of mutual trust.
(ii) In order to protect the integrity of investigations, asset holders should not be informed throughout the investigative and asset preservation procedures. However, this should not lead to a diminished level of due process rights and guarantees.
(iii) States should limit the grounds to refuse mutual legal assistance,

---

83 See para 13.5, and Sharman (2013).

84 For an in-depth illustration and critical assessment of this topical case see Longchamp and Herkenrath, 2013.

and avoid denying it for reasons of economic interest. Indeed, complications arising for the necessary use of mutual legal assistance mechanisms can cause further breakdowns in asset recovery cases, mainly because several developed countries do not provide effective and efficient support to requesting states in democratic transition. Quite the contrary, they rather prefer to rely on an outdated notion on the passive relationship between the requested and requesting States (Wyss, 2013). As a matter of fact, such strategy ignores the very fundamental core of any international asset recovery process: cross-border problems call for cross-border solutions.[85]

(iv) Another useful measure in this context is to extend the statutes of limitations.

(v) Finally, with regards to international cases involving offenses provided for by the UNCAC and the UNTOC, States should work to lift bank secrecy.

In light of the latter considerations, StAR (2011b: 3) calls for the removal of demanding legal barriers and thus states that "absent a clear and sound legal framework, asset recovery becomes, in a best-case scenario, arduous and, in a worst-case scenario, impossible."

17.4.2.3 Operational barriers

A whole set of problems within the asset recovery procedure may arise in the presence of an effective legal framework and is caused by the processes and communications between the parties. Among the numerous practical yet fundamental barriers which hinder the possibilities for States to repatriate the proceeds of corruption pursuant to the UNCAC, StAR (2011b) has pointed out the following ones: (i) the identification of focal points for mutual legal assistance requests; (ii) the establishment of a network of contacts to coordinate the asset recovery procedure; (iii) the timing to obtain the information requested for mutual legal assistance; and (iv) problems in the drafting of requests.

Further, operational barriers include the lack of a national bank registry which does not allow them to identify owners of bank accounts, but also the impossibility for some States to manage and preserve assets that have been restrained throughout the confiscation process. To fill in the latter gaps, it is suggested the establishment of a national bank registry,

---

85 As Raffray (2013: 48) remarks, "the recovery of stolen assets in accordance with the rule of law is intrinsically a cross-border problem calling for cross border solutions".

BOX 17.1 THE GLOBAL FOCAL POINT INITIATIVE AS A NETWORK OF ASSET RECOVERY EXPERTS

A recent joint initiative of StAR and INTERPOL to overcome the operational barriers is the Global Focal Point Platform which aims at promoting and increasing the cooperation among law enforcement agencies and anti-corruption entities around the world with regards to corruption data. The Platform was founded in 2009 and consists of a global network of asset recovery expert practitioners (so-called Focal Points) which can exchange information and ask for assistance through INTERPOL's network. More precisely, each INTERPOL member country may nominate a maximum of two Focal Points, one working in a law enforcement agency engaged with corruption, the second, either from the judiciary or another governmental entity responsible for anti-corruption and asset recovery. As of July 2013, a total of 181 national investigators and prosecutors from 99 countries had been nominated as Focal Points. Annual conferences and meetings bring together the Focal Points to discuss successes and lessons learned, and to ensure that the initiative constitutes an effective tool to fight corruption and recover stolen assets.[86]

The Global Focal Point Platform works on several fronts: not only does it aim at enhancing and strengthening trust among anti-corruption practitioners, but it also serves as a venue to assist practitioners and investigators in locating and recovering assets which have flown out of the country. Finally, it also provides a technical and strategic anti-corruption knowledge database, and constitutes a bridge by encouraging mutual understanding of the different systems.

To reach the latter objectives, the initiative makes use of the services provided by INTERPOL, and, in particular, of its secure communications network, which enables Focal Points to access:

---

86 More information on the conferences and meetings organized within the Global Focal Point Initiative see http://www.interpol.int/Crime-areas/Corruption/International-asset-recovery.

(i) information and contact details of Focal Points from other States;
(ii) legislative, administrative, investigative and judicial frameworks about asset recovery for each registered jurisdiction;
(iii) a secure e-mail platform (SECOM) exchange information concerning ongoing corruption and asset recovery cases;
(iv) a knowledge library on asset recovery and a library of best practices on anti-corruption produced by the INTERPOL Group of Experts on Corruption;
(v) all valid INTERPOL notices published for corruption-related offences;
(vi) INTERPOL notices to freeze assets, in order to alert immediately member countries to temporary asset freezing, while awaiting the long-term need to coordinate;
(vii) A 24-hour "initial action checklist" for asset recovery investigations: considering that time is crucial in recovering stolen assets, the checklist gives Focal Points a guide to use when initiating a stolen asset investigation, and to ensure that the crucial steps are taken (e.g. identifying and interviewing witnesses, freezing and seizing proceeds of crime, and obtaining relevant documents).

While the knowledge input to the concept, as well as the content for the Platform, is provided by StAR, financial support for the Platform comes from the US Department of State, through the Bureau of International Narcotics and Law Enforcement Affairs.

which is considered an effective tool to both trace assets and facilitate international cooperation in a more timely manner. In addition, the progressively effective implementation of financial disclosure laws is proving to be a remarkable element in both warning enforcement authorities to rapid and unexplained increases in the wealth of public office holders and in setting up the required level of evidence to secure corruption-related convictions (Messick 2013).

Insufficient guidance on the management of returned assets The appropriate management of restrained and seized assets is crucial in this context, where the risk of their depletion exists. A different set of issues concerns the management of assets once they have returned to the requesting State:

on this equally important phase of the asset recovery procedure, StAR has dedicated a policy note which explores and guides States on how to manage the repatriated funds and assets.[87] Starting from the assumption that the use of the latter resources is a sovereign decision of the State which has recovered them and that state sovereignty must be preserved,[88] StAR (2009c) aims at contributing to the understanding of these important issues in two ways. Firstly, it provides a quite extensive overview of the different policy options available to States (enhancing already existing national procedures, creating autonomous funds through the establishment of public entities, awarding the task to non-governmental organizations[89]) with the respective pros/cons and the considerations which should guide an accurate choice in light of the contextual circumstances.[90] Secondly, it puts forward substantive methodological guidance: an approach guided by openness and transparency in designing the arrangements to manage the returned assets is in fact considered desirable, especially in presence of high-profile returns.[91] In addition to that, a final part of the study highlights the importance of effectively monitoring performances of asset management: not only does it help identify strengths and weaknesses in the arrangements which have been put in place, but it is also deemed helpful to build confidence in the system and to foster the engagement of all the actors involved in the managerial process.[92]

Technical difficulties in identifying and quantifying the proceeds of corruption In the realm of operational barriers one could finally encompass the difficulties which courts face in identifying and quantifying the proceeds of corruption, especially the benefits obtained by the bribe payer. To help practitioners, but also legislators and policymakers to deal with such obstacles, the OECD and StAR have undertaken a joint study, which is intended to guide them by providing valuable practical information and examples on the technical issues which often constitute barriers in recovering assets.[93] Besides providing the legal framework for

---

87 StAR (2009c).

88 There exist ongoing debates over the extent to which States where stolen assets are located can determine the conditions under which money is returned to their State of origin, in particular, with regards to ensuring that the entrusted money is used transparently and for social or productive and developmental purposes.

89 In this respect see Jimu (2013).

90 StAR, 2009c: 11–20.

91 StAR (2009c: 2).

92 StAR (2009c: 23).

93 OECD and StAR (2012).

the treatment of the proceeds of bribery, the range of legal remedies available in several jurisdictions and the challenges linked to the interaction of remedies, it is the second part of the research which constitutes the most original contribution for the improvement of the asset recovery procedure. OECD and StAR (2012: 29 *et seq*) addresses, in fact, the methods deployable in practice to quantify the most common proceeds of active bribery.[94] Furthermore, it also provides concrete examples where such methods have been used,[95] as well as some comments on the practical challenges posed by some crucial factors like the relevant time period and the interest rates for the calculation of proceeds, agent fees, administrative costs, indirect benefits, partial transactions, and bribe payments. On the bright side, the analysis of OECD and StAR concludes by noting that the identification and quantification of the proceeds is neither too complicated nor expensive: rather, in many cases there are multiple alternatives and reasonable approaches.[96] The same could be said also for those jurisdictions which do not have extensive experience in this field: quite a few States have effectively developed their expertise by applying existing traditional legal principles that were already available to practitioners.[97] As a consequence, States can build quantification methods in different ways (applying existing legislation, enacting new legislation, as well as developing case law or guidelines), without renouncing to the legal certainty inherent in their laws, legal principles and established practices.

94 The study considers, in particular, (a) proceeds from contracts obtained through bribery; (b) business authorisations, permits or licenses to operate; (c) expenses or losses avoided; (d) expedition of delays; and (e) gains from using lax internal controls and inaccurate or incomplete books and records.

95 The detailed summaries of most of the cases which illustrate the findings of the study constitute the third and final part of the research.

96 OECD and StAR (2012: 69).

97 OECD and StAR (2012: 69), where it is also recalled that disgorgement initially grew out of case law in the United States, and that a mix of case law and statutes has led to remedies such as compensation for damages and contractual restitutions in the United Kingdom, South Africa and other jurisdictions.

Afterword

Leonardo S. Borlini

At the time of writing these pages Marco Arnone is no longer with us.

It is extremely difficult to find appropriate words to remember him and his work, and it may be that this is not the most suitable context to do so. What is relevant to me is stressing that the present book represents the outcome of a constant, open and lively dialogue between the two of us. And I am the one who has undoubtedly got the most out of such dialogue: Marco considered ethical commitment to be at the very heart of both his professional life and scientific works. But he also taught me that no credible research can be based solely on ethical passion. He made me clearly understand that in order to offer a meaningful contribution in the field of anti-corruption studies, we must distance ourselves from any sort of "illusion of purity".

Such legacy leads me to a first concluding remark. The very assumption of our entire work is that in order to assess whether and how to regulate a complex phenomenon like corruption, it is necessary to investigate its causes, its institutional and social effects along with its economic costs. Accordingly, we have shown that corruption is one of the most serious challenges to the rule of law and democratic society. Rampant corruption weakens the basic foundations, both of the representative mechanisms underlying the separation of powers and of human rights. As to its economic impact, suffice it here to remember that the economics of corruption has recently achieved a comprehensive understanding of its institutional consequences, economic effects at the macro and micro level, and developmental issues. Corruption is one of the most serious distortions of the competitive well-functioning of modern regulated markets, which typically creates and crystallizes asymmetric business environments, where outsiders are either excluded ex ante or forced to exit, as well as closed social systems, where the views of those without sufficient economic or political influence or enough visibility are simply without representation. Markets characterized by widespread corruption are dominated by operators with the least entrepreneurial capabilities, who need to break the rules, illegally impose their will, use (or be used by) political power to avoid competition. These operators may be good at rent-seeking, while they seek resources and parasitic advantages, but are not entrepreneurs as such. Corruption is often associated with poor and unequal legal enforcement, weakened regulatory oversight and, possibly, bad corporate governance, which, among other things, may allow management to easily divert resources from the firm and make use of such resources for their own private benefits, at the expense of bondholders (and other stakeholders like workers, clients, suppliers, and stockholders). Furthermore, empirical studies, which have explored the efficiency implications of corruption through its impact on growth and investment, composition of government expenditure, allocation of foreign direct investment, generally conclude that corruption reduces growth, and investment; skews expenditure towards public investment and away from operations and maintenance; and redirects foreign direct investment towards countries with lower corruption. Moreover, there is strong evidence of significant adverse distributional effects of corruption: high and rising corruption is associated with higher income inequality and poverty. Also, corruption should be looked at as huge developmental and distributive problem within the international scenario. Finally, when it hits financial markets, corruption affects, among the other things, asset prices and financial supervision.

Some of the cases we have analysed shows that, insofar as corruption is concerned, the emerging feature of globalization is the possibility of de-localising almost instantaneously activities for illicit purposes. In other words, the fact that globalization permits extreme contractions of the temporal and space dimensions, in which any human activity typically occurs offers, unprecedented opportunities for criminal actors and organisations able to fully exploit the chance to de-localise their activity. The resulting increased probability that corruption eludes state control and its effects spill over and resonate throughout the world economy has urged a response by the international community.

Only once the socio-institutional effects, economic costs and growing transnational dimension of the subject of our analysis has been clarified does it become possible for us to move to assess the achievements and shortcomings of the international.

In line with this approach, we have thus analysed the general patterns of the international instruments to curb corruption. Relevant steps have been undeniably made: to cite the most evident and significant examples, the array of provisions dealing with the criminalisation of corruption of foreign public officials and officials of international public organizations, liability of legal persons, disallowance of tax deductibility of bribes to foreign officials, and comprehensive apparatus of preventive measures, now represents a common patrimony of most of the anti-bribery treaties and, what is more, a solid basis upon which (sometimes rather) innovative national implementing pieces of legislation have been adopted and enforced. Furthermore, the very fact that five regional inter-governmental organizations and the UN have adopted hard law instruments against various forms of corruption is an event relevant in its own right. However, these initiatives have not been sufficiently coordinated and are characterised by (occasionally) considerable divergences: the scope *ratione materiae* varies noticeably, not to mention that some of the treaties contain numerous facultative provisions. It is, therefore, commendable to promote collective efforts in order to guarantee that the international anti-corruption movement does not paralyse itself, by duplicating efforts, setting conflicting standards and subjecting member States to ever-increasing reporting duties.

From yet another perspective, it is known far and wide that international provisions cannot produce any appreciable result without accurate implementation of national laws and, thereafter, rigorous application of such laws. This is why we argue that the State Parties of the various Conventions should maintain their follow-up mechanisms where functioning and effective. In a similar vein, they should find out ways to establish and/or strengthen effective follow-up procedures within the supervisory mechanisms envisaged by the anti-corruption treaties, in case the laws have not been effective. Such mechanisms represent, indeed, the main tool to thrust reluctant countries to accurately implement the Conventions themselves. Furthermore, they provide a unique instrument for the supervisory bodies to monitor whether the implementing laws are applied rigorously and consistently and to recommend the reforms being carried out.[1]

Other key findings emerge from our assessment of the main anti-corruption instruments developed by the international community in light of our previous economic analysis.

First, it is worth remarking that the impact of the main IFI's initiatives in the fields of anti-corruption and good governance policies is as important as the adoption of international treaties on the matter.

Second, when considering the different provisions contained in such treaties, we have highlighted that prevention and law enforcement are complements and not alternatives. Preventive policies are vain when they

---

[1] Implementation support and technical assistance must be further developed in order to help translate the results of monitoring, and the relevant recommendations in particular, into sustainable practical achievements. However, it goes without saying that national authorities have the ultimate responsibility for complying with the results of such monitoring.

are not backed up with firm action to counter impunity for abuses of official position (which corruption ultimately represents) and the conduct of those who bribe officials. Fighting impunity is crucial for the legitimacy of the political system, and so is a determined preventive approach. Similarly, in light of our analysis of the *Fininvest* case, we have concluded that civil remedies well complement criminal prosecution of corruption. Thus, international instruments establishing clear and detailed commitments to promote such remedies, like the CoE Civil Law Convention on Corruption, represent fundamental elements of a comprehensive anti-corruption strategy.

Third, the treaty-approach regarding criminalisation has unquestionably contributed to calibrate the national responses and, in some cases (e.g. the definition of the objective and subjective elements of the offence of "transnational corruption"; the design of innovative sanctions such as confiscation of equivalent value; and the promotion of forms *ex crimine* liability or legal entities) formulate them *ex novo*. Also, the efforts for harmonising the required elements of the different forms of corruption stand among the main achievements of anti-bribery treaties. As a matter of perspective, one can expect that the progressive harmonization of such elements and the other substantial aspects, such as the kind and level of sanctions, will increase where criminal co-operation is assuming closer and innovative forms (e.g. within the EU).

Fourth, a major and recent breakthrough of the international apparatus against corruption is represented by the asset recovery mechanism. With the adoption of the UNCAC the binding principle, according to which illicitly acquired assets are to be returned, has been ratified for the first time at a multilateral level. Thanks to the efforts of the StAR Initiative, States are substantially supported to further the required international cooperation to make the recovery of assets deprived by big corruption cases effective. Yes, as extensively illustrated, the path is not without obstacles.

Finally, our analysis has led us to account for the most remarkable shortcomings of the anti-corruption international instruments. Some forms of corruption, indeed, have been addressed with noticeable determination only by a few inter-governmental organizations. This is the case of private-to-private corruption, which is effectively tackled only by the Council Framework Decision 2003/568/JHA of 22 July 2003 on combating corruption in the private sector of the EU, whereas in the framework of the other international organizations private corruption is mainly addressed by facultative and/or non-criminal provisions. Another noticeable deficiency affecting the international apparatus against corruption concerns the treatment of financing of political parties. It no longer seems possible to dodge addressing this matter at domestic level. Some of the offences envisaged by the anti-corruption treaties may indirectly cover illicit funding of political parties. However, except for these provisions and, notwithstanding the efforts of some delegations in the negotiating proceedings of the OECD Convention and the UNCAC, the resulting scenario is still unsatisfying. Furthermore, despite the provisions on responsibility of legal entities involved in corruption cases, the misuse of corporate vehicles in different jurisdictions still represents an issue of particular concern. Coordinated initiatives to "pierce the corporate veil" cannot be procrastinated any longer. Also, there still seems to be a chasm between the well-recognised need of concerted criminal strategies, the challenges posed by transnational dynamics of corruption crimes, and the determination of States to maintain their criminal prerogatives: the emergence of causal chains stretching across national jurisdictional boundaries with effects that transgress one or more national criminal norms poses serious jurisdictional challenges. With regards to this issue, the treaty-mechanism seems to have favoured the relative States' freedom on the matter, rather than imposing binding commitments where the traditional territoriality approach plainly fails, *i.e.* when the crime is perpetrated through multi-jurisdictional corporate schemes. In cases where States refrain from reaching appropriate levels of criminal cooperation/integration, it is customary to recall what Weber long ago stressed. Each State is monopolist of legitimate violence; to cede the exercise of this power to States or polity other than the territorial State concerned represents a switch of allegiance from that State to other States or polities. Where criminal law faces the challenge of de-localised conduct, however, the lack of precise and binding commitments might affect the inherent efficiency of the entire apparatus. Such consideration shows the way for a more general conclusion: whereas the old *nomos* – as Carl Schmitt used to say – linked law to territories, at this moment in time, when law has to face de-localised phenomena like the new forms of rampant corruption, the new *nomos* has to stretch with them, take their extension, leave its old ties, and fully exploit its own artificial character.

Bibliography

Abbott, K.W. (2001), Rule-Making in the WTO: Lessons from the Case of Bribery and Corruption, *Journal of International Economic Law*, 4, p. 275.

Abbott, K.W. and Snidal, D. (2002), Filling in the Folk Theorem: The Role of Gradualism and Legalization in International Cooperation to Combat Corruption, Paper presented at the American Political Science Association Meeting, Boston, 30 August.

Abed, G. and Gupta, S. (2002), *Governance, Corruption & Economic Performance*, Washington, DC: IMF.

Abrams, N. (1989), The New Ancillary Offences, *Criminal Law Forum*, 1(1): 1–39.

Acquaviva, G. (2003), Il FCPA statunitense e il dilemma della lotta alla corruzione internazionale: azione unilaterale o cooperazione internazionale?, in Sacerdoti, G. (ed.), *Responsabilità d'impresa e strumenti internazionali anticorruzione. Dalla Convenzione OCSE 1997 al Decreto n. 231/2001*, Milan: Egea, p. 167.

Adam, R. (1998), La cooperazione in materia di giustizia e di affari interni tra comunitarizzazione e metodo intergovernativo, *Diritto dell'Unione Europea*, p. 481.

Adam, R. and Tizzano, A. (2008), *Lineamenti di diritto dell'Unione Europea*, Turin: Giappichelli.

Adams, R. (2008), Black Sunday at Wall Street, *The Guardian*, 15 September 2008.

Aderinwale, A. (ed.) (1995), *Corruption, Democracy and Human Rights in Eastern and Central Africa: Summary Report of the Seminar Organized by the Africa Leadership Forum*, Entebbe and Ibadan, Uganda: ALF Publications.

Aggarwal, R.K., Meschke, E.F. and Wang, T.Y. (2007), Corporate Political Contributions: Investment or Agency, Working Paper, the University of Minnesota.

Agrawal, A. and Knoeber, C. (2001), Do Some Outside Directors Play a Political Role?, *Journal of Law and Economics*, 44(1): 179–98.

Aidt, T. S. (2003), Economic Analysis of Corruption: A Survey, *The Economic Journal*, 113(491): F632–52.

Ajani, G. (2004), Ma la "rule of law" è lo Stato di diritto?, *Il Sole 24 ore*, 25 April.

Akehurst, M. (1972–73), Jurisdiction in International Law, *British Yearbook of International Law*, 46: 145.

Akehurst, M. (1974–5), Custom as a Source of International Law, *British Yearbook of International Law*, 47: 1.

Akerlof, George A. and Shiller, Robert J. (2009), *Animal Spirits: How Human Psychology Drives the Economy, and Why It Matters for Global Capitalism*, Princeton, NJ: Princeton University Press.

Akre, J.L. (2007), Overcoming Chad's Oil Curse: The African Union Convention on Preventing and Combating Corruption as a Framework for Securing Foreign Investments, available at: http://works.bepress.com/jennifer_akre/1.

Alam, M.S. (1989), Anatomy of Corruption: an Approach to the Political Economy of Underdevelopment, *American Journal of Economics and Sociology*, 48: 441.

Alesina, A. and Giavazzi, F. (2006), *The Future of Europe: Reform or Decline*, Cambridge, MA: The MIT Press.

Alessandri, A. (2003), La responsabilità amministrativa delle persone giuridiche: osservazioni generali, in Sacerdoti, G. (ed.), *Responsabilità d'impresa e strumenti internazionali anticorruzione. Dalla Convenzione OCSE 1997 al Decreto n. 231/2001*, Milan: Egea, p. 147.

Alessandri, A. (2005), Attività d'impresa e responsabilità penali, *Riv. dir. proc. pen.*, 2005: 534.

Alessandri, A. (2013), I reati di riciclaggio e corruzione nell'ordinamento italiano: linee generali di riforma, *Riciclaggio e corruzione: prevenzione e controllo tra fonti interne e internazionali* Acts of the Conference organized by Centro Nazionale di Prevenzione e Difesa Sociale (Courmayeur, 28 September 2012), Milan: Giuffrè, p. 57.

Alvarez, J. (2005), *International Organizations as Law-makers*, Oxford: Oxford University Press.

Andemicael, B. and Davidson, N. (1974), The OAU: Primacy in Seeking African Solutions within the UN Charter, in El-Ayouty, Y. and Zartman, I. W. (eds.), *The OAU after Twenty Years*, New York: Praeger Press, p. 101.

Anderson, M., Cullen, P., Gilmore, W., Raab, C. and Walker, N. (1995), *Policing the European Union*, Oxford: Clarendon.

Anechiarico, F. and Jacobs, J. (1996), *The Pursuit of Absolute Integrity. How Corruption Control Makes Government Ineffective*, Chicago: University of Chicago Press.

Ang, J. and Boyer, C.M. (2000), Finance and Politics: Special Interest Group Influence during the Nationalization and Privatization of

Conrail. Clarkson University, Economic and Financial Studies Working Paper, A-4.

Anon. (2003), Money Laundering, *American Criminal Law Review*, 40: 847.

Anon. (2004), *Conventión Interamerican contra la Corruptión. Implementación de un eficaz instrumento contra internacional de lucha contra la corruptión*, Buenos Aires: Oficina anticorruptión.

Anzilotti, D. (1928), *Corso di diritto internazionale*, Padua: Cedam.

Archer, C. (1993), *Organising Europe*, London: Macmillan.

Archer, C. (1994), *Organizing Europe*, London: Edward Arnold.

Argandon A. (2007), The United Nations Convention Against Corruption and its Impact on International Companies, *Journal of Business Ethics*, 74: 481.

Aristotle (1988), *The Politics*, Cambridge: Cambridge University Press.

Arnone, M., Bellavite Pellegrini, C. and Graziadei, F. (2006), *Il venture capital per lo sviluppo: un'analisi delle Economie Emergenti*, Milan: Vita e Pensiero.

Arnone, M., Bellavite Pellegrini, C. and Messa, A. (2010), Microfinance Institutions in Asia, Latin America and Africa: Empirical Analysis on the Operational Efficiency, Mimeo.

Arnone, M. and Borlini, L. (2010), International Anti-Money Laundering Programs: Empirical Assessment and Issues of Criminal Regulation, *Journal of Anti-Money Laundering Control*, 13(2): 226–71.

Arnone, M., Darbar, S. and Gambini, A. (2007), Financial Sector Governance in Banking Supervision: Theory and Practices, in Masciandaro, D., and Quintyn, M., *Designing Institutions for Financial Stability: Independence, Accountability and Governance*, Cheltenham, UK and Northampton, MA, USA: Edward Elgar.

Arnone, M. and Davigo, P. (2005), Arriva la Crisi Economica? Subito Spunta la Corruzione, *Vita e Pensiero*, 5 (September/October 2005): 44–51.

Arnone, Marco, and Gambini, A. (2006a), Architecture of Financial Supervisory Authorities and the Basel Core Principles, Institute for Economic Policy Working Paper, no. 48, Catholic University of Milan, March 2006.

Arnone, Marco, and Gambini, A. (2006b), Financial Supervisors Architecture and Banking Supervision, in Masciandaro, D., and Quintyn, M. (eds.), (2007), *Designing Institutions for Financial Stability: Independence, Accountability and Governance*, Cheltenham, UK and Northampton, MA, USA: Edward Elgar.

Arnone, M. and Iliopulos, E. (2005), *La Corruzione Costa: effetti economici, istituzionali e sociali*, Milan: Vita e Pensiero.

Arnone, Marco, Laurens, B. and Segalotto, J.F. (2006a), The Measurement of Central Bank Autonomy: Survey of Models, Indicators, and Empirical Evidence, IMF Working Paper, 227/06, Washington, DC.

Arnone, M., Laurens, B. and Segalotto, J.F. (2006b), Measures of Central Bank Autonomy: Empirical Evidence for OECD and Developing Countries, and Emerging Market Economies, IMF Working Paper, 228/06, Washington, DC.

Arnone, M. and Padoan, P.C. (2008), Anti-Money Laundering by International Institutions: A Preliminary Assessment, *European Journal of Law and Economics*, 26: 361–86.

Arnone, M. and Presbitero, A.F. (2010), *Debt Relief Initiatives: Policy Design and Outcomes*, Global Finance Series, Farnham, UK: Ashgate Publishing.

Arnull, A., Dashwood, A., Dougan, M., Ross, M., Spaventa, E. and Wyatt, D. (2006), *European Union Law*, 5th edn., London: Sweet and Maxwell.

Aronoff, A. (1994), The Commerce Department Speaks on International Trade and Investment, *Antibribery Provisions of the Foreign Corrupt Practices Act*, PLI Corporate Law & Practice Course Handbook Series 863.

Ashworth, A. (1999), *Principles of Criminal Law*, Oxford: Oxford University Press.

Auger, J. (2003), International Survey Sheds Light on Corruption Blackspots, *World Markets Analysis*, 7 July.

Aust, A. (2007), *Modern Treaty Law and Practice*, 2nd edn., Cambridge: Cambridge University Press.

Baderin Mashood, A. and Abass, A. (2002), Towards Effective Collective Security and Human Rights Protection in Africa: An Assessment of the Constitutive Act of the New African Union, *Netherland International Law Review*, 2002: 1.

Bai, J. and Ng, S. (2006), Confidence Intervals for Diffusion Index Forecasts and Inference for Factor Augmented Regressions, *Econometrica*, 74(4), 1133–50.

Baldassarre, A. (2002), *Globalizzazione contro democrazia*, Rome and Bari: Laterza.

Baldassarre, A. (2004), La Convenzione del Consiglio d'Europa sul riciclaggio, la ricerca, il sequestro, e la Confisca dei proventi di reato e sul finanziamento del terrorismo, *Diritto del Commercio Internazionale*, 20(3–4), July/December: 607.

Balmelli, T. (2004), La restitution internationale des avoirs acquis par la corruption: de l'obligation morale à l'obligation juridique, in Balmelli, T., and Jaggy, B., *Les Traités internationaux contre la corruption*, Lausanne: Editions interuniversitaires suisses, p. 63.

Bantekas, I. (2006), Corruption as an International Crime and Crime against Humanity, *Journal of International Criminal Justice*, 3: 466.

Banz, R.W. (1981), The Relationships between Return and Market Value of Common Stocks, *Journal of Financial Economics*, 9: 3–18.

Barberini, R. (2003), L'entrata in vigore della Convenzione contro il crimine organizzato transnazionale, *Questione Giustizia*, 4: 1034.

Barberis, M. (2006), *Etica per giuristi*, Rome and Bari: Laterza.

Bardhan, Pranab (1997), Corruption and Development: A Review of Issues, *Journal of Economic Literature*, 35(3): 1320–46.

Bardhan, P. and Mookherjee, D. (2006), Decentralization, Corruption and Government Accountability: An Overview, in Susan Rose-Ackerman (ed.), *International Handbook of the Economics of Corruption*, Cheltenham, UK and Northampton, MA, USA: Edward Elgar, 161–88.

Barro, R. (1990), Government Expenditure in a Simple Model of Endogenous Growth, *Journal of Political Economy*, 98: 103.

Barron, G. (2005), The World Bank & Rule of Law Reforms, 2005, London School of Economics and Political Sciences, Working Paper series no. 05–70, Development Studies Institute, London.

Basdevant, J. (1960), *Dictionnaire de la terminologie du droit international public*, Paris: Sirey.

Bassiouni, M.C. (1999a), Crimes against Humanity, in Bassiouni, M.C., *International Criminal Law*, vol. III, 2nd edn., Ardsley, NY: Transnational Publisher, p. 94.

Bassiouni, M.C. (1999b), *International Criminal Law. Procedural and Enforcement Mechanisms*, vol. II, 2nd edn., Ardsley, NY: Transnational Publisher.

Bassiouni, M.C. (1999c), *Le fonti e il contenuto del diritto penale internazionale*, Milan: Giuffrè.

Bassiouni, M.C. (2003), *Introduction to International Criminal Law*, New York: Transnational Publisher.

Basu, S. (1977), Investment Performances of Common Stocks in Relation to their Price Earnings Ratios: A Test of the Efficient Market Hypothesis, *Journal of Finance*, June: 663–82.

Bauman, Z. (1998), *Globalization. The Human Consequences*, New York: Columbia University Press

Bauman, Z. (1999), *La società dell'incertezza*, Bologna: Il Mulino.

Bauman, Z. (2002), *Society under Siege*, Cambridge: Cambridge University Press.

Baumann, T. (2004), Pro-poor Microcredit in South Africa: Cost-efficiency and Productivity of South African Pro-poor Microfinance Institutions, *Development Southern Africa*, 21(5): 785–98.

Beccaria, C. (1995), *Dei delitti e delle pene*, Milan: Mondadori.

Beck, M. and O'Brien M. (2000), Corporate Criminal Law Liability, *American Criminal Law Review*, 37(2): 261.

Beck, P.J. and Maher, M.W. (1986), A Comparison of Bribery and Bidding in Thin Markets, *Economics Letters*, 20: 1–5.

Beck, U. (1997), *Was ist Globalisierung? Irrtumer des Globalismus-Antworten auf Globalisierung*, Frankfurt am Main: Suhrkamp; Italian translation: *Che cos'è la globalizzazione. Rischi e prospettive della società planetaria* (1999), Rome: Carocci.

Becker, G. and Stigler, G. (1974), 'Law Enforcement, Malfeasance, and the Compensation of Enforcers', *Journal of Legal Studies*, 3: 1–19.

Bellavite Pellegrini, C. (2008), *Modelli d'equilibrio e fondamentali d'impresa. I rendimenti azionari nell'area dell'Euro*, Rome: Carocci Editore.

Bellavite Pellegrini, C. and Belcredi, M. (2002), Difese antiscalata e acquisizioni cross border in Europa: situazione e prospettive, *Rivista Bancaria Minerva Bancaria*, July–August: 17–58.

Bentham, J. (1843), Principles of Morals and Legislation, in *The Works of Jeremy Bentham*, published under the superintendence of his executor, John Bowring, Edinburgh: William Tait, 11 vols. Vol. 1.

Berenson, A. (2008), Markets Are Falling. But When They Hit the Bottom? *New York Times*, 22 September: I.

Bergbohm, C. (1877), *Staatsverträge und Gesetze als Quellen des Völkerrechts*, Dorpat: C. Mattiesen.

Bergman, D. (2000), *The Case for Corporate Responsibility: Corporate Violence and the Criminal Justice System*, London: Disaster Action.

Berman, F. (2003), Jurisdiction: The State, in Capps, P., Evans, M., and Kostadinidis, S. (eds.), *Asserting Jurisdiction: International and European Legal Perspectives*, Oxford: Oxford University Press, p. 5.

Bernardi, A. (2002), Il diritto penale tra globalizzazione e multiculuralismo, *Riv. it. dir. pubbl. Comunitario*, p. 533.

Bernardi, A. (2004a), Entre la pyramide et le résau: les effets de l'européanisation du droit sur le systeme penal, *Revue interdisciplinare d'etudes juridique*, p. 5.

Bernardi, A. (2004b), *L'europerizzazione del diritto e della scienza penale*, Turin: Giappichelli.

Bernardi, A. (2006), *Modelli penali e società multiculturali*, Turin: Giappichelli.

Bernasconi, P. (ed.) (2000), *Responding to Corruption: Social Defence and the Protection of the Public Administration and the Independence of Justice*, Naples: La città del sole.

Bertrand, M., Kramarz, F., Schoar, A. and Thesmar, D. (2004), Politically Connected CEOs and Corporate Outcomes: Evidence from France, Working Paper, University of Chicago.

Bhagwati, J. (1982), Directly Unproductive Profit-Seeking (DUP) Activities. *Journal of Political Economy*, 90(October): 988–1002.

Bhandari, L. (1988), Debt/Equity Ratio and Expected Common Stock Returns: Empirical Evidence, *Journal of Finance*: 507–28.

Bieber, R. and Monar, J. (ed.) (1995), *Justice and Home Affairs in the European Union: The Development of the Third Pillars*, Brussels: European University Press.

Black, F., Jensen, M.C. and Scholes, M. (1972) The Capital Asset Pricing Model: Some Empirical Tests, in Jensen, M. (ed.), *Studies in the Theory of Capital Markets*, New York, Praeger, pp. 79–121.

Blanchard, O. (1997), *Macroeconomics*, New Jersey, USA: Prentice Hall International; Italian translation edited by Giavazzi, F. (1998), *Macroeconomia*, Bologna: Il Mulino.

Bobbio, N. (1993), *Teoria generale del diritto*, Turin: Giappichelli.

Bobbio, N. (1997), *L'età dei diritti*, 3rd edn., Turin: Einaudi.

Bobbio, N., Matteucci, N. and Pasquino, G. (2004), *Il Dizionario di politca*, Turin: UTET.

Boeri, T. (2008), Il numero. 45, *Internazionale*, no. 37, 2008, p. 81.

Bogdandy, A. Von (2004), Globalization and Europe: How to square Democracy. Globalization and International Law, *European Journal of International Law*, 15: 885.

Bogdandy, A. Von, Dann, P. and Goldmann, M. (2008), Developing the Publicness of Public International Law: Towards a Legal Framework for Global Governance Activities, *German Law Journal*, 9: 1375.

Boister, N. (2003), Transnational Criminal Law?, *European Journal of International Law*, 14: 953.

Bone, J. (2003), Saddam's Billions from Oil for Food Corruption, *The Times* (London), 23 April.

Bonucci, N. (2007a), Articles 12: Monitoring and Follow-up, in Pieth, M., Low, L.A., and Cullen, P. (eds.), *The OECD Convention in Bribery: A Commentary*, Cambridge: Cambridge University Press, p. 445.

Bonucci, N. (2007b), Articles 13–17: Final Provisions, in Pieth, M., Low, L.A., and Cullen, P. (eds.), *The OECD Convention in Bribery: A Commentary*, Cambridge: Cambridge University Press, p. 476.

Bonucci, N. (2012), The Fight Against Transnational Bribery: The Value of Collective Action Seen From an International Organization's Perspective, in Pieth, M. (ed.), *Collective Action: Innovative Strategies to Prevent Corruption*, Zurich/St. Gall: Dike, p. 67.

Borghi M. and Meyer-Bisch, P. (eds.) (1995), *La corruption, l'envers de droits de l'homme. Corruption, the Reverse of Human Rights*, Fribourg: Editiones Universitaires Fribourg Suisse.

Borlini, L. (2003), Strumenti e iniziative di lotta alla corruzione nel commercio internazionale, in Sacerdoti, G. (ed.), *Responsabilità d'impresa e strumenti internazionali anticorruzione. Dalla Convenzione OCSE 1997 al Decreto n. 231/2001*, Milan: Egea, p. 5.

Borlini, L. (2005), La lotta alla corruzione internazionale: Le Convenzioni dell' OCSE e delle Nazioni Unite, il caso Enelpower, la "tangentopoli" irachena, *La Comunità Internazionale*, LX(1): 75.

Borlini, L. (2006), Una Convenzione ONU a 360 gradi, ma l'Italia tarda nella ratifica, *Guida al diritto. Comunitario e Internazionale. Il Sole 24 ore*, June–July, p. 18.

Borlini, L. (2007), Issues of the International Criminal Regulation of Money Laundering in the Context of Economic Globalization, *Diritto del Commercio Internazionale*, XXII(1): 37.

Borlini, L. (2008), Il "salto di qualità" nel contrasto con le sanzioni alle persone giuridiche, *Guida la diritto. Diritto internazionale e comunitario*, 1, January–February.

Borlini, L. (2013), Corruzione. Impatto sistemico e normativa internazionale, *Riciclaggio e corruzione: prevenzione e controllo tra fonti interne e internazionali*, Acts of the Conference organized by Centro Nazionale di Prevenzione e Difesa Sociale (Courmayeur, 28 September 2012), Milan: Giuffrè, p. 37.

Borlini, L. and Magrini, P. (2007), La lotta alla corruzione internazionale. Dall'ambito OCSE alla dimensione ONU, *Diritto del Commercio Internazionale*, XXI(1): 15.

Bossard, A. (1988), La Criminalité transfrontalière multidisciplinaire, *Revue de science criminelle et de droit pénal comparé*, 1988, p. 756.

Bossard, A. (1990), *Transnational Crime and Criminal Law*, Chicago: University of Illinois Press.

Bouckaert, B. (1996), La corruzione politica e il suo controllo. Istituzioni e morale, *Biblioteca della libertà*, 137, p. 33.

Braguinsky, S. (1996), Corruption and Schumpeterian Growth in Different Economic Environments, *Contemporary Economic Policy*, 14: 14.

Brau, J.C. and Woller, G.M. (2004), Microfinance: A Comprehensive Review of the Existing Literature, *Journal of Entrepreneurial Finance and Business Ventures*, 9(1): 1–26.

Brickey, K. (2003), From Enron to WorldCom and Beyond. Life and Crime after the Sarbanes-Oxley, *Washington University Law Quarterly*, 81: 357.

Brierly, J.I. (1928), The Lotus Case, *Law Quarterly Review*, 44: 154.

Brooks, R.C. (1970), The Nature of Political Corruption, in Heidenheimer, A.J. (ed.), *Political Corruption: Reading in Comparative Analysis*, New York: Holt, Reinhart and Winston, p. 58.

Brownlie, I. (2003), *Principles of Public International Law*, 6th edn., Oxford: Oxford University Press.

Brownlie, I. (2008), *Principles of Public International Law*, 7th edn., Oxford: Oxford University Press.

Brun, J.P., Gray, L. et al. (2011), *Asset Recovery Handbook: A Guide for Practitioners*, Washington, DC: World Bank.

Bruti Liberati, E. (2000), The Fight against Fraud and Corruption, in Alvazzi del Frate, A. and Pasqua, G. (eds.), *Responding to the Challenges of Corruption*, Acts of the International Conference (Milan, 19–20 November 1999), Rome/Milan: UNICRI publication No. 63, p. 57.

Bruton, W.F. (1999), Money Laundering: Is It Now a Corporate Problem?, *Dickinson Journal of International Law*, 17: 3.

Buergenthal, T. (1992), Self-executing and Non-Self Executing Treaties, in National and International Law, *Recueil des Cours*, 235: 303.

Buergenthal, T. and Shelton, D. (1995), *Protecting Human Rights in the Americas*, 4th edn., Arlington, VA: Engel.

Buergenthal, T. (2001), Proliferation of International Courts and Tribunals: Is It Good or Bad?, *Leiden Journal of International Law*, 14: 267.

Buzzard, J. (1978), Intent, *Criminal Law Review*, 1978: 5.

Cahn, E. (1949), *The Sense of Injustice*, Bloomington: Indiana University Press.

Caiden, G.E. (2004), Symposium: A Cautionary Tale. Ten Major Flaws in Combating Corruption, *South-western Journal of Law and Trade in the Americas*, 10: 269.

Calderone, C.F. (2001), La lotta alla corruzione in campo comunitario e internazionale, *Riv. trim. dir. pen. econ.*, 2001, p. 607.

Calderoni, F. (2008), A Definition that Could Not Work: The EU Framework Decision on the Fight Against Organized Crime, *European Journal of Crime, Criminal Law and Criminal Justice*, 16: 265.

Calvino, I. (2006), *Lezioni Americane. Sei proposte per il prossimo millennio*, Verona: Mondadori.

Campos, J.E. and Bhargava, V. (2007a), Introduction, in Campos, J.E., and Pradhan, S. (eds.), *The Many Faces of Corruption: Tracking Vulnerabilities at the Sector Level*, Washington, DC: The World Bank.

Campos, J.E. and Bhargava, V. (2007b), Tackling a Social Pandemic, in Campos, J.E., and Pradhan, S. (eds.), *Many Faces of Corruption: Tracking Vulnerabilities at the Sector Level*, Washington, DC: World Bank.

Campos, J.E. and Pradhan, S. (2007), *The Many Faces of Corruption: Tracking Vulnerabilities at the Sector Level*, Washington, DC: The World Bank.

Caracciolo, I. (2000), *Dal diritto penale internazionale al diritto internazionale penale. Il Rafforzamento delle garanzie giurisdizionali*, Naples: Editoriale scientifica.

Carino, L.V. (1986), *Bureaucratic Corruption in Asia: Causes, Consequences and Controls*, Manila, The Philippines: JMC Press.

Carrington, P. (2009), American Law and Transnational Corruption: Is There a Need for Lincoln's Law Abroad?, in Mayer, O. (ed.), *The Civil Law Consequences of Corruption*, Bremen: Nomos Auflage.

Carrington, P.D. (2007), Law and Transnational Corruption: The Need for Lincoln's Law Abroad?, *Law and Contemporary Problems*, 70: 109–38. Available at: http://scholarship.law.duke.edu/lcp/vol70/iss4/2.

Cartier-Bresson, J. (1997a), The Economics of Corruption, in Della Porta, D., and Meny, Y. (eds.), *Democracy and Corruption in Europe*, London: Pinter.

Cartier-Bresson, J. (1997b), Corruption Networks, Transaction Security and Illegal Social Exchange, *Political Studies*, 45(3): 463.

Cartier-Bresson, J. (2000), *The Causes and Consequences of Corruption: Economic Analyses and Lessons Learnt, No Longer Business As Usual*, Paris: Organisation for Economic Co-operation and Development, pp. 11–28.

Carver, J. (2003), Combating Corruption: The Emergence of New International Law, *International Law Forum*, 5(2): 119.

Cassani, U. (1996), Die Anwendung des schweizerischen Strafrecths auf internationale Wirtschafdelikte (Art. 3–7 StGB), *Schweizerische Zeitschrift für Strafrecth*, 114: 237.

Cassese, A. (1971), *Il controllo internazionale. Contributo alla teoria delle funzioni di organizzazione dell'ordinamento internazionale*, Milan: Giuffrè.

Cassese, A. (1990), Remarks on Scelle's Theory of Role Splitting (dédoublement functionnel) in International Law, *European Journal of International Law*, p. 219.

Cassese, A. (2001), *International Law*, Oxford: Oxford University Press.

Cassese A. (2002), Y-a-t-il un conflit insurmontable entre souveraineté des Etats et justice pénale internationale?, in Cassese, A., and Delmas-Marty, M., *Crimes internationaux et jurisdictions internationales*, Paris: PUF.

Cassese, A. (2003a), *International Criminal Law*, Oxford: Oxford University Press.

Cassese, A. (2003b), Crimes Against Humanity, in Cassese, A., Gaeta, P. and Jones, J.R.W.D., *The Rome Statute of the International Criminal Court*, Oxford: Oxford University Press.

Cassese, A. (2005a), *I diritti umani oggi*, Rome and Bari: Laterza.

Cassese, A. (2005b), *International Law*, 2nd edn., Oxford: Oxford University Press.

Cassese, A. (2006), *Diritto internazionale*, published under the superintendence of Gaeta, P., Bologna: Il Mulino.

Cassese, A., Chiavario, M. and De Francesco, G. (eds) (2005), *Problemi attuali della giustizia penale internazionale*, Turin: Giappichelli.

Cassese, A. and Gaeta, P. (2008), *Le sfide attuali del diritto internazionale*, Bologna: Il Mulino.

Cassese, S. (2005), *Universalità del diritto*, Naples: Editoriale Scientifica.

Cassese, S. (2006), *Oltre lo Stato*, Rome and Bari: Laterza.

Cassese, A. (2008), *International Criminal Law*, 2nd edn., Oxford: Oxford University Press.

Cassin, R.L. (2012), Marubeni Pays $546 Million to Settle TSKJ Nigeria Case, available at http://www.fcpablog.com/blog/2012/1/17/marubeni-pays-546-million-to-settletskj-nigeria-case.html.

Castellaneta, M. (2007a), Rafforzato il principio di sussidiarietà: protagonisti i parlamenti nazionali, *Guida al diritto. Diritto Comunitario e Internazionale. Il Sole 24 ore*, 6 (November–December): 15.

Castellaneta, M. (2007b), Si riducono i tempi per l'adozione degli atti di cooperazione penale, *Guida al diritto. Diritto Comunitario e Internazionale. Il Sole 24 ore*, 6 (November–December): 18.

Castronovo, V. (1986), *L'Industria Italiana dall'Ottocento ad oggi*, Milan: Arnoldo Mondatori Editore S.p.A, p. 410.

Cervenka, Z. (1969), *The Organization of the African Unity and its Charter*, London: C. Hurst.

Cervenka, Z. (1977), *The Unfinished Quest for Unity*, London: Julian Friedmann.

Chalmers, D. and Monti, G. (2008), *European Union Law. Updating Supplement*, Cambridge: Cambridge University Press.

Chalmers, D., Davies, G. and Monti, G. (2011), *European Union Law*, Cambridge: Cambridge University Press.

Chalmers, D., Hadjiemmanuil, C., Monti, G. and Tomkins, A. (2007), *European Union Law*, Cambridge: Cambridge University Press.

Chaves, M. (2009), *European Criminal Law: Reshaping Criminal Justice Across the European Union?*, London: Mimeo.

Chen, C.J.P., Ding, Y. and Kim, C. (2006), Political Connection, Legal Enforcement and Analysts' Forecast Characteristics, First draft, Old Dominion University, Norfolk, VA.

Chen, D.-H., Fan, J.P.H. and Wong, T.J. (2004), Politically Connected CEOs, Corporate Governance and Post-IPO Performance of China's Partially Privatized Firms, University of Shanghai, Centre for Economic Institutions (CEI), Working Paper series, 2004–05.

Chen, N.F. (1983), Some Empirical Tests of the Theory of Arbitrage Pricing, *The Journal of Finance*, XXXVIII(5): 1393–414.

Chen, N.F., Roll, R. and Ross, S. (1986), Economic Forces and the Stock

Market: Testing the APT and Alternative Asset Pricing Theories, *Journal of Business*, (59): 383–403.

Cheng, T.-M. and Reinhardt, U.E. (2012), Perspective on the Appropriate Role of the Private Sector in Meeting Health Care Needs, in Clements, B., Coady, D., and Gupta, S. (eds.), *The Economics of Public Health Care Reform in Advanced and Emerging Economies*, Washington, DC: International Monetary Fund.

Chiu, M.M. and Joh, S.W. (2004), Loans to Distressed Firms: Political Connections, Related Lending, Business Group Affiliations and Bank Governance, Chinese University of Hong Kong, Working Paper.

Ciocchini, F., Durbin, E. and Ng, D. (2003), Does Corruption Increase Emerging Market Bond Spreads?, *Journal of Economics and Business*, 55: 503–28.

Cissé H., Bradlow D. D. and Kingsbury B. (eds.) (2012), *International Financial Institutions and Global Legal Governance*, Washington DC, The World Bank.

Claessens, S., Feijen, E. and Laeven, L. (2008), Political Connections and Preferential Access to Finance: The Role of Campaign Contributions, *Journal of Financial Economics*, 88(3): 554–80.

Clapham, A. (2006), *Human Rights Obligations and Non-State Actors*, Oxford: Oxford University Press.

Clark, K.A. and Drew, K. (2005), Corporate Criminal Liability, *American Criminal Law Review*, 42: 325.

Clark, Nicola (2004), Appeal Hearings Open for 2 former Elf Chiefs Court to Review Corruption Convictions, *International Herald Tribune*, 7 October.

Clark, R.S. (1998), Countering Transnational and International Crime: Defining the Agenda, in Cullen, P.J. and Gilmore, W.C. (eds.), *Crime Sans Frontières: International and European Legal Approaches*, Edinburgh: Edinburgh University Press.

Clark, R.S. *Crime Against Humanity and the Rome Statute of the International Criminal Court*, in Politi M. and Nesi G. (eds) (2001), *The Rome Statute of the International Criminal Court*, Aldershot: Ashgate, p. 75.

Clements, B., Coady, D. and Gupta, S. (eds.) (2012), *The Economics of Public Health Care Reform in Advanced and Emerging Economies*, Washington, DC: International Monetary Fund.

Cockayne, J. (2005), Book Reviews – Review Essay. On the Cosmopolitanization of Criminal Jurisdiction, *Journal of International Criminal Justice*, 3: 514.

Coffee, J.C., Jr. (1983), Corporate Criminal Liability, in Kadish, Sanford H. (ed.), *Encyclopaedia of Criminal Justice*, vol. I, New York: Macmillan, p. 253.

Coffee, J.C., Jr. (1999), Corporate Criminal Liability: An Introduction and Comparative Survey, in Eser, A., Heine, G., and Huber, B. (eds.), *Criminal Responsibility of Legal and Collective Entities*, Freiburg: Edition Iuscrim, p. 9.

Collier, P. and Dollar, D. (1985), *A Matter of Principle*, Cambridge, MA: Harvard University Press.

Colombo, G. (1994), Stato di diritto e corruzione. I risultati delle indagini Milanesi sui reati contro la pubblica ammininstrazione, in *Cassazione penale*, 1994.

Colombo, G. (1997), Monitoring the Assets and the Lifestyle of Public Decision-makers. Can It be Made to Work?, Presented at VIII International Anti-Corruption Congress, Lima, 9 September.

Colombo, G. (2007), UNCAC: A Way of Life. The Role of the Judiciary, in Passas, N. and Vlassis, D. (eds.), *The United Nations Convention Against Corruption as a Way of Life*, Selected papers and contributions from the International Conference on 'The United Nations Convention Against Corruption as a Way of Life' (Courmayeur, 15–17 December 2006), Milan: ISPAC, p. 43.

Colombo, G. (2008), *Sulle regole*, Milan: Feltrinelli.

Condinanzi, M. (2004), sub Articolo 34, in Tizzano A. (ed.), *Trattati dell'Unione Europea e della Comunità Europea*, Milan: Giuffrè, p. 130.

Conforti, B. (2005), *Le Nazioni Unite*, 7th edn., Padua: Cedam.

Conforti, B. (2006), *Diritto internazionale*, 7th edn., Naples: Editoriale scientifica.

Conso, G. and Grevi, V. (2008), *Compendio di procedura penale*, 4th edn., Padua: Cedam.

Cooetze, J.M. (2008), *Diario di un anno difficile*, Turin: Einaudi.

Cooper, M.J., Gulen, H.M.C. and Ovtchinnikov, A. (2010), Corporate Political Contributions and Stock Returns, *Journal of Finance*, 65(2): 687–724.

Cordero, F. (2004), *Nere lune d'Italia. Segnali di un anno difficile*, Milan: Garzanti.

Cordero, F. (2006), *Procedura Penale*, 8th edn., Milan: Giuffrè.

Corr, F. and Lawler, J. (1999), Damned if You Do, Damned if You Don't? The OECD Convention and the Globalisation of Antibribery Measures, in *Vanderbilt Journal of Transnational Law*, 32: 1249.

Corstens, G.J.M. and Pradel, J. (2002), *European Criminal Law*, Paris: Dalloz.

Corstens, G.J.M. (2003), Criminal Law in the First Pillar?, *European Journal of Crime, Criminal Law, and Criminal Justice*, 11: 131.

Cosseddu, A. (2005), Responsabilità da reato degli enti collettivi: criteri di imputazione e tipologia delle sanzioni, *Riv. trim. dir. pen. ec.*, p. 1.

Costanzo, P. (2013), The risk-based approach to anti-money laundering and counter-terrorist financing in international and EU standards: What it is, what it entails, in Unger, B., and van der Linde, D. (eds), *Research Handbook On Money Laundering*, Cheltenham, UK and Northampton, MA, USA: Edward Elgar, p. 349.

Craig, P. and De Búrca, G. (2011), *EU Law: Text, Cases, and Materials*, Oxford: Oxford University Press.

Craufurd Smith, R. (1999), Remedies for Breaches of EC Law in National Courts: Legal Variations and Selections, in Craig, P., and de Bùrca, G. (eds.), *The Evolution of EU Law*, Oxford: Oxford University Press, p. 287.

Crespi, A., Stella, F. and Zuccalà, G. (eds.) (2004), *Commentario breve al codice penale*, Padua: Cedam.

Criminal Division of the U.S. Department of Justice, and Enforcement Division of the U.S. Securities and Exchange Commission (2012), *A Resource Guide to the U.S. Foreign Corrupt Practices Act*, available at http://www.justice.gov/criminal/fraud/fcpa/guide.pdf.

Csonka, P. (1999a), Civil Law and Corruption, Paper presented at 9th International Anti-Corruption Conference, available at www.transparency.org/iacc/papers/day3/ws1/d3ws1_pcsonka.html.

Csonka, P. (1999b), The Council of Europe's Anti-Corruption Treaties, Paper presented at 9th International Anti-Corruption Conference, available at: www.transparency.org/content/download/2523/14725.

Cull, R., Demirguc-Kunt, A. and Morduch, J. (2007), Financial Performance and Outreach: A Global Analysis of Leading Microbanks, *The Economic Journal*, 117(517): F107–33.

Cull, R. and Xu, L.C. (2005), Institutions, Ownership and Finance: The Determinants of Profit Reinvestment among Chinese Firms, *Journal of Financial Economics*, 77: 117–46.

Cullen, P.J. (2007), Article 6. Statute of Limitations, in Pieth, M., Low, L.A., and Cullen, P. (eds.), *The OECD Convention in Bribery. A Commentary*, Cambridge: Cambridge University Press, p. 353.

Daams, C. (2003), *Criminal Asset Forifeiture: One of the Most Effective Weapons against (Organised) Crime?*, Basel: Wolf Legal Publisher.

Dabbah, M. (2003), *The Internationalisation of Antitrust Policy*, Cambridge: Cambridge University Press.

Dabla-Norris, Era and Paul, Elisabeth (2006), What Transparency Can Do When Incentives Fail: An Analysis of Rent Capture, IMF Working Paper, 06/146, Washington, DC.

Dabla-Norris, Era and Wade, Paul (2002), Production, Rent Seeking and Wealth Distribution, in Abed, George T., and Gupta, Sanjeev (eds.), *Governance, Corruption and Economic Performance*, Washington, DC: IMF.

Daniel, T. (2004), Repatriation of Looted State Assets: Selected Case Studies and the UN Convention against Corruption, in Hodess, R., Inowlocki, T., Rodriguez, D., and Wolfe, T. (eds.), *The Global Corruption Report*, London: Pluto Press/Berlin: Transparency International, pp. 100–07.

Daniele, L. (2007), Trattato di Lisbona: addio all'idea federalista per superare gli ostacoli degli euroscettici, *Guida al diritto. Diritto Comunitario e Internazionale, Il Sole 24 ore*, November–December, p. 11.

Davies, M. (2013), An Ongoing Dialogue, in Fenner Zinkernagel, G., Monteith, C. and Gomes Pereira, P. (eds.), *Emerging Trends in Asset Recovery*, Bern: Peter Lang, p. 117.

Davigo, P.C. (2003), Gli intatti meccanismi della corruzione sistemica, in Forti, G. (ed.), *Il prezzo della tangente, La corruzione come sistema a dieci anni da "mani pulite"*, Milan: Vita e Pensiero.

Davigo, P.C. (2004), La giubba del re. Intervista sulla corruzione, in Pinardi, D. (ed.), Rome and Bari: Laterza.

Davigo, P. and Mannozzi, G. (2007), *La corruzione in Italia. Percezione sociale e controllo penale*, Rome and Bari: Laterza.

De Amicis, G. (2007), *Cooperazione giudiziaria e corruzione internazionale. Verso un sistema integrato di forme e strumenti di collaborazione tra le autorità giudiziarie*, Milan: Giuffrè.

De Amicis, G. and Iuzzolino, G. (2004), Lo spazio comune di libertà, sicurezza e giustizia nelle disposizioni penali del Trattato che istiuisce una Costituzione per l'Europa, in *Cass. Pen.*, p. 3070.

De Cecco, M. (2008), Fed&Congresso, Impero al declino, *la Repubblica, Affari & Finanza*, 22 September, p. 1.

De Franchis, F. (1996), *Dizionario giuridico-Law Dictionary*, vol. I, Milan: Giuffrè.

De Guttry, A. and Pagani, F. (eds.) (1995), *La cooperazione degli Stati in materia di confisca dei proventi di reato e lotta al riciclaggio*, Padua: Cedam.

De Maglie, C. (2002), *L'etica e il mercato. La responsabilità penale delle società*, Milan: Giuffrè.

De Maglie, C. (2003), In difesa della responsabilità penale delle persone giuridiche, *Legisl. pen.*, p. 349.

De Soto, H. (1989), *The Other Path: The Invisible Revolution in the Third World*, New York: Harper and Row Publishers.

De Soto, H. (2000), *The Mystery of Capital: Why Capitalism Triumphs in the West and Fails Everywhere Else*, New York: Basic Books.

De Speville, B. (1997), *Reversing the Onus of Proof: Is It Compatible with Respect for Human Rights Norms?*, Paper presented at the Eight International Anti-Corruption Conference, Lima, 7–11 September.

De Vitte, B. (1998), The Pillar Structure and the Nature of the European Union: Greek Temple or French Gothic Cathedral?, in Heukels, T.,

Blokker, N., and Brus, M. (eds.), *The European Union after Amsterdam: A Legal Analysis*, The Hague: Kluwer, p. 51.

Della Porta, D. (1992), *Lo Scambio Occulto*, Bologna: Il Mulino.

Della Porta, D. and Vannucci, A. (1994), *Corruzione Politica e Amministrazione Pubblica*, Bologna: Il Mulino.

Della Porta, D. and Vannucci, A. (2007), *Mani impunite. Vecchia e nuova corruzione in Italia*, Rome and Bari: Laterza.

Delmas-Marty, M. (1993a), Incompatibilities between Legal Systems and Harmonisation Measures: Final Report of the Working Party on a Comparative Study on the Protection of the Financial Interests of the Community, in European Commission (ed.), *The Legal Protection of the Financial Interests of the Community: Progress and Prospects since the Brussels Seminar of 1989, Brussels, 25 and 26 November 1993*, Brussels: European Commission, p. 59.

Delmas-Marty, M. (ed.) (1993b), *Quelle politique pénal pour l'Europe*, Paris: Economica.

Delmas-Marty, M. (1994), Le crime contre l'humanité, les droits de l'homme et l'irréductible humain, *RSCDPC*, 11(1994).

Delmas-Marty, M. (1996), Introduction, in Delmas-Marty, M., and De Leyssac, C.L. (eds.), *Libertés et droits fondamentaux. Introduction, textes et commentaires*, Paris: Seuil.

Delmas-Marty, M. (ed.) (1997a), *Corpus Juris: Introducing Penal Provisions for the Purpose of the Financial Interests of the European Community*, Paris: Economica.

Delmas-Marty, M. (1997b), Verso un diritto penale comune europeo?, in *Riv. It. Dir. Proc. Pen.*, p. 543.

Delmas-Marty, M. (2004a), *Studi giuridici comparati e internazionalizzazione del diritto*, Turin: Giappichelli.

Delmas-Marty, M. (2004b), Le droit pénal comme l'éthique de la mondialisation, *Revue de science criminelle et de droit pénal comparé*, p. 2.

Delmas-Marty, M. and Manacorda, S. (1997), La corruption: un dèfi pour l'Etat de droit et la société démocratique, *Revue de science criminelle et de droit penal comparé*, p. 696.

Delmas-Marty, M. and Vervaele, J.A.E. (eds.) (2000), *The Implementation of the Corpus Juris in the Member States*, vol. 1, Antwerp, Oxford: Intersentia.

Deming, S.H. (2005), *The Foreign Corrupt Practices Act and the New International Norms*, Chicago: International Practitioners' Deskbook Series.

Denza, E. (2002), *The Intergovernmental Pillars of the European Union*, Oxford: Oxford University Press.

Depaak, L. (1985), The Poverty of "Development Economics", A Book Review, *The Journal of Political Economy*, 95(4) (August): 885–7.

Di Martino, A. (2006), *La frontiera del diritto penale. Natura e contesto di diritto penale transnazionale*, Turin: Giappichelli.

Di Stefano, A. (2008a), Nel buio della crisi. Subito nuove regole, *Valori. Mensile di economia sociale, finanza etica e sostenibilità*, 8(62) (September): 3.

Di Stefano, A. (2008b), Abbassiamo la leva, *Valori. Mensile di economia sociale, finanza etica e sostenibilità*, 8(62) (September): 8.

Dimson, E. and Marsh, P. (1987), *The Hoare Govett Smaller Companies Index for the UK*, London: Hoare Govett Limited.

Dimson, E., Marsh, P. and Staunton, M. (2002a), *Triumph of the Optimists: 101 Years of Global Investments Returns*, Princeton, NJ and Oxford: Princeton University Press.

Dimson, E., Marsh, P. and Staunton, M. (2002b), The Worldwide Equity Premium: A Smaller Puzzle, Mimeo, London Business School.

Dinç, I. Serdar (2004), Politicians and Banks: Political Influences on Government-Owned Banks in Emerging Countries, *Journal of Financial Economics*, 77: 453–79.

Dioma, C.A. (2007), Aiutare l'Africa?, *Internazionale*, 729 (1–7 February 2007): 66.

Donahue, J.D. (1989), *The Privatization Decision*, New York: Basic Books.

Donat-Cattin, D. (1998), Crimes Against Humanity, in Lattanzi F. (ed.), *The International Criminal Court. Comments on the Draft Statute*, Naples: Scientifica, pp. 49–77.

Donini, M. (2004), *Il volto attuale dell'illecito penale*, Milan: Giuffrè.

Dornbierer, A. and Fenner Zinkernagel, G. (2013), Introduction, in Fenner Zinkernagel, G., Monteith, C. and Gomes Pereira, P. (eds.), *Emerging Trends in Asset Recovery*, Bern: Peter Lang, p. xv.

Draetta, U. (1995), Spunti per un'azione comunitaria contro la corruzione nel commercio internazionale, *Diritto del Commercio Internazionale*, (1995): 333.

Draetta, U. (1998a), La lotta alla corruzione nel commercio internazionale, *Impresa e Stato*, 47: 3.

Draetta, U. (1998b), La nuova Convenzione OECD e la lotta alla corruzione nelle operazioni commerciali internazionali, *Diritto del Commercio Internazionale*, (1998): 969.

Draetta, U. (2003), The OECD Convention on Bribery of Foreign Public Officials and the Bribes Paid by Foreign Subsidiaries, *Diritto del commercio internazionale*, 4: 649.

Du Plessis, L.M. (1999), The Evolution of Constitutionalism and the Emergence of a Constitutional Jurisprudence in South Africa: An

Evaluation of the South African Constitutional Court's Approach to Constitutional Interpretation, *Saskatchewan Law Review*, 62: 299.

Dubois, P. H. and Nowlan, A. E. (2010), Global Administrative Law and the Legitimacy of Sanctions Regimes in International Law, *Yale Journal of International Law Online*, 36: 15.

Duff, R.A. (1990), *Intention, Agency and Criminal Liability: Philosophy of Action and the Criminal Law*, Oxford: Blackwell.

Dugard, J. and van den Wyangaert, C. (eds.) (1996), *International Criminal Law, Procedural and Enforcement Mechanisms*, Dartmouth: Aldershot.

Duncan, J.W. (1982), Modifying the Foreign Corrupt Practices Act: The Search for a Practical Standard, *Northwestern Journal of International Law and Business*, 4: 203.

Dunn, C. (2012), Can't they Cooperate?, Available at http://www.law.com/corporatecounsel/PubArticleCC.jsp?id=1202541462077.

Dupuy, P.M. (1998), International Law: Torn between Coexistence, Co-operation, and Globalization. General Conclusions, *European Journal of International Law*, (1998): 278.

Dupuy, P.M. (1999), The Danger of Fragmentation or Unification of the International Legal System and the International Court of Justice, available for download at: http://www.pict-pcti.org/publications/PICT_articles/JILP/Dupuy.pdf.

Dupuy, P.M. (2004), *Droit international public*, Paris: Dalloz.

Durbin, E. and Ng, D. (2005), The Soverign Ceiling and Emerging Market Corporate Bond Spreads, *Journal of International Money and Finance*, 24: 631–49.

Dworkin, R. (1977), *Taking Rights Seriously*, Cambridge, MA: Harvard University Press.

Earle, B. (1996), The United States Foreign Corrupt Practices Act and the OECD Antibribery Recommendation: When Moral Suasion Won't Work, Try the Money Argument, *Dickson Journal of International Law*, 14: 207.

Easterly, William (2002), *The Elusive Quest for Growth*, Cambridge, MA: The MIT Press.

Ehrlich, I. and Lui, F.T. (1999), Bureaucratic Corruption and Endogenous Economic Growth, *Journal of Political Economy*, 107(S6) (December): S270–93.

Ehrmann, M. (2002), Procedures of Compliance Control in International Environmental Treaty, *Colorado Journal of International Law and Policy*, 13: 377.

Eiras, A.I. (2003), Ethics, Corruption, and Economic Freedom, Heritage Lecture No. 813, 9 December, available at: www.heritagefoundation.org.

El-Ayouty, Y. and Zartman, I.W. (eds.) (1974), *The OAU after Twenty Years*, New York: Praeger Press, pp. 101–19.

Elliot, K.A. (ed.) (1997), *Corruption and the Global Economy*, Washington, DC: Institute for International Economics.

Emberland, M. (2006), *The Human Rights of Company. Exploring the Structure of the ECHR Protection*, Oxford: Oxford University Press.

Eser, A. and Logodny, O. (eds.) (1992), *Principles and Procedures for a New Transnational Criminal Law*, Freiburg: Herstellung Barth.

Eser, A., Heine, G. and Huber, B. (eds.) (1999), *Criminal Responsibility of Legal and Collective*, Freiburg: Edition Iuscrim.

Esposito, G. (2013), L'evoluzione della normativa internazionale e l'adozione dell'approccio basato sul rischio, *Riciclaggio e corruzione: prevenzione e controllo tra fonti interne e internazionali*, Acts of the Conference organized by Centro Nazionale di Prevenzione e Difesa Sociale (Courmayeur, 28 September 2012), Milan: Giuffrè, p. 99.

Evans, M. and Murray, R. (eds.) (2008), *The African Charter on Human and Peoples' Rights: The System in Practice, 1986–2006*, Cambridge: Cambridge University Press.

Evans, M.D. (ed.) (2003), *International Law*, Oxford: Oxford University Press.

Evans, P. (1997), The Eclipse of State? Reflections on Stateness in an Era of Globalization, *World Politics*, 50: 62–87.

Evans, T. (ed.) (1998), *Human Rights Fifty Years On: A Reappraisal*, Manchester: Manchester University Press.

Faccio, M. (2006), Politically Connected Firms, *American Economic Review*, 96: 369–86.

Faccio, M. (2007), The Characteristics of Politically Connected Firms, Krannert School of Management, Purdue University, Working Paper no. 2007–006.

Faccio, M. and Parsley, D. (2006), Sudden Deaths: Taking Stock of Political Connections, Discussion Paper Series, no. 5460, Financial Economics, CEPR.

Fama, E. and French, K.R. (1992), The Cross Section of Expected Stock Returns, *Journal of Finance*, 47(2): 427–65.

Fama, E. and French, K.R. (1993), Common Risk Factors in the Returns on Stocks and Bonds, *Journal of Financial Economics*, 33: 3–56.

Fama, E. and French, K.R. (1995) Size and Book to Market Factors in Earnings and Returns, *Journal of Finance*, 50: 131–55.

Fama, E. and French, K.R. (1996), Multifactor Explanations of Asset Pricing Anomalies, *Journal of Finance*, 51: 55–84.

Fama, E. and French, K. (1997), Value versus Growth: The International Evidence, Working paper.

Fama, E. and French, K. (2002), The Equity Premium, *Journal of Finance*, 57: 637–59.

Fama, E.F. and Jensen, M.C. (1983a), Agency Problems and Residual Claims, *Journal of Law and Economics*, 26(2): 327–49.

Fama, E.F. and Jensen, M.C. (1983b), Separation of Ownership and Control, *Journal of Law and Economics*, 26(2): 301–25.

Fama, E. and MacBeth, J.D. (1973), Risk, Return and Equilibrium: Empirical Tests, *Journal of Political Economy*, 3(81): 607–36.

Farlane, J. and McLennan, K. (1996), Transnational Crime: The New Security Paradigm, Working Paper No. 294, Australia: Australian National University.

FATF (2006), The Misuse of Corporate Vehicles, Including Trust and Company Service Providers, FATF-GAFI, 13 October.

FATF (2010), Money Laundering Using New Payment Methods, available at: http://www.ctifcfi.be/website/images/EN/typo_fatf/46705859.pdf

FATF (2012), International Standards On Combating Money Laundering and the Financing of Terrorism & Proliferation. The FAFT Recommendations, available at: http://www.fatf-gafi.org/media/fatf/documents/recommendations/pdfs/FATF_Recommendations.pdf.

FATF, Evaluation of Law and System, in FATF Members Dealing with Asset Confiscation and Provisional Measures, available at: http://www.faft-gafi.org/dataoecd/32/48/34047135.pdf (last accessed 10 November 2011).

Fenner Zinkernagel, G., Monteith, C. and Gomes Pereira, P. (2013), *Emerging Trends in Asset Recovery*, Bern: Peter Lang.

Fenyk, J. (2007), The Level of Implementation of the Convention on the Protection of the EC's Financial Interests and of the Follow-up Protocols in the Czech Republic, *European Law and National Criminal Legislation*, 1: 116–21.

Ferola, L. (1999), La cooperazione giudiziaria in materia penale: origine problemi e prospettive, *RDE*, (1999): 49.

Ferola, L. (2003), *Le misure anticorruzione nello spazio giuridico europeo tra repressione prevenzione. Strategie, problemi interpretativi e prospettive*, in Sacerdoti, G. (ed.), *Responsabilità d'impresa e strumenti internazionali anticorruzione. Dalla Convenzione OCSE 1997 al Decreto n. 231/2001*, Milan: Egea, p. 188.

Ferola, L. (2004), Profili evolutivi del crimine organizzato e problemi definitori nel panorama normativo internazionale ed europeo: un caso ancora insoluto?, *Grotius*, (2004): 28.

Ferola, L. (2005), *Il Riciclaggio di proventi illeciti nel diritto internazionale*, Milan: Giuffrè.

Ferrarese, M.R. (2002), *Il Diritto al presente. Globalizzazione e tempo delle istituzioni*, Bologna: Il Mulino.

Ferrarese, M.R. (2006), *Diritto sconfinato*, Rome and Bari: Laterza.

Ferrarese, M.R. (2007), Globalizzazione, in Pomarici, U. (ed.), *Filosofia del diritto. Concetti Fondamentali*, Turin: Giappichelli.

Fiandaca, G. (2006), Il contributo della scienza penalistico alla costruzione di un diritto del penale europeo, *Nuove autonomie*, 1 (2006): 59.

Fiandaca, G. and Musco, E. (2001), *Diritto penale. Parte generale*, 4th edn., Bologna: Zanichelli.

Fiandaca, G. and Musco, E. (2002), *Diritto penale. Parte speciale*, 3th. edn., vol. I, Bologna: Zanichelli.

Fijnaut, C. (2000), Transnational Crime and the Role of the United Nations in Its Containment through International Cooperation: A Challenge for the 21st Century, *European Journal of Crime, Criminal Law and Criminal Justice*, 8(2): 119–27.

Fishman, M., Barr, D.S. and Heaver, E. (1991), A New Perspective on Conflict Resolution in Market Forecasting, *Proceedings The 1st International Conference on Artificial Intelligence Applications on Wall Street*, New York, pp. 97–102.

Fishman, M., Barr, D.S. and Loick, W.J. (1991), Using Neural Nets in Market Analysis, *Technical Analysis of Stocks & Commodities*, pp. 18–20.

Fisman, R. (2001), Estimating the Value of Political Connections, *American Economic Review*, 91(4): 1095–102.

Fitzmaurice, G. (1957), The Law and the Procedure of the International Court of Justice 1951–4, *British Yearbook of International Law*, p. 207.

Fitzmaurice, G. (1958), Some Problems Regarding the Formal Sources of International Law, *Symbolae Verzijl*, 153–7.

Flick, G.M. (1999), Lo spazio giudiziario europeo: risultati raggiunti e prospettive, *Rivista della Guardia di Finanza*, 2: 513.

Flick, G.M. (2000), Globalizzazione dei mercati e globalizzazione della giustizia, *Rivista di diritto penale dell'economia*, 3: 591.

Forti, G. (1995), Prospettive attuali del "diritto penale comunitario", in Corapi, D. (ed.), *Saggi di diritto commerciale europeo*, Naples: ESI, p. 32.

Forti, G. (2002), Basic Features of the Legislation for Combating Corruption and Bribery in Member States of the European Union, in B. Huber (ed.), *Combating Corruption in the European Union*, Series of Publications by the Academy of European Law in Trier, vol. 31, Cologne: Bundesanzeiger Verlag.

Forti, G. (ed.) (2003a), *Il prezzo della tangente, La corruzione come sistema a dieci anni da "mani pulite"*, Milan: Vita e Pensiero.

Forti, G. (2003b), La corruzione tra privati nell'orbita della disciplina della corruzione pubblica: un contributo alla tematizzazione, *Rivista Italiana di Diritto e Procedura Penale*, 46(4).

Forti, G. (2005), *La televisione del crimine*, Milan: Vita e Pensiero.

Francioni, F. (1988), sub voce, Crimini Internazionali, in *Digesto delle dottrine Pubblicistiche*, 3th edn., Turin: Utet, p. 226.

Freeman, K. (2004), Repatriation of Looted State Assets, Selected Case Studies and the UN Convention against Corruption; available at: http://www.assetrecovery.org/kc/node/4e75f561-a340–11dc-bf1b-335d0754ba85.1.

Freeman, K. (2005), The UN Convention against Corruption. Governmental Perspectives in Developing Countries, available at: http://www.kendallfreeman.com.

Freud, S. (2006), Il disagio della civiltà, in Freud, S., *Il disagio della civiltà e altri saggi*, Turin: Bollati Boringhieri, p. 199.

Friederich, C. (1972), *The Pathology of Politics: Violence, Betrayal, Corruption, Secrecy, and Propaganda*, New York: Harper & Row.

Friedman, M. (1970), The Social Responsibility of Business Is to Increase its Profits, *New York Times Magazine*, 13 September.

Frigo, M. (2001), *La circolazione internazionale dei beni culturali*, Milan: Giuffrè.

Fumagalli, C. and Motta, M. (2008), Buyers' Miscoordination, Entry and Downstream Competition, Economic Journal, 118(531): 1196–222.

G7 Finance Ministers (2000), *Actions against Abuse of the Global Financial System*, Report from G7 Finance Ministers to the Heads of State and Government, Okinawa, 21 July 2000.

Gaeta, P. (2005), Un'analisi dell'applicazione dei principi di territorialità e nazionalità attiva, in Cassese, A., Chiavario, M., and De Francesco, G. (eds.), *Problemi attuali della giustizia penale internazionale*, Turin: Giappichelli.

Gaeta, P. (2006), sub voce, Crimini Internazionali, in Cassese, S. (ed.), *Dizionario di diritto pubblico*, vol. 2., Milan: Giuffrè.

Gaines, L.K. and Miller, R.L. (2006), *Criminal Justice in Action: The Core*, Belmont, CA: Thomson-Wadsworth Publishing.

Gaja, G. (1987), *Unruly Treaty Reservations. Le Droit International à l'Heure de sa Codifications*, Milan: Giuffrè.

Gaja, G. (1998), How Flexible is Flexibility under the Amsterdam Treaty?, *Common Market Law Review*, 35: 855–70.

Galimberti, U. (2000), *Psiche e techne. L'uomo nell'età della tecnica*, Milan: Feltrinelli.

Galimberti, U. (2008), *La casa di psiche. Dalla psicoanalisi alla pratica filosofica*, Milan: Feltrinelli.

Gamble, J.K. (1980), Reservation to Multilateral Treaties: A Macroscopic

View of State Practices, *American Journal of International Law*, 74: 372.

Gandini, F. and Iuzzolino, G. (2006), L'entrata in vigore della Convenzione O.N.U. contro la corruzione e i problemi di adeguamento dell'ordinamento giuridico italiano, *Dir. Giust.*, 7: 96.

Gantz, D.A. (1988), Globalizing Sanctions against Foreign Bribery: The Emergence of a New International Legal Consensus, in *Journal of International Law and Business*, 18: 457.

Garulé, J. and Guerra, S. (1998), *The Law of Asset Forfeiture*, Charlottesville: Lexis Law.

Gavouneli, M. (2007), Enhancing the Impact of the Convention: A Reflection Paper, presented at the Expert Meeting "The OECD Anti-Bribery Convention: The Road Ahead", held in Rome, 21 November 2007; manuscript.

Gelos, R.G. and Wei, S.J. (2005), Transparency and International Portfolio Holdings, *Journal of Finance*, 60(6): 2987–3020.

George, B. and Lacey, K.A. (2000), A Coalition of Industrialized Nations, Developing Nations, Multilateral Development Bank, and Non-governmental Organizations: A Pivotal Complement to Current Anti-corruption Initiatives, *Cornell International Law Journal*, 33(3): 547.

George, B.C. and Lacey, K.A. (2006), Investigation of Halliburton Co./TSKJ's Nigerian Business Practices: Model for Analysis of the Current Anti-Corruption Environment on Foreign Corrupt Practices Act Enforcement, *Journal of Criminal Law and Criminology*, 96(2): 503–26.

Gerschenkron, A. (1962), *Economic Backwardness in Historical Perspective: A Book of Essays*, Cambridge, MA: Belknap Press of Harvard University Press.

Ghione, L. (2007), The Reform of the European Union, *Eucrim*, 3(4): 73.

Ghura, D. (2002), Tax Revenue in Sub-Sahara Africa: Effects of Economic Policies on Corruption, in Abed, G., and Gupta, S., *Governance, Corruption & Economic Performance*, Washington, DC: IMF, p. 369.

Gilmore, W.C. (ed.) (1995), *Mutual Legal Assistance in Criminal and Business Regulatory Matters*, Cambridge: Cambridge University Press.

Gilmore, W.C. (2004), *Dirty Money. The Evolution of International Measures to Counter Money Laundering and the Financing Act of Terrorism*, 3rd edn., Strasbourg: Council of Europe.

Gimein, M. (2002), You Bought They Sold, *Fortune*, no. 16 (2 September): 38.

Gino Naldi, J. (1999), *The Organization of African Unity: An Analysis of its Role*, 2nd edn., New York: Mansell Publishing Ltd.

Gino Naldi J. (2008), The African Union and the Regional Human Rights System, in Evans, M., and Murray, R. (eds.), *The African Charter on Human and Peoples' Right: The System in Practice, 1986–2006*, Cambridge: Cambridge University Press, p. 20.

Giovanoli, A. (2003), *Storia e globalizzazione*, Rome and Bari: Laterza.

Giuliano, M. (1956), *I diritti e gli obblighi degli Stati. Volume I. L'ambiente dell'attività degli Stati*, Padua: Cedam.

Glaeser, L. Edward and Saks, Raven (2004), Corruption in America, Harvard Institute of Economic Research Discussion Paper, no. 2043.

Glaser, S. (1960), Culpabilité en droit international pénal, *Recueil de Cours de l'Académie de droit international de La Haye*, 99: 473.

Glaser S. (1947–8), Le principe de la légalité des délites et des peines et les procès de criminel de guerre, *Revue générale de droit pénal et de criminologie*, 28: 230.

Global Witness (2012), *Grave Secrecy: How a Dead Man Can Own a UK Company and Other Hair-Raising Stories about Hidden Company Ownership from Kyrgyzstan and Beyond*, London: Global Witness.

Glynn, P., Kobrin, S.J. and Naìm M. (1997), The Globalization of Corruption, in Elliot, K.A. (ed.), *Corruption and the Global Economy*, Washington, DC: Institute for International Economics, p. 7.

Gobert, J. (1994), Corporate Criminality: New Crimes for the Times, *Criminal Law Review*, (1994): 772.

Gobert, J. and Mugnai, E. (2002), Coping with Corporate Criminality. Some Lessons from Italy, *Criminal Law Review*, (2002): 617.

Gobert, J. and Punch, M. (2003), *Rethinking Corporate Crime*, London: Butterworths.

Goldman, E., Rocholl, J. and So, J. (2006). Do Politically Connected Boards Affect Firms Value? University of North Carolina at Chapel Hill, Working Paper.

Gordon, G. (2000), *The Criminal Law of Scotland*, Edinburgh: W. Green.

Gosset, W.S. (1921), An Experimental Determination of the Probable Error of Dr Spearman's Correlation Coefficients, *Biometrika*, 13(2–3): 263–82.

Goudies, A. and Stasavage, D. (2000), Corruption, the Issue, Development Centres Technical Paper, no. 122, Paris: OECD.

Goy, R. (1979), Le retour et la restitution des biens culturels à leur Pays d'origine en cas d'appropriation illégale, *RGDIP*, p. 962.

Graham, C., Litan, R. and Sukhtankar, S. (2002), The Bigger They Are The Harder They Fall: An Estimate of the Costs of the Crisis in Corporate Governance, Washington, DC, available at: http://www.brookings.edu/Views/Papers/Graham/20020722Graham.pdf.

Grasso, G. (2006), La Costituzione per l'Europa e la formazione di un diritto penale dell'Unione Europea, in Dolcini, E. and Paliero, C.E. (eds.), *Studi in onore di G. Marinucci*, Milan: Giuffrè, p. 3070.

Graziano, L. (1990), *Clientelismo e Sistema Politico. Il Caso dell'Italia*, Milan: Franco Angeli.

Green, L.C. (2000), *The Contemporary Law of Armed Conflict*, 2nd edn., Manchester and New York: Manchester University Press.

Green, S.P. (2008), *Lying, Cheating, and Stealing. A Moral Theory of White-Collar Crime*, Italian translation: *I crimini dei colletti bianchi*, Milan: Egea.

Greene, W. (2000), *Econometric Analysis*, New York: Prentice Hall.

Grevi, V. (2006), Linee di cooperazione giudiziaria in materia penale nella Costituzione europea, in Dolcini, E. and Paliero, C.E. (eds.), *Studi in onore di G. Marinucci*, Milan: Giuffrè, p. 2783.

Grevi, V. (2007), Prefazione. Fenomeno corruttivo e contesto sociale, in Davigo, P.C. and Mennozzi, G., *La corruzione in Italia. Percezione sociale e controllo penale*, Rome and Bari: Laterza, p. iii.

Groenhuijsen, M.S. (2004), Criminal Law in the European Union: A Giant Leap or a Small Step?, in Moore, A. (ed.), *Police and Judicial Co-operation in the European Union*, Cambridge: Cambridge University Press, p. 221.

Grossman, S.J. and Hart, O.D. (1982), Corporate Financial Structure and Managerial Incentives, in John McCall (ed.), *The Economics of Information and Uncertainty*, Chicago, University Chicago Press.

Grosso, C.F. (1988), sub Dolo (diritto penale), in *Enciclopedia Giuridica Treccani*, vol. XII, Rome: Treccani.

Grote, R. (1999), Rule of Law, Rechtsstaat and Etat de Droit, in Starck, C. (ed.), *Constitutionalism, Universalism and Democracy – A Comparative Analysis*, Baden-Baden: Nomos Verlagsgesellschaft.

Gualtieri, C. (2007), Joint Investigation Team, available at: http://www.springerlink.com/content/t0k0846487178k22/fulltext.pdf.

Guerini, U. (2004), sub Articolo 29, in Tizzano, A. (ed.), *Trattati dell'Unione Europea e della Comunità Europea*, Milan: Giuffrè.

Guest, A. (ed.) (1961), *Oxford Essay in Jurisprudence*, Oxford: Oxford University Press.

Gupta, S., Davoodi, H.R. and Alonso-Terme, R. (2002), Does Corruption Affect Income Distribution and Poverty?, in Abed, G.T., and Gupta, S. (eds.), *Governance, Corruption and Economic Performances*, Washington, DC: IMF, p. 459.

Gupta, Sanjeev, Davoodi, Hamid R. and Tjongson, Erwin R. (2002), Corruption and the Provision of Health Care and Education Services, in Abed, George T., and Gupta, Sanjeev (eds.), *Governance, Corruption and Economic Performance*, Washington, DC: IMF.

Gupta, Sanjeev, de Mello, Luiz and Sharan, Raju (2002), Corruption and Military Spending, in Abed, George T. and Gupta, Sanjeev (eds.),

Governance, Corruption and Economic Performance, Washington, DC: IMF.

Gutierrez-Nieto, B., Serrano-Cinca, C. and Mar Molinero, C. (2007), Microfinance Institutions and Efficiency, *Omega*, 35: 131–42.

Habermas, J. (2001), *Morale, diritto, politica*, Italian translation, Milan: Edizioni di Comunità.

Haekkerup, N. (2001), *Controls & Sanctions in the EU Law*, Copenhagen: Djoef Publishing.

Hameed, Farhan (2005), Fiscal Transparency and Economic Outcomes, IMF Working Paper, 05/225, Washington, DC.

Hao, Y. and Johnston, M. (1995), Reform at the Crossroads: An Analysis of Chinese Corruption, *Asian Perspectives*, 9: 117.

Harari, M. and Berthod, A.V.J. (2007), Articles 9, 10 and 11. International Co-operation, in Pieth, M., Low, L.A., and Cullen, P. (eds.), *The OECD Convention in Bribery. A Commentary*, Cambridge: Cambridge University Press, p. 407.

Harding, C. (1996), Criminal Liability of Corporations – United Kingdom, in De Doelder, H., and Tiedemann, K. (eds.), *La Criminalisation du comportement Collectif*, The Hague, Netherlands: Kluwer Law International, p. 374.

Harms, B.C. (2000), Holding Public Officials Accountable in the International Realm: A New Multi-layered Strategy to Combat Corruption, *Cornell International Law Journal*, 33 (2000):159.

Harris, D.J. (2004), *Cases and Materials on International Law*, London: Sweet & Maxwell.

Harris, D.J., O'Boyle, M. and Warbrick, C. (1995), *Law of the European Convention on Human Rights*, London: Butterworth.

Harris, M. and Raviv, A. (1988), Corporate Governance, Voting Rights and Majority Rule, *Journal of Financial Economics*, 20: 203–35.

Hart, H.L.A. (1958), Positivism and the Separation between Law and Morals, *Harvard Law Review*, 71: 593.

Hart, H.L.A. (1961), Negligence, Mens Rea and Criminal Responsibility, in Guest, A. (ed.), *Oxford Essay in Jurisprudence*, Oxford: Oxford University Press, p. 29.

Hartmann, J.M. (1997), Government by Thieves: Revealing the Monsters Behind the Kleptocratic Masks, *Syracuse Journal of International Law and Commerce*, 24 (1997), p. 157.

Harvard Law School Research in International Law (1935), Jurisdiction with Respect to Crime, *American Journal of International Law Supplement*, 28: 435.

Hatchard, J., Ndulo, M. and Slinn, P. (2004), *Comparative Constitutionalism and Good Governance in the Commonwealth: An Eastern and Southern African Perspective*, Cambridge: Cambridge University Press.

Hausman, J.A. (1978), Specification Tests in Econometrics, *Econometrica*, 46(6): 1251–71.

Hausmann, R., Rodrik, D. and Velasco, A. (2005), Growth Diagnostics, John F. Kennedy School of Government, Harvard University, Mimeo.

Hausmann, R., Rodrik, D. and Velasco, A. (2006), Getting the Diagnosis Right, *Finance & Development*, 43(1).

Hayek, F.A.V. (1960), *The Constitution of Liberty*, Chicago: University of Chicago Press.

Hazlitt, W. (1901), *Table Talk: Essays on Men and Manner* (first published 1821–2), Oxford: Oxford University Press.

Heidenheimer, A.J. (ed.) (1970), *Political Corruption: Reading in Comparative Analysis*, New York: Holt, Reinhart, and Winston.

Heidenheimer, A.J. (1989), Perspective of the Perception of Corruption, in Heidenheimer, A.J., Johnston, M., and Le Vine, V. (eds), *Political Corruption: A Handbook*, New Brunswick, NJ: Transaction, p. 161.

Heimann, F.F. (1997), Combating Corruption: The Role of the Business Community, in Elliot, K.A. (ed.), *Corruption and the Global Economy*, Washington, DC: Institute for International Economics, p. 149.

Herlin-Karnell, E. (2012), EU Competence in Criminal Law After Lisbon, in Biondi, A., Eeckhout, P., and Ripley, S., *EU Law After Lisbon*, Oxford: Oxford University Press.

Hirsch, F. (1978), The Ideological Underlay of Inflation, in Hirsch, F., and Goldthorpe, J. (eds.), *The Political Economy of Inflation*, London: Martin Robinson, p. 284.

Hirschman, A.O. (1970), *Exit, Voice, and Loyalty: Responses to Decline in Firms, Organizations, and States*, Cambridge, MA: Harvard University Press.

Hirst, M. (2003), *Jurisdiction and the Ambit of the Criminal Law*, Oxford: Oxford University Press.

Hirst, P. and Thomson, G. (1996), *Globalisation in Question*, Cambridge: Cambridge University Press.

Hobbes, T. (1996), *Leviathan*, edited by Tuck, R., Cambridge: Cambridge University Press.

Hoffman, H. (2006), *Introduzione alla filosofia del diritto e della politica*, 4th edn., Rome and Bari: Laterza.

Hoffman, W.M. et al. (eds.) (1994), *Emerging Global Business Ethics*, Westport, CT: Quorum Books.

Holden, P. and Sobotka, J. (2000), Corruption: An Economic Perspective, in Bernasconi, P. (ed.), *Responding to Corruption. Social Defence and the*

Protection of the Public Administration and the Independence of Justice, Naples: La città del sole, p. 45.

Hootnick, A. (2003), Improvised Justice: Constitution vs. Reality in South Africa, in *American Scholar*, (winter 2003): 53.

Horder, J. (1995), Intention in the Criminal Law – A Rejoinder, *Modern Law Review*, 58: 678.

Hossain, K. and Giuliano, M. (1987), La Carta dei Diritti e Doveri Economici degli Stati: un tentativo improprio di codificazione del diritto internazionale, in *Le Droit International à l'heure de sa codification, Etudies en l'honneur de Roberto Ago*, vol. IV, Milan: Giuffré, p. 217. Available at: http://star.worldbank.org/star/sites/star/files/StAR_Partnership_Charter_0.pdf.

Huber, B. (ed.) (2002), *Corruption: Acts and Attitudes, Combating Corruption in the European Union*, vol. 31, Cologne: Bundesanzeiger Verlag.

Huber, P.J. (1967), The Behavior of Maximum Likelihood Estimates under Nonstandard Conditions, *Proceedings of Fifth Berkeley Symposium*, Berkeley, CA: University of California Press.

Huet, A. and Joering-Joulin, R. (2001), *Droit pénal international*, Paris: Thémis, PUF.

Huet, A. and Joering-Joulin, R. (2005), *Droit pénal international*, 3rd edn., Paris: PUF.

Huntington, S.P. (1968), *Political Order in Changing Society*, New Haven, CT: Yale University Press.

Huntington, S.P. (1989), Modernization and Corruption, in Heideheimer, A.J., Johnston, M., and Le Vine, V. (eds.), *Political Corruption: A Handbook*, New Brunswick, NJ: Transaction Publishers, p. 377.

Hurt, L. (2007), The Undercivilization of Corporate Law, University of Illinois Law & Economics Research Paper, LE07–005.

Iannone, C. (2004), sub Articolo 10, in Tizzano A. (ed.), *Trattati dell'Unione Europea e della Comunità Europea*, Milan: Giuffrè, p. 218.

Ibbotson Associates (1999), *Stocks, Bonds, Bills and Inflation: 1999 Yearbook, Market Results for 1926–1998*, Chicago: Ibbotson Associates.

Ielo, P. (2008), Commissione Greco: dall'usura alla frode verso una responsabilità ampia degli enti, *Guida al diritto. Diritto Comunitario e Internazionale*, (1): 22.

Ige, B. (2002), Abacha and the Bankers: Cracking the Conspiracy, *Forum on Crime and Society*, 2(1) (December): 111.

Ignatieff, M. (2001), *Human Rights as Politics and Idolatry*, Princeton, NJ: Princeton University Press.

Independent Inquiry Committee into the Oil-For-Food Programme (2005),

Report on the Impact of the UN Oil-for-Food Programme on the Iraqi people, 7 September 2005, available at: http://www.iic-offp.org.

International Association of Insurance Supervisors (IAIS) (1999), Principles Applicable to the Supervision of International Insurers and Insurance Groups and their Cross-Border Business Operations (Insurance Concordat), Basel.

International Association of Insurance Supervisors (IAIS) (2003), Insurance Core Principles and Methodology, revised by the Task Force on the Revisions of the Insurance Core Principles, Basel.

International Monetary Fund (1944), Articles of Agreement of the International Monetary Fund (amended last in 2011), available at http://www.imf.org/external/pubs/ft/aa/index.htm.

International Monetary Fund (1997), The Role of the IMF in Governance Issues – Guidance Note EBS/97/125 of July 2, 1997, Washington, DC, available at http://www.imf.org/external/pubs/ft/exrp/govern/govindex.htm.

International Monetary Fund (1998), Code of Good Practices in Fiscal Transparency, Washington, DC.

International Organization of Securities Commissions (IOSCO) (2003), *Objectives and Principles of Securities Regulation*, Madrid, available at www.iosco.org.

Irti, N. (2004), *Nichilismo giuridico*, Naples: Laterza.

Irti, N. (2007), *Il diritto nell'età della tecnica*, Naples: Editoriale Scientifica.

Irti, N. and Severino, E. (2001), *Dialogo su diritto e tecnica*, Rome and Bari: Laterza.

Irti, N. (2006), S-Confinatezza, in Dolcini, E., and Paliero, C.E. (eds.), *Studi in onore di Giorgio Marinucci. Parte speciale del diritto penale e legislazione penale*, Milano: Giuffrè

Ishrat H. and Faruqee, R. (1994), *Adjustments in Africa, Lessons from Country Case Studies*, Washington, DC: World Bank.

Jayawickrama, N., Pope, J. and Stolpe, O. (2002), Legal Provisions to Facilitate the Gathering of Evidence in Corruption Cases: Easing the Burden of Proof, *Forum on Crime and Society*, 2(1) (December): 23.

Jellinek, G. (2002), *La Dichiarazione dei diritti dell'uomo e del cittadino*, Italian translation, Rome and Bari: Laterza.

Jennings, R. and Watts, A. (eds.) (1992), *Oppenheim's International Law. Volume I. Peace*, London and New York: Longman Group UK.

Jennings, R. (1957), Extraterritorial Jurisdiction and the United States Antitrust Laws, *British Yearbook of International Law*, p. 146.

Jensen, M.C. and Meckling, W.H. (1976), Theory of the Firm: Managerial Behaviour, Agency Costs and Ownership Structure, *Journal of Financial Economics*, (3): 305–60.

Jescheck, H.H. (1971), L'oggetto del diritto penale internazionale e la sua più recente evoluzione, *Riv. it. dir. proc. pen.*, p. 634.

Jescheck, H.H. and Weigend, T. (1996), *Lehrbuch des Strafrechts: Allgemeiner Teil*, 5th edn., Berlin: Aufbau der Straftat, 8. Aufl.

Johnson, R.A. and Sharma, S. (2004), About Corruption: A Comparative Study, in Johnson, R.A. (ed.), *The Struggle Against Corruption: A Comparative Study*, New York: Palgrave Macmillan.

Johnson, S. and Mitton, T. (2003), Cronyism and Capital Controls: Evidence from Malaysia, *Journal of Financial Economics*, 67: 351–82.

Jorge, G. (2003), Notes on Asset Recovery in the U.N. Convention Against Corruption, available at: www.abanet.org/intlaw/hubs/programs/Annual0316.03–16.06.pdf.

Jorion, P. and Goetzmann, W.N. (1995), A Longer Look at Dividend Yields, *Journal of Business*, 68: 483–508.

Jorion, P. and Goetzmann, W.N. (1999), Global Stock Markets in the Twentieth Century, *Journal of Finance*, 54(3): 953–80.

Joseph, S., Shultz, J. and Castan, M. (2000), *The International Covenant on Civil and Political Rights*, Oxford: Oxford University Press.

Kalchiem, C. (2004), White Corruption in Israel, in Johnson, R.A. (ed.), *The Struggle Against Corruption: A Comparative Study*, New York: Palgrave Macmillan, p. 70.

Kallas, S. (2007), Editorial, *Eucrim*, 3(4): 65.

Kane, I. and Motala, A.C. (2008), The Creation of a New African Court of Justice and Human Rights, in Evans, M., and Murray, R. (eds.), *The African Charter on Human and Peoples' Right: The System in Practice, 1986–2006*, Cambridge: Cambridge University Press, p. 406.

Karimoun, N. (2002), *La corruption des fonctionnaires au Niger*, available at: http://unpan1.un.org/intradoc/groups/public/documents/ofpa/unpan002842.pdf.

Kaufmann, D. (1997), The Missing Pillar of a Growth Strategy for Ukraine: Reforms for Private Sector Development, in Cornelius, P. and Lenain, P. (eds.), *Ukraine: Accelerating the Transition to the Market*, Washington, DC: IMF, p. 234.

Kaufmann, D. (2004), Corruption, Governance and Security: Challenges for the Rich Countries and the World, *Global Competitiveness Report 2004/2005*, Washington, DC: The World Bank Institute, pp. 83–102.

Kaufmann, D. (2009), Mad Money, Legal Corruption, and the Financial Crisis, *The Kaufmann Governance Post*, http://thekaufmannpost.net/mad-money-legal-corruptionand-the-financial-crisis-cramer-vs-stewart-in-comedy-central/.

Kaufmann, D., Kraay, A. and Mastruzzi, M. (2004), Governance Matters

III: Governance Indicators for 1996–2002, Washington, DC: The World Bank.

Kaufmann, D., Kraay, A. and Mastruzzi, M. (2005), Governance Matters IV: Governance Indicators for 1996–2004, Washington, DC: The World Bank.

Kaufmann, D., Kraay, A. and Mastruzzi, M (2006), Governance Matters V: Governance Indicators for 1996–2005, Mimeo, World Bank.

Kaufmann, D., Kraay, A. and Mastruzzi M. (2007), Measuring Corruption: Myths and Realities, in Transparency International, *Global Corruption Report 2007. Corruption in Judicial Systems*, Cambridge: Cambridge University Press, p. 319.

Kaufmann, D., Kraay, A. and Mastruzzi, M. (2009), Governance Matters VIII: Aggregate and Individual Governance Indicators 1996–2008, Policy Research Working Paper Series 4978, The World Bank.

Kaufmann, D., Kraay, A. and Mastruzzi, M. (2010), The Worldwide Governance Indicators: Methodology and Analytical Issues. World Bank Policy Research Working Paper 5430, available at SSRN: http://ssrn.com/abstract=1682130.

Kaufmann, D. and Wei, S.-J. (1999), Does "Grease Money" Speed Up the Wheels of Commerce?, NBER Working Papers 7093, National Bureau of Economic Research, Inc.

Kaveny, M.C. (2004), Inferring Intention from Foresight, *Law Quarterly Review*, 120: 81.

Kelsen, H. (1966a), *General Theory of Law and State*, Cambridge, MA: Harvard University Press, 1946, Italian translation: *Teoria generale del diritto e dello Stato*, 5th edn., Milan: Comunità.

Kelsen, H. (1966b), *Principles of International Law*, 2nd edn., revised and edited by Tucker, R.W., New York: Holt, Rinehart & Winston, Inc.

Kelsen, H. (1975), *La dottrina pura del diritto*, Turin: Einaudi.

Keynes, J.M. (1936), *The General Theory of Employment, Interest and Money*, London: Macmillan.

Khan, M. (2006), Role of Audit in Fighting Corruption, Paper prepared for the conference, Ethics, Integrity, and Accountability in the Public Sector: Re-building Public Trust in Government through the Implementation of the UN Convention against Corruption, 26–7 September 2006, St Petersburg, Russia.

Khwaja, K. and Mian, A. (2005) Do Lenders Favour Politically Connected Firms? Rent Provision in an Emerging Financial Market, *Quarterly Journal of Economics*, 120: 1371–411.

Killander, M. (2008), The African Peer Review Mechanism and Human Rights: The First Reviews and the Way Forward, *Human Rights Quarterly*, 30(1): 41.

Kindiki, K. (2003), The Normative and Institutional Framework of the African Union Relating to the Protection of Human Rights and the Maintenance of International Peace and Security: A Critical Appraisal, *African Human Rights Law Journal*, 3(1); available at: http://www.chr.up.ac.za/centre_publications/ahrlj/ahrlj_contents.html#fiveBaimu.

Kingsbury, B., Krisch, N. and Stewart, R. (2005), The Emergence of Global Administrative Law, *Law and Contemporary Problems*, 16: 15.

Kip Viscusi, W. and Zeckhauser, R.J. (2005), Recollection Bias and the Combat of Terrorism, *The Journal of Legal Studies*, 34(1): 27–55.

Kittichaisaree, K. (2001), *International Criminal Law*, Oxford: Oxford University Press.

Klein, N. (2008), Interview, *L'espresso*, 39(LIV) (3 October): 57.

Klein, P. and Sands, P. (2001), *Bowett's International Institutions*, 5th edn., London: Sweet & Maxwell.

Klein, R.W. and Bawa, V.S. (1977), The Effect of Limited Information and Estimation Risk on Optimal Portfolio Diversification, *Journal of Financial Economics*, (5): 89–111.

Klitgaard, R. (1988), *Controlling Corruption*, Berkeley, CA: University of California Press; 2nd edn., 1991.

Klitgaard, R. (1989), Incentive Myopia, *World Development*, 17: 447.

Klitgaard, R. (1991), Gifts and Bribes, in Richard Zeckhauser (ed.), *Strategy and Choice*, Cambridge, MA: MIT Press.

Knack, S. and Keefer, P. (1995), Institutions and Economic Performance: Cross-Country Tests Using Alternative Institutional Measures, *Economics and Politics*, 7(3): 207.

Kofele-Kale, N. (1995a), *International Law of Responsibility for Economic Crimes. Holding Heads of State and Other High Ranking State Officials Individually Liable for Acts of Fraudulent Enrichment*, London and New York: Kluwer Law International.

Kofele-Kale, N. (1995b), Patrimonicide: The International Economic Crime of Indigenous Spoliation, *Vanderbilt Journal of Transnational Law*, 28: 45.

Koh, H.H. (1997), Why Do Nations Obey International Law?, *Yale Law Journal*, 106: 2599.

Kohlenberg, K. (2008), Die global Zocker, *Die Zeit* (31 July); I padroni del mondo, Italian translation published in *Internazionale*, (752) (19–25 September 2008): 30.

Kohn, S.M. (2012), *Sarbanes-Oxley Act: Legal Protection for Corporate Whistleblowers*, available at: http://www.whisteblowers.org/index.php?option=com_content&task=view&id=27

Kopelmanas, L. (1950), Le contrôle international, *Recueil des Cours* (1950-II): 77.

Koskenniemi, M. and Leino, P. (2002) Fragmentation of International Law? Postmodern Anxieties, *Leiden Journal of International Law*, 15: 553.

Krasner, S.D. (ed.) (1983), *International Regimes*, Ithaca, NY: Cornell University Press.

Kroszner, R.S. and Strahan, P.E. (1998), What Drives Deregulation?: Economics and Politics of the Relaxation of Bank Branching Restrictions, NBER Working Paper 6637, available at http://www.nber.org/w6637.

Kroszner, R.S. and Stratmann, T. (1998), Interest Group Competition and the Organization of Congress: Theory and Evidence from Financial Services' Political Action Committees, *American Economic Review*, 88: 1163–88.

Krueger, A.O. (1974), The Political Economy of the Rent Seeking Society, *American Economic Review*, 64 (June): 291–303.

Krugman, P. (2008a), The Crisis Endgame, *The New York Times* (18 September).

Krugman, P. (2008b), The 3 A.M. Call, *The New York Times* (26 September).

Krugman, P. (2008c), Where Are the Grown Ups?, *The New York Times* (22 September).

Krugman, P., Wells, R. and Graddy, K. (2007), *Economics: European Edition*, Worth Publishers.

Kuhl, L. (2005), Le pouvoirs de l'OLAF, in Ruggeri, F. (ed.), *La protection des intérêts financiaires de l'Union et le rôle de l'Olaf vis-à-vis la responsabilité des personnes morales et des chefs d'entreprises et admissibilité mutuelle des preuves*, Actes des Journées d'études de Inverigo-Como – 2005, cordonée avec Centre Etudes Droit Penal Européen, p. 87.

Kuhl, L. and Killman, B.R. (2006), The Community Competence for a Directive on Criminal Law Protection of the Financial Interests, *Eucrim*, 3(4): 101.

Kumar, C.R. (2006), Corruption as a Human Rights Issue in South Asia: Law, Development and Governance, available for download at: www.law.monash.edu.au/castancentre/events/2006/conf-06-kumar-paper.html.

Kunicová, J. (2006), Democratic Institutions and Corruption: Incentives and Constraints in Politics, in Rose-Ackerman, S. (ed.), *International Handbook on the Economics of Corruption*, Cheltenham, UK and Northampton, MA, USA: Edward Elgar, pp. 140–60.

Kyriakakis, J. (2007), Australian Prosecution of Corporations for International Crimes, *Journal of Criminal Justice*, 5: 809.

La Porta, R., De Silanes, F.L., Shleifer, A. and Vishny, R.W. (1997), Trust in Large Organizations, *American Economic Review*, 87(2): 333.

Lacey, N. (1993), A Clear Concept of Intention, *Modern Law Review*, 56: 621.

Lacey, N. (1995), In(de)terminable Intentions, *Modern Law Review*, 58: 69.

Lagos, E. (2000), The Future of the Inter-American Convention against Corruption. Interamerican Development Bank Conference: Transparency and Development in Latin America and the Caribbean, May, available at: http://www.iadb.org/leg/Documents/Lagos%20Eng.pdf.

Lahaye, E. (2009), The Evolution of the African Microfinance Sector, CGAP Microfinance Blog.

Laing, R.D. (1974), *Knots*; Italian translation, *Nodi. Paradigmi di rapporti intrapsichici e interpersonali*, Turin: Einaudi.

Lambrechts, B.D. (2004), Bribery & Corruption: A Legal Perspective, available at: http://www.servamus.co.za/july_04/bribery1.htm.

Lambsdorff, J.G. (2006), Consequences and Causes of Corruption – What do We Know from a Cross-Section of Countries?, in Rose-Ackerman, S. (ed.), *International Handbook on the Economics of Corruption*, Cheltenham, UK and Northampton, MA, USA: Edward Elgar, pp. 3–52.

Lambsdorff, J.G. (2008), The Big Picture: Measuring Corruption and Benchmarking Progress in the Fight against Corruption. Corruption Perception Index 2007, in Transparency International, *Global Corruption Report 2008. Corruption in the Water Sector*, Cambridge: Cambridge University Press, p. 296.

Lambsdorff, Johann Graf, and Schinke, Michael (2002), Non-Benevolent Central Banks, Goettingen University, CeGe Discussion Paper 16.

Landers, J. and Whittle, R. (2004), Bribery Case Findings Detailed; Halliburton Says Incidents Predate Ownership of Firm, *Dallas Morning News*, 3 September.

Landmeier, L.M. (2002), Anti-Corruption International Legal Developments, *International Lawyer*, 36: 589.

Landy, E.A. (1966), *The Effectiveness of International Supervision: Thirty Years of ILO Experience*, New York: Stevens & Sons.

Latouche, S. (2008), *Breve trattato sulla decrescita serena*, Turin: Bollati Boringhieri.

Laufer, W.S. (1999), Corporate Liability, Risk Shifting, and the Paradox of Compliance, *Vanderbilt Law Review*, 52(5): 1343.

Laurens, B., Arnone, M. and Segalotto, J.F. (2009), *Central Bank Independence, Accountability and Transparency: A Global Perspective*, International Monetary Fund Series, Basingstoke, UK and New York: Palgrave Macmillan.

Lauria, F. (1999), Tutela degli interessi finanziari e lotta alla corruzione dell'Unione Europea, in *Riv. trim. dir. pub. comp.*, p. 435.

Lee, C.D.H.C. and Ng, D. (2006), Capital Market Governance: How Do Securities Laws Affect Market Performance?, *Journal of Corporate Finance*, 12: 560–93.

Leff, N.H. (1964), Economic Development through Bureaucratic Corruption, *American Behavioral Scientist*, 8(3): 8–14.

Leigh, L.H. (1969), *The Criminal Liability of Corporations in English Law*, London: London School of Economics and Political Science.

Leite, C. and Weidmann, J. (2002), Does Mother Nature Corrupt? Natural Resources, Corruption, and Economic Growth, in Abed, G.T., and Gupta, S. (eds.), *Governance, Corruption and Economic Performance*, Washington, DC: IMF, pp. 71–99.

Leonhard, D. (2008), Bills Come Due for Excesses of Past Years, *The New York Times* (29 September): I.

Leroy, A. and Fariello, F. (2012), *The World Bank Group Sanctions Process and Its Recent Reforms*, Washington, DC: The World Bank.

Levi, M., Dakolias, M. and Greenberg, T.S. (2007), Money Laundering and Corruption, in Campos, J.E., and Pradham, S., *The Many Faces of Corruption. Tracking Vulnerabilities at the Sector Level*, Washington, DC: The World Bank, p. 389.

Lien, D.H.D. (1986), A Note on Competitive Bribery Games, *Economic Letters*, 22: 337–41.

Lintner, J. (1965), The Valuation of Risk Assets and the Selection of Risky Investment in Stock Portfolios and Capital Budgets, *Review of Economics and Statistics*, 47(1): 13–37.

Litzenberger, R. and Ramaswany, K. (1979), The Relationship between Return and Market Value of Common Stocks, *Journal of Financial Economics*, 9: 3–18.

Locati, G. (2003), Le convenzioni del Consiglio d'Europa, il monitoraggio del GRECO e gli adempimenti nazionali, in Sacerdoti, G. (ed.), *Responsabilità d'impresa e strumenti internazionali anticorruzione. Dalla Convenzione OCSE 1997 al Decreto n. 231/2001*, Milan: Egea, p. 217.

Lochner, S.J. (1980–81), The Criminalisation of American Extraterritorial Bribery: The Effect of the Foreign Corrupt Practices Act of 1977, *NYU Journal of International Law and Politics*, 13: 645.

Longchamp. O. and Herkenrath, M. (2013), Money Laundering, Liability and Sanctions for Financial Intermediaries – the Issue of Having the Assets of Politically Exposed Persons in Switzerland, in Fenner Zinkernagel, G., Monteith, C. and Gomes Pereira, P. (eds.), *Emerging Trends in Asset Recovery*, Bern: Peter Lang, p. 127.

Low, L.A. (2005), Enforcement of the FCPA in the United States, Trends and the Effects of International Standards, Paper presented at the

International Bar Association 3rd Annual Conference, The Awakening Giant of Anti-Corruption Enforcement, Paris, France, 4–6 May.

Low, L.A. (2008), The United Nations Against Corruption: The Globalization of Anticorruption Standard, Paper prepared for a Conference of the International Bar Association, The Awakening Giant of Anticorruption Enforcement, Paris, France, 25–6 April.

Low, L.A., Bjorklund, A. and Atkinson, C.K. (1998), The Inter-American Convention Against Corruption. A Comparison with the United States Foreign Corrupt Practices Act, *Vanderbilt Journal International Law*, 38: 243.

Lowe, V. (2003), Jurisdiction, in Evans, M.D. (ed.), *International Law*, Oxford: Oxford University Press, p. 329.

Lowell Brown, H. (2003), *Bribery in International Commerce*, USA: Thomson West.

Lucchini, R. (1995), Universalisme et relativisme dans l'approche de la corruption. Réflexions sociologiques, in Borghi, M. and Meyer-Bisch, P., *La corruption. L'envers des droits de l'homme*, Fribourg: Editions Universitaires Fribourg Suisse, pp. 51 ff.

Lui, F.T. (1985), An Equilibrium Queuing Model of Bribery, *Journal of Political Economy*, 93: 760–81.

Lui, F.T. (1996), Three Aspects of Corruption, *Contemporary Economic Policy*, 14(3): 26–9.

MacGregor, D. (2001), Jobs in the Public and Private Sectors: Presenting Data (updated to June 2000) on Jobs in the Public and Private Sectors, *Economic Trends*, Working Paper No. 571, p. 1.

Maffettone, S. and Veca, S. (eds.) (2003), *L'idea di giustizia da Platone a Rawls*, 4th edn., Rome and Bari: Laterza.

Magliveras, K. and Naldi, G.J. (2002), The African Union – A New Dawn for Africa?, *International and Comparative Law Quarterly*, 51: 415.

Magrini, P. (2001), L' evoluzione delle politiche europee nel settore della giustizia e degli affari interni: da Shengen a Tampere via Amsterdam, *Diritto pubblico comparato ed europeo*, 4: 1817.

Magrini, P. (2003), L'attuazione della Convenzione OCSE contro la corruzione negli Stati membri: il quadro comparato, in Sacerdoti, G. (ed.), *Responsabilità d'impresa e strumenti internazionali anticorruzione. Dalla Convenzione OCSE 1997 al Decreto n. 231/2001*, Milan: Egea.

Makinda, S.M. and Okumu, F.W. (2008), *The African Union: Challenges of Globalization, Security, and Governance*, London: Routledge.

Makinwa, A. (2007), The Rules Regulating Transnational Bribery: Achieving a Common Standard?, *Revue de droit des affaires internationals*, 1: 17.

Malem Seña, J.F. (2000), *Globalizaciòn, comercio internacionale y corrupciòn*, Barcelona: Gedisa.

Malkin, E. (2008), Microfinance Success Sets Off a Debate in Mexico, *The New York Times*, 5 April.

Mammarella, G. (2000), *L'Italia Contemporanea. 1943–1998*, Bologna: Il Mulino.

Manacorda, S. (1997), Unione Europea e diritto penale: stato della questione e prospettive di sviluppo, *Studium iuris*, p. 951.

Manacorda, S. (1999), *La corruzione internazionale del pubblico ufficiale. Linee di indagine penalistica*, Naples: Ed. Jovene.

Manacorda, S. (2005), Corruzione internazionale e tutela penale degli interessi finanziari. Il commento, *Diritto penale e processo*, 4: 415.

Mann, F.A. (1964), The Doctrine of Jurisdiction in International Law, *RCDAI*, 1 (1964-I): 111.

Manna, A. (2005), Imputazione dell'illecito penale e "responsabilità amministrativa" nella teoria della persona giuridica, *Riv. soc.*, p. 1314.

Marcelo, S.V. (2008), The Long Road from Zurich to Manila: The Recovery of the Marcos Swiss Dollar Deposits, in Pieth, M. (ed.) *Recovering Stolen Assets*, Bern: Peter Lang.

Mariani, P. (2003), La Convenzione civile del Consiglio d'Europa sulla Corruzione: un nuovo versante della cooperazione giuridica internazionale nella lotta alla corruzione, in Sacerdoti, G. (ed.), *Responsabilità d'impresa e strumenti internazionali anticorruzione. Dalla Convenzione OCSE 1997 al Decreto n. 231/2001*, Milan: Egea, p. 244.

Mariani, P. (2006), sub voce, OECD, in Cassese, G., *Dizionario di diritto pubblico*, Milan: Giuffrè, p. 3897.

Mariani, P. (2013), How Damages Recovery Actions Can Improve the Fight Against Corruption: The Crisis of Criminal Law Policies and the Role of Private Enforcement in an Italian Case of Judicial Corruption, *Crime, Law and Social Change*, 60(2): 209–26.

Marinucci, G. and Dolcini, E. (2001), *Corso di diritto penale, Le norme penale penali: fonti e limiti di applicabilità Il reato: struttura e sistematica*, Milan: Giuffrè.

Markovitz, H.M. (1959), *Portfolio Selection: Efficient Diversification of Investments*, New Haven, CT: Yale University Press.

Marques, S.A. (2013), Political Immunities: Obstacles in the Fight of Corruption, in Fenner Zinkernagel, G., Monteith, C. and Gomes Pereira, P. (eds.), *Emerging Trends in Asset Recovery*, Bern: Peter Lang, p. 93.

Mastroianni, R. (2004), sub Articolo 47, in Tizzano, A. (ed.), *Trattati dell'Unione Europea e della Comunità Europea*, Milan: Giuffrè, p. 167.

Mauro, P. (1997), The Effects of Corruption on Growth, Investment, and

Government Expenditure: A Cross-Country Analysis, in Elliot, K.A (ed.), *Corruption and the Global Economy*, Washington, DC: Institute for International Economics, p. 8.

Mauro, Paolo (1995), Corruption and Growth, *Quarterly Journal of Economics*, 110 (August): 681–712.

Mauro, Paolo (1998), Corruption and the Composition of Government Expenditure, *Journal of Public Economics*, 69: 263–79.

Mauro, Paolo (2002), The Persistence of Corruption and Slow Economic Growth, IMF Working Paper, 02/213, Washington, DC.

Mavroidis, P.C. and Neven, D.J. (1999), Some Reflections on Extraterritoriality in International Economic Law. A Law and Economic Analysis, in *Mélanges en hommage à Michel Walbroeck*, II, Brussels: Bruylant.

Mays, T.M. (2002), *Africa's First Peacekeeping Operation: The OAU in Chad, 1981–1982*, New York: Praeger.

McClean, D. (2002), *International Co-operation in Civil and Criminal Matters*, Oxford: Oxford University Press.

McClean, D. (2007), *Transnational Organized Crime. A Commentary on the UN Conventions and its Protocols*, Oxford: Oxford University Press.

McCord, J.W.H. and McCord, S.L. (2006), *Criminal Law and Procedure for the Paralegal: A Systems Approach*, 3rd edn., USA: Thomson Delmar Learning.

McCoy, J. and Heckel, H. (2001), The Emergence of a Global Anti-Corruption Norm, *International Politics*, 38: 65.

Mehra, R. and Prescott, E.C. (1985), The Equity Premium: A Puzzle, *Journal of Monetary Economics*, 15: 145–62.

Mendelson, M. (1999), The Formation of Customary International Law, *Hague Academy of International Law, Recueil des Cours*, 272: 159.

Merton, R. (1973), An Intertemporal Capital Asset Pricing Model, *Econometrica*, 411: 867–87.

Merton, T.M. (2002), The Year Nobody Will Survive, 5 September, available at: http://www.worldpress.org/Africa/703.cfm.

Messick, R. (2013), How Financial Disclosure Laws Help in the Recovery of Stolen Assets, in Fenner Zinkernagel, G., Monteith, C. and Gomes Pereira, P. (eds.), *Emerging Trends in Asset Recovery*, Bern: Peter Lang, p. 235.

Metcalfe, D. (2000), The OECD Agreement to Criminalize Bribery: A Negotiation Analytic Perspective, *International Negotiation*, 5: 129.

Michael, B. (2003), What does the UN Convention against Corruption Teach Us About International Regulatory Harmonization?, Paper presented at the Japanese Economic Association Conference in Nagoya, 2003.

Michael, B. (2007), Drafting Implementing Regulations for International Anti-Corruption Conventions, Working Paper Number 150, QEH Working Paper Series – QEHWPS150, available at: http://citeseerx.ist.psu.edu/viewdoc/download?doi=10.1.1.164.7862&rep=rep1&type=pdf.

Michael, B. and Hajredini, H. (2007), The Effective Implementation of International Anti-Corruption Conventions, *Eucrim*, 3(4): 128.

Militello, V. (2003), Partecipazione all'organizzazione criminale e standards internazionali di incrimininazione, in *Riv. it. dir. proc. pen.*, p. 83.

Militello, V. (2007), "Ripensare" la giustizia penale europea: potenzialità e limiti di un progetto alternativo, in Schünemann, B. (ed.), *Un progetto alternativo di giustizia penale europea*, Milan: Giuffrè, p. 129.

Miller, J. (1963), The OECD, in *Yearbook of World Affairs*, p. 80.

Miller, S.K. (1998), Piercing the Corporate Veil among Affiliated Companies in the European Community and in the US: A Comparative Analysis of US, German, and UK Veil-piercing Attitudes, *American Business Law Journal*, 73: 109.

Millet-Einbinder, M. (2000), No More Tax Breaks for Bribes, in OECD (ed.), *No Longer Business as Usual*, Paris: OECD, p. 67.

Mirri, M.B. (2005), sub Corruzione, in *Enciclopedia Giuridica Treccani*, vol. XI, Rome: Treccani, p. 7.

Mitsilegas, V. (2003), *Money Laundering Counter-measures in the European Union. A New Paradigm of Security Governance Versus Fundamental Legal Principles*, London and New York: Kluwer Law International.

Mitsilegas, V. (2009), *EU Criminal Law*, Oxford and Portland: Hart.

Molloy, R.T. (1940), Application of the Anti-Trust Laws to Extra-Territorial Conspiracies, *Yale Law Journal*, 49: 1312.

Monar, J. (1998), JHA in the Treaty of Amsterdam: Reform at the Price of Fragmentation, *European Law Review*, 23: 320.

Moneta, F. (2005), Gli elementi costituivi dei crimini internazionali: uno sguardo d'insieme, in Cassese, A., Chiavario, M.G., and De Francesco, G. (eds.), *Problemi della giustizia penale internazionale*, Turin: Giappichelli, p. 23.

Monfrini, E. (2008), in Pieth, M. (ed.) (2008), The Abacha Case, *Recovering Stolen Assets*, Bern: Peter Lang.

Monks, R.A.G. and Minow, N. (2008), *Corporate Governance*, Chichester, UK: John Wiley & Sons.

Monteith, C. (2013), Case and Investigation Strategy, in Fenner Zinkernagel, G., Monteith, C. and Gomes Pereira, P. (eds.), *Emerging Trends in Asset Recovery*, Bern: Peter Lang, p. 183.

Montesqueiu, C. de Secondat, (1989), *De L'esprit de lois*; *The Spirit of the Laws*, translated and edited by Cohler, A.M., Miller, B.C., and Stone, H.S., Cambridge: Cambridge University Press.

Monyal, P.Y. (2005), Reconnaissance d'une compétence pénale communautaire pour la CJCE, *Recueil Dalloz*, 44: 3064.

Moody-Stuart, G. (1997), *Grand Corruption*, Oxford: WorldView Publications.

Morduch, J. (1999a), The Microfinance Promise, *Journal of Economic Literature*, 37(4): 1569–614.

Morduch, J. (1999b), The Role of Subsidies in Microfinance: Evidence from the Grameen Bank, *Journal of Development Economics*, 60: 229–48.

Morduch. J. (2000), The Microfinance Schism, *World Development*, 28(4): 617–29.

Morrisey, D. (2007), The Fight Against Corruption by International Organizations, *The George Washington International Law Review*, 39: 165.

Motta, M. and Ruta, M. (2008), A Political Economy Model of Merger Policy in International Markets, CEPR Discussion Paper 6894.

Mueller, G.O.W. (1998), Transnational Crime: Definitions and Concepts, in Williams, P., and Vlasis, D. (eds.), *Combating Transnational Crime, a Special Issue of Transnational Organized Crime*, 4(3–4) (autumn/winter): 18.

Muna, A. (2004), The Africa Union Convention against Corruption, available at: http://www.transparency.org/content/download/8549/55114/file/Muna2004_introduction_AUconvention.pdf.

Munk, Gerardo L. (2003), Measures of Democracy, Governance and Rule of Law: An Overview of Cross-National Data Sets, Paper prepared for the World Bank workshop, Understanding Growth and Freedom from the Bottom Up, Washington, DC, 15–17 July.

Munk, Gerardo L. and Verkuilen, Jay (2002), Conceptualizing and Measuring Democracy: Evaluating Alternative Indices, *Comparative Political Studies*, 35(1): 5–34.

Murphy, Kevin M., Shleifer, Andrei, and Vishny, Robert (1991), The Allocation of Talent: Implications for Growth, *Quarterly Journal of Economics*, 106: 503–30.

Murray, R. (2004), *Human Rights in Africa: From the OAU to the African Union*, Cambridge: Cambridge University Press.

Muzila, L., Morales, M., Matthias, M. and Berger, T. (2012), *On the Take. Criminalizing Illicit Enrichment to Fight Corruption*, Washington DC, USA: International Bank for Reconstruction and Development/The World Bank.

Muzila, L., Morales, M., Matthias, M. and Berger, T. (2013), Illicit Enrichment: An Emerging Tool in the Asset Recovery Process, in Fenner Zinkernagel, G., Monteith, C. and Gomes Pereira, P. (eds.), *Emerging Trends in Asset Recovery*, Bern: Peter Lang, p. 245.

Nadelmann, E. (1990), Global Prohibition Regime: The Evolution of Norms in International Society, *International Organisation*, 44: 479.

Nagle, L.E. (2003), The Challenges of Fighting Global Organized Crime in Latin America, *Fordham International Law Journal*, 26: 1649.

Ng, D. (2006), The Impact of Corruption on Financial Market, *Managerial Finance*, 32: 822–36.

Ng, D. and Lee, C. (2003), Corruption and International Valuation: Does Virtue Pay?, Paper presented at Western Finance Association Annual Meeting.

Nichols, P.M. (1999), Regulating Transnational Bribery in Times of Globalisation and Fragmentation, *Yale Journal of International Law*, 24: 257.

Nietzsche, F. (2001), *La Gaia scienza*, translated into Italian by Masini, F. and edited by Cozza, D., 13th edn., Milan: Adelphi.

Nietzsche, F. (2007), *On the Genealogy of Morality*, edited by Ansell-Pearson, K., revised edn., Cambridge: Cambridge University Press.

Nigerian House of Representatives Petition Commission (2004), *Interim Report: The Halliburton/Tskj/Lng Investigation*, available at http://halliburtonwatch.org/news/nigeria_parliament_report.pdf.

Noonan J.T., Jr. (1984), *Bribes*, New York: Macmillan.

Nozick, R. (1974), *Anarchy, State and Utopia*, Oxford: Basil Blackwell.

Nye, J.S. (1967), Corruption and Political Development: A Cost-Benefit Analysis, *American Political Science Review*, 61(2): 417.

O'Driscoll, G.P., Feulner, E., Jr., and O'Grady, M.A. (2003), *Index of Economic Freedom*, Washington, DC: The Heritage Foundation and Dow Jones & Company Inc.

O'Keefe, D. (1995), *Recasting the Third Pillar*, *Common Market Law Review*, 32: 893–920.

O'Keefe, D. (1997), La cooperazione intergovernativa e il terzo pilastro sul Trattato dell'Unione Europea, *RIDPC*, p. 665.

O'Keefe, D. (2004), Universal Jurisdiction: Clarifying the Basic Concept, *Journal of International Criminal Justice*, 2: 735.

O'Keefe, D. and Twomey, P. (1999), *Legal Issues of the Amsterdam Treaty*, Oxford: Oxford University Press.

OECD (2000a), Working Group on Bribery in International Business Transactions, Corporate Liability Rules in Common Law Jurisdictions, DAFFE/IME/BR/2000/22.

OECD (2000b), Working Group on Bribery in International Business Transactions, Corporate Liability Rules in Civil Law Countries, DAFFE/IME/BR/2000/23.

OECD (2001), *Behind the Corporate Veil: Using Corporate Entities for Illicit Purposes*, Paris: OECD.

OECD (2010), *Good Practice Guidance on Internal Controls, Ethics, and Compliance*, Paris: OECD, available at http://www.oecd.org/investment/anti-bribery/anti-briberyconvention/44884389.pdf.

OECD (2012), CleanGovBiz. *Toolkit for Integrity*, available at: http://www.oecd.org/cleangovbiz/49891354.pdf

OECD Working Group on Bribery (2012), *Annual Report 2012*, Paris: OECD, available at: http://www.oecd.org/ctp/crime/oecdworkinggrouponbribery-annualreport.htm.

OECD Working Group on Bribery (2013), *Annual Report 2012*, Paris: OECD, available at: http://www.oecd.org/ctp/crime/oecdworkinggrouponbribery-annualreport.htm.

OECD and StAR (2012), *Identification and Quantification of the Proceeds of Bribery: Revised edition*, Paris: OECD.

Offe, C. (2004), Political Corruption: Conceptual and Practical Issues, in Kornai, J., and Rose-Ackerman, S. (eds.), *Problems of Post Socialist Transition: Building a Trustworthy State*, vol. 1, NewYork: Palgrave Macmillan, p. 290.

Ofria, F. (ed.) (2006), *Effetti distorsivi sull'economia legale: la corruzione*, Soveria Mannelli: Rubbettino.

Ogbu, A. (2004), House Probes Halliburton Bribery Scandal, *This Day, Nigeria*, 16 February.

Okoth-Ogendo, W.O. (1993), *Constitutions Without Constitutionalism: Reflections on an African Political Paradox*, in Greenberg, D. et al. (eds.), *Constitutionalism and Democracy: Transitions in the Contemporary World*, Oxford: Oxford University Press, p. 65.

Olaniyan, K. (2004a), Introductory Note to African Union (AU): Convention on Preventing and Combating Corruption, *International Legal Materials*, 43: 1.

Olaniyan, K. (2004b), The Africa Union Convention on Preventing and Combating Corruption: A Critical Appraisal, *African Human Rights Law Journal*, 4(1): 74.

Ormerod, D. (2005), *Smith & Hogan Criminal Law*, 11th edn., Oxford: Oxford University Press.

Osborne, D. (1997), Corruption as Counter-Culture: Attitudes to Bribery in Local and Global Society, in Rider, B. (ed.), *Corruption: The Enemy Within*, The Hague and Boston: Kluwer Law International, p. 11.

Oxford Dictionary of English (2006), revised 2nd edn., Oxford: Oxford University Press.

Oxman, B. (1997), Jurisdiction of States, in *Encyclopaedia of Public International Law*, vol. III, Amsterdam: Elsevier Science Publishers, p. 55.

Packer, A. and Rukare, S. (2002), The New African Union and its Constitutive Act, *American Journal of International Law*, 96: 365.

Palatano, V. and Vogliotti, M. (2001), La metamorfosi dell'incriminazione. Verso un nuovo paradigma in campo penale, *Pol. Dir.*, (2001): 665.

Palatano, V. (2003), Profili problematici della corruzione internazionale, in Palatano, V., *Nuove trategie per la lotta al crimine organizzato transnazionale*, Turin: Giappichelli, p. 393.

Paliero, C.E. (2000), La fabbrica del Golem. Progettualità e metodologia per la "Parte generale" di un codice penale dell'Unione Europea, *Rivista it. dir. proc. Pen.*, (2000): 466.

Palmer, R.W. (2002), *Fighting International and National Corruption by Means of Criminal Law*, South African national report to the XVI International Congress of Comparative Law, 2002.

Paradiso, P. (1983), *La corruzione negli affari. Un approccio criminologico*, Padua: Cedam.

Parisi, N. and Rinoldi, D. (eds) (1998), *Giustizia e affari interni nell'Unione Europea: il "terzo pilastro" del Trattato di Maastricht*, Turin: Giappichelli.

Parisi, N. and Rinoldi, D. (2003), Pluralità di strumenti pattizi internazionali di lotta alla corruzione adattamento all'ordinamento italiano, in Sacerdoti, G. (ed.), *Responsabilità d'impresa e strumenti internazionali anticorruzione. Dalla Convenzione OCSE 1997 al Decreto n. 231/2001*, Milan: Egea, p. 256.

Passas, N. (1994), I Cheat Therefore I Exist? The BCCI Scandal in Context, in Hoffman, W.M. et al. (eds.), *Emerging Global Business Ethics*, Westport, CT: Quorum Books, p. 75.

Passas, N. (2007), Introduction, in Passas, N. and Vlassis, D. (eds.), *The United Nations Convention against Corruption as a way of life*, Selected papers and contributions from the International Conference on "The United Nations Convention against Corruption as a way of life" (Courmayeur, 15–17 December 2006), Milan: ISPAC, p. 9.

Paust, J. (1988), Self-Executing Treaties, *American Journal of International Law*, (1988): 760.

Pecoraro, M.L. (2005), La tutela internazionale dei beni culturali alla luce della Convenzione UNIDROIT sulla restituzione dei beni culturali rubati o illecitamente esportati, in Albano, A., Lanzaro, A., and Pecoraro, M.L., *Legislazione internazionale e comunitaria dei beni culturali*, Naples: Esselibri Simone, p. 159.

Pedrazzi, C. (1968), Millantato credito, trafic d'influence, influence peddling, *Riv. it. dir. proc. pen.*, p. 913.

Pedrazzi, C. (2000), Tramonto del dolo?, *Riv. it. dir. proc. pen.*, p. 1265.

Perdriel-Vaissiere, M. (2012), The accumulation of unexplained wealth by public officials: Making the offence of illicit enrichment enforceable, Bergen: Chr. Michelsen Institute (U4 Brief 2012:1) available at http://

www.u4.no/publications/the-accumulation-of-unexplained-wealth-by-public-officials-making-the-offence-of-illicit-enrichment-enforceable/.

Peers, S. (1998), Who's Judging the Watchmen? The Judicial System of the "Area of Freedom, Security, and Justice", *Yearbook of European Law*, p. 337.

Peers, S. (2011), EU Justice and Home Affairs Law (Non-Civil), in Craig, P. and De Búrca, G., *The evolution of EU Law*, Oxford: Oxford University Press, p. 269.

Pellegrini, L. and Gerlagh, Reyer (2004), Corruption's Effect on Growth and its Transmission Channels, *Kuklos*, 57(3): 429–56.

Pellet, A. (1995), *Reports on the Law and Practices Relating to Reservations to Treaties, e.g., First Report*, Report of the International Law Commission, 1995.

Perduca, A. and Prato, F. (2006), Le indagini dell'Uffficio europeo per la lotta antifrode (OLAF) ed i rapporti con le autorità giudiziarie, *Cassazione Penale*, (2006): 4246.

Picone, P. (1989), L'appicazione extraterritoriale delle regole sulla concorrenza e il diritto internazionale, in Capotorti, F. (ed.), *Il fenomeno della concentrazione di imprese nel diritto interno e internazionale*, Padua: Cedam, p. 81.

Picotti L. (2006), L'attuazione in Italia degli strumenti dell'Unione Europea per la protezione penale degli interessi finaziari comunitari, *Riv. trim. dir. pen. proc.*, (2006): 615.

Pierros, P. and Hudson, C. (1998), The Hard Graft of Tackling Corruption in International Business Transactions. Progress in International Co-operation and the OCDE Convention, *Journal of World Trade*, (1998): 77.

Pieth, M. (1997), *International Cooperation to Combat Corruption, Corruption and the Global Economy*, Washington, DC: Institute for International Economics, p. 120.

Pieth, M. (2000), The Coordination of International Initiatives against Corruption: A Perspective for the Future?, in Bernasconi, P. (ed.), *Responding to Corruption. Social Defence and the Protection of the Public Administration and the Independence of Justice*, Naples: La città del sole, p. 389.

Pieth, M. (2002), International Efforts to Combat Corruption, in Huber, B. (ed.), *Corruption: Acts and Attitudes: Combating Corruption in the European Union*, vol. 31, Series of Publications by the Academy of European Law in Trier, Cologne: Bundesanzeiger Verlag, p. 132.

Pieth, M. (2004), International Standards against Money Laundering, in Pieth, M., and Aiolfi, G. (eds.), *A Comparative Guide to Anti-Money Laundering: A Critical Analysis of Systems in Singapore, Switzerland, the UK and the USA*, Cheltenham, UK and Northampton, MA, USA: Edward Elgar, p. 4.

Pieth, M. (2007a), Article 2: The Responsibility of Legal Persons, in Pieth, M., Low, L.A., and Cullen, P., *The OECD Convention in Bribery: A Commentary*, Cambridge: Cambridge University Press, p. 173.

Pieth M. (2007b), Article 3(3): Seizure and Confiscation, in Pieth, M., Low, L.A., and Cullen, P., *The OECD Convention in Bribery: A Commentary*, Cambridge: Cambridge University Press.

Pieth M. (2007c), Article 4: Jurisdiction, in Pieth, M., Low, L.A., and Cullen, P., *The OECD Convention in Bribery: A Commentary*, Cambridge: Cambridge University Press, p. 267.

Pieth, M. (2007d), Article 7: Money Laundering, in Pieth, M., Low, L.A., and Cullen, P., *The OECD Convention in Bribery: A Commentary*, Cambridge: Cambridge University Press, p. 355.

Pieth, M. (2007e), Introduction, in Pieth, M., Low, L.A., and Cullen, P., *The OECD Convention in Bribery: A Commentary*, Cambridge: Cambridge University Press, p. 5.

Pieth, M. (ed.) (2008), *Recovering Stolen Assets*, Bern: Peter Lang.

Pieth, M. (2009), From Ideal to Reality: Making the New Global Standard Stick, in OECD (ed.), *No Longer Business as Usual*, Paris: OECD, p. 57.

Pieth, M. (2011), *Harmonising Anti-Corruption Compliance. The OECD Good Practice Guidance 2010*, Zurich/St. Gall: Dike.

Pieth, M. (2013), Preface: Are We Recovering Any Assets Yet?, in Fenner Zinkernagel, G., Monteith, C. and Gomes Pereira, P. (eds.), *Emerging Trends in Asset Recovery*, Bern: Peter Lang, p. xi.

Pieth, M. and Lelieur, J. (2007), Strengthening International Coordination and Cooperation, Paper presented at the Experts Meeting of the OECD Anti-Bribery Convention: The Road Ahead, Rome, 21 November 2007.

Pilapitiya, T. (2004), The Impact of Corruption on the Human Rights Based Approach to Development, The Democratic Governance Fellowship Programme, United Nations Development Programme, Oslo Governance Centre, September, available at: http://www.undp.org/oslocentre/docs05/Thusitha_final.pdf.

Pirenne, H. (2010), *Storia d'Europa dalle invasioni al XVI secolo*, Rome: Newton Compton.

Pityana, N.B. (2004), Reflections on the African Court on Human and Peoples' Rights, *African Human Rights Law Journal*, 4(1) (2004): 121.

Pocar, F. (2008), Trattato di Lisbona: strumenti insufficienti per garantire unità sulla scena internazionale, *Guida al diritto. Diritto Comunitario e Internazionale*, 2 (March–April).

Poelemans, M. (2004), *La sanction dans l'ordre juridique communautaire*, Brussels: Bruylant.

Pope J. (1995), Corruption in Africa: The Role for Transparency International, in Aderinwale, A. (ed.), *Corruption, Democracy and Human Rights in Eastern and Central Africa: Summary Report of the Seminar Organized by the Africa Leadership Forum*, Entebbe and Ibadan, Uganda: ALF Publications, p. 14.

Posadas, A. (2000), Combating Corruption under International Law, *Duke Journal of Comparative and International Law*, 10 (2000): 345.

Post, D. (1995), E-Cash: Can't Live with It, Can't Live without It, *The American Lawyer*, 17 (1995): 116.

Powell, K. (2005), *Opportunities and Challenges for Delivering on the Responsibility to Protect: The African Union's Emerging Peace and Security Regime*, Ottawa, Canada: The North-South Institute, Monograph No. 119.

Prost, K. (1998), Breaking Down the Barriers: International Co-operation in Combating Transnational Crime, available at: http://www.oas.org/juridico/mla/en/can/en_can_prost.en.html.

Quinones, E. (2000), The Promise and the Reality: Monitoring Compliance with the OECD Convention, in OECD (ed.), *No Longer Business as Usual*, Paris: OECD, p. 101.

Raffray, F. (2013), The Rule of Law and 'Tommy Suharto' son of (former) President Suharto, in Fenner Zinkernagel, G., Monteith, C. and Gomes Pereira, P. (eds.), *Emerging Trends in Asset Recovery*, Bern: Peter Lang, p. 29.

Rajan, R. (2006), Has Finance Made the World Riskier?, *European Financial Management*, 12(4): pp. 499–533.

Rajan, R. and Zingales, L. (1998), Power in a Theory of the Firm, *Quarterly Journal of Economics*, 113(2): 387–432.

Rajan, R. and Zingales, L. (2001), The Firm as a Dedicated Hierarchy: A Theory of the Origins and Growth of Firms, *Quarterly Journal of Economics*, 116(3): 805–51.

Rajan, R. and Zingales, L. (2003), The Great Reversals: The Politics of Financial Development in the Twentieth Century, *Journal of Financial Economics*, 69(1): 5–50.

Rajesh Babu, R. (2006), The United Nations Convention Against Corruption: A Critical Overview, (1 March), available at SSRN: http://ssrn.com/abstract=891898.

Ramonet, I. (1997), La mutation du monde, *Le Monde Diplomatique*, October.

Rampini, F. (2008a), Il mondo in frantumi della finanza Usa, *la Repubblica*, (22 September): 1.

Rampini, F. (2008b), Una cambiale in bianco che costa quanto la Guerra in Iraq; Un fragile scudo alla prova dei mercati, *la Repubblica*, (21 September): 1.

Raphael, M. (2008), UK Global Update – Global Disappointment, Paper for The International Bar Association's 6th Annual Anticorruption Conference: The Awakening Giant of Anticorruption Enforcement, Paris, April 2008.

Rasmusen, E.B. and Ramseyer, J.M. (1994), Cheap Bribes and the Corruption Ban: A Coordination Game among Rational Legislators, *Public Choice*, 78: 305.

Rasmusen, E.B. and Ramseyer, J.M. (1999), Cheap Bribes and the Corruption Ban: A Coordination Game among Rational Legislators, in Fiorentini, Gianluca, and Zamagni, Stefano (eds.), *The Economics of Corruption and Illegal Markets*, Cheltenham, UK and Northampton, MA, USA: Edward Elgar.

Rawls, J. (1999), *A Theory of Justice*, revised edn., Cambridge, MA: Harvard University Press.

Rawls, J. (2004), *Lezioni di storia della filosofia morale*, Italian translation, Milan: Feltrinelli.

Recanatini, F. (2013), I costi della corruzione per i cittadini e le imprese, *Riciclaggio e corruzione: prevenzione e controllo tra fonti interne e internazionali*, Acts of the Conference organized by Centro Nazionale di Prevenzione e Difesa Sociale (Courmayeur, 28 September 2012), Milan: Giuffrè, p. 63.

Redgwell, C. (1993), Universality or Integrity? Some Reflections on Reservation to General Multilateral Treaties, *British Yearbook of International Law*, 64: 245.

Rehman, J. (2003), *International Human Rights Law*, London: Longman.

Reich, R.B. (2008), *Supercapitalism: The Transformation of Business, Democracy, and Everyday life*, Italian translation: *Supercapitalismo: Come cambia l'economia globale e rischi per la democrazia*, Rome: Fazi Editore.

Reisman, W.M. (1979), *Folded Lies: Bribery, Crusades and Reforms*, New York: Free Press.

Reisman, W.M. (1989), Comment, Harnessing International Law To Restrain and Recapture Indigenous Spoliation, *American Journal of International Law*, 83: 56.

Revelli, M. (1996), *Le due Destre*, Turin: Bollati Boringhieri.

Riahi-Belkaoui, A. (2004) Politically-Connected Firms: Are they Connected to Earning Opacity?, *Research in Accounting Regulation*, 17: 25–38.

Ribadu, N. (2008), Challenges and Opportunities of Asset Recovery in a Developing Economy, in Pieth, M. (ed.), *Recovering Stolen Assets*, Bern: Peter Lang, 2008, p. 29.

Rifkin, J. (2008), Credito, energia e global warming: tre crisi mondiali in un colpo solo, *La Repubblica*, 30 September.

Robbins, L. (1932), *An Essay on the Nature and Significance of Economic Science*, London: Macmillan.

Roberts. B. (1990), A Dead Senator Tells No Lies: Seniority and the Distribution of Federal Benefits, *American Journal of Political Sciences*, 34: 31–58.

Robinson, D. (1999), Defining "Crime Against Humanity" at the Rome Conference, *American Journal of International Law*, 93(1): 43–57.

Rodrik, D. (1997), Comments: Dani Rodrik and James E. Rauch, in Elliot, K.A. (ed.), *Corruption and the Global Economy*, Washington, DC: Institute for International Economics.

Rodrik, D. (1998), Why Do More Open Economies Have Bigger Governments? *Journal of Political Economy*, 106: 997–1032.

Rodrik, D. (1999), Institutions for High Quality Growth: What They Are and How To Acquire Them, Unpublished.

Rodrik, D. (2007), *One Economics, Many Recipes*, Princeton, NJ: Princeton University Press.

Roll, R. (1977), A Critique of the Asset Pricing Theory's Tests, *Journal of Financial Economics*, 4: 129–76.

Roll, R. and Ross, S. (1980), An Empirical Investigation of the Arbitrage Pricing Theory, *Journal of Finance*, 35: 1073–103.

Rooke, P. (2003), The UN Convention against Corruption, in Transparency International (ed.), *Global Corruption Report 2003*, Cambridge: Cambridge University Press, p. 111.

Rose-Ackerman, S. (1978), *Corruption: A Study in Political Economy*, New York: Academic Press.

Rose-Ackerman. S. (1997), The Political Economy of Corruption, in Elliot, K.A. (ed.), *Corruption and the Global Economy*, Washington, DC: Institute for International Economics, p. 31.

Rose-Ackerman, S. (1999), *Corruption and Government: Causes, Consequences, and Reform*, Cambridge: Cambridge University Press.

Rose-Ackerman, S. (2002), Corruption and the Global Corporation: Ethical Obligation and Workable Strategies, in Likosky, M. (ed.), *Transnational Legal Process*, London: Butterworth, p. 148.

Rose-Ackerman, S. (2004), Establishing the Rule of Law, in Rotberg, R. (ed.), *When States Fail: Causes and Consequences*, Princeton, NJ: Princeton University Press, p. 182.

Rosett, C. (2003), Oil, Food and a Whole Lot of Questions, *The New York*

Times, 18 April, available at: www.defenddemocracy.org/in_the_media/in_the_media_show.htm?doc_id=218141.

Rosi, E. (2003), Problematiche di accertamento delle indagini corruttive, in Forti, G. (ed.), *Il prezzo della tangente, La corruzione come sistema a dieci anni da "mani pulite"*, Milan: Vita e Pensiero, p. 233.

Rosi, E. (ed.) (2007), *Criminalità organizzata transnazionale e sistema penale italiano. La convenzione ONU di Palermo*, Milan: Ipsoa.

Rosi, E. (2008), Reati transnazionali e conflitti di giurisdizione: verso una "determinazione transnazionale della giurisdizione", Report to the Italian Superior Judicial Council, Rome 7–9 July, 2008, manuscript.

Ross, A. (1965), *On Law and Justice*, Italian translation, *Diritto e giustizia*, Turin: Einaudi.

Ross, S.A. (1976), The Arbitrage Theory of Capital Asset Pricing, *Journal of Economic Theory*, 13: 341–60.

Rossi, G. (2003), *Il conflitto epidemico*, Milan: Adelphi.

Rossi, G. (2006), *Il gioco delle regole*, Milan: Adelphi.

Rotberg, R.I. (2007), The Challenge of Weak, Failing, and Collapsed States, in Crocker, C.A. et al. (eds.), *Leashing the Dogs of War: Conflict Management in a Divided World*, Washington, DC: US Institute of Peace Press, p. 87.

Roubini, N. (2008), The Shadow Banking System is Unravelling, *The Financial Times*, 21 September.

Roubini, N. (2009), Seeing Crisis Clearly, *Finance & Development*, IMF, Relations Departments, (March 2009): 4–7, www.imf.org.

Rousseau, J.J. (1963–4), *Du contrat social*, Paris: Clavreuil.

Ruffolo, G. (2008), *Il capitalismo ha i secoli contati*, Turin: Einaudi.

Ruggie, J.G. (1983), International Regimes, Transnations and Change: Embedded Liberalism in the Post-war Economic Order, in Krasner, S.D. (ed.), *International Regimes*, Ithaca, NY: Cornell University Press.

Sacerdoti, G. (1995), Les aspects internationaux de la corruption, Rapport présente au Groupe Multidisciplinaire sur la Corruption du Conseil de l'Europe (GMC), (7), (24 January).

Sacerdoti, G. (1998), La Convenzione OCSE del 1997 sulla lotta contro la corruzione dei pubblici ufficiali stranieri nelle transazioni internazionali, *Rivista italiana di diritto e procedura penale*, (1998): 1349.

Sacerdoti G. (1999), The 1997 OECD Convention on Combating Bribery in Transnational Business,Transactions. An Example of Piece-Meal Regulation of Globalization, *IX Italian Yearbook of International Law*, (1999): 26.

Sacerdoti, G. (2000), To bribe or Not to Bribe?, in OECD (ed.), *No Longer Business as Usual*, Paris: OECD, p. 29.

Sacerdoti, G. (ed.) (2003), *Responsabilità d'impresa e strumenti internazionali anticorruzione. Dalla Convenzione OCSE 1997 al Decreto n. 231/2001*, Milan: Egea.

Sacerdoti, G. (2008), Nelle classifiche internazionali sul malaffare l'Italia resta indietro per lassismo e intolleranza, *Guida al diritto. Diritto internazionale e comunitario*, (1) (January–February): 9.

Sachs, S. (2004), Hussein's Regime Skimmed Billions from Aid Program, *The New York Times*, 29 February, available at: www.nytimes.com/2004/02/29/international/middleeast/29FOOD.html.

Sacucci, A. (2000), Nominato in Europa il super-investigatore antifrode, *Diritto penale e processo*, 1: 117.

Sacucci, A. (2005), *Profili di tutela dei diritti umani tra Nazioni Unite e Consiglio d'Europa*, Padua: Cedam.

Salazar, L. (1998a), Les projets législatifs de l'Union Européenne sur la lutte contre la corruption, in Corruption de fonctionnaires et fraude européenne, Actes du colloque de Bruxelles, 21 et 22/11/96, Brussels, 1998.

Salazar, L. (1998b), Recenti sviluppi internazionali nella lotta alla corruzione (. . . e conseguenti obblighi di recepimento da parte italiana), *Cassazione Penale*, (1998): 1537.

Salazar, L. (2003), La costruzione di uno spazio di libertà, sicurezza e giustizia dopo il Consiglio di Tampere, *Cassazione penale*, 4: 1114.

Salazar, L. (2004), sub Articolo 280, in Tizzano, A. (ed.) *Trattati dell'Unione Europea e della Comunità Europea*, Milan: Giuffrè, p. 1255.

Salbu, S.R. (1997), Bribery in the Global Market: A Critical Analysis of the Foreign Corrupt Practices Act, *Washington and Lee Law* Review, (1997): 229.

Salvioni, S. (2008), *Recovering the Proceeds of Corruption: Ferdinand Marcos of the Phillipines*, in Pieth, M. (ed.) *Recovering Stolen Assets*, Bern: Peter Lang, p. 79.

Samuel, L.M. (2005), Repatriation Obligations Under the United Nations Convention against Corruption, *Resource Material Series*, 65: 58–65.

Sanchez, N. and Waters, A.R. (1974), Controlling Corruption in Africa and Latin America, in Furubotn, Eirik G., and Pejovich, Svetozar (eds.), *The Economics of Property Rights*, Cambridge, MA: Ballinger, p. 279.

Sandel, M. (2009), *Justice: What's the Right Thing to Do?*, New York: Farrar, Straus and Giroux.

Saxon, D. (2002), Robbery against Humanity: the Treatment in International Humanitarian Law of Economic Crime as a Basis for Persecution and Genocide, *Forum on Crime and Society*, 2(1) (December).

Sayer, S. and Waldron, J. (2002), Corruption in International Projects: the International Legislative Framework and its Implementation, *International Business Law*, (October 2002): 387.

Scelle. G. (1932), *Prècis de droit des gens: Principes et systèmatique*, I, Paris: Recueil Sirey.

Schwelb, E. (1946), Crimes against Humanity, *British Yearbook of International Law*, 23: 178.

Shleifer, A. and Vishny, R. (1993), Corruption, *Quarterly Journal of Economics*, 109: 599.

Schloenhardt, A. (2005), Transnational Organised Crime and the International Criminal Court. Developments and Debates, *University of Queensland Law Journal*, 4, available at: http://www.austlii.edu.au.

Schmitt, C. (2001), *Der Nomos der Erde im Völkerrecht des Jus Publicum Europeum*, Berlin, 1974; Italian translation: *Il Nomos della terra nel diritto internazionale dello "jus publicum europaeum"*, 4th edn., Milan: Adelphi.

Schroth, P.W. (2002), The United States and International Bribery Conventions, *American Journal of Comparative Law*, 50: 593.

Schroth, P.W. (2003a), National and International Constitutional Law Aspects of African Treaties and Laws Against Corruption, *Transnational Law and Contemporary Problems*, 13: 83.

Schroth, P.W. (2003b), Symposium: The African Union and the New Pan-Africanism: Rushing to Organize or Timely Shift: National and International Constitutional Law Aspects of African Treaties and Laws Against Corruption, *Transnational Law and Contemporary Problems*, 13: 88.

Schroth, P.W. (2005a), The African Union Convention on Preventing and Combating Corruption, *Journal of African Law*, 49(1): 24.

Schroth, P.W. (2005b), The United Nations Convention against Doing Anything Serious about Corruption, *Journal of Legal Studies in Business*, 12: 2.

Schroth, P.W. and Bostan, A.D. (forthcoming), International Constitutional Law and Anti-Corruption Measures in the European Union's Accession Negotiations: Romania in Comparative Perspective, *American Journal of Comparative Law*.

Schumpeter, J.A. (1942), *Capitalism, Socialism and Democracy*, New York: Harper and Row.

Scott, J. (1972), *Comparative Political Corruption*, Englewood Cliffs, NJ: Prentice Hall.

Scott, V. (1998), International Lawyers: Handmaidens, Chefs, or Birth Attendants? A Response to Philip Alston, *European Journal of International Law*, 9: 750.

Seminara, S. (1993), Gli interessi tutelati nei reati di corruzione, *Rivista Italiana di diritto e procedura penale*, 3: 992.

Seminara, S. (2004), sub Art. 322 ter, in Crespi, A., Stella, F., and

Ziccalà, G. (eds), *Commentario breve al codice penale*, Padua: Cedam, p. 1202.

Sen, A.K. (1987), *On Ethics and Economics*, Oxford: Oxford University Press.

Sen, A.K. (1992), *Inequality Re-examined*, Oxford: Oxford University Press.

Sen, A.K. (2003), *Globalizzazione e libertà*, Italian translation, Milan: Mondadori.

Senior, I. (2006), *Corruption – The World's Big C. Causes, Consequences, Cures*, London: Institute of Economic Affairs.

Sevenster, H.G. (1992), Criminal Law and EC, *Common Market Law Review*, 29: 29.

Severino, E. (2007), *Il declino del capitalismo*, 2nd edn., Milan: BUR.

Shamir, R. (2005), Corporate Global Responsibility: A Case of Hegemony and Counter Hegemony, in De Sousa Santos, B. and Rodriguez-Garavito, C.A. (eds.), *Law and Globalisation from Below: Towards a Cosmopolitan Legality*, Cambridge: Cambridge University Press, p. 92.

Shams, H. (2001), The Fight against Extraterritorial Corruption and the Use of Money Laundering, *NAFTA Law and Business Review of the Americas*, (winter/spring 2001): 86.

Shams, H. (2004), *Legal Globalization. Money Laundering Law and Other Cases*, London: British Institute of International and Comparative Law.

Sharman, J. (2012), Tackling shell companies: Limiting the opportunities to hide proceeds of corruption, *U4 BRIEF December 2012 No 10*, Bergen: CMI-U4.

Sharman, J. (2013), Preventing the misuse of shell companies by regulating corporate service providers, *U4 Brief October 2013 No 7*, Bergen: CMI-U4.

Sharman, J. (2013), Shell Companies and Asset Recovery: Piercing the Corporate Veil, in Fenner Zinkernagel, G., Monteith, C. and Gomes Pereira, P. (eds.), *Emerging Trends in Asset Recovery*, Bern: Peter Lang, p. 67.

Sharpe, W.F. (1964), Capital Asset Prices: A Theory of Market Equilibrium under Conditions of Risks, *Journal of Finance*, 29(3): 425–42.

Sharpe, W.F. and Cooper, G.M. (1972), Risk-return Classes of New York Stock Exchange Common Stocks 1931–1967, *Financial Analyst Journal*, 28: 46–52.

Shaw, B. (2000), The Foreign Corrupt Practices Act and Progeny: Morally Unassailable, *Cornell International Law Journal*, 33: 689.

Shaw, M.N. (1994), *Global Society and International Relations*, Oxford: Oxford University Press.

Shaw, M.N. (2003), *International Law*, 5th edn., Cambridge: Cambridge University Press.

Shaw, M.N. (2008), *International Law*, 6th edn., Cambridge: Cambridge University Press.

Shihata, I.F.I. (1991), *The World Bank in a Changing World: Selected Essays*, edited by Tschofen, F. and Parra, A.R., Dordrecht, Boston and London: M. Nijhoff.

Shiller, R.J. (2000). *Euforia irrazionale: analisi dei boom di Borsa*, Bologna: Il Mulino.

Shleifer, A. (1996), Government in Transition, HIER Discussion Paper No. 1783, Harvard Institute for Economic Research.

Shleifer, A. and Vishny, R.W. (1986), Large Shareholders and Corporate Control, *Journal of Political Economy*, 94(3): 461–88.

Shleifer, A. and Vishny, R.W. (1993), Corruption, *Quarterly Journal of Economics*, 108(3): 599–617.

Shleifer, A. and Vishny, R.W. (1994), Politicians and Firms, *The Quarterly Journal of Economics*, 109(4): 95–1025.

Shleifer, A. and Vishny, R.W. (1995), The Limits of Arbritage, NBER, Working Paper, NW5167.

Shleifer, A. and Vishny, R. (1997), A Survey of Corporate Governance, *Journal of Finance*, 52: 737–83.

Sicurella, R. (2005), *Diritto penale e competenze del'Unione Europea*, Milan: Giuffrè.

Siegel, D. (2007), Governance/Anti-corruption. Legal Issues in the Work of the IMF, in Passas, N. and Vlassis, D. (eds.), *The United Nations Convention Against Corruption as a Way of Life*, Selected papers and contributions from the International Conference on 'The United Nations Convention Against Corruption as a Way of Life' (Courmayeur, 15–17 December 2006), Milan: ISPAC, p. 47.

Siegel, J. (2002), *Stocks for the Long Run*, New York: McGraw-Hill.

Sjaifudian, S. (1997), Graft and the Small Business, *Far Eastern Economic Review*, 16: 32.

Slaughter, A.M. (1997), The Real New World Order, *Foreign Affairs*, 76: 183.

Slaughter, A.M. (2000), Governing the Global Economy through Government Networks, in Byers, M. (ed.), *The Role of Law in International Politics*, Oxford: Oxford University Press, p. 193.

Smith, A. (1976), *Theory of Moral Sentiments*, edited by Raphael, D.D., and Macfie, A.L., Oxford: Oxford University Press.

Smith, A. (1998), *An Inquiry into the Nature and Causes of the Wealth of Nations*, Oxford: Oxford University Press.

Smith, D.M. (2002), *Storia d'Italia dal 1961 al 1997*, 2nd edn., Rome and Bari: Editori Laterza.

Smith, J.J.C. (1974), Intention in Criminal Law, *Current Legal Problems*, 27: 93.

Smith. J.J.C. (1978), A Reply, in *Criminal Law Review*, (1978): 14.

Snider, T.R. and Kidane, W. (2007), Combating Corruption through International Law in Africa: A Comparative Analysis, *Cornell International Law Journal*, 40: 691.

Sotis, C. (2007), *Il diritto senza codice. Uno studio sul diritto penale europeo vigente*, Milan: Giuffrè.

Spahn, E. (2012), Multi-Jurisdictional Bribery Law Enforcement: The OECD Anti-Bribery Convention, *Virginia Journal of International Law*, 53(1), (September): 26.

Speckbacher, C. (2009), The Protection of Whistleblowers in the Light of the GRECO's Work, available at: http://www.batory.org.pl/doc/Whistleblowing%20mechanisms%20REV2%20for%20Batory%20Foundation%20Conf%20of%2030March09.pdf

Sperber, M. (2002), Foreign Corrupt Practices Act, *American Criminal Law Review*, 39(2): 679.

Sporkin, S. (1997–8), The Worldwide Banning of Schmiergeld: A Look at the Foreign Corrupt Practices Act on its Twentieth Birthday, *Northwestern Journal of International Law and Business*, 18: 269.

StAR (2007), *Stolen Asset Recovery (StAR) Initiative: Challenges, Opportunities, and Action Plan*, Washington, DC: World Bank, available at: http://siteresources.worldbank.org/NEWS/Resources/Star-rep-full.pdf.

StAR (2008), World Bank and UNODC. Partnership Charter, 7 November, available at: http://star.worldbank.org/star/sites/star/files/StAR_Partnership_Charter_0.pdf.

StAR (2009a), *Towards a Global Architecture for Asset Recovery*, Washington, DC: World Bank, available at: http://star.worldbank.org/star/publication/towards-global-architecture-asset-recovery.

StAR (2009b), *Good Practices Guide for Non-Conviction Based Asset Forfeiture*, Washington, DC: World Bank, available at: http://star.worldbank.org/star/publication/good-practice-guide-non-conviction-based-asset-forfeiture.

StAR (2009c), *Management of Returned Assets: Policy Considerations*, Washington, DC: World Bank, available at: http://star.worldbank.org/star/publication/management-returned-assets.

StAR (2010), *Politically Exposed Persons: Preventive Measures for the Banking Sector*, Washington, DC: World Bank, available at: http://star.worldbank.org/star/publication/politically-exposed-persons.

StAR (2011a), *The Puppet Masters. How the Corrupt Use Legal Structures to Hide Stolen Assets and What to Do About It*, Washington, DC:

World Bank, available at: http://star.worldbank.org/star/publication/puppet-masters.
StAR (2011b), *Barriers to Asset Recovery. An Analysis of the Key Barriers and Recommendations for Action*, Washington, DC: World Bank, available at: http://star.worldbank.org/star/publication/barriers-asset-recovery.
StAR (2012), *Public Office, Private Interests. Accountability through Income and Asset Disclosure*, Washington, DC: World Bank, available at: http://star.worldbank.org/star/publication/public-office-private-interests.
StAR (2013), *Left out of the Bargain: Settlements in Foreign Bribery Cases and Implications for Asset Recovery*, Washington, DC: World Bank, available at: https://star.worldbank.org/star/publication/left-out-bargain-settlements-foreign-bribery-cases-and-implications-asset-recovery.
Stattman, D. (1980), Book Values and Expected Stock Returns, unpublished MBA honors paper.
Stella, F. (1998), Criminalità d'impresa: lotta di sumo o lotta di judo, *Riv. it. dir. proc. pen.*, (1998): 458.
Stella, F. (2002), Il mercato senza etica, in De Maglie, C., *L'etica e il mercato*, Milan: Giuffrè.
Stella, F. (2006), *La giustizia e le ingiustizie*, Bologna: Il Mulino.
Stern, B. (1980), The Legal Character of Emerging Norms Relating to the New International Economic Order: Some Comments, in Hossain, K. (ed.), *Legal Aspects of the New International Economic Order*, 69, London: Pinter, p. 70.
Stiglitz, J.E. (1993), *Principles of Macroeconomics*, New York: W.W. Norton & Company, Inc.
Stiglitz, J.E. (2001), Information and the Change in the Paradigm of Economics, Nobel Prize Lecture, 8 December.
Stiglitz, J.E. (2002), *Globalization and its Discontents*, New York: W.W. Norton and Company.
Stiglitz, J.E. (2003), *The Roaring Nineties*, New York: W.W. Norton and Company; Italian translation: *I ruggenti anni novanta*, Turin: Einaudi.
Stiglitz, J.E. (2008), Interview, *L'espresso*, 39(LIV) (3 October): 51.
Summers, A. (2000), *The Arrogance of Power: The Secret World of Richard Nixon*, New York: Viking Penguin.
Sur, S. (2007), The State between Fragmentation and Globalization, *European Journal of International Law*, 8: 278.
Szasz, P. (2002), The Security Council Starts Legislating, *American Journal of International Law*, 96: 901.
Talmon, S. (2005), The Security Council as World Legislature, *American Journal of International Law*, 99: 175.
Tamaha, B.Z. (2004), *On the Rule of Law: History, Politics, Theory*, Cambridge: Cambridge University Press.

Tanzi, V. (1994), Corruption, Governmental Activities, and Markets, IMF Working Paper, 94/99, Washington, DC.

Tanzi, V. (1998), Corruption Around the World – Causes, Consequences, Scopes, and Cures, IMF Working Paper, 98/63, Washington, DC.

Tanzi, V. (2002), Corruption Around the World: Causes, Consequences, Scope and Cures, in Abed, George T., and Gupta, Sanjeev (eds.), *Governance, Corruption and Economic Performance*, Washington, DC: IMF.

Tanzi, V. (2006), Corruption and Economic Activity, Distinguished Lecture Series 26, The Egyptian Center for Economic Studies, Cairo, December 2006.

Tanzi, V. and Davoodi, R.H. (1998), Corruption, Public Investment and Growth, IMF Working Paper, 97/139, Washington, DC.

Tanzi, V. and Davoodi, R.H. (2000), Corruption, Growth, and Public Finances, IMF Working Paper, 00/182, Washington, DC.

Tanzi, V. and Davoodi, R.H. (2002a), Corruption, Growth and Public Finances, in Abed, George T., and Gupta, Sanjeev (eds.), *Governance, Corruption and Economic Performance*, Washington, DC: IMF.

Tanzi, Vito, and Davoodi, R.H. (2002b), Corruption, Public Investment and Growth, in Abed, George T. and Gupta, Sanjeev (eds.), *Governance, Corruption and Economic Performance*, Washington, DC: IMF.

Tarullo, D.K. (2004), The Limits of Institutional Design: Implementing the OECD Anti-Bribery Convention, *Vanderbilt Journal of International Law*, 44: 665.

Tesauro, G. (2007), Un testo di revisione stilato a tempo di record che sacrifica partecipazione e valori condivisi, *Guida al diritto. Diritto Comunitario e Internazionale*, 6 (November–December): 8.

Tesauro, G. (2008), *Diritto Comunitario*, 5th edn., Padua: Cedam.

The Short Arm of the Law (2002), *The Economist*, 28 February.

Thomas, C. (1998), International Financial Institutions and Social and Economic Rights: An Exploration, in Evans, T. (ed.), *Human Rights Fifty Years On: A Reappraisal*, Manchester: Manchester University Press.

Thomas, J.W. and Grindle, M.S. (1990), After the Decision: Implementing Policy Reforms in developing Countries, *World Development*, 18(8): 1163.

Tiedeman, K. (1998), L'europizzazione del diritto penale, *Riv. it. dir. proc. pen.*, (1998): 1.

Tillman, R. and Indergaard, M. (2007), Corporate Corruption in the New Economy, in Pontell, H.N. and Geis, G. (eds.), *International Handbook of White Collar Crime*, New York: Springer, p. 474.

Tizzano, A. (1996), Brevi note sul "terzo pilastro" del Trattato di Maastricht, in *Diritto dell'Unione Europea*, (1996): 391.

Tizzano, A. (ed.) (2004), *Trattati dell'Unione Europea e della Comunità Europea*, Milan: Giuffrè.
Tjetje, C. (2002), Global Governance and Inter-Agency Co-operation in International Economic Law, *Journal of World Trade*, 3: 515.
Tobler, C. (2005), *Remedies and Sanctioning in EC Non-discrimination Law: Effective, Proportional and Dissuasive Sanctions and Remedies, with Particular Reference to Upper Limits on Compensation of Victims of Discrimination*, Luxembourg: Office for the Official Publications of the European Communities, p. 15.
Tomuschat, C. (1993), Obligations arising for States Without or Against their Will, *Recueil Des Courts*, 241(IV): 195.
Transparency International (1995), *1995 Corruption Index*, Cambridge: Cambridge University Press.
Transparency International (2003), Overcoming Obstacles to Enforcement of the OECD Convention on Combating Bribery of Foreign Public Officials, Report on Paris Meeting of 2–3 October.
Transparency International (2007), *Global Corruption Report 2007. Corruption in Judicial Systems*, Cambridge: Cambridge University Press.
Transparency International (2008), *Global Corruption Report 2008. Corruption in the Water Sector*, Cambridge: Cambridge University Press.
Transparency International (2011a), Promoting Revenue Transparency: 2011 Report on Oil and Gas Companies, available at: http://www.transparency.org/whatwedo/pub/promoting_revenue_transparency_2011_report_on_oil_and_gas_companies.
Transparency International (2011b), 2011 Progress Report on Enforcement of the OECD Anti-bribery Convention, available at http://www.transparency.org/whatwedo/pub/progress_report_2011_enforcement_of_the_oecd_anti_bribery_convention/.
Transparency International (2012), 2012 Progress Report on Enforcement of the OECD Anti-bribery Convention, available at: http://www.transparency.org/whatwedo/pub/exporting_corruption_country_enforcement_of_the_oecd_anti_bribery_convention/.
Transparency International (2013a), 2013 Progress Report on Enforcement of the OECD Anti-bribery Convention, available at: http://www.transparency.org/whatwedo/pub/exporting_corruption_progress_report_2013_assessing_enforcement_of_the_oecd.
Transparency International (2013b), *UN Convention Against Corruption. Progress Report 2013*, Berlin: Transparency International.
Transparency International (2013c), *Whistleblower Protection and the UN Convention Against Corruption*, Berlin: Transparency International.
Treisman, D. (2000), The Causes of Corruption: A Cross-national Study, *Journal of Public Economics*, 76 (2000): 399–457.

Trenor, J.A. (1995), Jurisdiction and Extraterritorial Application of Antitrust Laws after Harford Fire, *University of Chicago Law Review*, 62: 1583.

Treves, T. (1973), *La giurisdizione nel diritto penale internazionale*, Padua: Cedam.

Treves, T. (2005), *Diritto internazionale. Problemi fondamentali*, Milan: Giuffrè.

Triepel, H. (1899), *Völkerrecht und Landerrecht*, Leipzig: Hirschfield.

Trujillo, I. (2006), sub voce, Mondialismo, *Enciclopedia filosofica*, Milan: Bompiani.

Trujillo, I. (2007), *Giustizia globale. Le nuove frontiere dell'eguaglianza*, Bologna: Il Mulino.

Tullock, G. (1996), Corruption Theory and Practice, *Contemporary Economic Policy*, 14(3): 6–13.

Uckmar, V. (1995), Il settore privato e la corruzione dell'applicazione dei tributi, *Dir. Prat. Trib.*, (1995): 1410.

Udombana, N. (2004), Between Promise and Performance: Revisiting States' Obligations under the African Human Rights Charter, *Stanford Journal of International Law*, 40: 105.

Ulrich, M. (2007), UNCAC: A Way of Life. The Role of the Legislative Branch, in Passas, N. and Vlassis, D. (eds.), *The United Nations Convention Against Corruption as a Way of Life*, Selected papers and contributions from the International Conference on 'The United Nations Convention Against Corruption as a Way of Life' (Courmayeur, 15–17 December 2006), Milan: ISPAC, p. 33.

Unger, B. (2013), Money Laundering Regulation: From Al Capone to Al Qaeda, in Unger, B. and van der Linde, D. (eds.), *Research Handbook on Money Laundering*, Cheltenham, UK and Northampton, MA, USA: Edward Elgar Publishing.

United Nations Office of the High Commissioner for Human Rights, *CCPR General Comment No. 13: Article 14 (Administration of Justice), Equality before the Courts and the Right to a Fair and Public Hearing by an Independent Court Established by Law*, 13 April 1984, available at: http://www.refworld.org/docid/453883f90.html

UNODC (2006), *Legislative Guide for the Implementation of the United Nations Convention against Corruption*, Vienna: UNODC.

UNODC and World Bank (2007), *Stolen Asset Recovery (StAR) Initiative: Challenges, Opportunities and Action Plan*, Washington, DC: World Bank, available at: http://siteresources.worldbank.org/NEWS/Resources/Star-rep-full.pdf.

UNODC (2009), *Technical Guide to The United Nations Convention Against Corruption*, Vienna: UNODC.

UNODC (2013), *An Anti-Corruption Ethics and Compliance Programme for Business: A Practical Guide*, New York: UN.

US Department of Justice (DOJ) and Securities and Exchange Commission (SEC) (2012), *Resource Guide to the U.S. Foreign Corrupt Practices Act by the Criminal Division of the U.S. Department of Justice and the Enforcement Division of the U.S. Securities and Exchange Commission*, available at: http://www.justice.gov/opa/pr/2012/November/12-crm-1354.html.

Valenti, M. (2003), I criteri di giurisdizione nelle convenzioni internazionali contro la corruzione, in Sacerdoti, G. (ed.), *Responsabilità d'impresa e strumenti internazionali anticorruzione. Dalla Convenzione OCSE 1997 al Decreto n. 231*/2001, Milan: Egea, p. 57.

Van den Wyngaert, C. and Stessens, G. (1999), The International Ne Bis in Idem Principle: Resolving Some of the Unanswered Questions, *International and Comparative Law Quarterly*, 48: 779.

Van Walraven, K. (1999), *Dreams of Power: The Role of the Organization of African Unity in the Politics of Africa 1963–1993*, Aldershot: Ashgate.

Vander Beken, T. (2003), The Council of Europe's Criminal Law Convention on Corruption. Joint Programme of the Council of Europe and the European Union for Ukraine, Paper presented at the Seminar on the Anti-corruption Conventions and GRECO held in Kiev – 23 April 2003.

Vassalli, G. (1965), Nullum crimen sine lege, *Novissimo Digesto*, XI: 493.

Vattimo, G. (2003), *Nichilismo ed emancipazione. Etica, politica, diritto*, Milan: Garzanti.

Venzel, M. (1920), *Juristische Grundproblem – Zugleich eine Untersuchung zum Begriff des Staates und Problem des Völkerrechts*, Berlin: F. Dümmlers.

Veron, M. (2001), *Corruption et Trafic d'influence*, *Droit Pénal* (July 2001): 10.

Vervaele, J.A.E. (1994), Administrative Sanctioning Powers of and in the Community. Towards a System of European Administrative Sanctions?, in Vervaele, J.A.E. (ed.), *Administrative Law Application and Enforcement of Community Law in the Netherlands*, Deventer and Boston: Kluwer, p. 161.

Vervaele, J.A.E. (1999), Towards an Independent European Agency to Fight Fraud and corruption in the EU?, *European Journal of Crime, Criminal Law, and Criminal Justice*, 3: 331.

Vervaele, J.A.E. (2005a), The Transnational Ne Bis in Idem Principle: Mutual Recognition and Equivalent Protection of Human Rights, *Utrecht Law Review*, 1(2): 110.

Vervaele, J.A.E. (2005b), Europeanisation of Criminal Law and the Criminal

Law Dimension of European Integration, in Demaret, P., Govaere, I., and Hanf, D. (eds.), *30 Years of European Legal Studies at the College of Europe*, Brussels: Liber Professorum, P.I.E.-Peter Lang, p. 227.

Vervaele, J.A.E. (2006), The European Community and Harmonization of the Criminal Law Enforcement of Community Policy, *Eucrim*, 3(4): 87.

Vervaele, J.A.E. (2013), Economic crimes and money laundering: a new paradigm for the criminal justice system?, in Unger, B. and van der Linde, D. (eds.), *Research Handbook On Money Laundering*, Cheltenham, UK and Northampton, MA, USA: Edward Elgar.

Viljoen, F. and Louw, L. (2004), The Status of the Findings of the African Commission: From Moral Suasion to Legal Obligation, *Journal of African Law*, 48: 1.

Villinger M.E. (2009), *Commentary on the 1969 Vienna Convention on the law of Treaties*, Leiden, Holland and Boston, US: Martinus Nijhoff Publishers.

Vlasic, M.V. and Cooper, G. (2011), Beyond the Duvalier Legacy: What New "Arab Spring" Governments Can Learn from Haiti and the Benefits of Stolen Assets Recovery, *Northwestern University Journal of International Human Rights*, Vol. 10(19).

Vlassis, D. (ed.) (1998), *Combating Transnational Crime, a Special Issue of Transnational Organized Crime*, 4(3–4) (autumn/winter): 18.

Vlassis, D. (2007), The United Nations Convention against Corruption: a Way of Life, in Passas, N. and Vlassis, D. (eds.), *The United Nations Convention against Corruption as a way of life*, Selected papers and contributions from the International Conference on "The United Nations Convention against Corruption as a way of life" (Courmayeur, 15–17 December 2006), Milan: ISPAC, p. 15.

Von Hayek, F. (2006), *The Constitution of Liberty*, Abingdon, Oxon: Routledge Classics.

Wahl, T., Löhr, C. and Kiesel, S. (2007), Reform of the European Union, *Eucrim*, 1(2) (2007): 20.

Wallance, C.D. (2002), *The Multinational Enterprise and Legal Control. Host State Sovereignty in an Era of Economic Globalisation*, The Hague, London and New York: Kluwer Law International.

Wasmeier, M. and Thwaites, N. (2004), The "Battle" of the Pillars: Does the European Community Have the Power to Approximate National Criminal Laws?, *European Law Review*, 29: 613.

Waterbury, J. (1973), Endemic and Planned Corruption in a Monarchic Regime, *World Politics*, XXV(4): 533.

Webb, P. (2005), The United Nations Convention Against Corruption. Global Achievement or Missed Opportunity?, *Journal of International Economic Law*, (March): 191.

Wei, S.J. (2000), How Taxing is Corruption on International Investors, *Review of Economics and Statistics*, 82(1): 1.

Wei, Shan Jin (1997), Why is Corruption so Much More Taxing than Tax?, NBER Working Paper 2048.

Weiler, J.H.H. (2004), The Geology of International Law: Governance, Democracy, and Legitimacy, *Zeitschift für ausländiche öffentliches Recht und Völkerrecht*, 64(3): 547.

Wells, C. (1993), *Corporations and Criminal Liability*, Oxford: Oxford University Press.

Wells. C. (1994), Corporate Criminality: New Crimes for the Times, *Criminal Law Review*, (1994): 732.

Welsh, R. (1946), The Criminal Liability of Corporations, *Law Quarterly Review*, 62: 345.

White, H. (1980), A Heteroskedasticity-consistent Covariance Matrix Estimator and a Direct Test for Heteroskedasticity, *Econometrica*, 48: 817–38.

White, R.C.A. (2001), *Jacobs and White: The European Convention on Human Rights*, 3rd edn., Oxford: Oxford University Press.

White, S. (1996), Proposed Measures against Corruption in the European Union, *European Law Review*, (1996): 466.

Wilkitzky, P. (1992), Development of an Effective International Crime and Justice Programme – a European View, in Eser, A. and Logodny, O. (eds.), *Principles and Procedures for a New Transnational Criminal Law*, Freiburg: Herstellung Barth, p. 270.

Williams, P. and Murithi, T. (2005), *The African Union: Pan-Africanism, Peace-building and Development*, Aldershot: Ashgate Publishing Ltd.

Williams, R.J., Theobald, R., Moran, J., Flanery, R. and Doing, A. (eds.) (2001), *The Politics of Corruption*, 4 volumes, Cheltenham, UK and Northampton, MA, USA: Edward Elgar.

Wilsher, D. (2006), Inexplicable Wealth and Illicit Enrichment of Public Officials: A Model Draft that Respects Human Rights in Corruption Cases, *Crime, Law and Social Change*, 45(1): 27.

Winkler, M.M. (2008), *Imprese multinazionali e ordinamento internazionale nell'era della globalizzazione*, Milan: Giuffrè.

Wise, E.M. (1999), Aut Dedere Aut Judicare: The Duty to Prosecute or Extradite, in Bassiouni, M.C., *International Criminal Law: Procedural and Enforcement Mechanisms*, vol. 2, 2nd edn., Ardsley, NY: Transnational Publisher, p. 15.

Wisploz, C. (2008), La tempesta perfetta ha vendicato il mercato, *la Repubblica. Affari e finanza*, (29 September): 4.

Wolfers, M. (1976), *Politics of the Organization of Africa Unity*, London: Methuen.

Wolfsberg Group (2000), Global Anti Money Laundering Guidelines for Private Banking, available at http://www.wolfsberg-principles.com.

Wooldridge, J.M. (2002), *Econometric Analysis of Cross Section and Panel Data*, Cambridge, MA: MIT Press.

World Bank (2002a, 2003a, 2004a), World Development Report, available at: http://web.worldbank.org/WBSITE/EXTERNAL/EXTDEC/EXTRESEARCH/EXTWDRS/0,,contentMDK:20227703~pagePK:478093~piPK:477627~theSitePK:477624,00.html.

World Bank (2002b), *Globalization Growth, and Poverty, Building an Inclusive World Economy*, Washington, DC: World Bank; New York: Oxford University Press.

World Bank (2003b), Land Policies for Growth and Poverty Reduction, Report by K. Deininger, Development Research Group.

World Bank (2004b), *Globalization, Growth, and Poverty: Building an Inclusive World Economy* (paperback), Washington, DC: World Bank; New York: Oxford University Press.

World Bank (2006), *Guidelines on Preventing and Combating Fraud and Corruption in Projects Financed by IBRD Loans and IDA Credits and Grants* (last revised in January 2011), Washington, DC: World Bank, available at http://siteresources.worldbank.org/INTLAWJUSTICE/Resources/AnticorruptionGuidelinesOct2006RevisedJan2011.pdf.

World Bank (2007), *Strengthening World Bank Group Engagement on Governance and Anti-corruption*, Washington, DC: World Bank.

World Bank (2010a), *Integrity Vice Presidency Annual Report Fiscal 2010*, Washington, DC: World Bank, available at http://siteresources.worldbank.org/INTDOII/Resources/588889–1286308793420/WBG_IntegrityReport2010_final_LO-RES.pdf.

World Bank (2010b), *World Bank Group Sanction Regime: An Overview*, Washington, DC: World Bank, available at: www.worldbank.org/sanctions.

World Bank (2010c), *World Bank Sanctions Board Statute*, Washington, DC: World Bank, available at: http://go.worldbank.org/CVUUIS7HZ0.

World Bank (2010d), *Agreement on Mutual Enforcement of Debarment Decisions Among Multilateral Development Bank*, M2010–0358, IDA/SecM201010–0429, available at http://www.ebrd.com/downloads/integrity/Debar.pdf.

World Bank (2010e), *World Bank Group Integrity Compliance Guidelines*, available at: http://siteresources.worldbank.org/INTDOII/Resources/Integrity_Compliance_Guidelines.pdf

World Bank (2011a), *Integrity Vice Presidency Annual Report Fiscal 2011*, Washington, DC: World Bank, available at http://siteresources.

worldbank.org/INTDOII/Resources/588889–1316720250792/INT_AR_FY11_web.pdf.

World Bank (2011b), *Guidelines: Procurement of Goods, Works, and Non-Consulting Services under IBRD Loans and IDA Credits & Grants*, Washington, DC: World Bank, available at: http://go.worldbank.org/1KKD1KNT40.

World Bank (2011c), *Guidelines: Selection and Employment of Consultants under IBRD Loans & IDA Credits & Grants by World Bank Borrowers*, Washington, DC: World Bank, available at: http://go.worldbank.org/U9IPSLUDC0.

World Bank (2011d), Terms of Reference of the World Bank (IBRD/IDA) Evaluation Officer, Washington, DC: World Bank, available at: http://siteresources.worldbank.org/EXTOFFEVASUS/Resources/EO_Terms_of_Reference.pdf.

World Bank (2011e), *World Bank Sanctioning Guidelines*, Washington, DC: World Bank, available at http://siteresources.worldbank.org EXTOFFEVASUS/Resources/WorldBankSanctioningGuidelines.pdf.

World Bank (2012a), *World Bank Achievements in Governance and Anti-Corruption: Moving the Agenda Forward* (factsheet), Washington, DC: World Bank, available at http://siteresources.worldbank.org/EXTPREMNET/Resources/GAC_FACT_SHEET.pdf.

World Bank (2012b), *Integrity Vice Presidency Annual Report Fiscal 2012*, Washington, DC: World Bank, available at http://siteresources.worldbank.org/EXTDOII/Resources/WBG_IntegrityReport2012.pdf.

World Bank (2012c), World Bank Sanctions Procedures as adopted by the World Bank as of April 15, 2012, available at: www.worldbank.org/sanctions.

World Bank (2012d), MDB Harmonized Principles on Treatment of Corporate Groups, available at: http://lnadbg4.adb.org/oai001p.nsf/0/A7912C61C52A85AD48257ACC002DB7EE/$FILE/MDB%20Harmonized%20Principles%20on%20Treatment%20of%20Corporate%20Groups.pdf.

World Bank (2013), *Integrity Vice Presidency FY13 Annual Update*, Washington, DC: World Bank, available at http://siteresources.worldbank.org/INTDOII/Resources/588889–1381352645465/INT_Annual_Update_FY13_WEB.pdf.

Wraith, R. and Simpkins, E. (1963), *Corruption in Developing Countries*, London: G. Allen and Unwin.

Zacharias, J. (2008), An Investigation of Economies of Scale in Microfinance Institutions, The Leonard N. Stern School of Business.

Zagaris, B. (2004), French Investigate Halliburton & Technip's Energy

Payments in Nigeria, *International Enforcement Law Reporter*, 96(4).

Zagrebelsky. G. (2006), Corti costituzionali e diritti universali, *Riv. trim. dir. pubbl.*, (2006): 310.

Zampaglione, A. (2008), Finanza americana i giorni dell'Iri, *la Repubblica, Affari & Finanza*, 22 September

Zander, M. (1999), *Cases and Materials on the English Legal System*, 8th edn., London: Butterworths.

Zanghì, C. (1988), Controlli internazionali, *Enc. Giur.*, XII, Rome: Treccani.

Zanghì, C. (2006), *La protezione internazionale dei diritti dell'uomo*, Turin: Giappichelli.

Zarin, D. (2012), *Doing Business under the Foreign Corrupt Practices Act*, New York: Practising Law Institute.

Zedalis, R.J. (1998), How Does the New OECD Convention on Bribery Stack Up against the Foreign Corrupt Practices Act?, *Journal of World Trade*, 32: 169.

Zerbes, I. (2007), Article 1. Offence of Bribery of Foreign Public Officials, in Pieth, M., Low, L.A. and Cullen, P., *The OECD Convention in Bribery: A Commentary*, Cambridge: Cambridge University Press, p. 45.

Zerbes, I. (2008), The Future of European Criminal Justice under the Lisbon Treaty Report from the ERA Conference in Trier, 11–12 February 2008, *Eucrim*, 3(4): 75.

Ziccardi, P. (1950), Intorno ai limiti della legge penale e della giurisdizione penale italiana, *Rivista italiana di diritto penale*, (1950): 462.

Ziegler, J. (2003), *Les nouveaux maîtres du monde et ceux qui leur résistent*; Italian translation: *La privatizzazione del mondo*, Milan: Marco Tropea Editore.

Ziller, J. (2007), *Il nuovo Trattato europeo*, Bologna: Il Mulino.

Zimmerman S.S. and Fariello F.A. Jr., (2012), Coordinating the Fight against Fraud and Corruption: Agreement on Cross-Debarment among Multilateral Development Banks, in Cissé H., Bradlow D. D. and Kingsbury B. (eds.), *International Financial Institutions and Global Legal Governance*, Washington DC, The World Bank, p. 189.

Zimring, F.E. and Johnson, D.T. (2007), On the Comparative Study of Corruption, in Pontell, H.N., and Geis, G. (eds.), *International Handbook of White Collar Crime*, New York: Springer, p. 456.

Žižek, S. (2005), *Against Human Rights*; Italian translation, *Contro i diritto umani*, Milan: Il Saggiatore.

Zoller, E. (1998), La definition des crime contre l'humanité, *Journal du droit international*, (1998): 549.

Zorn, A. (1903), *Grundzüge und Völkerrechts*, 2nd edn., Leipzig: J.J. Weber.

Datasets Used

"Il Taccuino dell'Azionista", SASIP, Databank, 1987–2006.
"Il Calepino dell'Azionista", edited by Mediobanca, 1987–2006.
Consob website.
Official list of Parliament (1987–2006).
Company websites (of all the listed Italian firms considered in the sample).

Index